BIBLIOGRAPHY OF
EUROPEAN ECONOMIC AND SOCIAL HISTORY

ALSO AVAILABLE

Bibliography of British Economic and Social History
compiled by W. H. Chaloner
and R. C. Richardson

BIBLIOGRAPHY OF
EUROPEAN ECONOMIC AND SOCIAL HISTORY

COMPILED BY

DEREK H. ALDCROFT

AND

RICHARD RODGER

MANCHESTER
UNIVERSITY PRESS

PUBLISHED BY
MANCHESTER UNIVERSITY PRESS
Oxford Road, Manchester M13 9PL, U.K.
51 Washington Street, Dover, N.H. 03820, U.S.A.

BRITISH LIBRARY CATALOGUING IN PUBLICATION DATA

Aldcroft, Derek H.
  Bibliography of European economic and social history.
  1. Europe—Social conditions—Bibliography
  I. Title   II. Rodger, Richard
  016.9402
  ISBN 0-7190-0944-8

LIBRARY OF CONGRESS CATALOGING IN PUBLICATION DATA

Aldcroft, Derek Howard.
  Bibliography of European economic and social history.
  Includes index.
    1. Europe—Economic conditions—Bibliography.
  2. Europe—Social conditions—Bibliography. I. Rodger,
  Richard.   II. Title.
  Z7165.E8A4 1983 [HC240]   016.306′094   83-12049
  ISBN 0-7190-0944-8

PHOTOTYPESET
BY Elliott Brothers & Yeoman Limited, Liverpool

PRINTED IN GREAT BRITAIN
BY Bell & Bain Limited, Glasgow

CONTENTS

Preface—*ix*

EUROPE

General economic and social history—*1*
Agriculture and rural society—*9*
Industry and internal trade—*12*
Transport and communications—*15*
Money, banking and finance—*16*
Overseas trade and commercial relations—*19*
Population and migration—*23*
Labour conditions and organisation—*27*

Incomes, wages and prices—*29*
Urban history—*30*
Social structure and social conditions—*31*
Economic policy and thought—*35*
Theories and typologies—*35*
Economic aspects of war—*36*
Historiography and bibliography—*38*
Statistical series—*39*

WESTERN EUROPE

FRANCE
General economic and social history—*42*
Agriculture and rural society—*45*
Industry and internal trade—*47*
Transport and communications—*50*
Money, banking and finance—*51*
Overseas trade and commercial relations—*53*
Population and migration—*56*
Labour conditions and organisation—*57*
Incomes, wages and prices—*60*
Urban history—*60*
Social structure and social conditions—*61*
Economic policy and thought—*68*
Education, science and technology—*70*
Historiography and bibliography—*71*

GERMANY
General economic and social history—*72*
Agriculture and rural society—*76*
Industry and internal trade—*77*
Transport and communications—*82*

Money, banking and finance—*82*
Overseas trade and commercial relations—*84*
Population and migration—*87*
Labour conditions and organisation—*88*
Incomes, wages and prices—*90*
Urban history—*91*
Social structure and social conditions—*92*
Economic policy and thought—*96*
Treaty settlement and reparations—*97*
Economic aspects of Fascism—*98*
Historiography and bibliography—*99*

BELGIUM
General economic and social history—*100*
Agriculture and rural society—*101*
Industry and internal trade—*102*
Transport and communications—*102*
Money, banking and finance—*102*
Overseas trade and commercial relations—*102*
Population and migration—*102*
Labour conditions and organisation—*103*

CONTENTS

Incomes, wages and prices—*103*
Urban history—*103*
Social structure and social conditions—*104*
Economic policy and thought—*104*
Historiography and bibliography—*104*

THE NETHERLANDS
General economic and social history—*105*
Agriculture and rural society—*106*
Industry and internal trade—*106*
Transport and communications—*107*

Money, banking and finance—*107*
Overseas trade and commercial relations—*108*
Population and migration—*109*
Labour conditions and organisation—*110*
Incomes, wages and prices—*110*
Urban history—*110*
Social structure and social conditions—*111*
Economic policy and thought—*111*
Historiography and bibliography—*111*

SWITZERLAND—*112*

EAST CENTRAL AND SOUTH · EASTERN EUROPE

GENERAL WORKS
General economic and social history—*114*
Agriculture and rural society—*116*
Industry and internal trade—*116*
Transport and communications—*117*
Money, banking and finance—*117*
Overseas trade and commercial relations—*117*
Population and migration—*117*
Labour conditions and organisation—*118*
Incomes, wages and prices—*118*
Urban history—*118*
Social structure and social conditions—*118*
Historiography and bibliography—*119*

AUSTRIA
General economic and social history—*119*
Agriculture and rural society—*120*
Industry and internal trade—*120*
Transport and communications—*120*
Money, banking and finance—*120*
Overseas trade and commercial relations—*121*
Population and migration—*121*
Labour conditions and organisation—*122*
Incomes, wages and prices—*122*
Urban history—*122*
Social structure and social conditions—*122*
Historiography and bibliography—*123*

HUNGARY
General economic and social history—*123*
Agriculture and rural society—*124*
Industry and internal trade—*124*
Money, banking and finance—*125*
Overseas trade and commercial relations—*125*
Population and migration—*125*
Labour conditions and organisation—*126*
Incomes, wages and prices—*126*
Urban history—*126*
Social structure and social conditions—*126*
Historiography and bibliography—*126*

CZECHOSLOVAKIA
General economic and social history—*127*

Agriculture and rural society—*127*
Industry and internal trade—*127*
Transport and communications—*128*
Money, banking and finance—*128*
Overseas trade and commercial relations—*128*
Population and migration—*128*
Labour conditions and organisation—*128*
Urban history—*129*
Social structure and social conditions—*129*
Historiography and bibliography—*129*

POLAND
General economic and social history—*129*
Agriculture and rural society—*130*
Industry and internal trade—*130*
Transport and communications—*131*
Money, banking and finance—*131*
Overseas trade and commercial relations—*131*
Population and migration—*131*
Labour conditions and organisation—*132*
Urban history—*132*
Social structure and social conditions—*132*
Historiography and bibliography—*133*

YUGOSLAVIA
General economic and social history—*133*
Agriculture and rural history—*134*
Industry and internal trade—*135*
Transport and communications—*135*
Money, banking and finance—*135*
Overseas trade and commercial relations—*135*
Population and migration—*135*
Labour conditions and organisation—*135*
Urban history—*135*
Social structure and social conditions—*136*
Historiography and bibliography—*136*

BULGARIA—*136*

ROMANIA—*137*

RUSSIA/SOVIET UNION
General economic and social history—*139*

CONTENTS

Agriculture and rural society—*145*
Industry and internal trade—*150*
Transport and communications—*154*
Money, banking and finance—*155*
Overseas trade and commercial relations—*157*
Population and migration—*160*
Labour conditions and organisation—*161*

Incomes, wages and prices—*164*
Urban history—*166*
Social structure and social conditions—*167*
Economic policy and administration—*171*
Soviet economic planning—*173*
Co-operative movements—*174*
Historiography and bibliography—*174*

SOUTHERN EUROPE

ITALY
General economic and social history—*176*
Agriculture and rural society—*178*
Industry and internal trade—*178*
Transport and communications—*178*
Money, banking and finance—*178*
Overseas trade and commercial relations—*179*
Population and migration—*180*
Labour conditions and organisation—*180*
Incomes, wages and prices—*181*
Urban history—*181*
Social structure and social conditions—*181*
Economic policy and administration—*182*
Historiography and bibliography—*182*

SPAIN
General economic and social history—*182*
Agriculture and rural society—*183*
Industry and internal trade—*184*
Transport and communications—*184*
Money, banking and finance—*184*
Overseas trade and commercial relations—*185*
Population and migration—*185*
Incomes, wages and prices—*185*

Urban history—*186*
Social structure and social conditions—*186*
Economic policy and thought—*186*
Historiography and bibliography—*187*

TURKEY
General economic and social history—*187*
Agriculture and rural society—*188*
Industry and internal trade—*188*
Transport and communications—*188*
Money, banking and finance—*188*
Overseas trade and commercial relations—*188*
Population and migration—*188*
Labour conditions and organisation—*189*
Urban history—*189*
Social structure and social conditions—*189*
Historiography and bibliography—*189*

GREECE—*189*

PORTUGAL—*190*

MALTA—*191*

SCANDINAVIA

GENERAL WORKS
General economic and social history—*193*
Agriculture and rural society—*193*
Industry and internal trade—*194*
Money, banking and finance—*194*
Overseas trade and commercial relations—*194*
Population and migration—*194*
Labour conditions and organisation—*195*
Incomes, wages and prices—*195*
Urban history—*195*
Social structure and social conditions—*195*
Historiography and bibliography—*195*

NORWAY
General economic and social history—*195*
Agriculture and rural society—*196*
Industry and internal trade—*196*
Transport and communications—*197*

Money, banking and finance—*197*
Overseas trade and commercial relations—*197*
Population and migration—*197*
Labour conditions and organisation—*198*
Incomes, wages and prices—*198*
Urban history—*198*
Social structure and social conditions—*198*
Historiography and bibliography—*198*

SWEDEN
General economic and social history—*199*
Agriculture and rural society—*200*
Industry and internal trade—*200*
Transport and communications—*201*
Money, banking and finance—*202*
Overseas trade and commercial relations—*202*
Population and migration—*203*
Labour conditions and organisation—*205*

CONTENTS

Incomes, wages and prices—*205*
Urban history—*206*
Social structure and social conditions—*206*
Economic policy and thought—*207*
Historiography and bibliography—*207*

DENMARK
General economic and social history—*207*
Agriculture and rural society—*208*
Industry and internal trade—*208*
Transport and communications—*208*
Money, banking and finance—*208*
Overseas trade and commercial relations—*209*
Population and migration—*209*
Labour conditions and organisation—*210*
Incomes, wages and prices—*210*
Urban history—*210*
Social structure and social conditions—*211*

Economic policy and thought—*211*
Historiography and bibliography—*211*

FINLAND
General economic and social history—*211*
Agriculture and rural society—*212*
Industry and internal trade—*212*
Transport and communications—*213*
Money, banking and finance—*213*
Overseas trade and commercial relations—*213*
Population and migration—*213*
Labour conditions and organisation—*214*
Incomes, wages and prices—*214*
Urban history—*214*
Social structure and social conditions—*214*
Historiography and bibliography—*215*

ICELAND—*215*

THE BALTIC STATES

GENERAL WORKS—*216*

ESTONIA—*217*

LATVIA—*218*

LITHUANIA—*218*

Index—*221*

PREFACE

A generation ago it was virtually possible, even as a student, to read most, if not all, of the literature written in English on European economic and social history. Since that time the volume of writing has been quite prodigious, such that it is now getting difficult to master the literature on any one country, while the task of cataloguing it for the whole of Europe is an arduous one, as the compilers of the present volume will readily testify.

What then are the main aims and achievements of the volume? The main objective has been to provide a handy reference guide for teachers, students and researchers of modern European economic and social history. Since the bibliography covers only works written in the English language it will probably be of less use to the last named group, at least in so far as those within it are already seasoned researchers on a particular country or topic. However, it would have been quite impossible from the point of view of length to have included all the literature in foreign languages, while to have done so would have defeated the main aim of the volume, namely that of providing a reasonably convenient guide for those who teach and study the subject but who are not primarily specialists in the field.

A word about the coverage is required. Geographically the volume encompasses the whole of continental Europe, including Turkey in Europe. (For Britain see *Bibliography of British Economic and Social History* by W. H. Chaloner and R. C. Richardson, Manchester University Press, 1984.) The bibliography covers writings on the period 1700 to 1939 and includes most of the literature published during the twentieth century and a small selection of the important, and still relevant, writings which appeared in the nineteenth century. In so far as the rapid growth in the volume of literature is of fairly recent origin, the incidence of post-second world war writings is of course much higher than that for the earlier period. The selection is confined largely to books and journal articles; for the most part it does not include annual publications or government reports, though a number of publications of important public, semi-public and/or international organisations – for example, the League of Nations – have been included.

For each entry full details are given regarding the date of publication, publisher and place of publication in the case of books, and the volume number and year of publication for journal articles. Normally the first edition of books is listed, except in cases where later editions include substantial revisions. Where practical the UK edition of books is given, and the publishers are specified; in America the corresponding US publishers can if necessary be found from *Books in Print*. The titles of journals are given in full for each entry to obviate the tiresome business of referring to an abbreviations list.

The classification is by area and country, with a breakdown into a dozen or so subject headings for most countries and regions. As far as practicable the subject headings have been kept uniform throughout in order to facilitate cross-reference between countries and subjects. The detailed listing of the headings in the contents pages should prove helpful to those wishing to utilise the bibliography in this way.

As might be expected, a number of problems cropped up when the authors were classifying the entries. In some cases the subject matter of a work is not readily apparent from the title, and hence a short annotation has been added in square brackets to clarify the situation. Another difficulty arose with those works covering more than one country. Here the issue was resolved by producing a duplicate entry for publications covering two nations. Where more than two countries are involved – for example, Norway, Sweden and Denmark, or Germany, France and Belgium – then the entries appear only once under the broader geographical categories of Scandinavia and Europe respectively.

Subject classification proved a more difficult problem, however. In some cases, especially journal articles, there seemed at first glance to be three or four possible points of location, such is the ingenuity of authors when selecting their titles. However, on closer inspection it was usually found that the work in question focused attention on one subject rather than several and hence it was classified accordingly. Inevitably, however, a few arbitrary decisions had to be made from time to time. But perhaps the most irritating matter is the way authors change their nomenclature. Variations in the use of initials is one thing, but when the same author records four different spellings of his name it is getting beyond a joke! We have done our best to standardise the offenders.

It would probably be difficult to find any bibliography which was fully comprehensive, foolproof and free from error. We have done our best to cover as wide a range of sources as possible and also to check the accuracy of the entries. No doubt readers and reviewers will spot errors, omissions and misclassifications. Should this be the case we would be very grateful to receive relevant details so that amendments may be made to any future editions.

Entries were still being made in the latter half of 1982 but the coverage for that particular year is inevitably incomplete, owing to the delay in receiving journals.

We should like to thank David Welding of Leicester University Library for valuable assistance in tracking down references. David Turnock of the Geography Department and Philip Cottrell of the Economic and Social History Department, Leicester University, kindly offered guidance and provided references on Eastern Europe and Western Europe respectively. Gillian Austen, with the assistance of Margaret Christie and Charlotte Kitson, has undertaken the mammoth task of supervising the typing and arrangement of 6,000 entries. Her patience, skill and energy were invaluable in facilitating the progress of the work. We are sincerely grateful to Gillian and her co-workers for their endeavours.

Derek H. Aldcroft   *University of Leicester*
Richard Rodger   *February 1983*

EUROPE

GENERAL ECONOMIC AND SOCIAL HISTORY

Adelman, I., and C. T. Morris, 'Patterns of indus-trialization in the nineteenth and early twentieth centuries. A cross-sectional quantitative study', in P. Uselding, ed., *Research in economic history*, JAI Press, Greenwich, Conn. 5 (1980)

Aitken, H. G. J., ed., *The state and economic growth*, Social Science Research Council, New York (1959)

Aldcroft, D. H., *From Versailles to Wall Street, 1919-29*, Allen Lane, London (1977)

Aldcroft, D. H., *The European economy, 1914-80*, Croom Helm, London (1980)

Allen, G. C., 'The economic map of the world. Population, commerce and industries', in D. Thomson, ed., *The era of violence, 1898-1945. The New Cambridge Modern History*, vol. 12, Cambridge University Press, Cambridge (1960)

Alpert, P., *Twentieth century economic history of Europe*, Schuman, New York (1951)

Arndt, H. W., *The economic lessons of the nineteen-thirties*, Oxford University Press, London (1944)

Ashworth, W., 'Industrialization and the economic integration of nineteenth century Europe', *European Studies Review*, 4 (1974)

Ashworth, W., *A short history of the international economy since 1850*, Longmans Green, London (3rd edn. 1975)

Aubert, L., *The reconstruction of Europe*, Yale University Press, New Haven, Conn. (1925)

Bairoch, P., 'Original characteristics and conse-quences of the industrial revolution', *Diogenes*, 54 (1966)

Bairoch, P., 'Europe's gross national product, 1800-1975', *Journal of European Economic History*, 5 (1976)

Bairoch, P., 'International industrialization levels from 1750 to 1980', *Journal of European Economic History*, 11 (1982)

Bairoch, P., and M. Levy-Leboyer, eds, *Disparities in economic development since the industrial revolution*, Macmillan, London (1981)

Baldwin, R. E., *Economic development and growth*, John Wiley, New York (1957)

Barbera, H., *Rich nations and poor in peace and war. Continuity and change in the development hierarchy of seventy nations from 1913 through 1952*, D. C. Heath, Lexington, Mass. (1973)

Barnes, T. G., and G. D. Feldman, *Nationalism, industrialisation and democracy, 1815-1914*, Little Brown and Co., Boston (1972)

Baster, A. S. J., 'Some economic aspects of rear-mament', parts 1 and 2, *International Labour Review*, 37 (1938)

Baudet, H., and H. van der Meulen, *Consumer behaviour and economic growth in the modern economy*, Croom Helm, London (1982)

Baudhuin, F., 'Europe and the great crisis', in H. van der Wee, ed., *The great depression revisited. Essays on the economics of the thirties*, Nijhoff, The Hague (1972)

Berend, I. T., and G. Ránki, 'Underdevelopment in Europe in the context of east-west relations in the nineteenth century', *Etudes Historiques Hon-groises*, 1 (1980)

Berend, I. T., and G. Ránki, 'Foreign trade and the industrialization of the European periphery in the nineteenth century', *Journal of European Economic History*, 9 (1980)

Berend, I. T., and G. Ránki, *The European periphery and industrialization 1780-1914*, Cambridge University Press, Cambridge (1982)

Bićanić, R., 'The threshold of economic growth', *Kyklos*, 15 (1962)

Birnie, A., *An economic history of Europe, 1760–1930*, Dial Press, New York (2nd edn 1931)

Blodgett, R. H., and D. L. Kemmerer, *Comparative economic development*, McGraw-Hill, New York (1956)

Blum, J., *et al.*, *The emergence of the European world*, Routledge and Kegan Paul, London (1975)

Blum, J., *et al.*, *The European world since 1815. Triumph and transition*, Routledge and Kegan Paul, London (1975)

Boettler, H. E., 'Significant economic developments since the armistice', *Journal of Accountancy*, 41 (1926)

Bowden, W., *et al.*, *An economic history of Europe since 1750*, H. Fertig, New York (1970)

Bowman, M. J., and C. A. Anderson, 'Human capital and economic modernization. An historical perspective', *Papers presented to the Fourth International Conference of Economic History, Bloomington, 1968*, Mouton, Paris (1973)

Braudel, F., *Capitalism and material life, 1400–1800*, Weidenfeld and Nicholson, London (1973)

Brenner, Y. S., *A short history of economic progress*, Frank Cass, London (1969)

Briggs, A., 'Economic interdependence and planning economies', in D. Thomson, ed., *The era of violence, 1898–1945. The New Cambridge Modern History*, vol. 12, Cambridge University Press, Cambridge (1960)

Briggs, A., 'The world economy. Interdependence and planning', in C. L. Mowat, ed.; *The shifting balance of world forces, 1898–1945*, The New Cambridge Modern History, vol. 12, Cambridge University Press, Cambridge (rev. 2nd edn 1968)

Brunn, G., *Nineteenth century European civilization, 1815–1914*, Oxford University Press, London (1959)

Brunner, K., ed., *The great depression revisited*, Nijhoff, The Hague (1980)

Buchanan, N. S., and H. S. Ellis, *Approaches to economic development*, Twentieth Century Fund, New York (1955)

Bury, J. P. T., ed., *The zenith of European power, 1830–70. The New Cambridge Modern History*, vol. 10, Cambridge University Press, Cambridge (1960)

Cairncross, A. K., *Factors in economic development*, Allen and Unwin, London (1962)

Cameron, R. E., *France and the economic develop-*

ment of Europe, 1800–1914, Princeton University Press, Princeton, N.J. (1961)

Carnegie Endowment for International Peace and the International Chamber of Commerce (Joint Committee), *International economic reconstruction*, Carnegie and International Chamber of Commerce, Paris (1936)

Cipolla, C. M., *Literacy and development in the West*, Penguin, Harmondsworth (1969)

Cipolla, C.M., ed., *The industrial revolution*, Fontana Economic History of Europe, vol. 3, Collins/Fontana, Glasgow (1973)

Cipolla, C.M., ed., *The emergence of industrial societies*, Fontana Economic History of Europe, vol. 4, parts 1 and 2, Collins/Fontana, Glasgow (1973)

Cipolla, C.M., ed., *The twentieth century*, Fontana Economic History of Europe, vol. 5, parts 1 and 2, Collins/Fontana, Glasgow (1976)

Cipolla, C.M., ed., *Contemporary economies*, Fontana Economic History of Europe, vol. 6, parts 1 and 2, Collins/Fontana, Glasgow (1976)

Clark, C., *The conditions of economic progress*, Macmillan, London (3rd edn 1957)

Clough, S. B., *The rise and fall of civilization*, McGraw-Hill, New York (1951)

Clough, S. B., *The economic development of Western civilization*, McGraw-Hill, New York (1968)

Clough, S. B., and C. W. Cole, *Economic history of Europe*, D. C. Heath, Boston, Mass. (1941)

Clough, S. B., *et al.*, *Economic history of Europe. Twentieth century*, Macmillan, London (1969)

Cole, G. D. H. and M., *The intelligent man's review of Europe today*, Gollancz, London (1933)

Cole, W. A., and P. Deane, 'The growth of national incomes', in H. J. Habakkuk, and M. M. Postan, eds., *Cambridge economic history of Europe*, vol. 6(1), Cambridge University Press, Cambridge (1965)

Craig, G. A., *Europe since 1815*, Holt, London (3rd edn 1971)

Crawley, C. W., ed., *War and peace in an age of upheaval, 1793–1830*, The New Cambridge Modern History, vol. 9, Cambridge University Press, Cambridge (1965)

Crouzet, F., 'The economic history of modern Europe', *Journal of Economic History*, 31 (1971)

Crouzet, F., 'Western Europe and Great Britain. "Catching up" in the first half of the nineteenth century', in A. J. Youngson, ed., *Economic development in the long run*, Allen and Unwin, London (1972)

Crouzet, F., *et al.*, *Essays in European economic*

history, 1789–1914, Edward Arnold, London (1969)

Csernok, A., *et al.*, 'Numerical results of an international comparison of infrastructure development over the last 100 years', *European Economic Review*, 4 (1973)

Darby, H. C., and H. Fullard, eds., *The New Cambridge Modern History*, vol. 14, *Atlas*, Cambridge University Press, Cambridge (1970)

Davis, J. S., 'Economic and financial progress in Europe', *Review of Economic Statistics*, 5 (1923)

Davis, J. S., 'Economic and financial progress in Europe, 1923–24', *Review of Economic Statistics*, 6 (1924)

Davis, J. S., 'Economic and financial progress in Europe, 1924–25', *Review of Economics and Statistics*, 7 (1925)

Davis, J. S., *The world between the wars, 1919–39. An economist's view*, Johns Hopkins University Press, Baltimore, Mass. (1975)

Davis, R., *The rise of the Atlantic economies*, Weidenfeld and Nicholson, London (1973)

Davisson, W. I., and J. E. Harper, *European economic history*, Appleton-Century-Crofts, New York (1972)

Day, C., *Economic development in Europe*, Macmillan, New York (1949)

Day, J. P., *An introduction to world economic history since the Great War*, Macmillan, London (1939)

de Vries, J., *The economy of Europe in an age of crisis, 1600–1750*, Cambridge University Press, Cambridge (1976)

Degler, C. N., *Age of the economic revolution, 1876–1901*, Scott Foresman, Glenview, Ill. (1967)

Deutsch, K. W., and A. Eckstein, 'National industrialisation and the declining share of the international economic sector, 1890–1959', *World Politics*, 13 (1961)

Dobb, M., *Studies in the development of capitalism*, Routledge and Kegan Paul, London (1946)

Dowd, D. F., 'Economic stagnation in Europe in the interwar period', *Journal of Economic History*, 15 (1955) [review of Svennilson's work]

Earle, P., ed., *Essays in European economic history, 1500–1800*, Clarendon Press, Oxford (1974)

Einzig, P., *The world economic crisis, 1929–31*, Macmillan, London (1931)

Einzig, P., *The world economic crisis, 1929–32*, Macmillan, London (1932)

Einzig, P., *The economic foundations of fascism*, Macmillan, London (1933)

Einzig, P., *Europe in chains*, Penguin Books, Harmondsworth, Middlesex (1940)

Ellsworth, P. T., *The international economy*, Macmillan, New York (3rd edn 1964)

Elster, J., 'The motivation of economic agents in the past', in M. W. Flinn, ed., *Proceedings of the seventh International Economic History Association conference, Edinburgh, 1978*, Edinburgh University Press, Edinburgh (1978)

Emsley, C., ed., *Conflict and stability in Europe*, Open University Press, London (1979)

Eyre, E., ed., *European civilisation*, vol. 5, Economic History of Europe since the Reformation, Oxford University Press, London (1934–39)

Falkus, M. E., ed., *Readings in the history of economic growth*, Oxford University Press, London (1968)

Fearon, P., *The origins of the great slump, 1929–32*, Macmillan, London (1979)

Feis, H., *The changing pattern of international economic affairs*, Harper Bros., New York (1941)

Feld, M. D., 'Revolution and reaction in early modern Europe', *Journal of the History of Ideas*, 38 (1977)

Feldman, G. R., 'Socio-economic structures in the industrial sector and revolutionary potentialities 1917–22', in C. L. Bertrand, ed., *Revolutionary situations in Europe, 1917–22. Germany, Italy, Austria, Hungary*, Interuniversity Centre for European Studies, Montreal (1977)

Fieldhouse, D. K., *Economics and empire, 1830–1914*, Cornell University Press, Ithaca, N.Y. (1973)

Fisk, H. E., 'Some new estimates of national incomes', *American Economic Review*, 20 (1930) [compilation of early estimates of national income for most European countries]

Fleisig, H., 'War-related debts and the great depression', *American Economic Review, Papers and Proceedings*, 66 (1976)

Florinsky, M. T., *Fascism and national socialism. A study of the economic and social policies of the totalitarian state*, Macmillan, New York (1936)

Frank, A. G., 'Multilateral merchandise trade imbalances and uneven economic development', *Journal of European Economic History*, 5 (1976)

Frank, A. G., *World accumulation, 1492–1789*, Monthly Review Press, New York (1978)

Friedman, P., *The impact of trade destruction on national incomes. A study of Europe, 1924–38*, University Presses of Florida, Gainesville, Fla. (1974)

Friedman, P., 'An econometric model of national income, commercial policy and the level of international trade. The open economies of Europe, 1924–38', *Journal of Economic History*, 38 (1978)

Galbraith, J. K., *The great crash*, Hamish Hamilton, London (1955)

Gerschenkron, A., *Continuity in history and other essays*, Harvard University Press, Cambridge, Mass. (1968)

Gilbert, M., *First world war atlas*, Weidenfeld and Nicolson, London (1970)

Glamann, K., and H. van der Wee, eds., *Acts and proceedings of the sixth International Conference on Economic History, Copenhagen, 1974*, Akademisk Forlag, Copenhagen (1978)

Goodwin, A., ed., *The American and French revolutions, 1763–93*, The New Cambridge Modern History, vol. 8, Cambridge University Press, London (1968)

Gould, J. D., *Economic growth in history. Survey and analysis*, Methuen, London (1972)

Gramm, W. P., 'The real-balance effect in the great depression', *Journal of Economic History*, 32 (1972)

Habakkuk, H. J., 'The historical experience on the basic conditions of economic progress', *International Social Science Bulletin*, 6, (1954)

Habakkuk, H. J., 'Economic history of modern Europe', *Journal of Economic History*, 18 (1958)

Habakkuk, H. J., and M. M. Postan, eds., *The industrial revolution and after. Incomes, population and technological change*, vol. 6, The Cambridge Economic History of Europe, 2 vols., Cambridge University Press, Cambridge (1965 [bibliography in vol. 6(2)]

Haberler, G., *International trade and economic development*, National Bank of Egypt, Cairo (1959)

Haberler, G., *The world economy, money and the great depression, 1919–39*, American Enterprise Institute for Public Policy, Washington D.C. (1976)

Haider, C., *Capital and labor under fascism*, P. S. King, London (1930)

Hansen, A. H., *Economic stabilisation in an unbalanced world*, Harcourt Brace, New York (1932)

Harrison, A., *The framework of economic activity*, Macmillan, London (1968)

Hartwell, R. M., 'Economic change in England and Europe, 1780–1830', in C. W. Crawley, ed., *War and peace in an age of upheaval, 1793–1830*. The New Cambridge Modern History, vol. 9, Cambridge University Press, Cambridge (1965)

Heaton, H., *Economic history of Europe*, Harper Bros., New York (rev. edn 1948)

Heaton, H., 'Economic change and growth', in J. P. T. Bury, ed., *The zenith of European power, 1830–70*. The New Cambridge Modern History, vol. 10, Cambridge University Press, Cambridge (1960)

Heckscher, E. F., *The continental system. An economic interpretation*, Clarendon Press, Oxford (1922)

Henderson, W. O., 'Trade cycle in the nineteenth century', *History*, 18 (1933–34)

Hilferding, R., *Finance capital. A study of the latest phase of capitalist development*, Routledge and Kegan Paul, London (1981) [originally published in Vienna in 1910)

Hill, M., *The economic and financial organization of the League of Nations. A survey of twenty-five years' experience*, Carnegie Endowment for International Peace, Washington, D.C. (1946)

Hinsley, F. H., ed., *Material progress and world-wide problems, 1870–98*. The New Cambridge Modern History, vol. 11, Cambridge University Press, Cambridge (1962)

Hobsbawm, E. J., *The age of revolution. Europe 1789–1848*, Weidenfeld and Nicolson, London (1962)

Hobsbawm, E. J., *The age of capital*, Weidenfeld and Nicolson, London (1975)

Hobson, J. A., *The evolution of modern capitalism*, W. Scott, London (4th edn 1926)

Hodson, W. V., *Slump and recovery, 1929–37. A survey of world economic affairs*, Oxford University Press, London (1938)

Hoffmann, W. G., *The growth of industrial economics*, Manchester University Press, Manchester (1958)

Hohenberg, P. M., *A primer on the economic history of Europe*, Random House, New York (1968)

Hughes, J. R. T., *Industrialization and economic history. Theses and conjectures*, McGraw-Hill, New York (1970)

Hughes, J. R. T., 'Economic growth and change. How and why', *Journal of Interdisciplinary History*, 2 (1972)

International Conference of Economic Services, *International abstract of economic statistics, 1919–30*, International Conference of Economic Services, London (1934)

International Economic History Association, Proceedings of, *First international conference of economic history, Stockholm, 1960*, Mouton, Paris

(1960). *Second international conference of economic history, Aix-en-Provence, 1962,* Mouton, Paris (1965). *Third international conference of economic history, Munich, 1965,* Mouton, Paris (1968). *Fourth international conference of economic history, Bloomington, 1968,* Mouton, Paris (1973). *Fifth international conference of economic history, Leningrad, 1970,* Mouton, Paris (1979). *Sixth international congress on economic history, Copenhagen, 1974,* Akademisk Forlag, Copenhagen (1978). *Seventh international congress on economic history,* Edinburgh, 1978, Edinburgh University Press, Edinburgh (1978). *Eighth international congress on economic history, Budapest, 1982,* Akadémiai Kiadó, Budapest (1982)

International Labour Office, 'Public works as a factor in economic stabilisation', *International Labour Review,* 58 (1938)

International Labour Office, *Public investment and full employment,* International Labour Office, Geneva (1946)

Jewkes, J., 'The growth of world industry', *Oxford Economic Papers,* 3 (1951)

Jones, E. L., 'Environment, agriculture, and industrialisation in Europe', *Agricultural History,* 51 (1977)

Jones, E. L., 'Disaster management and resource saving in Europe, 1400–1800', in M. W. Flinn, ed., *Proceedings of the seventh international economic history congress, Edinburgh, 1978,* Edinburgh University Press, Edinburgh (1978)

Kapp, K. W., *The League of Nations and raw materials, 1919–39,* Geneva Research Centre, Geneva (1941)

Kemp, T., *Industrialization in nineteenth century Europe,* Longman, London (1969)

Kemp, T., *Historical patterns of industrialization,* Longman Group, London (1978)

Kenwood, A. G., and A. L. Lougheed, *The growth of the international economy, 1820–1960,* Allen and Unwin, London (1971)

Kindleberger, C. P., *Economic development,* McGraw-Hill, New York (1958)

Kindleberger, C. P., *The world in depression, 1929–39,* Allen Lane, London (1973)

Kindleberger, C. P., *Economic response. Comparative studies in trade, finance and growth,* Harvard University Press, Cambridge, Mass. (1978)

Knight, M. M., *et al., Economic history of Europe,* Houghton Mifflin, Boston, Mass. (1982)

Knowles, L., *Economic development in the nineteenth century. France, Germany, Russia and the United States of America,* Routledge, London (1932)

Kooy, M., ed., *Studies in economics and economic history. Essays in honour of Prof. H. M. Robertson,* Macmillan, London (1972)

Kranzberg, M., and C. Pursell, eds., *Technology and Western civilization,* 2 vols, Oxford University Press, New York (1967)

Kuznets, S., 'Retardation of economic growth', *Journal of Economic and Business History,* 1 (1929)

Kuznets, S., 'Population, income and capital', *International Social Science Bulletin,* 6 (1954)

Kuznets, S., 'Quantitative aspects of the economic growth of nations. Levels and variability of rates of growth', *Economic Development and Cultural Change,* 5 (1956–57)

Kuznets, S., 'Quantitative aspects of the economic growth of nations. Industrial distribution of national product and labor force', *Economic Development and Cultural Change,* Supplement, 5 (1956–57)

Kuznets, S., 'Quantitative aspects of the economic growth of nations. Distribution of national income factor shares', *Economic Development and Cultural Change,* Supplement, 7 (1958–59)

Kuznets, S., *Six lectures on economic growth,* Free Press, Glencoe, Ill. (1959)

Kuznets, S., *Economic growth and structure. Selected essays,* Heinemann, London (1965)

Kuznets, S., *Modern economic growth. Rate, structure and spread,* Yale University Press, New Haven, Conn. (1966)

Kuznets, S., *Economic gowth of nations. Total output and production structure,* Harvard University Press, Cambridge, Mass. (1971)

Lander, J. E., *International economic history. Industrialisation in the world economy, 1830–1950,* Macdonald and Evans, London (1967)

Landes, D. S., 'Japan and Europe. Contrasts in industrialisation', in W. W. Lockwood, ed., *The state and economic enterprise in Japan,* Macmillan, London (1965)

Landes, D. S., ed., *The rise of capitalism,* Macmillan, New York (1966)

Lawley, F. E., *The growth of collective economy,* 2 vols., P. S. King (1938)

League of Nations, *Report on certain aspects of the raw materials problems,* 2 vols., League of Nations, Geneva (1922)

League of Nations, *World production and prices, 1933–39,* from 1926 to 1932 published as *Memorandum on production and trade,* and in

1932 as *Review of world production, 1925–31*, League of Nations, Geneva

League of Nations, *Report and proceedings of the world economic conference,* 2 vols., League of Nations, Geneva (1927)

League of Nations, *Statistical Yearbook,* 1927 onwards, League of Nations, Geneva

League of Nations, *Ten Years of world co-operation,* League of Nations, Geneva (1930)

League of Nations, *The course and phases of the world economic depression,* League of Nations, Geneva (1931)

League of Nations, *World economic survey, 1931–32,* League of Nations, Geneva (1932, annually)

League of Nations, *Report of the committee for the study of the problem of raw materials,* League of Nations, Geneva (1937)

League of Nations, *Economic stability in the postwar world. Report of the delegation on economic depression,* League of Nations, Geneva (1945)

League of Nations, *League of Nations' reconstruction schemes in the inter-war period,* League of Nations, Geneva (1945)

League of Nations, *Raw materials problems and policies,* League of Nations, Geneva (1946)

Leffler, M. P., *The elusive quest. America's pursuit of European stability and French security, 1919–33,* University of North Carolina Press, Chapel Hill, N.C. (1979)

Lévy-Leboyer, M., and P. Bairoch, *Disparities in economic development since the industrial revolution,* Macmillan, London (1981)

Lewis, W. A., *Economic survey, 1919–39,* Allen and Unwin, London (1949)

Lewis, W. A., 'World production, prices and trade, 1870–1960', *Manchester School,* 20 (1952)

Lewis, W. A., *The evolution of the international economic order,* Princeton University Press, Princeton, N.J. (1978)

Lewis, W. A., *Growth and fluctuations, 1870–1913,* Allen and Unwin, London (1978)

Lewis, W. A., and P. J. O'Leary, 'Secular swings in production and trade, 1870–1913', *Manchester School,* 23 (1955)

Lieberman, S., ed., *Europe and the industrial revolution,* General Learning Press, Morristown, N.Y. (1972)

Lindsay, J. O., ed., *The old regime, 1713–63.* The New Cambridge Modern History, vol. 7, Cambridge University Press, Cambridge (1957)

Lundberg, E., *Instability and economic growth,* Yale University Press, New Haven, Conn. (1968) [early chapters have some interesting comments on the

inter-war years]

MacIver, R. M., *et al., Economic reconstruction. Report of the Columbia University Commission,* Columbia University Press, New York (1964)

Maczak, A., 'Natural resources and economic development. The pre-industrial period', in M. W. Flinn, ed., *Proceedings of the seventh international economic history congress, Edinburgh, 1978,* Edinburgh University Press, Edinburgh (1978)

Maczak, A., and W. N. Parker, *Natural resources in European history,* Johns Hopkins University Press, Baltimore, Md. (1979)

Maddison, A., 'Economic growth in western Europe, 1870–1957', *Banca Nazionale del Lavoro Quarterly Review,* 12 (1959)

Maddison, A., 'Growth and fluctuation in the world economy, 1870–1960', *Banca Nazionale del Lavoro Quarterly Review,* 15 (1962)

Maddison, A., *Economic growth in the West,* Allen and Unwin, London (1964)

Maddison, A., 'Phases of capitalist development', *Banca Nazionale del Lavoro Quarterly Review,* 121 (1977)

Maddison, A., 'Long run dynamics of productivity growth', *Banca Nazionale del Lavoro Quarterly Review,* 128 (1979)

Maddison, A., *Phases of capitalist development,* Oxford University Press, London (1982)

Maier, C. S., *Recasting bourgeois Europe. Stabilization in France, Germany and Italy in the decade after World War I,* Princeton University Press, Princeton, N.J. (1975)

Maier, C. S., 'The two postwar eras and the conditions for stability in twentieth century western Europe', *American Historical Review,* 86 (1981)

Maitra, P., *The mainspring of economic development,* Croom Helm, London (1979)

Mandel, E., *Long waves of capitalist development. The Marxist interpretation,* Cambridge University Press, Cambridge (1981)

Mathias, P., and M. M. Postan, eds., *The industrial economies. Capital, labour and enterprise,* vol. 7, part 1, *Britain, France, Germany and Scandinavia;* part 2, *United States, Japan and Russia.* The Cambridge Economic History of Europe, Cambridge University Press, Cambridge (1978)

Mayer, A. J., *The persistence of the old regime. Europe to the Great War,* Pantheon, New York (1981)

Meier, G. M., ed., *Leading issues in development economics,* Oxford University Press, New York (1964) [deals with development in historical perspective]

Meier, G. M., and R. O. Baldwin, *Economic development. Theory, history, policy,* John Wiley, New York (1957)

Mendels, F. F., 'Seasons and regions in agriculture and industry during the process of industrialization', in S. Pollard, ed., *Region und industrialisierung,* Vandenhoeck and Ruprecht, Göttingen (1980)

Meuvret, J., 'Prices, population and economic activities in Europe, 1688–1715. A note', in J. S. Bromley, ed., *New Cambridge Modern History,* vol. 6, Cambridge University Press, Cambridge (1970)

Milward, A., and S. B. Saul, *The economic development of continental Europe, 1780–1870,* Allen and Unwin, London (1973)

Milward, A., and S. B. Saul, *The development of the economies of continental Europe, 1850–1914,* Allen and Unwin, London (1977)

Mitchell, B. R., 'Statistical appendix, 1700–1914', in C. M. Cipolla, ed., *The emergence of industrial societies,* Fontana Economic History of Europe, vol. 4, part 2, Collins/Fontana, Glasgow (1973)

Mitchell, B. R., *European historical statistics, 1750–1970,* Cambridge University Press, Cambridge (1975)

Mitchell, B. R., 'Statistical appendix, 1920–1970', in C. M. Cipolla, ed., *Contemporary economies,* Fontana Economic History of Europe, vol. 6, part 2, Collins/Fontana, Glasgow (1976)

Mokyr, J., 'Growing up and the industrial revolution in Europe', *Explorations in Economic History,* 13 (1976)

Mokyr, J., 'Demand vs. supply in the industrial revolution', *Journal of Economic History,* 37 (1977)

Moulton, H. G., 'Economic conditions in Europe', *American Economic Review,* 13 (1923)

Mowat, C. L., ed., *The shifting balance of world forces, 1898–1945.* The New Cambridge Modern History, vol. 12, Cambridge University Press, Cambridge (rev. 2nd edn 1968)

Myrdal, G., *An international economy,* Harper, New York (1956)

Nef, J. U., 'The industrial revolution reconsidered', *Journal of Economic History,* 3 (1943)

Nef, J. U., *War and human progress. An essay on the rise of industrial civilisation,* Routledge and Kegan Paul, London (1950)

Neisser, H., *Some international aspects of the business cycle,* University of Pennsylvania Press, Philadelphia, Pa. (1936)

Newbold, J. T. W., 'The beginnings of the world crisis, 1873–96', *Economic History,* 2 (1930–33)

Nurkse, R., *Patterns of trade and development,* Blackwell, Oxford (1961)

O'Brien, P. K., 'European economic development. The contribution of the periphery', *Economic History Review,* 35 (1982)

Okun, B., and R. W. Richardson, *Studies in economic development,* Holt Rinehart and Winston, New York (1965)

Paige, D. C., *et al.,* 'Economic growth. The last hundred years', *National Institute Economic Review,* 16 (1961)

Parker, W. N., 'Growth and stagnation in the European economy', *Scandinavian Economic History Review,* 3 (1955) [review of Svennilson's work]

Parker, W. N., 'Economic development in historical perspective', *Economic Development and Cultural Change,* 10 (1961–62)

Parker, W. N., 'National resources and economic development. The nineteenth and twentieth centuries', in M. W. Flinn, ed., *Proceedings of the seventh international economic history congress, Edinburgh, 1978,* Edinburgh University Press, Edinburgh (1978)

Pinder, J., 'Europe in the world economy, 1920–70', in C. M. Cipolla, ed., *Contemporary economies.* Fontana Economic History of Europe, vol. 6, part 1, Collins/Fontana, Glasgow (1976)

Pollard, S., 'Industrialisation and the European economy', *Economic History Review,* 26 (1973)

Pollard, S., *European economic integration, 1815–1970,* Harcourt, Brace, New York (1974)

Pollard, S., 'Industrialization and integration of the European economy', in O. Büsch, *et al.,* eds., *Industrialisierung und europäische Wirtschaft im 19. Jahrhundert. Ein Togungsbericht,* W. de Gruyter, Berlin (1976)

Pollard, S., *The integration of the European economy since 1815,* Allen and Unwin, London (1981)

Pollard, S., *Peaceful conquest. The industrialization of Europe, 1760–1970,* Oxford University Press, London (1981)

Pounds, N. J. G., *An historical geography of Europe, 1500–1840,* Cambridge University Press, Cambridge (1980)

Pringle, W. H., ed., *Economic problems in Europe today,* A. and C. Black, London (1927)

Rees, G., *The great slump. Capitalism in crisis, 1929–33,* Weidenfeld and Nicolson, London (1970)

Reimann, G., *The myth of the total state. Europe's last bid for world rule,* W. Morrow, New York (1941)

Rich, E. E., and C. H. Wilson, eds., *The economy of Europe in the sixteenth and seventeenth centuries.* Cambridge economic history of Europe, vol. 4, Cambridge University Press, Cambridge (1967)

Rich, E. E., and C. H. Wilson, eds., *The economic organization of early modern Europe.* Cambridge Economic History of Europe, vol. 5, Cambridge University Press, Cambridge (1977)

Rimlinger, G. V., 'Production factors in economic development. A review article', *Business History Review,* 54 (1980)

Robbins, L., *The great depression,* Macmillan, London (1934)

Robinson, R. A. H., 'Histories of twentieth century Europe', *History,* 59 (1974)

Röpke, W., *Crises and cycles,* W. Hodge, London (1936)

Röpke, W., *International economic disintegration,* W. Hodge, London (1942)

Rostow, W. W., *How it all began. Origins of the modern economy,* Methuen, London (1975)

Rostow, W. W., 'Growth rates at different levels of income and stage of growth. Reflections on why the poor get richer and the rich slow down', in P. Uselding, ed., *Research in economic history,* JAI Press, Greenwich, Conn. 3 (1978)

Rostow, W. W., *The world economy. History and prospect,* Macmillan, London (1978)

Salter, A., *et al., The world economic crisis,* Kennikat Press, New York (1932)

Saville, L., 'Statistical sampling. An adaptation to Italian economic development', *Economic History Review,* 9 (1956–57)

Schmookler, J., *Invention and economic growth,* Harvard University Press, Cambridge, Mass. (1966)

Schumpeter, J. A., *Business cycles. A theoretical, historical and statistical analysis of the capitalist process,* 2 vols., McGraw-Hill, New York (1939)

Scoville, W. C., and J. C. la Force, eds., *The economic development of western Europe from 1914 to the present,* D. C. Heath, Lexington, Mass. (1969)

Siepmann, H. A., 'The Brussels conference', *Economic Journal,* 30 (1920)

Silverman, D. P., *Reconstructing Europe after the Great War,* Harvard University Press, Cambridge, Mass. (1982)

Singer, H., *International development. Growth and change,* McGraw-Hill, New York (1964)

Singer, J. D., and M. Small, *The wages of war, 1816–1965. A statistical handbook,* J. Wiley, New York (1972)

Smith-Gordon, L., and C. O'Brien, *Co-operation in many lands,* Co-operative Union, Manchester (1919)

Staley, E., *World economy in transition,* Council on Foreign Relations, New York (1939)

Staley, E., *World economic development. Effects on advanced industrial countries,* International Labour Office, Montreal (1945)

Studenski, P., *The income of nations. Theory, measurement and analysis, past and present. A study in applied economics and statistics,* New York University Press, New York (1958)

Supple, B., 'The state and the industrial revolution, 1700–1914', in C. M. Cipolla, ed., *The industrial revolution.* Fontana Economic History of Europe, vol. 3, Collins/Fontana, Glasgow (1973)

Supple, B. E., ed., *The experience of economic growth. Case studies in economic history,* Random House, New York (1963)

Svennilson, I., *Growth and stagnation in the European economy,* United Nations, Geneva (1954)

Thomson, D., ed., *The era of violence, 1898–1945,* The New Cambridge Modern History, vol. 12, Cambridge University Press, Cambridge (1960)

Thomson, D., *Europe since Napoleon,* Penguin, Harmondsworth (1966)

Tilly, C., ed., *The formation of national states in western Europe,* Princeton University Press, Princeton, N.J. (1975)

Tiltman, H. H., *Slump? A study of stricken Europe today,* Jarrolds, London (1932)

Topolski, J., 'Cases of dualism in the economic development of modern Europe', *Studia Historiae Oeconomicae,* 3 (1968)

Trebilcock, C., 'Economic backwardness and military forwardness', *Historical Journal,* 20 (1977)

Trebilcock, C., *The industrialisation of the continental powers, 1780–1914,* Longman, London (1981)

Trescott, M. M., ed., *Dynamos and virgins revisited. Women and technological change in history,* Scarecrow Press, Metuchen, N.J. (1979)

Tuma, E. H., *European economic history, tenth century to the present. Theory and history of economic change,* Harper and Row, New York (1971)

Usher, A. P., *et al., An economic history of Europe since 1750,* American Book Company, New York (1937)

Vaizey, J., *Capitalism and socialism. A history of industrial growth,* Weidenfeld and Nicolson, London (1980)

van der Wee, H., ed., *The great depression revisited.*

Essays on the economics of the thirties, Nijhoff, The Hague (1972)

Vilar, P., 'Problems of the formation of capitalism', *Past and Present,* 10 (1956)

Viljoen, S., *Economic systems in world history,* Longman, London (1974)

Vissering, G., *International economic and financial problems,* Macmillan, London (1970)

Wallerstein, I. M., 'The rise and future demise of the world capitalist system', *Comparative Studies in Society and History,* 16 (1974)

Wallerstein, I. M., *The modern world system. Mercantilism and the consolidation of the European world economy, 1600–1750,* Academic Press, New York (1980)

Webb, A. D., *The new dictionary of recent statistics of the world to the year 1911,* Routledge, London (1911)

Wilson, C. H., 'Economic conditions', in F. H. Hinsley, ed., *Material progress and world-wide problems, 1870–98.* The New Cambridge Modern History, vol. 11, Cambridge Press, Cambridge (1962)

Wilson, C. H., 'The historical study of economic growth and decline in early modern history', in E. E. Rich and C. H. Wilson, eds., *The economic organization of early modern Europe.* The Cambridge Economic History of Europe, vol. 5, Cambridge University Press, Cambridge (1977)

Woodruff, W., *Impact of Western man. A study of Europe's role in the world economy, 1750–1960,* Macmillan, London (1966)

Woodruff, W., 'The emergence of an international economy, 1700–1914', in C. M. Cipolla, ed., *The emergence of industrial societies.* Fontana Economic History of Europe, vol. 4, part 2, Collins/Fontana, Glasgow (1973)

Woolf, S. J., ed., *The nature of fascism,* Weidenfeld and Nicolson, London (1968)

Woytinsky, W. S. and E.S., *World population and production. Trends and outlook,* Twentieth Century Fund, New York (1953)

Woytinsky, W. S. and E.S., *World commerce and governments,* Twentieth Century Fund, New York (1955)

Youngson, A. J., ed., *Economic development in the long run,* Allen and Unwin, London (1972)

Zimmerman, L. J., 'The distribution of world income, 1860–1960', in E. de Vries, ed., *Essays on unbalanced growth,* Mouton, The Hague (1962)

Zimmerman, L. J., *Poor lands, rich lands. The widening gap,* Random House, New York (1965)

AGRICULTURE AND RURAL SOCIETY

Abel, W., *Agricultural fluctuations in Europe from the thirteenth to the twentieth centuries,* St Martin's Press, New York (1980)

Adelman, I., and C. T. Morris, 'The role of institutional influences in patterns of agricultural development', *Journal of Economic History,* 39 (1979)

Anderson, J. L., 'Climate change in European economic history', in P. Uselding, ed., *Research in economic history,* JAI Press, Greenwich, Conn. 6 (1981)

Ankarloo, B. 'Agriculture and women's work. Directions of change in the West, 1700–1900', *Journal of Family History,* 4 (1979)

Bairoch, P., 'Agriculture and the industrial revolution, 1700–1914', in C. M. Cipolla, ed., *The industrial revolution.* Fontana Economic History of Europe, vol. 3, Collins/Fontana, Glasgow (1973)

Bennett, M. K., 'World wheat crops, 1885–1932', *Wheat Studies,* 9 (1933)

Blum, J., 'The European village as community. Origins and functions', *Agricultural History,* 45 (1971)

Blum, J., 'The internal structure and polity of the European village community from the fifteenth to the nineteenth century', *Journal of Modern History,* 43 (1971)

Blum, J., 'The conditions of the European peasantry on the eve of emancipation', *Journal of Modern History,* 46 (1974)

Blum, J., *The end of the old order in rural Europe,* Princeton University Press, Princeton, N.J. (1978)

Brandt, K., 'Public control of land use in Europe', *Journal of Farm Economics,* 21 (1939)

Brenner, R., 'Agrarian class structure and economic development in pre-industrial Europe', *Past and Present,* 70 (1976)

Chorley, G. P. H., 'The agricultural revolution in northern Europe, 1750–1880, Nitrogen, legumes, and crop productivity', *Economic History Review,* 34 (1981)

Collins, E. J. T., 'Labour supply and demand in European agriculture, 1800–80', in E. L. Jones and S. J. Woolf, eds., *Agrarian change and economic development,* Methuen, London (1969)

Cooper, J. P., 'In search of agrarian capitalism', *Past and Present,* 80 (1978) [mainly eighteenth century]

Danhof, C. H., 'American evaluations of European agriculture', *Journal of Economic History,* supplement, 9 (1949)

Dovring, F., *Land and labour in Europe, 1900–50,* Nijhoff, The Hague (1964) [revised as *Land and labour in Europe in the twentieth century,* Nijhoff, The Hague (1965)]

Dovring, F., 'The transformation of European agriculture', in H. J. Habakkuk and M. M. Postan, eds., *Cambridge Economic History of Europe,* vol. 6(2), Cambridge University Press, Cambridge (1965)

Friedmann, H., 'World market, state and family farm. Social bases of household production in the era of wage labor', *Comparative Studies in Society and History,* 20 (1978)

Fussell, G. E., 'Ploughs and ploughing before 1800', *Agricultural History,* 40 (1966)

Fussell, G. E., 'Dairy farming, 1600–1900', *Papers presented to the third international conference of economic history, Munich, 1965,* Mouton, Paris (1973)

Fussell, G. E., 'Agricultural science and experiment in the eighteenth century. An attempt at a definition', *Agricultural History Review,* 24 (1976)

Goldin, C. D., 'The economics of emancipation', *Journal of Economic History,* 33 (1973)

Goy, J., and E. Le Roy Ladurie, *Tithe and agrarian history from the fourteenth to the nineteenth century. An essay in comparative history,* Cambridge University Press, Cambridge (1982)

Gras, N. S. B., *A history of agriculture in Europe and America,* Crofts, New York (1925)

Grigg, D. B., 'Population pressure and agricultural change', *Progress in Geography,* 8 (1976)

Gunst, P., 'The comparative impact of industrialization on western and eastern European agriculture in the nineteenth and early twentieth century', *Agrartorteneti Szemle,* 18 (1976)

Huggett, F. E., *The land question and European society since 1650,* Harcourt Brace Jovanovich, New York (1975)

Jones, E. L., and S. J. Woolf, eds., *Agrarian change and economic development. The historical problems,* Methuen, London (1969)

International Institute of Agriculture, *The agrarian reform,* vol. 1, *Austria, Finland, Latvia, Lithuania and Poland,* International Institute of Agriculture, Rome (1930)

International Institute of Agriculture, *The agricultural situation in 1930–31,* International Institute of Agriculture, Rome (1932)

International Institute of Agriculture, *The course of the agricultural depression in 1931–32,* International Institute of Agriculture, Rome (1933)

Kahan, A., 'Notes on serfdom in western and eastern Europe', *Journal of Economic History,* 33 (1973)

Kain, R., 'Tithe as an index of pre-industrial agricultural production', *Agricultural History Review,* 27 (1979)

Landsberger, H. A., ed., *Rural protest. Peasant movements and social change,* Macmillan, London (1974)

League of Nations, *The agricultural crisis,* 2 vols., League of Nations, Geneva (1931)

League of Nations, *European conference on rural life, 1939. Contributions by the International Institute of Agriculture,* six reports, League of Nations, Geneva (1939) [wealth of factual information on agriculture]

League of Nations, *Agricultural production in continental Europe during the 1914–18 war and the reconstruction period,* League of Nations, Geneva (1943)

Le Roy Ladurie, E., *Times of feast, times of famine. A history of climate since the year 1000,* Allen and Unwin, London (1972)

Le Roy Ladurie, E., 'Peasants', in P. Burke, ed., *Companion volume.* The New Cambridge Modern History, vol. 13, Cambridge University Press, Cambridge (1979)

Le Roy Ladurie, E., and M. Baulant, 'Grape harvests from the fifteenth through the nineteenth centuries', *Journal of Interdisciplinary History,* 10 (1979–80) [see also the note by B. Bell in the same issue]

Le Roy Ladurie, E., and J. Goy, *Tithe and agrarian history from the fourteenth to the nineteenth centuries. An essay in comparative history,* Cambridge University Press, Cambridge (1981)

Meij, J. L., ed., *Mechanisation in agriculture,* North-Holland, Amsterdam (1960)

Mellor, J. W., *The economics of agricultural development,* Cornell University Press, Ithaca, N.Y. (1966)

Mitchell, A. R., 'The European fisheries in early modern history', in E. E. Rich and C. H. Wilson, eds., *The economic organization of early modern Europe,* The Cambridge Economic History of Europe, vol. 5, Cambridge University Press, Cambridge (1977)

Moody, V. A., 'Agrarian reform before the post-war European constituent assemblies', *Agricultural History,* 7 (1933)

Parker, W. N., and E. L. Jones, eds., *European peasants and their markets. Essays in agrarian economic history,* Princeton University Press, Princeton, N.J. (1975)

Post, J. D., 'A study in meteorological and trade cycle

history. The economic crisis following the Napoleonic wars', *Journal of Economic History*, 34 (1974)

Post, J. D., *The last great subsistence crisis in the Western world*, Johns Hopkins University Press, Baltimore, Md. (1977)

Postan, M. M., and J. Hatcher, 'Population and class relations in feudal society', *Past and Present*, 78 (1978)

Priebe, H., The changing role of agriculture, 1920–70', in C. M. Cipolla, ed., *The twentieth century*. Fontana Economic History of Europe, vol. 5, part 2, Collins/Fontana, Glasgow (1976)

Probyn, J. W., ed., *Systems of land tenure in various countries*, Cobden Club, London (1881)

Roberts, M., 'Sickles and scythes. Women's work and men's work at harvest time', *History Workshop Journal*, 7 (1979)

Rossiter, M. W., *The emergence of agricultural science. Justus Liebig and the Americas, 1840–80*, Yale University Press, New Haven, Conn. (1975)

Royal Institute of International Affairs, *World agriculture. An international survey*, Oxford University Press, London (1932)

Sabean, D., 'Markets, uprisings and leadership in peasant societies. Western Europe, 1381–1789', *Peasant Studies Newsletter*, 2 (1973)

Schore, D. J., 'European raininess since A.D. 1700', *Quarterly Journal of the Royal Meteorological Society*, 75 (1949) [see also the author's article on temperature in the same volume]

Shanahan, E. W., 'The prospective food supplies of western Europe', *Economic Journal*, 29 (1919)

Slicher van Bath, B. H., 'The influence of economic conditions on the development of agricultural tools and machines in history', in J. L. Meij, ed., *Mechanisation in agriculture*, North-Holland, Amsterdam (1960)

Slicher van Bath, B. H., *The agrarian history of western Europe, A.D. 500–1850*, Edward Arnold, London (1963)

Slicher van Bath, B. H., 'The yield of different crops (mainly cereals) in relation to the seed *c.* 1810–20', *Acta Historiae Neerlandicae*, 2 (1967)

Slicher van Bath, B. H., 'Eighteenth century agriculture on the continent of Europe. Evolution or revolution', *Agricultural History*, 43 (1969) [comment by F. Dovring in the same issue]

Slicher van Bath, B. H., 'Agriculture in the vital revolution', in E. E. Rich and C. H. Wilson, eds., *The economic organization of early modern Europe*. The Cambridge Economic History of Europe, vol. 5, Cambridge University Press, Cam-

bridge (1977)

Smith, A. E., and D. M. Secoy, 'Salt as a pesticide, manure and seed steep', *Agricultural History*, 50 (1976)

Spring, D., ed., *European landed elites in the nineteenth century*, Johns Hopkins University Press, Baltimore, Md. (1977)

Stankiewicz, Z., 'Some remarks on the typology of transition from feudalism to capitalism in agriculture', *Acta Poloniae Historica*, 28 (1973)

Thirsk, J., 'The European debate on customs of inheritance, 1500–1700', in J. Goody *et al.*, eds., *Family and inheritance. Rural society in western Europe, 1200–1800*, Cambridge University Press, Cambridge (1976)

Thorner, D., 'Peasant economy as a category in economic history', *Papers presented to the second international economic history conference, Aix-en-Provence, 1962*, Mouton, Paris (1965)

Tilly, C., 'Food supply and state-making in Europe', *Peasant Studies Newsletter*, 2 (1973)

Timoshenko, V. P., *World agriculture and the depression*, University of Michigan, Ann Arbor, Mich. (1933)

Tracy, M., *Agriculture in western Europe. Crisis and adaptation since 1880*, Cape, London (1964)

Trow-Smith, R., *Life from the land. The growth of farming in western Europe*, Longmans, London (1967)

Tuma, E. H., *Twenty-six centuries of agrarian reform. A comparative analysis*, University of California Press, Berkeley, Cal. (1965)

Vandenbroeke, C., 'Cultivation and consumption of the potato in the seventeenth and eighteenth century', *Acta Historiae Neerlandicae*, 5 (1971)

Warner, C. K., ed., *Agrarian conditions in modern European history*, Macmillan, New York (1966)

Warriner, D., 'Some controversial issues in the history of agrarian Europe', *Slavonic and East European Review*, 32 (1953–54)

Wellmann, I., 'Village community and industrialization. Economic and social changes', *Agrartorteneti Szemle*, 18 (1976)

Yates, P. L., *Food production in western Europe*, Longmans, London (1940)

Yates, P. L., *Food, land and manpower in western Europe*, Macmillan, London (1960)

Yates, P. L., and D. Warriner, *Food and farming in postwar Europe*, Oxford University Press, London (1943)

INDUSTRY AND INTERNAL TRADE

Ahlström, G., *Engineers and industrial growth*, Croom Helm, London (1982)

Barker, E., *The development of public services in western Europe, 1660–1930*, Oxford University Press, London (1944)

Benham, F., 'The iron and steel industry of Germany, France, Belgium, Luxemburg and the Saar', *London and Cambridge Economic Service*, 39 (1934)

Bogucka, M., 'North European commerce as a solution factor of resource shortage in the sixteenth–eighteenth centuries', in A. Maczak, and W. N. Parker, *Natural resources in European history*, Resources for the Future, Washington, D.C. (1978) [papers prepared for International Economic History Conference, Edinburgh 1978]

Bogucka, M., 'The role of Baltic trade in European development from the sixteenth to the eighteenth centuries', *Journal of European Economic History*, 9 (1980)

Briggs, A., 'Technology and economic development', *Scientific American*, 209 (1963)

Brondel, G., 'The sources of energy, 1920–70', in C. M. Cipolla, ed., *The twentieth century*. Fontana Economic History of Europe, vol. 5, part 1, Collins/Fontana, Glasgow (1976)

Brown, R., 'History of accountants. The continent of Europe', in R. Brown, ed., *A history of accounting and accountants*, Cass, London (1968)

Cameron, R. E., 'The international diffusion of technology and economic development in the modern economic epoch', *Papers presented to the sixth International Economic History Association conference, Copenhagen, 1974*, Akademisk Forlag, Copenhagen (1978)

Carden, G. L., *Machine tool trade in Germany, France, Switzerland, Italy and the United Kingdom*, U.S. Government Printing Office, Washington, D.C. (1909)

Censer, J. R., 'Publishing in early modern Europe', *Journal of Social History*, 13 (1980)

Chamberlin, W. H., *The world's iron age*, Macmillan, New York (1941)

Chandler, A. D., 'Institutional integration. An approach to comparative studies in the history of large-scale business enterprise', *Revue Economique*, 27 (1976)

Chandler, A. D., and H. Daems, 'Administrative co-ordination, allocation and monitoring. Concepts and comparisons', in N. Horn and J. Kocka, eds., *Recht und Entwicklung der Grossunternehmen im 19. und frühen 20. Jahrhundert*, Vandenhoeck und Ruprecht, Göttingen (1979) [cartels, trusts in nineteenth and early twentieth centuries]

Clapp, V. W., 'The story of permanent/durable book-paper, 1115–1970', *Scholarly Publishing*, 2 (1971)

Cornish, W. R., 'Legal controls over cartels and monopolization, 1880–1914. A comparison', in N. Horn and J. Kocka, eds., *Recht und Entwicklung der Grossunternehmen im 19. und frühen 20. Jahrhundert*, Vandenhoeck und Ruprecht, Göttingen (1979)

Daems, H., and H. van der Wee, eds., *The rise of managerial capitalism*, Nijhoff, The Hague (1974)

Derry, T. K., and T. I. Williams, *A short history of technology from the earliest times to A.D. 1900*, Clarendon Press, Oxford (1960)

Dietrich, E. B., 'The present status of the cotton textile industry', *International Labour Review*, 22 (1930)

Dietrich, E. B., 'The present status of the wool textile industry', *International Labour Review*, 22 (1930)

Eastman, M., 'The European coal crisis, 1926–27' *International Labour Review*, 17 (1928)

Fischer, W., 'Rural industrialization and population change', *Comparative Studies in Society and History*, 15 (1973)

Foreman-Peck, J., 'The American challenge of the twenties. Multinationals and the European motor industry', *Journal of Economic History*, 42 (1982)

Franko, L. G., 'The origins of multinational manufacturing by continental European firms', *Business History Review*, 48 (1974)

Franko, L. G., *The European multinationals*, Greylock Publishers, Stanford, Conn. (1976)

Freudenberger, H., 'The mercantilist proto-factories', *Business History Review*, 40, (1966)

Freudenberger, H., and F. Redlich, 'The industrial development of Europe. Reality, symbols, images', *Kyklos*, 17 (1964)

Grebler, L., 'House building, the business cycle and state intervention', parts 1 and 2, *International Labour Review*, 33 (1936)

Guye, R., 'Post-war building difficulties and housing policy in Europe', *International Labour Review*, 24 (1931)

Guyot, Y., 'The sugar industry on the continent', *Journal of the Royal Statistical Society*, 65 (1902)

Haber, L. F., *The chemical industry in the*

nineteenth century, Clarendon Press, Oxford (1958)

Haber, L. F., *The chemical industry 1900–30. International growth and technological change*, Clarendon Press, Oxford (1971)

Hamilton, E. J., 'Profit inflation and the industrial revolution, 1751–1800', *Quarterly Journal of Economics*, 56 (1942)

Hannah, L., 'Mergers, cartels and concentration. Legal factors in the U.S. and European experience', in N. Horn and J. Kocka, eds., *Recht und Entwicklung der Grossunternehmen im 19. und frühen 20. Jahrhundert*, Vanderhoeck und Ruprecht, Göttingen (1979)

Hartwell, R. M., 'The service revolution. The growth of services in modern economy, 1700–1914', in C. M. Cipolla, ed., *The industrial revolution.* Fontana Economic History of Europe, vol. 3, Collins/Fontana, Glasgow (1973)

Henderson, W. O., 'The cotton famine on the continent, 1861–5', *Economic History Review*, 4 (1933)

Henderson, W. O., *Britain and industrial Europe, 1750–1870*, Liverpool University Press, Liverpool (1954)

Henderson, W. O., *The industrial revolution on the continent. Germany, France, Russia, 1800–1914*, Frank Cass, London (1961)

Henderson, W. O., *The genesis of the Common Market*, Frank Cass, London (1962)

Henderson, W. O., *The industrialization of Europe, 1790–1914*, Thames and Hudson, London (1969)

Hexner, E., *International cartels*, University of North Carolina Press, Chapel Hill, N.C. (1945)

Hilgerdt, F., *Industrialization and foreign trade*, League of Nations, Geneva (1945)

Hohenberg, P. M., *Chemicals in western Europe, 1850–1914. An economic study of technical change*, Rand-McNally and North-Holland, Chicago, Ill. (1967)

Horn, N., and J. Kocka, eds., *Recht und Entwicklung der Grossunternehmen im 19. und frühen 20. Jahrhundert*, Vandenhoeck und Ruprecht, Göttingen (1979) [articles in English and English summaries to essays in German]

Horner, J., *The linen trade of Europe during the spinning wheel period*, McCaw Stevenson and Orr, Belfast (1920)

International Labour Office, 'The European lignite industry', parts 1 and 2, *International Labour Review*, 22 (1930), 23 (1931)

International Labour Office, 'The present state of the lignite industry in the various European countries',
International Labour Review, 23 (1931)

Jones, E., 'The agricultural origins of industry', *Past and Present*, 40 (1968)

Kellenbenz, H., 'Rural industries in the West from the end of the Middle Ages to the eighteenth century', in P. Earle, ed., *Essays in European economic history, 1500–1800*, Clarendon Press, Oxford (1974)

Kellenbenz, H., 'The organization of industrial production', in E. E. Rich and C. H. Wilson, eds., *The Cambridge Economic History of Europe*, vol. 5, Cambridge University Press, Cambridge (1977)

Keller, M., 'Public policy and large enterprise. Comparative historical perspectives', in N. Horn and J. Kocka, eds., *Recht und Entwicklung der Grossunternehmen im 19. und frühen 20. Jahrhundert*, Vandenhoeck und Ruprecht, Göttingen (1979)

Kenwood, A. G., and A. L. Lougheed, *Technological diffusion and industrialisation before 1914*, Croom Helm, London (1982)

Kindleberger, C. P., 'Commercial expansion and the industrial revolution', *Journal of European Economic History*, 4 (1975)

Klima, A., 'The domestic industry and the putting-out system (*Verlagssystem*) in the period of transition from feudalism to capitalism', *Papers presented to the second international economic history conference, Aix-en-Provence, 1962*, Mouton, Paris (1965)

Koistinen, P. A. C., 'The "industrial-military complex" in historical perspective. World War I', *Business History Review*, 41 (1967)

Kriedte, P., *et al.*, *Industrialisation before industrialisation. Rural industry in the genesis of capitalism*, Cambridge University Press, Cambridge (1981)

Landes, D. S., 'Technological change and development in western Europe, 1750–1914', in H. J. Habakkuk and M. M. Postan, eds., *Cambridge Economic History of Europe*, vol. 6(1), Cambridge University Press, Cambridge (1965)

Landes, D. S., 'The structure of enterprise in the nineteenth century', in D. S. Landes, ed., *The rise of capitalism*, Collier-Macmillan, London (1966)

Landes, D. S., *The unbound Prometheus. Technological change and industrial development in western Europe from 1750 to the present*, Cambridge University Press, Cambridge (1969)

Landes, D. S., 'Watchmaking. A case study in enterprise and change', *Business History Review*, 53 (1979)

Lane, F. C., and J. C. Riemersma, eds., *Enterprise and secular change. Readings in economic his-*

tory, R. D. Irwin, Homewood, Ill. (1953)

League of Nations, *The problem of the coal industry. Interim report on its international aspects,* League of Nations, Geneva (1929)

Levy, H., *The new industrial system,* Routledge, London (1936)

Lewis, M. J. T., 'Industrial archaeology', in C. M. Cipolla, ed., *The industrial revolution.* Fontana Economic History of Europe, vol. 3, Collins/ Fontana, Glasgow (1973)

Leifmann, R., *Cartels, concerns and trusts,* Methuen, London (1932)

Lilley, S., 'Technological progress and the industrial revolution, 1700–1914', in C. M. Cipolla, ed., *The industrial revolution.* Fontana Economic History of Europe, vol. 3, Collins/Fontana, Glasgow (1973)

Macleod, R. and K., 'The social relations of science and technology, 1914–39', in C. M. Cipolla, ed., *The twentieth century.* Fontana Economic History of Europe, vol. 5, part 1, Collins/Fontana, Glasgow (1976)

McNeill, W. H., 'The industrialization of war', *Southern Humanities Review,* 13 (1979) [armaments industry 1700–1900]

Maddison, A., 'Industrial productivity growth in Europe and in the U.S.', *Economica,* 21 (1954)

Maier, C. S., 'Between Taylorism and technocracy. European ideologies and the vision of industrial productivity in the 1920s'. *Journal of Contemporary History,* 5 (1970)

Mathias, P., 'Who unbound Prometheus? Science and technical change, 1600–1800', *Yorkshire Bulletin of Economic and Social Research,* 21 (1969)

Mathias, P., 'British industrialisation. Unique or not?' in P. Leon *et al., L' Industrialisation en Europe au XIXe siècle,* Centre for National Scientific Research, Paris (1972)

Mathias, P., 'Industrial structure in the twentieth century. Economies not centrally planned', *Papers presented to the fourth international conference of economic history, Bloomington, 1968,* Mouton, Paris (1973)

Mathias, P., 'Skills and diffusion of innovations from Britain in the eighteenth century', *Transactions of the Royal Historical Society,* 25 (1975)

Mathias, P., 'Science and technology in processes of industrialisation, 1700–1914', *Papers presented to the sixth International Economic History Association conference, Copenhagen, 1974,* Akademisk Forlag, Copenhagen (1978)

Meakin, W., *The new industrial revolution,* Gollancz, London (1928)

Mendels, F. F., 'Proto-industrialization. The first phase of the industrialization process', *Journal of Economic History,* 32 (1972)

Mendershausen, H., 'The elimination of seasonal fluctuations in the building industry', *International Labour Review,* 36 (1937)

Mori, G., 'The process of industrialization in general and the process of industrialization in Italy', *Journal of European Economic History,* 8 (1979)

Multhauf, R. P., 'Geology, chemistry and the production of common salt', *Technology and Culture,* 17 (1976)

Neal, L., 'Factoring out industrialization', *Journal of Economic History,* 39 (1979)

Nef, J. U., 'Impact of war on science and technology', *Papers presented to the fourth international conference of economic history, Bloomington, 1968,* Mouton, Paris (1973)

Okochi, A., and H. Vchida, eds., *Development and diffusion of technology,* University of Tokyo Press, Tokyo (1980)

Organisation for Economic Co-operation and Development, *Basic statistics of industrial production, 1913–60,* OECD, Paris (1962)

Paretti, V., and G. Bloch, 'Industrial production in western Europe and the United States, 1901–55', *Banca Nazionale del Lavoro Quarterly Review,* 9 (1956)

Parker, W. N., *Coal and steel in western Europe,* Faber and Faber, London (1952)

Parker, W. N., 'Entrepreneurship, industrial organization and economic growth,' *Journal of Economic History,* 14 (1954)

Parker, W. N., 'Coal and steel output movements in western Europe, 1880–1956', *Explorations in Entrepreneurial History,* 9 (1957)

Patel, S. J., 'Rates of industrial growth in the last century, 1860–1958', *Economic Development and Cultural Change,* 9 (1961)

Pellicelli, G., 'Management, 1920–70', in C. M. Cipolla, ed., *The twentieth century.* Fontana Economic History of Europe, vol. 5, part 1, Collins/Fontana, Glasgow (1976)

Pesek, B. P., 'Kuznets' incremental capital-output ratios', *Economic Development and Cultural Change,* 12 (1963–64)

Plummer, A., *International combines in modern industry,* Pitman, London (1951)

Pounds, N. J. G., and W. N. Parker, *Coal and steel in western Europe,* Faber and Faber, London (1957)

Rabinowitch, H., 'The handicraftsman and modern industry', *International Labour Review,* 17 (1928)

Redlich, F., 'Business leadership. Diverse origins and

variant forms', *Economic Development and Cultural Change*, 6 (1957–58)

Redlich, F, and H. Freudenberger, 'The industrial development of Europe. Reality, symbols, images', *Kyklos*, 17 (1964)

Reed, I. H., 'The European hard-paste porcelain manufacture of the eighteenth century', *Journal of Modern History*, 8 (1936)

Reingold, N., and A. Molella, 'The interaction of science and technology in the industrial age', *Technology and Culture*, 17 (1976)

Rosenberg, N., ed., *The economics of technological change*, Penguin, Harmondsworth (1971)

Salin, E., 'European entrepreneurship', *Journal of Economic History*, 12 (1952)

Saul, S. B., 'The nature and diffusion of technology', in A. J. Youngson, ed., *Economic development in the long run*, Allen and Unwin, London (1972)

Schremmer, E., 'Proto-industrialisation. A step towards industrialisation?', *Journal of European Economic History*, 10 (1981)

Schulze Gaevernitz, G. von, *The cotton trade in England and on the continent*, Simpkin Marshall Hamilton Kent, London (1895)

Siengenthaler, J. K., 'A scale analysis of nineteenth century industrialization', *Explorations in Economic History*, 10 (1972–73)

Singer, C., *et al.*, *A history of technology*, vol. 4. *The industrial revolution, c. 1750–c. 1850*, vol. 5. *The late nineteenth century, c. 1850–c. 1900*, Clarendon Press, Oxford (1958)

Southard, F. A., *American industry in Europe*, Houghton Mifflin, Boston, Mass. (1931)

Supple, B., 'The nature of enterprise', in E. E. Rich and C. H. Wilson, eds., *The economic organization of early modern Europe*, The Cambridge Economic History of Europe, vol. 5, Cambridge University Press, Cambridge (1977)

Takayama, S., 'Development of the theory of the steam engine', *Japanese Studies in the History of Science*, 18 (1979)

Tann, J., and M. J. Breckin, 'The international diffusion of the Watt engine, 1775–1825', *Economic History Review*, 31 (1978)

Teich, M., 'Science and technology in the twentieth century', *Papers presented to the fourth international conference of economic history, Bloomington, 1968*, Mouton, Paris (1973)

Temin, P., 'A time-series test of patterns of industrial growth', *Economic Development and Cultural Change*, 15 (1966–67)

Todd, J. A., *The cotton world. A survey of the world's cotton supplies and consumption*, Pitman, London (1927)

Trebilcock, C., 'British armaments and European industrialization, 1890–1914', *Economic History Review*, 26 (1973)

United Nations, *International cartels*, United Nations, New York (1947)

van Stuyvenberg, J. H., *Margarine. An economic, social and scientific history, 1869–1969*, Liverpool University Press, Liverpool (1969)

Vernon, R., ed., *Big business and the state. Changing relations in western Europe*, Macmillan, London (1974)

Wilken, P. H., *Entrepreneurship. A comparative and historical study*, Ablex Publishing Corporation, Norwood, N.J. (1979)

Wilkins, M., 'An American enterprise abroad. American Radiation Company in Europe, 1895–1914', *Business History Review*, 43 (1969)

Wilkins, M., 'Modern European economic history and the multinationals', *Journal of European Economic History*, 6 (1977)

Wilson, C. H., 'The multinational in historical perspective', in K. Nakagawa, ed., *Strategy and structure of big business*, University of Tokyo, Tokyo (1976)

Woodruff, W., 'An inquiry into the origins of invention and the intercontinental diffusion of techniques of production in the rubber industry', *Economic Record*, 38 (1962)

Woodruff, W. and H., 'Economic growth. Myth or reality? The interrelatedness of continents and the diffusion of technology, 1860–1960', *Technology and Culture*, 7 (1966)

Wrigley, E. A., *Industrial growth and population change. A regional study of the coalfield areas of north-west Europe in the later nineteenth century*, Cambridge University Press, Cambridge (1961)

TRANSPORT AND COMMUNICATIONS

Berghouse, E., *The history of railways*, Barrie and Rockliff, London (1964)

Chartres, J., 'L'homme et la route. A conference report', *Journal of Transport History*, 2 (1981)

Cohn, G., 'On the nationalization of railways', *Economic Journal*, 18 (1908)

Dunham, A. L., *The pioneer period of European railroads*, Harvard Graduate School of Business Administration, Cambridge, Mass. (1946)

French, C. J., 'Eighteenth century shipping tonnage measurements', *Journal of Economic History*, 33 (1973)

Girard, L., 'Transport', in H. J. Habakkuk and M. M. Postan, eds., *Cambridge Economic History of Europe*, vol. 6(1), Cambridge University Press, Cambridge (1965)

Gomez-Mendoza, A., 'Railways and Western economic development', *Transport History*, 11 (1980)

Jackson, R. V., 'The decline of the wool clippers', *Great Circle*, 2 (1980)

Kellenbenz, H., 'The economic significance of the Archangel route (from the late sixteenth to the late eighteenth century)', *Journal of European Economic History*, 2 (1973)

League of Nations, *The general transport situation in 1921*, League of Nations, Geneva (1922)

League of Nations, *Transport problems which arose from the war of 1914–18 and the work of restoration undertaken in this field by the League of Nations*, League of Nations, Geneva (1945)

McKay, J. P., *Tramways and trolleys. The rise of urban mass transport in Europe*, Princeton University Press, Princeton, N.J. (1976)

O'Brien, P. K., *Railways and the economic development of western Europe, 1830–1914*, Macmillan, London (1982)

O'Brien, P. K., 'Transport and economic growth in western Europe, 1830–1914', *Journal of European Economic History*, 11 (1982)

Roberts, R. O., 'Comparative shipping and shipbuilding costs', *Economica*, 14 (1947)

Salvemini, B., 'Transport and economic development', *Journal of European Economic History*, 2 (1973)

Wilson, C. H., 'Transport as a factor in the history of economic development', *Journal of European Economic History*, 2 (1973)

MONEY, BANKING AND FINANCE

Adler, J. H., ed., *Capital movements and economic development*, Macmillan, London (1967)

Agherli, B. B., 'The balance of payments and the money supply under the gold standard regime, 1879–1914', *American Economic Review*, 65 (1975)

Aliber, R. Z., 'Speculation in the foreign exchanges. The European experience, 1919–26', *Yale Economic Essays*, 2 (1962)

Bartel, R. J., 'International monetary unions. The nineteenth century experience', *Journal of European Economic History*, 3 (1974)

Baster, A. S. J., *The international banks*, P. S. King, London (1935)

Beyen, J. W., *Money in a maelstrom*, Macmillan, London (1951)

Bidwell, R. L., *Currency conversion tables. A hundred years of change*, Rex Collings, London (1970)

Bloomfield, A. I., *Monetary policy under the international gold standard, 1880–1914*, Federal Reserve Bank of New York, New York (1959)

Bloomfield, A. I., *Short term capital movements under the pre-1914 gold standard*, Princeton University Press, Princeton, N.J. (1963)

Bloomfield, A. I., *Patterns of fluctuation in international investment before 1914*, Princeton University Press, Princeton, N.J. (1968)

Brown, W. A., *The international gold standard reinterpreted, 1914–34*, 2 vols., National Bureau of Economic Research, New York (1940)

Buist, M. G., *At spes non fracta. Hope and Co., 1770–1815. Merchant bankers and diplomats at work*, Nijhoff, The Hague (1974) [international banking in seven European countries]

Cagan, P., 'The monetary dynamics of hyperinflation', in M. Friedman, ed., *Studies in the quantity theory of money*, University of Chicago Press, Chicago, Ill. (1956)

Cameron, R. E., 'The Crédit Mobilier and the economic development of Europe', *Journal of Political Economy*, 61 (1953)

Cameron, R. E., 'The banker as entrepreneur', *Explorations in Entrepreneurial History*, (1963–64)

Cameron, R. E., 'Theoretical bases of a comparative study of the role of financial institutions in the early stages of industrialization', *Papers presented to the second international conference of economic history, Aix-en-Provence, 1962*, Mouton, Paris (1965)

Cameron, R. E., et al., *Banking in the early stages of industrialization*, Oxford University Press, New York (1967)

Cameron, R. E., *Banking and economic development. Some lessons of history*, Oxford University Press, London (1972)

Carroll, M. B., *Taxation of securities in Europe*, U.S. Government Printing Office, Washington, D.C. (1925)

Cassel, G., *The world's monetary problems*, Constable, London (1921)

Cassel, G., *Post-war monetary stabilisation*, Columbia University Press, New York (1928)

Cassel, G., *The crisis in the world's monetary system*, Oxford University Press, Oxford (1932)

Cassel, G., *The downfall of the gold standard*, Oxford University Press, London (1936)

Choudhri, E. U., and L. A. Kochin, 'The exchange rate and the international transmission of business cycle disturbances. Some evidence from the great depression', *Journal of Money, Credit and Banking,* 12 (1980)

Clarke, S. V. O., *Central bank co-operation, 1924–31,* Federal Reserve Bank of New York, N.Y. (1967)

Clarke, S. V. O., *The reconstruction of the international monetary system. The attempts of 1922 and 1933,* Princeton Studies in International Finance No. 33, International Finance Section, Department of Economics, Princeton University, Princeton, N.J. (1973)

Corti, E. C., *The reign of the house of Rothschild,* Cosmopolitan Book Corporation, New York (1928)

Corti, E. C., *The rise of the house of Rothschild,* Gollancz, London (1928)

Crouzet, F., ed., *Capital formation in the industrial revolution,* Methuen, London (1972)

Crowley, R. W., 'Long swings in the role of government. An analysis of wars and government expenditures in western Europe since the eleventh century', *Public Finance,* 26 (1971)

Davis, J. S., 'World currency expansion during the war and in 1919', *Review of Economic Statistics,* 2 (1920)

Davis, J. S., 'Recent developments in world finance', *Review of Economic Statistics,* 4 (1922)

De Cecco, M., *Money and empire. The international gold standard, 1890–1914,* Blackwell, London (1976)

Einzig, P., *The Bank for International Settlements,* Macmillan, London (1930)

Einzig, P., *Behind the scenes of international finance,* Macmillan, London (1931)

Einzig, P., *The fight for financial supremacy,* Macmillan, London (1931)

Einzig, P., *World finance, 1914–1935,* Macmillan, New York (1935)

Einzig, P., *World finance since 1914,* Kegan Paul Trench Trubner, London (1935)

Einzig, P., *World finance, 1935–37,* Kegan Paul Trench Trubner, London (1937)

Einzig, P., *World finance, 1937–38,* Kegan Paul, Trench Trubner, London (1938)

Einzig, P., *World finance, 1938–39,* Kegan Paul Trench Trubner, London (1939)

Einzig, P., *World finance, 1939–40,* Kegan Paul Trench Trubner, London (1940)

Emden, P. H., *Money powers of Europe in the nineteenth and twentieth centuries,* Appleton-Century, London (1938)

Falkus, M. E., 'United States economic policy and the "dollar gap" of the 1920s', *Economic History Review,* 24 (1971)

Fanno, M., *Normal and abnormal international capital transfers,* University of Minnesota Press, Minneapolis, Minn. (1939)

Feis, H., *Europe, the world's banker, 1870–1914,* Oxford University Press, London (1930)

Frenkel, J. A., 'Purchasing power parity. Doctrinal perspective and evidence from the 1920s', *Journal of International Economics,* 8 (1978)

Frenkel, J. A., 'Exchange rates, prices and money. Lessons from the 1920s', *American Economic Review,* 70 (1980)

Frenkel, J. A., and K. W. Clements, 'Exchange rates in the 1920s. A monetary approach', in M. J. Flanders and A. Razin, eds., *Development in an inflationary world,* Academic Press, New York (1981)

Gayer, A. D., *Monetary policy and economic stabilization. A study of the gold standard,* A. and C. Black, London (1937)

Gayer, A. D., ed., *The lessons of monetary experience. Essays in honour of Irving Fisher,* Farrer and Rinehart, New York (1937)

Gilbert, M., *Currency depreciation,* University of Pennsylvania Press, Philadelphia, Pa. (1939)

Gille, B., 'Banking and industrialization in Europe, 1730–1914', in C. M. Cipolla, ed., *The industrial revolution.* Fontana Economic History of Europe, vol. 3, Collins/Fontana, Glasgow (1973)

Glynn, S., and A. L. Lougheed, 'A comment on United States economic policy and the "dollar gap" of the 1920s', *Economic History Review,* 26 (1973) [European dollar gap]

Good, D. F., 'Backwardness and the role of banking in the nineteenth century European industrialisation', *Journal of Economic History,* 33 (1973)

Gregory, T. E., *The gold standard and its future,* Methuen, London (3rd edn 1934)

Gupta, S. P., 'Public expenditure and economic growth. A time-series analysis', *Public Finance,* 22 (1967)

Harris, S. E., *Exchange depreciation. Its theory and history, 1931–35, with some consideration of related domestic policies,* Harvard University Press, Cambridge, Mass. (1936)

Hawtrey, R. G., 'The Genoa resolutions on currency', *Economic Journal,* 32 (1922)

Hawtrey, R. G., *Monetary reconstruction,* Longman, London (2nd edn 1926)

Hawtrey, R. G., *The gold standard in theory and practice,* Longmans, London (5th edn 1947)

Hill, R. L., 'The role of rigidities in the failure of the gold standard', *Weltwirtschaftliches Archiv*, 77 (1956)

Hirsch, F., and P. Oppenheimer, 'The trial of managed money. Currency, credit and prices, 1920–70', in C. M. Cipolla, ed., *The twentieth century*. Fontana Economic History of Europe, vol. 5, part 2, Collins/Fontana, Glasgow (1976)

Horsefield, J. K., 'Currency devaluation and public finance', 1929–37', *Economica*, 6 (1939)

Iverson, C., *Aspects of the theory of international capital movements*, Oxford University Press, London (1935)

Jack, D. T., *The economics of the gold standard*, P. S. King, London (1925)

Jack, D. T., *The restoration of European currencies*, P. S. King, London (1927)

Jacobsson, P., *Some monetary problems. International and national*, Oxford University Press, London (1958)

Kindleberger, C. P., *International short-term capital movements*, Columbia University Press, New York (1937)

Kindleberger, C. P., *The formation of financial centres. A study in comparative economic history*, Princeton Studies in International Finance, No. 36, International Finance Section, Department of Economics, Princeton University, Princeton, N.J. (1974)

Kindleberger, C. P., *A history of financial panics*, Macmillan, London (1978)

Kindleberger, C. P., and J.-P. Laffargue, eds., *Financial Crises. Theory, history and policy*, Cambridge University Press, Cambridge (1982)

Kriz, M. A., *Postwar international lending*, Princeton University Press, Princeton, N.J. (1947)

Kuznets, S., 'Quantitative aspects of the economic growth of nations. The long term trends in capital formation proportions', *Economic Development and Cultural Change*, 9 (1960–61)

League of Nations, *Money and banking*, vol. I, *Monetary review*, vol. II, *Commercial and central banks since 1931*, in continuation of *Memorandum on commercial banks, 1913–29 and 1925–33* (1931 and 1934), *Commercial banks, 1929–34* (1935) and *Memoranda on currencies and central banks* (1922–26), League of Nations, Geneva

League of Nations, *Public finance, 1928–35* (1936); similar titles published intermittently in the 1920s under the title of *Memorandum on Public Finance*, League of Nations, Geneva

League of Nations, *Currencies after the war. A survey of conditions in various countries*, League of Nations, Geneva (1920)

League of Nations, *International financial conference, Brussels, 1920*, vol. I, *Report of the conference*, vol. 2, *Statements on the financial situation of the countries represented at the conference*, League of Nations, Geneva (1920–21)

League of Nations, *The functioning of the gold standard*, League of Nations, Geneva (1931)

League of Nations, *Second interim report of the gold delegation of the financial committee*, League of Nations, Geneva (1931)

League of Nations, *Final report of the gold delegation of the financial committee*, League of Nations, Geneva (1932)

League of Nations, *Relief deliveries and relief loans, 1919–23*, League of Nations, Geneva (1943)

League of Nations, *International currency experience. Lessons of the inter-war period*, League of Nations, Geneva (1944)

Lehfeldt, R. A., *Restoration of the world's currencies*, P. S. King, London (1923)

Lindert, P., *Key currencies and gold, 1900–13*, Princeton University Press, Princeton, N.J. (1969)

McCusker, J. J., *Money and exchange in Europe and America, 1600–1775. A handbook*, Macmillan, London (1978)

Martin, D. A., 'The impact of mid-nineteenth century gold depreciation upon Western monetary standards', *Journal of European Economic History*, 6 (1977)

Meyer, R. H., *Bankers' diplomacy. Monetary stabilisation in the twenties*, Columbia University Press, New York (1970)

Moggridge, D. E. 'Financial crises and lenders of last resort. Policy in the crises of 1920 and 1929', *Journal of European Economic History*, 10 (1981)

Morgenstern, O., *International financial transactions and business cycles*, Princeton University Press, Princeton, N.J. (1959)

Myers, M. G., 'The League loans', *Political Science Quarterly*, 60 (1945)

National Bureau of Economic Research, *Capital formation and economic growth*, Princeton University Press, Princeton, N.J. (1955)

Neuburger, H. M., and H. H. Stokes, 'The relationship between interest rates and gold flows under the gold standard. A new empirical approach', *Economica*, 46 (1979)

North, D. C., 'International capital movements in historical perspective', in R. F. Mikesell, ed., *U.S. private and government investment abroad*, University of Oregon Books, Eugene, Or. (1962)

Nugent, J. B., 'Exchange rate movements and economic development in the late nineteenth century', *Journal of Political Economy*, 81 (1973)

Otsuka, H., 'The early history of banking in Europe and Japan. An introductory study in comparative history', *International Review of the History of Banking*, 3 (1970)

Palgrave, R., *Bank rate and money market in England, France, Germany, Holland and Belgium, 1844–1900*, J. Murray, London (1903)

Palyi, M., *The twilight of gold, 1914–36. Myths and realities*, Henry Regnery, Chicago, Ill. (1972)

Pasvolsky, L., *Current monetary issues*, Brookings Institution, Washington, D.C. (1933)

Pelaez, C. M., 'A comparison of long-term monetary behaviour and institutions in Brazil, Europe and the United States', *Journal of European Economic History*, 5 (1976)

Polak, J. J., 'European exchange depreciation in the early twenties', *Econometrica*, 2 (1943)

Preston, H. H., 'Europe's return to gold', *Harvard Business Review*, 11 (1931)

Redlich, F., 'Payments between nations in the eighteenth and early nineteenth centuries', *Quarterly Journal of Economics*, 50 (1936)

Rowland, B. M., ed., *Balance of power or hegemony. The interwar monetary system*, New York University Press, New York (1976)

Royal Institute of International Affairs, *The international gold problems. Collected papers*, Oxford University Press, London (1932)

Royal Institute of International Affairs, *Monetary policy and the depression*, Oxford University Press, London (1933)

Royal Institute of International Affairs, *The problem of international investment*, Oxford University Press, London (1937)

Sperling, J. G., 'The international payments mechanism in the seventeenth and eighteenth centuries', *Economic History Review*, 14 (1961–62)

Stern, S., *Fourteen years of European investments, 1914–28*, Bankers Publishing Company, New York (1929)

Strandh, J., 'Some notes on the history of international capital movements, 1930–32', *Economy and History*, 5 (1962)

Temin, P., *Did monetary forces cause the great depression?* W. W. Norton, New York (1976) [concentrates on America but relevant material on Europe, especially Germany]

Thomas, L. B., 'Some evidence on international currency experience, 1919–25', *Nebraska Journal of Economics and Business*, 11 (1972)

Traynor, D. E., *International monetary and financial conferences in the interwar period*. Catholic University of America Press, Washington, D.C. (1949)

Triffin, R., *The evolution of the international monetary system. Historical reappraisal and future perspectives*, Princeton University Press, Princeton, N.J. (1964)

Triffin, R., *Our international monetary system. Yesterday, today and tomorrow*, Random House, New York (1968)

Tsiang, S. C., 'Fluctuating exchange rates in countries with relatively stable economies. Some European experiences after World War I', *International Monetary Fund Staff Papers*, 7 (1959–60)

United Nations, *Public debt, 1914–46*, United Nations, New York (1948)

United Nations, *International capital movements during the inter-war period*, United Nations, New York (1949)

van der Wee, H., 'Money, credit and banking systems', in E. E. Rich and C. H. Wilson, eds., *The economic organization of early modern Europe. The Cambridge Economic History of Europe, vol. 5*, Cambridge University Press, Cambridge (1977)

van Dillen, J. G., ed., *History of the principal public banks*, Nijhoff, The Hague (1934)

Vilar, P., *A history of gold and money, 1450–1920*, New Left Books, London (1976)

Williams, D., 'The 1931 financial crisis', *Yorkshire Bulletin of Economic and Social Research*, 15 (1963)

Willis, H. P., and B. H. Beckhart, eds., *Foreign banking systems*, H. Holt and Co., New York (1929)

Wirth, M., ed., *A history of banking in all the leading nations*, Journal of Commerce and Commercial Bulletin, New York (1896)

Wright, P. Q., ed., *Gold and monetary stabilization*, University of Chicago Press, Chicago, Ill. (1932)

Yeager, L. B., *International monetary relations. Theory, history and policy*, Harper and Row, New York (1966, 2nd edn 1976)

Young, J. P., *European currency and finance*, U.S. Government Printing Office, Washington, D.C. (1925)

OVERSEAS TRADE AND COMMERCIAL RELATIONS

Anstey, R., 'The slave trade of the continental powers, 1760–1810', *Economic History Review*, 30 (1977)

Austen, R. A., 'Economic imperialism revisited. Late nineteenth century Europe and Africa. A review article', *Journal of Modern History*, 47 (1975)

Bacon, L. B., and F. C. Schloemer, *World trade in agricultural products*, Institute of Agriculture, Rome (1940)

Bairoch, P., 'Free trade and European economic development in the nineteenth century', *European Economic Review*, 3 (1972)

Bairoch, P., 'European foreign trade in the nineteenth century. The development of the value and volume of exports (preliminary results)', *Journal of European Economic History*, 2 (1973)

Bairoch, P., 'Geographical structure and trade balance of European foreign trade from 1800 to 1970', *Journal of European Economic History*, 3 (1974)

Bairoch, P., *The economic development of the Third World since 1900*, Methuen, London (1975) [European economic relations with the Third World]

Baldwin, R. E., 'The commodity composition of trade. Selected industrial countries, 1900–54', *Review of Economics and Statistics*, 40 (1958)

Berov, L., 'Changes in price conditions in trade between Turkey and Europe in the sixteenth to nineteenth century', *Etudes Balkaniques*, 2–3 (1974)

Berrill, K., 'International trade and the rate of economic growth,' *Economic History Review*, 12 (1959–60)

Blusse, L., and F. Gaastra, eds., *Companies and trade. Essays on overseas trading companies during the Ancien Regime*, Leiden University Press, Leiden (1981)

Broeze, F. J., 'The new economic history, the navigation Acts, and the continental tobacco market, 1770–90', *Economic History Review*, 26 (1973)

Buckley, P. J., and B. R. Roberts, *European direct investment in the U.S.A. before World War I*, Macmillan, London (1982)

Cain, P. J., 'European expansion overseas, 1830–1914', *History*, 59 (1974)

Cairncross, A. K., 'World trade in manufactures since 1900', *Economia Internazionale*, 8 (1955)

Cairncross, A. K., and J. Faaland, 'Long-term trends in Europe's trade', *Economic Journal*, 62 (1952)

Chapman, S. D., 'The international houses. The continental contribution to British commerce, 1800–60', *Journal of European Economic History*, 6 (1977)

Chauduri, K. N., 'The economic and monetary problem of European trade with Asia during the seventeenth and eighteenth centuries', *Journal of European Economic History*, 4 (1975)

Clark, G. N., 'War trade and trade war, 1701–13', *Economic History Review*, 1 (1927–28)

Commission of Enquiry into National Policy in International Economic Relations, *International economic relations*, University of Minnesota Press, Minneapolis, Minn. (1934)

Condliffe, J. B., *The reconstruction of world trade*, Allen and Unwin, London (1941)

Condliffe, J. B., *The commerce of nations*, Allen and Unwin, London (1951)

Davies, R. B., *Peacefully working to conquer the world. Singer sewing machines in foreign markets*, Arno Press, New York (1974)

Day, C., *A history of commerce*, Longmans Green, London (4th edn 1938)

de Groot, A. H., 'The organization of western European trade in the Levant, 1500–1800', in L. Blusse and F. Gaastra, eds., *Companies and trade*, Leiden University Press, Leiden (1981)

Delle Donne, O., *European tariff policies since the world war*, Adelphi, New York (1928)

Dillard, D., *Economic development of the north Atlantic community*, Prentice-Hall, New York (1967)

Donaldson, J., *International economic relations. A treatise on world economy and world politics*, Longmans Green, London (1978)

Dunn, R. E., 'Bu Himara's European connexion. The commercial relations of a Moroccan warlord', *Journal of African History*, 21 (1980)

Dunning, J. H., 'Capital movements in the twentieth century', *Lloyds Bank Review*, 72 (1964)

Dunning, J. H., *Studies in international investment*, Allen and Unwin, London (1970)

Engerman, S. L., 'Comments on Richardson and Boulle and the "Williams thesis" ', *Revue Francaise d' Histoire d'Outre-Mer*, 62 (1975)

Fage, J. D., 'Europe's economic and political relations with tropical Africa', in C. W. Crowley, ed., *War and peace in an age of upheaval, 1793–1830*. The New Cambridge Modern History, Cambridge University Press, Cambridge (1965)

Fay, H. van V., 'Commercial policy in post-war Europe. Reciprocity versus most-favoured-nation treatment', *Quarterly Journal of Economics*, 41 (1927)

Fieldhouse, D. K., 'Imperialism. An historiographical revision', *Economic History Review*, 11 (1961–62)

Fieldhouse, D. K., *The colonial empires. A comparative survey from the eighteenth century*, Macmillan, London (1982)

Fornari, H. D., 'U.S. grain exports. A bicentennial overview', *Agricultural History*, 50 (1976)

Fursenko, A., 'The beginnings of international competition in oil', in M. W. Flinn, ed., *Proceedings of the seventh International Economic History Association conference, Edinburgh, 1978*, Edinburgh University Press, Edinburgh (1978)

Gignilliat, J. L., 'Pigs, politics and protection. The European boycott of American pork, 1879–91', *Agricultural History*, 35 (1961)

Glamann, K., 'European trade, 1500–1750', in C. M. Cipolla, ed., *The sixteenth and seventeenth centuries*. Fontana Economic History of Europe, vol. 2, Collins/Fontana, Glasgow (1971)

Glamann, K., 'The changing pattern of trade', in E. E. Rich and C. H. Wilson, eds., *The Cambridge Economic History of Europe*, vol. 5, Cambridge University Press, Cambridge (1977)

Gordon, M. S., *Barriers to world trade. A study of recent commercial policy*, Macmillan, New York (1941)

Goutalier, R., 'Privateering and piracy', *Journal of European Economic History*, 6 (1977)

Grassman, S., 'Long-term trends in openness of national economies', *Oxford Economic Papers*, 32 (1980)

Green, A., and M. C. Urquhart, 'Factor and commodity flows in the international economy of 1870–1914. A multi-country view', *Journal of Economic History*, 36 (1976)

Hamilton, E. J., 'The role of monopoly in the overseas expansion and colonial trade of Europe before 1800', *American Economic Review*, 38 (1948)

Harris, R. C., 'The simplification of Europe overseas', *Annals of the Association of American Geographers*, 67 (1977) [refers to colonial, land and family aspects]

Headrick, D. R., 'The tools of imperialism. Technology and the expansion of European colonial empires in the nineteenth century', *Journal of Modern History*, 51 (1979)

Headrick, D. R., *The tools of empire. Technology and European imperialism in the nineteenth century*, Oxford University Press, New York (1981)

Heckscher, E. F., 'Multilateralism, Baltic trade and the mercantilists', *Economic History Review*, 3 (1950–51)

Hooker, A. A., *The international grain trade*, Pitman, London (1936)

Houmanidis, L., 'Europe's contribution to world economy', *The Piraeus Srodrate School of Industrial Studies*, Piraeus (1977)

Kiernan, V., *European empires from the conquest to collapse, 1815–1960*, Fontana, London (1982)

Kindleberger, C. P., 'Industrial Europe's terms of trade on current account', *Economic Journal*, 65 (1955)

Kindleberger, C. P., *The terms of trade. A European case study*, Chapman and Hall, London (1956)

Kindleberger, C. P., *Foreign trade and the national economy*, Yale University Press, New Haven, Conn. (1962)

Kindleberger, C. P., 'The rise of free trade in western Europe, 1820–75' *Journal of Economic History*, 35 (1975)

Kirchner, W., *Commercial relations between Russia and Europe, 1400–1800. Collected essays*, Indiana University Publications, Bloomington, Ind. (1966)

Koebner, R., 'The concept of economic imperialism', *Economic History Review*, 2 (1949)

Kravis, I. B., 'Trade as a handmaiden of growth. Similarities between the nineteenth and twentieth centuries', *Economic Journal*, 80 (1970)

Kuznets, S., 'Quantitative aspects of the economic growth of nations. Level and structure of foreign trade. Long term trends', *Economic Development and Cultural Change*, 15 (1966–67)

League of Nations, *Balance of payments, 1933–38*. From 1924–26 published as vol. I of *Memorandum on balance of payments and foreign trade balances*. From 1927–28 as vol. I of *Memorandum on international trade and balances of payments*. From 1929–30 as vol. II of *Memorandum on international trade and balances of payments*. In 1931 as vol. II of *Memorandum on trade and balances of payments*, League of Nations, Geneva

League of Nations, *International trade statistics, 1933–38*. From 1924–26 published as vol. II of *Memorandum on balance of payments and foreign trade balances*. From 1927–28 as vol. II of *Memorandum on international trade and balances of payments*. From 1929–30 as vol. III of *Memorandum on international trade and balances of payments*. In 1931 as vol. III of *Memorandum on trade and balances of payments*, League of Nations, Geneva

League of Nations, *Review of world trade, 1933–38*. From 1924–26 published as vol. I of *Memorandum on balance of payments and foreign trade balances*. For 1931–32 as vol. I of *Memorandum on trade and balances of payments*, League of Nations, Geneva

League of Nations, *International economic conference. Final report of the trade barriers committee of the International Chamber of Commerce*, League of Nations, Geneva (1927)

League of Nations, *Tariff level indices*, League of Nations, Geneva (1927)

League of Nations, *Interim report of the gold delega-*

tion of the financial committee, League of Nations, Geneva (1930)

League of Nations, *Legislation on gold*, League of Nations, Geneva (1930)

League of Nations, *Principles and methods of financial reconstruction work undertaken under the auspices of the League of Nations*, League of Nations, Geneva (1930)

League of Nations, *International trade in certain raw materials and foodstuffs*, League of Nations, Geneva (1938)

League of Nations, *Europe's trade*, League of Nations, Geneva (1941)

League of Nations, *Commercial policy in the interwar period*, League of Nations, Geneva (1942)

League of Nations, *The network of world trade*, League of Nations, Geneva (1942)

League of Nations, *Europe's overseas needs, 1919–20, and how they were met*, League of Nations, Geneva (1943)

League of Nations, *Quantitative trade controls. Their causes and nature*, League of Nations, Geneva (1943)

Lewis, C., *America's stake in international investment*, Brookings Institution, Washington, D.C. (1938)

Lewis, C., *Nazi Europe and world trade*, Brookings Institution, Washington, D.C. (1941)

Lewis, W. A., 'International competition in manufactures', *American Economic Review*, 47 (1957)

Liepman, H., *Tariff levels and the economic unity of Europe*, Allen and Unwin, London (1938)

Loveday, A., 'Tariff level indices', *Journal of the Royal Statistical Society*, 112 (1928)

Loveday, A., *Britain and world trade*, Longmans Green, London (1931)

Luthy, H., 'Colonisation and the making of mankind', *Journal of Economic History*, 21 (1961)

Maczak, A., 'Continental east-west trade as a factor of development in central Europe from the middle of the sixteenth to the eighteenth century', *Papers presented to the fifth international economic history conference, Leningrad, 1970*, Mouton, Paris (1979)

Maizels, A., *Industrial growth and world trade*, Cambridge University Press, Cambridge (1963)

Malenbaum, W., *The world wheat economy, 1885–1939*, Harvard University Press, Cambridge, Mass. (1953)

Martin, K., and F. G. Thackeray, 'The terms of trade of selected countries, 1870–1938,' *Bulletin of the Oxford University Institute of Statistics*, 10 (1948)

Mauro, F., 'Towards an "intercontinental model". European overseas expansion between 1500 and 1800', *Economic History Review*, 14 (1961–62)

Mauro, F., and J. O'Leary, 'Tensions and the transmission of tensions in the European expansion to America (1500–1900)', *Plantation Society in the Americas*, 1 (1979)

Minchinton, W. E., 'Western Europe and the Atlantic economy in the eighteenth century', *Bijdragen en Medelingen Betreffende de Geschiedenis der Nederlanden*, 91 (1976)

Nourse, E. G., *American agriculture and the European market*, McGraw-Hill, New York (1924)

Novack, D., and M. Simon, 'Commercial responses to the American export invasion, 1871–1914. An essay in attitudinal history', *Explorations in Entrepreneurial History*, 3 (1965–66)

Nzemeke, A. D., 'The cowrie and the development of Euro-African trade in Lagos, 1851–61', *Bulletin de l'Institut Fondamental d'Afrique Noire*, 39 (1977)

Oudendijk, J. K., 'Blockaded seaports in the history of international law', *Tijdschrift voor Rechtsgeschiedenis*, 42 (1974)

Parrini, C. P., *Heir to empire. United States economic diplomacy, 1916–23*, University of Pittsburg Press, Pittsburg, Pa. (1969)

Peet, R., 'Influence of the British market on agriculture and related economic development in Europe before 1860', *Institute of British Geographers*, 56 (1972)

Political and Economic Planning, *Report on international trade*, PEP, London (1937)

Rappard, W. E., *Post-war efforts for freer trade*, Geneva Research Centre, Geneva (1938)

Sanderson, G. N., 'The European partition of Africa. Coincidence or conjuncture', *Journal of Imperial and Commonwealth History*, 3 (1974)

Schoonover, T., 'Costa Rican trade and navigation ties with the United States, Germany and Europe, 1840–85', *Jahrbuch für Geschichte von Staat Wirtschaft und Gesellschaft Lateinamerikas*, 14 (1977)

Senkowska-Gluck, M., 'Effects of Napoleonic legislation on the development of nineteenth century Europe', *Acta Poloniae Historica*, 38 (1978)

Stern, R. M., 'A century of food exports, *Kyklos*, 13 (1960)

Svennilson, I., 'The transfer of industrial know-how to non-industrialized countries', in K. Berrill, ed., *Economic development, with special reference to east Asia*, Macmillan, London (1964)

Tasca, H. J., *World trading systems*, League of

Nations, Paris (1939)

Taylor, H. C. and A. D., *World trade in agricultural products*, Macmillan, New York (1943)

Thayer, G., *The war business. The international trade in armaments*, Weidenfeld and Nicolson, London (1969)

Tyszynski, H., 'World trade in manufactured commodities, 1899–1950', *Manchester School*, 19 (1951)

Vasudevan, C. P. A., 'The nature of the European expansion', *Journal of Indian History*, 53 (1975), 54 (1976)

Wax, D. D., ' "A people of beastly living". Europe, Africa and the Atlantic slave trade', *Phylon*, 41 (1980)

Wesseling, H. L., ed., *Expansion and reaction. Essays on European expansion and reactions in Asia and Africa*, Leiden University Press, Leiden (1978)

Williams, G., *The expansion of Europe in the eighteenth century. Overseas rivalry, discovery and exploitation*, Blandford Press, London (1966)

Williams, G., ' "Savages noble and ignoble". European attitudes towards the wider world before 1800', *Journal of Imperial and Commonwealth History*, 6 (1978)

Wilson, C. H., 'The growth of overseas commerce and European manufacture', in J. O. Lindsay, ed., *The old regime, 1713–63*. The New Cambridge Modern History, vol. 7, Cambridge University Press, Cambridge (1957)

Wolfe, M., ed., *The economic causes of imperialism*, John Wiley, New York (1972)

Woodruff, W., *America's impact on the world. A study of the role of the United States in the world economy, 1750–1970*, Macmillan, London (1974)

Yates, P. L., *Forty years of foreign trade*, Allen and Unwin, London (1959)

Youngson, A. J., 'The opening up of new territories', in H. J. Habakkuk and M. M. Postan, eds., *The industrial revolution and after*. Cambridge Economic History of Europe, vol. 6(1), Cambridge University Press, Cambridge (1965)

Zacchia, C., 'International trade and capital movements, 1920–70', in C. M. Cipolla, ed., *The twentieth century*. Fontana Economic History of Europe, vol. 5, part 2, Collins/Fontana, Glasgow (1976)

POPULATION AND MIGRATION

Ackerman, S., 'Towards an understanding of emigrational processes', *Scandinavian Journal of History*, 3 (1978)

Appleby, A. B., 'Famine, mortality, and epidemic disease. A comment', *Economic History Review*, 30 (1977)

Appleby, A. B., 'Epidemics and famines in the little ice age', *Journal of Interdisciplinary History*, 10 (1979–80) [eighteenth century]

Armengaud, A., 'Population in Europe, 1700–1914', in C. M. Cipolla, ed., *The industrial revolution*. Fontana Economic History of Europe, vol. 3, Collins/Fontana, Glasgow (1973)

Berkner, L., and F. F. Mendels, 'Inheritance systems, family structure and demographic patterns in western Europe, 1700–1900', in C. Tilly, ed., *Historical studies of changing fertility*, Princeton University Press, Princeton, N.J. (1978)

Bremer, S., *et al.*, 'The population density and war proneness of European nations, 1816–1965', *Comparative Political Studies*, 6 (1973)

Burch, T. K., 'Some demographic determinants of average household size. An analytical approach', in P. Laslett, ed., *Household and family in past time*, Cambridge University Press, Cambridge (1972)

Caldwell, J. C., 'The mechanisms of demographic change in historical perspective', *Population Studies*, 35 (1981)

Carlsson, G., 'The decline of fertility. Innovation or adjustment process', *Population Studies*, 20 (1966–67)

Carlsson, G., 'Nineteenth century fertility oscillations', *Population Studies*, 24 (1970)

Chevalier, L., 'Towards a history of population', in D. V. Glass and D. E. C. Eversley, eds., *Population in history. Essays in historical demography*, Edward Arnold, London (1965)

Chojnacka, H., 'Nuptiality patterns in agrarian society', *Population Studies*, 30 (1976)

Cipolla, C. M., *The economic history of world population*, Penguin, Harmondsworth (1962)

Citroen, H. A., *European emigration overseas, past and future*, Nijhoff, The Hague (1951)

Coale, A. J., 'The decline of fertility in Europe from the French revolution to World War II', in S. J. Behrman *et al.*, *Fertility and family planning. A world view*, University of Michigan Press, Ann Arbor, Mich. (1970)

Coale, A. J., 'The demographic transition reconsidered', in *Proceedings of the international population conference, London 1969*, vol. 1, International Union for the Scientific Study of the Population, Liège (1971)

Coale, A. J., 'Remarriage and the matrimonial market. A methodological approach', in J. Dupaquier *et al.*, *Marriage and remarriage in populations of the past*, Academic Press, London (1981)

Cohen, J. E., 'Childhood mortality, family size and birth order in pre-industrial Europe', *Demography*, 12 (1975)

Davis, K., and J. E. Isaac, *People on the move*, Bureau of Current Affairs, London (1950)

Deprez, P., ed., *Population and economics*, University of Manitoba Press, Winnipeg (1970)

Dovring, F., 'European reactions to the Homestead Act', *Journal of Economic History*, 22 (1962)

Drake, M., 'Age at marriage in the pre-industrial West', in F. Bechhofer, ed., *Population growth and the brain drain*, Edinburgh University Press, Edinburgh (1969)

Drake, M., ed., *Population in industrialisation*, Methuen, London (1969)

Dunlevy, J. A., 'Nineteenth-century European immigration to the United States. Intended versus lifetime settlement patterns', *Economic Development and Cultural Change*, 29 (1980–81)

Dupaquier, J., 'Population', in P. Burke, ed., *Companion volume. The New Cambridge Modern History*, vol. 13, Cambridge University Press, Cambridge (1979)

Dupaquier, J., *et al.*, *Marriage and remarriage in populations of the past*, Academic Press, London (1981)

Easterlin, R., 'Influences on European overseas emigration before World War I', *Economic Development and Cultural Change*, 9 (1960–61)

Eldridge, H. T., 'Population growth and economic development', *Land Economics*, 28 (1952)

Engerman, S. L., 'The study of the European fertility decline', *Journal of Family History*, 1 (1976)

Erickson, C., ed., *Emigration from Europe, 1815–1914. Selected documents*, A. and C. Black, London (1976)

Eversley, D. E. C., *Social theories of fertility and the Malthusian debate*, Oxford University Press, London (1959)

Eversley, D. E. C., 'Demography and economics. A summary report', *Papers presented to the third international conference of economic history, Munich, 1965*, Mouton, Paris (1972) [see also report of discussions in the same volume]

Ferenczi, I., 'A historical study of migration statistics', *International Labour Review*, 20 (1929)

Finlay, R., 'Natural decrease in early modern cities', *Past and Present*, 92 (1981) [reply by A. Sharlin]

Flinn, M. W., 'The stabilization of mortality in pre-industrial western Eruope', *Journal of European Economic History*, 3 (1974)

Flinn, M. W., 'Plague in Europe and the Mediterranean countries', *Journal of European Economic History*, 8 (1979)

Flinn, M. W., *The European demographic system, 1500–1820*, Harvester Press, Brighton (1981)

Fourastié, J., 'From the traditional to the "tertiary" life cycle', in W. Petersen, ed., *Readings in population*, Macmillan, New York (1972)

Gaskin, K., 'Age at first marriage in Europe before 1850', *Journal of Family History*, 3 (1978)

Glass, D. V., *Population policies and movements in Europe*, Clarendon Press, Oxford (1940)

Glass, D. V., and D. E. C. Eversley, eds, *Population in history. Essays in historical demography*, Edward Arnold, London (1965)

Glass, D. V., and E. Grebenik, 'World population, 1800–1950', in H. J. Habakkuk and M. M. Postan, eds, *Cambridge Economic History of Europe*, vol. 6(1), Cambridge University Press, Cambridge (1965)

Glass, D. V., and R. Revelle, eds, *Population and social change*, Edward Arnold, London (1972)

Goldsheider, C., *Population, modernization and social structure*, Little Brown and Co., Boston, Mass. (1971)

Gould, J. D., 'European intercontinental emigration, 1815–1914. Patterns and causes', *Journal of European Economic History*, 8 (1979)

Gould, J. D., 'European intercontinental emigration. The road home. Return migration from the USA', *Journal of European Economic History*, 9 (1980)

Gould, J. D., 'European international emigration. The role of "diffusion" and "feedback" ', *Journal of European Economic History*, 9 (1980)

Guillet, E. C., *The great migration. The Atlantic crossing by sailing ship since 1770*, Nelson, London (1937)

Habakkuk, H. J., 'Population problems and European economic development in the late eighteenth and nineteenth centuries', *American Economic Review, Papers and Proceedings*, 53 (1963)

Habakkuk, H. J., *Population growth and economic development since 1750*, Leicester University Press, Leicester (1971)

Hagen, E. E., 'Population and economic growth', *American Economic Review*, 49 (1959)

Haines, M. R., *Fertility and occupation. Population. Patterns in industrialization*, Academic Press, New York (1979)

Hajnal, J., 'The marriage boom', *Population Index*, 19 (1953)

Hajnal, J., 'European marriage patterns in perspective', in D. V. Glass and D. E. C. Eversley, eds, *Population in history. Essays in historical demography*, Edward Arnold, London (1965)

Hansen, A. H., 'Economic progress and declining population', *American Economic Review*, 29 (1939)

Hauser, P. M., 'Demographic indicators of economic development', *Economic Development and Cultural Change*, 7 (1959)

Helleiner, K. F., 'The vital revolution reconsidered', *Canadian Journal of Economics and Political Science*, 23 (1957)

Helleiner, K. F., 'The population of Europe from the Black Death to the eve of the vital revolution', in E. E. Rich and C. H. Wilson, eds, *The Cambridge Economic History of Europe*, vol. 4, Cambridge University Press, Cambridge (1967)

Herlitz, F., 'The *tableau économique* and the doctrine of sterility', *Scandinavian Economic History Review*, 9 (1961)

Hersch, L., 'International migration of the Jews', in W. F. Willcox, ed., *International migrations*, National Bureau of Economic Research, New York (1931)

Hersch, L., 'The fall of the birth rate and its effects on social policy', *International Labour Review*, 28 (1933)

Hutchinson, E. P., 'Notes on immigration statistics of the United States', *American Statistical Association Journal*, 53 (1958)

Hvidt, K., 'Emigration agents. The development of a business and its methods', *Scandinavian Journal of History*, 3 (1978)

International Labour Office, 'Population and social problems', *International Labour Review*, 39 (1939)

Isaac, J. E., *Economics of migration*, Kegan Paul Trench Trubner, London (1947)

Isaac, J. E., *The effect of European migration on the economy of sending and receiving countries*, Research Group for European Migration Problems, The Hague (1953)

Jerome, H., *Migration and business cycles*, National Bureau of Economic Research, New York (1926)

Kelley, A. C., 'Demographic cycles and economic growth. The long swing reconsidered', *Journal of Economic History*, 29 (1969)

Kindleberger, C. P., 'Emigration and economic growth', Banca Nazionale del Lavoro Quarterly Review, 18 (1965)

Kirk, D., *Europe's population in the inter-war years*, United Nations, Geneva (1946)

Knodel, J., 'Family limitation and the fertility transition. Evidence from the age patterns of fertility in Europe and Asia', *Population Studies*, 31 (1977)

Knodel, J., 'European populations in the past. Family-level relations', in S. H. Preston, ed., *The effects of infant and child mortality on fertility*, Academic Press, New York (1978)

Knodel, J., *et al.*, 'The decline of non-marital fertility in Europe, 1880–1941', *Population Studies*, 25 (1971)

Kovacsics, J., 'World population after 1800', in *International population conference, London, 1969*, vol. 4, International Union for the Scientific Study of the Population, Liège (1971)

Kuczynski, R. R., *Population movements*, Clarendon Press, Oxford (1936)

Kuczynski, R. R., *Living space and population problems*, Farrer and Rinehart, New York (1939)

Kulischer, E. M., *Europe on the move. War and population changes, 1917-47*, Columbia University Press, New York (1948)

Kuznets, S., 'Population and economic growth', *Proceedings of the American Philosophical Society*, 3 (1967)

Langer, W. L., 'Europe's initial population explosion', *American Historical Review*, 69 (1963–64)

Langer, W. L., 'American foods and Europe's population growth, 1750–1850', *Journal of Social History*, 8 (1976)

Laslett, P., 'Age at menarche in Europe since the eighteenth century', *Journal of Interdisciplinary History*, 2 (1971)

Laslett, P., *Family life and illicit love in earlier generations. Essays in historical sociology*, Cambridge University Press, Cambridge (1977)

Laslett, P., *et al.*, *Bastardy and its comparative history*, Edward Arnold, London (1980)

Lee, E. S., 'A theory of migration', *Demography*, 3 (1966)

Lee, R. D., *et al.*, *Population patterns in the past*, Academic Press, New York (1977)

Lee, W. R., ed., *European demography and economic growth*, Croom Helm, London (1979)

Leibenstein, H., 'Population growth and the take-off hypothesis', in W. W. Rostow, ed., *The economics of take-off into sustained growth*, Macmillan, London (1963)

Lochore, R. A., *From Europe to New Zealand. An account of our continental European settlers*, A. H. and A. W. Reed, Wellington (1951)

Lockridge, K. A., 'Historical demography', in C. F. Delzell, ed., *The failure of history*, Vanderbilt University Press, Nashville, Tenn. (1977)

McKeown, T., *The modern rise of population,* Edward Arnold, London (1976)

McKeown, T., et al., 'An interpretation of the modern rise of population in Europe', *Population Studies,* 26 (1972)

McNeill, W. H., *Europe's steppe frontier, 1500–1880. A study of the eastward movement in Europe,* University of Chicago Press, Chicago, Ill. (1974)

McNeill, W. H., 'Historical patterns of migration', *Current Anthropology,* 20 (1979)

McNeill, W. H., and R. S. Adams, eds, *Human migration. Patterns and policies,* Indiana University Press, Bloomington, Ind. (1978)

Macura, M., 'Population in Europe, 1920–70', in C. M. Cipolla, ed., *The twentieth century.* Fontana Economic History of Europe, vol. 5, part 1, Collins/Fontana, Glasgow (1976)

Marschalk, P., 'Social and economic conditions of European emigration to South America in the nineteenth and twentieth centuries', *Jahrbuch für Geschichte von Staat Wirtschaft und Gesellschaft Lateinamerikas,* 13 (1976)

Matthiessen, P. C., and J. C. McCann, 'The role of mortality in the European fertility transition. Aggregate level relations', in S. H. Preston, ed., *The effects of infant and child mortality on fertility,* Academic Press, New York (1978)

Mendels, F., 'Notes on the age of maternity, population growth, and family structure in the past', *Journal of Family History,* 3 (1978)

Moller, H., ed., *Population movements in modern European history,* Macmillan, London (1964)

Morner, M., 'Immigration from the mid-nineteenth century onwards. A new Latin America', *Cultures,* 5 (1978)

National Bureau of Economic Research, *Demographic and economic change in developed countries,* Princeton University Press, Princeton, N.J. (1976)

Neal, L., 'Cross-spectral analysis of long swings in Atlantic migration', in P. Uselding, ed., *Research in economic history,* JAI Press, Greenwich, Conn. 1 (1976)

Notestein, F. W., et al., *The future population of Europe and the Soviet Union,* League of Nations, Geneva (1944)

Parish, W. L., 'Internal migration and modernization. The European case', *Economic Development and Cultural Change,* 21 (1972–73)

Peller, S., 'Mortality, past and future', *Population Studies,* 1 (1947–48)

Post, J. D., 'Famine, mortality and epidemic disease in the process of modernization', *Economic History Review,* 29 (1976)

Poulson, B. W., and J. Holyfield, 'A note on European migration to the United States. A cross-spectral analysis', *Explorations in Economic History,* 11 (1973–74)

Preston, S. H., 'The changing relation between mortality and level of economic development', *Population Studies,* 29 (1975)

Razzell, P. E., 'An interpretation of the modern rise of population in Europe. A critique', *Population Studies,* 23 (1974)

Ravenhold, H., 'A quantitative concept of the international mobility of population and its application to certain European countries in the period 1851–1935', *Théorie Générale de la Population,* 1 (1937)

Rose, A. M., *Migrants in Europe. Problems of acceptance and adjustment,* University of Minnesota Press, Minneapolis, Minn. (1969)

Rotberg, R. I., and T. K. Rabb, *Marriage and fertility. Studies in interdisciplinary history,* Princeton University Press, Princeton, N.J. (1980)

Schofield, R., 'Comparative fertility analysis of various types of marriage', in J. Dupaquier *et al., Marriage and remarriage in populations of the past,* Academic Press, London (1981)

Scott, F. D., 'The study of the effects of emigration', *Scandinavian Economic History Review,* 8 (1960)

Semmingsen, I., 'Emigration and the image of America in Europe', in H. S. Commager, ed., *Immigration and American history,* University of Minnesota Press, Minneapolis, Minn. (1961)

Shorter, E., 'Female emancipation, birth control, and fertility in European history', *American Historical Review,* 78 (1973)

Shorter, E., *et al.,* 'The decline of non-marital fertility in Europe, 1880–1940', *Population Studies,* 25 (1971)

Smith, D. S., 'A homeostatic demographic regime. Patterns in west European family reconstitution studies', in R. D. Lee, ed., *Population patterns in the past,* Academic Press, London (1977)

Smith, J. E., 'How first marriage and remarriage markets mediate the effects of declining mortality on fertility', in J. Dupaquier *et al., Marriage and remarriage in populations of the past,* Academic Press, London (1981)

Spengler, J. J., 'Population change. Cause, effect, indicator', *Economic Development and cultural Change,* 9 (1961)

Stolnitz, G. J., 'A century of international mortality

trends', *Population Studies*, 9 (1955–56), 10 (1956–57)

Taylor, P., *The distant magnet. European emigration to the USA*, Eyre and Spottiswoode, London (1971)

Thistlethwaite, F., 'Migration from Europe overseas in the nineteenth and twentieth centuries', in the *Report of the eleventh Congrès international des sciences historiques*, vol. 5, Uppsala, 1960, reprinted in H. Moller, ed., *Population movements in modern European history*, Macmillan, New York (1964)

Thomas, B., *Migration and economic growth. A study of Great Britain and the Atlantic economy*, Cambridge University Press, Cambridge (1954) [mostly concerned with Britain but wider European implications and some Swedish data]

Thomas, B., ed., *Economics of international migration*, Macmillan, London (1958)

Tilly, C., 'The historical study of vital processes', in C. Tilly, ed., *Historical studies of changing fertility*, Princeton University Press, Princeton, N.J. (1978)

Tilly, C., 'Migration in modern European history', in W. H. McNeill and R. S. Adams, eds, *Human migration. Patterns and policies*, Indiana University Press, Bloomington, Ind. (1978)

Tilly, C., and E. A. Wrigley, eds, *Historical studies of changing fertility*, Princeton University Press, Princeton, N.J. (1978)

Tilly, L. A., *et al.*, 'Women's work and European fertility patterns', *Journal of Interdisciplinary History*, 6 (1976)

Tomaske, J. A., 'The determinants of inter-country differences in European emigration, 1881–1900', *Journal of Economic History*, 31 (1971)

United Nations, *The determinants and consequences of population trends*, United Nations, New York (1953)

Vacher, L. C., 'A nineteenth century assessment of causes of European mortality decline', *Population and Development Review*, 5 (1979)

van der Woude, A., 'Illegitimate fertility and the marriage market', in J. Dupaquier *et al.*, *Marriage and remarriage in populations of the past*, Academic Press, London (1981)

Watkins, S. C., 'Regional patterns of nuptiality in Europe, 1870–1960', *Population Studies*, 35 (1981)

Wilkinson, M., 'European migration to the United States. An econometric analysis of aggregate labor supply and demand', *Review of Economics and Statistics*, 52 (1970)

Willcox, W. F., ed., *International migrations*, 2 vols, National Bureau of Economic Research, New York (1929, 1931)

Williamson, J. G., 'Migration to the New World. Long-term influences and impact', *Explorations in Economic History*, 11 (1974)

Winter, J. M., 'Aspects of the demographic effects of the two world wars, with special reference to western Europe', in M. W. Flinn, ed., *Proceedings of the seventh International Economic History Association conference, Edinburgh, 1978*, Edinburgh University Press, Edinburgh (1978)

Wischnitzer, M., *To dwell in safety. The story of Jewish migration since 1800*, Jewish Publication Society of America, Philadelphia, Pa. (1948)

Zolberg, A. R., 'International migration policies in a changing world system', in W. H. McNeill and R. S. Adams, eds, *Human migration. Patterns and policies*, Indiana University Press, Bloomington, Ind. (1978)

LABOUR CONDITIONS AND ORGANISATION

Bairoch, P., and J. M. Limbor, 'Changes in the industrial distribution of the world labour force, by region, 1880–1960', *International Labour Review*, 98 (1968)

Bergier, J. F., 'The industrial bourgeoisie and the rise of the working class, 1700–1914', in C. M. Cipolla, ed., *The industrial revolution*. Fontana Economic History of Europe, vol. 3, Collins/Fontana, Glasgow (1973)

Conacher, H. M., 'The regulation of agricultural labour conditions in continental Europe', *International Labour Review*, 8 (1923)

Deldycke, T., *et al.*, *The working population and its structure. International historical statistics*, Université Libre de Bruxelles, Brussels (1968)

Dhondt, J., 'Government labour and trade unions', in H. van der Wee, ed., *The great depression revisited. Essays on the economics of the thirties*, Nijhoff, The Hague (1972)

Estey, J. A., *Revolutionary syndication. An exposition and a criticism*, P. S. King, London (1913)

Frumkin, G., 'Pre-war and post-war trends in manpower of European countries', *Population Studies*, 4 (1950–51)

Fuss, H., 'Unemployment in 1925', *International Labour Review*, 14 (1926)

Fuss, H., 'Money and unemployment', *International Labour Review*, 16 (1927)

Fuss, H., 'Unemployment and employment among women', *International Labour Review*, 31 (1935)

Galenson, W., 'The labour force and labour problems in Europe, 1920–70', in C. M. Cipolla, ed., *The twentieth century.* Fontana Economic History of Europe, vol. 5, part 1, Collins/Fontana, Glasgow (1976)

Garraty, J. A., *Unemployment in history. Economic thought and public policy,* Harper and Row, New York (1978)

Geary, D., *European labour protest 1848–1939,* Croom Helm, London (1981)

Geremek, B., 'Men without masters. Marginal society during the pre-industrial era', *Diogenes,* 98 (1977)

Gompers, S., *Labor in Europe and America,* Harper Bros., New York (1910)

Gottschalk, M., 'Employment and unemployment in some great European ports', *International Labour Review,* 21 (1930)

Halstead, J. L., 'The national question and the workers' movement in Europe, 1848–1946', *Bulletin of the Society for the Study of Labour History,* 36 (1978)

Henderson, W. O., 'The labour force in the textile industries', *Archiv für Sozialgeschichte,* 16 (1976)

Hersch, L., 'Seasonal unemployment in the building industry in certain European countries', *International Labour Review,* 19 (1929)

Hunt, V. R., 'A brief history of women workers and hazards in the workplace', *Feminist Studies,* 5 (1979)

Jemnitz, J., 'Between revolution and reformism. The European working class movement in 1917', in *Etudes historiques hongroises,* 1975, Proceedings of the fourteenth Congress of Historical Sciences, Akademici Kiado, Budapest (1975)

International Labour Office, 'Control of the employment of children in agriculture in Europe', *International Labour Review,* 4 (1921)

International Labour Office, 'The three-shift system in the iron and steel industry', *International Labour Review,* 6 (1922)

International Labour Office, *Remedies for unemployment,* International Labour Organization, Geneva (1923)

International Labour Office, 'Trade unionism in 1922. A survey', *International Labour Review,* 7 (1923)

International Labour Office, 'Unemployment in 1924 and the beginning of 1925', *International Labour Review,* 12 (1925)

International Labour Office, 'Remedies for unemployment among professional workers', *International Labour Review,* 33 (1936)

Knapp, V. J., 'Popular participation in the European general strikes prior to 1914', *Studies in History and Society,* 5 (1973)

Knapp, V. J., 'Europe's textile artisans and the early stages of the industrial revolution', *Studies in Modern European History and Culture,* 3 (1977)

Kuczynski, J., *Labour conditions in western Europe, 1820–1935,* Lawrence and Wishart, London (1937)

Kuczynski, J., *The rise of the working class,* Weidenfeld and Nicolson, London (1967)

Lindberg, J., 'An attempt to construct international measures of unemployment', *International Labour Review,* 26 (1932)

Lindberg, J., 'Some problems of international employment statistics', *International Labour Review,* 35 (1937)

Lorwin, V. R., 'Working-class politics and economic development in western Europe', *American Historical Review,* 63 (1957–58)

Lorwin, V. R., ed., *Labor and working conditions in modern Europe,* Macmillan, New York (1967)

Lynch, K. A., 'The consequences of the industrial revolution for the European working class', in H. T. Parker, ed., *Problems in European history,* Moore Publications, Durham, N.C. (1979)

Magnus, E., 'The social, economic, and legal conditions of domestic servants', parts 1 and 2, *International Labour Review,* 30 (1934)

Maurette, F., 'An inqiry into working conditions in coal mines', *International Labour Review,* 17 (1928)

Mishinsky, M., 'The Jewish labor movement and European socialism', *Cahiers d'Histoire Mondiale,* 11 (1968)

Mitchell, H., and P. N. Stearns, eds, *Workers and protest. The European labour movement, the working classes, and the origins of social democracy, 1890–1914,* F. E. Peacock, Itasca, Ill. (1971)

Paine, S., 'The changing role of migrant labour in the advanced capitalist economies of western Europe', in R. T. Griffiths, ed., *Government, business and labour in European capitalism,* papers presented at the January 1977 conference of the University Association for Contemporary European Studies, Europotentials Press, London (1977)

Palmer, B. D., 'Most uncommon common men. Craft and culture in historical perspective', *Labour,* 1 (1976) [deals with artisans during seventeenth to twentieth centuries]

Rager, F., 'Provision for prolonged unemployment in certain industrial states', *International Labour Review,* 16 (1927)

Rimlinger, G. V., 'The legitimation of protest. A comparative study in labour history', *Comparative Studies in Society and History,* 2 (1960)

Rimlinger, G. V., 'Labour and government. A comparative historical perspective', *Journal of Economic History,* 37 (1977)

Royal Institute of International Affairs, *Unemployment. An international problem,* Oxford University Press, London (1935)

Somogyi, S., 'Is there a relation between the fall of the birth rate and unemployment?', *International Labour Review,* 31 (1935)

Spengler, J. J., 'Right to work. A backward glance', *Journal of Economic History,* 28 (1968)

Stearns, P. N., 'National character and European labour history', *Journal of Social History,* 4 (1970)

Stearns, P. N., ed., *The impact of the industrial revolution. Protest and alienation,* Prentice-Hall, Englewood Cliffs, N.J. (1972)

Stearns, P. N., 'Measuring the evolution of strike movements', *International Review of Social History,* 19 (1974)

Stearns, P. N., *Lives of labour. Work in a maturing industrial society,* Croom Helm, London (1975)

Stearns, P. N., 'The effort at continuity in working-class culture', *Journal of Modern History,* 52 (1980)

Sternberg, F., 'Prolonged unemployment, technical progress and the conquest of new markets', *International Labour Review,* 36 (1937)

Sturmthal, A. F., *The tragedy of European labour, 1918–39,* Gollancz, London (1944)

Thibert, M., 'The economic depression and the employment of women', parts 1 and 2, *International Labour Review,* 27 (1933)

Vallentin, A., 'The employment of women since the war', *International Labour Review,* 25 (1932)

Wagenfuhr, R., and W. Voss, 'Trade unions and the world economic crisis', in H. van der Wee, ed., *The great depression revisited. Essays on the economics of the thirties,* Nijhoff, The Hague (1972)

Wheeler, R. F., 'Organized sport and organized labour. The workers' sports movement', *Journal of Contemporary History,* 13 (1978)

Wright, P. Q., *Unemployment as a world problem,* University of Chicago Press, Chicago, Ill. (1931)

Young, E., *Labour in Europe and America,* U.S. Bureau of Statistics, Philadelphia, Pa. (1875)

INCOMES, WAGES AND PRICES

Braudel, F., and F. C. Spooner, 'Prices in Europe from 1450 to 1750', in E. E. Rich and C. H. Wilson, eds, *The economy of expanding Europe in the sixteenth and seventeenth centuries,* The Cambridge Economic History of Europe, vol. 4, Cambridge University Press, Cambridge (1967)

Deaton, A. S., 'The structure of demand, 1920–70', in C. M. Cipolla, ed., *The twentieth century.* Fontana Economic History of Europe, vol. 5, part 1, Collins/Fontana, Glasgow (1976)

Farnsworth, H. C., 'Decline and recovery of wheat prices in the nineties', *Wheat Studies,* 10 (1934)

Galenson, W., 'Social security and economic development', *Industrial and Labour Relations Review,* 21 (1968)

Heilperin, M. A., *Postwar European inflation, World War I. A study of selected cases,* National Bureau of Economic Research, New York (1945)

Hoffner, C., 'The compulsory payment of family allowances in Belgium, France and Italy', *International Labour Review,* 32 (1935)

International Labour Office, 'Food consumption of working-class families in certain countries', *International Labour Review,* 28 (1933)

International Labour Office, 'Recent family budget enquiries', *International Labour Review,* 28 (1933)

International Labour Office, 'An international survey of recent family living studies', parts 1 and 2, *International Labour Review,* 39 (1939)

Jefferson, M., 'A record of inflation', in M. Jefferson, ed., *Inflation,* John Calder, London (1977)

Kiss, I. N., 'Money, prices, values and purchasing power from the sixteenth to the eighteenth century', *Journal of European Economic History,* 9 (1980)

Kuznets, S., 'Quantitative aspects of the economic growth nations. The share and structure of consumption', *Economic Development and Cultural Change,* 10 (1961–62)

League of Nations, *The course and control of inflation. A review of monetary experience in Europe after World War I,* League of Nations, Geneva (1946)

Maier, C. S., 'The politics of inflation in the twentieth century', in F. Hirsch and J. Goldthorpe, eds, *The political economy of inflation,* Martin Robertson, London (1978)

Minchinton, W. E., 'Patterns of demand, 1750–1914', in C. M. Cipolla, ed., *The industrial revolution.* Fontana Economic History of Europe, vol. 3, Collins/Fontana, Glasgow (1973)

Phelps Brown, E. H., 'Levels and movements of industrial productivity and real wages internationally compared', *Economic Journal,* 83 (1973)

Phelps Brown, E. H., and M. H. Browne, *A century of pay. The course of pay and production in*

France, Germany and Sweden, the United Kingdom and the United States of America, 1860–1960, Macmillan, London (1968)

Phelps Brown, E. H., and S. V. Hopkins, 'The course of wage rates in five countries, 1860–1939', *Oxford Economic Papers*, 2 (1950)

Richardson, J. H., 'Some aspects of recent wage movements and tendencies in various countries', *International Labour Review*, 17 (1928)

Roberts, C. A., 'Interregional *per capita* income differentials and convergence, 1880–1950', *Journal of Economic History*, 39 (1979)

Schwartz, A. J., 'Secular price change in historical perspective', *Journal of Money, Credit and Banking*, 5 (1973)

Spooner, F. C., 'Secular price movements and problems in capital formation', *Papers presented to the second international conference of economic history, Aix-en-Provence, 1962*, Mouton, Paris (1965)

Staehle, H., 'An international enquiry into living costs', *International Labour Review*, 26 (1932)

Turnau, I., 'Consumption of clothes in Europe between the sixteenth and the eighteenth centuries', *Journal of European Economic History*, 5 (1976)

Uselding, P., 'Wage and consumption levels in England and on the continent in the 1830s', *Journal of European Economic History*, 4 (1975)

URBAN HISTORY

Bairoch, P., 'Urbanisation and economic development in the Western world. Some provisional conclusions of an empirical study', in H. Schmal, ed., *Patterns of European urbanisation since 1500*, Croom Helm, London (1981)

Barley, M. W., ed., *European towns. Their archaeology and early history*, Academic Press, London (1977)

Benevolo, L., *The origins of modern town planning*, Routledge, London (1967)

Blackwell, W. L., 'Geography, history and the city in Europe and Russia', *Journal of Urban History*, 6 (1980)

Blumenfeld, H., *The modern metropolis. Its origins, growth, characteristics and planning*, Massachusetts Institute of Technology Press, Cambridge, Mass. (1967)

Burke, P., 'Some reflections on the pre-industrial city', *Urban History Yearbook* (1975)

Choay, F., *The modern city. Planning in the nineteenth century*, Studio Vista, London (1969)

Collins, G. R., *The modern city. Planning in the twentieth century*, Studio Vista, London (n.d.)

Collins, G. R., and C. C., *Camillo Sitte and the birth of modern city planning*, Phaidon Press, London (1965)

Collins, G. R. and C. C., 'Camillo Sitte reappraised', in R. Kain, ed., *Planning for conservation*, Mansell, London (1981)

Conrads, U., and H. G. Sperlich, *Fantastic architecture. Utopian building and planning in modern times*, Architectural Press, London (1963)

Curl, J. S., *European cities and society. A study of the influence of political climate on town design*, Leonard Hill, London (1970)

de Vries, J., 'Patterns of urbanization in pre-industrial Europe', in H. Schmal, ed., *Patterns of European urbanisation since 1500*, Croom Helm, London (1981)

Diederiks, H., 'Patterns of urban growth since 1500, mainly in western Europe', in H. Schmal, ed., *Patterns of European urbanisation since 1500*, Croom Helm, London (1981)

Geretsegger, H., and M. Peintner, *Otto Wagner, 1841–1918. The expanding city. The beginning of modern architecture*, Pall Mall Press, London (1970)

Gutkind, E. A., *International history of city development*, 8 vols, Collier-Macmillan, London (1964–72)

Hammarström, I., and T. Hall, eds, *Growth and transformation of the modern city*, Swedish Council for Building Research, Stockholm (1979)

Herlihy, D., 'Urbanisation and social change. Report', in M. W. Flinn, ed., *Proceedings of the seventh International Economic History Association conference, Edinburgh, 1978*, Edinburgh University Press, Edinburgh (1978)

Kaelble, H., 'Social mobility in America and Europe. A comparison of nineteenth century cities', *Urban History* (1980)

Kooij, P., 'Urbanisation. What's in a name?', in H. Schmal, ed., *Patterns of European urbanisation since 1500*, Croom Helm, London (1981)

Lampard, E. E., 'Urbanization and social change. An overview', in M. W. Flinn, ed., *Proceedings of the seventh International Economic History Association conference, Edinburgh, 1978*, Edinburgh University Press, Edinburgh (1978)

Lane, B. M., 'Changing attitudes to monumentality. An interpretation of European architecture and urban form, 1880–1914', in I. Hammerström and T. Hall, eds *Growth and transformation of the modern city*, Swedish Council for Building

Research, Stockholm (1979)

Lees, A. and L., eds, *The urbanization of European society in the nineteenth century*, D. C. Heath, Lexington, Mass. (1976)

Meller, H. 'Cities and evolution. Patrick Geddes as an internation prophet of town planning before 1914', in A. Sutcliffe, ed., *The rise of modern urban planning, 1800–1914*, Mansell, London (1981)

Merrington, J., 'Town and country in the transition to capitalism', *New Left Review*, 93 (1975)

Munro, W. B., *The government of European cities*, Macmillan, New York (1909)

Peets, E., *On the art of designing cities*, Massachusetts Institute of Technology Press, Cambridge, Mass. (1968)

Rude, G., 'Urbanization and popular protest in eighteenth century western Europe', *Eighteenth Century Life*, 2 (1976)

Schmal, H., ed., *Patterns of European urbanization since 1500*, Croom Helm, London (1981)

Schorske, C., 'The idea of the city in European thought. Voltaire to Spengler', in O. Handlin, and J. Burchard, eds, *The historian and the city*, Massachusetts Institute of Technology Press, Cambridge, Mass. (1963)

Sitte, C., *The art of building cities*, Reinhold, New York (1945)

Sitte, C., *City planning according to artistic principles*, Phaidon Press, London (1965)

Sutcliffe, A., *A history of modern town planning. A bibliographic guide*, University of Birmingham Centre for Urban and Regional Studies, Research Memorandum No. 57, Birmingham (1977)

Sutcliffe, A., ed., *The rise of modern urban planning, 1800–1914*, Mansell, London (1980)

Weber, A. F., *The growth of cities in the nineteenth century. A study in statistics*, Macmillan, New York (1899)

SOCIAL STRUCTURE AND SOCIAL CONDITIONS

Abramson, P. R., 'Social class and political change in western Europe', *Comparative Political Studies*, 4 (1971)

Anderson, E. N. and P. R., *Political institutions and social change in continental Europe in the nineteenth century*, University of California Press, Berkeley, Cal. (1967)

Anderson, M., *Approaches to the history of the Western family, 1500–1914*, Macmillan, London (1980)

Aries, P., 'Laws and customs relating to remarriage', in J. Dupaquier *et al.*, *Marriage and remarriage in populations of the past*, Academic Press, London (1981)

Arriaza, A. J., 'Mousnier and Barber. The theoretical underpinning of the "Society of Orders" in early modern Europe', *Past and Present*, 89 (1980)

Athey, L. L., 'From social conscience to social action. The consumers' leagues in Europe, 1900–14', *Social Science Review*, 52 (1978)

Behrens, B., 'Government and society', in E. E. Rich and C. H. Wilson, eds, *The Cambridge Economic History of Europe*, vol. 5, Cambridge University Press, Cambridge (1977)

Berkner, L. K., 'Rural family organisation in Europe. A problem in comparative history', *Peasant Studies Newsletter*, 1 (1972) [comment by A. Plakans, 2 (1973)]

Bezucha, R. J., ed., *Modern European social history*, D. C. Heath, Lexington, Mass. (1972)

Biziere, J. M., 'Hot beverages and the enterprising spirit in eighteenth century Europe', *Journal of Psychohistory*, 7 (1979) [nutrition and social customs]

Boxer, M. J., and J. H. Quataert, eds, *Socialist women. European socialist feminism in the nineteenth and twentieth centuries*, Elsevier, New York (1978)

Branca, P., 'A new perspective on women's work. A comparative typology', *Journal of Social History*, 9 (1975)

Branca, P., *Women in Europe since 1750*, Croom Helm, London (1978)

Bridenthal, R., and C. Koonz, eds, *Becoming visible. Women in European history*, Houghton Mifflin, Boston, Mass. (1977)

Bruford, W. H., 'German constitutional and social development, 1795–1830', in C. W. Crawley, ed., *War and peace in an age of upheaval, 1793–1830. The New Cambridge Modern History*, vol. 9, Cambridge University Press, Cambridge (1965)

Callahan, W. J., and D. Higgs, eds, *Church and society in Catholic Europe of the eighteenth century*, Cambridge University Press, Cambridge (1979)

Chapin, F. S., *An historical introduction to social economy*, Century, New York (1917)

Chirot, D., *Social change in the twentieth century*, Harcourt Brace Jovanovich, New York (1977)

Davis, G. H., 'Prisoners of war in twentieth century economies', *Journal of Contemporary History*, 12 (1977)

Denby, E., *Europe re-housed*, Allen and Unwin, London (1938)

Dixon, R. A., and E. K. Eberhart, *Economics and cultural change*, McGraw-Hill, London (1938)

Eager, J. M., 'The early history of quarantine', *Bulletin of the Yellow Fever Institute*, 12 (1903)

Eley, G., 'Nationalism and social history', *Social History*, 6 (1981)

Evans, R. J., *The feminists. Women's emancipation movements in Europe, America and Australasia, 1840–1920*, Croom Helm, London (1977)

Fischer, W., 'Social tensions at early stages of industrialization', *Comparative Studies in Society and History*, 9 (1966)

Flandrin, J. L., *Families in former times. Kinship, household and sexuality*, Cambridge University Press, Cambridge (1979)

Forster, E. and R., *European diet from pre-industrial to modern times*, Harper and Row, New York (1975)

Forster, R. and E., eds, *European society in the eighteenth century*, Macmillan, London (1969)

Futugawa, Y., *Wooden houses in Europe*, A.D.A. Edita, Tokyo (1978)

Gattrell, V. A. C., *Crime and the law. The social history of crime in western Europe since 1500*, Europa, London (1980)

Gerschenkron, A., 'Social attitudes, entrepreneurship and economic development', *Explorations in Entrepreneurial History*, 6 (1953–54) [comments also by T. C. Cochran, D. S. Landes, J. E. Sawyer and Gerschenkron also in 6 (1953–54) and 7 (1954–55)]

Gerschenkron, A., 'Social attitudes, entrepreneurship and economic development', *International Social Science Bulletin*, 6 (1954)

Gillis, J. R., *Youth in history. Tradition and change in European age relations, 1770 to the present*, Academic Press, New York (1974)

Gillis, J. R., *The development of European society, 1770–1870*, Houghton Mifflin, Boston, Mass. (1977)

Goodwin, A., ed., *The European nobility in the eighteenth century*, A. and C. Black, London (1953)

Goody, J., *et al.*, *Family and inheritance. Rural society in western Europe, 1200–1800*, Cambridge University Press, Cambridge (1976)

Gordon, E., *The anti-alcohol movement in Europe*, Revell, New York (1913)

Graff, H. J., *Literacy and social development in the West. A reader*, Cambridge University Press, Cambridge (1981)

Guye, R., 'A further contribution to the international comparison of rents', *International Labour Review*, 34 (1936)

Habakkuk, H. J., 'Family structure and economic change in nineteenth century Europe', *Journal of Economic History*, 15 (1955)

Haines, M. R., 'Industrial work and the family life cycle, 1889–90', *Research in Economic History*, 4 (1979)

Harris, P. M. G., 'Family and household across time and culture', *Journal of European Economic History*, 3 (1974)

Hechter, M., 'Ethnicity and industrialization. On the proliferation of the cultural division of labor', *Ethnicity*, 3 (1976)

Hobsbawm, E. J., and J. W. Scott, 'Political shoemaker', *Past and Present*, 89 (1980)

Holton, R. J., 'The crowd in history. Some problems of theory and method', *Social History*, 3 (1978)

Hufton, O., *Europe. Privilege and protest, 1730–89*, Fontana, London (1980)

Hurwitz, E. F., 'The international sisterhood', in R. Bridenthal and C. Koonz, eds, *Becoming visible. Women in European history*, Houghton Mifflin, Boston, Mass. (1977)

Jones, E. L., 'The environment and the economy', in P. Burke, ed., *Companion volume. The New Cambridge Modern History*, vol. 13, Cambridge University Press, Cambridge (1979)

International Labour Office, 'Housing as a post-war western Europe, 1700–1900', in C. Tilly and E. A. *Review*, 10 (1924)

Kamenka, E., and F. B. Smith, *Intellectuals and revolution. Socialism and the experience of 1848*, St Martin's Press, New York (1979)

Laslett, P., ed., *Household and family in past time*, Cambridge University Press, Cambridge (1972)

Laslett, P., 'The family as a public and private institution. A historical perspective', *Journal of Marriage and the Family*, 35 (1973)

Liepmann, K., 'Public utility housing', parts 1 and 2, *International Labour Review*, 20 (1929)

Lindsay, J. O., 'The social classes and the foundations of the states', in J. O. Lindsay, ed., *The old regime, 1713–63. The New Cambridge Modern History*, vol. 7, Cambridge University Press, Cambridge (1957)

Lis, C., and H. Soly, *Poverty and capitalism in pre-industrial Europe*, Harvester Press, Brighton (1979)

Lopes, R. P., 'The economic depression and public health', *International Labour Review*, 29 (1934)

Lorch, A., *Trends in European social legislation between the two world wars*, Editions de la Maison Française, New York (1943)

Lorence, B. W., 'Parents and children in eighteenth century Europe', *History of Childhood Quarterly,* 2 (1974)

Malcolmson, R. W., 'Popular culture and social change', *Journal of Popular Culture,* 4 (1971)

Martin, E. W., ed., *Comparative development in social welfare,* Allen and Unwin, London (1972)

Mathias, P., 'Adam's burden. Diagnoses of poverty in post-medieval Europe and the Third World now', *Tijdschrift voor Geschiedenis,* 89 (1976)

Mayer, A. J., *The persistence of the old regime. Europe to the Great War,* Pantheon, New York (1981)

Maynes, M. J., 'The virtues of archaism. The political economy of schooling in Europe, 1750–1850', *Comparative Studies in Society and History,* 21 (1979)

Medick, H., 'The proto-industrial family economy. The structural function of household and family during the transition from peasant to industrial capitalism', *Social History,* 1 (1976)

Mendels, F. F., 'Social mobility and phases of industrialization', *Journal of Interdisciplinary History,* 7 (1976–77)

Mendels, F. F., and L. K. Berkner, 'Inheritance systems, family structure and demographic patterns in western Europe, 1700–1900', in C. Tilly and E. A. Wrigley, eds, *Historical studies of changing fertility,* Princeton University Press, Princeton, N.J. (1978)

Méquet, G., 'Housing problems and the depression', *International Labour Review,* 27 (1933)

Merriman, J. M., ed., *Consciousness and class experience in nineteenth century Europe,* Holmes and Meier, New York (1979)

Mileykovsky, A., 'Coexistence of two systems and transformation of social structures', *Papers presented to the fourth international conference of economic history, Bloomington, 1968,* Mouton, Paris (1973)

Minge-Kalman, W., 'The industrial revolution and the European family. The industrialization of "childhood" as a market for family labour', *Comparative Studies in Society and History,* 20 (1978)

Mitterauer, M., and R. Sieder, *The European family. Patriarchy to partnership from the Middle Ages to the present,* Blackwell, Oxford (1982)

Mommsen, W. J., and G. Hirschfeld, *Social protest, violence and terror in nineteenth and twentieth century Europe,* Macmillan, London (1982)

Nicholson, M., 'Economy, society and environment, 1920–70', in C. M. Cipolla, ed., *The twentieth century.* Fontana Economic History of Europe, vol. 5, part 2, Collins/Fontana, Glasgow (1976)

O'Boyle, L., 'The middle class in western Europe', *American Historical Review,* 71 (1966)

O'Boyle, L., 'The problem of an excess of educated men in western Europe, 1800–50', *Journal of Modern History,* 42 (1970)

O'Boyle, L., 'A possible model for the study of nineteenth century secondary education in Europe', *Journal of Social History,* 12 (1978)

Parker, G., 'An educational revolution? The growth of literacy and schooling in early modern Europe', *Tijdschrift voor Geschiedenis,* 93 (1980)

Pelenski, J., ed., *The American and European revolutions, 1776–1848. Sociopolitical and ideological aspects,* University of Iowa Press, Iowa (1980)

Phayer, J. M., *Sexual liberation and religion in nineteenth century Europe,* Croom Helm, London (1977)

Plakans, A., 'The study of social structure from listings of inhabitants', *Journal of Family History,* 4 (1979)

Rabb, T. K., and R. I. Rotberg, eds, *The family in history. Interdisciplinary essays,* Harper and Row, New York (1973)

Raeff, M., 'The well ordered police state and the development of modernity in seventeenth- and eighteenth-century Europe. An attempt at a comparative approach', *American Historical Review,* 80 (1975)

Rimlinger, G. V., 'Welfare policy and economic development. A comparative historical perspective', *Journal of Economic History,* 26 (1966)

Rimlinger, G. V., *Welfare policy and industrialization in Europe, America and Russia,* John Wiley, New York (1971)

Ringer, F. K., *Education and society in modern Europe,* Indiana University Press, Bloomington, Ind. (1979)

Robbins, H. H., and F. Deak, 'The familial property rights of illegitimate children. A comparative study', *Columbia Law Review,* 30 (1930)

Rosenberg, C., 'Cholera in nineteenth century Europe. A tool for social and economic analysis', *Comparative Studies in Society and History,* 8 (1966)

Rowbotham, S., *Hidden from history. Rediscovering women in history from the seventeenth century to the present.* Pantheon Books, New York (1975)

Rudé, G., *The crowd in history, 1730–1848,* John Wiley, New York (1964)

Rudé, G., *Europe in the eighteenth century. Aristoc-*

racy and the bourgeois challenge, Prager, New York (1972)

Ruud, C. A., 'Limits on the "freed" press of eighteenth and nineteenth century Europe', *Journalism Quarterly,* 56 (1979)

Russell, C., *Science and social change, 1700–1900,* Macmillan, London (1982)

Sabean, D., 'Aspects of kinship behaviour and property in rural western Europe before 1800', in J. Goody *et al., Family and inheritance. Rural society in western Europe, 1200–1800,* Cambridge University Press, Cambridge (1976)

Schieder, T., 'Political and social developments in Europe', in F. H. Hinsley, ed., *Material progress and world-wide problems, 1870–98.* The New Cambridge Modern History, vol. 11, Cambridge University Press, Cambridge (1962)

Scott, J. W., and L. A. Tilly, 'Woman's work and the family in nineteenth century Europe', in R. I. Rothberg, ed., *The family in history,* Harper and Row, New York (1973)

Scott, J. W., and L. A. Tilly, 'Women's work and the family in nineteenth century Europe', *Comparative Studies in Society and History,* 17 (1975)

Scull, A. T., 'Madness and segregative control. The rise of the insane asylum', *Social Problems,* 24 (1977)

Segalen, M., *Women in peasant societies from the later Middle Ages to the present,* Blackwell, Oxford (1982)

Shorter, E., 'Illegitimacy, sexual revolution and social change in modern Europe', *Journal of Interdisciplinary History,* 2 (1971–72)

Shorter, E., *The making of the modern family,* Collins, Glasgow (1975)

Soman, A., 'Deviance and criminal justice in western Europe, 1300–1800. An essay in structure', *Criminal Justice History,* 1 (1980) [attention devoted mainly to Paris]

Stearns, P. N., *European society in upheaval,* Macmillan, London (1967)

Stevenson, J. A., 'Daniel de Leon and European socialism, 1890–1914', *Science and Society,* 44 (1980)

Sturmer, M., 'An economy of delight. Court artisans of the eighteenth century', *Business History Review,* 53 (1979)

Tenfelde, K., 'Mining festivals in the nineteenth century', *Journal of Contemporary History,* 13 (1978)

Teuteberg, H. J., 'The general relationship between diet and industrialization', in E. and R. Forster, eds, *European diet from pre-industrial to modern*

times, Harper and Row, New York (1975)

Thomas, W. L., *et al., Man's role in changing the face of the earth,* University of Chicago Press, Chicago, Ill. (1956)

Thomson, D., 'The transformation of social life', in D. Thomson, ed., *The era of violence, 1898–1945.* The New Cambridge Modern History, vol. 12, Cambridge University Press, Cambridge (1960)

Thomson, D., 'The transformation of social life', in C. L. Mowat, ed., *The shifting balance of forces, 1898–1945.* The New Cambridge Modern History, vol. 12, Cambridge University Press, Cambridge (rev. 2nd edn 1968)

Tilly, C., 'Food supply and public order in modern Europe', in C. Tilly, ed., *The formation of national states in western Europe,* Princeton University Press, Princeton, N.J. (1975)

Tilly, C., 'Revolutions and collective violence', in F. T. Greenstein and N. Polsby, eds, *Handbook of political science,* vol. 3, Addison-Wesley, Reading, Mass. (1975)

Tilly, C., *et al., The rebellious century, 1830–1920,* Harvard University Press, Cambridge, Mass. (1975)

Tilly, L. A., 'Women and collective action in Europe', in D. McGuigan, ed., *The role of women in conflict and peace,* Center for Continuing Education of Women, Ann Arbor, Mich. (1977)

Tilly, L. A., and J. W. Scott, *Women, work and family,* Holt Rinehart and Winston, New York (1978)

Tilly, L. A. and C., eds, *Class conflict and collective action,* Sage Publications, Beverly Hills, Cal. (1981)

Tipps, D. C., 'Modernization and the comparative study of societies', *Comparative Studies in Society and History,* 15 (1973)

van den Berg, G. van B., 'The interconnection between processes of state and class formation', *Acta Politica,* 3 (1976)

Vann, R. T., 'Toward a new life style. Women in pre-industrial capitalism', in R. Bridenthal and C. Koonz, eds, *Becoming visible. Women in European history,* Houghton Mifflin, Boston, Mass. (1977)

Wachter, K. W., *et al., Statistical studies of historical social structure,* Academic Press, London (1978)

Weber, E. J., *A modern history of Europe. Men, cultures and societies from the Renaissance to the present,* Hale, London (1973)

Wechsberg, J., *The lost world of the great spas,* Harper and Row, New York (1979)

Weisser, M. R., *Crime and punishment in early modern Europe,* Humanities Press, Atlantic Highlands, N.J. (1979)

Wheaton, R., 'Family and kinship in western Europe. The problem of the joint family household', *Journal of Interdisciplinary History,* 5 (1974–75)

Williams, E. N., *The ancien régime in Europe. Government and society in the major states, 1648–1789,* Harper and Row, New York (1970)

Woytinsky, W. S., *The social consequences of the economic depression,* International Labour Office, Geneva (1936)

Wrigley, E. A., 'Reflections on the history of the family', *Daedalus,* 106 (1977)

ECONOMIC POLICY AND THOUGHT

Aldcroft, D. H., 'The development of the managed economy before 1939', *Journal of Contemporary History,* 4 (1969)

Blaug, M., 'A case of emperor's clothes. Perroux theories of economic domination', *Kyklos,* 17 (1964)

Blitz, R. C., 'Mercantilist policies and the pattern of world trade, 1500–1750', *Journal of Economic History,* 27 (1967)

Cocks, P., 'Towards a Marxist theory of European integration', *International Organization,* 34 (1980)

Day, R. B., *The "crisis" and the "crash". Soviet studies of the West, 1917–39,* N.L.B., London (1981)

Edwards, G. W., 'Government control of foreign investments', *American Economic Review,* 18 (1928)

Gerschenkron, A., 'History of economic doctrines and economic history', *American Economic Review,* 59 (1969)

Habakkuk, H. J., 'Population, commerce and economic ideas', in A. Goodwin, ed., *The American and French revolutions, 1763–93.* The New Cambridge Modern History, vol. 8, Cambridge University Press, Cambridge (1965)

Hocevar, T., 'Monetary theory in J. F. Kryger's second Ljubljana essay (1779)', *Economy and History,* 18 (1975)

Johnson, H. G., 'Mercantilism. Past, present and future', *Manchester School of Economic and Social Studies,* 42 (1974)

Kahan, A., 'Nineteenth century European experience with policies of economic nationalism', in H. G. Johnson, ed., *Economic nationalism in old and new states,* University of Chicago Press, Chicago, Ill. (1967)

Lane, F. C., 'The role of governments in economic growth in early modern times', *Journal of Economic History,* 35 (1975)

Lorwin, L. L., *Planning in western Europe,* University of Chicago Press, Chicago, Ill. (1932)

Maddison, A., 'Economic policy and performance in Europe, 1913–70', in C. M. Cipolla, ed., *The twentieth century.* Fontana Economic History of Europe, vol. 5, part 2, Collins/Fontana, Glasgow (1976)

Martin, P. W., 'The present status of economic planning', *International Labour Review,* 35 (1937)

Nussbaum, F. L., *A history of the economic institutions of Europe. An introduction to Der moderne Kapitalismus of Werner Sombart,* Crofts, New York (1937)

Spengler, J. J., 'Institutions, institutionalism, 1776–1974', *Journal of Economic Issues,* 8 (1974)

Viner, J., 'The economist in history', *American Economic Review,* 53 (1963)

Ward, B., 'National economic planning and policies in twentieth century Europe, 1920–70', in C. M. Cipolla, ed., *The twentieth century.* Fontana Economic History of Europe, vol. 5, part 2, Collins/Fontana, Glasgow (1976)

Winch, D., 'The emergence of economics as a science, 1750–1870', in C. M. Cipolla, ed., *The industrial revolution.* Fontana Economic History of Europe, vol. 3, Collins/Fontana, Glasgow (1973)

Woytinsky, W. S., 'International measures to create employment. A remedy for the depression', *International Labour Review,* 25 (1925)

THEORIES AND TYPOLOGIES

Adelman, I., and C. T. Morris, 'Patterns of industrialization in the nineteenth and early twentieth centuries. A cross-sectional quantitative study', in P. Uselding, ed., *Research in economic history,* vol. 5, JAI Press, London (1980)

Almquist, E. L., 'Pre-famine Ireland and the theory of European proto-industrialization', *Journal of Economic History,* 39 (1979)

Ashworth, W., 'Backwardness, discontinuity, and industrial development', *Economic History Review,* 23 (1970)

Ashworth, W., 'Typologies and evidence. Has nineteenth-century Europe a guide to economic growth?', *Economic History Review,* 30 (1977)

Barsby, S. L., 'Economic backwardness and the characteristics of development', *Journal of*

Economic History, 29 (1969)

Cairncross, A. K., 'The stages of economic growth', *Economic History Review*, 13 (1961)

Cameron, R. E., 'The logistics of European economic growth. A note on historical periodization', *Journal of European Economic History*, 2 (1973)

Checkland, S. G., 'Theories of economic and social evolution. The Rostow challenge', *Scottish Journal of Political Economy*, 7 (1960)

Chenery, H. B., 'Patterns of industrial growth', *American Economic Review*, 50 (1960)

Chenery, H. B., and L. Taylor, 'Development patterns. Among countries and over time', *Review of Economics and Statistics*, 50 (1968)

Clemhout, S., 'Types of industrialization and their forecasting value', *Papers presented to the second international conference of economic history, Aix-en-Provence, 1962*, Mouton, Paris (1965)

Gerschenkron, A., *Economic backwardness in historical perspective*, Harvard University Press, Cambridge, Mass. (1968)

Gerschenkron, A., *Continuity in history and other essays*, Harvard University Press, Cambridge, Mass. (1968)

Hershlag, Z. Y., 'Theory of stages of economic growth in historical perspective', *Kyklos*, 22 (1969)

Hoselitz, B. F., 'Patterns of economic growth', *Canadian Journal of Economics and Political Science*, 21 (1955)

Hoselitz, B. F., ed., *Theories of economic growth*, The Free Press, New York (1960)

Hughes, J. R. T., 'Balanced economic growth in history. A critique. Foreign trade and balanced growth. The historical framework', *American Economic Review. Papers and Proceedings*, 49 (1959)

Jones, E. L., 'Institutional determinism and the rise of the Western world', *Economic Enquiry*, 12 (1974)

Jones, E. L., 'A new essay on Western civilization in its economic aspects', *Australian Economic History Review*, 16 (1976)

Lago, A. M., 'The Hoffman industrial growth development path. An international comparison', *Weltwirtschaftliches Archiv*, 103 (1969)

North, D. C., 'A note on Professor Rostow's "take-off" into self-sustained economic growth', *Manchester School*, 26 (1958)

North, D. C., 'Institutional change and economic growth', *Journal of Economic History*, 21 (1971)

North, D. C., and R. P. Thomas, 'An economic theory of the growth of the Western world', *Economic History Review*, 23 (1970)

North, D. C., and R. P. Thomas, *The rise of the Western world*, Cambridge University Press, London (1973)

Ohlin, B., 'Balanced economic growth in history', *American Economic Review, Papers and Proceedings*, 49 (1959)

Ringrose, D. R., 'European economic growth. Comments on the North–Thomas theory', *Economic History Review*, 26 (1973)

Robinson, S., 'Theories of economic growth and development. Methodology and content', *Economic Development and Cultural Change*, 21 (1972)

Rostow, W. W., 'The take-off into self-sustained growth', *Economic Journal*, 66 (1956)

Rostow, W. W., 'Industrialization and economic growth', *Papers presented to the first international economic history conference, Stockholm, 1960*, Mouton, Paris (1960)

Rostow, W. W., *The stages of economic growth*, Cambridge University Press, Cambridge (1960)

Rostow, W. W., ed., *The economics of take-off into sustained growth*, Macmillan, London (1963)

Rostow, W. W., 'The beginnings of modern growth in Europe. An essay in synthesis', *Journal of Economic History*, 33 (1973)

Rostow, W. W., 'Kondratieff, Schumpeter, and Kuznets. Trend periods revisited', *Journal of Economic History*, 35 (1975)

Weaver, F. S., 'Relative backwardness and cumulative change. A comparative approach to European industrialization', *Studies in Comparative International Development*, 9 (1974)

Williamson, J. G., 'Regional inequality and the process of national development. A description of the patterns', *Economic Development and Cultural Change*, 13 (1965)

ECONOMIC ASPECTS OF WAR

Abrahams, P., 'American bankers and the economic tactics of peace, 1919', *Journal of American History*, 56 (1969)

Anderson, O., 'Economic warfare in the Crimean war', *Economic History Review*, 14 (1961–62)

Bakeless, J., *The economic causes of modern war. A study of the period 1878–1918*, Moffat Yard and Co., New York (1921)

Bane, S. L., and R. H. Lutz, eds, *Organization of American relief in Europe, 1918–19. Selected documents*, Stanford University Press, Stanford, Cal. (1943)

Baruch, B. M., *The making of the reparation and economic sections of the treaty*, Harper and Row,

New York (1920)

Bell, A. C., *A history of the blockade of Germany, Austria–Hungary, Bulgaria and Turkey, 1914–18*, HMSO, London (1937)

Bogart, E. L., *Direct and indirect costs of the Great War*, Oxford University Press, London (1919)

Boswell, J. L., 'Some neglected aspects of the world war debt payments', *American Economic Review*, 21 (1931)

Boulding, K. E., *The economics of peace*, Prentice-Hall, New York (1945)

Bowley, A. L., *Some economic consequences of the Great War*, Thornton Butterworth, London (1930)

Brown, W. A., 'German reparations and the international flow of capital. Discussion', *American Economic Review, Papers and Proceedings*, 20 (1930)

Butler, R., 'The peace treaty settlement of Versailles, 1918–33', in C. L. Mowat, ed., *The shifting balance of world forces, 1898–1945*. The New Cambridge Modern History, vol. 12, Cambridge University Press, Cambridge (1968)

Clapham, J. H., 'Europe after the great wars, 1816 and 1920', *Economic Journal*, 30 (1920)

Clark, J. M., *et al.*, *Readings in the economics of war*, University of Chicago Press, Chicago, Ill. (1918)

Cooper, J. M., *Causes and consequences of World War I*, Croom Helm, London (1975)

Crouzet, F., 'Wars blockade and economic change in Europe, 1792–1815', *Journal of Economic History*, 24 (1964) [see also comment by R. Tilly in same issue]

Dawes, R. C., *The Dawes Plan in the making*, Bobbs-Merrill, Indianapolis, Ind. (1925)

Dickson, P. G. M., and J. Sperling, 'War finance, 1689–1714', in J. S. Bromley, ed., *The rise of Great Britain and Russia, 1688–1715*. The New Cambridge Modern History, vol. 6, Cambridge University Press, Cambridge (1970)

Ebersole, J. F., 'Deflationary indemnity hopes and war debts', *Harvard Business Review*, 10 (1931)

Einzig, P., *The economics of rearmament*, Kegan Paul Trench Trubner, London (1934)

Einzig, P., *Economic problems of the next war*, Macmillan, London (1939)

Einzig, P., *Appeasement before, during and after the war*, Macmillan, London (1941)

Fisk, H. E., *The inter-ally debts. An analysis of war and post-war public finance, 1914–23*, Bankers Trust Company, New York (1924)

Gilbert, C., *American financing of World War I*, Greenwood Press, Westport, Conn. (1970)

Gottlieb, L. R., 'Indebtedness of principal belligerents', *Quarterly Journal of Economics*, 33 (1918–19)

Hardach, G., *The first world war, 1914–18*, Allen Lane, London (1977)

Hogan, M. J., 'The United States and the problem of international economic control. American attitudes toward European reconstruction, 1918–20', *Pacific Historical Review*, 44 (1975)

Kaiser, D. E., *Economic diplomacy and the origins of the second world war. Germany, Britain, France and Eastern Europe, 1930–39*, Princeton University Press, Princeton, N.J. (1980)

Keynes, J. M., *The economic consequences of the peace*, Macmillan, London (1919)

Keynes, J. M., *A revision of the treaty*, Macmillan, London (1922)

Kiraly, B. K., 'War and society in western and east central Europe during the eighteenth and nineteenth centuries. Similarities and contrasts', in B. K. Kiraly and G. E. Rothenburg, eds, *War and society in west central Europe*, Brooklyn College Press, New York (1979)

League of Nations, *The transition from war to peace economy. Report of the delegation on economic depressions*, League of Nations, Geneva (1943)

Lloyd George, D., *The truth about reparations and war debts*, Heinemann, London (1932)

Lutz, H. L., 'Inter-allied debts, reparations and national policy', *Journal of Political Economy*, 38 (1930)

Maier, C. S., 'The truth about the treaties?', *Journal of Modern History*, 51 (1979)

Marwick, A., *War and social change in the twentieth century. A comparative study of Britain, France, Germany, Russia and the United States*, Macmillan, London (1974)

Mason, T. W., 'Some origins of the second world war', *Past and Present*, 29 (1964)

Mendershausen, H., *The economics of war*, Prentice-Hall, New York (1940)

Moulton, H. G., 'Economic problems involved in the payment of international debts', *American Economic Review, Papers and Proceedings*, 16 (1926)

Moulton, H. G., and L. Pasvolsky, *World war debt settlements*, Macmillan, London (1926)

Moulton, H. G., and L. Pasvolsky, *War debts and world prosperity*, Brookings Institution, Washington, D.C. (1932)

Oberle, W. E., 'War debts and international trade theory', *American Economic Review*, 15 (1925)

Philips, A., *Economic aspects of reparations and inter-allied debts*, S. C. van Doesburgh, Leiden

(1930)

Robbins, L., *The economic causes of war*, Cape, London (1939)

Saucerman, S. A., *International transfers of territory in Europe with the names of the affected political subdivisions as of 1910–14 and the present*, U.S. Government Printing Office, Washington, D.C. (1937)

Schulz, G., *Revolutions and peace treaties*, Methuen, London (1972)

Scott, J. B., ed., *The Paris peace conference. History and documents*, 6 vols, Columbia University Press, New York (1934–42)

Seligman, E. R. A., 'The cost of the war and how it was met', *American Economic Review*, 9 (1919)

Staley, E., *War and the private investor. A study of the relations of international politics and international private investment*, Doubleday Doran, Garden City, N.Y. (1935)

Staley, E., *Raw materials in peace and war*, Council on Foreign Relations, New York (1937)

Stamp, J., *Taxation during the war*, Oxford University Press, London (1932)

Stamp, J., *The financial aftermath of war*, Benn, London (1932)

Temperley, H. W. V., ed., *A history of the peace conference of Paris*, 6 vols, Oxford University Press, London (1920–24)

Trouton, R., 'Cancellation of inter-allied debts', *Economic Journal*, 31 (1921)

Viner, J., 'Who paid for the war?', *Journal of Political Economy*, 28 (1920)

Winter, J. M., ed., *War and economic development. Essays in memory of David Joslin*, Cambridge University Press, Cambridge (1975)

Wood, G. L., 'Reparations and war debts', *Economic Record, Supplement*, 8 (1932)

HISTORIOGRAPHY AND BIBLIOGRAPHY

Becker, W., 'Methodological aspects in describing bourgeois and industrial revolutions', in P. Bairoch and M. Levy-Leboyer, eds, *Disparities in economic development since the industrial revolution*, Macmillan, London (1981)

Berend, I. T., 'The indivisibility of the social and economic factors of economic growth. A methodological study', in M. W. Flinn, ed., *Proceedings of the seventh international economic history conference, Edinburgh, 1978*, Edinburgh University Press, Edinburgh (1978)

Berkner, L. K., 'The use and misuse of census data for the historical analysis of family structure', *Journal of Interdisciplinary History*, 5 (1974–75)

Cameron, R. E., 'Comparative economic history', in R. E. Gallman, ed., *Recent developments in the study of economic and business history. Essays in memory of Herman E. Kroos*, JAI Press, Greenwich, Conn. (1977)

Clough, S. B., and C. G. Moodie, eds, *European economic history. Documents and readings. Major developments from the end of the Middle Ages to the present*, Van Nostrand, Princeton, N.J. (1965)

Diephouse, D. J., 'Clio's mirror and modern consciousness', *Fides et Histoire*, 13 (1980)

Dovring, F., 'Development as history. A review article', *Comparative Studies in Society and History*, 21 (1979)

Fischer, W., 'Some recent developments of business history in Germany, Austria and Switzerland', *Business History Review*, 37 (1963)

Frey, S. L., *et al., Women in western European history. A select chronological, geographical and topical bibliography*, Harvester Press, Brighton (1982)

Gerschenkron, A., 'Typology of industrial development as a tool of analysis', *Papers presented to the second international conference of economic history, Aix-en-Provence, 1962*, Mouton, Paris (1965)

Gunnarsson, G., 'A study in the historiography of prices', *Economy and History*, 19 (1976)

Iggers, G. G., and H. T. Parker, eds, *International handbook of historical studies. Contemporary research and theory*, Greenwood Press, Westport, Conn. (1979) [individual country studies for most European nations]

Joll, J., 'Europe. An historian's view', *History of European ideas*, 1 (1980)

Kaelble, H., *Historical research on social mobility. Western Europe and the USA in the nineteenth and twentieth centuries*, Croom Helm, London (1981)

Kuznets, S., 'The state as a unit in study of economic growth', *Journal of Economic History*, 11 (1951)

Le Roy Ladurie, E., *et al., The mind and method of the historian*, University of Chicago Press, Chicago (1981)

McNeill, W. H., and M. Kammen, 'Modern European history', in M. Kammen, ed., *The past before us. Contemporary historical writing in the United States*, Cornell University Press, Ithaca, N.Y. (1980)

Mendels, F. F., 'Recent research in European historical demography', *American Historical Review*, 75

(1970)

North, D. C., 'Innovation and diffusion of technology. A theoretical framework', *Papers presented to the fourth international conference of economic history, Bloomington, 1968,* Mouton, Paris (1973) [see also contribution by L. Makkai in the same volume]

Outhwaite, R. B., 'New approaches to European agrarian history', *Historical Journal,* 20 (1977)

Pollard, S., and C. Holmes, eds, *Documents of European economic history,* vol. 1, *The process of industrialisation, 1750–1870* (1968), vol. 2, *Industrial power and national rivalry, 1870–1914* (1972), vol. 3, *The end of the old Europe, 1914–39* (1973), Edward Arnold, London

Reinke, H., 'Archiving machine-readable historical data. Data services of the Center for Historical Social Research', *Historical Social Research,* 12 (1979)

Schaeper, T. J., 'Interuniversity centre for European studies', *French Historical Studies,* 12 (1981)

Schofer, L., 'The history of European Jewry. Search for a method', *Leo Baeck Institute Yearbook,* 24 (1979)

Schorsch, L. L., 'Direct producers and the rise of the factory system', *Science and Society,* 44 (1980–81)

Sutcliffe, A., *The history of urban and regional planning. An annotated bibliography,* Facts on File, New York (1981)

Vivarelli, R., '1870 in European history and historiography' *Journal of Modern History,* 53 (1981)

Wilson, C. H., and G. Parker, eds, *An introduction to the sources of European economic history, 1500–1800,* vol. 1, *Western Europe,* Weidenfeld and Nocolson, London (1977)

STATISTICAL SERIES

Bairoch, P., 'European foreign trade in the nineteenth century. The development of the value and volume of exports (preliminary results)', *Journal of European Economic History,* 2 (1973)

Bairoch, P., 'Geographical structure and trade balance of European foreign trade from 1800 to 1970', *Journal of European Economic History,* 3 (1974)

Bairoch, P., 'Europe's gross national product, 1800–1975', *Journal of European Economic History,* 5 (1976)

Bairoch, P., and J. M. Limbor, 'Changes in the industrial distribution of the world labour force. By region, 1880–1960', *International Labour Review,* 98 (1968)

Baldwin, R. E., 'The commodity composition of trade. Selected industrial countries, 1900–54', *Review of Economics and Statistics,* 40 (1958)

Bidwell, R. L., *Currency conversion tables. A hundred years of change,* Rex Collings, London (1970)

Cairncross, A. K., 'World trade in manufactures since 1900', *Economia Internazionale,* 8 (1955)

Cairncross, A. K., and J. Faaland, 'Long-term trends in Europe's trade', *Economic Journal,* 62 (1952)

Deldlycke, T., *et al., The working population and its structure. International historical statistics,* Université Libre de Bruxelles, Brussels (1968)

Ferenczi, I., 'A historical study of migration statistics', *International Labour Review,* 20 (1929)

Fisk, H. E., 'Some new estimates of national incomes', *American Economic Review,* 20 (1930)

International Conference of Economic Services, *International abstract of economic statistics, 1919–30,* International Conference of Economic Services, London (1934)

Jefferson, M., 'A record of inflation', in M. Jefferson, ed., *Inflation,* John Calder, London (1977)

Kuznets, S., 'Quantitative aspects of the economic growth of nations. Levels and variability of rates of growth', *Economic Development and Cultural Change,* 5 (1956–57)

Kuznets, S., 'Quantitative aspects of the economic growth of nations. Industrial distribution of national product and labor force', *Economic Development and Cultural Change,* Supplement, 5 (1956–57)

Kuznets, S., 'Quantitative aspects of the economic growth of nations. Distribution of national income factor shares', *Economic Development and Cultural Change,* Supplement, 7 (1958–59)

Kuznets, S., 'Quantitative aspects of the economic growth of nations. Long-term trends in capital formation proportions', *Economic Development and Cultural Change,* 9 (1960–61)

Kuznets, S., 'Quantitative aspects of the economic growth of nations. The share and structure of consumption', *Economic Development and Cultural Change,* 10 (1961–62)

Kuznets, S., 'Quantitative aspects of the economic growth of nations. Level and structure of foreign trade. Long-term trends', *Economic Development and Cultural Change,* 15 (1966–67)

Kuznets, S., *Economic growth of nations. Total output and production structure,* Harvard University Press, Cambridge, Mass. (1971)

League of Nations, *Tariff level indices,* League of Nations, Geneva (1927)

League of Nations, *Balances of payments, 1933–38,*

from 1924–26 published as vol. I of *Memorandum on balance of payments and foreign trade balances*, from 1927–28 as vol. I of *Memorandum on international trade and balances of payments*, from 1929–30 as vol. II of *Memorandum on international trade and balances of payments*, in 1931 as vol. II of *Memorandum on trade and balances of payments*, League of Nations, Geneva

League of Nations, *International trade statistics, 1933–38,* from 1924–26 published as vol. II of *Memorandum on balance of payments and foreign trade balances,* from 1927–28 as vol. II of *Memorandum on international trade and balances of payments,* from 1929–30 as vol. III of *Memorandum on international trade and balances of payments,* in 1931 as vol. III of *Memorandum on trade and balances of payments,* League of Nations, Geneva

League of Nations, *Money and Banking,* vol. I, *Monetary Review,* vol. II, *Commercial and central banks since 1931,* in continuation of *Memorandum on commercial banks, 1913–29 and 1925–33* (1931 and 1934), *Commercial banks, 1929–34* (1935) and *Memoranda on currencies and central banks* (1922–26), League of Nations, Geneva

League of Nations, *Public finance, 1928–35* (1936). Similar studies published intermittently in the 1920s under the title of *Memorandum on public finance,* League of Nations, Geneva

League of Nations, *Review of world trade, 1933–38,* from 1924–26 published as vol. I of *Memorandum on balance of payments and foreign trade balances,* for 1931–32 as vol. I of *Memorandum on trade and balances of payments,* League of Nations, Geneva

League of Nations, *Statistical Yearbook* (1927 onwards), League of Nations, Geneva

League of Nations, *World production and prices, 1933–39,* from 1926–32 published as *Memorandum on production and trade* and in 1932 as *Review of world production, 1925–31,* League of Nations, Geneva

Lewis, W. A., 'World production, prices and trade, 1870–1960', *Manchester School,* 20 (1952)

Lewis, W. A., and P. J. O'Leary, 'Secular swings in production and trade, 1870–1913', *Manchester School,* 23 (1955)

Maddison, A., 'Industrial productivity growth in Europe and in the US', *Economica,* 21 (1954)

Maddison, A., 'Economic growth in western Europe, 1870–1957', *Banca Nazionale del Lavoro Quarterly Review,* 12 (1959)

Maddison, A., 'Growth and fluctuation in the world economy, 1870–1960', *Banca Nazionale del Lavoro Quarterly Review,* 15 (1962)

Maddison, A., 'Phases of capitalist development', *Banca Nazionale del Lavoro Quarterly Review,* 121 (1977)

Maddison, A., 'Long run dynamics of productivity growth', *Banca Nazionale del Lavoro Quarterly Review,* 128 (1979)

McCusker, J. J., *Money and exchange in Europe and America, 1600–1775. A handbook,* Macmillan, London (1978)

Mitchell, B. R., 'Statistical appendix, 1700–1914', in C. M. Cipolla, ed., *The emergence of industrial societies.* Fontana Economic History of Europe, vol. 4, part 2, Collins/Fontana, Glasgow (1973)

Mitchell, B. R., *European historical statistics, 1750–1970,* Cambridge University Press, Cambridge (1975)

Mitchell, B. R., 'Statistical appendix 1920–70', in C. M. Cipolla, ed., *Contemporary economies.* Fontana Economic History of Europe, vol. 6, part 2, Collins/Fontana, Glasgow (1976)

Organisation for Economic Co-operation and Development, *Basic statistics of industrial production, 1913–60,* OECD, Paris (1962)

Patel, S. J., 'Rates of industrial growth in the last century, 1860–1958', *Economic Development and Cultural Change,* 9 (1961)

Paretti, V., and G. Bloch, 'Industrial production in western Europe and the United States, 1901–55', *Banca Nazionale del Lavoro Quarterly Review,* 9 (1956)

Pesek, B. P., 'Kuznets' incremental capital-output ratios', *Economic Development and Cultural Change,* 12 (1963–64)

Phelps Brown, E. H., 'Levels and movements of industrial productivity and real wages internationally compared', *Economic Journal,* 83 (1973)

Phelps Brown, E. H., and M. H. Browne, *A century of pay. The course of pay and production in France, Germany, Sweden, the United Kingdom, and the United States of America, 1860–1960,* Macmillan, London (1968)

Phelps Brown, E. H., and S. V. Hopkins, 'The course of wage rates in five countries, 1860–1939', *Oxford Economic Papers,* 2 (1950)

Schwartz, A. J., 'Secular price change in historical perspective', *Journal of Money, Credit and Banking,* 5 (1973)

Singer, J. D., and M. Small, *The wages of war, 1816–1965. A statistical handbook,* Wiley, New York (1972)

Tyszynski, H., 'World trade in manufactured commodities, 1899–1950', *Manchester School,* 19 (1951)

United Nations, *Public debt, 1914–46,* United Nations, New York (1948)

United Nations, *International capital movements during the inter-war period,* United Nations, New York (1949)

Wachter, K. W., *et al., Statistical studies of historical social structure,* Academic Press, London (1978)

Webb, A. D., *The new dictionary of recent statistics of the world to the year 1911,* Routledge, London (1911)

Weber, H. F., *The growth of cities in the nineteenth century. A study in statistics,* Macmillan, New York (1899)

Willcox, W. F., *International migrations,* 2 vols, National Bureau of Economic Research, New York (1929–31)

Zimmerman, L. J., 'The distribution of world income, 1860–1960', in E. de Vries, ed., *Essays on unbalanced growth,* Mouton, The Hague (1962)

WESTERN EUROPE

FRANCE

GENERAL ECONOMIC AND SOCIAL HISTORY

Albrecht-Carrié, R., *France, Europe and the two world wars*, Minard, Paris (1960)

Artz, F. B., *France under the Bourbon restoration, 1814–30*, Russell and Russell, New York (1963)

Bergeron, L., *France under Napoleon*, Princeton University Press, Princeton, N.J. (1981)

Cahill, J. R., *Report on economic and industrial conditions in France in 1928*, H.M.S.O., London (1928)

Cahill, J. R., *Report on economic conditions in France*, H.M.S.O., London (1934)

Cameron, R. E., 'Economic growth and stagnation in France, 1815–1914', *Journal of Modern History*, 30 (1958)

Cameron, R. E., *France and the economic development of Europe*, Princeton University Press, Princeton, N.J. (1961)

Cameron, R. E., 'Economic growth and stagnation in France', in B. E. Supple, ed., *The experience of economic growth. Case studies in economic history*, Random House, New York (1963)

Cameron, R. E., éd., *Essays in French economic history*, Richard D. Irwin, Homewood, Ill. (1970)

Caron, F., *An economic history of modern France*, Columbia University Press, New York (1979)

Chang, H. J., 'Industrialisation in France and in Germany', *Ssu yu Yen*, 11 (1973)

Clapham, J. H., *The economic development of France and Germany, 1815–1914*, Cambridge University Press, Cambridge (1936)

Clark, J. J., 'The nationalisation of war industries in France, 1936–37. A case study', *Journal of Modern History*, 49 (1977)

Clough, S. B., *France. A history of national economics, 1789–1939*, Scribner, New York (1939)

Clough, S. B., 'The crisis in the French economy at the beginning of the revolution', *Journal of Economic History*, 6 (1946)

Clough, S. B., 'Retardative factors in French economic development in the nineteenth and twentieth centuries', *Journal of Economic History*, Supplement 3 (1943)

Clout, H. D., ed., *Themes in the historical geography of France*, Academic Press, London (1977)

Cobban, A., *A history of modern France*, 3 vols., Cape, London (1962–65)

Cowan, L. G., *France and the Saar, 1680–1948*, Columbia University Press, New York (1950)

Croot, P., and D. Parker, 'Agrarian class structure and economic development', *Past and Present*, 78 (1978)

Crouzet, F., 'Wars, blockade and economic change in Europe, 1792–1815', *Journal of Economic History*, 24 (1964)

Crouzet, F., 'England and France in the eighteenth century. A comparative analysis of two economic growths', in R. M. Hartwell, ed., *The causes of the industrial revolution in England*, Methuen, London (1967)

Crouzet, F., 'An annual index of French industrial production in the nineteenth century', in R. E. Cameron, ed., *Essays in French economic history*, Richard D. Irwin, Homewood, Ill. (1970)

Crouzet, F., 'French economic growth in the nineteenth century reconsidered', *History*, 59 (1974)

Davis, J. S., 'Recent economic and financial progress in France', *Review of Economic Statistics*, 3 (1921)

Dunham, A. L., *The Anglo-French treaty of commerce of 1860 and the progress of the industrial revolution in France,* University of Michigan Press, Ann Arbor, Mich. (1930)

Dunham, A. L., *The industrial revolution in France, 1815–48,* Exposition Press, New York (1955)

Eagly, R. V., 'Business cycle trends in France and Germany, 1869–79. A new appraisal', *Weltwirtschaftliches Archiv,* 99 (1967)

Earle, E. M., ed., *Modern France. Problems of the Third and Fourth Republics,* Princeton University Press, Princeton, N.J. (1951)

Farrar, M. M., 'Preclusive purchases. Politics and economic warfare in France during the first world war', *Economic History Review,* 26 (1973)

Florinsky, M. T., *The Saar struggle,* Macmillan, New York (1934)

Fohlen, C., 'The industrial revolution in France', in R. E. Cameron, ed., *Essays in French economic history,* Richard J. Irwin, Homewood, Ill. (1970)

Fohlen, C., 'The industrial revolution in France, 1700–1914', in C. M. Cipolla, ed., *The emergence of industrial societies.* Fontana Economic History of Europe, vol. 4, part 1, Collins/Fontana, Glasgow (1973)

Fohlen, C., 'France 1920–70', in C. M. Cipolla, ed., *Contemporary economies.* Fontana Economic History of Europe, vol. 6, part 1, Collins/Fontana, Glasgow (1976)

Gerschenkron, A., 'Social attitudes, entrepreneurship and economic development', *Explorations in Entrepreneurial History,* 6 (1953–54) [comments by T. C. Cochran, D. S. Landes, J. E. Sawyer and Gerschenkron in 6 (1953–54) and 7 (1954–55)]

Gide, C., *Effects of the war upon French economic life,* Oxford University Press, Oxford (1923)

Goodwin, A., ed., *The American and French revolutions, 1763–93,* The New Cambridge Modern History, vol. 8, Cambridge University Press, Cambridge (1965)

Goreux, L. M., *Agricultural productivity and economic development in France, 1852–1950,* Arno Press, New York (1977)

Guerlac, H., 'Science and French national strengths', in E. M. Earle, ed., *Modern France. Problems of the Third and Fourth Republics,* Princeton University Press, Princeton, N.J. (1951)

Hauser, H., 'The characteristic features of French economic history from the middle of the sixteenth to the middle of the eighteenth century', *Economic History Review,* 4 (1932–34)

Heckscher, E., *The continental system. An economic interpretation,* Clarendon Press, Oxford (1922)

Henderson, W. O., 'The genesis of the industrial revolution in France and Germany in the eighteenth century', *Kyklos,* 9 (1956)

Hoffman, S. R., ed., *France. Change and tradition,* Gollancz, London (1963)

Kaplan, S. L., *Bread, politics and political economy in the reign of Louis XV,* 2 vols., Nijhoff, The Hague (1976)

Kawana, K., 'The French revolution and the progress of capitalism', *Kyoto University Economic Review,* 30 (1960)

Kemp, T., 'Structural factors in the retardation of French economic growth', *Kyklos,* 15 (1962)

Kemp, T., 'Aspects of French capitalism between the wars', *Science and Society,* 33 (1969)

Kemp, T., *Economic forces in French history. An essay on the development of the French economy, 1760–1914,* Dobson, London (1971)

Kemp, T., 'The French economy under the Franc Poincaré', *Economic History Review,* 24 (1971)

Kemp, T., *The French economy, 1919–39. The history of a decline,* Longmans, London (1972)

Kemp, T., 'Tariff policy and French economic growth, 1815–1914', *International Review of the History of Banking,* 12 (1976)

Kindleberger, C. P., 'Foreign trade and economic growth. Lessons from Britain and France, 1850–1913', *Economic History Review,* 14 (1961–62)

Kindleberger, C. P., *Economic growth in France and Britain, 1851–1950,* Harvard University Press, Cambridge, Mass. (1964)

Knowles, L., 'New light on the economic causes of the French revolution', *Economic Journal,* 29 (1919)

Kuisel, R. F., *Capitalism and the state in modern France. Renovation and economic management in the twentieth century,* Cambridge University Press, Cambridge (1981)

Labrousse, E., '1848–1830–1789. How revolutions are born', in F. Crouzet *et al., Essays in European economic history, 1789–1914,* Edward Arnold, London (1969)

Landes, D. S., 'French entrepreneurship and industrial growth in the nineteenth century', *Journal of Economic History,* 9 (1949)

Landes, D. S., 'The statistical study of French crises', *Journal of Economic History,* 10 (1950)

Leet, D. R., and D. A. Shaw, 'French economic stagnation, 1700–1960. Old economic history revisited', *Journal of Interdisciplinary History,* 8 (1977–78)

Lefebvre, G., *The coming of the French revolution,*

Princeton University Press, Princeton, N.J. (1947)

Leffler, M. P., *The elusive quest. America's pursuit of European stability and French security, 1919–33,* University of North Carolina Press, Chapel Hill, N.C. (1979)

Levy-Leboyer, M., 'Capital investment and economic growth in France, 1820–1930', in P. Mathias and M. M. Postan, eds, *The industrial economies. Capital, labour and enterprise,* Cambridge Economic History of Europe, vol. 7, part 1, Cambridge University Press, Cambridge (1978)

Liebowitz, J. J., 'Economic strength and diplomatic attitudes. The formation of French hostility before World War I', *Social Science History,* 3 (1978)

McDougall, W. A., *France's Rhineland diplomacy, 1914–24,* Princeton University Press, Princeton, N.J. (1978)

Marczewski, J., 'Some aspects of the economic growth of France, 1660–1958', *Economic Development and Cultural Change,* 9 (1961)

Marczewski, J., 'The take-off hypothesis and French experience', in W. W. Rostow, ed., *The economics of take-off into sustained growth,* Macmillan, London (1963)

Martin, G., 'The industrial reconstruction of France since the war', *Harvard Business Review,* 5 (1927)

Meuvret, J., 'The condition of France, 1688–1715', in J. S. Bromley, ed., *The rise of Great Britain and Russia, 1688–1715/25,* The New Cambridge Modern History, vol. 6, Cambridge University Press, Cambridge (1970)

Müller, K. J., 'French fascism and modernisation', *Journal of Contemporary History,* 11 (1976)

Newell, W. H., *Population change and agricultural development in nineteenth century France,* Arno Press, New York (1977)

O'Brien, P. K., and C. Keyder, *Economic growth in Britain and France, 1780–1914. Two paths to the twentieth century,* Allen and Unwin, London (1978)

Ogborn, W. F., and W. Jaffé, *The economic development of postwar France. A survey of production,* Columbia University Press, New York (1929)

Palmade, G. P., *French capitalism in the nineteenth century,* David and Charles, Newton Abbot (1972)

Pitts, J. R., 'Continuity and change in bourgeois France', in S. Hoffman, ed., *France. Change and tradition,* Gollancz, London (1963)

Post, J. D., 'A study in meteorological and trade cycle history. The economic crisis following the Napoleonic wars', *Journal of Economic History,* 34 (1974)

Price, R., *The economic modernisation of France, 1730–1880,* Croom Helm, London (1975)

Price, R., *An economic history of modern France, 1730–1914,* Macmillan, London (1981)

Roehl, R., 'French industrialisation. A reconsideration', *Explorations in Economic History,* 13 (1976)

Rudé, G. E., 'The outbreak of the French revolution', *Past and Present,* 8 (1955)

Rudé, G. E., *Interpretations of the French revolution,* Historical Association Pamphlets, General Series, No. 47, London (1961)

Sauvy, A., 'The economic crisis of the 1930s in France', *Journal of Contemporary History,* 4 (1969)

Sawyer, J. E., 'Social structure and economic progress. General propositions and some French examples', *American Economic Review, Papers and Proceedings,* 41 (1951)

Scoville, W. C., 'The Huguenots in the French economy, 1650–1750', *Quarterly Journal of Economics,* 67 (1953)

Scoville, W. C., *The persecution of the Huguenots and French economic development, 1680–1720,* University of California Press, Berkeley, Cal. (1960)

Scoville, W. C., 'The French economy in 1700–01. An appraisal by the Deputies of Trade', *Journal of Economic History,* 22 (1962)

Sée, H., *Economic and social conditions in France during the eighteenth century,* A. A. Knopf, New York (1927)

Sée, H., 'The economic and social origins of the French revolution', *Economic History Review,* 3 (1931–32)

Silver, J., 'French peasant demands for popular leadership in the Vendomois (Loir-et-Cher), 1852–90', *Journal of Social History,* 14 (1980)

Silverman, D. P., 'The economic consequences of annexation. Alsace-Lorraine and imperial Germany, 1871–1918', *Central European History,* 4 (1971)

Stockder, A. H., 'The legality of the blockades instituted by Napoleon's decrees and the British orders in council, 1806–13', *American Journal of International Law,* 10 (1916)

Taylor, G. V., 'Types of capitalism in eighteenth century France', *English Historical Review,* 79 (1964)

Taylor, G. V., 'Non-capitalist wealth and the origins of the French revolution', *American Historical Review,* 72 (1967)

Thomson, D., *Democracy in France since 1870,*

Oxford University Press, London (5th edn 1969)

Wright, G., *France in modern times. 1760 to the present,* Murray, London (1962) [sections on economic development]

Zeldin, T., *France, 1848–1945.* vol. 1. *Ambition, love and politics,* Clarendon Press, Oxford (1973)

AGRICULTURE AND RURAL SOCIETY

Appleby, A. B., 'Grain prices and subsistence crises in England and France, 1590–1740', *Journal of Economic History,* 39 (1979)

Auffret, M., *et al.,* 'Regional inequalities and economic development. French agriculture in the nineteenth and twentieth centuries', in P. Bairoch and M. Levy-Leboyer, eds., *Disparities in economic development since the industrial revolution,* Macmillan, London (1981)

Bamford, P. W., *Forests and French sea power, 1660–1789,* Toronto University Press, Toronto (1956)

Beauroy, J., 'The pre-revolutionary crises in Bergerac, 1770–89', *Proceedings of the Annual Meeting of the Western Society for French History,* 1 (1973)

Behrens, B., 'Nobles, privileges and taxes in France at the end of the *ancien régime*', *Economic History Review,* 15 (1962–63)

Behrens, B., 'A revision defended. Nobles, privileges and taxes in France', *French Historical Studies,* 9 (1975–76)

Berenson, E., 'The modernisation of rural France', *Journal of European Economic History,* 8 (1979)

Berger, S., *Peasants against politics. Rural organisations in Brittany, 1911–67,* Harvard University Press, Cambridge, Mass. (1972)

Bloch, M., *French rural history. An essay in its basic characteristics,* Routledge, London (1966)

Blum, J., 'The condition of the European peasantry on the eve of emancipation', *Journal of Modern History,* 46 (1974)

Bourde, A. J., *The influence of England on the French agronomes, 1756–89,* Cambridge University Press, Cambridge (1953)

Cavanaugh, G. J., 'Nobles, privileges and taxes in France. A revision reviewed', *French Historical Studies,* 8 (1973–74)

Clout, H., 'Land-use in Finistère during the eighteenth and nineteenth centuries', *Etudes Rurales,* 73 (1979)

Clout, H. D., *Agriculture in France on the eve of the railway age,* Croom Helm, London (1980)

Cooper, J. P., 'In search of agrarian capitalism', *Past and Present,* 80 (1978)

Cullen, L. M., and F. Furet, eds, *Ireland and France, 1600–1900. Towards a comparative study of rural history,* Editions de l'Ecole des Hautes Etudes en Sciences Sociales, Paris (1980)

Dallas, G., *The imperfect peasant economy. The Loire country, 1800–1914,* Cambridge University Press, Cambridge (1982)

Davies, A., 'The new agriculture in lower Normandy', *Transactions of the Royal Historical Society,* 8 (1958)

Davies, A., 'The origins of the French peasant revolution', *History,* 46 (1964)

Davies, A., 'Agricultural production in Calvados at the end of the old regime', *Proceedings of the third international economic history conference, Munich, 1965,* Mouton, Paris (1973)

Debien, G., 'Land clearings and artificial meadows in eighteenth century Poitou', *Agricultural History,* 19 (1945)

Dumas, J., 'The present state of the land system in France', *Economic Journal,* 19 (1909)

Flaningam, M. L., 'The rural economy of north-eastern France and the Bavarian Palatinate, 1815 to 1830', *Agricultural History,* 24 (1950)

Forster, R., 'The noble as landlord in the region of Toulouse at the end of the old regime', *Journal of Economic History,* 17 (1957)

Forster, R., 'The noble wine producers of the Bordelais in the eighteenth century', *Economic History Review,* 14 (1961–62)

Forster, R., 'Obstacles to agricultural growth in eighteenth century France', *American Historical Review,* 75 (1969–70)

Gide, C., 'The union between agricultural syndicates and co-operative societies in France', *Economic Journal,* 5 (1895)

Gide, C., 'The wine crisis in south France', *Economic Journal,* 17 (1907)

Goldberg, H., 'The myth of the French peasant', *American Journal of Economics and Sociology,* 13 (1954)

Grantham, G. W., 'Scale and organisation in French farming, 1840–89', in W. N. Parker and E. L. Jones, eds, *European peasants and their markets. Essays in agrarian economic history,* Princeton University Press, Princeton, N.J. (1975)

Grantham, G. W., 'The diffusion of the new husbandry in northern France, 1815–40', *Journal of*

Economic History, 38 (1978)

Grantham, G. W., 'The persistence of open field farming in nineteenth century France', *Journal of Economic History*, 40 (1980)

Guillot-Lageat, G., 'Growth and regional inequalities in agriculture. France during the nineteenth century', *Proceedings of the third international economic history conference, Munich, 1965*, Mouton, Paris (1974)

Higgs, D., 'Politics and land-ownership among the French nobility after the revolution', *European Studies Review*, 1 (1971)

Higgs, H., '*Métayage* in western France', *Economic Journal*, 4 (1894)

Hohenberg, P. M., 'Change in rural France in the period of industrialisation, 1830–1914', *Journal of Economic History*, 32 (1972)

Hohenberg, P. M., 'Maize in French agriculture', *Journal of European Economic History*, 6 (1977)

Hohenberg, P. M., 'The transformation of agricultural labour supply in nineteenth century France', *Economic History Review*, 32 (1979) [comment by R. Price in same issue]

Hufton, O., 'The seigneur and the rural community in eighteenth century France. The seigneurial reaction. A reappraisal', *Transactions of the Royal Historical Society*, 29 (1979)

Johnson, C. H., 'Some recent French village studies', *Peasant Studies Newsletter*, 2 (1973)

Jolas, T., and F. Zonabend, 'Tillers of the fields and woodspeople', in R. Forster and O. Ranum, eds, *Rural society in France*, Johns Hopkins University Press, Baltimore, Md. (1977)

Jones, P. M., 'Political commitment and rural society in the southern Massif Central', *European Studies Review*, 10 (1980) [eighteenth and nineteenth century study]

Judt, T., 'The origins of rural socialism in Europe. Economic change and the Provençal peasantry, 1870–1914', *Social History*, 1 (1976)

Kaplan, S. L., 'Lean years, fat years. The "community" granary system and the search for abundance in eighteenth century Paris', *French Historical Studies*, 10 (1977–78)

Labrousse, E., 'The evolution of peasant society in France', in E. M. Acomb and M. L. Brown, eds, *French society and culture since the old regime*, Holt Rinehart and Winston, New York (1966)

Lefebvre, G., 'The place of the revolution in the agrarian history of France', in R. Forster and O. Ranum, eds, *Rural society in France*, Johns Hopkins University Press, Baltimore, Md. (1977)

Le Goff, T. J. A., and D. M. G. Sutherland, 'The revolution and the rural community in eighteenth century Brittany', *Past and Present*, 62 (1974)

Le Guin, C. A., 'Jean-Marie Roland and Arthur Young. An essay in parallel history', in C. C. Sturgill, ed., *The consortium on revolutionary Europe, 1750–1850*, University Presses of Florida, Gainesville, Fla. (1975)

Le Roy Ladurie, E., *The peasants of Languedoc*, University of Illinois Press, Urbana, Ill. (1974)

Le Roy Ladurie, E., and J. Goy, *Tithe and agrarian history from the fourteenth to the nineteenth centuries. An essay in comparative history*, Cambridge University Press, Cambridge (1981)

Leslie, T. E. C., 'The land system in France', in J. W. Probyn, ed., *Systems of land tenure in various countries*, Cobden Press, London (1881)

Loubère, L. A., *The red and the white. The history of wine in France and Italy in the nineteenth century*, New York State University Press, Albany, N.Y. (1978)

Ludkiewicz, Z., 'The agrarian structure of Poland and France from the point of view of emigration', *International Labour Review*, 22 (1931)

McDonald, F., 'The relation of the French peasant veterans of the American revolution to the fall of feudalism in France, 1789–92', *Agricultural History*, 25 (1951)

Mackrell, J. Q. C., *The attack on 'feudalism' in eighteenth century France*, Routledge and Kegan Paul, London (1973)

Margadant, T. W., 'French rural society in the nineteenth century. A review essay', *Agricultural History*, 53 (1979)

Mendras, H., *Vanishing peasant. Innovation and change in French agriculture*, Massachusetts Institute of Technology Press, Cambridge Mass. (1970)

Morineau, M., 'Was there an agricultural revolution in eighteenth century France?', in R. E. Cameron, ed., *Essays in French economic history*, Richard D. Irwin, Homewood, Ill. (1970)

Morineau, M., 'The agricultural revolution in nineteenth century France. Comment', *Journal of Economic History*, 36 (1976)

Newell, W. H., 'The agriculture revolution in nineteenth century France', *Journal of Economic History*, 33 (1973)

O'Brien, P. K., *et al.*, 'Agricultural efficiency in Britain and France, 1815–1914', *Journal of European Economic History*, 6 (1977)

Palmer, R. S., 'George Lefebvre. The peasants and the French revolution', *Journal of Modern History*, 31 (1959)

Pesez, J.-M., and E. Le Roy Ladurie, 'The deserted villages of France. An overview', in R. Forster and O. Ranum, eds, *Rural society in France,* Johns Hopkins University Press, Baltimore, Md. (1977)

Price, R., 'The onset of labour shortage in nineteenth century French agriculture', *Economic History Review,* 28 (1975)

Pundt, A. G., 'French agriculture and the industrial crisis of 1788', *Journal of Political Economy,* 49 (1941)

Rogers, J. W., 'Subsistence crises and the political economy in France at the end of the *ancien régime*', in P. Uselding, ed., *Research in economic history,* vol. 5, JAI Press, Greenwich, Conn. (1980)

Rutten, V. W., 'Structural retardation and the modernisation of French agriculture. A skeptical view', *Journal of Economic History,* 38 (1978)

Sargent, F. O., 'The persistence of communal tenure in French agriculture', *Agricultural History,* 32 (1958)

Sargent, F. O., 'Feudalism to family farms in France, *Agricultural History,* 35 (1961)

Seebohm, F., 'French peasant proprietorship under the open field system of husbandry', *Economic Journal,* 1 (1891)

Sexauer, B., 'English and French agriculture in the late eighteenth century', *Agricultural History,* 50 (1976)

Shaffer, J. W., *Family and farm. Agrarian change and household organisation in the Loire valley, 1500–1900,* State University of New York Press, Albany, N.Y. (1982)

Sheppard, T. F., *Lourmarin in the eighteenth century. A study of a French village,* Johns Hopkins University Press, Baltimore, Md. (1971)

Simoni, P., 'Agricultural change and landlord-tenant relations in nineteenth century France. The canton of Apt (Vaucluse)', *Journal of Social History,* 13 (1979)

Soboul, A., 'The French rural community in the eighteenth and nineteenth centuries', *Past and Present,* 10 (1956)

Soboul, A., 'Persistence of "feudalism" in the rural society of nineteenth century France', in R. Forster and O. Ranum, eds, *Rural society in France,* Johns Hopkins University Press, Baltimore, Md. (1977)

Sokoloff, S., 'Land tenure and political tendency in rural France. The case for sharecropping', *European Studies Review,* 10 (1980)

Soubeyroux, N., 'Changes in French agriculture between 1862 and 1962', *Journal of European History,* 9 (1980)

Soubeyroux, N., 'The spread of agricultural growth over the departments of France from the mid-nineteenth to the mid-twentieth century', in P. Bairoch and M. Lévy-Leboyer, eds, *Disparities in economic development since the industrial revolution,* Macmillan, London (1981)

Stevenson, I., 'The diffusion of disaster. The phylloxera outbreak in the department of Hérault, 1826–80', *Journal of Historical Geography,* 6 (1980)

Usher, A. P., *The history of the grain trade in France, 1400–1710,* Harvard University Press, Cambridge, Mass. (1913)

Warner, C. K., *The wine growers of France and the government since 1875,* Columbia University Press, New York (1960)

Weber, E., *From peasants into Frenchmen. The modernisation of rural France, 1870–1914,* Stanford University Press, Stanford, Cal. (1976)

Weber, E., 'The Second Republic. Politics and peasants', *French Historical . Studies,* 11 (1979–80)

Wright, G., *Rural revolution in France,* Stanford University Press, Stanford, Cal. (1964)

INDUSTRY AND INTERNAL TRADE

Adelson, J., 'The early evolution of business organisation in France', *Business History Review,* 31 (1957)

Andrew, C. M., and A. S. Kanya-Forstner, 'French business and the French colonialists', *Historical Journal,* 19 (1976)

Bamford, P. W., 'Entrepreneurship in seventeenth and eighteenth century France', *Explorations in Entrepreneurial History,* 9 (1951)

Barker, R. J., 'French entrepreneurship during the Restoration. The record of a single firm, the Anzin Mining Company', *Journal of Economic History,* 21 (1961)

Barker, R. J., 'The Conseil Général des Manufactures under Napoleon, 1810–14', *French Historical Studies,* 7 (1969–70)

Bergeron, L., 'Investment and industry in Lorraine', in S. Pollard, ed., *Region und Industrialisierung,* Vandenhoeck und Ruprecht, Göttingen (1980)

Boime, A., 'Entrepreneurial patronage in nineteenth century France', in E. C. Carter *et al., Enterprise and entrepreneurship in nineteenth and twentieth century France,* Johns Hopkins University Press,

Baltimore, Md. (1976)

Bosher, J. F., 'The Paris business world and the seaports under Louis XV', *Social History,* 12 (1979)

Bradley, M., 'Franco-Prussian engineering links. The careers of Lamé and Clapeyron, 1820–30', *Annals of Science,* 38 (1981)

Byrnes, R. F., 'The French publishing industry and its crisis in the 1890s', *Journal of Modern History,* 23 (1951)

Caron, F., 'Investment strategy in France', in H. Daems and H. Van der Wee, eds, *The rise of managerial capitalism,* Nijhoff, The Hague (1974)

Carter, E. C., *et al., Enterprise and entrepreneurs in nineteenth and twentieth century France,* Johns Hopkins University Press, Baltimore, Md. (1976)

Chapman, S. D., and S. Chassagne, *European textile printers in the eighteenth century. A study of Peel and Oberkampf,* Heinemann, London (1981)

Christofferson, T. R., 'The French national workshops of 1848. The view from the provinces', *French Historical Studies,* 11 (1979–80)

Crafts, N. F. R., 'Industrial revolution in England and France. Some thoughts on the question "Why was England first" ', *Economic History Review,* 30 (1977) [comments by W. W. Rostow and reply by Crafts in 31 (1978)]

Deyon, P., and P. Guignet, 'The royal manufactures and economic progress in France before the industrial revolution', *Journal of European Economic History,* 9 (1980)

Dubreuil, H., and J. P. Lugrin, 'Scientific management in a food preserving establishment. The "Géo factory", Paris', *International Labour Review,* 33 (1936)

Dunham, A. L., 'Government aid to industry in the French economic reforms of 1860', *Economic History,* 2 (1927)

Dunham, A. L., 'The development of the cotton industry in France and the Anglo-French Treaty of Commerce of 1860', *Economic History Review,* 1 (1927–28)

Ehrmann, H. W., *Organised business in France,* Princeton University Press, Princeton, N.J. (1957)

Fohlen, C., 'Entrepreneurship and management in France in the nineteenth century', in P. Mathias and M. M. Postan, eds, *The industrial economies. Capital, labour and enterprise,* Cambridge Economic History of Europe, vol. 7, part 1, Cambridge University Press, Cambridge (1978)

Forrester, R. B., *The cotton industry in France,* Longmans, London (1921)

Freedeman, C. E., 'Joint stock business organisation in France, 1807–67', *Business History Review,* 39 (1965)

Freedeman, C. E., 'The coming of free enterprise in France, 1850–67', *Explorations in Entrepreneurial History,* 4 (1966–67)

Freedeman, C. E., *Joint stock enterprise in France, 1807–67. From privileged company to modern corporation,* University of North Carolina Press, Chapel Hill, N.C. (1979)

Geiger, R. G., *The Anzin Coal Company, 1800–33. Big business in the early stages of the French industrial revolution,* University of Delware Press, Newark, Del. (1974)

Gillet, M., 'The coal age and the rise of coalfields in the Nord and the Pas-de-Calais', in F. Crouzet *et al., Essays in European economic history,* Edward Arnold, London (1969)

Greer, G., *The Ruhr-Lorraine industrial problem. A study of the economic interdependence of the two regions and their relation to the reparation question,* Macmillan, New York (1925)

Hafter, D. M., 'The programmed brocade loom and the "decline of the drawgirl" ', in M. M. Trescott, ed., *Dynamos and virgins revisited. Women and technological change in history,* Scarecrow Press, Metuchen, N.J. (1979) [eighteenth century French brocade industry]

Harris, J. R., 'Technological divergence and industrial development in Britain and France before 1800', *Proceedings of the fifth international Economic history conference, Leningrad, 1970,* Mouton, Paris (1979)

Harris, J. R., 'Saint-Gobain and Ravenhead', in B. M. Ratcliffe, ed., *Great Britain and her world, 1750–1914. Essays in honour of W. O. Henderson,* Manchester University Press, Manchester (1975)

Harris, J. R., 'Attempts to transfer English steel techniques to France in the eighteenth century', in S. Marriner, ed., *Business and businessmen. Studies in business, economic and accounting history,* Liverpool University Press, Liverpool (1978)

Harris, J. R., and Pris, C., 'The memoirs of Delannay Deslandes', *Technology and Culture,* 17 (1976) [glassmaking, 1750–1800]

Henderson, W. O., and W. H. Chaloner, 'The Manbys and the industrial revolution in France', *Transactions of the Newcomen Society,* 30 (1955–57)

Heywood, C. M., 'The rural hosiery industry of the lower Champagne region, 1750–1850,' *Textile History,* 7 (1976)

Heywood, C. M., 'The launching of an "import industry". The cotton industry of Troyes under protectionism, 1793–1860', *Journal of European Economic History*, 10 (1981)

Horn, N., and J. Kocka, *Law and the formation of the big enterprise in the nineteenth and early twentieth centuries. Studies in the history of industrialisation in Germany, France, Great Britain and the United States,* Vandenhoeck und Ruprecht, Göttingen (1979)

Hoselitz, B., 'Entrepreneurship and capital formation in France and Britain since 1700', in M. Abramovitz, ed., *Capital formation and economic growth,* National Bureau of Economic Research, New York (1955)

Hoselitz, B., 'Entrepreneurship and capital formation in France and Britain since 1700', in M. E. Falkus, ed., *Readings in the history of economic growth,* Oxford University Press, London (1968)

International Labour Office, 'Employers' organisations in France', *International Labour Review,* 16 (1927)

Kaelble, H., 'Long term changes in the recruitment of the business elite. Germany compared with the United States, Great Britain and France since the industrial revolution', *Journal of Social History,* 13 (1980)

Keller, M., 'Public policy and large enterprise. Comparative historical perspectives', in N. Horn and J. Kocka, eds, *Recht und Entwicklung der Grossunternehmen im 19. und frühen 20. Jahrhundert,* Vandenhoeck und Ruprecht, Göttingen (1979)

Kisch, H., 'The impact of the French revolution on the lower Rhine textile districts – some comments on economic development and social change', *Economic History Review,* 15 (1962–63)

Koepke, R. L., 'The Lois des Patentes of 1844', *French Historical Studies,* 11 (1979–80)

Kuisel, R. F., *Ernest Mercier, French technocrat,* University of California Press, Berkeley, Cal. (1967)

Kuisel, R. F., 'Auguste Detoeuf, conscience of French industry, 1926–47', *International Review of Social History,* 20 (1975)

Landes, D. S., 'Business and businessmen. A social and cultural analysis', in E. M. Earle, ed., *Modern France. Problems of the Third and Fourth Republics,* Princeton University Press, Princeton, N.J. (1951)

Landes, D. S., 'New model entrepreneurship in France and problems of historical explanation', *Explorations in Entrepreneurial History,* 5 (1963)

Landes, D. S., 'Religion and enterprise. The case of the French textile industry', in E. C. Carter *et al.,*

Enterprise and entrepreneurs in nineteenth and twentieth century France, Johns Hopkins University Press, Baltimore, Md. (1976)

Lanthier, P., 'The relationship between state and private electric industry, France, 1880–1920', in N. Horn and J. Kocka, eds, *Recht und Entwicklung der Grossunternehmen im 19. und frühen 20. Jahrhundert,* Vandenhoeck und Ruprecht, Göttingen (1979)

Laux, J. M., 'Some notes on entrepreneurship in the early French automobile industry', *French Historical Studies,* 3 (1963)

Laux, J. M., 'Heroic days in the French automobile industries', *French Review,* 37 (1964)

Laux, J. M., 'Rochet-Schneider and the French motor industry to 1914', *Business History,* 8 (1966)

Laux, J. M., 'The rise and fall of Armand Deperdussin', *French Historical Studies,* 8 (1973–74)

Laux, J. M., *In first gear. The French automobile industry to 1914,* Liverpool University Press, Liverpool (1976)

Laux, J. M., 'Gnome et Rhone. An aviation engine firm in the first world war', *Aerospace History,* 27 (1980)

Le Goff, T. J. A., 'An eighteenth century grain merchant. Ignace Advisse Desruisseaux', in J. F. Bosher, ed., *French government and society, 1500–1850. Essays in memory of Alfred Cobban,* Athlone Press, London (1973)

Lévy-Leboyer, M., 'Innovation and business strategies in nineteenth and twentieth century France', in E. C. Carter *et al., Enterprise and entrepreneurs in nineteenth and twentieth century France,* Johns Hopkins University Press, Baltimore, Md. (1976)

Lévy-Leboyer, M., 'Hierarchical structure, rewards and incentives in a large corporation. The early managerial experience of Saint-Gobain, 1872–1912', in N. Horn and J. Kocka, eds, *Recht und Entwicklung der Grossunternehmen im 19. und frühen 20. Jahrhundert,* Vandenhoeck und Ruprecht, Göttingen (1979)

Locke, R. R., 'A method for identifying French corporate businessmen (the Second Empire)', *French Historical Studies,* 10 (1977–78)

McKay, D. C., *The national workshops. A study in the French revolution of 1848,* Oxford University Press, London (1933)

Markovitch, T. J., 'The dominant sectors of French industry', in R. E. Cameron, ed., *Essays in French economic history,* Richard D. Irwin, Homewood, Ill. (1970)

Neumeyer, F., 'A contribution to the history of modern patent legislation in the United States and in France', *Scandinavian Economic History Review*, 4 (1956)

Parker, H. T., *The Bureau of Commerce in 1781 and its policies with respect to French industry*, Carolina Academic Press, Durham, N.C. (1979)

Paulin, V., 'Home work in France. Its origin, evolution and future', *International Labour Review*, 37 (1938)

Peiter, H., 'Institutions and attitudes. The consolidation of the business community in bourgeois France, 1880–1914', *Journal of Social History*, 9 (1976)

Schaeper, T. J., 'The creation of the French Council of Commerce in 1700', *European Studies Review*, 9 (1979)

Schmilt, J. M., 'The origins of textile industry in Alsace. The beginnings of the manufacture of printed cloth at Wesserling (1762–1802)', *Textile History*, 13 (1982)

Scoville, W. C., 'Technology and the French glass industry, 1640–1740', *Journal of Economic History*, 1 (1941)

Scoville, W. C., 'Large-scale production in the French plate-glass industry, 1665–1789', *Journal of Political Economy*, 50 (1942)

Scoville, W. C., 'State policy and the French glass industry, 1640–1789', *Quarterly Journal of Economics*, 56 (1942)

Sée, H., 'Hat manufacturing in Rennes, 1776–89. Its financial and commercial organisation', *Journal of Economic and Business History*, 1 (1928–29)

Sheridan, G. J., 'Household and craft in an industrialising economy. The case of the silk weavers of Lyon', in J. M. Merriman, ed., *Consciousness and class experience in nineteenth century Europe*, Holmes and Meier, New York (1979)

Sheridan, G. J., 'The political economy of artisan industry. Government and the people in the silk trade of Lyon, 1830–70', *French Historical Studies*, 11 (1979–80)

Smith, J. G., *The origins of early development of the heavy chemical industry in France*, Clarendon Press, Oxford (1979)

Smith, M. S., 'The *haute bourgeoisie capitaliste* in the late nineteenth century. A prosopographic inquiry', *Proceedings of the Annual Meeting of the Western Society for French History*, 3, (1975)

Smith, M. S., 'Thoughts on the evolution of the French capitalist community in the nineteenth century', *Journal of European Economic History*, 7 (1978)

Sonenscher, M., 'The hosiery industry of Nimes and

lower Languedoc in the eighteenth century', *Textile History*, 10 (1979)

Stearns, P. N., 'British industry through the eyes of French industrialists (1820–48)', *Journal of Modern History*, 37 (1965)

Stearns, P. N., 'Individualism and association in French industry, 1820–48', *Business History Review*, 40 (1966)

Stein, R. L., 'The French sugar business in the eighteenth century. A quantitative study', *Business History*, 22 (1980)

Taylor, G. V., 'Some business partnerships at Lyon, 1785–93', *Journal of Economic History*, 23 (1963)

Taylor, G. V., 'Notes on commercial transfers in eighteenth century France', *Business History Review*, 38 (1964)

Wasserman, M. J., 'Inflation and enterprise in France, 1919–26', *Journal of Political Economy*, 42 (1934)

Wiebenson, D., 'Building technology in France (1685–1786)', *Journal of the Society of Architectural Historians*, 39 (1980)

Wilks, P., 'An entrepreneur at the court of Napoleon III', *Explorations in Entrepreneurial History*, 7 (1955)

Young, D. B., 'Forest, mines, and fuel. The question of wood and coal in eighteenth century France', *Proceedings of the Annual Meeting of the Western Society for French History*, 3 (1975)

Zupko, R. E., *French weights and measures before revolution*, Indiana University Press, Bloomington, Ind. (1978)

TRANSPORT AND COMMUNICATIONS

Bamford, P. W., 'French shipping in northern European trade, 1660–1789', *Journal of Modern History*, 26 (1954)

Blanchard, M., 'The railway policy of the Second Empire', in F. Crouzet *et al.*, *Essays in European economic history*, Edward Arnold, London (1969)

Caron, F., 'French railroad investment, 1850–1914', in R. E. Cameron, ed., *Essays in French economic history*, Richard D. Irwin, Homewood, Ill. (1970)

Cermakian, J., *The Moselle. River and canal from the Roman Empire to the European Economic Community*, Toronto University Press, Toronto (1975)

Chaloner, W. H., 'De Lesseps and the Suez canal', *History Today* (1956)

Crouzet, F., 'When the railways were built. A French

engineering firm during the "Great Depression" and after', in S. Marriner, ed., *Business and businessmen. Studies in business, economic and accounting history*, Liverpool University Press, Liverpool (1978)

Crowhurst, R. P., 'Profitability in French privateering, 1793–1815', *Business History*, 24 (1982)

Dougall, H. E., 'The French solution for the railway problem', *Journal of Political Economy*, 42 (1934)

Dougall, H. E., 'Railway rates and rate-making in France since 1921', *Journal of Political Economy*, 41 (1933)

Dougall, H. E., 'Railway nationalisation and transport co-ordination in France', *Journal of Political Economy*, 46 (1938)

Doukas, K. A., *The French railroads and the state*, Columbia University Press, New York (1945)

Dunham, A. L., 'How the first French railways were planned', *Journal of Economic History*, 1 (1941)

Hammond, W. E., 'The development of the Marne-Rhine canal and the Zollverein', *French Historical Studies*, 3 (1964)

Hansen, B., and K. Tourk, 'The profitability of the Suez canal as a private enterprise, 1859–1956', *Journal of Economic History*, 38 (1978)

Lefranc, G., 'The French railroads, 1823–42', *Journal of Economic and Business History*, 2 (1929–30)

Melvin, F. E., *Napoleon's navigation system. A study of trade control during the continental blockade*, D. Appleton, New York (1919)

Prestwich, P. E., 'French businessmen and the Channel tunnel project of 1913', *French Historical Studies*, 9 (1975–76)

Pritchard, J.-S., 'The pattern of French colonial shipping to Canada before 1760', *Revue Française d'Histoire d'Outre-mer*, 63 (1976)

Ram, K. V., 'British government, finance capitalists and the French Jibuti-Addis Ababa railway, 1898–1913', *Journal of Imperial and Commonwealth History*, 9 (1981)

Ratcliffe, B. M., 'The origins of the Paris–Saint-Germain railway', *Journal of Transport History*, 1 (1972)

Ratcliffe, B. M., 'The building of the Paris–Saint-Germain railway', *Journal of Transport History*, 2 (1973)

Ratcliffe, B. M., 'Railway imperialism. The example of the Pereires' Paris–Saint-Germain company, 1835–46', *Business History*, 18 (1976)

Rivet, F., 'American technique and steam navigation on the Saône and the Rhône, 1827–50', *Journal of*

Economic History, 16 (1956)

MONEY, BANKING AND FINANCE

Anderson, B. M., *Effects of the war on money, credit and banking in France and the United States*, Oxford University Press, New York (1919)

Armstrong, A. F., 'France and the Hoover plan', *Foreign Affairs*, 10 (1931)

Balogh, T., 'The import of gold into France', *Economic Journal*, 40 (1930)

Barker, R. J., 'The Perier Bank during the Restoration (1815–30)', *Journal of European Economic History*, 2 (1973)

Baughman, J. J., 'Financial resources of Louis Philippe', *French Historical Studies*, 4 (1965)

Bloch, J. F., 'The financial effort of France during the war', *Annals of the American Academy of Political and Social Science*, 75 (1918)

Bosher, J. F., 'The Premiers Commis des Finances in the reign of Louis XVI', *French Historical Studies*, 3 (1964)

Blumberg, A., 'The Second French Empire, Eugen Rouher, and the Italian railroads. Documents illustrative of economic imperialism', *Economy and History*, 8 (1965)

Bosher, J. F., 'French administration and public finance in their European setting', in A. Goodwin, ed., *The American and French revolutions, 1763–93*. The New Cambridge Modern History, vol. 8, Cambridge University Press, Cambridge (1965)

Bosher, J. F., *French finances 1770–95. From business to bureaucracy*, Cambridge University Press, London (1970)

Bouvier, J., 'The banking mechanism in France in the late nineteenth century', in R. E. Cameron, ed., *Essays in French economic history*, Richard D. Irwin, Homewood, Ill. (1970)

Bradley, M., 'The financial basis of French scientific education and scientific institutions in Paris, 1790–1815', *Annals of Science*, 36 (1969)

Cameron, R. E., 'The Crédit Mobilier and the economic development of Europe', *Journal of Political Economy*, 61 (1953)

Cameron, R. E., 'France, 1800–70', in R. E. Cameron, ed., *Banking in the early stages of industrialisation. Some lessons of history*, Oxford University Press, London (1967)

Carroll, M. B., *Taxation of business in France*, U.S. Government Printing Office, Washington, D.C. (1931)

Clark, J. G., 'Marine insurance in eighteenth century

La Rochelle', *French Historical Studies*, 10 (1977–78)

Clarke, S. V. O., *Exchange-rate stabilisation in the mid-1930s. Negotiating the Tripartite Agreement*, Princeton Studies in International Finance, No. 41, International Finance Section, Department of Economics, Princeton University, Princeton, N.J. (1977)

Clough, S. B., 'Taxation and capital formation since 1870 in France, Italy and the United States', *Proceedings of the third international economic history conference, Munich, 1965*, Mouton, Paris (1968)

Cottrell, P. L., 'Anglo-French financial co-operation, 1850–80', *Journal of European Economic History*, 3 (1974)

Drummond, I. M., *London, Washington and the management of the franc, 1936–39*, Princeton Studies in International Finance, No. 45, International Finance Section, Department of Economics, Princeton University, Princeton, N.J. (1979)

Dulles, E. L., *The French franc, 1914–28. The facts and their interpretation*, Macmillan, New York (1929)

Dulles, E. L., *The dollar, the franc and inflation*, Macmillan, New York (1933)

Einzig, P., *The sterling-dollar-franc tangle*, Kegan Paul Trench Trubner, London (1933)

Einzig, P., *France's crisis*, Macmillan, London (1934)

Gide, C., 'French war budgets for 1919–20', *Economic Journal*, 29 (1919)

Grice, J. W., *National and local finance. A review between the central and local authorities in England, France, Belgium and Prussia during the nineteenth century*, P. S. King, London (1910)

Haig, R. M., *The public finances of post-war France*, Columbia University Press, New York (1929)

Haig, R. M., 'The national budget of France, 1928–37', *Proceedings of the Academy of Political Science*, 17 (1937)

Harris, R. D., 'French finances and the American war, 1777–83', *Journal of Modern History*, 48 (1976)

Harris, R. D., 'The reform of the *ancien régime* in France', in H. T. Parker, ed., *Problems in European history*, Moore Publications, Durham, N.C. (1979)

Harris, R. D., *Necker. Reform statesman of the ancien régime*, University of California Press, Berkeley, Cal. (1979)

Harris, S. E., 'The *assignats*', *Harvard Economic Studies*, 33 (1930)

Hawtrey, R. G., 'The collapse of the French *assig-nats*', *Economic Journal*, 23 (1918)

Hawtrey, R. G., 'French monetary policy', *Economica*, 3 (1936)

Jèze, G., 'The economic and financial position of France in 1920', *Quarterly Journal of Economics*, 35 (1921)

Kindleberger, C. P., 'Origins of United States direct investment in France', *Business History Review*, 48 (1974)

Labordère, M., 'The mechanism of foreign investment in France and its outcome, 1890–1914', *Economic Journal*, 24 (1914)

Landes, D. S., *Bankers and pashas. International finance and economic imperialism in Egypt*, Heinemann, London (1958) [French foreign investment and imperialism in Egypt]

Landes, D. S., 'A chapter in the financial revolution of the nineteenth century. The rise of French deposit banking', *Journal of Economic History*, 23 (1963)

Landes, D. S., 'The old bank and the new. The financial revolution of the nineteenth century', in F. Crouzet *et al.*, *Essays in European economic history*, Edward Arnold, London (1969)

Liesse, A., *Evolution of credit and banks in France from the founding of the Bank of France to the present time*, U.S. Government Printing Office, Washington, D.C. (1909)

Long, J. W., 'Organised protest against the 1906 Russian loan', *Cahiers du Monde Russe et Soviétique*, 13 (1972)

MacClintock, S., 'French finances and economic resources', *Journal of Political Economy*, 30 (1922)

McCloskey, D. N., 'A mismeasurement of the incidence of taxation in Britain and France, 1715–1810', *Journal of European Economic History*, 7 (1978) [reply by P. Mathias and P. O'Brien in the same issue]

McCollim, G., 'Council versus minister. The Controller General of Finances, 1661–1715', *Proceedings of the Annual Meeting of the Western Society for French History*, 6 (1978)

Mackenzie, K., *The banking systems of Great Britain, France, Germany and the United States of America*, Macmillan, London (1932)

Mathias, P., and P. O'Brien, 'Taxation in Britain and France, 1715–1810. A comparison of the social and economic incidence of taxes collected for the central governments', *Journal of European Economic History*, 5 (1976)

Matthews, G. T., *The royal general farms in eighteenth century France*, Columbia University Press,

New York (1958)

Miller, H. E., 'The franc in war and reconstruction', *Quarterly Journal of Economics,* 44 (1930)

Monroe, A. E., 'The French indemnity of 1871 and its effects', *Review of Economic Statistics,* 1 (1919)

Moulton, H. G., and C. Lewis, *The French debt problem,* Macmillan, New York (1925)

Myers, M. G., *Paris as a financial centre,* P. S. King, London (1936)

Nicolle, A., 'The problem of reparations after the hundred days', *Journal of Modern History,* 25 (1953) [French treaty obligations of 1815 and their financial effects]

O'Farrell, H. H., *The Franco-German war indemnity and its economic results,* Harrison, London (1913)

Parker, W., *The Paris bourse and French finance,* Columbia University Press, New York (1920)

Peel, A. G. V., *The financial crisis of France,* Macmillan, London (1925)

Ratcliffe, B. M., 'Some banking ideas in France in the 1830s. The writings of Emile and Isaac Pereire, 1830–35', *International Review of the History of Banking,* 6 (1973)

Ratcliffe, B. M., 'Some ideas on public finance in France in the 1830s. The writings of Emile and Isaac Pereire, 1830–35', *International Review of the History of Banking,* 10 (1975)

Redlich, F., 'Jacques Laffitte and the beginnings of investment banking in France', *Bulletin of the Business Historical Society,* 22 (1948)

Redlich, F., 'Two nineteenth century financiers and autobiographers. A comparative study in creative destructiveness and business failure', *Economy and History,* 10 (1967)

Rhodes, B., 'Reassessing "Uncle Shylock". The United States and the French war debt, 1917–29', *Journal of American History,* 55 (1969)

Riley, J. C., 'Dutch investment in France, 1781–87', *Journal of Economic History,* 33 (1973)

Robisheaux, E., 'The "private army" of the tax farms. The men and their origins', *Social History,* 6 (1973)

Rose, R. B., 'Tax revolt and popular organisation in Picardy, 1789–91', *Past and Present,* 43 (1969)

Samuel, H. B., *The French default. An analysis of the problems involved in the debt repudiation of the French Republic,* E. Wilson, London (1930)

Schmidt, G. C., 'The politics of currency stabilisation. The French franc, 1926', *Journal of European Economic History,* 3 (1974)

Schrecker, E., *The hired money. The French debt to the United States, 1917–29,* Arno Press, New York (1978)

Schuker, S. A., *The end of French predominance in Europe. The financial crisis of 1924 and the adoption of the Dawes plan,* University of North Carolina Press, Chapel Hill, N.C. (1976)

Schuker, S. A., 'Finance and foreign policy in the era of German inflation. British, French and German strategies for economic reconstruction after the first world war', in O. Büsch and G. D. Feldman, eds, *Historische Prozesse der deutschen Inflation. Ein Tagungsbericht,* Colloquium Verlag, Berlin (1978)

Spooner, F. C. *The international economy and monetary movements in France, 1493–1725,* Harvard University Press, Cambridge, Mass. (1972)

Taylor, G. V., 'The Paris *bourse* on the eve of the revolution, 1781–89', *American Historical Review,* 67 (1961–62)

Thompson, D. G., 'The fate of the French Jesuits' creditors under the *ancien régime, English Historical Review,* 91 (1976)

Trachtenberg, M., *Reparation in world politics. France and European economic diplomacy, 1916–23,* Columbia University Press, New York (1980)

White, A. D., 'Fiat money in France', in M. Jefferson, ed., *Inflation,* John Calder, London (1977)

Wolfe, M., *The French franc between the wars, 1919–39,* Columbia University Press, New York (1957)

Wynne, W. H., 'The French franc, June 1928–February 1937', *Journal of Political Economy,* 45 (1937)

OVERSEAS TRADE AND COMMERCIAL RELATIONS

Andrew, C. M., 'The French colonialist movement during the Third Republic. The unofficial mind of imperialism', *Transactions of the Royal Historical Society,* 26 (1976)

Ashley, P. W. L., *Modern tariff history. Germany—United States—France,* J. Murray, London (3rd edn 1926)

Bamford, P. W., 'France and the American market in naval timber and masts, 1776–86', *Journal of Economic History,* 12 (1952)

Bosher, J. F., *The single duty project. A study of the movement for a French customs union in the eighteenth century,* Athlone Press, London (1964)

Bosher, J. F., 'French Protestant families in Canadian trade, 1740–60', *Social History,* 7 (1974)

Bosher, J. F., 'A Quebec merchant's trading circles in

France and Canada. Jean-André Lamaletie before 1763', *Social History*, 10 (1977)

Boulle, P. H., 'Patterns of French colonial trade and the Seven Years' War', *Social History*, 7 (1974)

Boulle, P. H., 'French mercantilism, commercial companies and colonial profitability', in L. Blusse and F. Gaastra, eds, *Companies and trade*, Leiden University Press, Leiden (1981)

Broder, A., 'French consular reports', *Business History*, 23 (1981)

Browning, O., 'The treaty of commerce between England and France in 1786', *Transactions of the Royal Historical Society*, 2 (1885)

Buckley, R. N., 'Business as usual. A review essay of Robert Louis Stein's *The French slave trade in the eighteenth century. An Old Regime business*', *Umoja. A Scholarly Journal of Black Studies*, 4 (1980)

Cameron, R. E., 'Some French contributions to the industrial development of Germany, 1840–70', *Journal of Economic History*, 16 (1956)

Cameron, R. E., 'Problems of French investment in Italian railways. A document of 1868', *Business History Review*, 35 (1961)

Cameron, R. E., 'Economic relations of France with central and eastern Europe, 1800–1914', *Journal of European Economic History*, 10 (1981)

Cieslak, E., 'Seaborne trade between France and Poland in the eighteenth century', *Journal of European Economic History*, 6 (1977)

Collins, D. N., 'The Franco-Russian alliance and Russian railways, 1891–1914', *Historical Journal*, 16 (1973)

Crisp, O., 'Some problems of French investment in Russian joint stock companies, 1894–1914', *Slavonic and East European Review*, 35 (1956–57)

Crisp, O., 'French investment in Russian joint stock companies, 1894–1914', *Business History*, 2 (1960)

Crisp, O., 'The Russo-Chinese Bank. An episode in Franco-Russian relations', *Slavonic and East European Review*, 52 (1974)

Dietrich, E. B., 'French import quotas', *American Economic Review*, 23 (1933)

Doerflinger, T. M., 'The Antilles trade of the old regime. A statistical overview', *Journal of Interdisciplinary History*, 6 (1976)

Donaghay, M., 'Calonne and the Anglo-French commercial treaty of 1786', *Journal of Modern History*, 50 (1978)

Donaghay, M., 'The Maréchal de Castries and the Anglo-French commercial negotiations of 1786–87', *Historical Journal*, 22 (1979)

Dunham, A. L., 'Chevalier's plan of 1859. The basis of the new commercial policy of Napoleon III', *American Historical Review*, 30 (1924–25)

Dunham, A. L., 'The influence of the Anglo-French Treaty of Commerce of 1860 on the development of the iron industry in France', *Quarterly Journal of Economics*, 41 (1927)

Dunham, A. L., 'The attempt of President Thiers to restore high protection in France (1871–73)', *Journal of Economic and Business History*, 1 (1928–29)

Ellis, G., *Napoleon's continental blockade. The case of Alsace*, Clarendon Press, Oxford (1981)

Fisher, H. A. L., 'The protectionist reaction in France', *Economic Journal*, 6 (1896)

Fox-Genovese, E., 'France and the Chesapeake. A history of the French tobacco monopoly, 1674–1791', *Journal of Modern History*, 46 (1974)

Gagnier, D., 'French loans to China, 1895–1914. The alliance of international finance and diplomacy', *Australian Journal of Politics and History*, 18 (1972)

Gide, C., 'The commercial policy of France after the war', *Economic Journal*, 26 (1916)

Girault, A., *The colonial tariff policy of France*, Clarendon Press, Oxford (1916)

Golob, E. O., *The Méline tariff. French agriculture and nationalist economic policy*, Columbia University Press, New York (1944)

Gourevitch, P. A., 'International trade, domestic coalitions and liberty. Comparative responses to the crisis of 1873–96', *Journal of Interdisciplinary History*, 8 (1977–78)

Guyot, Y., 'The amount, direction and nature of French investments', *Annals of the American Academy of Political and Social Science*, 68 (1916)

Haight, F. A., *A history of French commercial policies*, Macmillan, New York (1941)

Hamilton, K. A., 'An attempt to form an Anglo-French "industrial *entente*"', *Middle Eastern Studies*, 11 (1975)

Harkins, J. R., 'The dissolution of the maximums and trade controls in the Department of the Somme in 1795', *French Historical Studies*, 6 (1969–70)

Henderson, W. O., 'The Anglo-French commercial treaty of 1786', *Economic History Review*, 10 (1957–58)

Iliasu, A. A., 'The Cobden-Chevalier commercial treaty of 1860', *Historical Journal*, 14 (1971)

Jennings, L. C., 'French policy towards trading with African and Brazilian slave merchants, 1840–53',

Journal of African History, 17 (1976)

Jennings, L. C., 'France, Great Britain and the repression of the slave trade, 1841–45', *French Historical Studies*, 10 (1977–78)

Jordan, W. M., *Great Britain, France and the German problem, 1918–39. A study of Anglo-French relations in the making and maintenance of the Versailles settlement,* Oxford University Press, Oxford, (1943)

Laffey, J. F., 'The Lyon Chamber of Commerce and Indochina during the Third Republic', *Canadian Journal of History*, 10 (1975)

Lokke, C. L., *France and the colonial question. A study of contemporary French opinion, 1763–1801,* P. S. King, London (1932)

Long, D. C., 'The Austro-French commercial treaty of 1866', *American Historical Review*, 41 (1935–36)

Meredith, H. O., *Protection in France,* P. S. King, London (1904)

Miquelon, D., *Dugard of Rouen. French trade to Canada and the West Indies, 1729–70,* McGill-Queen's University Press, Montreal (1978)

Murphy, O. T., 'Dupont de Nemours and the Anglo-French commercial treaty of 1786', *Economic History Review*, 19 (1966)

Newbury, C. W., 'The protectionist revival in French colonial trade. The case of Senegal', *Economic History Review*, 21 (1968)

Persell, S. M., 'Joseph Chailly-Bert and the importance of the Union Coloniale Française', *Historical Journal*, 51 (1974)

Prochaska, D. R., 'Fourierism and the colonisation of Algeria. L'Union Agricole d'Afrique, 1846–53', *Proceedings of the Annual Meeting of the Western Society for French History*, 1 (1973)

Raccagni, M., 'The French economic interests in the Ottoman empire', *International Journal of Middle East Studies*, 11 (1980)

Ratcliffe, B. M., 'Napoleon III and the Anglo-French commercial treaty of 1860. A reconsideration', *Journal of European Economic History*, 2 (1973)

Ratcliffe, B. M., 'The origins of the Anglo-French commercial treaty of 1860. A reassessment', in B. M. Ratcliffe, ed., *Great Britain and her world, 1750–1914. Essays in honour of W. O. Henderson,* Manchester University Press, Manchester (1975)

Ratcliffe, B. M., 'The tariff reform campaign in France, 1831–36', *Journal of European Economic History*, 7 (1978)

Ratcliffe, B. M., 'The politics of tariff reform in the 1830s', *Proceedings of the Annual Meeting of the*

Western Society for French History, 6 (1978)

Rist, M., 'A French experiment with free trade. The treaty of 1860', in R. E. Cameron, ed., *Essays in French economic history,* Richard D. Irwin, Homewood, Ill. (1970)

Rose, J. H., 'The Franco-British commercial treaty of 1786', *English Historical Review*, 23 (1908)

Russell, D., 'Fredric Bastiat and the free trade movement in France and England, 1840–50', *Economic History Review*, 14 (1962)

Schneider, J., 'Terms of trade between France and Latin America, 1826–56', in P. Bairoch and M. Levy-Leboyer, eds, *Disparities in economic development since the industrial revolution,* Macmillan, London (1981)

Sée, H., 'The Normandy Chamber of Commerce and the commercial treaty of 1786', *Economic History Review*, 2 (1929–30)

Shields, R. A., 'The Canadian tariff and the Franco-Canadian treaty negotiations of 1901–09. A study in imperial relations', *Dalhousie Review*, 57 (1977)

Shorrock, W. I., *French imperialism in the Middle East. The failure of policy in Syria and Lebanon, 1900–14,* University of Wisconsin Press, Madison, Wis. (1976)

Smith, M. S., 'Free trade versus protection in the early Third Republic. Economic interests, tariff policy, and the making of the Republican synthesis', *French Historical Studies*, 10 (1977–78)

Smith, M. S., 'The free trade revolution reconsidered. Economic interests and the making of French tariff policy under the Second Empire', *Proceedings of the Annual Meeting of the Western Society for French History*, 6 (1978)

Smith, M. S., *Tariff reform in France, 1860–1900. The politics of economic interest,* Cornell University Press, Ithaca, N.Y. (1980)

Stein, R. L., 'The profitability of the Nantes slave trade, 1783–92', *Journal of Economic History*, 35 (1975)

Stein, R. L., 'Measuring the French slave trade, 1713–92/3', *Journal of African History*, 19 (1978)

Stein, R. L., *The French slave trade in the eighteenth century. An Old Regime business,* University of Wisconsin Press, Madison, Wis. (1979)

Stein, R. L., 'Mortality in the eighteenth century French slave trade', *Journal of African History*, 21 (1980)

Viles, P., 'The slaving interest in the Atlantic ports, 1763–92', *French Historical Studies*, 7 (1971–72)

Webster, J. H., 'The concerns of Bordeaux's merchants and the formation of royal commercial policy for the West Indies', *Proceedings of the Annual Meeting of the Western Society for French History*, 2 (1974)

Weiller, J. S., 'Long-run tendencies in foreign trade, with a statistical study of French foreign trade structure, 1871–1939', *Journal of Economic History*, 31 (1971)

Weiskel, T. C., *French colonial rule and the Baule people. Resistance and collaboration*, Oxford University Press, New York (1981)

White, H. D., *The French international accounts, 1880–1913*, Harvard University Press, Cambridge, Mass. (1933)

Wright, G., 'The origins of Napoleon III's free trade', *Economic History Review*, 9 (1938–39)

POPULATION AND MIGRATION

Bidean, A., 'A demographic and social analysis of widowhood and remarriage. The example of the Castellany of Thoissey-en-Dombes, 1670–1840', *Journal of Family History*, 5 (1980)

Biraben, J. N., 'Certain demographic characteristics of the plague epidemic in France, 1720–22'', *Daedalus*, 97 (1968)

Bourgeois-Pichat, J., 'The general development of the population of France since the eighteenth century', in D. V. Glass and D. E. C. Eversley, eds, *Population in history. Essays in historical demography*, Edward Arnold, London (1965)

Bunle, H., 'Migratory movements between France and foreign lands', in W. F. Willcox, ed., *International migrations*, vol. 2, National Bureau of Economic Research, New York (1931)

Castelot, E., 'Stationary population in France', *Economic Journal*, 14 (1904)

Cross, G. S., 'The politics of immigration in France during the era of World War I', *French Historical Studies*, 11 (1979–80)

Dupaquier, J., 'French population in the seventeenth and eighteenth centuries', in R. E. Cameron, ed., *Essays in French economic history*, Richard D. Irwin, Homewood, Ill. (1970)

Dupeux, G., 'The impact of immigration on the occupational structure in the city of Bordeaux', *Historical Methods Newsletter*, 7 (1974)

Etienne, B., 'The Europeans of Algeria', *Tarikh*, 6 (1979)

Goubert, P., 'Historical demography and the reinterpretation of early modern French history', *Journal of Interdisciplinary History*, 1 (1970–71)

Greer, D., *The incidence of emigration during the French revolution*, Harvard University Press, Cambridge, Mass. (1951)

Henry, L., 'The population of France in the eighteenth century', in D. V. Glass and D. E. C. Eversley, eds, *Population in history. Essays in historical demography*, Edward Arnold, London (1965)

Hermalin, A. I., and E. Van de Walle, 'The civil code and nuptiality. Empirical investigation of a hypotheses', in R. D. Lee *et al.*, *Population patterns in the past*, Academic Press, New York (1977)

Hunter, J. C., 'The problem of the French birth rate on the eve of World War I', *French Historical Studies*, 2 (1962)

Kirk, D., 'Populations and population trends in modern France', in E. M. Earle, ed., *Modern France. Problems of the Third and Fourth Republics*, Princeton University Press, Princeton, N.J. (1951)

Mauco, G., 'Immigration in France', *International Labour Review*, 27 (1933)

Meuvret, J., 'Demographic crisis in France from the late sixteenth to the eighteenth century', in D. V. Glass and D. E. C. Eversley, eds, *Population in history. Essays in historical demography*, Edward Arnold, London (1965)

Moch, L. P., 'Adolescence and migration. Nimes, France, 1906', *Social Science History*, 5 (1981)

Moch, L. P., 'Marriage, migration and urban demographic structure. A case from France in the *belle époque*', *Journal of Family History*, 6 (1981)

Pinkney, D. H., 'Migrations to Paris during the Second Empire', *Journal of Modern History*, 25 (1953)

Preston, S. H., and E. Van de Walle, 'Urban French mortality in the nineteenth century', *Population Studies*, 32 (1978)

Serra, E., 'Italian emigration to France during Crispi's first government (1887–91)', *Journal of European Economic History*, 7 (1978)

Spagnoli, P. G., 'High fertility in mid-nineteenth century France. A multivariate analysis of fertility patterns in the *arrondissement* of Lille', in P. Uselding, ed., *Research in economic history*, JAI Press, Greenwich, Conn. 2 (1977)

Spagnoli, P. G., 'Population history from parish monographs. The problem of local demographic variations', *Journal of Interdisciplinary History*, 7 (1977)

Spengler, J. J., *France faces depopulation*, Duke University Press, Durham, N.C. (1938)

Spengler, J. J., 'Note on France's response to her declining rate of demographic growth', *Journal of Economic History*, 11 (1951)

Tilly, C., 'Population and pedagogy in France', *His-*

tory of Education Quarterly, 13 (1973)

Van de Walle, E., *Alone in Europe. The French fertility decline since 1850,* Office of Population Research Publications, Princeton, N.J. (1974)

Van de Walle, E., *The female population of France in the nineteenth century. A reconstruction of 82 départements,* Princeton University Press, Princeton, N.J. (1974)

Van de Walle, E., 'France', in W. R. Lee, ed., *European demography and economic growth,* Croom Helm, London (1979)

Van de Walle, E., 'Motivations and technology in the decline of French fertility', in R. Wheaton and T. K. Hareven, eds, *Family and sexuality in French history,* University of Pennsylvania Press, Philadelphia, Pa. (1980)

Vincent, P. E., 'French demography in the eighteenth century', *Population Studies,* 1 (1947–48)

Weitman, S., *et al.,* 'Statistical recycling of documentary information. Estimating regional variations in a pre-censual population', *Social Forces,* 55 (1976)

Winchester, H. P. M., *Changing patterns of French internal migration, 1891–1968,* University of Oxford, School of Geography, Research Paper 17 (1977)

LABOUR CONDITIONS AND ORGANISATION

Aminzade, R., 'French strike development and class struggle. The development of the strike in mid-nineteenth century Toulouse', *Social Science History,* 4 (1980)

Augé-Laribé, M., 'Labour conditions in French agriculture', *International Labour Review,* 25 (1932)

Baker, A. R. H., 'Ideological change and settlement continuity in the French countryside. The development of agricultural syndicalism in Loir-et-Cher during the late nineteenth century', *Journal of Historical Geography,* 6 (1980)

Bezucha, R. J., *The Lyon uprising of 1834. A social and political conflict in the early July monarchy,* Harvard University Press, Cambridge, Mass. (1974)

Bezucha, R. J., 'The "pre-industrial" worker movement. The *Canuts* of Lyon', in C. Emsley, ed., *Conflict and stability in Europe,* Oxford University Press, London (1979)

Borghese, A., 'Industrial paternalism and lower class agitation. The case of Mulhouse, 1848–51', *Social History,* 13 (1980)

Caldwell, T. B., 'The Syndicat des Employés du Commerce et de l'Industrie (1887–1919). A pioneer French Catholic trade mission of white-collar workers', *Internation Review of Social History,* 11 (1966)

Collinet, M., 'The structure of the employee class in France during the last fifty years', *International Labour Review,* 67 (1953)

Colton, J. G., *Compulsory labor arbitration in France, 1936–39,* King's Crown Press, New York (1950)

Dunham, A. L., 'Industrial life and labour in France, 1815–48', *Journal of Economic History,* 3 (1943)

Dunham, A. L., 'Unrest in France in 1848', *Journal of Economic History,* 8 (1948)

Elwitt, S., 'Politics and ideology in the French labour movement', *Journal of Modern History,* 49 (1977)

Elwitt, S., 'Two points of view in French labour history', *Marxist Perspectives,* 1 (1978)

Elwitt, S., *Economie sociale and the discipline of labour. Social science and social engineering in France, 1860–1900,* Europa, London (1979)

Fairchilds, C. C., 'Masters and servants in eighteenth century Toulouse', *Journal of Social History,* 12 (1979)

Fasel, G., 'Urban workers in provincial France, February–June, 1848', *International Review of Social History,* 17 (1972)

Forer, P. S., 'The French trade union delegation to the Philadelphia Centennial Exposition, 1876', *Science and Society,* 40 (1976)

Frader, L. L., 'Grapes of wrath. Vineyard workers, labour unions and strike activity in the Aude, 1860–1913', in L. A. and C. Tilly, eds, *Class conflict and collective action,* Sage Publications, Beverley Hills, Cal. (1981)

Griffiths, R., 'Anti-capitalism and the French extra-parliamentary right, 1870–1940', *Journal of Contemporary History,* 13 (1978)

Guignet, P., 'The lacemakers of Valenciennes in the eighteenth century. An economic and social study of a group of female workers under the *ancien régime*', *Textile History,* 10 (1979)

Gullickson, G. L., 'The sexual division of labour in cottage industry and agriculture in the Pays de Caux, Auffay, 1750–1850', *French Historical Studies,* 12 (1980)

Hanagan, M. P., *The logic of solidarity. Artisans and industrial workers in three French towns, 1871–1914,* University of Illinois Press, Urbana, Ill. (1980)

Heywood, C., 'The market for child labour in nineteenth century France', *History,* 66 (1981)

Hunt, P., 'French teachers and their unions', *History of Education Quarterly,* 13 (1973) [covers the period 1800–1972]

Johnson, C. H., 'Patterns of proletarianization. Parisian taylors and Lodève woolens workers', in J. M. Mirriman, ed., *Consciousness and class experience in nineteenth century Europe,* Holmes and Meier, New York (1979)

Judt, T., *Socialism in Provence, 1871–1914. A study in the origins of the modern French left,* Cambridge University Press, Cambridge (1979)

Kelso, M. R., 'The inception of modern French labour movement (1871–79). A reappraisal', *Journal of Modern History,* 8 (1936)

Kuczynski, J., *A short history of labour conditions under industrial capitalism,* vol. 4. *France, 1700 to the present day,* Muller, London (1946)

Kulstein, D. I., 'Economic instruction for workers during the Second Empire', *French Historical Studies,* 1 (1959)

Kulstein, D. I., 'The attitude of French workers towards the Second Empire', *French Historical Studies,* 2 (1962)

Kulstein, D. I., 'Bonapartist workers during the Second Empire', *International Review of Social History,* 9 (1964)

Lequin, Y., 'Labour in the French economy since the revolution', in P. Mathias and M. M. Postan, eds, *Cambridge Economic History of Europe,* vol. 7, part 1. Cambridge University Press, Cambridge (1978)

Liebman, R., 'Repressive strategies and working-class protest. Lyon, 1848–52', *Social Science History',* 4 (1980)

Lifka, M. L., 'Thiers, the July monarchy and the "troubles of April" 1834', *Studies in Modern European History and Culture,* 2 (1976) [the working class and poor relief in 1834]

Longfellow, D., 'Silk weavers and the social struggle in Lyon during the French revolution, 1789–94', *French Historical Studies,* 12 (1981–82)

Lorwin, L. L., *The labour movement in France. A study in revolutionary syndicalism,* P. S. King, London (1912)

Lorwin, V. R., *The French labour movement,* Harvard University Press, Cambridge, Mass. (1954)

Lorwin, V. R., 'Reflections on the history of the French and American labour movements', *Journal of Economic History,* 17 (1957)

Loubère, L. A., 'Left-wing radicals, strikes and the military, 1880–1907', *French Historical Studies,* 3 (1963)

Loubère, L. A., 'The emergence of the extreme left in lower Languedoc 1848–51. Social and economic factors in politics', *American Historical Review,* 73 (1967–68)

McBride, T. M., 'A woman's world. Department stores and the evolution of women's employment, 1870–1920', *French Historical Studies,* 10 (1977–78)

McConagha, W. A., *Development of the labour movement in Great Britain, France and Germany,* University of North Carolina Press, Chapel Hill, N.C. (1942)

McDougall, M. L., 'Consciousness and community. The workers of Lyon, 1830–50', *Journal of Social History,* 12 (1978)

McDougall, M. L., 'Women's work in industrialising Britain and France', *Atlantis,* 4 (1979)

Margadant, T. W., 'Peasant protest in the Second Republic', *Journal of Interdisciplinary History,* 5 (1974)

Mauco, G., 'Alien workers in France', *International Labour Review,* 33 (1936)

Merriman, J. M., 'Incident at the statue of the Virgin Mary. The conflict of old and new in nineteenth century Limoges', in J. M. Merriman, ed., *Consciousness and class experience in nineteenth century Europe,* Holmes and Meier, New York (1979)

Mitzman, A., 'The French working class and the Blum government', *International Review of Social History,* 9 (1964)

Montgomery, B. G., *British and continental labour policy. The political labour movement and labour legislation in Great Britain, France and the Scandinavian countries, 1920–22,* Kegan Paul Trench Trubner, London (1922)

Moon, S. J., 'The Saint-Simonian Association of working class women, 1830–50', *Proceedings of the Annual Meeting of the Western Society for French History,* 5 (1977)

Moss, B. H., 'Parisian producers' associations. The socialism of skilled workers, 1830–51', *Proceedings of the Annual Meeting of the Western Society for French History,* 1 (1973)

Moss, B. H., 'Producers' associations and the origins of French socialism. Ideology from below', *Journal of Modern History,* 48 (1976)

Moss, B. H., *The origins of the French labour movement. The socialism of skilled workers, 1830–1914',* University of California Press, Berkeley, Cal. (1976)

Moss, B. H., 'Urban workers and utopian socialism in France', *Journal of Urban History,* 3 (1977)

Neville, R. G., 'The Courrières colliery disaster, 1906', *Journal of Contemporary History,* 13

(1978)

Oualid, W., 'The occupational distribution and status of foreign workers in France', *International Labour Review,* 20 (1929)

Papayanis, N., 'Alphonse Merrheim and the strike of Hennebont. The struggle for the eight-hour day in France', *International Review of Social History,* 16 (1971)

Perrot, M., 'Workers and machines in France during the first half of the nineteenth century', *Proceedings of the Annual Meeting of the Western Society for French History,* 5 (1977)

Perrot, M., *et al.,* 'The three ages of industrial discipline in nineteenth century France', in J. M. Merriman, ed., *Consciousness and class experience in nineteenth century Europe,* Holmes and Meier, New York (1979)

Picard, R., 'Labour legislation in France during and after the war', *International Labour Review,* 3 (1921)

Pinkney, D. H., '*Laissez-faire* or intervention? Labour policy in the first months of the July monarchy', *French Historical Studies,* 3 (1963)

Reardon, J. A., 'Colonisation in reverse. The legal position of foreign workers in Roubaix, France, in the nineteenth century', *Proceedings of the Annual Meeting of the Western Society for French History,* 7 (1979)

Reardon, J. A., 'Belgian and French workers in nineteenth century Roubaix', in L. A. and C. Tilly, eds, *Class conflict and collective action,* Sage Publications, Beverley Hills, Cal. (1981)

Reddy, W. M., 'Family and factory. French linen weavers in the *belle èpoque*', *Journal of Social History,* 8 (1975)

Reddy, W. M., 'The Batteurs and the informer's eye. A labour dispute under the French Second Empire', *History Workshop Journal,* 7 (1979)

Reid, D., 'The role of mine safety in the development of working-class consciousness and organisation. The case of the Aubin coal basin, 1867–1914', *French Historical Studies,* 12 (1981–82)

Rimlinger, G. V., 'Labour and the government. A comparative historical perspective', *Journal of Economic History,* 37 (1977)

Scott, J. W., *The glassmakers of Carmaux. French craftsmen and political action in a nineteenth century city,* Harvard University Press, Cambridge, Mass. (1974)

Scoville, W. C., 'Labour and labour conditions in the French glass industry, 1643–1789', *Journal of Modern History,* 15 (1943)

Seidman, M., 'The birth of the weekend and the revolts against work. The workers of the Paris region during the Popular Front (1936–38)', *French Historical Studies,* 12 (1981–82)

Sewell, W. H., 'Social change and the rise of working-class politics in nineteenth century Marseilles', *Past and Present,* 65 (1974)

Sewell, W. H., 'Property, labour and the emergence of socialism in France, 1789–1848', in J. M. Merriman, ed., *Consciousness and class experience in nineteenth century Europe,* Holmes and Meier, New York (1979)

Shorter, E., and C. Tilly, *Strikes in France, 1830–1968,* Cambridge University Press, London (1974)

Sibalis, M. D., 'Workers' organisations in Napoleonic Paris', *Proceedings of the Annual Meeting of the Western Society for French History,* 5 (1977)

Smith, J. H., 'Agricultural workers and the French wine growers' revolt of 1907', *Past and Present,* 79 (1978)

Snyder, D. S., 'Institutional setting and industrial conflict. Comparative analyses of France, Italy and the United States', *American Sociological Review,* 40 (1975)

Stearns, P. N., 'Patterns of industrial strike activity in France during the July monarchy', *American Historical Review,* 70 (1965)

Stearns, P. N., 'Against the strike threat. Employer policy toward labour agitation in France, 1900–14', *Journal of Modern History,* 40 (1968)

Stearns, P. N., 'National character and European labour history', *Journal of Social History,* 4 (1970)

Stearns, P. N., *Revolutionary syndicalism and French labour. A cause without rebels,* Rutgers University Press, New Brunswick, N.J. (1971)

Stearns, P. N., *Paths to authority. The middle class and the industrial labour force in France, 1820–48.* University of Illinois Press, Urbana, Ill. (1978)

Strumingher, L. S., ' "A bas les prêtres! A bas les couvents!" The Church and the workers in nineteenth century Lyon', *Journal of Social History,* 11 (1978)

Truant, C. M., 'Solidarity and symbolism among journeymen artisans. The case of Compagnonnage', *Comparative Studies in Society and History,* 21 (1979)

Waelbroek, P., 'Industrial relations in the French state mines of the Saar basin', parts 1 and 2, *International Labour Review,* 21 (1930); 22 (1930)

Willoughby, W. F., 'The French workmen's compensation Act', *Quarterly Journal of Economics,* 12

(1898)

Willoughby, W. F., 'The study of practical labour problems in France', *Quarterly Journal of Economics,* 13 (1899)

Willoughby, W. F., 'Labour legislation in France under the Third Republic', parts 1 and 2, *Quarterly Journal of Economics,* 15 (1900–01)

INCOMES, WAGES AND PRICES

Danière, A., 'Feudal incomes and demand elasticity for bread in late eighteenth century France', *Journal of Economic History,* 18 (1958) [see also D. S. Landes's reply and following discussion in same issue]

Daumard, A., 'Wealth and affluence in France since the beginning of the nineteenth century', in W. D. Rubinstein, ed., *Wealth and the wealthy in the Western world,* Croom Helm, London (1980)

Douglas, P. H., 'Family allowances and clearing funds in France', *Quarterly Journal of Economics,* 38 (1924)

Palyi, M., *A lesson in French inflation,* Economists' National Committee on Monetary Policy, New York (1959)

Rogers, J. H., *The process of inflation in France, 1914–27,* Columbia University Press, New York (1929)

Toutain, J. C., 'The uneven growth of regional incomes in France from 1840 to 1970', in P. Bairoch and M. Levy-Leboyer, eds, *Disparities in economic development since the industrial revolution,* Macmillan, London (1981)

Van der Wee, H., 'Real wage income during the *ancien régime* in the light of economic growth. Methodological and statistical problems', *Proceedings of the fourth international economic history conference, Bloomington, 1968,* Mouton, Paris (1973)

Wasserman, M. J., 'The compression of French wholesale prices during inflation, 1919–26', *American Economic Review,* 26 (1936)

URBAN HISTORY

Abercrombie, P., 'Paris. Some influences that have shaped its growth', *Town Planning Review,* 2 (1911–12)

Ackermann, E. B., 'The social and economic development of Bonnières-sur-Seine in the nineteenth century', *Proceedings of the Annual Meeing of the Western Society for French History,* 2 (1974)

Ackermann, E. B., 'The commune of Bonnières-sur Seine in the eighteenth and nineteenth centuries', *Annales,* (1977)

Ackermann, E. B., 'Alternative to rural exodus. The development of the commune of Bonnières-sur-Seine in the nineteenth century', *French Historical Studies,* 10 (1977–78)

Ackermann, E. B., *Village on the Seine. Tradition and change in Bonnières, 1815–1914,* Cornell University Press, Ithaca, N.Y. (1978)

Boulle, P. H., 'Slave trade, commercial organisation and industrial growth in eighteenth century Nantes', *Revue Française d'Histoire d'Outre-Mer,* 59 (1972)

Chapman, B., 'Baron Haussmann and the planning of Paris', *Town Planning Review,* 24 (1953–54)

Christofferson, T. R., 'Urbanisation and political change. The political transformation of Marseilles under the Second Republic', *Historian,* 36 (1974)

Couperie, P., *Paris through the ages. An illustrated atlas of urbanism and architecture,* Barrie and Jenkins, London (1970)

Evenson, N., 'The city as an artifact. Building control grand design, Studio Vista, London (1970?)

Evenson, N., *Paris. A century of change,* Yale University Press, New Haven, Conn. (1979)

Evanson, N., 'The city as an artifact. Building control in modern Paris', in R. Kain, ed., *Planning for conservation,* Mansell, London (1981)

Gutkind, E. A., *International history of city development.* vol. 5. *Urban development in western Europe. France and Belgium,* Collier-Macmillan, London (1970)

Haug, C. J., 'The population dynamics of a tourist city. Nice, 1872–1911', *Proceedings of the Annual Meeting of the Western Society for French History,* 3 (1975)

Hufton, O., *Bayeux in the late eighteenth century,* Cornell University Press, Ithaca, N.Y. (1963)

Jones, A. N., ' "Artisanal" production. A case study of Paris, 1847–60. A quantitative view', *Melbourne Historical Journal,* 12 (1977)

Laffey, J. F., 'Municipal imperialism in nineteenth century France', *Historical Reflections,* 1 (1974)

Laffey, J. F., 'Municipal imperialism in France. The Lyon Chamber of Commerce, 1900–14', *Proceedings of the American Philosophical Society,* 119 (1975)

Laffey, J. F., 'Municipal imperialism. The Lyon Chamber of Commerce, 1914–25', *Journal of European Economic History,* 4 (1975)

Laffey, J. F., 'Municipal imperialism in decline. The Lyon Chamber of Commerce, 1925–38', *French*

Historical Studies, 9 (1975–76)

Lees, L., 'Metropolitan types. London and Paris compared', in H. J. Dyos and M. Wolff, eds, *The Victorian city*, vol. 1, Routledge and Kegan Paul, London (1973)

Lefebvre, G., 'Urban society in the Orléanais in the late eighteenth century', *Past and Present*, 19 (1961)

Le Goff, T. J. A., *Vannes and its region. A study of town and country in eighteenth century France*, Oxford University Press, Oxford (1981)

Leonard, C. M., *Lyon transformed. Public works of the Second Empire, 1853–64*, University of California Press, Berkeley, Cal. (1961)

McPhee, P., 'Social change and political conflict in Mediterranean France. Canet in the nineteenth century', *French Historical Review*, 12 (1981–82)

Merriman, J. M., ed., *French cities in the nineteenth century*, Hutchinson, London (1982)

O'Brien, P. K., 'Urban growth and social control. The municipal police of Paris in the first half of the nineteenth century', *Proceedings of the Annual Meeting of the Western Society for French History*, 3 (1975)

Olivieri, A., 'An urban case history. Bordeaux', *Journal of European Economic History*, 2 (1973)

Peets, E., 'Haussmann', *Town Planning Review*, 12 (1927) [development of nineteenth century Paris]

Pinkney, D. H., 'Napoleon III's transformation of Paris. The origins and development of the idea', *Journal of Modern History*, 27 (1955)

Pinkney, D. H., 'Money and politics in the rebuilding of Paris, 1860–70', *Journal of Economic History*, 17 (1957)

Pinkney, D. H., *Napoleon III and the rebuilding of Paris*, Princeton University Press, Princeton, N.Y. (1958)

Ranum, O., *Paris in the age of absolution*, Indiana University Press, Bloomington, Ind. (1979)

Saalman, H., *Haussmann. Paris transformed*, G. Brazillier, New York (1971)

Sutcliffe, A., *The autumn of central Paris. The defeat of town planning, 1850–1970*, Edward Arnold, London (1970)

Sutcliffe, A., 'Environmental control and planning in European capitals, 1850–1914. London, Paris and Berlin', in I. Hammerström and T. Hall, eds, *Growth and transformation of the modern city*, Swedish Council for Building Research, Stockholm (1979)

Sutcliffe, A., 'Architecture and civic design in nineteenth century Paris', in I. Hammerström and T. Hall, eds, *Growth and transformation of the modern city*, Swedish Council for Building Research, Stockholm (1979)

Sutcliffe, A., *Towards the planned city. Germany, Britain, the United States and France, 1780–1914*, Blackwell, Oxford (1981)

Thomson, J. K. J., *Clermont-de-Lodève, 1633–1789. Fluctuations in the prosperity of a Languedocian cloth-making town*, Cambridge University Press, Cambridge (1982)

Uninsky, P. B., and C.A. Tamason, 'French cities in the eighteenth and nineteenth centuries', *Trends in History*, 2 (1981)

Williams, A., 'The police and public welfare in eighteenth century Paris', *Social Science Quarterly*, 56 (1975)

Williams, A., 'The police and the administration of eighteenth century Paris', *Journal of Urban History*, 4 (1978)

Williams, A., 'Patterns of deviance in eighteenth century Paris', *Proceedings of the Annual Meeting of the Western Society for French History*, 6 (1978)

Willis, F. R., 'Development planning in eighteenth century France. Corsica's Plan Terrier', *French Historical Studies*, 11 (1979–80)

Wolf, P. M., *Eugène Hénard and the beginning of urbanism in Paris, 1900–14*. Centre de Recherche d'Urbanisme, Paris (1968)

SOCIAL STRUCTURE AND SOCIAL CONDITIONS

Ackerknecht, E. H., and C. E. Rosenberg, 'German Jews, English dissenters, French Protestants. Nineteenth-century pioneers of modern medicine and science', in C. E. Rosenberg, ed., *Healing and History. Essays for George Rosen*, Science History Publications, New York (1979)

Ackermann, E. B., and E. A. Lang, 'Use by patients of a French provincial hospital, 1895–1923', *Bulletin of the History of Medicine*, 54 (1980)

Acomb, E. M., and M. L. Brown, eds, *French society and culture since the old regime*, Holt Rinehart and Winston, New York (1966)

Adams, T. M., 'From old regime to new. Business, bureaucracy, and social change in eighteenth century France', *Business History Review*, 55 (1981)

Agulhon, M., *The Republic in the village. The people of the Var from the French revolution to the Second Republic*, Cambridge University Press, Cambridge (1982)

Aminzade, R., 'The transformation of social solidarities in nineteenth century Toulouse', in J. M.

Merriman, ed., *Consciousness and class experience in nineteenth century Europe,* Holmes and Meier, New York (1979)

Aminzade, R., *Class, politics and early industrial capitalism. A study of mid-nineteenth century Toulouse,* State University of New York Press, Albany, N.Y. (1981)

Barber, E. D., *The bourgeoisie in eighteenth century France,* Princeton University Press, Princeton,. N.J. (1955)

Barrows, S., *Distorting mirrors. Visions of the crowd in late nineteenth century France,* Yale University Press, New Haven, Conn. (1981)

Beck, T. D., *French legislators, 1800–34. A study in quantitative history,* University of California Press, Berkeley, Cal. (1974)

Berker, L. K., and J. W. Shaffer, 'The joint family in the Nivernais', *Journal of Family History,* 3 (1978)

Berlanstein, L. R., 'Vagrants, beggars and thieves. Delinquent boys in mid-nineteenth century Paris', *Journal of Social History,* 12 (1979)

Berlanstein, L. R., 'Growing up as workers in nineteenth century Paris. The case of the orphans of the Prince Imperial', *French Historical Studies,* 11 (1979–80)

Berlanstein, L. R., 'Illegitimacy, concubinage and proletarianisation in a French rural town, 1760–1914', *Journal of Family History,* 5 (1980)

Blacker, J. G. C., 'Social ambitions of the bourgeoisie in eighteenth century France and their relation to family limitation', *Population Studies,* 11 (1957–58)

Blayo, Y., 'Size and structure of households in a northern French village between 1836 and 1861', in P. Laslett, ed., *Household and family in past time,* Cambridge University Press, Cambridge (1972)

Bosher, J. F., ed., *French government and society, 1500–1850. Essays in memory of Alfred Cobban,* Athlone Press, London (1973)

Boxer, M. J., 'Foyer or factory. Working class women in nineteenth century France', *Proceedings of the Annual Meeting of the Western Society for French History,* 2 (1974)

Boxer, M. J., 'French socialism, feminism and the family', *Third Republic,* 3–4 (1977)

Bynum, W. F., 'Chronic alcoholism in the first half of the nineteenth century', *Bulletin of the History of Medicine,* 42 (1968)

Cahm, E., *Politics and society in contemporary France (1789–1971). A documentary history,* Harrap, London (1972)

Cameron, I. A., 'The police of eighteenth century France', *European Studies Review,* 7 (1977)

Cameron, I. A., *Crime and repression in the Auvergne and the Guyenne, 1720–90,* Cambridge University Press, Cambridge (1981)

Castan, N., 'Crime and justice in Languedoc. The critical years (1750–90)', *Criminal Justice History,* 1 (1980)

Censer, J. R., *Prelude to power. The Parisian radical press, 1789–91,* Johns Hopkins University Press, Baltimore, Md. (1976)

Chamoux, A., 'Town and child in eighteenth century Rheims', *Local Population Studies,* 13 (1974)

Chevalier, L., *Labouring classes and dangerous classes in Paris during the first half of the nineteenth century,* Howard Fertig, New York (1973)

Chevalier, L., 'Crime and social pathology among the Parisian lower classes', in A. and L. Lees, eds, *The urbanisation of European society in the nineteenth century',* D. C. Heath, Lexington, Mass. (1976)

Christopher, J. C., 'The dessication of the bourgeois spirit', in E. M. Earle, ed., *Modern France. Problems of the Third and Fourth Republics,* Oxford University Press, London (1951)

Clark, L. L., 'Social Darwinism in France, *Journal of Modern History,* 53 (1981)

Cobb, R. C., *The police and the people. French popular protest, 1789–1820,* Oxford University Press, London (1970)

Cobban, A., *The social interpretation of the French revolution,* Cambridge University Press, Cambridge (1964)

Coleman, W., 'Health and hygiene in the *Encyclopédie.* A medical doctrine for the bourgeoisie', *Journal of the History of Medicine and Allied Sciences,* 29 (1974)

Corcia, J. di, 'Bourg, bourgeois, bourgeois de Paris from the eleventh to the eighteenth century', *Journal of Modern History,* 50 (1978)

Coward, D. A., 'Attitudes to homosexuality in eighteenth century France', *Journal of European Studies,* 10 (1980)

Cummings, M., 'The social impact of the Paulette. The case of the Parlement of Paris', *Canadian Journal of History,* 15 (1980)

Daumard, A., 'The Parisian bourgeoisie, 1815–48', in A. and L. Lees, eds, *The urbanisation of European society in the nineteenth century,* D. C. Heath, Lexington, Mass. (1976)

Drescher, S., 'Two variations of anti-slavery. Religious organisation and social mobilisation in Britain and France, 1780–1870', in C. Bolt and S. Drescher, eds, *Anti-slavery, religion and reform. Essays in memory of Roger Anstey*, Dawson, Folkestone (1980)

Dupaquier, J., 'Naming practices, godparenthood, and kinship in the Vexin, 1540–1900', *Journal of Family History*, 6 (1981)

Dupeux, G., *French society, 1789–1970*, Methuen, London (1976)

Edwards, S., *The Paris commune, 1871*, Quadrangle Books, Chicago, Ill. (1973)

Elwitt, S., 'Social reform and social order in late nineteenth century France. The *musée social* and its friends', *French Historical Studies*, 11 (1979–80)

Fairchilds, C. C., *Poverty and charity in Aix-en-Provence, 1640–1789*, Johns Hopkins University Press, Baltimore, Md. (1976)

Fairchilds, C. C., 'Female sexual attitudes and the rise of illegitimacy. A case study', *Journal of Interdisciplinary History*, 8 (1977–78)

Faure, O., 'Physicians in Lyon during the nineteenth century. An exceptional social success', *Journal of Social History*, 10 (1977)

Feeley, D., 'Women in the Paris commune', *International Socialist Review*, 32 (1971)

Feinerman, F. M., 'What aided France in the 1750s? Mirabeau presents the nobility's diagnosis', *Proceedings of the Western Society for French History*, 7 (1979)

Ford, F. L., *Robe and sword. The regrouping of the French aristocracy after Louis XIV*, Harvard University Press, Cambridge, Mass. (1953)

Forrest, A., 'The conditions of the poor in revolutionary Bordeaux', *Past and Present*, 59 (1973)

Forrest, A., *The French revolution and the poor*, Blackwell, Oxford (1981)

Forstenzer, T. R., *French provincial police and the fall of the Second Republic. Social fear and counter-revolution*, Princeton University Press, Princeton, N.J. (1981)

Forster, R., *The nobility of Toulouse in the eighteenth century. A social and economic study*, Johns Hopkins University Press, Baltimore, Md. (1960)

Forster, R., 'The survival of the nobility during the French revolution', *Past and Present*, 37 (1967)

Forster, R., *The house of Saulx-Tavanes, Versailles and Burgundy, 1700–1830*, Johns Hopkins University Press, Baltimore, Md. (1971)

Forster, R., 'The French revolution and the "new" elite, 1800–50', in J. Pelenski, ed., *The American and European revolutions, 1776–1848. Socio-political and ideological aspects*, University of Iowa Press, Iowa City, Iowa (1980)

Forster, R., *Merchants, landlords, magistrates. The Dupont family in eighteenth century France*, Johns Hopkins University Press, Baltimore, Md. (1980)

Forster, R., and O. Ranum, eds, *Rural society in France*, Johns Hopkins University Press, Baltimore, Md. (1977)

Forty, A., 'The modern hospital in England and France. The social and medical uses of architecture', in A. D. King, ed., *Buildings and society. Essays on the social development of the built environment*, Routledge and Kegan Paul, London (1980)

Fox, R., 'Learning, politics and polite culture in provincial France. The *sociétés savantes* in the nineteenth century', *Historical Reflections*, 7 (1980)

Furet, F., and J. Ozouf, 'Three centuries of cultural cross-fertilisation. France', in H. J. Graff, ed., *Literacy and social development in the West. A reader*, Cambridge University Press, Cambridge (1981)

Gargan, E. T., and R. A. Hanneman, 'Recruitment to the clergy in nineteenth century France. "Modernisation" and "decline" ', *Journal of Interdisciplinary History*, 9 (1978–79)

Gelfand, T., 'Gestation of the clinic', *Medical History*, 25 (1981) [Parisian hospitals and surgeons in the late eighteenth century]

Gibson, R., 'The French nobility in the nineteenth century – particularly in the Dordogne', in J. Howorth and P. G. Cerny, eds, *Elites in France. Origins, reproduction and power*, Frances Pinter, London (1981)

Giesey, R. E., 'Rules of inheritance and strategies of mobility in pre-revolutionary France', *American Historical Review*, 82 (1977)

Gildea, R., 'Education and the *classes moyennes* in the nineteenth century', *Historical Reflections*, 7 (1980)

Godechot, J., 'The business classes and the revolution outside France', *American Historical Review*, 64 (1958–59)

Goubert, P., 'Family and province. A contribution to the knowledge of family structures in early modern France', *Journal of Family History*, 2 (1977)

Goubert, P., 'The extent of medical practice in France around 1780', *Journal of Social History*, 10 (1977)

Grassby, R. B., 'Social status and commercial enterprise under Louis XIV', *Economic History*

Review, 13 (1960–61)

Greenbaum, L. S., 'Scientists and politicians. Hospital reform in Paris on the eve of the French revolution', in C. C. Sturgill, ed., *The consortium on revolutionary Europe, 1750–1850*, University Presses of Florida, Gainesville, Fla. (1975)

Greenbaum, L. S., 'Science, medicine, religion. Three views of health care in France on the eve of the French revolution', *Studies in Eighteenth Century Culture*, 20 (1981)

Gurvitch, G., 'Social structure in pre-war France', *American Journal of Sociology*, 48 (1943)

Hampson, N., *A social history of the French revolution*, Routledge and Kegan Paul, London (1963)

Hanagan, M. P., 'The logic of solidarity. Social structure in Le Chambon-Feugerolles', *Journal of Urban History*, 3 (1977)

Hanagan, M. P., 'The politics of proletarianisation. A review article', *Comparative Studies in Society and History*, 21 (1979)

Harrigan, P. J., *Mobility, elites and education in French society of the Second Empire*, Wilfred Laurier University Press, Waterloo, Ontario (1980)

Hartman, M. S., 'Crime and the respectable woman. Towards a pattern of middle-class female criminality in nineteenth century France and England', *Feminist Studies*, 2 (1974)

Hellerstein, E., *et al.*, *Victorian women. A documentary account of women's lives in nineteenth-century England, France and the United States*, Harvester Press, Brighton (1982)

Holt, R., *Sport and society in modern France*, Archon, Hamden, Conn. (1981)

Howorth, J., and P. G. Cerny, eds, *Elites in France. Origins, reproduction and power*, Frances Pinter, London (1981)

Hufton, O., 'Begging, vagrancy and vagabondage and the law. An aspect of the problem of poverty in eighteenth century France', *European Studies Review*, 2 (1972)

Hufton, O., *The poor of eighteenth century France, 1750–89*, Oxford University Press, London (1974)

Hufton, O., 'Women and family economy in eighteenth century France', *French Historical Studies*, 9 (1975–76)

Hunt, D., *Parents and children in history. The psychology of family life in early modern France*, Basic Books, London (1970)

Hunt, D., 'The people and Pierre Dolivier. Popular uprisings in the Seine-et-Oise Department', *French Historical Studies*, 11 (1979–80)

Ingraham, B. L., *Political crime in Europe. A comparative study of France, Germany and England*,

University of California Press, Berkeley, Cal. (1979)

Isherwood, R. M., 'Entertainment in the Parisian fairs in the eighteenth century', *Journal of Modern History*, 53 (1981)

Jensen, C., and D. Bitton, 'Social mobility in Clairac', *Proceedings of the Annual Meeting of the Western Society for French History*, 7 (1979)

Johnson, D., ed., *French society and the revolution*, Cambridge University Press, Cambridge (1976)

Jones, C., *Charity and bienfaisance. The treatment of the poor in the Montpellier region, 1740–1815*, Cambridge University Press, Cambridge (1982)

Jones, P. M., 'The rural bourgeoisie of the southern Massif Central. A contribution to the study of the social structure of *ancien régime* France', *Social History*, 4 (1979)

Jones, P. M., 'Political commitment and rural society in the southern Massif Central', *European Studies Review*, 10 (1980)

Jones, P. M., 'Parish, *seigneurie* and the community of inhabitants in southern central France during the eighteenth and nineteenth centuries', *Past and Present*, 91 (1981)

Kagan, R. L., 'Law students and legal careers in eighteenth century France', *Past and Present*, 68 (1975)

Kaiser, C., 'The deflation in the volume of litigation at Paris in the eighteenth century and the waning of the old judicial order', *European Studies Review*, 10 (1980)

Kanipe, E. S., 'Working class women and the social question in late nineteenth century France', *Proceedings of the Annual Meeting of the Western Society for French History*, 6 (1978)

Kaplan, S. L., 'Religion, subsistence and social control. The uses of Saint Geneviève', *Eighteenth Century Studies*, 13 (1979–80)

Kaplow, J., *The names of kings. The Parisian labouring poor in the eighteenth century*, Basic Books, New York (1972)

La Berge, A. F., 'The French public health movement, 1815–48', *Proceedings of the Annual Meeting of the Western Society for French History*, 3 (1975)

La Berge, A. F., 'A. J. B. Parent-Duchatelet. Hygienist of Paris, 1821–36', *Clio Medica*, 12 (1977)

La Berge, A. F., 'A restoration prefect and public health. Alban de Villeneuve-Bargemont at Nantes and Lille, 1824–30', *Proceedings of the Annual Meeting of the Western Society for French History*, 5 (1977)

Lehning, J. R., *The peasants of Marlhes. Economic*

development and family organisation in nineteenth century France, University of North Carolina Press, Chapel Hill, N.C. (1980)

Lemey, E., 'Thomas Herier, a country surgeon outside Angoulême at the end of the eighteenth century. A contribution to social history', *Journal of Society History*, 10 (1977)

Lerch, O., 'Itinerants, modernisation and the development of popular culture in France, 1870–1914', *Proceedings of the Annual Meeting of the Western Society for French History*, 6 (1978)

Litchfield, R. B., and D. Gordon, 'Closing the "Tour". A close look at the marriage market, unwed mothers and abandoned children in mid-nineteenth century Amiens', *Journal of Social History*, 13 (1980)

Lodhi, A. Q., and C. Tilly, 'Urbanisation, crime and collective violence in nineteenth century France', *American Journal of Sociology*, 79 (1973)

Lynch, K. A., 'The problem of child labour reform and the working class family in France during the July monarchy', *Proceedings of the Annual Meeting of the Western Society for French History*, 5 (1977)

McBride, T. M., 'Social mobility for the lower class. Domestic servants in France', *Journal of Social History*, 8 (1974)

McBride, T. M., ' "Women's work". Mistress and servant in the nineteenth century', *Proceedings of the Annual Meeting of the Western Society for French History*, 3 (1975)

McBride, T. M., *The domestic revolution. The modernisation of household service in England and France, 1820–1920*, Croom Helm, London (1976)

McBride, T. M., 'The modernisation of "women's work" ', *Journal of Modern History*, 49 (1977)

McBride, T. M., *'Ni bourgeoises, ni proletaires.* Women sales clerks, 1870–1920', *Proceedings of the Annual Meeting of the Western Society for French History*, 5 (1977)

McCloy, S. T., *The humanitarian movement in eighteenth century France*, University of Kentucky Press, Lexington, Ky. (1957)

McDougall, M. L., 'Working class women during the industrial revolution, 1780–1914', in R. Bridenthal and C. Koonz, eds, *Becoming visible. Women in European history'*, Houghton Mifflin, Boston, Mass. (1977)

McLaren, A., 'Doctor in the house. Medicine and private morality in France, 1800–50', *Feminist Studies*, 2 (1975)

McLaren, A., 'Abortion in France. Women and the regulation of family size, 1800–1914', *French Historical Studies*, 10 (1977–78)

McLaren, A., 'Some secular attitudes towards sexual behaviour in France, 1760–1860', *French Historical Studies*, 8 (1973–74)

McLaren, A., 'A prehistory of the social sciences. Phrenology in France', *Comparative Studies in Society and History*, 23 (1981)

McMillan, J. F., *Housewife or harlot. The place of women in French society*, St Martin's, New York (1981)

McPhee, P., 'Social change and political conflict in Mediterranean France. Canet in the nineteenth century', *French Historical Studies*, 12 (1981)

Manceron, C., *Their gracious pleasure. Last days of the aristocracy, 1782–85*, Knopf, New York (1981)

Margadant, T. W., 'The Paris commune. A revolution that failed', *Journal of Interdisciplinary History*, 7 (1976–77)

Marrus, M. R., 'Social drinking in the *belle époque*', *Journal of Social History*, 7 (1974)

Martin, B. F., 'Law and order in France, 1980 and 1912', *Contemporary French Civilisation*, 5 (1981)

Matossian, M. K., and W. D. Schafer, 'Family, fertility and political violence, 1700–1900', *Journal of Social History*, 11 (1977)

Mayeur, F., 'Women and elites from the nineteenth to the twentieth century', in J. Howorth and P. G. Cerny, eds, *Elites in France. Origins, reproduction and power*, Frances Pinter, London (1981)

Maynes, M. J., 'Work or school? Youth and the family in the Midi in the early nineteenth century', *Historical Reflections*, 7 (1980)

Merriman, J. M., 'Social conflict in France and the Limôges revolution of April 27, 1848', *Societàs*, 4 (1974)

Mitchell, H., 'Resistance to the revolution in western France', *Past and Present*, 63 (1974)

Mitchell, H., 'Politics in the service of knowledge. The debate over the administration of medicine and welfare in late eighteenth century France', *Social History*, 6 (1981)

Mogensen, W., 'Crimes and punishments in eighteenth century France. The example of the Pays d'Auge', *Social History*, 10 (1977)

Monaco, P., *Cinema and society. France and Germany during the twenties*, Elsevier, New York (1976)

Mousnier, R., and B. Pearce, *The institutions of France under the absolute monarchy, 1598–1789. Society and the state*, University of Chicago Press, Chicago, Ill. (1979)

Murphy, T. D., 'The French medical profession's perception of its social function between 1776 and 1830', *Medical History*, 23 (1979)

Offen, K. M., 'The "woman question" as a social issue in nineteenth century France. A bibliographical guide', *Third Republic*, 3–4 (1977)

Osborne, T. R., 'Social science at the Sciences Po. Training the bureaucratic elite in the early Third Republic', *Historical Reflections*, 8 (1981)

Parish, W. L., and M. Schwartz, 'Household complexity in eighteenth century France', *American Sociological Review*, 37 (1972)

Payne, H. C., 'Elite versus popular mentality in the eighteenth century', *Studies in Eighteenth Century Culture*, 8 (1979) [social reform 1750–89]

Peter, J. P., 'Disease and the sick at the end of the eighteenth century', in R. Forster and O. Ranum, eds, *Biology of man in history*, Johns Hopkins University Press, Baltimore, Md. (1975)

Phillips, R., 'Women and family breakdown in eighteenth century France. Rouen, 1780–1800', *Social History*, 2 (1976)

Phillips, R., 'Women's emancipation, the family and social change in eighteenth century France', *Journal of Social History*, 12 (1979)

Phillips, R., 'Gender solidarities in late eighteenth century urban France. The example of Rouen', *Social History*, 13 (1980)

Phillips, R., *Family breakdown in late eighteenth century France. Divorces in Rouen*, Oxford University Press, New York (1981)

Pilbeam, P., 'Popular violence in provincial France after the 1830 revolution', *English Historical Review*, 91 (1976)

Pope, B. C., 'Angels in the devil's workshop. Leisured and charitable women in nineteenth century England and France', in R. Bridenthal and C. Koonz, eds, *Becoming visible. Women in European history*, Houghton Mifflin, Boston, Mass. (1977)

Pope, B. C., 'Revolution and retreat. Upper class French women after 1789', in C. R. Berkin and C. M. Lovett, eds, *Women, war and revolution*, Holmes and Meier, New York (1980)

Prestwich, P. E., 'Temperance in France. The curious case of Absinth', *Historical Reflections*, 6 (1979)

Prestwich, P. E., 'French workers and the temperance movement', *International Review of Social History*, 25 (1980)

Price, R., 'Popular disturbances in the French provinces after the July revolution of 1830', *European Studies Review*, 1 (1971)

Price, R., 'Conservative reactions to social disorder. The Paris commune of 1871', *Journal of European Studies*, 1 (1971)

Price, R., *The French Second Republic. A social history*, Batsford, London (1981)

Przeworski, A., *et al.*, 'The evolution of the class structure in France, 1901–68', *Economic Development and Cultural Change*, 28 (1979–80)

Reddy, W. M., 'The textile trade and the language of the crowd at Rouen, 1752–1871', *Past and Present*, 74 (1977)

Reddy, W. M., 'Skeins, scales, discounts, steam and other objects of crowd justice in early French textile mills', *Comparative Studies in Society and History*, 21 (1979)

Redlich, F., 'Science and charity. Count Rumford and his followers', *International Review of Social History*, 16 (1971) [soup kitchens and nutrition in the nineteenth century]

Riley, P. F., 'Police and the search for *bon ordre* in Louis XIV's Paris', *Proceedings of the Annual Meeting of the Western Society for French History*, 7 (1979)

Rose, R. B., 'Eighteenth century price riots. The French revolution and the Jacobin maximum', *International Review of Social History*, 3 (1959)

Roubin, L., 'Male space and female space within within the Provençal community', in R. Forster and O. Ranum, eds, *Rural society in France*, Johns Hopkins University Press, Baltimore, Md. (1977)

Rudé, G. E., 'The motives of popular insurrections in Paris during the French revolution', *Bulletin of the Institute of Historical Research*, 26 (1953)

Rudé, G. E., 'Prices, wages and popular movements in Paris during the French revolution', *Economic History Review*, 6 (1954)

Rudé, G. E., *The crowd in the French revolution*, Clarendon Press, Oxford (1959)

Rudé, G. E., *Paris and London in the eighteenth century. Studies in popular protest*, Viking Press, New York (1971)

Rudé, G. E., 'Urbanisation and popular protest in eighteenth century western Europe', *Eighteenth Century Life*, 2 (1976)

Rudé, G. E., 'Ideology and popular protest in revolutionary France, 1789–1871', *Proceedings of the Annual Meeting of the Western Society for French History*, 6 (1978)

Ruff, J., 'Law and order in eighteenth century France. The Maréchaussée of Guyenne', *Proceedings of the Annual Meeting of the Western Society for French History*, 4 (1976)

Salmon, J. H. M., 'Storm over the *noblesse*', *Journal of Modern History*, 53 (1981)

Sawyer, J. E., 'The entrepreneur and the social order. France and the United States', in W. Miller, ed., *Men in business*, Harvard University Press, Cambridge, Mass. (1952)

Scott, J. W., 'Socialisation in two French villages', *History of Education Quarterly*, 13 (1973)

Scott, J. W., 'The history of the family as an affective unit', *Social History*, 4 (1979)

Scott, J. W., 'Social history and the history of socialism. French socialist municipalities in the 1890s', *Mouvement Social*, 111 (1980)

Segalen, M., 'The family cycle and household structure. Five generations in a French village', in R. Wheaton and T. K. Hareven, eds, *Family and sexuality in French history*, University of Pennsylvania Press, Philadelphia, Pa. (1980)

Sewell, W. H., 'Social mobility in a nineteenth century city. Some findings and implications', *Journal of Interdisciplinary History*, 7 (1976–77)

Shaffer, J. W., 'Family, class and young women. Occupational expectations in nineteenth century Paris', *Journal of Family History*, 3 (1978)

Shapiro, A. L., 'Private rights, public interest and professional jurisdiction. The French public health law of 1902', *Bulletin of the History of Medicine*, 54 (1980)

Silver, J., 'French peasant demands for popular leadership in the Vendômois (Loir-et-Cher), 1852–90', *Journal of Social History*, 14 (1980)

Singer, B., 'The teacher as notable in Brittany, 1880–1914', *French Historical Studies*, 9 (1975–76)

Singer, B., *Village notables in nineteenth century France. Priests, mayors, schoolmasters*, State University of New York Press, Albany, N.Y. (1982)

Sirinelli, J. F., 'The Ecole Normale Supérieure and elite formation and selection during the Third Republic', in J. Howorth and P. G. Cerny, eds, *Elites in France. Origins, reproduction and power*, Frances Pinter, London (1981)

Skocpol, T., 'France, Russia, China. A structural analysis of social revolutions', *Comparative Studies in Society and History*, 18 (1976)

Smith, B. G., *Ladies of the leisure class. The bourgeoisie of northern France during the nineteenth century*, Princeton University Press, Princeton, N.J. (1981)

Smith, J. H., 'Work routine and social structure in a French village. Cruzy Hérault in the nineteenth century', *Journal of Interdisciplinary History*, 5 (1974–75)

Smith, R. L., 'The rise of the mass press in nineteenth century France', *Journalism Quarterly*, 53 (1976)

Sorlin, P., 'French society, 1840–1914. The big cities', in A. and L. Lees, eds, *The urbanisation of European society in the nineteenth century*, D. C. Heath, Lexington, Mass. (1976)

Sowerwine, C., *Sisters or citizens? Women and socialism in France since 1876*, Cambridge University Press, Cambridge (1982)

Spears, J., 'Folk medicine and popular attitudes toward disease in the high Alps, 1780–1870', *Bulletin of the History of Medicine*, 54 (1980)

Stearns, P. N., *Old age in European society. The case of France*, Croom Helm, London (1977)

Strebel, E. G., 'French social cinema and the popular front', *Journal of Contemporary History*, 12 (1977)

Strieter, T. W., 'The French army's cadre, a mirror of French civilian society? Some aspects of the family among the professional cadre, 1848–1895' *Proceedings of the Annual Meeting of the Western Society for French History*, 7 (1979)

Strumingher, L. S., 'Women's work and consciousness. Lyon, 1830–50', *Societàs*, 6 (1976)

Strumingher, L. S., 'The artisan family. Traditions and transition in nineteenth century Lyon', *Journal of Family History*, 2 (1977)

Strumingher, L. S., *Women and the making of the working class. Lyon, 1830–70*, Eden Press, St Albans, Vt. (1979)

Suleiman, E. N., *Elites in French society*, Princeton University Press, Princeton, N.J. (1978)

Sussman, G. D., 'Carriers of cholera and poison rumours in France in 1832', *Societàs*, 3 (1973)

Sussman, G. D., 'The wet-nursing business in Paris, 1769–1876', *Proceedings of the Annual Meeting of the Western Society for French History*, 1 (1973)

Sussman, G. D., 'The wet-nursing business in nineteenth century France', *French Historical Studies*, 9 (1975–76)

Sussman, G. D., 'Parisian infants and Norman wet-nurses in the early nineteenth century. A statistical study', *Journal of Interdisciplinary History*, 7 (1976–77)

Sussman, G. D., 'Enlightened health reform, professional medicine and traditional society. The cantonal physicians of the Bas-Rhin, 1810–70', *Bulletin of the History of Medicine*, 51 (1977)

Sussman, G. D., 'The end of the wet-nursing business in France, 1874–1914', *Journal of Family History*, 2 (1977)

Sussman, G. D., 'The end of the wet-nursing business in France, 1874–1914', in R. Wheaton and T. K.

Hareven, eds, *Family and sexuality in French history*, University of Pennsylvania Press, Philadelphia, Pa. (1980)

Talbott, J., 'Private lives and public affairs in nineteenth century France', *Journal of Interdisciplinary History*, 7 (1976–77)

Tamason, C. A., 'From mortuary to cemetery. Funeral riots and funeral demonstrations in Lille, 1779–1870', *Social Science History*, 4 (1980)

Tilly, C., 'Local conflicts in the Vendée before the rebellion of 1793', *French Historical Studies*, 2 (1961)

Tilly, C., *The Vendée. A sociological analysis of the counter-revolution of 1793*, Harvard University Press, Cambridge, Mass. (1964)

Tilly, C., 'How protest modernised in France, 1845–55', in W. O. Aydelotte *et al., The dimensions of quantitative research in history*, Princeton University Press, Princeton, N.J. (1972)

Tilly, C., 'Getting it together in Burgundy, 1675–1975', *Theory and Society*, 4 (1977)

Tilly, C., 'Did the cake of custom break?', in J. M. Merriman, ed., *Consciousness and class experience in nineteenth century Europe*, Holmes and Meier, New York (1979)

Tilly, C., The web of contention in eighteenth century cities', in L. A. and C. Tilly, eds, *Class conflict and collective action*, Sage Publications, Beverley Hills, Cal. (1981)

Tilly, L. A., 'The food riot as a form of political conflict in France', *Journal of Interdisciplinary History*, 2 (1971)

Tilly, L. A., 'Industrial lives and family strategies in the French proletariat', *Journal of Family History*, 4 (1979)

Tilly, L. A., 'The family wage economy of a French textile city. Roubaix, 1872–1906', *Journal of Family History*, 4 (1979)

Tilly, L. A., 'Women's collective action and feminism in France, 1870–1914', in L. A. and C. Tilly, eds, *Class conflict and collective action*, Sage Publications, Beverley Hills, Cal. (1981)

Tomlos, R., 'Revolt and repression in France', *Historical Journal*, 24 (1981)

Vess, D. M., 'French medical institutions during the revolution', in L. Kennett, ed., *The consortium on revolutionary Europe, 1750–1850*, University of Florida Press, Gainesville, Fla. (1973)

Vess, D. M., *Medical revolution in France, 1789–1896*, Florida State University Press, Gainesville, Fla. (1975)

Weary, W. A., 'The house of Trémoille. Fifteenth through eighteenth centuries. Change and adaptation in a French noble family', *Journal of Modern History*, 49 (1977)

Weiner, D., 'François-Vincent Raspail. Doctor and champion of the poor', *French Historical Studies*, 1 (1959)

Wheaton, R., and T. K. Hareven, eds, *Family and sexuality in French history*, University of Pennsylvania Press, Philadelphia, Pa. (1980)

Wilkins, W. H., 'The debate over secondary and higher education for women in nineteenth century France', *North Dakota Quarterly*, 49 (1981)

Wilson, L. C., 'Fevers and science in early nineteenth century medicine', *Journal of the History of Medicine and Allied Science*, 33 (1978)

Wilson, S., 'Conflict and its causes in southern Corsica, 1800–35', *Social History*, 6 (1981)

Woloch, I., 'War widows' pensions. Social policy in revolutionary and Napoleonic France', *Societàs*, 6 (1976)

Zehr, H., 'The modernisation of crime in Germany and France, 1830–1913', *Journal of Social History*, 8 (1975)

Zehr, H., *Crime and the development of modern society. Patterns of criminality in nineteenth century Germany and France*, Croom Helm, London (1976)

ECONOMIC POLICY AND THOUGHT

Bernstein, P., 'The economic aspect of Napoleon III's Rhine policy', *French Historical Studies*, 1 (1960)

Brinton, C., *French revolutionary legislation on illegitimacy, 1789–1804*, Harvard University Press, Cambridge, Mass. (1936)

Carlisle, R. B., 'Metropolis and cosmopolis. The Saint-Simonian synthesis', *Proceedings of the Annual Meeting of the Western Society for French History*, 5 (1977)

Clark, L. L., 'Social Darwinism in France, 1860–1915. Some reactions from political quarters', *Proceedings of the Annual Meeting of the Western Society for French History*, 4 (1976)

Clark, L. L., 'Social Darwinism in France', *Journal of Modern History*, 53 (1981)

Clark, T. N., *Prophets and patrons. The French university and the emergence of the social sciences*, Harvard University Press, Cambridge, Mass. (1973)

Clarke, S.V.O., 'The influence of the economists on the tripartite agreement of September, 1936', in M. W. Flinn, ed., *Proceedings of the seventh international congress on economic history, Edinburgh,*

1978, Edinburgh University Press, Edinburgh (1978)

Cohen, D. K., 'Lemontey. An early critic of industrialism', *French Historical Studies*, 4 (1966)

Cole, C. W., *Colbert and a century of French mercantilism*, 2 vols, Columbia University Press, New York (1939)

Du Boff, R. B., 'Economic thought in revolutionary France, 1789–92. The question of poverty and unemployment', *French Historical Studies*, 4 (1966)

Fox-Genovese, E., 'The physiocratic model and the transition from feudalism to capitalism', *Journal of European Economic History*, 4 (1975)

Fox-Genovese, E., *The origins of physiocracy. Economic revolution and social order in eighteenth century France*, Cornell University Press, Ithaca, N.Y. (1976)

Grabau, T. W., 'Visions of the future. Wartime perceptions of the goals of postwar reconstruction in France, 1914–19', *Proceedings of the Annual Meeting of the Western Society for French History*, 7 (1979)

Hill, M. J., 'The French perception of and reaction to early nineteenth century industrialisation', *Proceedings of the Annual Meeting of the Western Society for French History*, 1 (1973)

Jones, R. A., and R. M. Anservitz, 'Saint-Simon and Saint-Simonism. A Weberian view', *American Journal of Sociology*, 80 (1975)

Kalecki, M., 'The lesson of the Blum experiment', *Economic Journal*, 48 (1938)

Katzenback, E. L., 'Liberals at war. The economic policies of the government of national defence, 1870–71', *American Historical Review*, 56 (1950–51)

Kindleberger, C. P., 'Keynesianism versus monetarism in eighteenth and nineteenth century France', *History of Political Economy*, 12 (1980)

Kuisel, R. F., 'Technocrats and public economic policy. From the Third to the Fourth Republics', *Journal of European Economic History*, 2 (1973)

Lodge, E. C., *Sully, Colbert and Turgot. A chapter in French economic history*, Methuen, London (1931)

McCloy, S. T., 'Government assistance during the plague of 1720–22 in south-eastern France', *Social Service Review*, 12 (1938)

McCloy, S. T., 'Flood relief and control in eighteenth century France', *Journal of Modern History*, 13 (1941)

McCloy, S. T., *Government assistance in eighteenth*

century France, Duke University Press, Durham, N.C. (1946)

McLaren, A., 'A prehistory of the social sciences. Phrenology in France', *Comparative Studies in Society and History*, 23 (1981) [French social policy, 1800–50]

Marjolin, R., 'Reflections on the Blum experiment', *Economica*, 5 (1938)

Maurette, F., 'A year of experiment in France', parts 1 and 2, *International Labour Review*, 36 (1937)

Monnet, G., 'The place of agriculture in the economic policy of the French government', *International Affairs*, 16 (1937)

Oualid, W., 'National social insurance in France', *Journal of Political Economy*, 42 (1934)

Parker, H. T., 'Two administrative bureaux under the Directory and Napoleon', *French Historical Studies*, 4 (1965)

Peel, A. G. V., *The economic policy of France*, Macmillan, London (1937)

Picard, R., 'The German and French national economic councils', *International Labour Review*, 11 (1925)

Rappaport, R., 'Government patronage of science in eighteenth century France. An essay review', *History of Science*, 8 (1969)

Ratcliffe, B. M., 'The economic influence of the Saint-Simonians. Myth or reality', *Proceedings of the Annual Meeting of the Western Society for French History*, 5 (1977)

Schwob, P., 'French monetary policy and its critics', *Economica*, 2 (1935)

Seeber, E. D., *Anti-slavery opinion in France during the second half of the eighteenth century*, Johns Hopkins University Press, Baltimore, Md. (1937)

Sherman, D., 'The meaning of economic liberalism in mid-nineteenth century France', *History of Political Economy*, 6 (1974)

Sherman, D., 'Government policy toward joint-stock business organisations in mid-nineteenth century France', *Journal of European Economic History*, 3 (1974)

Sherman, D., 'Governmental responses to economic modernisation in mid-nineteenth century France', *Journal of European Economic History*, 6 (1977)

Spengler, J. J., *French predecessors of Malthus. A study in eighteenth century wage and population theory*, Duke University Press, Durham, N.C. (1942)

Trachtenberg, M., 'A "new economic order". Etienne Clementel and French economic diplomacy during the first world war', *French Histori-*

cal Studies, 10 (1977–78)

Tugwell, R. G., 'The agricultural policy of France', *Political Science Quarterly,* 45 (1930)

Watson, C., 'Recent developments in French immigration policy', *Population Studies,* 6 (1952–53)

EDUCATION, SCIENCE AND TECHNOLOGY

Ahlstrom, G., 'Higher technical education and the engineering profession in France and Germany during the nineteenth century', *Economy and History,* 21 (1978)

Artz, F. B., *The development of technical education in France, 1500–1850,* Massachusetts Institute of Technology Press, Cambridge, Mass. (1966)

Baker, D. N., and P. J. Harrigan, eds, *The making of Frenchmen. Current directions in the history of education in France, 1679–1979,* Historical Reflections Press, Waterloo, Ontario (1980)

Bradley, M., 'Scientific education for a new society. The Ecole Polytechnique, 1795–1830', *History of Education,* 5 (1976)

Bush, J. W., 'Education and social status. The Jesuit College in the early Third Republic', *French Historical Studies,* 9 (1975–76)

Chisick, H., 'Institutional innovation in popular education in eighteenth century France. Two examples', *French Historical Studies,* 10 (1977–78)

Crosland, M., 'Science and the Franco-Prussian war', *Social Studies of Science,* 6 (1976)

Day, C. R., 'Technical and professional education in France. The rise and fall of l'Enseignement Secondaire Spécial, 1865–1902', *Journal of Social History,* 6 (1972–73)

Day, C. R., 'Education, technology and social change in France. The short unhappy life of the Cluny School, 1866–91', *French Historical Studies,* 8 (1973–74)

Day, C. R., 'Social advancement and the primary school teacher. The making of Normal School directors in France, 1815–80', *Social History,* 7 (1974)

Day, C. R., 'The development of higher primary and intermediate technical education in France, 1800–70', *Historical Reflections,* 3 (1976)

Day, C. R., 'The Third Republic and the development of intermediate education in France, 1870–1914', *Proceedings of the Annual Meeting of the Western Society for French History,* 4 (1976)

Day, C. R., 'The making of mechanical engineers in France. The Ecoles d'Arts et Métiers, 1803–14', *French Historical Studies,* 10 (1977–78)

Day, C. R., 'Making men and training technicians. Boarding schools of the Ecoles d'Arts et Métiers during the nineteenth century', *Historical Reflections,* 7 (1980)

Fox, R., and G. Weisz, eds, *The organisation of science and technology in France, 1808–1914,* Cambridge University Press, Cambridge (1980)

Furet, F., and J. Ozouf, 'Literacy and industrialisation. The case of the Département du Nord in France', *Journal of European Economic History,* 5 (1976)

Gerbod, P., 'The *baccalauréat* and its role in the recruitment and promotion of French elites in the nineteenth century', in J. Howorth and P. G. Cerny, eds, *Elites in France. Origins, reproduction and power,* Frances Pinter, London (1981)

Gillespie, C. C., *Science and polity in France at the end of the old regime,* Princeton University Press, Princeton, N.J. (1980)

Harrigan, P. J., 'Elites, education and social mobility in France during the Second Empire', *Proceedings of the Annual Meeting of the Western Society for French History,* 4 (1976)

Harrigan, P. J., *Mobility, elites and education in French society of the Second Empire,* Wilfred Laurier University Press, Waterloo, Ontario (1980)

Helmreich, J. E., 'The establishment of primary schools in France under the Directory', *French Historical Studies,* 2 (1961)

Henderson, W. O., 'The growth of technical education in France and the activities of French mining engineers on the Continent in the age of Napoleon', in K. H. Manegold, ed., *Wissenschaft, Wirtschaft und Technik. Studien zur Geschichte. Wilhelm Treue zum 60. Geburtstag,* Bruckmann, Munich (1969)

Jefferson, C., 'Worker education in England and France, 1800–1914', *Comparative Studies in Sociology,* 6 (1964)

Karady, V., 'Scientists and class structure. Social recruitment of students at the Parisian Ecole Normale Supérieure in the nineteenth century', *History of Education,* 8 (1979)

Kindleberger, C. P., 'Technical education and the French entrepreneurs', in E. C. Carter *et al., Enterprise and entrepreneurs in nineteenth and twentieth century France,* Johns Hopkins University Press, Baltimore, Md. (1976)

Laqueur, T. W., 'English and French education in the nineteenth century', *History of Education Quarterly,* 13 (1973)

Louges, C. C., 'Noblesse, domesticity and social reform. The education of girls by Fénelon and Saint-Cyr', *History of Education Quarterly,* 14

(1974)

McCloy, S. T., *French inventions of the eighteenth century*. University of Kentucky Press, Lexington, Ky. (1952)

Margadant, T. W., 'Primary schools and youth groups in pre-war Paris. Les "Petites A's" ', *Journal of Contemporary History*, 13 (1978)

Maynes, M. J., 'The virtues of archaism. The political economy of schooling in Europe, 1750–1850', *Comparative Studies in Society and History*, 21 (1979)

Meyers, P. V., 'Professionalisation and societal change. Rural teachers in nineteenth century France', *Journal of Social History*, 9 (1976)

Paul, H. W., 'The issues of decline in nineteenth century French science', *French Historical Studies*, 7 (1971–72)

Paul, H. W., *The sorcerer's apprentice. The French scientist's image of German science, 1840–1919*, University of Florida Press, Gainesville, Fla. (1972)

Scoville, W. C., 'The Huguenots and the diffusion of technology', *Journal of Political Economy*, 60 (1952)

Smith, R. J., *The Ecole Normale Supérieure and the Third Republic*, State University of New York Press, Albany, N.Y. (1981)

Strumingher, L. S., *What were little girls and boys made of? Primary education in rural France, 1830–80*, State University of New York Press, Albany, N.Y. (1982)

Vaughan, M., 'The Grandes Ecoles', in R. Wilkinson, ed., *Governing elites. Studies in training and selection*, Oxford University Press, New York (1969)

Vaughan, M., and M. S. Archer, *Social conflict and educational change in England and France, 1789–1848*, Cambridge University Press, Cambridge (1971)

Weisz, G., 'The anatomy of university reform, 1863–1914', *Historical Reflections*, 7 (1980)

Wilkins, W. H., 'The debate over secondary and higher education for women in nineteenth century France', *North Dakota Quarterly*, 49 (1981)

HISTORIOGRAPHY AND BIBLIOGRAPHY

Adams, P. V., 'Historical demography by aggregative methods. Nineteenth century France', *Journal of Interdisciplinary History*, 7 (1976)

Adams, P. V., 'Towards a geography of French historical demography. Problems and sources', *French Historical Studies*, 11 (1979–80)

Aymard, M., 'The Annales and French historiography', *Journal of European Economic History*, 1 (1972)

Beck, T. D., 'A data bank. France, 1800–47', *Social Science History*, 4 (1980)

Bedarida, F., 'The growth of urban history in France. Some methodological trends', in H. J. Dyos, ed., *The study of urban history*, Edward Arnold, London (1968)

Bezucha, R. J., 'Current research on the social history of nineteenth century France', in C. C. Sturgill, ed., *The consortium on revolutionary Europe, 1750–1850*, University Presses of Florida, Gainesville, Fla. (1975)

Bosher, J. F., 'Current writing on administration and finance in eighteenth century France', *Journal of Modern History*, 53 (1981)

Clout, H. D., and K. Sutton, 'The *cadastre* as a source for French rural studies', *Agricultural History*, 43 (1969)

Crosland, M., 'The history of French science. Recent publications and perspectives', *French Historical Studies*, 8 (1973–74)

Dunham, A. L., 'The economic history of France, 1815–70', *Journal of Modern History*, 21 (1949) [bibliographical article]

Dunne, J., 'What difference does a decade make? Recent works in Napoleonic studies', *European Studies Review*, 10 (1980)

Ehrmann, H. W., 'Recent writings on the French labour movement', *Journal of Modern History*, 22 (1950)

Ends, T., 'Recent studies on business history of France. Series on the business history of banking and steelmaking in the nineteenth century', *Keieishigaku*, 3 (1968)

Fohlen, C., 'A critical evaluation of recent research and publications on the economic history of nineteenth century France', *Journal of Economic History*, 18 (1958)

Fohlen, C., 'The present state of business history in France', *Business History Review*, 41 (1967)

Forster, R., 'Achievements of the Annales school', *Journal of Economic History*, 38 (1978) [discussion by D. C. North in the same issue]

Freedeman, C. E., 'French economic and social history from the revolution to the 1880s', *Journal of Economic History*, 38 (1978)

Gottlieb, B., 'France and Germany (1500–1800). Let us bless our countings', *Trends in History*, 1 (1979)

Goubert, P., 'Recent theories and research in French population between 1500 and 1700', in D. V. Glass and D. E. C. Eversley, eds, *Population in history. Essays in historical demography,* Edward Arnold, London (1965)

Harrigan, P. J., 'Historians and compilers joined. The historiography of the 1970s and the French *enquêtes* of the nineteenth century', *Historical Reflections,* 7 (1980)

Haug, C. J., 'Manuscript census materials in France. The use and availability of the *listes nominatives*', *French Historical Studies,* 11 (1979–80)

Hellerstein, E., *et al., Victorian women. A documentary account of women's lives in nineteenth century England, France and the United States,* Harvester Press, Brighton (1982)

Johnson, C. H., 'The revolution of 1830 in French economic history', in J. M. Merriman, ed., *1830 [eighteen-thirty] in France,* New Viewpoints, New York (1975)

Knapton, D. R., 'The archives and library of the Assistance Publique de Paris', *French Historical Studies,* 8 (1973–74)

Labrousse, E., 'Observations on a new history of modern France', *New Left Review,* 86 (1974) [social classes, 1848–1945]

Landes, D. S., 'Recent work in the economic history of modern France', *French Historical Studies,* 1 (1958)

Laurent, R., 'Octroi archives as source of urban, social and economic history', in R. E. Cameron, ed., *Essays in French economic history,* Richard D. Irwin, Homewood, Ill. (1970)

Leuilliot, P., 'Recent French writings in the social and economic history of modern France', *Economic History Review,* 2 (1949–50); 5 (1952–53)

Leuilliot, P., 'The industrial revolution in France. Some reflections inspired by a recent study by Arthur Louis Dunham', *Journal of Economic History,* 17 (1957)

Lévi-Strauss, L., and H. Mendras, 'Survey of peasant studies. Rural studies in France', *Journal of Peasant Studies,* 1 (1974)

Perrot, M., 'The strengths and weaknesses of French social history', *Journal of Social History,* 10 (1976)

Pillorget, R., 'From classical to a serial and quantitative study of history. Some new directions in French historical research', *Durham University Journal,* 69 (1977)

Roche, D., 'Urban history in France. Achievements, tendencies and objectives', *Urban History Yearbook* (1980)

Sée, H., 'Recent work in French economic history (1905–25)', *Economic History Review,* 1 (1927–28)

Spengler, J. J., 'French population theory since 1800', *Journal of Political Economy,* 44 (1936)

Tilly, L. A., 'The social sciences and the study of women. A review article', *Comparative Studies in Society and History,* 20 (1978)

Tonsor, S. J., 'Feudalism, revolution and neo-fascism. A review article', *Comparative Studies in Society and History,* 21 (1979)

Veit-Brause, I., 'The place of local and regional history in German and French historiography. Some general reflections', *Australian Journal of French Studies,* 16 (1979)

Weiss, J. H., 'The history of higher education in nineteenth century France. A survey of recent writings', *Journal of Social History,* 3 (1969–70)

Wilson, S., 'Proust's *A la recherche du temps perdu* as a document of social history', *Journal of European Studies,* (1971)

Woloch, I., 'French economic and social history. A review article', *Journal of Interdisciplinary History,* 4 (1973–74)

GERMANY

GENERAL ECONOMIC AND SOCIAL HISTORY

Abraham, D., *The collapse of the Weimar republic. Political economy and crisis,* Princeton University Press, Princeton, N.J. (1981)

Angell, J. W., *The recovery of Germany,* Yale University Press, New Haven, Conn. (1932)

Axe, E. W., and H. M. Flinn, 'An index of general business conditions for Germany, 1898–1914', *Review of Economics and Statistics,* 7 (1925)

Baade, F., 'Fighting depression in Germany', in E. S. Woytinsky, ed., *So much alive. The life and work of Wladimir S. Woytinsky,* Vanguard Press, New York (1962)

Balderston, T., 'The German business cycle in the 1920s. A comment', *Economic History Review,* 30 (1977)

Balogh, T., 'The national economy of Germany', *Economic Journal*, 48 (1938)

Bane, S. L., and R. H. Lutz, eds, *The blockade of Germany after the armistice, 1918–19. Selected documents*, Stanford University Press, Stanford, Cal. (1942)

Baster, A. S. J., 'Some economic aspects of rearmament', *International Labour Review*, 37 (1938)

Bennathan, E., 'German national income 1850–1960', *Business History*, 5 (1962–63)

Bennett, E. W., *German rearmament and the West, 1932–33*, Princeton University Press, Princeton, N.J. (1979)

Bessel, R., 'Eastern Germany as a structural problem in the Weimar republic', *Social History*, 3 (1978)

Böhme, H., *An introduction to the social and economic history of Germany. Political and economic change in the nineteenth and twentieth centuries*, Blackwell, Oxford (1978)

Borchardt, K., 'The industrial revolution in Germany, 1700–1914', in C. M. Cipolla, ed., *The emergence of industrial societies*. Fontana Economic History of Europe, vol. 4, part 1, Collins/Fontana, Glasgow (1973)

Borchardt, K., 'Regional differentiation in development of Germany throughout the nineteenth century with special regard to the east/west differential', *Papers presented to the third international conference of economic history, Munich, 1965*, Mouton, Paris (1974)

Brady, R. A., *Business as a system of power*, Columbia University Press, New York (1943)

Brinkmann, C., 'The place of Germany in the economic history of the nineteenth century', *Economic History Review*, 4 (1933)

Brück, W. F., *Social and economic history of Germany from William II to Hitler, 1888–1938*, University Press Board, Cardiff (1938)

Cassel, G., *Germany's economic power of resistance*, Jackson Press, New York (1916)

Chang, H. J., 'Industrialization in France and Germany', *Ssu yu Yen*, 11 (1973)

Clapham, J. H., *The economic development of France and Germany, 1815–1914*, Cambridge University Press, Cambridge (1936)

Costigliola, F., 'The United States and the reconstruction of Germany in the 1920s', *Business History Review*, 50 (1976)

Davis, J. S., 'Recent economic and financial progress in Germany', *Review of Economic Statistics*, 3 (1921)

Dawson, W. H., *The revolution of modern Germany*, T. Fisher Unwin, London (1908)

Dawson, W. H., *What is wrong with Germany?* Longmans Green, London (1915)

Dickinson, R. E., *The regions of Germany*, Kegan Paul Trench Trubner, London (1945)

Dorn, W. L., 'The Prussian bureaucracy in the eighteenth century', *Political Science Quarterly*, 46 (1931); 47 (1932)

Eagly, R. V., 'Business cycle trends in France and Germany, 1869–79. A new appraisal', *Weltwirtschaftliches Archiv*, 99 (1967)

Falkus, M. E., 'The German business cycle in the 1920s', *Economic History Review*, 28 (1975)

Feldman, G. D., *Army, industry and labour in Germany, 1914–18*, Princeton University Press, Princeton, N.J. (1966)

Feldman, G. D., 'Economic and social problems of German demobilisation, 1918–19', *Journal of Modern History*, 48 (1975)

Fischer, W., 'Government activity and industrialisation in Germany, 1815–70', in W. W. Rostow, ed., *The economics of take-off into sustained growth*, Macmillan, London (1963)

Fletcher, R., 'Revisionism and empire. Joseph Bloch, the *Sozialistische Monatshefte* and German nationalism, 1907–14', *European Studies Review*, 10 (1980)

Flink, J., *The German Reichsbank and economic recovery. A study of the policies of the Reichsbank in their relation to the economic development of Germany, with special reference to the period after 1923*, Columbia University Press, New York (1930)

Fremdling, R., and R. Tilly, 'German banks, German growth and econometric history', *Journal of Economic History*, 36 (1976)

Grünig, F., 'An estimate of the national capital account of the Federal German Republic', in R. Goldsmith and C. Saunders, eds, *Income and wealth*, No. 8, Bowes and Bowes, London (1959) [data back to 1913]

Guillebaud, C. W., *The economic recovery of Germany from 1933 to the incorporation of Austria in March 1938*, Macmillan, London (1939)

Guttsman, W. L., *The German Social Democratic Party. From Ghetto to government*, Allen and Unwin, London (1981)

Hamerow, T. S., *Restoration, revolution, reaction. Economics and politics in Germany, 1815–71*, Princeton University Press, Princeton, N.J. (1958)

Hammen, O. J., 'Economic and social factors in the Prussian Rhineland in 1848', *American Historical Review*, 54 (1948–49)

Hansen, A. H., *Cycles of prosperity and depression in*

the United States, Great Britain and Germany. A study of monthly data 1902–08, University of Wisconsin, Madison, Wis. (1921)

Hardach, K., 'Germany, 1914–70, in C. M. Cipolla, ed., Contemporary economies. Fontana Economic History of Europe, vol. 6, part 1, Collins/Fontana, Glasgow (1976)

Hardach, K., The political economy of Germany in the twentieth century, University of California Press, Berkeley, Cal. (1980)

Hayashi, K., 'Japan and Germany in the interwar period', in J. W. Morley, ed., Dilemmas of growth in pre-war Japan, Princeton University Press, Princeton, N.J. (1971)

Henderson, W. O., 'Economic development in Germany, 1815–1914', Naval Intelligence Division, Geographical Handbook series, Germany, vol. 2, History and administration, London (1944)

Henderson, W. O., 'The economic development of Germany, 1918–39', Naval Intelligence Division, Geographic Handbook series, Germany, vol. 3, Economic geography, London (1944)

Henderson, W. O., 'The genesis of the industrial revolution in France and Germany in the eighteenth century, Kyklos, 2 (1956)

Henderson, W. O., The state and the industrial revolution in Prussia, 1740–1870, Liverpool University Press, Liverpool (1958)

Hiden, J. W., The Weimar Republic, Longman, London (1974)

Hiden, J. W., Germany and Europe, 1919–39, Longman, London (1977)

Hoffmann, W. G., 'The take-off in Germany', in W. W. Rostow, ed., The economics of take-off into sustained growth, Macmillan, London (1963)

Holborn, H., A history of modern Germany, 2 vols, Eyre and Spottiswoode, London, (1969)

Horn, N., and J. Kocka, 'Development of company law and economic growth, especially in Germany, 1800–1914', in M. W. Flinn, ed., Proceedings of the seventh International Economic History Association conference, Edinburgh, 1978, Edinburgh University Press, Edinburgh (1978)

Huston, J. A., 'The Allied blockade of Germany, 1918–19', Journal of Central European Affairs, 10 (1950)

Jostock, P., 'The long-term growth of national income in Germany', in S. Kuznets, ed., Income and wealth, No. 5, Bowes and Bowes, London (1955)

Kehr, E., Economic interest, militarism, and foreign policy, University of California Press, Berkeley, Cal. (1977)

Keynes, J. M., 'The economics of war in Germany', Economic Journal, 25 (1915)

Kimmich, C. M., Germany and the League of Nations, University of Chicago Press, Chicago, Ill. (1976)

Kindleberger, C. P., 'Germany's overtaking of England, 1806–1914', parts 1 and 2, Weltwirtschaftliches Archiv, 111 (1975)

Kitchen, M., The political economy of Germany, 1815–1914, Croom Helm, London (1978)

Klein, B. H., 'Germany's preparation for war. A re-examination', American Economic Review, 38 (1948)

Klein, B. H., Germany's economic preparations for war, Harvard University Press, Cambridge, Mass. (1959)

Knight-Patterson, W. M., Germany. From defeat to conquest, 1913–33, Allen and Unwin, London (1945)

Kuczynski, J., Germany's economic position. Germany today, London (1939)

Landes, D. S., 'Industrialization and economic development in nineteenth century Germany', Papers presented to the first international economic history conference, Stockholm, 1960, Mouton, Paris (1960)

Landes, D. S., 'Industrialization and economic development in nineteenth century Germany', in M. E. Falkus, ed., Readings in the history of economic growth, Oxford University Press, London (1968)

Lebovics, H., ' "Agrarians" versus "industrializers". Social conservative resistance to industrialism and capitalism in late nineteenth century Germany', International Review of Social History, 12 (1967)

Lee, W. R., 'Tax structure and economic growth in Germany (1750–1850)', Journal of European Economic History, 4 (1975)

Lee, W. R., Population growth, economic development, and social change in Bavaria, 1750–1850, Arno Press, New York (1977)

Liebowitz, J. J., 'Economic strength and diplomatic attitudes. A model of hostility formation', Proceedings of the Annual Meeting of the Western Society for French History, 3 (1975)

Liebowitz, J. J., 'Economic strength and diplomatic attitudes. The formation of French hostility before World War I', Social Science History, 3 (1978)

MacDonald, C. A., 'Economic appeasement and the German "moderates", 1937–39', Past and Present, 56 (1972)

Maier, C., 'Coal and economic power in the Weimar Republic. The effects of the coal crisis of 1920', in

H. Mommsen, *et al.*, *Industrielles system und politische Entwicklung in der Weimarer Republik. Verhandlungen des internationalen Symposiums in Bochum vom 12–17 Juni 1973*, Droste, Düsseldorf, (1974)

Mandelbaum, K., 'An experiment in full employment. Controls in the German economy, 1933–38', in Oxford University Institute of Statistics, *The economics of full employment*, Blackwell, Oxford (1944)

Mendershausen, H., *Two postwar recoveries of the German economy*, North-Holland Publishing Co., Amsterdam (1955)

Milward, A. S., *The German economy at war*, Athlone Press, London (1965)

Nathan, O., *The Nazi economic system. Germany's mobilization for war*, Duke University Press, Durham, N.C. (1944)

Nelson, K. L., *Victors divided. America and the Allies in Germany, 1918–23*, University of California Press, Berkeley, Cal. (1975)

Nipperday, T., 'Mass education and modernization. The case of Germany, 1780–1850', *Transactions of the Royal Historical Society*, 27 (1977)

Ohno, E., 'The historical stage of German capitalism', *Kyoto University Economic Review*, 40 (1970)

Overy, R. J., 'Transportation and rearmament in the Third Reich', *Historical Journal*, 16 (1973)

Overy, R. J., 'Cars, roads and economic recovery in Germany, 1932–38', *Economic History Review*, 28 (1975)

Overy, R. J., 'The German *Motorisierung* and rearmament. A reply', *Economic History Review*, 32 (1979)

Overy, R. J., 'Hitler's war and the German economy. A reinterpretation', *Economic History Review*, 35 (1982)

Overy, R. J., *The German economic recovery*, Macmillan, London (1982)

Paret, P., *Yorck and the era of Prussian reform, 1807–15*, Princeton University Press, Princeton, N.J. (1966)

Passant, E. J., *A short history of Germany, 1815–1945*, Cambridge University Press, Cambridge (1959) [economic sections by W. O. Henderson]

Peterson, E. N., *Hjalmar Schacht. For and against Hitler. A political-economic study of Germany, 1923–45*, Christopher Publishing House, Boston, Mass. (1954)

Petzina, D., 'Germany and the great depression', *Journal of Contemporary History*, 4 (1969)

Pounds, N. J. G., 'Economic growth in Germany', in

H. G. J. Aitken, ed., *The state and economic growth*, Social Science Research Council, New York (1959)

Pyle, K. B., 'Advantages of followership. German economists and Japanese bureaucrats, 1890–1925', *Journal of Japanese Studies*, 1 (1974)

Quigley, H., and R. T. Clark, *Republican Germany. A political and economic study*, Methuen, London (1928)

Rawlins, D., *Economic conditions in Germany to March 1936*, H.M.S.O., London (1936)

Redlich, F., 'German economic planning for war and peace', *Review of Politics*, 6 (1944)

Reinhold, P., *The economic, financial and political state of Germany since the war*, Yale University Press, New Haven, Conn. (1928)

Ridley, F. F., 'The economic causes of the German empire', *Business History*, 10 (1968)

Roll, E., *Spotlight on Germany. A survey of her economic and political problems*, Faber and Faber, London (1933)

Rosenberg, H., *Bureaucracy, aristocracy, and autocracy. The Prussian experience, 1660–1815*, Harvard University Press, Cambridge, Mass. (1958)

Scheele, G., *The Weimar Republic. Overture to the Third Reich*, Faber and Faber, London (1946) [considerable attention to economic matters]

Schmidt, C. T., *German business cycles, 1924–33*, National Bureau of Economic Research, New York (1934)

Schuker, S., 'Finance and foreign policy in the era of German inflation. British, French and German strategies for economic reconstruction after the first world war', in O. Büsch, and G. D. Feldman, eds, *Historische Prozesse der deutschen Inflation. Ein Togungsbericht*, Colloquim Verlag, Berlin (1978)

Sheehan, J. J., ed., *Imperial Germany. New viewpoints*, New York (1976)

Silverman, D. P., 'The economic consequences of annexation. Alsace-Lorraine and imperial Germany, 1871–1918', *Central European History*, 4 (1971)

Silverman, D. P., *Reluctant union. Alsace-Lorraine and imperial Germany, 1871–1918*, Pennsylvania State University Press, University Park, Pa. (1972)

Simpson, A. E., 'The struggle for control of the German economy, 1936–37', *Journal of Modern History*, 31 (1959)

Spenceley, G. F. R., 'R. J. Overy and the *Motorisierung*. A comment', *Economic History Review*, 32 (1979)

Stolper, G., *et al.*, *The German economy, 1870 to the* *present*, Weidenfeld and Nicolson, London (2nd edn 1967)

Temin, P., 'The beginning of the depression in Germany', *Economic History Review*, 24 (1971)

Thelwall, J. W. F., and C. J. Kavanagh, *Report on the economic and financial conditions in Germany to March 1922*, H.M.S.O., London (1922)

Thelwall, J. W. F., and C. J. Kavanagh. *Report on the economic and financial conditions in Germany, revised to April 1924*, H.M.S.O., London (1924)

Tilly, R., 'German industrialization in the nineteenth century', *Zeitschrift für die gesamte Staatswissenschaft*, 124 (1968)

Tilly, R., 'Soll und Haben. Recent German economic history and the problem of economic development', *Journal of Economic History*, 29 (1969)

Tipton, F. B., *Regional variations in the economic development of Germany during the nineteenth century*, Wesleyan University Press, Middletown, Conn. (1976)

Treue, W., 'Germany between capitalism and socialism, 1918–19', *Proceedings of the fifth international economic history conference, Leningrad, 1970*, Mouton, Paris (1979)

Trivanovich, V., *The situation in Germany at the beginning of 1933*, National Industrial Conference Board, New York (1933)

Turner, H. A., *Stresemann and the politics of the Weimar Republic*, Princeton University Press, Princeton, N.J. (1963)

Veblen, T., *Imperial Germany and the industrial revolution*, Macmillan, London (rev. edn 1939)

Wehler, H. U., 'Bismark's imperialism, 1862–90', *Past and Present*, 48 (1970)

Zielinski, H., 'The role of Silesia in central Europe in the nineteenth and twentieth centuries', *Acta Poloniae Historica*, 22 (1970)

AGRICULTURE AND RURAL SOCIETY

Berdahl, R. M., 'Conservative politics and aristocratic landholders in Bismarckian Germany', *Journal of Modern History*, 44 (1972)

Berkner, L. K., 'Inheritance, land tenure and peasant family structure. A German regional comparison', in J. Goody *et al.*, *Family and inheritance. Rural society in western Europe, 1200–1800*, Cambridge University Press, Cambridge (1976)

Brandt, K., 'Farm relief in Germany', *Social Research*, 1 (1934)

Brandt, K., 'The German back-to-the-land move-

ment', *Land Economics*, 11 (1935)

Brandt, K., 'Land valuation in Germany', *Journal of Farm Economics*, 19 (1937)

Brentano, L., 'Agrarian reform in Prussia', *Economic Journal*, 7 (1897)

Dawson, W. H., 'Agricultural co-operative credit associations', *Economic Journal*, 12 (1902)

Dickler, R. A., 'Organisation and change in productivity in Eastern Prussia', in W. N. Parker, and E. L. Jones, eds, *European peasants and their markets*, Princeton University Press, Princeton, N.J. (1975)

Farquharson, J. E., *The plough and the swastika. The NSDAP and agriculture in Germany, 1928–45*, Sage Publications, London (1976)

Flaningham, M. L., 'The rural economy of northeastern France and the Bavarian Palatinate, 1815–30', *Agricultural History*, 24 (1950)

Fleischer, M. P., 'The first German agricultural manuals', *Agricultural History*, 55 (1981)

Gagliardo, J. G., 'Moralism, rural ideology, and the German peasant in the late eighteenth century', *Agricultural History*, 42 (1968)

Gagliardo, J. G., *From pariah to patriot. The changing image of the German peasant, 1770–1840*, University Press of Kentucky Lexington, Ky. (1969)

Gerschenkron, A., *Bread and democracy in Germany*, University of California Press, Berkeley, Cal. (1943)

Gessner, D., 'Agrarian protectionism in the Weimar Republic', *Journal of Contemporary History*, 12 (1977)

Haines, M. R., 'Agriculture and development in Prussian Upper Silesia, 1846–1913', *Journal of Economic History*, 42 (1982)

Hunt, J. C., 'The "egalitarianism" of the right. The Agrarian League in south-west Germany 1893–1914', *Journal of Contemporary History*, 10 (1975)

International Labour Office, 'Scientific management and German agriculture', *International Labour Review*, 15 (1927)

Jasney, M. P., 'Some aspects of German agricultural settlement', *Political Science Quarterly*, 52 (1937)

Lambi, I. N., 'The agrarian industrial front in Bismarckian politics, 1873–79', *Journal of Central European Affairs*, 20 (1961)

Long, J. W., 'Agricultural conditions in the German colonies of Novouzensk district, Samara province, 1861–1914', *Slavic Review*, 57 (1979)

Lovin, C. R., 'Agricultural reorganization in the Third Reich. The Reich Food Corporation (Reichsnährstand), 1933–36', *Agricultural History*, 43 (1969)

Mayhew, A., *Rural settlement and farming in Germany*, Barnes and Noble, New York (1963)

Moeller, R. G., 'Peasants and tariffs in the *Kaiserreich*. How backwards were the *Bauern*?', *Agricultural History*, 55 (1981)

Moeller, R. G., 'Winners as losers in the German inflation. Peasant protest over the controlled economy, 1920–23', in G. D. Feldman *et al.*, eds, *Die deutsche Inflation. Eine Zwischenbilanz*, de Gruyter, Berlin (1982)

Morier, R. D. B., 'The agrarian legislation of Prussia during the present century. Also a report on the tenure of land in the Grand Duchy of Hesse', in J. W. Probyn, ed., *Systems of land tenure in various countries*, Cobden Club, London (1881)

Muth, H., 'Farmers' movements and political parties, 1862–1920', *Cahiers Internationaux d'Histoire Economique et Sociale*, 6, (1976)

Osmond, J., 'German peasant farmers in war and inflation, 1914–24. Stability or stagnation?', in G. D. Feldman *et al.*, eds, *Die deutsche Inflation. Eine Zwischenbilanz*, de Gruyter, Berlin (1982)

Perkins, J. A., 'The agricultural revolution in Germany, 1850–1914', *Journal of European Economic History*, 10 (1981)

Richard, A. R., 'The political economy of *Gutswirtschaft*. A comparative analysis of east Elbian Germany, Egypt and Chile', *Comparative Studies in Society and History*, 21 (1979)

Sabean, D., 'Small peasant agriculture in Germany at the beginning of the nineteenth century. Changing work patterns', *Peasant Studies*, 7 (1978)

Smith, R. S., 'Land prices and tax policy. An historical review', *American Journal of Economics and Sociology*, 36 (1977)

Tipton, F. B., 'Farm labour and power politics in Germany, 1850–1914', *Journal of Economic History*, 34 (1974)

Tirrell, S. R., *German agrarian politics after Bismarck's fall. The formation of the Farmers' League*, Columbia University Press, New York (1951)

Webb, S. B., 'Agricultural protection in Wilhelminian Germany. Forging an empire with pork and rye', *Journal of Economic History*, 42 (1982)

White, D. S., 'The German peasant', *Journal of Interdisciplinary History*, 1 (1970–71)

Wolf, E., 'The inheritance of land among Bavarian and Tyrolese peasants', *Anthropologica*, 12 (1970)

INDUSTRY AND INTERNAL TRADE

Adelmann, G., 'Structural change in the Rhenish linen and cotton trades at the outset of industrialization', in F. Crouzet *et al.*, *Essays in European economic history*, Edward Arnold, London (1969)

Angel-Volkov, S., 'The "decline of the German handicrafts". Another reappraisal', *Vierteljahrschrift für Sozial- und Wirtschaftsgeschichte*, 61 (1974)

Armeson, R. B., *Total warfare and compulsory labour. A study of the military-industrial complex in Germany during World War I*, Nijhoff, The Hague (1964)

Banfield, T. C., *Industry of the Rhine*, Kelley, New York (1969)

Barkhausen, M., 'Government control and free enterprise in West Germany and the Low Countries in the eighteenth century', in P. Earle, ed., *Essays in European economic history, 1500–1800*, Clarendon Press, Oxford (1974)

Barkin, K. D., 'Adolf Wagner and German industrial development', *Journal of Modern History*, 41 (1969)

Barkin, K. D., *The controversy over German industrialisation, 1890–1902*, University of Chicago Press, Chicago, Ill. (1970)

Batty, P., *The house of Krupp*, Secker and Warburg, London (1966)

Beer, J. J., *The emergence of the German dye industry*, University of Illinois Press, Urbana, Ill. (1959)

Berdrow, W., ed., *Alfred Krupp, 1812–87. A great businessman seen through his letters*, Dial Press, New York (1930)

Berdrow, W., *The Krupps. 150 years' Krupp history, 1787–1937, based on documents and work archives*, P. Schmidt, Berlin (1937)

Block, H., 'Industrial combination vs. small business. The trend of Nazi policy', *Social Research*, 10 (1943)

Bowen, R. H., 'The roles of government and private enterprise in German industrial growth, 1870–1914', *Journal of Economic History*, Supplement 10 (1950)

Brady, R. A., *The rationalization movement in German industry. A study in the evolution of economic planning*, University of California Press, Berkeley, Cal. (1933)

Brady, R. A., 'Modernized cameralism in the Third Reich. The case of the national industry group', *Journal of Political Economy*, 50 (1942)

British Electrical and Allied Manufacturers' Association. *The electrical industry in Germany,*

BEAMA, London (1926)

Cameron, R. E., 'Some French contributions to the industrial development of Germany, 1840–70', *Journal of Economic History*, 16 (1956)

Campbell, F. G., 'The struggle for Upper Silesia, 1919–22', *Journal of Modern History*, 42 (1970)

Cecil, L., *Albert Ballin. Business and politics in imperial Germany, 1888–1918*, Princeton University Press, Princeton, N.J. (1967)

Cowan, L. G., *France and the Saar, 1680–1948*, Columbia University Press, New York (1950)

Dawson, P., *Germany's industrial revival*, Williams and Norgate, London (1926)

Dawson, W. H., *Industrial Germany*, Collins, London (1912)

Dehn, R. M. R., *The German cotton industry*, Manchester University Press, Manchester (1913)

Dumke, R. H., 'Intra-German trade in 1837 and regional economic development', *Vierteljahrschrift für Sozial- und Wirtschaftsgeschichte*, 64 (1977)

Egle, W., 'The progress of mass production and the German small-scale industries', *Journal of Political Economy*, 46 (1938)

Engels, W., and H. Pohl, eds, *German yearbook on business history, 1981*, Springer-Verlag, Berlin (1982)

Feldman, G. D., 'The social and economic policies of German big business, 1918–29', *American Historical Review*, 75 (1969–70)

Feldman, G. D., 'German business between war and revolution. The origins of the Stinnes-Legien agreement', in G. A. Rilter, ed., *Entstehung und Wandel der modernen Gesellschaft. Festschrift für Hans Rosenberg zum 65. Geburtstag*, de Gruyter, Berlin (1970)

Feldman, G. D., 'Big business and the Kapp *Putsch*', *Central European History*, 4 (1971)

Feldman, G. D., 'The origins of the Stinnes-Legien agreement. A documentation', *Internationale Wissenschaftliche Korrespondenz zur Geschichte der deutschen Arbeitsbewegung*, 19/20 (1972)

Feldman, G. D., 'The collapse of the Steelworks Association, 1912–19', in H. U. Wehler, ed., *Sozialgeschichte heute. Festschrift für Hans Rosenberg zum 70. Geburtstag*, Vandenhoek and Ruprecht, Göttingen (1974)

Feldman, G. D., *Iron and steel in the German inflation, 1916–23*, Princeton University Press, Princeton, N.J. (1977)

Feldman, G. D., and U. Nocken, 'Trade associations and economic power. Interest group development in the German iron and steel and machine-building industries, 1900–33', *Business History Review*, 49 (1975)

Fischer, W., and P. Czada, 'Industrial structure in the twentieth century. Germany', *Papers presented to the fourth international conference of economic history, Bloomington, 1968*, Mouton, Paris (1973)

Friedrichs, C. R., 'Early capitalism and its enemies. The Wörner family and the weavers of Nördlingen', *Business History Review*, 50 (1976)

Fritz, M., *German steel and Swedish iron ore, 1939–45*, Gothenburg Institute of Economic History, Gothenburg (1974)

Fukuo, T., 'German industrialization and Prussian bureaucracy in the first half of the nineteenth century', *Keieishigaka*, 6 (1971)

Fullerton, R. A., 'Creating a mass book market in Germany. The story of the Colporteur novel, 1870–80', *Journal of Social History*, 10 (1977)

Hahn, A., 'Stabilisation of business in Germany', *Harvard Business Review*, 7 (1929)

Halle, E. von, 'The rise and tendencies of German enterprise', *Economic Journal*, 17 (1907)

Haller, W. M., 'Regional and national free trade associations in Germany, 1859–79', *European Studies Review*, 6 (1976)

Hallgarten, G. W. F., 'Adolf Hitler and German heavy industry, 1931–33', *Journal of Economic History*, 12 (1952)

Hamburger, L., *How Nazi Germany has controlled business*, Brookings Institution, Washington, D.C. (1943)

Hannah, L., 'Public policy and the advent of large-scale technology. The case of electricity supply in the U.S.A., Germany and Britain', in N. Horn and J. Kocka, eds, *Recht und Entwicklung der Grossunternehmen im 19. und frühen 20. Jahrhundert*, Vandenhoeck und Ruprecht, Göttingen (1979)

Hardie, D. W. F., 'The emergence of the German dye industry', *Business History*, 5 (1962–63)

Hartmann, H., *Education for business leadership. The role of the German 'Hochschulen'*, OEEC, Paris (1955)

Hartsough, M. L., 'Business leaders in Cologne in the nineteenth century', *Journal of Economic and Business History*, 2 (1929–30)

Hartsough, M. L., 'The rise and fall of the Stinnes combine', *Journal of Economic and Business History*, 3 (1930–31)

Hauser, H., *Economic Germany. German industry considered as a factor making for war*, Nelson, London (1915)

Henderson, W. O., 'William Thomas Mulvany. An Irish pioneer in the Ruhr', *Explorations in Entrepreneurial History*, 5 (1953)

Henderson, W. O., 'Peter Beuth and the rise of Prussian industry, 1810–45', *Economic History Review,* 8 (1955–56)

Henderson, W. O., 'The evolution of modern industrial organization', in A. Roberts, ed., *Management notebook,* Newman Neame, London (1957)

Henderson, W. O., 'The rise of the Berlin silk and porcelain industries', *Business History,* 1 (1958–59)

Henderson, W. O., 'The rise of the metal and armament industries in Berlin and Brandenberg, 1712–95', *Business History,* 3 (1960–61)

Henderson, W. O., 'The Berlin commercial crisis of 1763', *Economic History Review,* 15 (1962–63)

Henderson, W. O., *The rise of German industrial power, 1834–1914',* Temple Smith, London (1975)

Hesselbach, W., *Public, trade union and corporative enterprise in Germany. The commonweal idea,* Frank Cass, London (1976)

Hidy, R., 'The roles of government and private enterprise in German industrial growth, 1870–1914', *Journal of Economic History,* Supplement, 10 (1950)

Homze, E. L., *Arming the Luftwaffe. The Reich Air Ministry and the German aircraft industry, 1919–39,* University of Nebraska Press, Lincoln, Neb. (1976)

Hopfinger, K. B., *The Volkswagen story,* Foulis, Henley on Thames (rev. 3rd edn 1971)

Horn, N., and J. Kocka, *Law and the formation of the big enterprise in the nineteenth and early twentieth centuries. Studies in the history of industrialization in Germany, France, Great Britain and the United States,* Vandenhoeck und Ruprecht, Göttingen (1979)

Howard, E. D., *The cause and extent of the recent industrial progress of Germany,* Constable, London (1907)

Hughes, T. P., 'Technological momentum in history. Hydrogenation in Germany, 1898–1933', *Past and Present,* 44 (1969)

James, H., 'State, industry and depression in Weimar Germany', *Historical Journal,* 24 (1981)

Jankowski, M. D., 'Law, economic policy and private enterprise. The case of the early Ruhr mining region, 1766–1865', *Journal of European Economic History,* 2 (1973)

Jankowski, M. D., *Public policy and economic growth. The case of the early Ruhr mining region, 1766–1865,* Arno Press, New York (1977)

Kaelble, H., 'Long-term changes in the recruitment of the business elite. Germany compared with the U.S., Great Britain and France since the industrial

revolution', *Journal of Social History,* 13 (1980)

Kessler, W. C., 'German cartel regulation under the decree of 1923', *Quarterly Journal of Economics,* 50 (1936)

Kessler, W. C., 'The German corporation law of 1937', *American Economic Review,* 28 (1938)

Kisch, H., 'The textile industries in Silesia and the Rhineland. A comparative study in industrialisation', *Journal of Economic History,* 19 (1959)

Kisch, H., 'The impact of the French revolution on the Lower Rhine textile districts. Some comments on economic development and social change', *Economic History Review,* 15 (1962–63)

Kisch, H., 'Growth deterrents of a medieval heritage. The Aachen area woollen trades before 1790', *Journal of Economic History,* 24 (1964)

Kisch, H., 'Prussian mercantilism and the rise of the Krefeld silk industry. Variations upon an eighteenth century theme', *Transactions of the American Philosophical Society,* 58 (1968)

Kisch, H., 'From monopoly to *laissez-faire.* The early growth of the Wupper valley textile trades', *Journal of European Economic History,* 1 (1972)

Kitamura, J., 'Metamorphosis of the modern entrepreneur in Germany', *Keieishigaka,* 6 (1971)

Klass, G. von, *Krupps. The story of an industrial empire,* Sidgwick and Jackson, London (1954)

Klass, G. von, *Hugo Stinnes,* Wunderlich, Tübingen (1958)

Kocka, J., 'Family and bureaucracy in German industrial management, 1850–1914. Siemens in comparative perspective', *Business History Review,* 45 (1971)

Kocka, J., 'Entrepreneurs and managers in German industrialization', in P. Mathias and M. M. Postan, eds, *Cambridge Economic History of Europe,* vol. 7(1), Cambridge University Press, Cambridge (1978)

Kocka, J., 'Capitalism and bureaucracy in German industrialisation before 1914', *Economic History Review,* 34 (1981)

Köllmann, W., 'The merchants and manufacturers of Barmen', in A. and L. Lees, eds, *The urbanization of European society in the nineteenth century,* D. C. Heath, Lexington, Mass. (1976)

Lambi, I. N., 'The protectionist interests of the German iron and steel industry, 1873–79', *Journal of Economic History,* 22 (1962)

Landes, D. S., *The structure of enterprise in the nineteenth century. The cases of Britain and Germany,* University of California Press, Berkeley, Cal. (1960)

Levy, H., *Industrial Germany. A study of its monopoly organizations and their control by the state, Cambridge University Press, Cambridge (1935)

Liefmann, R., 'German industrial organization since the world war', *Quarterly Journal of Economics,* 40 (1926)

Lotz, W., 'The effect of protection on some German industries', *Economic Journal,* 14 (1904)

Lundgreen, P., 'Industrialization and the educational formation of manpower in Germany', *Journal of Social History,* 9 (1975)

Lundgreen, P., 'German technical associations between science, industry and the state, 1860–1914', *Historical Social Research,* 13 (1980)

Macgregor, D. H., 'The development of German syndicates', *Economic Journal,* 24 (1914)

Manchester, W., *The arms of Krupp, 1587–1968,* Michael Joseph, London (1969)

Maschke, E., 'Outline of the history of German cartels from 1873 to 1914', in F. Crouzet *et al.,* *Essays in European economic history,* Edward Arnold, London (1969)

Medalen, C., 'State monopoly capitalism in Germany. The Hibernia affair', *Past and Present,* 78 (1978)

Mendel, A., 'The debate between Prussian Junkerdom and the forces of urban industry, 1897–1902', *Jahrbuch des Instituts für Deutsche Geschichte,* 4 (1975)

Milkereit, G., 'The Thyssen company. A representative example of the interconnection between banking and industry at the beginning of the twentieth century', *Papers presented to the fifth international economic history conference, Leningrad, 1970,* Mouton, Paris (1979)

Morrow, J. H., 'Industrial mobilization in World War I. The Prussian army and the aircraft industry', *Journal of Economic History,* 37 (1977)

Musgrave, P. W., *Technical change, the labour force and education. A study of the British and German iron and steel industries, 1860–1964,* Pergamon, Oxford (1967)

National Industrial Conference Board, *Rationalization of German industry,* National Industrial Conference Board, New York (1931)

Nelson, W. H., *Small wonder. The amazing story of Volkswagen,* Hutchinson, London (1967)

Newman, P. C., 'Key German cartels under the Nazi regime', *Quarterly Journal of Economics,* 62 (1948)

Nolte, E., 'Big business and German politics. A comment', *American Historical Review,* 75 (1969–70)

Overy, R. J., 'The German pre-war aircraft production plans. November 1936–April 1939', *English Historical Review,* 90 (1975)

Overy, R. J., *The German economic recovery,* Macmillan, London (1982)

Parker, W. N., 'Entrepreneurial opportunities and response in the German economy', *Explorations in Entrepreneurial History,* 7 (1954)

Parker, W. N., 'Entrepreneurship, industrial organization and economic growth. A German example', *Journal of Economic History,* 14 (1954)

Parker, W. N., 'National states and national development in French and German ore mining in the late nineteenth century', in H. G. J. Aitken, ed., *The state and economic growth,* Social Science Research Council, New York (1959)

Pierenkemper, T., 'Entrepreneurs in heavy industry. Upper Silesia and the Westphalian Ruhr region, 1852–1913', *Business History Review,* 53 (1979)

Pounds, N. J. G., *The Ruhr. A study in historical and economic geography,* Faber, London (1952)

Pounds, N. J. G., *The Upper Silesian industrial region,* Indiana University Press, Bloomington, Ind. (1958)

Rabinbach, A. G., 'The aesthetics of production in the Third Reich', *Journal of Contemporary History,* 11 (1976)

Raumer, H. von, 'Walther Rathenau', *Deutsche Rundschau,* 78 (1952)

Redlich, F., 'The leaders of the German steam engine industry during the first hundred years', *Journal of Economic History,* 4 (1944)

Redlich, F., 'A German eighteenth century ironworks during its first hundred years', parts 1, 2 and 3, *Business History Review,* 27 (1953)

Redlich, F., 'Academic education for business. Its development and the contribution of Ignaz Jastrow (1856–1937)', *Business History Review,* 31 (1957)

Redlich, F., *The German military entrepreneur and his work. A study in European economic and social history,* 2 vols, Steiner, Wiesbaden (1964)

Reimann, G., *Patents for Hitler,* Gollancz, London (1945)

Rosenthal, B. M., 'Cartel, clan or dynasty? The Olschkis and the Rosenthals, 1859–1976', *Harvard Library Bulletin,* 25 (1977)

Rostas, L., 'Industrial production, productivity and distribution in Britain, Germany and the United States, 1935–37', *Economic Journal,* 53 (1943)

Schindler, E., 'Handicrafts in Germany', *International Labour Review,* 34 (1936)

Schmitz, C. J., 'German non-ferrous metal production in the early nineteenth century', *Journal of European Economic History,* 3 (1974)

Schremmer, E., 'The textile industry in southern

Germany, 1750–1850. Some causes for the technological backwardness during the industrial revolution. Investment approach and structure approach', *Textile History*, 7 (1976)

Schuster, E., 'The promotion of companies and the valuation of assets according to German law', *Economic Journal*, 10 (1900)

Schweitzer, A., 'Big business and the Nazi party in Germany', *Journal of Business*, 19 (1946)

Schweitzer, A., 'Big business and private property under the Nazis, *Journal of Business*, 19 (1946)

Schweitzer, A., 'Profits under Nazi planning', *Quarterly Journal of Economics*, 61 (1947)

Schweitzer, A., 'Business power under the Nazi regime', *Zeitschrift für Nationalökonomie*, 20 (1960)

Schweitzer, A., *Big business in the Third Reich*, Eyre and Spottiswoode, London (1964)

Sharlin, A., 'From the study of social mobility to the study of society', *American Journal of Sociology*, 85 (1979) [German retailing, 1840s and 1850s]

Showatter, D. E., 'Weapons technology and the military in Metternich's Germany. A study in stagnation', *Australian Journal of Politics and History*, 24 (1978)

Sichel, F. H., 'The rise and fall of the *Kasseler Tageblatt*', *Leo Baeck Institute Yearbook*, 19 (1974) [changing economic fortunes of a German newspaper]

Smith, C. N., 'The formation of the Sudetendeutsche Bergbau-A.G.', *Explorations in Economic History*, 7 (1969–70) [a corporation formed in 1938–39 by the Dresdner Bank)

Smith, C. N., 'Motivation and ownership. History of the ownership of the Gelsenkirchener Bergwerks-A.G.', *Business History*, 12 (1970)

Spencer, E. G., 'Between capital and labour. Supervisory personnel in Ruhr heavy industry before 1914', *Journal of Social History*, 9 (1975)

Spencer, E. G., 'Employer response to unionism. Ruhr coal industrialists before 1914', *Journal of Modern History*, 48 (1976)

Spencer, E. G., 'Rulers of the Ruhr. Leadership and authority in German big business before 1914', *Business History Review*, 53 (1979)

Stern, F., 'Gold and iron. The collaboration and friendship of Gerson Bleichröder and Otto von Bismarck', *American Historical Review*, 75 (1969–70)

Stern, G., *Gold and iron. Bismark, Bleichröder and the building of the German empire*, Random House, New York (1979)

Stockder, A. H., *German trade associations. The coal kartells*, H. Holt, New York (1924)

Stockder, A. H., *Regulating an industry. The Rhenish-Westphalian coal syndicate, 1893–1929*, Columbia University Press, New York (1932)

Sweezy, M. Y., 'German corporate profits, 1926–38', *Quarterly Journal of Economics*, 54 (1940)

Tampke, J., *The Ruhr and revolution. The revolutionary movement in the Rhenish-Westphalian industrial region 1912–19*, Croom Helm, London (1979)

Tilly, R., 'The growth of large-scale enterprise in Germany since the middle of the nineteenth century', in H. Daems and H. van der Wee, eds, *The rise of managerial capitalism*, Nijhoff, The Hague (1974)

Tipton, F. B., 'Small business and the rise of Hitler. A review article', *Business History Review*, 53 (1979)

Todsal, H. R., 'The German steel syndicate', *Quarterly Journal of Economics*, 32 (1917)

Trivanovitch, V., *Rationalization of German industry*, National Industrial Conference Board, New York (1931)

Turner, H. A., 'Hitler's secret pamphlet for industrialists, 1927', *Journal of Modern History*, 40 (1968)

Turner, H. A., 'Big business and the rise of Hitler', *American Historical Review*, 75 (1969–70)

Turner, H. A., 'The *Ruhrlade*. Secret cabinet of heavy industry in the Weimar Republic', *Central European History*, 3 (1970)

Visser, D., 'The German captain of enterprise. Veblen's *Imperial Germany* revisited', *Explorations in Entrepreneurial History*, 6 (1968–69)

Walker, F., 'The German steel syndicate', *Quarterly Journal of Economics*, 20 (1906)

Warriner, D., *Combines and rationalisation in Germany, 1924–28*, P. S. King, London (1931)

Webb, S. B., 'Tariffs, cartels, technology and growth in the German steel industry, 1879–1914', *Journal of Economic History*, 40 (1980)

Weisbrod, B., 'Economic power and political stability reconsidered. Heavy industry in Weimar Germany', *Social History*, 4 (1979)

Williams, E. E., *Made in Germany*, Heinemann, London (1896)

Winkler, H. A., 'From social protectionism to national socialism. The German small business movement in comparative perspective', *Journal of Modern History*, 48 (1976)

Wolff, K. H., 'Guildmaster to millhand. The industrialization of linen and cotton in Germany to 1850', *Textile History*, 10 (1979)

TRANSPORT AND COMMUNICATIONS

Bryant, L., 'The development of the diesel engine', *Technology and Culture*, 17 (1976)

Fremdling, R., 'Railroads and German economic growth. A leading sector analysis with a comparison to the United States and Great Britain', *Journal of Economic History*, 37 (1977)

Fremdling, R., 'Freight rates and state budget. The role of the national Prussian railways, 1880–1913', *Journal of European Economic History*, 9 (1980)

Hammond, W. E., 'The development of the Marne-Rhine canal and the Zollverein', *French Historical Studies*, 3 (1964)

Hart, H. W., 'Thomas Clarke Worsdell and the Leipzig and Dresden railway', *Journal of Transport History*, 3 (1976)

Henderson, W. O., 'Roads, inland waterways and ports in Germany', Naval Intelligence Division, Geographical Handbook series, *Germany*, vol. 4, *Ports and communications*, London (1945)

Knauerhase, R., 'The compound steam engine and productivity changes in the German merchant marine fleet, 1871–87', *Journal of Economic History*, 28 (1968)

Lamar, C., *Albert Ballin*, Princeton University Press, Princeton, N.J. (1967) [shipping magnate, late nineteenth century]

Martel, G., 'The Near East in the balance of power. The repercussions of the Kaulla incident in 1893', *Middle Eastern Studies*, 16 (1980)

Mork, G. R., 'The Prussian railway scandal of 1873. Economics and politics in the German empire', *European Studies Review*, 1 (1971)

Pick, P. W., 'German railway construction in the Middle East', *Jahrbuch des Instituts für Deutsche Geschichte*, 1 (1975)

Robbins, M., 'The Third Reich and its railways. A review article', *Journal of Transport History*, 5 (1979)

Vagts, D. F., 'Railroads, private enterprise and public policy. Germany and the United States, 1870–1920', in N. Horn and J. Kocka, eds, *Recht und Entwicklung der Grossunternehmen im 19. und frühen 20. Jahrhundert*, Vandenhoeck und Ruprecht, Göttingen (1979)

MONEY, BANKING AND FINANCE

Abel, A., *et al.*, 'Money demand during hyperinflation', *Journal of Monetary Economics*, 5 (1979)

Andic, S., and J. Veverka, 'The growth of government expenditure in Germany since the unification', *Finanzarchiv*, 23 (1964)

Bennett, E. W., *Germany and the diplomacy of the financial crisis, 1931*, Harvard University Press, Cambridge, Mass. (1962)

Bonn, M. J., *German war finance*, German University League, New York (1916)

Bonn, M. J., *Stabilization of the mark*, First National Bank of Chicago, Chicago, Ill. (1922)

Cameron, R. E., 'Founding of the Bank of Darmstadt', *Explorations in Entrepreneurial History*, 8 (1956)

Cohn, G., 'German experiments in fiscal legislation', *Economic Journal*, 23 (1913)

D'Abernon, Viscount, 'German currency, its collapse and recovery, 1920–26', *Journal of Royal Statistical Society*, 90 (1927)

Dietzel, H., 'The readjustment of German finance by means of a capital levy', *Economic Journal*, 29 (1919)

Ellis, H. S., *German monetary theory, 1905–33*, Harvard University Press, Cambridge, Mass. (1934)

Ellis, H. S., 'Exchange control in Germany', *Quarterly Journal of Economics*, Supplement, 54 (1940)

Elsas, M., 'The internal purchasing power of the German mark', *Economic Journal*, 31 (1921), 32 (1922)

Fergusson, A., *When money dies. The nightmare of the Weimar collapse*, William Kimber, London (1975)

Fischer, R., *Karl Helfferich*, Historische-Politischer Verlag, Berlin (1932) [financial statesman in Weimar Republic]

Fischer, W., 'The strategy of public investment in nineteenth century Germany', *Journal of European Economic History*, 6 (1977)

Frenkel, J. A., 'The forward exchange rate, expectations and the demand for money. The German hyperinflation', *American Economic Review*, 67 (1977)

Frenkel, J. A., 'Further evidence on expectations and the demand for money during the German hyperinflation', *Journal of Monetary Economics*, 5 (1979)

Frenkel, J. A., 'The forward exchange rate, expectations, and the demand for money. The German hyperinflation. Reply', *American Economic Review*, 70 (1980)

Grebler, L., and W. Winkler, *The cost of the war to Germany and Austria–Hungary*, Yale University

Press, New Haven, Conn. (1940)

Grice, J. W., *National and local finance. A review of the relations between the central and local authorities in England, France, Belgium and Prussia during the nineteenth century*, P. S. King, London (1910)

Grunwald, K., '*Pénétration pacifique*. The financial vehicles of Germany's "Drang nach dem Osten" ', *Jahrbuch des Instituts für Deutsche Geschichte*, 1 (1975)

Grunwald, K., 'Three chapters of German-Jewish banking history', *Leo Baeck Institute Yearbook*, 22 (1977)

Klein, J. J., 'German money and prices, 1932–44', in M. Friedman, ed., *Studies in the quantity theory of money*, University of Chicago Press, Chicago, Ill. (1956)

Knauerhase, R., 'Some observations on the institutional development of the Reichsbank, 1875–1910', *International Review of the History of Banking*, 8 (1974)

Komlos, J., 'The *Kreditbanken* and German growth. A postscript', *Journal of Economic History*, 38 (1978)

Kuczynski, R. R., *American loans to Germany*, Macmillan, New York (1927)

Kuczynski, R. R., *Bankers' profits from German loans*, Brookings Institution, Washington D.C. (1932)

Lawrence, P. A., 'Radicalism and the cash nexus', *American Journal of Sociology*, 86 (1980) [finance and industrialisation, 1870–1900]

Loveday, A., 'German war finance in 1914', *Economic Journal*, 26 (1916)

Lurie, S., *Private investment in a controlled economy. Germany, 1933–39*, Columbia University Press, New York (1947)

Mackenzie, K., *The banking systems of Great Britain, France, Germany and the United States of America*, Macmillan, London (1932)

Muhlen, N., *Schacht. Hitler's magician. The life and loans of Dr. H. Schacht*, Alliance Book Corporation, New York (1939)

Napier, E. S., *The German credit problem*, London General Press, London (1931)

Nathan, O., *Nazi war finance and banking*, National Bureau of Economic Research, New York (1944)

Neuberger, H. M., 'The industrial politics of the *Kreditbanken*, 1880–1914', *Business History Review*, 51 (1977)

Neuberger, H. M., and H. H. Stokes, 'German banks and German growth, 1833–1913. An empirical view', *Journal of Economic History*, 34 (1974)

Neuberger, H. M., and H. H. Stokes, 'German banking and Japanese banking. A comparative analysis', *Journal of Economic History*, 35 (1975)

Newcomer, M., *Central and local finance in Germany and England*, Columbia University Press, New York (1937)

Northrop, M. B., *The control policies of the Reichsbank, 1924–33*, P. S. King, London (1938)

O'Farrell, H. H., *The Franco-German war indemnity and its economic results*, Harrison, London (1913)

Pedersen, J., 'A chapter of the history of monetary theory and policy', in G. Bombach, ed., *Stabile Preise in wachsender Wirtschaft. Das Inflationsproblem*, J. C. B. Mohr, Tübingen (1960)

Peterson, E. N., *Hjalmar Schacht. For and against Hitler. A political-economic study of Germany, 1923–45*, Christopher Publishing House, Boston (1954)

Poole, K. E., *German financial policies, 1932–39*, Harvard University Press, Cambridge, Mass. (1939)

Redlich, F., 'Jewish enterprise and Prussian coinage in the eighteenth century', *Explorations in Entrepreneurial History*, 3 (1951)

Redlich, F., 'An eighteenth century German guide for investors', *Business History Review*, 26 (1952)

Redlich, F., 'Two nineteenth century financiers and autobiographers. A comparative study in creative destructiveness and business failure', *Economy and History*, 10 (1967)

Redlich, F., 'The eighteenth century trade in "light ducats". A profitable illegal business', *Economy and History*, 16 (1973)

Riesser, J., *The great German banks and their concentration in connection with the economic development of Germany*, National Monetary Commission, Washington, D.C. (3rd edn trans. 1911; reprinted Arno Press, New York 1977)

Rosenbaum, E., and A. J. Sherman, *M. M. Warburg & Co., 1798–1938, Merchant bankers of Hamburg*, C. Hurst, London (1979)

Row-Fogo, J., 'Local taxation in Germany', *Economic Journal*, 11 (1901)

Salemi, M. K., 'Expected exchange depreciation and the demand for money in hyperinflation Germany', *Journal of Money, Credit and Banking*, 12 (1980)

Schacht, H. H. G., *The stabilization of the mark*, Allen and Unwin, London (1927)

Schacht, H. H. G., *Account settled*, Weidenfeld and Nicolson, London (1949)

Schacht, H. H. G., *My first seventy-six years*, Allan Wingate, London (1955)

Schacht, H. H. G., *Confessions of 'the Old Wizard'*, Houghton Mifflin, Boston, Mass. (1956)

Schacht, H. H. G., *The magic of money*, Oldbourne, London (1967)

Schumacher, H., 'Germany's present currency system', in A. D. Gayer, ed., *The lessons of monetary experience. Essays in honor of Irving Fisher*, Farrer and Rinehart, New York (1937)

Schweitzer, A., 'Schacht's regulation of money and capital markets', *Journal of Finance*, 3 (1948)

Schweitzer, A., 'Foreign exchange crisis of 1936', *Zeitschrift für die gesamte Staatswissenschaft*, 118 (1962)

Simpson, A. E., *Hjalmar Schacht in perspective*, Mouton, The Hague (1969)

Tilly, R., *Financial institutions and industrialization in the Rhineland, 1815–70*, University of Wisconsin Press, Madison, Wis. (1966)

Tilly, R., 'The political economy of public finance and the industrialisation of Prussia, 1815–66', *Journal of Economic History*, 26 (1966), 27 (1967) [a corrective note also published 27 (1967)]

Tilly, R., 'Germany, 1815–70', in R. E. Cameron, ed., *Banking in the early stages of industrialisation*, Oxford University Press, New York (1967)

Tilly, R., 'Fiscal policy and Prussian economic development, 1815–66', *Papers presented to the third international conference of economic history, Munich, 1965*, Mouton, Paris (1968)

Tilly, R., 'Capital formation in Germany in the nineteenth century', in P. Mathias and M. M. Postan, eds, *Cambridge Economic History of Europe*, vol. 7(1), Cambridge University Press, Cambridge (1978)

Vagts, A., 'The golden chains. The Jew and Wilhelminic imperialism', *Maryland History*, 4 (1973) [German Jewish finance and banking]

Whale, P. B., *Joint stock banking in Germany. A study of the German credit banks before and after the war*, Macmillan, London (1930)

Williamson, J. G., *Karl Helfferich, 1872–1924. Economist, financier, politician*, Princeton University Press, Princeton, N.J. (1971)

Wolfe, M., 'The development of Nazi monetary policy', *Journal of Economic History*, 15 (1955)

OVERSEAS TRADE AND COMMERCIAL RELATIONS

Allen, R. C., 'International competition in iron and steel, 1850–1913', *Journal of Economic History*, 39 (1979)

Ashley, P. W. L., *Modern tariff history. Germany— United States—France*, J. Murray, London (3rd edn 1926)

Austen, R. A., 'Duala versus Germans in Cameroon. Economic dimensions of a political conflict, *Revue Française d' Histoire d'Outre-Mer*, 64 (1977)

Basch, A., *The Danube basin and the German economic sphere*, Kegan Paul Trench Trubner, London (1944)

Bog, I., 'Mercantilism in Germany', in D. C. Coleman, ed., *Revisions in mercantilism*, Methuen, London (1969)

Bohme, H., 'Big business pressure groups and Bismarck's turn to protectionism, 1873–79', *Historical Journal*, 10 (1967)

Bonnell, A. T., *German control over international economic relations, 1930–40*, University of Illinois Studies in Social Sciences, Urbana, Ill. (1940)

Braatz, W. E., 'German commercial interests in Palestine, 1933–34', *European Studies Review*, 9 (1979)

Buchheim, C., 'Aspects of nineteenth century Anglo-German trade rivalry reconsidered', *Journal of European Economic History*, 10 (1981)

Carr, W., *Arms, autarchy and aggression. A study in German foreign policy, 1933–39*, Edward Arnold, London (1972)

Child, F. C., *The theory and practice of exchange control in Germany. A study of monopolistic exploitation in international markets*, Nijhoff, The Hague (1958)

Dawson, W. H., 'The new German tariff', *Economic Journal*, 12 (1902)

Dawson, W. H., 'The genesis of the German tariff', *Economic Journal*, 14 (1904)

Dawson, W. H., *Protection in Germany. A history of German fiscal policy during the nineteenth century*, P. S. King, London (1904)

Dietzel, H., 'The German tariff controversy', *Quarterly Journal of Economics*, 17 (1903)

Einzig, P., *Bloodless invasion. German economic penetration into the Danubian states and the Balkans*, Duckworth, London (1938)

Fetter, B. S., 'Central Africa, 1914. German schemes and British designs', *Bulletin des Séances l'Académie Royale des Sciences d'Outre-Mer*, 4 (1972)

Firth, S., 'German rule. Ideology and practice', *Journal of Pacific History*, 12 (1977)

Firth, S., 'German labour policy in Nauru and Angaur, 1906–14', *Journal of Pacific History*, 13 (1978)

Fischer, W., 'The German Zollverein. A case study in customs union', *Kyklos*, 13 (1960)

Flaningham, M. L., 'German economic controls in Bulgaria, 1894–1914', *Slavic Review,* 20 (1961)

Flux, A. W., 'British trade and German competition', *Economic Journal,* 7 (1897)

Forbes, I. L. D., 'German informal imperialism in South America before 1914', *Economic History Review,* 31 (1978)

Foster, E. D., 'The trend of Soviet-German commercial relations and its significance', *Harvard Business Review,* 11 (1933)

Friedman, P., 'The welfare costs of bilateralism. German-Hungarian trade, 1933–38', *Explorations in Economic History,* 13 (1976)

Gehling, D., 'German consular reports', *Business History,* 23 (1981)

Geiss, I., 'The German empire and imperialism, 1871–1918', *Australian Journal of Politics and History,* 20 (1974)

Gordon, N. M., 'Britain and the Zollverein duties, 1842–45', *Economic History Review,* 22 (1969)

Gourevitch, P. A., 'International trade, domestic coalitions and liberty. Comparative responses to the crisis of 1873–96', *Journal of Interdisciplinary History,* 8 (1977–78)

Harper, G. T., *German economic policy in Spain during the Spanish civil war, 1936–39,* Mouton, Paris (1967)

Hauser, H., *Germany's commercial grip on the world. Her business methods explained,* Eveleigh Nash, London (1917)

Henderson, W. O., 'The Zollverein', *History,* 19 (1934)

Henderson, W. O., 'The German colonial empire, 1884–1918', *History,* 20 (1935)

Henderson, W. O., 'German colonisation', *German Life and Letters,* 1 (1937)

Henderson, W. O., 'Germany and Mitteleuropa', *German Life and Letters,* 2 (1938)

Henderson, W. O., 'Economic aspects of German imperial colonisation', *Scottish Geographical Magazine,* 54 (1938)

Henderson, W. O., 'Germany's trade with her colonies, 1884–1914', *Economic History Review,* 9 (1938–39)

Henderson, W. O., *The Zollverein,* Cambridge University Press, Cambridge (1939)

Henderson, W. O., 'Twenty years of mandate government. Some aspects of the development of the former German colonies, 1919–39', *The Highway,* 32 (1940)

Henderson, W. O., 'The pan-German movement', *History,* 26 (1941)

Henderson, W. O., 'The conquest of German colonies, 1914–18', *History,* 27 (1942)

Henderson, W. O., 'The war economy of German East Africa, 1914–17', *Economic History Review,* 13 (1943)

Henderson, W. O., 'British economic activity in the German colonies, 1884–1914', *Economic History Review,* 15 (1945)

Henderson, W. O., 'German economic penetration in the Middle East, 1870–1914', *Economic History Review,* 18 (1948)

Henderson, W. O., 'Prince Smith and free trade in Germany', *Economic History Review,* 2 (1949–50)

Henderson, W. O., 'A nineteenth century approach to a West European common market', *Kyklos,* 10 (1957)

Henderson, W. O., *Studies in German colonial history,* Frank Cass, London (1962)

Henderson, W. O., 'German East Africa, 1884–1918', in V. Harlow and E. M. Chilver, eds, *History of East Africa,* vol. 2, Oxford University Press, London (1965)

Hillmann, H. C., 'Analysis of Germany's foreign trade and the war', *Economica,* 7 (1940)

Himmer, R., 'Rathenau, Russia, and Rapallo', *Central European History,* 9 (1976) [Russian-German economic relations]

Hoeffding, W., 'German trade with the Soviet Union', *Slavonic and East European Review,* 14 (1936)

Hoffman, R. J. S., *Great Britain and the German trade rivalry, 1875–1914,* University of Philadelphia Press, Philadelphia, Pa. (1933)

Hunt, J. C., 'Peasants, grain tariffs, and meat quotas. Imperial German protectionism re-examined', *Central European History,* 7 (1974)

Johnston, C., 'The Russo-German tariff war', *Economic Journal,* 4 (1894)

Katzenellenbogen, S. E., 'British businessmen and German Africa, 1885–1919', in B. M. Ratcliffe, ed., *Great Britain and her world, 1750–1914. Essays in honour of W. O. Henderson,* Manchester University Press, Manchester (1975)

Kennedy, P. M., *The rise of the Anglo-German antagonism, 1860–1914,* Allen and Unwin, London (1980)

Kirchner, W., 'Russian tariffs and foreign industries before 1914. The German entrepreneur's perspective', *Journal of Economic History,* 41 (1981)

Kitamura, J., 'Historical roles of German colonial companies', *Keieishigaku,* 4 (1969)

Knoll, A. J., *Togo under imperial Germany, 1884–1914. A case study in colonial rule,* Hoover Institution Press, Stanford, Cal. (1978)

Lambi, I. N., *Free trade and protection in Germany, 1868–79*, F. Steiner, Wiesbaden (1963)

Laves, W. H. G., *German governmental influence on foreign investments 1871–1912*, Arno Press, New York (1977)

Lewis, C., and J. C. McClelland, *Nazi Europe and world trade*, Brookings Institution, Washington, D.C. (1941)

Long, D. C., 'Efforts to secure an Austro-German customs union in the nineteenth century, in A. E. R. Boak, ed., *University of Michigan historical essays*, University of Michigan Press, Ann Arbor, Mich. (1937)

Lorscheider, H. M., 'The commercial treaty between Germany and Serbia of 1904', *Central European History*, 9 (1976)

Luza, R., *Austro-German relations in the Anschluss era*, Princeton University Press, Princeton, N.J. (1975)

Meritt, H. P., 'Bismarck and the German interest in East Africa, 1884–85', *Historical Journal*, 21 (1978)

Minchinton, W. E., and E. E. Williams, '*Made in Germany* and after', *Vierteljahrschrift für sozial- und Wirtschaftsgeschichte*, 62 (1975)

Molodowsky, N., 'Germany's foreign trade terms in 1899–1913', *Quarterly Journal of Economics*, 41 (1927)

Mommsen, W. J., 'Domestic factors in German foreign policy before 1914', *Central European History*, 6 (1973)

Neal, L., 'The economics and finance of bilateral clearing agreements. Germany, 1934–38', *Economic History Review*, 32 (1979)

Neuburger, H. M., and H. H. Stokes. 'The Anglo-German trade rivalry, 1897–1913. A counterfactual outcome and its implications', *Social Science History*, 3 (1979)

Newman, M. D., 'Britain and the German-Austro customs union proposals of 1931', *European Studies Review*, 6 (1976)

O'Faurell, H. H., 'British and German export trade before the war', *Economic Journal*, 26 (1916)

Orde, A., 'The origins of the German-Austrian customs union affair of 1931', *Central European History*, 13 (1980)

Pierard, R. V., 'A case study in German economic imperialism. The Colonial Economic Committee, 1896–1914', *Scandinavian Economic History Review*, 16 (1968)

Pogge von Strandmann, H., 'Domestic origins of Germany's colonial expansion under Bismarck', *Past and Present*, 42 (1969)

Price, A. H., *The evolution of the Zollverein*, University of Michigan Press, Ann Arbor, Mich. (1949)

Rempel, D. G., 'The expropriation of the German colonists in south Russia during the Great War', *Journal of Modern History*, 4 (1932)

Robinson, N., 'German foreign trade and industry after the first world war', *Quarterly Journal of Economics*, 58 (1944)

Ronall, J., 'German and Austrian Jews in the financial modernization of the Middle East', *Leo Baeck Institute Yearbook*, 22 (1977)

Schiff, W., 'The influence of the German armed forces and war industry on Argentina, 1880–1914', *Hispanic American Historical Review*, 52 (1972)

Schweitzer, A., 'The role of foreign trade in the Nazi war economy', *Journal of Political Economy*, 51 (1943)

Smith, W. D., 'The ideology of German colonialism, 1840–1906', *Journal of Modern History*, 46 (1974)

Smith, W. D., *The German colonial empire*, University of North Carolina Press, Chapel Hill, N.C. (1978)

Snyder, L. L., 'The American-German hog dispute, 1879–91', *Journal of Modern History*, 18 (1945)

Stambrook, F. G., 'The German-Austrian customs union projects of 1931. A study of German methods and motives', *Journal of Central European Affairs*, 21 (1961)

Tobler, H. W., 'German colonies in South America. 'A new Germany in the Cono Sur?', *Journal of Interamerican Studies and World Affairs*, 22 (1980)

Townsend, M. E., 'The economic impact of imperial Germany. Commercial and colonial policies', *Journal of Economic History*, Supplement, 3 (1943)

Van Helten, J. J., 'German capital, the Netherlands Railway Company, and the political economy of the Transvaal, 1886–1900', *Journal of African History*, 23 (1978)

Waller, B., 'Bismarck, the dual alliance and economic central Europe, 1877–85', *Vierteljahrschrift für Sozial- und Wirtschaftsgeschichte*, 63 (1976)

Williams, M., 'German imperialism and Austria, 1938', *Journal of Contemporary History*, 14 (1979)

Wrigley, D. W., 'Germany and the Turco-Italian war, 1911–12', *International Journal of Middle East Studies*, 11 (1980)

POPULATION AND MIGRATION

Berkner, L. K., 'Peasant household organization and demographic change in lower Saxony (1689–1766)', in R. D. Lee *et al.*, *Population patterns in the past*, Academic Press, New York (1977)

Blaschke, K., 'The development of population in an area of early industrialization. Saxony from the sixteenth to the nineteenth century', *Papers presented to the third international conference of economic history, Munich, 1965*, Mouton, Paris (1972)

Bürgdorfer, F., 'Migration across the frontiers of Germany', in W. F. Willcox, ed., *International migrations*, vol. 2, National Bureau of Economic Research, New York (1931)

Cohn, G., 'The increase of population in Germany', *Economic Journal*, 22 (1912)

Haines, M. R., 'Population and economic change in nineteenth century eastern Europe. Prussian upper Silesia, 1840–1913', *Journal of Economic History*, 36 (1976)

Hansen, M. L., 'The revolutions of 1848 and German emigration', *Journal of Economic and Business History*, 2 (1929–30)

Imhof, A. E., 'The analysis of eighteenth century causes. Some methodological considerations', *Historical Methods Newsletter*, 2 (1978) [causes of eighteenth century deaths]

Imhof., A. E., 'Structure of reproduction in a west German village, 1690–1900', in S. Akerman *et al.*, *Chance and change. Social and economic studies in historical demography in the Baltic area*, Odense University Press, Odense (1978)

Imhof, A. E., 'Remarriage in rural populations and in urban middle and upper strata in Germany from the sixteenth to the twentieth century', in J. Dupaquier *et al.*, *Marriage and remarriage in populations of the past*, Academic Press, London (1981)

Kloberdanz, T. J., 'Plainsmen of three continents. Volga German adaptation to steppe, prairie and pampa', in F. C. Luebke, ed., *Ethnicity on the great plains*, University of Nebraska Press, Lincoln. Neb. (1980)

Knodel, J., 'Law, marriage and illegitimacy in nineteenth century Germany', *Population Studies*, 20 (1966–67)

Knodel, J., 'Infant mortality and fertility in three Bavarian villages. An analysis of family histories from the nineteenth century', *Population Studies*, 22 (1968)

Knodel, J., 'Two and a half centuries of demographic history in a Bavarian village', *Population Studies*, 24 (1970)

Knodel, J., 'Malthus minus. Marriage restrictions in nineteenth century Germany', *Social Science*, 27 (1972)

Knodel, J., *The decline of fertility in Germany, 1871–1939*, Princeton University Press, Princeton, N.J. (1974)

Knodel, J., 'Town and country in nineteenth century Germany. A review of urban–rural differentials in demographic behaviour', *Social Science History*, 1 (1977)

Knodel, J., 'Natural fertility in pre-industrial Germany', *Population Studies*, 32 (1978)

Knodel, J., 'Remarriage and marital fertility in Germany during the eighteenth and nineteenth centuries. An exploratory analysis based on German village genealogies', in J. Dupaquier *et al.*, *Marriage and remarriage in populations of the past*, Academic Press, London (1981)

Knodel, J., and S. DeVos, 'Preferences for sex of offspring and demographic behaviour in eighteenth and nineteenth century Germany. An examination of evidence from village genealogies', *Journal of Family History*, 5 (1980)

Knodel, J., and M. J. Maynes, 'Urban and rural marriage patterns in imperial Germany', *Journal of Family History*, 1 (1976)

Knodel, J., and E. Shorter, 'The reliability of family reconstitution data in German village genealogies (*Ortssippenbücher*)', *Annales de Demographie Historique* (1976)

Knodel, J., and E. van de Walle, 'Breast feeding, fertility and infant mortality. An analysis of some early German data', *Population Studies*, 21 (1967)

Knodel, J. and C. Wilson, 'The secular increase in fecundity in German village populations. An analysis of reproductive histories of couples married 1750–1899', *Population Studies*, 35 (1981)

Köllmann, W., 'The population of Germany in the age of industrialism', in H. Moller, ed., *Population movements in modern European history*, Macmillan, New York (1964)

Köllmann, W., 'The population of Barmen before and during the period of industrialization', in D. V. Glass and D. E. C. Eversley, eds, *Population in History. Essays in historical demography*, Edward Arnold, London (1965)

Köllmann, W., 'Population and labour force potential in Germany, 1815–65', in P. Deprez, ed., *Population and economics*, University of Manitoba Press, Winnipeg (1970)

Köllmann, W., *et al.*, 'German emigration to the United States', *Perspectives in American His-*

tory, 7 (1973)

Kuczynski, R. R., *The balance of births and deaths,* Macmillan, New York (1928)

Lee, W. R., 'Primary sector output and mortality changes in early nineteenth century Bavaria', *Journal of European Economic History,* 6 (1977)

Lee, W. R., 'Germany', in W. R. Lee, ed., *European demography and economic growth,* Croom Helm, London (1979)

Lee, W. R., 'Medicalisation and mortality trends in South Germany in the early nineteenth century', in A. E. Imhof, ed., *Mensch und Gesundheit in der Geschichte,* Matthiesen Verlag, Husum (1980)

Neuman, R. P., 'Working class birth control in Wilhelmine Germany', *Comparative Studies in Society and History,* 20 (1978)

Newman, A. R., 'A test of the Okun-Richardson model of internal migration', *Economic Development and Cultural Change,* 29 (1981) [uses results of imperial German census, 1871–1914]

Obermann, K., 'Population movements in Germany in the nineteenth century', in *International population conference, London* (1969), vol. 4, International Union for the Scientific Study of Population, Liège (1971)

Richards, T., 'Fertility decline in Germany. An econometric appraisal', *Population Studies,* 31 (1977)

Szajkowski, Z., 'Sufferings of Jewish emigrants to America in transit through Germany', *Jewish Social Studies,* 39 (1977)

von Hippel, H., 'Emigration from Wurtemberg in the eighteenth and nineteenth centuries', *Immigration History Newsletter,* 13 (1981)

Walker, M., *Germany and the emigration, 1816–85,* Harvard University Press, Cambridge, Mass. (1964)

LABOUR CONDITIONS AND ORGANISATION

Anderson, E., *Hammer or anvil. The story of the German working class movement,* Gollancz, London (1945)

Angel-Volkov, S., 'Popular anti-modernism. Ideology and sentiment among master-artisans during the 1890s', *Jahrbuch des Instituts für deutsche Geschichte,* 3 (1974)

Ashley, W. J., *The progress of the German working classes in the last quarter of a century,* Longmans, London (1904)

Bailey, S., 'The Berlin strike of January 1918', *Central European History,* 13 (1980)

Blessing, W. K., 'The cult of monarchy, political loyalty and the workers' movement in imperial Germany', *Journal of Contemporary History,* 13 (1978)

Braunthal, G., *Socialist labour and politics in Weimar Germany. The General Federation of German Trade Unions,* Archon Books, Hamden, Conn. (1978)

Brozek, A., 'Industrial labour force in a politically divided area. Formation and development of its structure. The upper Silesian example, 1870–1939', in M. W. Flinn, ed., *Proceedings of the seventh International Economic History Association conference, Edinburgh, 1978,* Edinburgh University Press, Edinburgh (1978)

Crew, D. F., 'Steel, sabotage and socialism. The strike at the Dortmund "Union" steelworks in 1911', in R. J. Evans, ed., *The German working class, 1888–1933,* Croom Helm, London (1982)

Cullity, J. P., 'The growth of governmental employment in Germany, 1882–1950', *Zeitschrift für die Gesamte Staatswissenschaft,* 123 (1967)

Dawson, W. H., *German socialism and Ferdinand Lassalle. A biographical history of German socialist movements during this century,* Swann Sonnenschein, London (1888)

Dawson, W. H., *The German working man. A study in national efficiency,* P. S. King, London (1906)

Evans, R. J., ' "Red Wednesday" in Hamburg. Social democrats, police and lumpenproletariat in the suffrage disturbances of 17 July 1906', *Social History,* 4 (1979)

Evans, R. J., 'The sociological interpretation of German labour history', in R. J. Evans, ed., *The German working class, 1888–1933,* Croom Helm, London (1982)

Evans, R. J., ed., *The German working class, 1888–1933. The politics of everyday life.* Croom Helm, London (1982)

Geary, D., 'The German labour movement, 1848–1918', *European Studies Review,* 6 (1976)

Geary, D., 'Radicalism and the German worker. Metal workers and revolution 1914–23', in R. J. Evans, ed., *Society and politics in Wilhelmine Germany,* Croom Helm, London (1978)

Geary, D., 'Identifying militancy. The assessment of working class attitudes towards state and society', in R. J. Evans, ed., *The German working class, 1888–1933,* Croom Helm, London (1982)

Grebing, H., *The history of the German labour movement. A survey,* Wolff, London (1969)

Grunberger, R., *Red rising in Bavaria,* Barker, London (1973)

Ham, W. T., 'Labour under the German Republic', *Quarterly Journal of Economics*, 48 (1934)

Ham, W. T., 'The organization of farm labourers in Germany', *Journal of Political Economy*, 44 (1936)

Hamburger, L., *How Nazi Germany has mobilized and controlled labour*, Brookings Institution, Washington D.C. (1940)

Herbst, J., 'White collar, blue collar and no collar. Comparison, anyone?', *Reviews in American History*, 6 (1978)

Hickey, S., 'The shaping of the German labour movement. Miners in the Ruhr', in R. J. Evans, ed., *Society and politics in Wilhelmine Germany*, Croom Helm, London (1978)

Homze, E. L., *Foreign labour in Nazi Germany*, Princeton University Press, Princeton, N.J. (1967)

International Labour Office, 'Collective agreements in Germany', *International Labour review*, 5 (1922)

International Labour Office, 'Hours of work in German industry', *International Labour Review*, 5 (1922)

International Labour Office, 'The reduction of the working week in Germany', *International Labour Review*, 29 (1934)

International Labour Office, 'Hours of work in Germany', *International Labour Review*, 39 (1939)

Kele, M. H., *Nazis and workers. The National Socialist appeals to German labour, 1919–33*, University of North Carolina Press, Chapel Hill, N.C. (1972)

Kocka, J., 'The study of social mobility and the formation of the working class in the nineteenth century', *Mouvement Social*, 111 (1980)

Kuczynski, J., *The conditions of the workers in Great Britain, Germany and the Soviet Union, 1932–38*, Gollancz, London (1939)

Kuczynski, J., *A short history of labour conditions under industrial capitalism*, vol. 3, *Germany*, Muller, London (1944)

Labisch, A., 'The Working Men's Samaritan Federation (Arbeiter-Samariterbund), 1888–1933', *Journal of Contemporary History*, 13 (1978)

Lee, J. J., 'Labour in German industrialization', in P. Mathias and M. M. Postan, eds, *Cambridge Economic History of Europe*, vol. 7(1), Cambridge University Press, Cambridge (1978)

Legman, D., 'The eight hour day and the problem of overtime in Germany', *International Labour Review*, 6 (1922)

Lloyd, G. I. H., 'Labour organisation in the cutlery trade of Solingen', *Economic Journal*, 18 (1908)

McConagha, W. A., *Development of the labour movement in Great Britain, France and Germany*, University of North Carolina Press, Chapel Hill, N.C. (1942)

Maehl, W. H., 'August Bebel. Shadow emperor of the German workers', *Memoirs of the American Philosophical Society* (1980)

Mason, T., 'Labour in the Third Reich, 1933–39', *Past and Present*, 33 (1966)

Mittelman, E. B., 'The German use of unemployment insurance funds for works purposes', *Journal of Political Economy*, 46 (1938)

Murphy, R. C., 'The Polish trade union in the Ruhr coalfield. Labor organization and ethnicity in Wilhelmian Germany', *Central European History*, 11 (1978)

Noyes, P. H., *Organization and revolution. Working class associations in the German revolutions of 1848–49*, Princeton University Press, Princeton, N.J. (1966)

Rimlinger, G. V., 'The legitimation of protest. A comparative study in labour history', *Comparative Studies in Society and History*, 2 (1960)

Roberts, J. S., 'Drink and the labour movement. The Schnapps boycott of 1909', in R. J. Evans, ed., *The German working class, 1888–1933*, Croom Helm, London (1982)

Rosenhaft, E., 'Organising the *Lumpenproletariat*. Cliques and communists in Berlin during the Weimar Republic', in R. J. Evans, ed., *The German working class, 1888–1933*, Croom Helm, London (1982)

Schofer, L., 'Patterns of worker protest. Upper Silesia, 1865–1914', *Journal of Social History*, 5 (1972)

Schofer, L., *The formation of a modern labor force. Upper Silesia, 1865–1914*, University of California Press, Berkeley, Cal. (1975)

Schweinitz, K. de, 'Industrialization, labor controls and democracy', *Economic Development and Cultural Change*, 7 (1959)

Shankleman, J., 'Women in labour', *Bulletin of the Society for the Study of Labour History*, 28 (1974) [female employment, seventeenth to twentieth century]

Sitzler, F., 'Recent emergency legislation in Germany, with special reference to wages and hours of work', *International Labour Review*, 25 (1932)

Spencer, E. G., 'Workers in Wilhelmine Germany. A review article', *Central European History*, 10 (1977)

Stearns, P. N., 'Adaptation to industrialization. German workers as a test case', *Central European*

History, 3 (1970)

Stearns, P. N., 'National character and European labour history', *Journal of Social History*, 4 (1970)

Steenson, G. P., *Not one man! Not one penny! German social democracy 1863–1914*, University of Pittsburgh Press, Pittsburgh, Pa. (1981)

Vollweiler, H., 'The mobilisation of labour reserves in Germany', parts 1 and 2, *International Labour Review*, 38 (1938)

Waelbroeck, P., 'Industrial relations in the French state mines of the Saar Basin', parts 1 and 2, *International Labour Review*, 21 (1930), 22 (1930)

Wagenführ, R., and W. Voss, 'Trade unions and the world economic crisis. The case of Germany', in H. van der Wee, ed., *The great depression revisited*, Nijhoff, The Hague (1972)

Wendel, H. C. M., *The evolution of industrial freedom in Prussia, 1845–49*, New York University Press, New York (1921)

Wiggs, K. I., *Unemployment in Germany since the war*, P. S. King, London (1933)

Woytinsky, W., 'New statistics of collective agreements in Germany', *International Labour Review*, 23 (1931)

Wunderlich, F., *Farm labor in Germany, 1810–1945*, Princeton University Press, Princeton, N.J. (1961)

Zielinski, H., 'The social and political background of the Silesian uprisings', *Acta Pononiae Historica*, 26 (1972)

Zucker, S., 'Ludwig Bamberger and the politics of the cold shoulder. German liberalism's response to working class legislation in the 1870s', *European Studies Review*, 2 (1972)

INCOMES, WAGES AND PRICES

Born, K. E., 'The German inflation after the first world war', *Journal of European Economic History*, 6 (1977)

Bresciani-Turroni, C., *The economics of inflation. A study of currency depreciation in post-war Germany*, Allen and Unwin, London (1937)

Bry, G., *Wages in Germany, 1871–1945*, Princeton University Press, Princeton, N.J. (1960)

Bry, G., and Boschan, C., 'Secular trends and recent changes in real wages and wage differentials in three Western industrial countries. The United States, Great Britain and Germany', *Papers presented to the second international conference of economic history, Aix-en-Provence, 1962*, Mouton, Paris (1965)

Childers, T., 'Inflation, stabilization, and political realignment in Germany, 1919–28, in G. D. Feldman *et al.*, eds, *Die deutsche Inflation. Eine Zwischenbilanz*, de Gruyter, Berlin (1982)

Desai, A. V., *Real wages in Germany, 1871–1913*, Clarendon Press, Oxford (1968)

Feldman, G. D., 'The political economy of Germany's relative stabilization during the 1920/21 depression', in G. D. Feldman *et al.*, eds, *Die deutsche Inflation. Eine Zwischenbilanz*, de Gruyter, Berlin (1982)

Geisenberger, S., and J. H. Müller, 'Changes in the structure of incomes in Prussia, 1874–1913', *German Economic Review*, 9 (1971)

Graham, F. D., *Exchange, prices and production in hyperinflation Germany, 1920–23*, Princeton University Press, Princeton, N.J. (1930)

Grünfeld, J., 'Rationalisation and the employment and wages of women in Germany', *International Labour Review*, 29 (1934)

Guttman, W., and P. Mechan, *The great inflation. Germany, 1919–23*, Saxon House, New York (1975)

Holtfrerich, C. L., 'Domestic and foreign expectations and the demand for money during the German inflation, 1920–23', in C. P. Kindleberger and J.-P. Laffargue, eds, *Financial crises. Theory, history and policy*, Cambridge University Press, Cambridge (1982)

Hughes, M., 'Economic interest, social attitudes, and creditor ideology. Popular responses to inflation', in G. D. Feldman *et al.*, eds, *Die deutsche Inflation. Eine Zwischenbilanz*, de Gruyter, Berlin (1982)

Jacobs, R. L., 'Hyperinflation and the supply of money', *Journal of Money, Credit and Banking*, 9 (1977)

Jones, L. E., 'Inflation, revaluation, and the crisis of middle-class politics. A study in the dissolution of the German party system', *Central European History*, 12 (1979) ·

Kieswetter, H., 'Regional disparities in wages. The cotton industry in nineteenth century Germany. Some methodological considerations', in P. Bairoch, and M. Levy-Leboyer, eds, *Disparities in economic development since the industrial revolution*, Macmillan, London (1981)

Kuczynski, R. R., *Trend of wages in Germany, 1898 to 1907*, U.S. Government Printing Office, Washington D.C. (1910)

Kuczynski, R. R., *Postwar labour conditions in Germany*, U.S. Government Printing Office, Washington D.C. (1925)

Laursen, K., and J. Pedersen, *The German inflation,*

1918–23, North-Holland Publishing Co., Amsterdam (1964)

Merkin, G., 'Towards a theory of the German inflation. Some preliminary observations', in G. D. Feldman *et al.*,eds, *Die deutsche Inflation. Eine Zwischenbilanz*, de Gruyter, Berlin (1982)

Midland Bank Review, 'The German inflation of 1923', *Midland Bank Review*, (1975)

Nathan, O., 'Consumption in Germany during the period of rearmament', *Quarterly Journal of Economics*, 56 (1942)

Neitzel, G., 'Hours and wages in the German heavy iron industry', *International Labour Review*, 17 (1928)

Oppenheimer-Bluhm, H., 'The standard of living of German labour under Nazi rule', *Social Research*, supplement, 5 (1943)

Orsagh, T. J., 'The probable geographical distribution of German income, 1882–1963', *Zeitschrift für die gesamte Staatswissenschaft*, 124 (1968)

Phillipi, G., 'Prices, wages and productivity in Germany from 1500 to the present day', *Konjunkturpolitik*, 12 (1966)

Ringer, F. K., ed., *The German inflation of 1923*, Oxford University Press, New York (1969)

Sargent, T. J., and N. Wallace, 'Rational expectations and the dynamics of hyperinflation', *International Economic Review*, 14 (1973)

Schmölders, G., 'The German experience. Essay on inflation', *Proceedings of the Academy of Political Science*, 31 (1975)

Sitzler, F., 'The adaptation of wages to the depreciation of the currency in Germany', *International Labour Review*, 9 (1924)

Sweezy, M. Y., 'Distribution of wealth and income under the Nazis', *Review of Economic Statistics*, 21 (1939)

Willis, H. P., and J. M. Chapman, *The economics of inflation*, Columbia University Press, New York (1935)

URBAN HISTORY

Abercrombie, P., 'Berlin. Its growth and present state. The nineteenth century', *Town Planning Review*, 4 (1914)

Albers, G., 'Town planning in Germany. Change and continuity under conditions of political turbulence', in G. E. Cherry, ed., *Shaping an urban world*, Mansell, London (1980)

Bollerey, F., and K. Hartmann, 'A patriarchal utopia. The garden city and housing reform in Germany at the turn of the century', in A. Sutcliffe, ed., *The rise of modern urban planning, 1800–1914*, Mansell, London (1980)

Breitling, P., 'The role of competition in the genesis of urban planning. Germany and Austria in the nineteenth century', in A. Stucliffe, ed., *The rise of modern urban planning, 1800–1914*, Mansell, London (1980)

Crew, D. F., 'Definitions of modernity. Social mobility in a German town. Bochum, 1880–1901', *Journal of Social History*, 7 (1973)

Crew, D. F., *Town in the Ruhr. A social history of Bochum, 1860–1914*, Columbia University Press, New York (1979)

Dawson, W. H., *Municipal life and government in Germany*, Longmans Green, London (1914)

Friedrichs, C. R., 'Capitalism, mobility and class formation in the early modern German city', *Past and Present*, 69 (1975)

Greene, E. T., *Politics and geography in postwar German city planning. A field study of four German cities. Hanover, Cologne, Kiel and Trier*, University Microfilms, Ann Arbor, Mich. (1960)

Gutkind, E. A., *International history of city development*, vol. 1, *Urban development in central Europe*, Collier-Macmillan, London (1964)

Hall, P., 'Rhine-Ruhr,' in P. Hall, *The world cities*, Weidenfeld and Nicolson, London (1966)

Hartsough, M. L., 'Cologne. The metropolis of western Germany', *Journal of Economic and Business History*, 3 (1930–31)

Köllmann, W., 'The process of urbanization in Germany at the height of the industrialization period', *Journal of Contemporary History*, 4 (1969)

Lane, B. M., *Architecture and politics in Germany, 1918–45*, Harvard University Press, Cambridge, Mass. (1968)

Lee, J. J., 'Aspects of urbanisation and economic development in Germany, 1815–1914', in P. Abrams and E. A. Wrigley, eds, *Towns in societies. Essays in economic history and historical sociology*, Cambridge University Press, Cambridge (1978)

Lees, A., 'Debates about the big city in Germany, 1890–1914', *Societas*, 5 (1975)

Liebel, H., '*Laissez-faire v.* mercantilism. The rise of Hamburg. The Hamburg bourgeoisie *v.* Frederick the Great in the crisis of 1763', *Vierteljahrschrift für Sozial- und Wirtschaftsgesichte*, 52 (1965)

Logan, T. H., 'The Americanization of German zoning', *Journal of the American Institute of Planners*, 42 (1976) [German city plans 1860–1968]

Masur, G., *Imperial Berlin*, Routledge and Kegan Paul, London (1971)

Matzerath, H., 'The influence of industrialization on urban growth in Prussia (1815–1914)', in H. Schmal, ed., *Patterns of European urbanisation since 1500,* Croom Helm, London (1981)

Mullin, J. R., 'American perceptions of German city planning at the turn of the century', *Urbanism Past and Present,* 3 (1976–77)

Mullin, J. R., 'City planning in Frankfurt, Germany, 1925–32. A study in practical utopianism', *Journal of Urban History,* 4 (1977)

Muthesius, S., 'The origins of the German conservation movement', in R. Kain, ed., *Planning for conservation,* Mansell, London (1981)

Peets, E., 'Camillo Sitte' and 'Haussmann', *Town Planning Review,* 12 (1927)

Poor, H. L., 'City versus country. Anti-urbanism in the Weimar republic', *Societas,* 6 (1976)

Rebentisch, D., 'Regional planning and its institutional framework. An illustration from the Rhine-Main area, 1890–1945', in G. E. Cherry, ed., *Shaping an urban world,* Mansell, London (1980)

Reulecke, J., 'Population growth and urbanization in Germany in the nineteenth century', *Urbanism Past and Present,* 4 (1977)

Sheehan, J. J., 'Liberalism and the city in nineteenth century Germany', *Past and Present,* 51 (1971)

Sutcliffe, A., 'Environmental control and planning in European capitals, 1850–1914. London, Paris and Berlin', in I. Hammarström and T. Hall, eds, *Growth and transformation of the modern city,* Swedish Council for Building Research, Stockholm (1979)

Sutcliffe, A., *Towards the planned city. Germany, Britain, the United States and France, 1780–1914,* Blackwell, Oxford (1981)

Weber, A., 'The cultural and social significance of the big city', in A. and L. Lees, eds, *The urbanization of European society in the nineteenth century,* D. C. Heath, Lexington, Mass. (1976)

Zophy, J. W., 'Reformation and war in the early modern German city', *Journal of Urban History,* 7 (1980)

SOCIAL STRUCTURE AND SOCIAL CONDITIONS

Abraham, D., 'Constituting hegemony. The bourgeois crisis of Weimar Germany', *Journal of Modern History,* 51 (1979)

Ackerknecht, E. H., and C. E. Rosenberg, 'German Jews, English dissenters, French Protestants. Nineteenth century pioneers of modern medicine and science', in C. E. Rosenberg, ed., *Healing and History. Essays for George Rosen,* Science History Publications, New York (1979)

Ahlstrom, G., 'Higher technical education and the engineering profession in France and Germany in the nineteenth century', *Economy and History,* 21 (1978)

Anderson, E. N., *The social and political conflict in Prussia, 1858–64,* University of Nebraska Press, Lincoln, Neb. (1954)

Anthony, K., *Feminism in Germany and Scandinavia,* Holt, New York (1915)

Bajohr, S., 'Illegitimacy and the working class. Illegitimate mothers in Brunswick, 1900–33', in R. J. Evans, ed., *The German working class, 1888–1933,* Croom Helm, London (1982)

Baumert, G., 'Changes in the family and the position of older persons in Germany', *International Journal of Comparative Sociology,* 1 (1960)

Bessel, R. J., and E. J. Feuchtwanger, *Social change and political development in Weimar Germany,* Croom Helm, London (1981)

Blackbourn, D., 'The *Mittelstand* in Germany. Society and politics, 1871–1914', *Social History,* 4 (1977)

Blanning, T. C. W., *Reform and revolution in Mainz, 1743–1803,* Cambridge University Press, Cambridge (1974)

Blanning, T. C. W., 'German Jacobins and the French revolution', *Historical Journal,* 23 (1980)

Bruford, W. H., *Germany in the eighteenth century. The social background of the literary revival,* Cambridge University Press, Cambridge (1935)

Buse, D. K., 'German revolutions. A different view of German history', *Dalhousie Review,* 52 (1972)

Bynum, W. F., 'Chronic alcoholism in the first half of the nineteenth century', *Bulletin of the History of Medicine,* 42 (1968)

Caplan, J., ' "The imaginary universality of particular interests". The "tradition" of the civil service in German history', *Social History,* 4 (1979)

Coyner, S., 'Class consciousness and consumption. The new middle class during the Weimar Republic', *Journal of Social History,* 10 (1977)

Dasey, R., 'Women's work and the family. Women garment workers in Berlin and Hamburg before the first world war', in R. J. Evans and W. R. Lee, eds, *The German family,* Croom Helm, London (1981)

Dawson, W. H., *German life in town and country,* Putnam, London (1901)

Demeter, K., *The German officer corps in society and state, 1650–1945,* Weidenfeld and Nicolson, London (1965)

Dibble, V., 'Political judgements and the perception of social relationships. An analysis of some applied social research in late nineteenth century Germany', *American Journal of Sociology*, 78 (1972)

Dominick, R., 'Democracy or socialism? A case study of Vorwarts in the 1890s', *Central European History,* 10 (1977) [role of the press]

Dowe, D., 'The working men's choral movement in Germany before the first world war', *Journal of Contemporary History,* 13 (1978)

Eley, G., 'Defining social imperialism. Use and abuse of an idea', *Social History,* 3 (1976)

Ende, A., 'Battering and neglect. Children in Germany, 1860–1978', *Journal of Psychohistory,* 7 (1979–80)

Engelsing, R., 'The economic and social differentiation of the German commercial clerks, 1690–1900', *Zeitschrift für die gesamte Staatswissenschaft,* 123 (1967)

Evans, R. J., *The feminist movement in Germany, 1894–1933,* Sage Publications, London (1976)

Evans, R. J., 'Prostitution, state and society in imperial Germany', *Past and Present,* 70 (1976)

Evans, R. J., *Society and politics in Wilhelmine Germany,* Croom Helm, London (1978)

Evans, R. J., 'German social democracy and women's suffrage, 1891–1918', *Journal of Contemporary History,* 15 (1980)

Evans, R. J., 'Politics and the family. Social democracy and the working class family in theory and practice before 1914', in R. J. Evans and W. R. Lee, eds, *The German family,* Croom Helm, London (1981)

Evans, R. J., and W. R. Lee, eds, *The German family. Essays on the social history of the family in nineteenth and twentieth century Germany,* Croom Helm, London (1981)

Forbes, I. D., 'Social imperialism and Wilhelmine Germany', *Historical Journal,* 22 (1979)

Forman, P., 'The financial support and political alignment of physicists in Weimar Germany', *Minerva,* 12 (1974)

Friedrichs, C. R., 'Marriage, family and social structure in an early modern German town', *Canadian Historical Association Historical Papers* (1975)

Friedrichs, C. R. *Urban society in an age of war. Nordlingen, 1580–1720,* Princeton University Press, Princeton, N.J. (1979)

Geary, D., 'The Ruhr. From social peace to social revolution', *European Studies Review,* 10 (1980)

Gellately, B., *The politics of economic despair. Shopkeepers and German politics, 1890–1914,* Sage Publications, London (1974)

Grunberger, R., *A social history of the Third Reich,* Weidenfeld and Nicolson, London (1971)

Gruttner, M., 'Working class crime and the labour movement. Pilfering in the Hamburg docks, 1888–1923', in R. J. Evans, ed., *The German working class, 1888–1933,* Croom Helm, London (1982)

Hamerow, T. S., *The social foundations of German unification, 1858–71,* vol. 1, *Ideas and institutions;* vol. 2, *Struggles and accommodation,* Princeton University Press, Princeton, N.J. (1969)

Hansen, K., 'Family and role division. The polarisation of sexual stereotypes in the nineteenth century. An aspect of the dissociation of work and family life', in R. J. Evans and W. R. Lee, eds, *The German family,* Croom Helm, London (1981)

Hardt, H., *Social theories of the press. Early German and American perspectives,* Sage Publications, Beverley Hills, Cal. (1979)

Hart, H., and H. Hertz, 'Expectation of life as an index of social progress', *American Sociological Review,* 9 (1944)

Henderson, W. O., 'Friedrich List and the social question', *Journal of European Economic History,* 10 (1981)

Herwig, H. H., 'The feudalization of the bourgeoisie. The role of the nobility in the German naval officer corps, 1890–1918', *Historian,* 38 (1976)

Honeycutt, K., 'Socialism and feminism in imperial Germany', *Signs,* 5 (1979)

Horsfall, T. C., *The improvement of dwellings and surroundings of the people. The example of Germany,* Manchester University Press, Manchester (1904)

Hughes, D. J., 'Occupational origins of Prussia's generals, 1871–1914', *Central European History,* 13 (1980)

Husi-Huey Liang, 'Lower-class immigrants in Wilhelmine Berlin', *Central European History,* 3 (1970)

Husi-Huey Liang, 'Lower-class immigrants in Wilhelmine Berlin', in A. and L. Lees, eds, *The urbanization of European society in the nineteenth century,* D. C. Heath, Lexington, Mass. (1976)

Imhof, A. E., 'The hospital in the eighteenth century. For whom? The Charité hospital in Berlin, the navy hospital in Copenhagen, the Königsberg hospital in Norway', *Journal of Social History,* 10 (1977)

Ingraham, B. L., *Political crime in Europe. A comparative study of France, Germany and England,* University of California Press, Berkeley, Cal. (1979)

Jackson, J. H., 'Overcrowding and family life. Working class families and the housing crisis in late nineteenth century Duisburg', in R. J. Evans, and W. R. Lee, eds, *The German family*, Croom Helm, London (1981)

Jacobs, N., 'The German Social Democratic Party school in Berlin, 1906–14', *History Workshop Journal*, 5 (1978)

Jarausch, K. H., 'Liberal education as illiberal socialization. The case of students in imperial Germany', *Journal of Modern History*, 50 (1978)

Kaelble, H., 'Social stratification in Germany in the nineteenth and twentieth centuries. A survey of research since 1945', *Journal of Social History*, 10 (1976)

Kaelble, H., 'Social mobility in Germany, 1900–60', *Journal of Modern History*, 50 (1978)

Kirkpatrick, C., *Nazi Germany. Its women and family life*, Bobbs-Merrill, New York (1938)

Landes, D. S., 'The Jewish merchant. Typology and stereotypology in Germany', *Leo Baeck Institute Yearbook*, 19 (1974)

Lee, W. R., 'Bastardy and the socioeconomic structure of south Germany', *Journal of Interdisciplinary History*, 7 (1977) [comment by E. Shorter and reply by W. R. Lee in 8 (1978)]

Lee, W. R., 'Family and "modernisation". The peasant family and social change in nineteenth century Bavaria', in R. J. Evans and W. R. Lee, eds, *The German family*, Croom Helm, London (1981)

Lees, A., 'Critics of urban society in Germany, 1854–1914', *Journal of the History of Ideas*, 40 (1979)

Lidtke, V., 'Social class and secularization in imperial Germany. The working classes', *Leo Baeck Institute Yearbook*, 25 (1980)

Liebel, H. P., 'The bourgeoisie in southwestern Germany, 1500–1789. A rising class?', *International Review of Social History*, 10 (1965)

Lowenstein, S. M., 'The rural community and the urbanization of German jewry', *Central European History*, 13 (1980)

McClelland, C., *State, society, and university in Germany, 1700–1914*, Cambridge University Press, Cambridge (1980)

McCormmach, R., 'On academic scientists in Wilhelmian Germany', *Daedalus*, 103 (1974)

McCreary, E. C., 'Social welfare and business. The Krupp welfare program, 1860–1914', *Business History Review*, 42 (1968)

McHale, V. E., and E. A. Johnson, 'Urbanization, industrialization and crime in imperial Germany', *Social Science History*, 1 (1976)

Maynes, M. J., 'The virtues of archaism. The political economy of schooling in Europe, 1750–1850',

Comparative Studies in Society and History, 21 (1979) [concerned with Baden]

Miringoll, M. L., 'The impact of population policy upon social welfare', *Social Service Review*, 54 (1980)

Mommsen, W. J., ed., *The emergence of the welfare state in Britain and Germany*, Croom Helm, London (1981)

Monaco, P., *Cinema and society. France and Germany during the twenties*, Elsevier, New York (1976)

Muller, D. K., 'The qualifications crisis and school reform in late nineteenth century Germany', *History of Education*, 9 (1980) [school selection by social class and comments on class structure in general]

Muncy, L., *The Junker in Prussian administration under William II, 1888–1914*, Brown University Press, Providence, R.I. (1944)

Neuman, R. P., 'Industrialization and sexual behaviour. Some aspects of working class life in imperial Germany', in R. J. Bezucha, ed., *Modern European social history*, D. C. Heath, Lexington, Mass. (1972)

Neuman, R. P., 'The sexual question and social democracy in imperial Germany', *Journal of Social History*, 7 (1974)

Nolan, M., *Social democracy and society. Working class radicalism in Düsseldorf, 1890–1920*, Cambridge University Press, Cambridge (1981)

Ohno, E., 'The social basis of Nazism', *Kyoto University Economic Review*, 42 (1972)

Olson, J. M., 'Radical social democracy and school reform in Wilhelmine Germany', *History of Education Quarterly*, 17 (1977)

Pachter, H. M., *Modern Germany. A social, cultural and political history*, Westview, Boulder, Col. (1979)

Phayer, J. M., 'Lower class morality. The case of Bavaria', *Journal of Social History*, 7 (1974)

Pyenson, L. and D. Skopp, 'Educating physicists in Germany c. 1900', *Social Studies of Science*, 7 (1977)

Quataert, J. H. 'Unequal partners in an uneasy alliance. Women and the working class in imperial Germany', in M. J. Boxer and J. H. Quataert, eds, *Socialist women. European socialist feminism in the nineteenth and early twentieth centuries*, Elsevier, New York (1978)

Quataert, J. H., *Reluctant feminists in German social democracy, 1855–1917*, Princeton University Press, Princeton, N.J. (1979)

Redlich, F., 'Science and charity. Count Rumford and

his followers', *International Review of Social History*, 16 (1971)

Richarz, M., 'Jewish social mobility in Germany during the time of emancipation (1790–1871)', *Leo Baeck Institute Yearbook*, 20 (1975)

Riehl, W. H., 'The city as a source of corruption', in A. and L. Lees, eds, *The urbanization of European society in the nineteenth century*, D. C. Heath, Lexington, Mass. (1976)

Ringee, F. K., *The decline of the German mandarins. The German academic community, 1890–1933*, Harvard University Press, Cambridge, Mass. (1969)

Ritter, G. A., 'Workers' culture in imperial Germany. Problems and points of departure for research', *Journal of Contemporary History*, 13 (1978)

Rohr, D. G., *The origins of social liberalism in Germany*, University of Chicago Press, Chicago (1963)

Rürup, R., 'Problems of the German revolution, 1918–19', *Journal of Contemporary History*, 3 (1968)

Sabean, D., 'Household formation and geographical mobility. A family register study for a Würtemberg village, 1760–1900', *Annales de Demographie Historiques*, 7 (1970)

Sagarra, E., *A social history of Germany, 1648–1914*, Methuen, London (1977)

Schlumbohm, J., ' "Traditional" collectivity and "modern" individuality. Some questions and suggestions for the historical study of socialization. The examples of the German lower and upper bourgeoisies around 1800', *Social History*, 5 (1980)

Schoenbaum, D., *Hitler's social revolution. Class and states in Nazi Germany, 1933–39*, Weidenfeld and Nicolson, London (1966)

Schomerus, H., 'The family life cycle. A study of factory workers in nineteenth century Würtemburg', in R. J. Evans and W. R. Lee, eds, *The German family*, Croom Helm, London (1981)

Schweitzer, A., 'The nazification of the lower middle class and peasants', in M. Baumont, ed., *The Third Reich*, Praeger, New York (1955)

Sheehan, J. J., *The career of Lujo Brentano. A study of liberalism and social reform in imperial Germany*, Chicago University Press, Chicago, Ill. (1966)

Sheehan, J. J., 'Liberalism and society in Germany, 1815–48', *Journal of Modern History*, 45 (1973)

Shefter, M., 'Party and patronage. Germany, England and Italy', *Politics and Society*, 7 (1977)

Shorter, E., 'Middle class anxiety in the German revolution of 1848', *Journal of Social History*, 2 (1969)

Silverman, D. P., 'A pledge unredeemed. The housing crisis in Weimar Germany', *Central European History*, 3 (1970)

Spree, R., 'The impact of the professionalization of physicians on social change in Germany during the late nineteenth and early twentieth century', *Historical Social Research*, 15 (1980)

Steinberg, H. J., 'Workers' libraries in Germany before 1914', *History Workshop Journal*, 1 (1976)

Steinberg, J., 'The Kaiser's navy and German society', *Past and Present*, 28 (1964)

Stephenson, J., *Women in Nazi society*, Croom Helm, London (1975)

Stephenson, J., *The Nazi organization of women*, Croom Helm, London (1980)

Tenfelde, K., 'Mining festivals in the nineteenth century', *Journal of Contemporary History*, 13 (1978)

Thomas, K., *Women in Nazi Germany*, Gollancz, London (1943)

Tilly, R., 'Popular disorders in nineteenth century Germany', *Journal of Social History*, 4 (1970–71)

Turk, E. L., 'The press of imperial Germany. A new role for a traditional resource', *Central European History*, 10 (1977)

Voeltz, R. A., 'Sport, culture and society in late imperial and Weimar Germany. Some suggestions for future research', *Journal of Sport History*, 4 (1977)

Volkov, S., *The rise of popular antimodernism in Germany. The urban master artisans, 1873–96*, Princeton University Press, Princeton, N.J. (1978)

Waeibroeck, P., and I. Bessling, 'Some aspects of German social policy under the National Socialist regime', *International Labour Review*, 43 (1941)

Walk, J., 'Profile of a local Zionist association, 1903–04. On the social history of German Zionism', *Leo Baeck Institute Yearbook*, 24 (1979)

Weber, M., 'Towards a sociology of the press', *Journal of Communication*, 26 (1976) [deals with period 1900–14]

Weisbrod, B., 'The crisis of German unemployment insurance, 1928–29, and its political repercussions', in W. J. Mommsen, ed., *The emergence of the welfare state in Britain and Germany*, Croom Helm, London (1981)

West, H., 'Göttingen and Weimar. The organization of knowledge and social theory in eighteenth century Germany', *Central European History*, 11 (1978)

Whaley, J., 'New light on the circulation of early

newspapers. The case of the *Hamburgischer Correspondent* in 1730', *Bulletin of the Institute of Historical Research*, 52 (1979)

Wiener, J. M., 'Working class consciousness in Germany, 1848–1933', *Marxist Perspectives*, 2 (1979–80)

Wilke, G., and K. Wagner, 'Family and household. Social structures in a German village between the two world wars', in R. J. Evans and W. R. Lee, eds, *The German family*, Croom Helm, London (1981)

Witt, T. E. J. de, 'The economics and politics of welfare in the Third Reich', *Central European History*, 11 (1978)

Zehr, H., 'The modernization of crime in Germany and France, 1830–1913', *Journal of Social History*, 8 (1975)

Zehr, H., *Crime and the development of modern society. Patterns of criminality in nineteenth century Germany and France*, Croom Helm, London (1976)

ECONOMIC POLICY AND THOUGHT

Baerweld, F., 'How Germany reduced unemployment', *American Economic Review*, 24 (1934)

Barclay, D. E., 'A Prussian socialism? Wichard von Moellendorff and the dilemmas of economic planning in Germany, 1918–19', *Central European History*, 11 (1978)

Blanning, T. C. W., 'German Jacobins and the French revolution', *Historical Journal*, 23 (1980)

Block, H., 'German methods of allocating raw materials', *Social Research*, 9 (1942)

Borkin, J., and C. A. Welsh, *Germany's master plan. The story of the industrial offensive*, Duell Sloan and Pearce, New York (1943)

Brady, R. A., 'The economic impact of imperial Germany. Industrial policy', *Journal of Economic History*, Supplement, 3 (1943)

Brandt, K., 'Recent agrarian policies in Germany, Great Britain and the United States', *Social Research*, 3 (1936)

Brandt, K., 'German agricultural policy. Some selected lessons', *Journal of Farm Economics*, 19 (1937)

Brandt, K., *The German fat plan and its economic setting*, Stanford University Press, Stanford, Cal. (1938)

Braun, H. J., 'Economic theory and policy in Germany, 1750–1800', *Journal of European Economic History*, 4 (1975)

Burchardt, L., 'Science policy in imperial Germany. A

progress report', *Historical Social Research*, 13 (1980)

Carroll, M. R., *Unemployment insurance in Germany*, Brookings Institution, Washington D.C. (1929)

Colm, G., 'Why the Papen plan of economic recovery failed', *Social Research*, 1 (1934)

Creamer, D., 'Unemployment insurance in Germany. Further considered', *Journal of Political Economy*, 42 (1934)

Dawson, W. H., *Bismarck and state socialism. An exposition of the social and economic legislation of Germany since 1870*, Swan Sonnenschein, London (1890)

Dawson, W. H., *Social insurance in Germany, 1883–1911. Its history, operation, results and a comparison with the National Insurance Act, 1911*, T. F. Unwin, London (1913)

Eucken, W., 'On the theory of the centrally administered economy. An analysis of the German experiment', *Economica*, 15 (1948)

Ficek, K. F., 'How Germany reduced unemployment', *American Economic Review*, 24 (1934)

Fischer, F., *War of illusions. German policies from 1911–14*, Chatto and Windus, London (1975)

Garraty, J. A., 'The New Deal, National Socialism and the great depression', *American Historical Review*, 78 (1973)

Garvy, G., 'Keynes and the economic activists of pre-Hitler Germany', *Journal of Political Economy*, 83 (1975)

Geck, L. H. A., 'New trends in social policy in Germany', *International Labour Review*, 36 (1937)

Grebler, L., 'Work creation policy in Germany, 1932–35', parts 1 and 2, *International Labour Review*, 35 (1937)

Guillebaud, C. W., *The social policy of Nazi Germany*, Cambridge University Press, Cambridge (1941)

Heath, J. S. C., 'German labour exchanges', *Economic Journal*, 20 (1910)

Heinemann, J. L., 'Count von Neurath and German policy at the London Economic Conference, 1933', *Journal of Modern History*, 31 (1969)

Henderson, W. O., 'Walter Rathenau. A pioneer of the planned economy', *Economic History Review*, 4 (1951–52)

Henderson, W. O., *Studies in the economic policy of Frederick the Great*, Frank Cass, London (1963)

Heyl, J. D., 'Hitler's economic thought. A reappraisal', *Central European History*, 6 (1973)

James, H., 'Rudolf Hilferding and the application of the political economy of the Second International',

Historical Journal, 24 (1981)

Jennison, E. W., 'Christian Garve and Garlieb Markel. Two theorists of peasant emancipation during the ages of enlightenment and revolution', *Journal of Baltic Studies*, 4 (1973)

John, B. H., *German agricultural policy, 1918–34. The development of a national philosophy toward agriculture in postwar Germany*, University of North Carolina Press, Chapel Hill, N.C. (1936)

Kohler, E. D., 'Revolutionary Pomerania 1919–20. A study in majority socialist agricultural policy and civil–military relations', *Central European History*, 9 (1976)

Lee, J. J., 'Administrators and agriculture. Aspects of German agricultural policy in the first world war', in J. M. Winter, ed., *War and economic development*, Cambridge University Press, Cambridge (1975)

Lewis, B. W., 'The German use of unemployment insurance funds for work purposes', *Journal of Political Economy*, 46 (1938)

Maehl, W. H., 'German social democratic agrarian policy, 1890–95', *Central European History*, 13 (1980)

Marburg, T. F., 'Government and business in Germany. Public policy toward cartels', *Business History Review*, 38 (1964)

Merlin, S., 'Trends in German economic control since 1933', *Quarterly Journal of Economics*, 57 (1943)

Miller, J. W., 'Pre-war Nazi agrarian policy', *Agricultural History*, 15 (1941)

Mosse, W. E., 'Judaism, Jews and capitalism. Weber, Sombart and beyond', *Leo Baeck Institute Yearbook*, 24 (1979)

Nathan, O., 'Some considerations on unemployment insurance in the light of German experience', *Journal of Political Economy*, 42 (1934)

Picard, R., 'The German and French National Economic Councils', *International Labour Review*, 11 (1925)

Rohrlich, G. F., 'Equalization schemes in German unemployment compensation', *Quarterly Journal of Economics*, 58 (1944)

Röpke, W., 'Trends in German business cycle policy', *Economic Journal*, 43 (1933)

Röpke, W., *German commercial policy*, Longmans Green, London (1934)

Rosenberg, H., 'Economic impact of imperial Germany. Agricultural policy', *Journal of Economic History*, Supplement, 3 (1943)

Sheehan, J. J., *German liberalism in the nineteenth century*, Methuen, London (1982)

Thies, J., 'Hitler's European building programme', *Journal of Contemporary History*, 13 (1978)

Tipton, F. B., 'The national consensus in German economic history', *Central European History*, 7 (1974)

Weigert, O., 'The development of unemployment relief in Germany', parts 1 and 2, *International Labour Review*, 28 (1933)

Wunderlich, F., 'The National Socialist agrarian programme', *Social Research*, 13 (1946)

TREATY SETTLEMENT AND REPARATIONS

Baruch, B. M., *The making of the reparation and economic sections of the treaty*, Harper, New York (1920)

Bergman, C., *The history of reparations*, E. Benn, London (1927)

Borsky, G., *The greatest swindle in the world. The story of German reparations*, New Europe, London (1942)

Burnett, P. M., *Reparations at the Paris peace conference*, 2 vols, Columbia University Press, New York (1940)

Comstock, A., 'Reparation payments in perspective', *American Economic Review*, 20 (1930)

Cornebise, A. E., 'Cuno, Germany, and the coming of the Ruhr occupation. A study in German–west European relations', *Proceedings of the American Philosophical Society*, 116 (1972)

Cornebise, A. E., 'Gustav Stresemann and the Ruhr occupation. The making of a statesman', *European Studies Review*, 2 (1972)

Dawson, W. H., *Germany under the treaty*, Allen and Unwin, London (1933)

Dulles, J. F., 'The reparation problem', *Economic Journal*, 31 (1921)

Felix, D., 'Reparations considered with a vengeance', *Central European History*, 4 (1971)

Felix, D., *Walter Rathenau and the Weimar Republic. The politics of reparations*, Johns Hopkins University Press, Baltimore, Md. (1971)

Fleisig, H., 'War-related debts and the great depression', *American Economic Review, Papers and Proceedings*, 66 (1976)

Florinsky, M. T., *The Saar struggle*, Macmillan, New York (1934)

Graham, F. D., 'Germany's capacity to pay and the reparation plan', *American Economic Review*, 15 (1925)

Greer, G., *The Ruhr-Lorraine industrial problem. A study of the economic interdependence of the two* *regions and their relation to the reparation question*, Macmillan, New York (1925)

Guillebaud, C. W:, 'The economics of the Dawes report', *Economic Journal*, 34 (1924)

Harris, C. R. S., *Germany's foreign indebtedness*, Oxford University Press, London (1935)

Henderson, W. O., 'The peace settlement of 1919', *History*, 26 (1941)

Johnson, H. G., 'The classical transfer problem. An alternative formulation', *Economica*, 42 (1975)

Jordan, W. M., *Great Britain, France and the German problem, 1918–39. A study of Anglo-French relations in the making and maintenance of the Versailles settlement*, Oxford University Press, Oxford (1943)

Keynes, J. M., 'The German transfer problem', *Economic Journal*, 39 (1929) [this volume includes discussion of transfer problem involving Keynes, B. Ohlin and J. Rueff]

Lamont, T., 'The reparations settlement and economic peace in Europe', *Political Science Quarterly*, 45 (1930)

Lloyd George, D., *The truth about reparations and war debts*, Heinemann, London (1932)

McDougall, W. A., 'Political economy versus national sovereignty. French structure for German economic integration after Versailles', *Journal of Modern History*, 51 (1979)

McIntosh, D. C., 'Mantoux versus Keynes. A note on German income and the reparations commission', *Economic Journal*, 87 (1977)

Mantoux, E., *The Carthaginian peace, or, The economic consequences of Mr. Keynes*, Oxford University Press, London (1946)

Marks, S., 'Reparations reconsidered. A reminder', *Central European History*, 2 (1969), 5 (1972)

Marks, S., 'The myths of reparations', *Central European History*, 11 (1978)

Moon, P. T., 'The Young plan in operation', *Proceedings of the Academy of Political Science*, 14 (1931)

Moulton, H. G., *The reparation plan. An interpretation of the reports of the expert committee appointed by the Reparation Commission*, McGraw-Hill, New York (1924)

Moulton, H. G., and C. E. McGuire, *Germany's capacity to pay*, McGraw-Hill, New York (1923)

Ohlin, B., 'The reparation problem. A discussion', *Economic Journal*, 39 (1929)

Rupieper, H. J., *The Cuno government and reparations, 1921–23. Politics and economics*, Nijhoff, The Hague (1979)

Schacht, H. H. G., *The end of reparations*, Jonathan Cape, London (1931)

Schmid, R. J., *Versailles and the Ruhr. Seedbed of World War II*, Nijhoff, The Hague (1968)

Schumacher, H., 'The situation in the Ruhr', *Economic Journal*, 33 (1923)

Sering, M., *Germany under the Dawes plan*, P. S. King, London (1929)

Tardieu, S., *The truth about the treaty*, Bobbs-Merrill, Indianapolis, Ind. (1921)

Trachtenberg, M., 'Reparations at the Paris peace conference', *Journal of Modern History*, 51 (1979)

Walker, G. 'The payment of reparations', *Economica*, 11 (1931)

Wheeler-Bennett, J., *The wreck of reparations. Being the political background of the Lausanne agreement, 1932*, Allen and Unwin, London (1933)

Wheeler-Bennett, J., and H. Latimer, *Information on the reparations settlement*, Allen and Unwin, London (1930)

Williams, J. H., 'Reparations and the flow of capital', *American Economic Review, Papers and Proceedings*, 20 (1930)

ECONOMIC ASPECTS OF FASCISM

Bracher, K. D., *The German dictatorship. Origins, structure and effects of National Socialism*, Weidenfeld and Nicolson, London (1971)

Brady, R. A., *The spirit and structure of German fascism*, Gollancz, London (1937)

Carroll, B. A., *Design for total war. Arms and economics in the Third Reich*, Mouton, The Hague (1969)

Carsten, F. L., *The rise of fascism*, Batsford, London (1967)

Crump, N., 'The economics of the Third Reich', *Journal of the Royal Statistical Society*, 102 (1939)

Ebenstein, W., *The Nazi state*, Farrar and Rinehart, New York (1943)

Einzig, P., *The economic foundations of fascism*, Macmillan, London (1933)

Einzig, P., *Germany's default. The economics of Hitlerism*, Macmillan, London (1934)

Einzig, P., *Hitler's new order in Europe*, Macmillan, London (1941)

Eucken, W., 'On the theory of the centrally administered economy. An analysis of the German experiment', *Economica*, 15 (1948)

Florinsky, M. T., *Fascism and national socialism. A study of the economic and social policies of the* *totalitarian state*, Macmillan, New York (1936)

Frank, L., 'An economic and social diagnosis of National Socialism', in M. Baumont, ed., *The Third Reich*, Praeger, New York (1955)

Gates, R. A., 'German socialism and the crisis of 1929–33', *Central European History*, 7 (1974)

Guerin, D., *Fascism and big business*, Pioneer Publishers, New York (1939)

Haider, C., *Capital and labour under fascism*, P. S. King, London (1930)

Hauner, M., 'Did Hitler want a world dominion?', *Journal of Contemporary History*, 13 (1978)

Henderson, W. O., 'Some economic aspects of National Socialism in Germany', *German Life and Letters*, 3 (1939)

Kitchen, M., *Fascism*, Macmillan, London (1976)

Knauerhase, R., *An introduction to National Socialism, 1920–39*, C. E. Merrill, Columbus, Ohio (1972)

Koehl, R. L., 'A prelude to Hitler's greater Germany', *American Historical Review*, 59 (1953–54)

Kuczynski, J., *Germany under fascism, 1933 to the present day*, F. Muller, London (1944)

Kuczynski, J., *Germany. Economic and labour conditions under fascism*, International Publishers, New York (1945)

Kuczynski, J., and M. Witt, *The economics of barbarism. Hitler's new economic order in Europe*, F. Muller, London (1942)

Lütge, F., 'An explanation of the economic conditions which contributed to the victory of National Socialism', in M. Baumont, ed., *The Third Reich*, Praeger, New York (1955)

Mason, T., 'The primacy of politics. Politics and economics in National Socialist Germany', in S. J. Woolf, ed., *The nature of fascism*, Weidenfeld and Nicolson, London (1968)

Mason, T., 'The legacy of 1918 for National Socialism', in A. Nicholls, and E. Mathias, eds, *German democracy and the triumph of Hitler*, Allen and Unwin, London (1971)

Neumann, F., *Behemoth. The structure and practice of National Socialism, 1933–44*, Oxford University Press, New York (1944)

Nicholls, A. J., *Weimar and the rise of Hitler*, Macmillan, London (1968)

Overy, R. J., 'Hitler and air strategy', *Journal of Contemporary History*, 15 (1980)

Palyi, M., 'Economic foundations of the German totalitarian state', *American Journal of Sociology*, 46 (1941)

Reimann, G., *Germany. World empire or world revolution*, Secker and Warburg, London (1938)

Reimann, G., *The vampire economy. Doing business under fascism*, The Vanguard Press, New York (1939)

Robertson, E. M., *Hitler's pre-war policy and military plan, 1933–39*, Longman, London (1963)

Sauer, W., 'National Socialism. Totalitarianism or fascism', *American Historical Review*, 73 (1967–68)

Schweitzer, A., 'On depression and war. Nazi phase', *Political Science Quarterly*, 62 (1947)

Sohn-Rethel, A., *Economy and class structure of German fascism*, C.S.E. Books, London (1978)

Speer, A., *Inside the Third Reich*, Weidenfeld and Nicolson, London (1970)

Thies, J., 'Hitler's European building programme', *Journal of Contemporary History*, 13 (1978)

Trivanovich, V., *Economic development of Germany under National Socialism*, National Industrial Conference Board, New York (1937)

Turner, H. A., 'Fascism and modernization', *World Politics*, 24 (1972)

Woolf, S. J., 'Did a fascist economic system exist?', in S. J. Woolf, ed., *The nature of fascism*, Weidenfeld and Nicolson, London (1968)

Woolston, M. B. Y. S., *The structure of the Nazi economy*, Harvard University Press, Cambridge, Mass. (1941)

Wunderlich, F., 'Germany's defense economy and the decay of capitalism', *Quarterly Journal of Economics*, 52 (1938)

HISTORIOGRAPHY AND BIBLIOGRAPHY

Conze, W., 'Writings in social and economic history in Germany (1939–49)', *Economic History Review*, 3 (1950–51)

Crew, D. F., and E. Rosenhaft, 'SSRC research group on modern German social history. First meeting. History of the family', *Social History*, 4 (1979)

Eley, G., 'Memories of underdevelopment. Social history in Germany', *Social History*, 2 (1977)

Eley, G., 'Capitalism and the Wilhelmine state. Industrial growth and political backwardness in recent German historiography, 1890–1918', *Historical Journal*, 21 (1978)

Eley, G., and K. Nield, 'Why does social history ignore politics?', *Social History*, 5 (1980)

Fischer, W., 'Some recent developments in the study of economic and business history in western Germany', in R. E. Gallman, ed., *Recent developments in the study of business and economic history. Essays in memory of H. E. Kroos*, JAI Press,

Greenwich, Conn. (1977)

Gottlieb, B., 'France and Germany (1500–1800). Let us bless our countings', *Trends in History*, 1 (1979)

Hardach, K., 'Some remarks on German economic historiography and its understanding of the industrial revolution in Germany', *Journal of European Economic History*, 1 (1972)

Imhof, A. E., 'Historical demography in Germany. A research note', *Historical Methods Newsletter*, 10 (1977)

Imhof, A. E., 'Historical demography as social history. Possibilities in Germany', *Journal of Family History*, 2 (1977)

Imhof, A. E., 'The computer in social history. Historical demography in Germany', *Computers and the Humanities*, 12 (1978)

Imhof, A. E., 'An approach to historical demography in Germany', *Social History*, 4 (1979)

Jaeger, H., 'Business history in Germany. A survey of recent developments', *Business History Review*, 48 (1974)

Kocka, J., 'Recent historiography of Germany and Austria. Theoretical approaches to social and economic history of modern Germany. Some recent trends, concepts, and problems in Western and Eastern Germany', *Journal of Modern History*, 47 (1975)

Kocka, J., 'Theory and social history. Recent developments in West Germany', *Social Research*, 47 (1980)

Lee, W. R., 'The German family. A critical survey of the current state of historical research', in R. J. Evans, and W. R. Lee, eds, *The German family*, Croom Helm, London (1981)

Lee, W. R., 'Past legacies and future prospects. Recent research on the history of the family in Germany', *Journal of Family History*, 6 (1981)

Peterson, L., 'From social democracy to communism. Recent contributions to the history of the German workers' movement, 1914–45', *Labour*, 5 (1980)

Puhle, H. J., 'Conservatism in modern German history', *Journal of Contemporary History*, 13 (1978)

Redlich, F., 'Research on German entrepreneurship', *Explorations in Entrepreneurial History*, 2 (1950), 4 (1951)

Redlich, F., 'The beginnings and development of German business history', *Business History Review*, 26 (1952)

Redlich, F., 'Recent developments in German economic history', *Journal of Economic History*, 18 (1958)

Sheehan, J. J., 'What is German history? Reflections on the role of the nation in German history and historiography', *Journal of Modern History*, 53 (1981)

Soliday, G. L., 'Marburg in upper Hesse. A research report', *Journal of Family History*, 2 (1977)

Stern, W. M., '*Wehrwirtschaft*. A German contribution to economics', *Economic History Review*, 13 (1960–61)

Vann, J. A., 'The comparative method and German urban history', *Comparative Studies in Society and History*, 15 (1973)

Veit-Brause, I., 'The place of local and regional history in German and French historiography. Some general reflections', *Australian Journal of French Studies*, 16 (1979)

BELGIUM

GENERAL ECONOMIC AND SOCIAL HISTORY

Barkhausen, M., 'Government control and free enterprise in West Germany and the Low Countries', in P. Earle, ed., *Essays in European Economic History, 1500–1800*, Clarendon Press, Oxford (1974)

Craeybeckx, J., 'The beginning of the industrial revolution in Belgium', in R. E. Cameron, ed., *Essays in French economic History*, Richard D. Irwin, Homewood, Ill. (1970)

de Brabander, G. L., *Regional specialisation, employment and economic growth in Belgium between 1846 and 1970*, Arno Press, New York (1981)

de Vries, J., 'Benelux, 1920–70', in C. M. Cipolla, ed., *Contemporary economies*, Fontana Economic History of Europe, vol. 6, part 1, Collins/Fontana, Glasgow (1976)

Dhondt, J., and M. Bruwier, 'The industrial revolution in the Low Countries, 1700–1914', in C. M. Cipolla, ed., *The emergence of industrial societies*, Fontana Economic History of Europe, vol. 4, part 1, Collins/Fontana, Glasgow (1973)

Kossman, E. H., *The Low Countries, 1780–1940*, Clarendon Press, Oxford (1978)

Mendels, F. F., 'Industrialisation and population pressure in eighteenth century Flanders', *Journal of Economic History*, 31 (1971)

Mokyr, J., 'The industrial revolution in the Low Countries in the first half of the nineteenth century. A comparative case study', *Journal of Economic History*, 34 (1974)

Mokyr, J., *Industrialisation in the Low Countries, 1795–1850*, Yale University Press, New Haven, Conn. (1976)

Van Houtte, J. A., 'Economic development of Belgium and the Netherlands from the beginning of the modern era', *Journal of European Economic History*, 1 (1972)

Van Houtte, J. A., *An economic history of the Low Countries, 800–1800*, Weidenfeld and Nicolson, London (1977)

AGRICULTURE AND RURAL SOCIETY

Daelemans, F., 'Tithe revenues in rural south-west Brabant, fifteenth to eighteenth centuries', in H. Van der Wee and E. Van Cauwenberghe, eds, *Productivity of land and agricultural innovation in the Low Countries (1250–1800)*, Leuven University Press, Leuven (1978)

Gutmann, M. P., *War and rural life in the early modern Low Countries*, Van Gorcum, Assen (1980)

Gutmann, M. P., 'War, the tithe and agricultural production. The Meuse basin north of Liège, 1661–1740', in H. Van der Wee and E. Van Cauwenberghe, eds, *Productivity of land and agricultural innovation in the Low Countries (1250–1800)*, Leuven University Press, Leuven (1978)

Jansen, J. C. G. M., 'Agrarian development and exploitation in south Limburg in the years 1650–1850', *Acta Historiae Neerlandica*, 5 (1971)

Jansen, J. C. G. M., 'Tithes and the productivity of land in the south of Limburg, 1348–1790', in H. Van der Wee and E. Van Cauwenberghe, eds, *Productivity of land and agricultural innovation in the Low Countries (1250–1800)*, Leuven University Press, Leuven (1978)

Laveleye, E. L. V. de, 'The land system of Belgium and Holland', in J. W. Probyn, ed., *Systems of land tenure*, Cobden Club, London (1881)

Mendels, F. F., 'Agriculture and peasant industry in eighteenth century Flanders', in W. N. Parker and E. L. Jones, eds, *European peasants and their markets*, Princeton University Press, Princeton, N.J. (1975)

Rowntree, S., *Land and labour. Lessons from Belgium*, Macmillan, London (1910)

Slicher van Bath, B. H., 'Agriculture in the Low Countries (c. 1600–1800)', *Relazioni del X⁰ congresso internazionale di scienze storiche, 4*, Storia Moderna, Florence (1955)

Tits-Dieuaide, M. J., 'Cereal yields around Louvain, 1404–1729', in H. Van der Wee and E. Van Cauwenberghe, eds, *Productivity of land and agricultural innovation in the Low Countries (1250–1800)*, Leuven University Press, Leuven (1978)

Tits-Dieuaide, M. J., 'Peasant dues in Brabant. The example of the Meldert farm near Tirlemont (1380–1787)', in H. Van der Wee and E. Van Cauwenberghe, eds, *Productivity of land and agricultural innovation in the Low Countries (1250–1800)*, Leuven University Press, Leuven (1978)

Vandenbroeke, C., 'Cultivation and consumption of the potato in the seventeenth and eighteenth century', *Acta Historiae Neerlandicae*, 5 (1971)

Vandenbroeke, C., and W. Vanderpijpen, 'The problem of the "agricultural revolution" in Flanders and in Belgium. Myth or reality?', in H. Van der Wee and E. Van Cauwenberghe, eds, *Productivity of land and agricultural innovation in the Low Countries (1250–1800)*, Leuven University Press, Leuven (1978)

Van Stuijvenberg, J. H., 'A reconsideration of the origins of the agricultural co-operative', *Low Countries Yearbook*, 13 (1980)

Van de Walle, E., 'Household dynamics in a Belgian village, 1847–66', *Journal of Family History*, 1 (1976)

Van der Wee, H., 'Agrarian development in the Low Countries as reflected in the tithe and rent statistics, 1250–1800', in M. W. Flinn, ed., *Proceedings of the seventh International Congress on Economic History, Edinburgh, 1978*, Edinburgh University Press, Edinburgh (1978)

Van der Wee, H., 'The agricultural development of the Low Countries as revealed by the tithe and rent statistics, 1250–1800', in H. Van der Wee and E. Van Cauwenberghe, eds, *Productivity of land and agricultural innovation in the Low Countries (1250–1800)*, Leuven University Press, Leuven (1978)

Van der Wee, H., and E. Van Cauwenberghe, eds,

Productivity of land and agricultural innovation in the Low Countries (1250–1800), Leuven University Press, Leuven (1978)

Wever, F. de, 'Rents and selling prices of land at Zele, sixteenth-eighteenth century', in H. Van der Wee and E. Van Cauwenberghe, eds, *Productivity of land and agricultural innovation in the Low Countries (1250–1800)*, Leuven University Press, Leuven (1978)

INDUSTRY AND INTERNAL TRADE

Carden, G. L., *Machine-tool trade in Belgium*, U.S. Government Printing Office, Washington, D.C. (1909)

Dhondt, J., 'The cotton industry in Ghent during the French occupation', in F. Crouzet *et al.*, *Essays in European economic history*, Edward Arnold, London (1969)

Gillingham, J., *Belgium business in the Nazi New Order*, Jan Dhondt Foundation, Ghent (1977)

Ishizaka, A., 'Genesis of the S.A. John Cockerill. International entrepreneurial activities in the Belgian industrial revolution', *Keieishigaku*, 4 (1969)

Lamfalussy, A., 'The patern of growth in Belgian manufacturing industry, 1937–56', *Journal of Industrial Economics*, 6 (1957–58)

Van der Wee, H., 'Investment strategy of Belgian industrial enterprise between 1830 and 1980, and its influence on the economic development of Europe', in *Belgium and Europe. Proceedings of the International Francqui-Colloquium*, Brussels (1981)

Van Noeske, P., 'Profit, inflation and Belgian industrial expansion, 1830–1914', *Tijdschrift voor Economie*, 9 (1963)

Van der Wee, H., and E. Aerts, 'The history of the textile industry in the Low Countries. Second list of publications, 1970–80', *Textile History*, 12 (1981)

TRANSPORT AND COMMUNICATIONS

Anonymous. 'The growth of commercial aviation in Belgium. SNETA, the King Albert Airline and SABENA', *Transport History*, 9 (1978)

MONEY, BANKING AND FINANCE

Ansiaux, M., 'The Belgian exchange since the war', *Economic Journal*, 30 (1920)

Cameron, R. E., 'Belgium, 1800–75', in R. E.

Cameron, ed., *Banking in the early stages of industrialisation*, Oxford University Press, New York (1967)

Daems, H., 'Property rights, agency relations and provincial intermediation. A reinterpretation of the Belgian banking legislation of 1934 and 1935', in M. W. Flinn, ed., *Proceedings of the seventh international congress on economic history, Edinburgh, 1978*, Edinburgh University Press, Edinburgh (1978)

Grice, J. W., *National and local finance. A review of the relations between central and local authorities in England, France, Belgium and Prussia during the nineteenth century*, P. S. King, London (1910)

Hurst, W., 'Holland, Switzerland and Belgium and the English gold crisis of 1931', *Journal of Political Economy*, 40 (1932)

Morrison, R. J., 'Financial intermediaries and economic development. The Belgian case', *Scandinavian Economic History Review*, 15 (1967)

Shepherd, H. L., *The monetary experience of Belgium, 1914–36*, Princeton University Press, Princeton, N.J. (1936)

Willoughby, W. F., 'The General Savings and Old Age Pension Bank of Belgium', *Journal of Political Economy*, 8 (1900)

OVERSEAS TRADE AND COMMERCIAL RELATIONS

Boucher, M., 'Flemish interlopers beyond the Cape of Good Hope, 1715–23', *Historia*, 21 (1976)

Harms, R., 'The end of red rubber. A reassessment', *Journal of African History*, 16 (1975) [overseas economic interests]

Jewsiewicki, B., 'The great depression and making of the colonial economic system in the Belgian Congo', *African Economic History*, 4 (1977)

Meade, J. E., *The Belgium-Luxembourg economic union, 1921–39. Lessons from an early experiment*, Princeton University Press, Princeton, N.J. (1956)

Stols, E., 'The southern Netherlands and the foundation of the Dutch East and West Indies Companies', *Acta Historiae Neerlandicae*, 9 (1976)

Tamse, C. A., 'The role of small countries in the international politics of the 1860s. The Netherlands and Belgium in Europe', *Acta Historiae Neerlandicae*, 9 (1976)

POPULATION AND MIGRATION

Deprez, P., 'The demographic development of Flanders in the eighteenth century', in D. V. Glass and D. E. C. Eversley, eds, *Population in history. Essays in historical demography*, Edward Arnold, London (1965)

Deprez, P., 'Problems of geographical mobility in Belgium in the eighteenth century', in *International Population Conference, London 1969*, vol. 4, International Union for the Scientific Study of the Population, Liège (1971)

Deprez, P., 'The Low Countries', in W. R. Lee, ed., *European demography and economic growth*, Croom Helm, London (1979)

Desama, C., 'Socio-demographical structures and the industrial revolution. Verviers, 1806–46', *Historical Methods Newsletter*, 7 (1974)

Desama, C., 'Industrial revolution and urban demography', *Urbanism Past and Present*, 2 (1976)

Gutmann, M. P., 'Why they stayed. The problem of wartime population loss', *Tijdschrift voor Geschiedenis*, 91 (1978) [demographic history of lower Meuse, 1600–1789]

Legouis, J., 'The problem of European settlement in the Belgian Congo', *International Labour Review*, 34 (1936)

Lesthaeghe, R. J., *Infant mortality and marital fertility decline in Belgium, 1880–1910. A short research note*, Vrije Universiteit Brussel Publications, Brussels (1975)

Lesthaeghe, R. J., *The decline of Belgian fertility, 1800–1970*, Princeton University Press, Princeton, N.J. (1978)

Mendels, F. F., 'Industry and marriages in Flanders before the industrial revolution', in P. Deprez, ed., *Population and economics*, University of Manitoba Press, Winnipeg, (1970)

Mendels, F. F., 'Industry and marriages in Flanders before the industrial revolution', in *Proceedings of the fourth international economic history conference, Bloomington, 1968*, Mouton, Paris (1973)

Sharlin, A., 'Methods of estimating population total, age distribution and vital rates in family reconstitution studies', *Population Studies*, 32 (1978) [covers nineteenth-century Belgium]

Spencer, B., 'Size of population and variability of demographic data (seventeenth and eighteenth centuries)', *Genus*, 32 (1976)

Spencer, B., *et al.*, 'Spectral analysis and the study of seasonal fluctuations in historical demography', *Journal of European Economic History*, 5 (1976)

Van Praag, P., 'The development of neo-Malthusian Flanders', *Population Studies*, 31 (1978)

Watkins, S. C., 'The female life cycle in a Belgian commune. La Halpe, 1847–66', *Journal of Family History*, 5 (1980)

LABOUR CONDITIONS AND ORGANISATION

Dechesne, L., 'Trade unions in Belgium', *Economic Journal*, 15 (1905)

Reardon, J. A., 'Belgian and French workers in nineteenth century Roubaix', in L. A. and C. Tilly, eds, *Class conflict and collective action*, Sage Publications, London (1981)

Stearns, P. N., 'National character and European labour history', *Journal of Social History*, 4 (1970)

INCOMES, WAGES AND PRICES

Balthazar, H., 'A study of wealth and income in the nineteenth and twentieth centuries', *Acta Historiae Neerlandicae*, 9 (1976) [general theory in a Belgian setting]

Goldsmidt, P., 'Family allowances in Belgium', *International Labour Review*, 34 (1936)

Gottschalk, M., 'The purchasing power and the consumption of Belgian workers at different periods', *International Labour Review*, 25 (1932)

Lis, C., and H. Soly, 'Food consumption in Antwerp between 1807 and 1859', *Economic History Review*, 30 (1977)

Soltow, L., 'The distribution of wealth in Belgium in 1814–15', *Journal of European Economic History*, 10 (1981)

Van der Wee, H., 'Prices and wages as development variables. A comparison between England and the southern Netherlands, 1400–1700', *Acta Historiae Neerlandicae*, 10 (1978)

Vries, J. de, 'An inquiry into the behaviour of wages in the Dutch Republic and the southern Netherlands, 1580–1800', *Acta Historiae Neerlandicae*, 10 (1978)

URBAN HISTORY

Gutkind, E. A., *International history of city development, vol. 5, Urban development in western Europe, France and Belgium*, Collier-Macmillan, London (1970)

Klep, P. W. W., 'Regional disparities in Brabantine urbanisation before and after the industrial revolution (1374–1970). Some aspects of measurement and explanation', in P. Bairoch and M. Levy-Leboyer, eds, *Disparities in economic develop-*

ment since the industrial revolution, Macmillan, London (1981)

Veraghtert, K., 'An analysis of the growth of the Antwerp port during the nineteenth century', in M. W. Flinn, ed., *Proceedings of the seventh international congress on economic history, Edinburgh, 1978,* Edinburgh University Press, Edinburgh (1978)

Vollans, E. C., 'Urban development in Belgium since 1830', in R. P. Beckinsale and J. M. Houston, eds, *Urbanisation and its problems. Essays in honour of E. W. Gilbert,* Blackwell, Oxford (1968)

SOCIAL STRUCTURE AND SOCIAL CONDITIONS

Beterams, F. G. C., *The high society Belgo-Luxembourgeoisie,* Cultura, Wettern (1973)

Craeybeckx, J., 'The Brabant revolution. A conservative revolt in a backward country', *Acta Historiae Neerlandicae* 4 (1970)

Helin, E., 'Size of households before the industrial revolution. The case of Liège in 1801', in P. Laslett, ed., *Household and family in past time,* Cambridge University Press, Cambridge (1972)

Van der Woude, A. M., 'Variations in the size and structure of the household in the United Provinces of the Netherlands in the seventeenth and eighteenth centuries', in P. Laslett, ed., *Household and family in past time,* Cambridge University Press, Cambridge (1972)

Witte, E., 'Political power struggle in and around the main Belgian cities, 1830–48', *Acta Historiae Neerlandicae,* 8 (1975)

Witte, E., 'Changes in the Belgian elite in 1830. A provisional study', *Low Countries Yearbook,* 13 (1980)

Zolberg, A. R., 'The making of Flemings and Walloons. Belgium, 1830–1914', *Journal of Interdisciplinary History,* 5 (1974)

ECONOMIC POLICY AND THOUGHT

Braunthal, A., 'The new economic policy in Belgium', *International Labour Review,* 33 (1936)

Hansen, E., 'Hendrik de Man and the theoretical foundations of economic planning. The Belgian experience, 1933–40', *European Studies Review,* 8 (1978)

Hansen, E., 'Depression decade crisis. Social democracy and *planisme* in Belgium and the Netherlands, 1929–39', *Journal of Contemporary History,* 16 (1981)

Roger, C., 'New deal for Belgium', *Foreign Affairs,* 13 (1933)

HISTORIOGRAPHY AND BIBLIOGRAPHY

Blockmans, W., *et al.,* 'Belgian historiography written in Dutch, 1971–73', *Acta Historiae Neerlandicae,* 7 (1974) [English summaries of Dutch works on Belgium]

Carter, A. C., 'Survey of recent historical works on Belgium and the Netherlands published in Dutch', *Acta Historiae Neerlandicae,* 8 (1975)

Craeybeckx, J., 'Economic history in Belgium and the Netherlands, 1939–48', *Journal of Economic History,* 10 (1950) [bibliographical article]

Dhondt, J., 'Belgian historiography written in Dutch, 1969–71', *Acta Historiae Neerlandicae,* 6 (1973) [English summaries of Dutch works on Belgium]

Emery, C. R., and K. W. Swart, 'Survey of recent historical works on Belgium and the Netherlands published in Dutch', *Low Countries Yearbook,* 11 (1978), 12 (1979); 13 (1980) [English summary of Dutch and Belgian historical writing]

Everaert, J., and C. Vandenbroeke, 'Thirty years of research in social and economic history. The Centre of Modern and Colonial History at the University of Ghent', *Journal of European History,* 5 (1976)

Gutmann, M. P., and E. Van de Walle, 'New sources for social and demographic history. The Belgian population register', *Social Science History,* 2 (1978)

Jones, R. L., and K. W. Swart, 'Survey of recent historical works on Belgium and the Netherlands published in Dutch', *Acta Historiae Neerlandicae,* 9 (1976); 10 (1978) [English summary of Dutch and Belgian historical writing]

Mokyr, J., 'Industrialisation in two languages', *Economic History Review,* 34 (1981)

THE NETHERLANDS

GENERAL ECONOMIC AND SOCIAL HISTORY

Aymard, M., ed., *Dutch capitalism and world capitalism,* Cambridge University Press, Cambridge (1982)

Blok, P. J., *History of the people of the Netherlands,* 5 vols, AMS Press, New York (1970)

Boogman, J. C., 'The Netherlands in the European scene, 1813–1913', in J. S. Bromley and E. H. Kossman, eds, *Britain and the Netherlands in Europe and Asia,* Macmillan, London (1968)

Bromley, J. S., and E. H. Kossman, eds, *Britain and the Netherlands in Europe and Asia,* Macmillan, London (1968)

Brugmans, I. J., 'Economic fluctuations in the Netherlands in the nineteenth century', in F. Crouzet *et al., Essays in European economic history,* Edward Arnold, London (1969)

de Jonge, J. A., 'The role of the outer provinces in the process of Dutch economic growth in the nineteenth century', in J. S. Bromley and E. H. Kossman, eds, *Britain and the Netherlands,* vol. 4, Nijhoff, The Hague (1971)

de Vries, J., 'Spiral and miracle. The Dutch economy since 1920', *Delta,* 13 (1970)

de Vries, J., 'Benelux, 1920–70', in C. M. Cipolla, ed., *Contemporary economies.* Fontana Economic History of Europe, vol. 6, part 1, Collins/Fontana, Glasgow (1976)

Dhondt, J., and M. Bruwier, 'The industrial revolution in the Low Countries, 1700–1914', in C. M. Cipolla, ed., *The emergence of industrial societies.* Fontana Economic History of Europe, vol. 4, part 1, Collins/Fontana, Glasgow (1973)

Faber, J. A., 'Population changes and economic development in the Netherlands. A historical survey', *A.A.G. Bijdragen,* 12 (1965)

Faber, J. A., *et al.,* 'Economic developments and population changes in the Netherlands up to 1800', *Papers presented to the third international conference of economic history, Munich, 1965,* Mouton, Paris (1972)

Griffiths, R. T., *Industrial retardation in the Netherlands, 1830–50,* Nijhoff, The Hague (1979)

Hansen, E., 'Depression decade crisis. Social democracy and *planisme* in Belgium and the Netherlands, 1929–39', *Journal of Contemporary History,* 16 (1981)

Jonge, J. A. de, *De industrialistie in Nederland tussen 1850 en 1914,* Scheltema and Holkema, Amsterdam (1968) [summary in English and translation of tabular material]

Jonge, J. A. de, 'Industrial growth in the Netherlands, 1850–1914', *Acta Historiae Neerlandicae,* 5 (1971)

Klein, P. W., 'Entrepreneurial behaviour and the economic rise and decline of the Netherlands in the seventeenth and eighteenth centuries', *Annales Cisalpines d' Histoire Sociale,* 1 (1970)

Klein, P. W., 'Depression and policy in the thirties', *Acta Historiae Neerlandicae,* 8 (1975)

Kossman, E. H., *The Low Countries, 1780–1940,* Clarendon Press, Oxford (1978)

Leach, R. H., 'The provinces in the Dutch system of government', *South Atlantic Quarterly,* 69 (1970)

Mokyr, J., 'The industrial revolution in the Low Countries in the first half of the nineteenth century. A comparative case study', *Journal of Economic History,* 34 (1974)

Mokyr, J., 'Capital, labour and the delay of the industrial revolution in the Netherlands', *Economisch en Sociaal Historische Jaarboek,* 38 (1975)

Mokyr, J., *Industrialization in the Low Countries, 1795–1850,* Yale University Press, New Haven, Conn. (1976)

Mokyr, J., 'Industrialization in two languages', *Economic History Review,* 34 (1981)

Newton, G., *The Netherlands. An historical and cultural survey, 1795–1977,* Ernest Benn, London (1978)

Schiff, E., *Industrialization without national patents. The Netherlands, 1869–1912. Switzerland, 1850–1907,* Princeton University Press, Princeton, N.J. (1971)

Slicher van Bath, B. H., 'Historical demography and the social and economic development of the Netherlands', *Daedalus – Historical Population Studies,* 43 (1968)

Tamse, C. A., 'The role of small countries in the international politics of the 1860s. The Netherlands and Belgium in Europe', *Acta Historiae Neerlandicae,* 9 (1976)

van Houtte, J. A., *An economic history of the Low Countries, 800–1800,* Weidenfeld and Nicolson, London (1977)

van Houtte, J. A., 'Economic development of Belgium and the Netherlands from the beginning of the modern era', *Journal of European Economic History,* 1 (1972)

Vries, J. de, 'Peasant demand patterns and economic development. Friesland, 1550–1750', in W. N.

Parker and E. L. Jones, eds, *European peasants and their markets*, Princeton University Press, Princeton, N.J. (1975)

Vries, J. de, *The Netherlands economy in the twentieth century*, Van Gorcum, Assen (1978)

Vries, J. de, 'Regional economic inequality in the Netherlands since 1600', in P. Bairoch and M. Levy-Leboyer, eds, *Disparities in economic development since the industrial revolution*, Macmillan, London (1981)

Wilson, C. H., 'The economic decline of the Netherlands', *Economic History Review*, 9 (1938–39)

Wilson, C. H., 'The decline of the Netherlands', in C. H. Wilson, *Economic History and the historians. Collected essays*, Weidenfeld and Nicolson, London (1969)

AGRICULTURAL AND RURAL SOCIETY

Faber, J. A., 'Cattle-plague in the Netherlands during the eighteenth century', *Mededelingen van de Landbouwhogeschool*, 62 (1962)

Faber, J. A., 'Dearth and famine in pre-industrial Netherlands', *Low Countries Yearbook*, 13 (1980)

Fussell, G. E., ' "Low countries" influence on English farming', *English Historical Review*, 84 (1959)

Jansen, J. C. G. M., 'Agrarian development and exploitation in South Limburg in the years 1650–1850', *Acta Historiae Neerlandicae*, 5 (1971)

Lambert, A. M., *The making of the Dutch landscape*, Seminar Press, London (1971)

Laveleye, E. L. V. de, 'The land system of Belgium and Holland', in J. W. Probyn, ed., *Systems of land tenure*, Cobden Club, London (1881)

Ristow, W. W., 'Dutch polder maps', *Quarterly Journal of the Library of Congress*, 31 (1974)

Robertson Scott, J. W., *A free farmer in a free state. A study of rural life and industry and agricultural politics in an agricultural country*, Heinemann, London (1912)

Roessingh, H. K., 'Village and hamlet in a sandy region of the Netherlands in the middle of the eighteenth century', *Acta Historiae Neerlandicae*, 4 (1970)

Roessingh, H. K., 'Tobacco growing in Holland in the seventeenth and eighteenth centuries. A case study of the innovative spirit of Dutch peasants', *Low Countries Yearbook*, 11 (1978)

Slicher van Bath, B. H., 'Manor, mark and village in the eastern Netherlands', *Speculum*, 21 (1946)

Slicher van Bath, B. H., 'Agriculture in the Low Countries (c. 1600–1800)', *Relazioni del X° congresso internazionale di scienze storiche*, 4, Storia Moderna, Florence (1955)

van der Poel, J. M. G., 'A hundred years' agricultural mechanization in the Netherlands', *Acta Historiae Neerlandicae*, 5 (1971)

van der Wee, H., 'The agricultural development of the Low Countries as revealed by the tithe and rent statistics, 1250–1800', in H. van der Wee and E. van Cauwenberghe, eds, *Productivity of land and agricultural innovation in the Low Countries (1250–1800)*, Leuven University Press, Leuven (1978)

van der Wee, H., 'Agrarian development in the Low Countries as reflected in the tithe and rent statistics, 1250–1800', in M. W. Flinn, ed., *Proceedings of the seventh international economic history congress, Edinburgh, 1978*, Edinburgh University Press, Edinburgh (1978)

van der Wee, H., and E. van Cauwenberghe, eds, *Productivity of land and agricultural innovation in the Low Countries (1200–1800)*, Leuven University Press, Leuven (1978)

van der Woude, A., 'The long-term movement of rent for pasture land in north Holland and the problem of profitability in agriculture (1570–1800)', in H. van der Wee and E. van Cauwenberghe, eds, *Productivity of land and agricultural innovation in the Low Countries (1250–1800)*, Leuven University Press, Leuven (1978)

Vries, J. de, *The Dutch rural economy in the golden age, 1500–1700*, Wiley, New York (1974)

INDUSTRY AND INTERNAL TRADE

Bouman, P. J., *Wilton-Fijenoord history. Dock and yard company Wilton-Fijenoord Ltd*, Wyt, Rotterdam (1954)

Bouman, P. J., *Philips of Eindhoven*, Macmillan, London (1958)

Bouman, P. J., *Growth of an interprise. The life of Anton Philips*, Macmillan, London (2nd edn 1970)

Gerretson, F., *History of the Royal Dutch*, 4 vols, E. J. Brill, Leiden (1953–57)

Griffiths, R. T., 'Eye-witnesses at the birth of the Dutch cotton industry, 1832–39', *Economisch en Sociaal Historisch Jaarboek*, 40 (1977)

Hackman, W. D., 'The growth of science in the Netherlands in the seventeenth and eighteenth centuries', in M. Crosland, ed., *The emergence of* science in Europe, Macmillan, London (1971)

Philips, F., *Forty-five years with Philips. An industrialist's life*, Blandford Press, Poole (1978)

Unger, R. W., 'Technology and industrial organization. Dutch shipbuilding to 1800', *Business History*, 17 (1975)

Unger, R. W., *Dutch shipbuilding before 1800. Ships and guilds*, Van Gorcum, Assen and Amsterdam (1978)

Unger, R. W., 'Dutch shipbuilding in the golden age', *History Today*, 31 (1981)

van der Pols, K., 'The introduction of the steam engine to the Netherlands', *Low Countries Yearbook*, 12 (1979)

van der Wee, H., and E. Aerts, 'The history of the textile industry in the Low Countries. Second list of publications, 1970–80', *Textile History*, 12 (1981)

Vries, J. de, 'From keystone to cornerstone. Hoogovens I Jmuiden, 1918–68. The birth and development of a basic industry in the Netherlands', *Acta Historiae Neerlandicae*, 6 (1973)

Yamey, B. S., 'Ralph Davison's accounting journals', *Economisch en Sociaal Historisch Jaarboek*, 39 (1976)

TRANSPORT AND COMMUNICATIONS

Lindblad, T., 'Swedish shipping with the Netherlands in the second half of the eighteenth century', *Scandinavian Economic History Review*, 27 (1979)

Pieters, L. J., 'A hundred years of sea communication between England and the Netherlands', *Journal of Transport History*, 6 (1964)

Vries, J. de, *Barges and capitalism. Passenger transportation in the Dutch economy, 1632–1839*, HES Publishers, Utrecht (1981)

Weber, R. E. J., 'Sea and land mail services to the former Netherlands East Indies', *Maritime History*, 3 (1973)

MONEY, BANKING AND FINANCE

Aalbers, J., 'Holland's financial problems (1713–33) and the wars against Louis XIV', in A. C. Duke and C. A. Tamse, eds, *Britain and the Netherlands*, vol. 6, *War and society*, Nijhoff, The Hague (1977)

Buist, M. G., 'Russia's entry on the Dutch capital market, 1770–1815', *Papers presented to the fifth international economic history conference, Leningrad, 1970*, Mouton, Paris (1979)

Buist, M. G., *At spes non fracta. Hope & Co., 1770–1815*, Nijhoff, The Hague (1974) [leading

Dutch international bank]

Buist, M. G., 'The sinews of war. The role of Dutch finance in European politics, c. 1750–1815', in A. C. Duke and C. A. Tamse, eds, *Britain and the Netherlands*, vol. 6, *War and society*, Nijhoff, The Hague (1977)

Carter, A. C., 'The Dutch and the English public debt in 1777', *Economica*, 20 (1953)

Carter, A. C., 'Financial activities of the Huguenots in London and Amsterdam in the mid-eighteenth century', *Proceedings of the Huguenots Society*, 19 (1959)

Carter, A. C., *Getting, spending and investing in early modern times. Essays on Dutch, English and Huguenot economic history*, Van Gorcum, Assem (1975)

de Jong, A. M., 'The origin and foundation of the Netherlands Bank', in J. G. van Dillen, ed., *History of the principal public banks*, Cass, London (1964)

Heckscher, E. F., 'The Bank of Sweden in its connection with the Bank of Amsterdam', in J. G. van Dillen, ed., *History of the principal public banks*, Cass, London (1964)

Hurst, W., 'Holland, Switzerland and Belgium and the English gold crisis of 1931', *Journal of Political Economy*, 40 (1932)

Riley, J. C., 'Life annuity-based loans on the Amsterdam capital market towards the end of the eighteenth century', *Economisch en Sociaal Historisch Jaarboek*, 36 (1973)

Riley, J. C., *International government finance and the Amsterdam capital market, 1740–1815*, Cambridge University Press, Cambridge (1980)

Schama, S., 'The exigencies of war and the politics of taxation in the Netherlands, 1795–1810', in J. M. Winter, ed., *War and economic development*, Cambridge University Press, Cambridge (1975)

Stuart, A. J. C., 'Progressive taxation in Holland', *Economic Journal*, 8 (1898)

van der Flier, M. J., *War finances of the Netherlands up to 1918–23*, Clarendon Press, Oxford (1923)

van Dillen, J. G., *The economic history of the Netherlands and the Bank of Amsterdam (1609–1820)*, J. H. de Bussy, Amsterdam (1929)

van Dillen, J. G., 'The Bank of Amsterdam', in J. G. van Dillen, ed., *History of the principal public banks*, Nijhoff, The Hague (1934)

van Winter, P. J., *American finance and Dutch investment 1780–1805. With an epilogue to 1840*, 2 vols, Arno Press, New York (1977)

Verrijn Stuart, G. M., 'The Netherlands during the recent depression', in A. D. Gayer, ed., *The les-*

sons of monetary experience. Essays in honor of Irving Fisher, Farrer and Rinehart, New York (1937)

Vissering, G., 'The Netherlands Bank and the war', *Economic Journal*, 27 (1917)

OVERSEAS TRADE AND COMMERCIAL RELATIONS

Arasaratnam, S., 'Monopoly and free trade in Dutch Asian commercial policy', *Journal of Southeast Asian Studies*, 4 (1972)

Arasaratnam, S., 'Dutch commercial policy and interests in the Malay peninsula, 1750–95', in B. B. Kling and M. N. Pearson, eds, *The age of partnership. Europeans in Asia before dominion*, University Press of Hawaii, Honolulu (1979)

Baudet, H., and I. J. Brugmans, 'Colonial policy weighed. The last fifty years of the Dutch East Indies in retrospect', *Acta Historiae Neerlandicae*, 1 (1966)

Boxer, C. R., *The Dutch seaborne empire, 1600–1800*, Hutchinson, London (1965)

Boxer, C. R., 'The Dutch East India Company and the China trade', *History Today*, 29 (1979)

Boxer, C. R., *Jan Compagnie in war and peace, 1602–1799. A short history of the Dutch East India Company*, Heinemann Asia, Hong Kong (1980)

Broeze, F. J. A., 'A challenge without response. Holland and the trans-Pacific route to east Asia after 1815', *Economisch en Sociaal Historisch Jaarboek*, 38 (1975)

Broeze, F. J. A., 'A second-hand discovery. The Netherlands and the Pacific in the first half of the nineteenth century', *Journal of Pacific History*, 10 (1975)

Broeze, F. J. A., 'Whaling in the southern oceans. The Dutch quest for whaling in the nineteenth century', *Economisch en Sociaal Historisch Jaarboek*, 40 (1977)

Broeze, F. J. A., 'Atlantic rivalry. The struggle for the Dutch tea market', *Low Countries Yearbook*, 11 (1978)

Bromley, J. S., 'The North Sea in wartime, 1688–1713', *Bijdragen en Mededelingen Betreffende de Geschiedenis der Nederlanden*, 92 (1977)

Bromley, J. S., and E. H. Kossman, eds, *Britain and the Netherlands. Metropolis, dominion and province*. Papers from the fourth Anglo-Dutch historical conference, Nijhoff, The Hague (1970)

Carter, A. C., 'Dutch foreign investment, 1738–1800', *Economica*, 20 (1953)

Carter, A. C., 'Dutch investment in eighteenth century England. Note on a note on yardsticks', *Economic History Review*, 12 (1959–60)

Carter, A. C., 'How to revise treaties without negotiating. Commonsense mutual fears and the Anglo-Dutch trade disputes of 1759', in R. M. Hatton and M. S. Anderson, eds, *Studies in diplomatic history. Essays in memory of D. B. Horn*, Longmans, London (1970)

Carter, A. C., *Neutrality or commitment. The evolution of Dutch foreign policy, 1667–1795*, Edward Arnold, London (1975)

Crowhurst, P., 'Marine insurance and the trade of Rotterdam, 1755–63', *Maritime History*, 2 (1972)

Debo, R. K., 'Dutch-Soviet relations, 1917–24. The role of finance and commerce in the foreign policy of Soviet Russia and the Netherlands', *Canadian-American Slavic Studies*, 4 (1970)

Emmer, P. C., 'The West India Company, 1621–1791. Dutch or Atlantic?', in L. Blusse and F. Gaastra, eds, *Companies and trade*, Leiden University Press, Leiden (1981)

Feldbaek, O., 'Dutch Batavia trade via Copenhagen, 1795–1807. A study of colonial trade and neutrality', *Scandinavian Economic History Review*, 21 (1973)

Glamann, K., 'The Dutch East India Company's trade in Japanese copper, 1645–1736', *Scandinavian Economic History Review*, 1 (1953)

Glamann, K., *Dutch-Asiatic trade, 1620–1740*, Nijhoff, The Hague (1958)

Jong, T. P. M. de, 'The Netherlands and Latin America, 1815–26', *Economic-Historical Yearbook*, 29 (1963)

Jong, T. P. M. de, 'The venture of making profit in a disordered market', *Economic-Historical Yearbook*, 31 (1967) [Dutch trade to Latin America, 1805–80]

Jong, T. P. M. de, 'Atlantis, 1780–1830', *Acta Historiae Neerlandicae*, 3 (1968)

Knoppers, J., 'The changing nature of eighteenth century Dutch trade with Russia', *New Review of European History*, 15–16 (1976)

Knoppers, J., *Dutch trade with Russia from the time of Peter I to Alexander I. A quantitative study in eighteenth century shipping*, 3 vols, Interuniversity Centre for European Studies, Montreal (1976)

Knoppers, J., 'A comparison of the Sound accounts and the Amsterdam Galjootsgeld registers', *Scandinavian Economic History Review*, 24 (1976)

Lequin, F., 'A new approach to the history of the Dutch expansion in Asia. The personnel of the Dutch East India Company in the eighteenth century', *Journal of European Economic History*, 8 (1979)

Muller, M., 'Ten years of guerilla warfare and slave rebellions in Surinam, 1750–59', *Acta Historiae Neerlandicae*, 8 (1975) [considers some effects on Dutch money market and trade]

Perkins, J. A., 'The Lincolnshire contraband tobacco trade after the Napoleonic wars', *Journal of Transport History*, 4 (1977) [trade with Holland]

Postma, J., 'The dimension of the Dutch slave trade from western Africa', *Journal of African History*, 13 (1972)

Postma, J., 'West African exports and the Dutch West India Company, 1675–1731', *Economisch en Sociaal Historisch Jaarboek*, 36 (1973)

Postma, J., 'Mortality in the Dutch slave trade, 1675–1795', in H. A. Gemery and J. S. Hogendorn, eds, *The uncommon market. Essays in the economic history of the Atlantic slave trade*, Academic Press, New York (1979)

Prakash, O., 'Bullion for goods. International trade and the economy of early eighteenth century Bengal', *Indian Economic and Social History Review*, 13 (1976) [Dutch East India Company trading interests]

Prakash, O., 'Asian trade and European impact. A study of the trade from Bengal, 1630–1720', in B. B. Kling and M. N. Pearson, eds, *The age of partnership. Europeans in Asia before dominion*, University Press of Hawaii, Honolulu (1979)

Raven-Hart, R., ed., *Cape of Good Hope, 1652–1702. The first fifty years of Dutch colonisation*, Balkema, Cape Town (1973)

Ricklefs, M. C., *Jogjakarta under Sultan Mangkubumi, 1749–92*, Oxford University Press, London (1974) [contains information on Dutch East India Company interests]

Riley, J. C., 'Dutch investment in France, 1781–87', *Journal of Economic History*, 33 (1973)

Riley, J. C., 'Foreign credit and fiscal stability. Dutch investment in the United States, 1781–94', *Journal of American History*, 65 (1978)

Schoffer, I., 'Dutch "expansion" and Indonesian reactions. Some dilemmas of modern colonial rule', in ·H. Wesseling, ed., *Expansion and reaction. Essays on European expansion and reactions in Asia and Africa*, Nijhoff, The Hague (1977)

Schutte, G., et al., 'Company and colonists at the Cape', in R. Elphick, and H. Giliomee, eds, *The shaping of South African society, 1652–1820*, Longman, Cape Town (1979)

Stols, E., 'The southern Netherlands and the foundation of the Dutch East and West India Companies',

Acta Historiae Neerlandicae, 9 (1976)

Tamse, C. A., 'The Netherlands consular service and the Dutch consular reports of the nineteenth and twentieth centuries', *Business History*, 23 (1981)

van der Wal, S. L., 'The Netherlands as an imperial power in south-east Asia in the nineteenth century and after', in J. S. Bromley, and E. H. Kossman, eds, *Britain and the Netherlands in Europe and Asia*, Macmillan, London (1968)

van Dillen, J. G., 'Economic fluctuations and trade in the Netherlands, 1650–1750', in P. Earle, ed., *Essays in European economic history, 1500–1800*, Clarendon Press, Oxford, (1974)

van Dongen, F., 'The cautious imperialists', *Acta Historiae Neerlandicae*, 4 (1970) [Dutch trading interests in the East Indies]

van Helten, J. J., 'German capital, the Netherlands Railway Company and the political economy of the Transvaal, 1886–1900', *Journal of African History*, 23 (1978)

Wilson, C. H., *Anglo-Dutch commerce and finance in the eighteenth century*, Cambridge University Press, Cambridge (1941)

Wilson, C., 'Dutch investment in eighteenth century England', *Economic History Review*, 12 (1959–60)

Wright, H. R. C., 'The Anglo-Dutch dispute in the East, 1814–24', *Economic History Review*, 3 (1950–51)

Wright, H. R. C., *Free trade and protection in the Netherlands, 1816–30. A study of the first Benelux*, Cambridge University Press, Cambridge (1955)

POPULATION AND MIGRATION

Angenot, L. H. J., 'The fertility of the female population of Rotterdam between 1870 and 1940', in *International population conference, London, 1969*, vol. 4, International Union for the Scientific Study of the Population, Liège (1971)

Buissink, J. D., 'Regional differences in marital fertility in the Netherlands in the second half of the nineteenth century', *Population Studies*, 25 (1971)

Deprez, P., 'The Low Countries', in W. R. Lee, ed., *European demography and economic growth*, Croom Helm, London (1979)

Deurbo, M. C., and G. A. Hoekveld, 'The population growth of the urban municipalities in the Netherlands between 1849 and 1970, with particular reference to the period 1899–1930', in H. Schmal, ed., *Patterns of European urbanisation since 1500*, Croom Helm, London (1981)

Ellemers, J. E., 'The determinants of emigration. An analysis of Dutch studies on migration', *Sociologica Neerlandica,* 2 (1964)

Hofstee, E. W., 'Population increase in the Netherlands', *Acta Historiae Neerlandicae,* 3 (1968)

Lucas, H. S., *Netherlanders in America. Dutch immigration to the United States and Canada, 1789–1950,* University of Michigan Press, Ann Arbor, Mich. (1955)

Methorst, H. W., 'Differential fertility in the Netherlands', *Population,* 1 (1935) [special memoir]

Petersen, W., 'The demographic transition in the Netherlands', *American Sociological Review,* 25 (1960)

Slicher van Bath, B. H., 'Report on the study of historical demography in the Netherlands', *A.A.G. Bijdragen,* 11 (1964)

Slicher van Bath, B. H., 'Contrasting demographic development in some parts of the Netherlands during the depression period of the seventeenth and eighteenth centuries', in F. Bechhofer, ed., *Population growth and the brain drain,* Edinburgh University Press, Edinburgh (1969)

Swierenga, R. P., 'Dutch immigrant demography, 1820–80', *Journal of Family History,* 5 (1980)

Swierenga, R. P., and H. S. Stout, 'Dutch immigration in the nineteenth century, 1820–77. A quantitative overview', *Indiana Social Studies Quarterly,* 28 (1975)

Swierenga, R. P., and H. S. Stout, 'Socio-economic patterns of migration from the Netherlands in the nineteenth century', in P. Uselding, ed., *Research in economic history,* JAI Press, Greenwich, Conn. (1976)

van den Brink, T., 'Birth rate trends and changes in marital fertility in the Netherlands after 1937', *Population Studies,* 4 (1950–51) [has considerable data on inter-war years]

van Praag, P., 'Views and concepts relating to population problems in the Netherlands, 1918–39', *Population Studies,* 31 (1977)

van Praag, P., 'The development of neo-Malthusianism in Flanders', *Population Studies,* 32 (1978)

Wabeke, B. H., *Dutch emigration to North America, 1624–1860. A short history,* Netherlands Information Bureau, New York City (1944)

LABOUR CONDITIONS AND ORGANISATION

Bruijn, J. R., 'Seamen in Dutch ports, *c.* 1700–1914', *Mariner's Mirror,* 65 (1979)

Bruyns, C. M., 'Rationalisation and the decasualisation of dock labour in the port of Rotterdam', *International Labour Review,* 37 (1938)

Carter, A. C., 'Some Huguenots in professional and administrative functions in the Netherlands in the eighteenth century', *Proceedings of the Huguenot Society of London,* 21 (1970)

Hansen, E., 'Workers and socialists. Relations between the Dutch trade union movement and social democracy, 1894–1914', *European Studies Review,* 7 (1977)

Hansen, E., and P. A. Prosper, 'Religion and the development of the Dutch trade union movement, 1872–1914', *Social History,* 9 (1976)

Hansen, E., and P. A. Prosper, 'The Nederlands Verbond van Vakverenigigen. The labour movement in the Netherlands, 1905–14', *Social History,* 10 (1977)

Hilgenga, J., 'The situation of agricultural and horticultural workers in the Netherlands', *International Labour Review,* 37 (1938)

van Tijn, T., 'A contribution to the scientific study of the history of trade unions', *International Review of Social History,* 21 (1976)

INCOMES, WAGES AND PRICES

International Labour Office, 'Social insurance in the Netherlands', *International Labour Review,* 40 (1939)

Middelhoven, P. J., 'Auctions at Amsterdam of northern European pinewood, 1717–1808. A contribution to the history of prices in the Netherlands', *Low Countries Yearbook,* 13 (1980)

Muinck, B. E. de, 'A regent's family budget about the year 1700', *Acta Historiae Neerlandicae,* 2 (1967)

Posthumus, N. W., *Inquiry into the history of prices in Holland,* E. J. Brill, Leiden (1946)

Vries, J. de, 'An inquiry into the behaviour of wages in the Dutch republic and the southern Netherlands', *Acta Historiae Neerlandicae,* 10 (1978)

URBAN HISTORY

Dougill, W., 'Amsterdam. Its town planning development', *Town Planning Review,* 14 (1931)

Gutkind, E. A., *International history of city development,* vol. 6, *Urban development in western Europe. The Netherlands and Great Britain,* Collier-Macmillan, London (1971)

Kruijt, B., 'The changing spatial pattern of firms in Amsterdam. Empirical evidence', *Tijdschrift voor Economishe en Sociale Geografie,* 70 (1979)

Steigenga, W., 'The urbanization of the Netherlands', Tijdschrift K.N.A.G. (1960)

van Dijk, H., 'Urbanization and social change in the Netherlands during the nineteenth century', in M. W. Flinn, ed., *Proceedings of the seventh international economic history congress, Edinburgh, 1978*, Edinburgh University Press, Edinburgh (1978)

van Engelsdorp Gastelaars, R., and M. Wagenaar, 'The rise of the *Ranstad, 1815–1930*', in H. Schmal, ed., *Patterns of European urbanisation since 1500*, Croom Helm, London (1981)

van Tijn, T., 'Twenty years in the history of Amsterdam. The social development of the Dutch capital from the mid-nineteenth century till 1876', *Acta Historiae Neerlandicae*, 3 (1968)

SOCIAL STRUCTURE AND SOCIAL CONDITIONS

Bergman, M., 'The potato blight in the Netherlands and its social consequences (1845–47)' *International Review of Social History*, 12 (1967)

Brake, W. Te, 'Revolution and the rural community in the eastern Netherlands', in L. A. and C. Tilly, eds, *Class conflict and collective action*, Sage Publications, London (1981)

Bruijn, J. R., 'Dutch men-of-war – those on board, *c.* 1700–50', *Acta Historiae Neerlandicae*, 7 (1974)

Daalder, H., 'Dutch Jews in a segmented society', *Acta Historiae Neerlandicae*, 10 (1978)

Diederiks, H., 'Patterns of criminality and law enforcement during the *ancien régime*. The Dutch case', *Criminal Justice History*, 1 (1980)

Jansen, P., 'Poverty in Amsterdam at the close of the eighteenth century', *Acta Historiae Neerlandicae*, 10 (1978)

Mokyr, J., 'Industrialization and poverty in Ireland and the Netherlands', *Journal of Interdisciplinary History*, 10 (1980)

Oerlemans, J. W., 'Authority and freedom, 1800–1914. A historical inquiry into resistance against industrial society', *Acta Historiae Neerlandicae*, 4 (1970)

Schama, S., 'School and politics in the Netherlands, 1796–1814', *Historical Journal*, 13 (1970)

Schama, S., 'Municipal government and the burden of the poor in south Holland during the Napoleonic wars', in A. C. Duke and C. A. Tamse, eds, *Britain and the Netherlands*, vol. 6, *War and society*, Nijhoff, The Hague (1977)

Schoffer, I., 'The Jews in the Netherlands. The position of a minority through three centuries', *Studia Rosenthaliana*, 15 (1981)

van Dijk, H., and D. J. Roorda, 'Social mobility under the Regents of the Republic', *Acta Historiae Neerlandicae*, 9 (1976)

van der Woude, A., 'Variations in the size and structure of the household in the United Provinces of the Netherlands in the seventeenth and eighteenth centuries', in P. Laslett, ed., *Household and family in past time*, Cambridge University Press, Cambridge (1972)

ECONOMIC POLICY AND THOUGHT

Barkhausen, M., 'Government control and free enterprise in west Germany and the Low Countries', in P. Earle, ed., *Essays in European economic history, 1500–1800*, Clarendon Press, Oxford (1974)

Butter, I. H., *Academic economics in Holland, 1800–70*, Nijhoff, The Hague (1970)

Gerritsz, J., 'Measures to combat unemployment in the Netherlands', *International Labour Review*, 7 (1923)

Hansen, E., 'Dutch social democracy, and agrarian policy, 1894–1906, *Agricultural History*, 50 (1976)

Hansen, E., 'Marxists and society. The emergence of Marxian social theory in the Netherlands, 1894–1914', *Journal of European Studies*, 6 (1976)

Schiff, E., 'Dutch foreign trade policy and the infant industry argument for protection', *Journal of Political Economy*, 50 (1942)

HISTORIOGRAPHY AND BIBLIOGRAPHY

Brugmans, I. J., 'The economic history of the Netherlands in the nineteenth and twentieth century', *Acta Historiae Neerlandicae*, 2 (1967)

Carter, A. C., 'Survey of recent Dutch historiography', *Acta Historiae Neerlandicae*, 6 (1973) [English summary of works on Dutch history]

Craeybeckx, J., 'Economic history in Belgium and the Netherlands, 1939–48', *Journal of Economic History*, 10 (1950) [bibliographical article]

Diedericks, H., and P. H. J. van der Laan, 'Urban history in the Netherlands', *Urban History Yearbook* (1976)

Emery, C. R., and K. W. Swart, 'Survey of recent historical works on Belgium and the Netherlands published in Dutch', *Low Countries Yearbook*, 11 (1978), 12 (1979), 13 (1980)

Fishman, J. S., 'Discovering and utilizing sources for the history of the Jews in the Netherlands', *Studia Rosenthaliana*, 15 (1981)

Hardenberg, H., 'Archives in the Netherlands', *Acta Historiae Neerlandicae*, 3 (1968)

Jones, R. L., and K. W. Swart, 'Survey of recent historical work on Belgium and the Netherlands published in Dutch', *Acta Historiae Neerlandicae*, 9 (1976), 10 (1978) [English summary of Dutch and Belgian historical writing]

Klompmaker, 'Business history in Holland', *Business History Review*, 38 (1964)

van der Woude, A., 'The *A.A.G. Bijdragen* and the study of Dutch rural history', *Journal of European Economic History*, 4 (1975)

Vries, P. de, 'The writing and study of history in the Netherlands in the nineteenth century', *Acta Historiae Neerlandicae*, 3 (1968)

SWITZERLAND

Altermatt, U., 'Conservatism in Switzerland. A study in anti-modernism', *Journal of Contemporary History*, 14 (1979)

Bachmann, G., 'The return to the gold standard in Switzerland', *American Economic Review*, 19 (1929)

Biucchi, B. M., 'The industrial revolution in Switzerland', in C. M. Cipolla, ed., *The emergence of industrial societies*. Fontana Economic History of Europe, vol. 4, part 2, Collins/Fontana, Glasgow (1973)

Borsel, A., 'The condition of agricultural workers in Switzerland', *International Labour Review*, 38 (1938)

Braun, R., 'The impact of cottage industry on an agricultural population', in D. S. Landes, ed., *The rise of capitalism*, Macmillan, New York (1966)

Braun, R., 'The rise of a rural class of industrial entrepreneurs', *Journal of World History*, 10 (1967) [nineteenth-century entrepreneurs in Zurich Oberland]

Braun, R., 'Early industrialization and demographic change in the canton of Zurich', in C. Tilly, ed., *Historical studies of changing fertility*, Princeton University Press, Princeton, N.J. (1978)

Burgin, A., 'The growth of the Swiss national economy', in H. G. J. Aitken, ed., *The state and economic growth*, Social Science Research Council, New York (1964)

Carroll, M. B., *Taxation of business in Switzerland*, U.S. Government Printing Office, Washington D.C. (1927)

Caspard, P., 'Illegitimacy and prenuptial pregnancy at Neuchâtel. (1678–1820)', *Annales*, 4 (1977)

Caspard, P., 'Manufacture and trade in calico printing at Neuchâtel. The example of Cortalloid (1752–1854)', *Textile History*, 8 (1977)

Church, R. A., 'Nineteenth century clock technology in Britain, the United States, and Switzerland', *Economic History Review*, 28 (1975)

Dawson, W. H., *Social Switzerland. Studies of present-day social movements and legislation in the Swiss republic,* Chapman and Hall, London (1897)

Gutkind, E. A., *International history of city development,* vol. 2, *Urban development in the Alpine and Scandinavian countries,* Collier-Macmillan, London (1965)

Henderson, W. O., 'J. C. Fischer, a Swiss industrial pioneer', *Zeitschrift für die gesamte Staatswissenschaft,* 119 (1963)

Hurst, W., 'Holland, Switzerland and Belgium and the English gold crisis of 1932', *Journal of Political Economy,* 40 (1932)

Imlah, A. G., *Britain and Switzerland, 1845–60. A study of Anglo-Swiss relations during some critical years of Swiss neutrality,* Longmans Green, London (1966)

International Labour Office, 'The scientific organisation of a department store and its effect on industrial relations. The "Globe Stores" at Zurich', *International Labour Review,* 33 (1936)

Jaffe, W., 'Leon Walras, an economic adviser *manqué*', *Economic Journal,* 85 (1975)

Jequier, F., 'Switzerland from the revolution of 1798 to the present day. A critical study of recent work in French on Swiss history of the last two centuries', *European Studies Review,* 6 (1976)

Landes, D. S., 'Watchmaking. A case study in enterprise and change', *Business History Review,* 53 (1979)

Mayer, K. B., *The population of Switzerland,* Columbia University Press, New York (1952)

Melting, R. M., 'Household dynamics in a nineteenth century Swiss village', *Journal of Family History,* 4 (1979)

Monter, E. W., 'Women in Calvinist Geneva (1550–1800)', *Signs,* 6 (1980)

Pfister, C., 'Climate and economy in eighteenth century Switzerland', *Journal of Interdisciplinary History,* 9 (1978–79)

Piuz, A.-M., 'Economic policy in Geneva and mercantile doctrine, *c.* 1690–1740', *Papers presented to the fifth international economic history conference, Leningrad, 1970,* Mouton, Paris (1979)

Rychner, J., 'Running a printing house in eighteenth century Switzerland. The workshop of the Société Typographique de Neuchâtel', *Library,* 1 (1979)

Schelbert, L., 'On becoming an emigrant. A structural view of the eighteenth and nineteenth century Swiss data', *Perspectives in American History,* 7 (1973)

Schiff, E., *Industrialization without national patents. The Netherlands, 1869–1912. Switzerland, 1850–1907,* Princeton University Press, Princeton, N.J. (1971)

Siegenthaler, H., 'Switzerland 1920–70', in C. M. Cipolla, ed., *Contemporary economies.* Fontana Economic History of Europe, vol. 6, part 2, Collins/Fontana, Glasgow (1976)

Siegenthaler, K., 'Producers' co-operatives in Switzerland', *International Labor and Working Class History,* (1977)

Steinberg, J., *Why Switzerland',* Cambridge University Press, Cambridge (1976)

EAST CENTRAL AND SOUTH-EASTERN EUROPE

GENERAL WORKS

GENERAL ECONOMIC AND SOCIAL HISTORY

Berend, I. T., and G. Ránki, 'Economic problems of the Danube region after the break-up of the Austro-Hungarian monarchy, *Journal of Contemporary History*, 4 (1969)

Berend, I. T., and G. Ránki, *Economic development in east central Europe in the nineteenth and twentieth centuries*, Columbia University Press, New York (1974)

Berend, I. T., and G. Ránki, 'Foreign trade and the industrialisation of the European periphery in the nineteenth century', *Journal of European Economic History*, 9 (1980)

Boia, L., *Relationships between Romanians, Czechs and Slovaks, 1848–1914*, Bucaresti Editura Academi Republicii Socialiste Romania, Bucharest (1977)

Carsten, F. L., *Revolution in central Europe, 1918–19*, Temple Smith, London (1972)

Carter, F. W., ed.; *An historical geography of the Balkans*, Academic Press, London (1977)

Good, D. F., *et al.*, 'Modern economic growth in the Habsburg monarchy', *East Central Europe*, 7 (1980)

Granick, D., 'The pattern of foreign trade in eastern Europe and its relation to economic development policy', *Quarterly Journal of Economics*, 68 (1954)

Gross, N. T., 'The industrial revolution in the Habsburg monarchy, 1750–1914', in C. M. Cipolla, ed., *The emergence of industrial societies*, Fontana Economic History of Europe, vol. 4, part 1, Collins/Fontana, Glasgow (1973)

Gunst, P., 'The comparative impact of industrialisation on western and eastern European agriculture in the nineteenth and early twentieth century', *Agrartorteneti Szemle*, Supplement, 18 (1976)

Halasz, A.,*New central Europe in economical maps*, R. Gergely, Budapest (1928)

Hertz, F., *The economic problems of the Danubian States. A study in economic nationalism*, Gollancz, London (1947)

Jelavich, B., 'The British traveller in the Balkans. The abuses of Ottoman administration in the Slavonic provinces',*Slavonic and East European Review*, 33 (1955)

Jelavich, B., 'The Balkan nations and the Czech war of independence', in N. P. Diamandouros *et al.*, *Hellenism and the first Greek war of liberation, (1821–30). Continuity and change*, Institute for Balkan Studies, Thessaloniki (1976)

Jelavich, C. and B., *The establishment of the Balkan National States, 1804–1920*, University of Washington Press, Seattle, Wash. (1977)

Kaser, M. C., and E. A. Radice, *The economic history of eastern Europe, 1919–75*, vol. 1, *Economic structure and performance between the two wars*, Oxford University Press, London (1982)

Kiraly, B. K., and G. E. Rothenberg, eds, *War and security in east central Europe. Special topics and generalisations on the eighteenth and nineteenth centuries*, Brooklyn College Press, New York (1979)

Lampe, J. R., 'Varieties of unsuccessful industrialisation. The Balkan states before 1914', *Journal of Economic History*, 35 (1975)

Lampe, J. R., and M. R. Jackson, *Balkan economic history, 1550–1950. From imperial borderlands to developing nations*, Indiana University Press, Bloomington, Ind. (1982)

League of Nations, *Report by the Stresa conference for the economic restoration of central and eastern Europe submitted to the Commission of Enquiry for European Union*, League of Nations, Stresa (1932)

Macartney, C. A., *National states and national minorities*, Oxford University Press, Oxford (1934)

Macartney, C. A., *The Danube Basin*, Clarendon Press, Oxford (1939)

Macartney, C. A., *Problems of the Danube Basin*, Cambridge University Press, Cambridge (1942)

Macartney, C. A., and A. W. Palmer, *Independent eastern Europe*, Macmillan, London (1962)

Macartney, C. A., *The Habsburg empire, 1790–1918*, Weidenfeld and Nicolson, London (1968)

McGowan, B., *Economic life in Ottoman Europe. Taxation, trade and the struggle for land, 1600–1800*, Cambridge University Press, Cambridge (1981)

McNeill, W. H., *Europe's Steppe frontier, 1500–1800*, University of Chicago Press, Chicago, Ill. (1964)

Maczak, A., 'Continental east-west trade as a factor of development in central Europe from the middle of the sixteenth to the eighteenth century', *Proceedings of the fifth international economic history conference, Leningrad, 1970*. Mouton, Paris (1978)

März, E., 'Some economic aspects of the nationality conflict in the Habsburg empire', *Journal of Central European Affairs*, 13 (1953)

Mitrany, D., *The effect of the war in south-eastern Europe*, Yale University Press, New Haven, Conn. (1936)

Moisue, V., and I. Calafeteanu, *Assertion of unitary independent national states in central and south-east Europe (1821–1923)*. Editura Academiei Republicii Socialiste Romania, Bucharest (1980)

Nagy, Z. L., 'The United States and the Danubian basin (1919–1939)', in *Etudes historiques hongroises, 1975. Proceedings of the Fourteenth Congress of Historical Sciences*, Akademiai Kiado, Budapest (1975)

Okey, R., *Eastern Europe, 1740–1980. Feudalism to communism*, Hutchinson, London (1982)

Pasvolsky, L., *Economic nationalism of the Danubian states*, Allen and Unwin, London (1928)

Peselz, B., *The industrialisation of peasant Europe*, Mid-European Studies Centre, New York (1953)

Political and Economic Planning, *Economic development in south-east Europe*, PEP, London (1945)

Polonsky, A., *The little dictators*, Routledge and Kegan Paul, London (1975)

Ránki, G., 'On the economic development of the Habsburg monarchy', in P. Bairoch and M. Levy-Leboyer, eds, *Disparities in economic development since the industrial revolution*, Macmillan, London (1981)

Raupach, H., 'The impact of the great depression on eastern Europe', *Journal of Contemporary History*, 4 (1969)

Raupach, H., 'The impact of the great depression on eastern Europe', in H. Van der Wee, ed., *The great depression revisited. Essays on the economics of the thirties*, Nijjoff, The Hague (1972)

Rosenberg, H., 'Political and social consequences of the great depression of 1873–1896 in central Europe', *Economic History Review*, 13 (1943)

Rosenstein-Rodan, P., 'Problems of industrialisation of eastern and south-eastern Europe', *Economic Journal*, 53 (1943)

Rothschild, J., *East central Europe between the two world wars*, American University Publishers Group, Washington, D.C. (1975)

Roucek, J. S., *Central eastern Europe, crucible of world wars*, Prentice-Hall, New York (1946)

Royal Institute of International Affairs, *The Balkan States. Economic. A review of the economic and financial development of Albania, Bulgaria, Greece, Roumania and Yugoslavia since 1919*, Oxford University Press, London (1936)

Royal Institute of International Affairs, *South-eastern Europe. A political and economic survey*, Oxford University Press, London (1939)

Royal Institute of International Affairs, *South-eastern Europe. A brief survey*, Oxford University Press, London (1940)

Rudolph, R. L., *et al.*, 'Social structure and the beginning of Austrian economic growth', *East Central Europe*, 7 (1980) [new approach to economic development in Habsburg empire]

Seton-Watson, H., *Eastern Europe between the wars, 1918–41*, Cambridge University Press, Cambridge (1945)

Shaw, S. J., 'The aims and achievements of Ottoman rule in the Balkans', *Slavic Review*, 21 (1962)

Spulber, N., 'The role of the state in economic growth in eastern Europe since 1860', in H. G. J. Aitken, ed., *The state and economic growth*, Social Science Research Council, New York (1959)

Spulber, N., '*The state and economic development*

in eastern Europe, Random House, New York (1966)

Stavrianos, L. S., *Balkan federation. A history of the movement toward the Balkan unity in modern times*, Department of History of Smith College, Northampton, Mass. (1944)

Stavrianos, L. S., *The Balkans, 1815–1914*, Holt Rinehart and Winston, New York (1963)

Stavrianos, L. S., *The Balkans since 1453*, Holt Rinehart and Winston, New York (1965)

Stojanovic, M. D., *The great powers and the Balkans, 1875–78*, Cambridge University Press, Cambridge (1939; reprinted 1968)

Sugar, P. F., *South-eastern Europe under the Ottoman empire, 1354–1804*, University of Washington Press, Seattle, Wash. (1977)

Teichova, A., 'Structural change and industrialisation in inter-war central east Europe', in P. Bairoch and M. Levy-Leboyer, eds, *Disparities in economic development since the industrial revolution*, Macmillan, London (1981)

Todorov, N., 'The genesis of capitalism in the Balkan provinces of the Ottoman empire in the nineteenth century', *Explorations in Economic History*, 7 (1969–70)

Turnock, D., *Studies in industrial geography. Eastern Europe*, Dawson, Folkestone (1978)

Wanklyn, H. G., *The eastern marchlands of Europe*, G. Philip, London (1941)

Warriner, D., ed., *Contrasts in emerging societies. Readings in the social and economic history of south-eastern Europe in the nineteenth century*, Athlone Press, London (1965)

Zauberman, A., 'Russia and eastern Europe, 1920–70', in C. M. Cipolla, ed., *Contemporary economies*. Fontana Economic History of Europe, vol. 6, part 2, Collins/Fontana, Glasgow (1976)

AGRICULTURE AND RURAL SOCIETY

Blum, J., 'The rise of serfdom in eastern Europe', *American Historical Review*, 62 (1957)

Conze, W., 'Agrarian reform in central Europe', in G. S. Metraux and F. Crouzet, eds, *The nineteenth century world*, New American Library, New York (1963)

Conze, W., 'The effects of nineteenth century liberal agrarian reforms on social structure in central Europe', in F. Crouzet *et al.*, *Essays in European economic history*, Edward Arnold, London (1969)

Djordjevic, D., 'Agrarian factors in nineteenth century Balkan revolutions', in B. K. Kiraly and G. E.

Rothenberg, eds, *War and society in east central Europe*, Brooklyn College Press, New York (1979)

International Labour Office, 'New agrarian legislation in central Europe. A comparative study', *International Labour Review*, 6 (1922)

Jackson, G. D., *Comintern and peasant in east Europe, 1919–30*, Columbia University Press, New York (1966)

Jedruszczak, H., 'Land reform and economic development in the people's democracies of Europe', *Studia Historiae Oeconomicae*, 7 (1972)

Kahan, A., 'Notes on serfdom in western and eastern Europe', *Journal of Economic History*, 33 (1973)

Kahan, A., 'The infringement of the market upon the serf economy in eastern Europe', *Peasant Studies Newsletter*, 3 (1974)

Makkai, L., 'Neo-serfdom. Its origins and nature in east central Europe', *Slavic Review*, 34 (1975)

Morgan, O. S., ed., *Agricultural systems of middle Europe*, Macmillan, London (1933)

Rondolsky, R., 'On the nature of peasant serfdom in central and eastern Europe', *Journal of Central European Affairs*, 12 (1952)

Rothenberg, J., 'Demythologizing the Shtetl', *Midstream*, 27 (1981) [agrarian society]

Stoianovich, T., 'Land tenure and related sectors of the Balkan economy, 1600–1800', *Journal of Economic History*, 13 (1953)

Völgyes, I., ed., *The east European peasantry*, Pergamon Press, New York (1979)

Warriner, D., *Economics of peasant farming*, Oxford University Press, London (1939)

Warriner, D., 'Some controversial issues in the history of agrarian Europe', *Slavonic and East European Review*, 32 (1953–54)

Wiatrowski, L., 'Modernised agricultural enterprise in central and eastern Europe in the nineteenth and at the beginning of the twentieth century, *Proceedings of the seventh international congress on economic history, Edinburgh, 1978*, Edinburgh University Press, Edinburgh (1978)

Zagoroff, S. D., *et al.*, *The agricultural economy of the Danubian countries, 1935–45*, Stanford University Press, Stanford, Cal. (1955)

INDUSTRY AND INTERNAL TRADE

Csato, T., 'The development of internal trade in east central and south-east Europe', *Acta Historica*, 23 (1977)

Dlugsborski, W., 'Peasant economy in the coal and

smelting regions of middle east Europe before and during the early period of industrialisation', *Studia Historiae Oeconomicae*, 10 (1975)

Endrei, W., 'Northern cloths and kerseys in eastern Europe, sixteenth-eighteenth centuries', *Textile History*, 5 (1974)

Klima, A., 'The domestic industry and the putting-out system (*Verlags-system*) in the period of transition from feudalism to capitalism', *Proceedings of the second international economic history conference, Aix-en-Provence, 1962*, Mouton, Paris (1965)

Minkes, A. L., 'Statistical evidence and the concept of tertiary industry', *Economic Development and Cultural Change*, 3 (1955)

Stoianovich, T., 'The conquering Balkan orthodox merchant', *Journal of Economic History*, 20 (1960)

Zauberman, A., *Industrial progress in Poland, Czechoslovakia and east Germany, 1937–62*, Oxford University Press, London (1964)

TRANSPORT AND COMMUNICATIONS

Berov, L., 'Transport costs and their role in trade in the Balkan lands in the sixteenth to nineteenth centuries', *Bulgarian Historical Review*, 3 (1975)

Hajnal, H., *The Danube. Its historical, political and economic importance*, Nijhoff, The Hague (1920)

Jensen, J. H., and G. Rosegger, 'Transferring technology to a peripheral economy. The case of the lower Danube transport development, 1856–1928', *Technology and Culture*, 19 (1978)

Karkar, Y. N., *Railway development in the Ottoman empire, 1856–1914*, Vintage Press, New York (1972)

May, A. J., 'Trans-Balkan railway schemes', *Journal of Modern History*, 24 (1952)

MONEY, BANKING AND FINANCE

Bandera, V. N., *Foreign capital as an instrument of national economic policy. A study based on the experience of east European countries between the world wars*, Nijhoff, The Hague (1964)

Berend, I. T., 'Investment strategies in east central Europe in the nineteenth and twentieth centuries', *Proceedings of the Sixth International Congress on Economic History, Copenhagen, 1974*, University of Copenhagen, Institute of Economic History, Copenhagen, (1974)

Berend, I. T., 'Investment strategy in east central Europe', in H. Daems and H. Van der Wee, eds,

The rise of managerial capitalism, Nijhoff, The Hague (1974)

Ellis, H. S., *Exchange control in central Europe*, Harvard University Press, Cambridge, Mass (1941)

Good, D. F., 'National bias in the Austrian capital market before World War I', *Explorations in Economic History*, 14 (1977) [concerned with five countries in east central and south-east Europe]

Nötel, R., 'International capital movements and finance in eastern Europe, 1919–49', *Vierteljahrschrift für Sozial- und Wirtschaftsgeschichte*, 61 (1974)

Paulat, V. J., 'Investment policy and the standard of living in east mid-European countries', *Journal of Central European Affairs*, 14 (1954)

Teichova, A., 'Versailles and the expansion of the Bank of England into central Europe', in N. Horn and J. Kocka, eds, *Reicht und Entwicklung der Grossunternehmen im 19. und frühen 20. Jahrhundert*, Vandenhoeck and Ruprecht, Göttingen (1979)

OVERSEAS TRADE AND COMMERCIAL RELATIONS

Basch, A., *The Danube Basin and the German economic sphere*, Kegan Paul Trench Trubner, London (1944)

Blaisdell, D. C., *European financial control and the Ottoman empire*, AMS Press, New York (1966)

Cameron, R. E., 'Economic relations of France with central and eastern Europe, 1800–1914', *Journal of European Economic History*, 10 (1981)

Carter, F. W., 'Balkan exports through Dubrovnik. A geographical analysis', *Journal of Croatian Studies*, 9–10 (1968–69)

Liebel, H. P., 'Free trade and protectionism under Maria Theresa and Joseph II', *Canadian Journal of History*, 14 (1979)

Meyer, H. C., 'German economic relations with south-eastern Europe, 1870–1914', *American Historical Review*, 57 (1951–52)

Momtchiloff, N., *Ten years of controlled trade in south-eastern Europe*, Cambridge University Press, Cambridge (1944)

Stambrook, F. G., 'A British proposal for the Danubian states. The customs union project of 1932', *Slavonic and East European Review*, 42 (1963)

Tamborra, A., 'The rise of Italian industry and the Balkans, 1900–14', *Journal of European Economic History*, 3 (1974)

Waller, B., 'Bismarck, the Dual Alliance and economic central Europe, 1877–85', *Vierteljahr-*

schrift für Sozial- und Wirtschaftsgeschichte, 63 (1976)

POPULATION AND MIGRATION

Lodge, O., 'Socio-biological studies in the Balkans', *Population*, I (1934) [family and population studies in nineteenth-century Balkan villages]

Moore, W. E., *Economic demography of eastern and southern Europe*, League of Nations, Geneva (1945)

Rosenstein-Rodan, P., 'Agricultural surplus population in eastern and south-eastern Europe', *Economic Journal*, 53 (1943)

Sklar, J. L., 'The role of marriage behaviour in the demographic transition. The case of eastern Europe around 1900', *Population Studies*, 28 (1974)

LABOUR CONDITIONS AND ORGANISATION

Balawyder, A., ed., *Co-operative movements in eastern Europe*, Macmillan, London (1980)

Berend, I. T., and G. Ránki, 'Peculiarities of industrial progress in eastern Europe and the development of the working class', *Proceedings of the third international economic history conference, Munich, 1965*, Mouton, Paris (1968)

Mendel, A. P., 'Peasant and worker on the eve of the first world war', *Slavic Review*, 24 (1965)

Polach, J. G., 'The beginning of trade unionism among the Slavs of the Austrian empire', *Slavic Review*, 14 (1955)

Rose, A., 'Agricultural workers and agrarian reform in central Europe', *International Labour Review*, 18 (1928)

INCOMES, WAGES AND PRICES

Berov, L., 'Wages in the Balkan lands during the period of manufacturing capitalism and the industrial revolution', *Bulgarian Historical Review*, 7 (1979)

URBAN HISTORY

Gutkind, E. A., *et al.*, *Urban development in east central Europe, Poland, Czechoslovakia and Hungary*, Collier-Macmillan, London (1972)

Gutkind, E. A., *et al.*, *Urban development in eastern Europe, Bulgaria, Romania and the USSR*, Collier-Macmillan, London (1972)

Kuklinska, K., 'Central European towns and the fac-

tors of economic growth in the transition from stagnation to expansion between the seventeenth and eighteenth centuries', *Journal of European Economic History*, II (1982)

Lampe, J. R., 'Modernisation and social structure. The case of the pre-1914 Balkan capitals', *South-eastern Europe*, 5 (1978)

Molenda, D., 'Mining towns in central eastern Europe in feudal times. Problem outline', *Acta Poloniae Historica*, 34 (1976)

Stoianovich, T., 'Model and mirror of the pre-modern Balkan city', *Studia Balcanica*, 3 (1970)

SOCIAL STRUCTURE AND SOCIAL CONDITIONS

Adler, P. J., 'Habsburg school reform among the orthodox minorities, 1770–1870', *Slavic Review*, 33 (1974)

Benkin, R. L., 'Ethnicity and organisation. Jewish communities in eastern Europe and the United States', *Sociological Quarterly*, 19 (1978)

Bohachevsky-Chomiak, M., 'Socialism and feminism The first stages of women's organisation in the eastern part of the Austrian empire', in T. Yedlin, ed., *Women in eastern Europe and the Soviet Union*, Praeger, New York (1980)

Chirot, D., *Social change in a peripheral society. The creation of a Balkan colony*, Academic Press, New York (1976)

Clogg, R., ed., *Balkan society in the age of Greek independence*, Macmillan, London (1981)

Durham, M. E., *Some tribal origins, laws and customs of the Balkans*, Allen and Unwin, London (1928)

Jelavich, C. and B., eds, *The Balkans in transition. Essays on the development of Balkan life and politics since the eighteenth century*, University of California Press, Berkeley, Cal. (1963)

Landsberger, H. A., ed., *Rural protest. Peasant movements and social change*, Macmillan, London (1974)

Niederhauser, E., 'The problem of bourgeois transformation in eastern and southern Europe', in S. Fischer-Galati, ed., *Man, state and society in east European history*, Pall Mall Press, London (1970)

Pelenski, J., 'The Haidamak insurrections and the old regimes in eastern Europe', in J. Pelenski, ed., *The American and European revolutions, 1776–1848. Sociopolitical and ideological aspects*, University of Iowa Press, Iowa City, Io. (1980)

Pfeifer, G., 'The quality of peasant living in central

Europe', in W. L. Thomas, ed., *Man's role in changing the face of the earth*, University of Chicago Press, Chicago, Ill. (1956) [relevant to inter-war years]

Sanders, I. T., 'Balkan rural societies and war', in B. K. Kiraly and G. E. Rothenberg, eds, *War and society in east central Europe*, Brooklyn College Press, New York (1979)

Stoianovich, T., 'Factors in the decline of Ottoman society in the Balkans', *Slavic Review*, 21 (1962)

Stoianovich, T., *A study in Balkan civilisation*, Knopf, New York (1967)

Sugar, P. F., 'The nature of non-Germanic societies under Habsburg rule', *Slavic Review*, 22 (1963) [see comments by S. Fischer-Galati and H. Kojn]

Vucinich, W. S., 'The nature of Balkan society under Ottoman rule', *Slavic Review*, 21 (1962)

Yedlin, T., ed., *Women in eastern Europe and the Soviet Union*, Praeger, New York (1980)

HISTORIOGRAPHY AND BIBLIOGRAPHY

Kerner, R. J., *Social sciences in the Balkans and Turkey. A survey of resources for study and research in the fields of knowledge*, University of California Press, Berkeley, Cal. (1930)

Lampe, J. R., 'Urban history in south-eastern Europe. Recent research on the capital cities', *Maryland Historian*, 11 (1980)

Lampe, J. R., and M. R. Jackson, 'An appraisal of recent Balkan historiography', *East European Quarterly*, 9 (1975)

Turnan, I., 'Recent publications on the history of costume and textile handicrafts in eastern Europe', *Textile History*, 10 (1979)

AUSTRIA

GENERAL ECONOMIC AND SOCIAL HISTORY

Freudenberger, H., 'State intervention as an obstacle to economic growth in the Hapsburg monarchy', *Journal of European History*, 27 (1967)

Gerschenkron, A., *The economic spurt that failed. Four lectures in Austrian history*, Princeton University Press, Princeton, N.J. (1977)

Good, D. F., 'Stagnation and "take-off" in Austria, 1873–1913', *Economic History Review*, 27 (1974)

Good, D. F., 'The great depression and Austrian growth after 1873', *Economic History Review*, 31 (1978)

Good, D. F., et al., 'Modern economic growth in the Habsburg monarchy', *East Central Europe*, 7 (1980)

Good, D. F., 'Economic integration and regional development in Austria-Hungary, 1867-1913', in P. Bairoch and M. Levy-Leboyer, eds., *Disparities in economic development since the industrial revolution*, Macmillan, London (1981)

Gross, N. T., 'Economic growth and the consumption of coal in Austria and Hungary, 1831–1913', *Journal of Economic History*, 31 (1971)

Gross, N. T., 'The industrial revolution in the Habsburg monarchy 1750–1914', in C. M. Cipolla, ed., *The emergence of industrial societies*, Fontana Economic History of Europe, vol. 4, part 1, Collins/Fontana, Glasgow (1976)

Gulik, C. A., *Austria from Habsburg to Hitler*, 2 vols, University of California Press, Berkeley, Cal. (1948)

Huertas, T. F., *Economic growth and economic policy in a multinational setting (The Habsburg monarchy, 1841–1865)*, Arno Press, New York (1977)

Kaldor, N., 'The economic situation of Austria', *Harvard Business Review*, 11 (1932–1933)

Kann, R. A., *The multinational empire. Nationalism and the national reform in the Habsburg monarchy, 1840–1918*, 2 vols, Columbia University Press, New York (1950)

Komlos, J., 'Is the depression in Austria after 1873 a "myth"?', *Economic History Review*, 31 (1978)

Layton, W., and C. Rist, *The economic situation of Austria*, League of Nations, Geneva (1925)

Lederer, M., 'Social legislation in the republic of Austria', *International Labour Review*, 2 (1921)

Lederer, M., 'The reform of social insurance in Austria', *International Labour Review*, 19 (1929)

Lovin, C. R., 'Food, Austria and the Supreme Economic Council, 1919', *East European Quarterly*, 12 (1979)

Macartney, C. A., *The House of Austria, 1790–1918*, Edinburgh University Press, Edinburgh (1978)

Marz, E., 'Some economic aspects of the nationality conflict in the Habsburg empire', *Journal of Central European Affairs*, 13 (1953)

May, A. J., *The Hapsburg monarchy, 1867–1914.*

Harvard University Press, Cambridge, Mass. (1951)

Rath, R. J., 'The Hapsburgs and the great depression in Lombardy-Venetia, 1814–18', *Journal of Modern History*, 13 (1941)

Remak, J., 'The healthy invalid: how doomed the Habsburg empire?' *Journal of Modern History*, 41 (1969)

Rothschild, K. W., *Austria's economic development between the two wars*, Muller, London (1947)

Rudolph, R. L., *et al.*, 'Social structure and the beginning of Austrian economic growth', *East Central Europe*, 7, (1980)

Stadler, K. R., 'The disintegration of the Austrian Empire', *Journal of Contemporary History*, 3 (1968)

Taylor, A. J. P., *The Hapsburg monarchy, 1809–1918. A history of the Austrian empire and Austria-Hungary*, Penguin, Harmondsworth (1964)

Wangermann, E., *Austrian achievement, 1700–1800*, Harcourt, New York (1973)

AGRICULTURE AND RURAL SOCIETY

Blum, J., 'Land tenure in the Austrian monarchy before 1848', *Agricultural History*, 19 (1945)

Blum, J., *Noble landowners and agriculture in Austria, 1815–48, A study of the origins of the peasant emancipation of 1848*, Johns Hopkins Press, Baltimore, Md. (1948)

Czekner, J., 'A comparison of the agricultural systems of Austria and Hungary in the two decades before World War I', *East European Quarterly*, 12 (1979)

Eddie, S. M., 'The terms of trade as a tax on agriculture. Hungary's trade with Austria, 1883–1913', *Journal of Economic History*, 32 (1972)

Komlos, J., 'Austro-Hungarian agricultural development, 1827–77', *Journal of European Economic History*, 8 (1979).

Lewis, G., 'The peasantry, rural change and conservative agrarianism. Lower Austria at the turn of the century', *Past and Present*, 81 (1978)

Link, E. M., *The emancipation of the Austrian peasant, 1740–98*, Columbia University Press, New York (1949)

INDUSTRY AND INTERNAL TRADE

Freudenberger, H., 'The woollen goods industry of the Hapsburg monarchy in the eighteenth century', *Journal of Economic History*, 20 (1960)

Gross, N. T., 'An estimate of industrial product in Austria in 1841', *Journal of Economic History*, 28 (1968)

Gross, N. T., 'Austrian industrial statistics, 1880–85 and 1911–1913', *Zeitschrift für die gesamte Staatswissenschaft*, 124 (1968)

Grull, G., 'The Poneggen hosiery enterprise, 1763–1818. A study of Austrian mercantalism', *Textile History*, 5 (1974)

Long, D. C., 'Philippe de Givard and the introduction of mechanical flax spinning in Austria', *Journal of Economic History*, 14 (1954)

Rudolph, R. L., 'The patterns of Austrian industrial growth from the eighteenth to the early twentieth century', *Austrian History Yearbook*, 11 (1975) [see comments by H. Mattis and E. Marz in the same issue]

TRANSPORT AND COMMUNICATIONS

Blum, J., 'Transportation and industry in Austria, 1815–48', *Journal of Modern History*, 15 (1943)

Coons, R. E., *Steamships, statesmen and bureaucrats. Austrian policy towards the steam navigation company of the Austrian Lloyd, 1836–48*, Franz Steiner, Wiesbaden (1975)

May, A. J., 'The Novibazar railway project', *Journal of Modern History*, 10 (1938)

MONEY, BANKING AND FINANCE

Amery, L. S., 'Austro-Hungarian financial relations', *Economic Journal*, 8 (1898)

Cottrell, P. L., 'London financiers and Austria, 1863–75'. The Anglo-Austrian Bank', *Business History*, 11 (1969)

Ellis, H. S., 'Exchange control in Austria and Hungary', *Quarterly Journal of Economics*, 54 (1939)

Good, D. F., 'Natural bias in the Austrian capital market before World War I', *Explorations in Economic History*, 14 (1977)

Good, D. F., 'Financial integration in late nineteenth century Austria', *Journal of Economic History*, 37 (1977)

Grebler, L., and W. Winkler, *The cost of the war to Germany and Austria-Hungary*, Yale University Press, New Haven, Conn. (1940)

Komlos, J., 'Discrimination in the Austrian capital market?', *Explorations in Economic History*, 17 (1980) [reply by D. F. Good in same issue]

League of Nations, *The financial reconstruction of*

Austria, League of Nations, Geneva (1926)

Mises, L. von, 'The foreign exchange policy of the Austro-Hungarian bank', *Economic Journal*, 19 (1909)

Petritsch, L., 'The fiscal question and the experience of the Austro-Hungarian empire', *Economic Journal*, 14 (1904)

Rudolph, R. L., 'Austria, 1800–1914', in R. E. Cameron, ed., *Banking and economic development. Some lessons of history*, Oxford University Press, New York (1972)

Rudolph, R. L., *Banking and industrialization in Austria-Hungary. The role of the bank in the industrialization of the Czech Crown lands, 1813–1914*, Cambridge University Press, Cambridge (1976)

Schlesinger, K., 'The disintegration of the Austro-Hungarian currency', *Economic Journal*, 30 (1920)

Sieghart, R., 'The reform of direct taxation in Austria', *Economic Journal*, 8 (1898)

Steefel, L. D., 'The Rothschilds and the Austrian loan of 1865', *Journal of Modern History*, 8 (1936)

Walre de Bordes, J. van, *The Austrian crown*, P. S. King, London (1924)

Yeager, L., 'Fluctuating exchange rates in the nineteenth century. The experience of Austria and Russia', in R. A. Mundell and A. K. Swoboda, eds., *Monetary problems of the international economy*, University of Chicago Press, Chicago, Ill. (1969)

OVERSEAS TRADE AND COMMERCIAL RELATIONS

Don, Y., 'Comparability of international trade statistics. Great Britain and Austria-Hungary before World War I', *Economic History Review*, 21 (1968)

Eddie, S. M., *et al.*, 'Austria in the dual monarchy. Her trade, within and without the customs union', *East Central Europe*, 7 (1980)

Gratz, G., and R. Schüller, *The economic policy of Austria-Hungary during the war in its external relations*, Oxford University Press, London (1928)

Helleiner, K. F., *Free trade and frustration. Anglo-Austrian negotiations, 1860–70*, University of Toronto Press, Toronto (1973)

Liebel, H. P., 'Free trade and protectionism under Maria Theresa and Joseph II', *Canadian Journal of History*, 14 (1979)

Long, D. C., 'The Austro-French commercial treaty of 1866', *American Historical Review*, 41 (1935–36)

Long, D. C., 'Efforts to secure an Austro-German customs union in the nineteenth century', in A. E. R. Boak, ed., *University of Michigan historical essays*, University of Michigan Press, Ann Arbor, Mich. (1937)

Luza, R., *Austro-German relations in the Anschluss era*, Princeton University Press, Princeton, N.J. (1975)

Mikoletzky, L., 'The interdependence of economics and politics. An example from the Austro-Russian alliance during the Napoleonic wars', *Journal of European Economic History*, 2 (1973)

Newman, M. D., 'Britain and the German-Austrian customs union proposal of 1931', *European Studies Review*, 6 (1976)

Orde, A., 'The origins of the German-Austrian customs union affair of 1931', *Central European History*, 13 (1980)

Philippovich, E. von, 'Austrian-Hungarian trade policy', *Economic Journal*, 12 (1902)

Radulescu-Zoner, S., 'Contributions to the history of the customs war between Roumania and Austria-Hungary', *Revue Romaines d'Etudes Internationales*, 1 (1972)

Ronall, J., 'German and Austrian Jews in the financial modernisation of the Middle East', *Leo Baeck Institute Yearbook*, 22 (1977)

Stambrook, F. G., 'The German-Austrian customs union projects of 1931. A study of German methods and motives', *Journal of Central European Affairs*, 21 (1961)

Williams, M., 'German imperialism and Austria, 1938', *Journal of Contemporary History*, 14 (1979)

POPULATION AND MIGRATION

Demeny, P., 'Early fertility decline in Austria-Hungary. A lesson in demographic transition', *Daedalus*, 97 (1968)

Demeny, P., 'Early fertility decline in Austria-Hungary. A lesson in demographic transition', in D. V. Glass and R. Revelle, eds, *Population and social change*, Edward Arnold, London (1972)

Helczmanovski, H., 'Austria-Hungary', in W. R. Lee, ed., *European demography and economic growth*, Croom Helm, London (1979)

Klezl, F., 'Austria', in W. F. Willcox, ed., *International migrations*, vol. 2, National Bureau of Economic Research, New York (1931)

Sharlin, A., 'Natural decrease in early modern cities. A reconsideration', *Past and present*, 79 (1978) [mainly Austrian material]

LABOUR CONDITIONS AND ORGANISATION

Polach, J. G., 'The beginnings of trade unionism among the Slavs of the Austrian empire', *Slavic Review,* 14 (1955)

Rager, F., 'The settlement of the unemployed on the land in Austria', *International Labour Review,* 29 (1934)

Spates, T. G., 'Industrial relations in the Zeiss works', *International Labour Review,* 22 (1930)

Zawadski, B., and P. F. Lazarsfeld, 'The psychological consequences of unemployment', *Journal of Social Psychology,* 6 (1935)

INCOMES, WAGES AND PRICES

Carroll, M. R., *Unemployment insurance in Austria,* Brookings Institution, Washington, D.C. (1932)

Forchheimer, C., 'Sliding wage scales in Austria', *International Labour Review,* 10 (1924)

Good, D. F., 'The cost of living in Austria, 1874–1913', *Journal of European Economic History,* 5 (1976)

URBAN HISTORY

Abercrombie, P., 'Vienna', *Town Planning Review,* 1 (1910–11)

Breitling, P., 'The role of competition in the genesis of urban planning. Germany and Austria in the nineteenth century', in A. Sutcliffe, ed., *The rise of modern urban planning, 1800–1914,* Mansell, London (1980)

Breitling, P., 'The origins and development of a conservation philosophy in Austria', in R. Kain, ed., *Planning for conservation,* Mansell, London (1981)

Gutkind, E. A., *International history of city development,* vol. 2, *Urban development in the Alpine and Scandinavian countries,* Collier-Macmillan, London (1965)

Herber, C. J., 'Economic and social aspects of Austrian baroque architecture', *Eighteenth Century Life,* 3 (1977)

Hubbard, W. H., 'Politics and society in the Central European city', Graz, Austria, 1861–1918', *Canadian Journal of History,* 5 (1970)

Hubbard, W. H., 'Aspects of social mobility in Graz, 1857–80', *Historical Social Research,* 14 (1980)

Schorske, C., 'Politics and the psyche in *fin de siècle* Vienna', *American Historical Review,* 61 (1961)

SOCIAL STRUCTURE AND SOCIAL CONDITIONS

Berkner, L. K., 'The stem family and the development cycle of the peasant household. An eighteenth century Austrian example', *American Historical Review,* 77 (1972)

Fischer, E., 'Seven Viennese Jewish families. From the ghettos to the holocaust and beyond', *Jewish Social Studies,* 42 (1980)

Gordon, B. M., 'The challenge of industrialization. The Catholic Church and the working class around Vienna, 1815–48', *Austrian History Yearbook,* 9–10 (1973–74)

Grunwald, M., *The history of Jews of Vienna,* Jewish Publication Society of Vienna, Philadelphia, Pa. (1936)

Jahoda, M., *et al., Marienthal. The sociography of an unemployed community,* Tavistock Publications, London (1972)

Kann, R. A., 'The social prestige of the officer corps in the Habsburg empire from the eighteenth century to 1918', in B. Kiraly and G. E. Rothenburg, eds, *War and society in Europe,* Brooklyn College Press, New York (1979)

Kimball, S. B., 'The Mormons in the Habsburg lands, 1841–1914', *Austrian History Yearbook,* 9–10 (1973–74)

Knapp, J., *Austrian social democracy, 1889–1914,* University Press of America, Washington, D.C. (1980)

Macartney, C. A., *The social revolution in Austria,* Cambridge University Press, Cambridge (1926)

Polisensky, J., *Aristocrats and the crowd in the revolutionary year 1848. A contribution to the history of revolution and counter-revolution in Austria,* State University of New York Press, Albany, N.Y. (1980)

Rothenburg, G. E., 'The Austrian sanitary cordon and the control of the bubonic plague, 1710–1871', *Journal of the History of Medicine and Allied Sciences,* 28 (1973)

Rutledge, J. S., 'The delayed reflex. Journalism in Josephinian Vienna', *Studies in Eighteenth Century Culture,* 9 (1979)

Schorske, C., 'The transformation of the garden. Ideal and society in Austrian literature', *American Historical Review,* 67 (1967)

Schorske, C., *Fin-de-siècle Vienna. Politics and culture,* Cambridge University Press, Cambridge (1981)

HISTORIOGRAPHY AND BIBLIOGRAPHY

Di Vittorio, A., 'Economic history in Austria over the last twenty-five years as represented in national and local historical review (1945–70)', *Journal of European Economic History,* 1 (1972)

Kocka, J., 'Recent historiography of Germany and Austria. Theoretical approaches to the social and economic history of modern Germany. Some recent trends, concepts and problems in western and eastern Germany', *Journal of Modern History,* 47 (1975)

Kolossa, T., 'The social structure and the peasant class in Austria-Hungary. Statistical sources and mehods of research', *East European Quarterly,* 3 (1970)

Rudolph, R. L., 'The new versus the old in Austrian economic history', *Austrian History Yearbook,* 11 (1975)

Schmidtbauer, P., 'The history of family structure in Austria. Sources and research problems', *Local Population Studies,* 23 (1979)

HUNGARY

GENERAL ECONOMIC AND SOCIAL HISTORY

Berend, I. T., 'The present in historical perspective', *New Hungarian Quarterly,* 17 (1976)

Berend, I. T., and G. Ránki, 'Economic factors in nationalism. The example of Hungary at the beginning of the twentieth century', *Austrian History Yearbook,* 3 (1967)

Berend, I. T., and G. Ránki, *Hungary. A century of economic development,* David and Charles, Newton Abbot (1974)

Cushing, G. F., *et al.,* 'Hungary', in D. Warriner, ed., *Contrasts in emerging societies,* Athlone Press, London (1965)

Donald, R., *The tragedy of Trianon,* Thornton Butterworth, London (1928)

Ecker-Racz, L., *The Hungarian economy, 1920–54,* Council for Economic Industry Research, Washington, D.C. (1954)

Eckhart, F., *A short history of the Hungarian people,* G. Richards, London (1931)

Eckstein, A., 'National income and capital formation in Hungary, 1900–50', in S. Kuznets, ed., *Income and Wealth,* No. 5, Bowes and Bowes, London (1955)

Good, D. F., 'Economic integration and regional development in Austria-Hungary, 1867–1913', in P. Bairoch and M. Levy-Leboyer, eds, *Disparities in economic development since the industrial revolution,* London (1981)

Good, D. F., *et al.,* 'Modern economic growth in the Habsburg monarchy', *East Central Europe,* 7 (1980)

Grátz, G., *The economical situation in Hungary,* Pallas Printing Co., Budapest (1925)

Grátz, G., ed., *The Hungarian economic yearbook,* Grill, Budapest (1939, 1940)

Gross, N. T., 'Economic growth and the consumption of coal in Austria and Hungary, 1831–1913', *Journal of Economic History,* 31 (1971)

Gross, N. T., 'The industrial revolution in the Habsburg monarchy, 1750–1914', in C. M. Cipolla, ed., *The emergence of industrial societies,* Fontana Economic History of Europe, vol. 4, part 1, Collins/Fontana, Glasgow (1973)

Hanák, P., 'Hungary in the Austro-Hungarian monarchy. Preponderancy or dependency', *Austrian History Yearbook,* 8 (1967)

Hanák, P., 'Economics, society, and sociopolitical thought in Hungary during the age of capitalism', *Austrian History Yearbook,* 11 (1975)

Horváth, J., *Modern Hungary, 1660–1920,* Magyar Kulugyi Tarsasag, Budapest (1922)

Horváth, R., 'The interdependence of economic and demographic development in Hungary (from the mid-eighteenth to the mid-nineteenth centuries)', *Proceedings of the fourth international economic history conference, Bloomington, 1968,* Mouton, Paris (1973)

Illés, A. E., and A. Halász, *The economics of Hungary in maps,* Magyarorszag Gazdasagi Terkepekben, Budapest (1920)

Illés, A. E., and A. Halász, eds, *Hungary before and after the war in economic-statistical maps,* Institute of Political Sciences of the Hungarian Statistical Society, Budapest (1926)

Ivanyi, B. G., 'From feudalism to capitalism. The economic background to Szechenyi's reform in Hungary', *Journal of Central European Affairs,*

20 (1960)

Kann, R. A., *The multinational empire. National-ism and reform in the Habsburg empire,* 2 vols, Columbia University Press, New York (1950)

Katus, L., 'Economic growth in Hungary during the age of dualism, 1867–1918', *Studia Historica,* 62 (1970)

Katus, L., 'Economic growth in Hungary during the age of dualism (1867–1913). A quantitative analysis', in E. Pamlényi, ed., *Social-economic researches on the history of east central Europe,* Akadémiai Kiadó, Budapest¹ (1970)

Kiraly, B. K., *Hungary in the late eighteenth cen-tury. The decline of enlightened despotism,* Col-umbia University Press, New York (1969)

Komlos, J., 'Economic growth and industrialisation in Hungary, 1880–1913', *Journal of European Economic History,* 10 (1981)

Macartney, C. A., *Hungary and her successors. The treaty of Trianon and its consequences, 1919–37,* Oxford University Press, London (1937)

Macartney, C. A., *A history of Hungary, 1929–45,* 2 vols, Praeger, New York (1956–57)

Macartney, C. A., *Hungary. A short history, 900–1956,* Edinburgh University Press, Edinburgh (1962)

McNeill, W. H., *Europe's steppe frontier, 1500–1800,* University of Chicago Press, Chicago, Ill. (1964)

Matolesy, M., and S. Varga, *The national income of Hungary, 1924/25–1936/37,* P. S. King, London (1938)

May, A. J., *The Hapsburg monarchy, 1867–1914,* Harvard University Press, Cambridge, Mass. (1951)

Mitnitzky, M., 'The economic and social effects of industrial development in Hungary', *Interna-tional Labour Review,* 39 (1939)

Nagy, T., 'The Hungarian economic reform. Past and future', *Austrian Economic Review,* 61 (1971)

Ránki, G., 'Some problems of capital accumulation and industrialisation in Hungary, 1867–1914', *Proceedings of the second international economic history conference, Aix-en-Provence, 1962,* Mouton, Paris (1965)

Rudolph, R. L., 'Austrian industrialisation. A case study in leisurely economic growth', in *Sozialis-mus Geschichte und Wirtschaft. Festschrift für Eduard Marz,* Europa Verlag, Vienna (1973)

AGRICULTURE AND RURAL SOCIETY

Benda, G., *et al., Technical innovation in Hun-garian peasant agriculture (nineteenth-twentieth centuries),* Akadémiai Kiadó, Budapest (1982)

Czekner, J., 'A comparison of the agricultural systems of Austria and Hungary in the two decades before World War I', *East European Quarterly,* 12 (1979)

Dymond, T. S., *Agricultural industry and education in Hungary, being an account of the Essex farmers' party to Hungary in May and June, 1902,* J. Dutton, Chelmsford (1902)

Eddie, S. M., 'The changing pattern of land ownership in Hungary, 1867–1914', *Economic History Review,* 20 (1967)

Eddie, S. M., 'Agricultural production and output per worker in Hungary, 1870–1913', *Journal of Economic History,* 28 (1968)

Eddie, S. M., 'Farmers' response to price in large estate agriculture. Hungary, 1870–1913', *Economic History Review,* 24 (1971)

Eddie, S. M., 'The terms of trade as a tax on agricul-ture. Hungary's trade with Austria, 1883–1913', *Journal of Economic History,* 32 (1972)

Held, J., ed., *The modernisation of agriculture. Rural transformation in Hungary, 1848–1975,* East European Monographs, Boulder, Col. (1980)

International Labour Office, 'Agrarian reform in Hungary', *International Labour Review,* 2 (1921)

Kally, I., 'Management of big estates in Hungary between 1711 and 1848', *Etudes Historiques Hongroises,* 1 (1980)

Kiraly, B. K., 'Neo-serfdom in Hungary', *Slavic Review,* 34 (1975)

Komlos, J., 'The emancipation of the peasantry and the development of Hungarian agriculture', in I. Volgyes, ed., *The east European peasantry,* Pergamon Press, New York (1978)

Komlos, J., 'Austro-Hungarian agricultural develop-ment, 1827–77', *Journal of European Economic History,* 8 (1979)

Szabo, E., 'The agrarian question in Hungary (1908)', *Peasant Studies,* 7 (1978)

Toth, T., 'Profitability and cost-efficiency in Hun-garian agriculture in the 1930s', *Journal of Euro-pean Economic History,* 11 (1982)

INDUSTRY AND INTERNAL TRADE

Berend, I. T., 'Industrial structure in the twentieth century. Hungary', *Proceedings of the fourth international economic history conference, Bloomington, 1968,* Mouton, Paris (1973)

Berend, I. T., and G. Ránki, *The development of manufacturing industry in Hungary, 1900–44,*

Akadémiai Kiadó, Budapest (1960)

Berend, I. T., and G. Ránki, *The Hungarian manufacturing industry. Its place in Europe, (1900–38),* Akadémiai Kiadó, Budapest (1960)

Berend, I. T., and G. Ránki, 'The Hungarian manufacturing industry. Its place in Europe (1900–38)', *Etudes Historiques,* 2 (1960)

Hollan, A., 'The results of the measures taken in Hungary for the development of industry', *Economic Journal,* 21 (1911)

Ránki, G., 'Problems of the development of Hungarian industry, 1900–44', *Journal of Economic History,* 24 (1964)

MONEY, BANKING AND FINANCE

Ecker, L. L., 'The Hungarian thrift crown', *American Economic Review,* 23 (1933) [a unit of account adopted by Hungary in 1924]

Ellis, H. S., 'Exchange control in Austria and Hungary', *Quarterly Journal of Economics,* 54 (1939)

League of Nations, *The financial reconstruction of Hungary,* League of Nations, Geneva (1926)

Mises, L. von, 'The foreign exchange policy of the Austro-Hungarian Bank', *Economic Journal,* 19 (1909)

Rudolph, R. L., *Banking and industrialisation in Austria-Hungary. The role of banks in the industrialisation of the Czech Crown lands, 1873–1914,* Cambridge University Press, Cambridge (1976)

OVERSEAS TRADE AND COMMERCIAL RELATIONS

Csöppus, J., 'The Rome pact and Hungarian agricultural exports to Italy (1920–44)', *Journal of European Economic History,* 11 (1982)

Don, Y., 'Comparability of international trade statistics. Great Britain and Austria-Hungary before World War I', *Economic History Review,* 21 (1968)

Eddie, S. M., 'The terms and patterns of Hungarian foreign trade, 1882–1913', The terms and patterns of Hungarian foreign trade, 1882–1913', *Journal of Economic History,* 37 (1977)

Friedman, P., 'The welfare costs of bilateralism. German-Hungarian trade, 1933–38', *Explorations in Economic History,* 13 (1976)

Grátz, G., and R. Schüller, *The economic policy of Austria-Hungary during the war in its external relations,* Oxford University Press, London (1928)

Philippovich, E. von, 'Austrian-Hungarian trade policy', *Economic Journal,* 12 (1902)

POPULATION AND MIGRATION ·

Andorka, R., 'Birth control in the eighteenth and nineteenth centuries in some Hungarian villages', *Local Population Studies,* 22 (1979)

Demeny, P., 'Early fertility decline in Austria-Hungary. A lesson in demographic transition', *Daedalus,* 97 (1968)

Demeny, P., 'Early fertility decline in Austria-Hungary. A lesson in demographic transition', in D. V. Glass and R. Revelle, eds, *Population and social change,* Edward Arnold, London (1972)

Helczmanovski, H., 'Austria-Hungary', in W. R. Lee, ed., *European demography and economic growth,* Croom Helm, London (1979)

Horváth, R., 'The scientific study of mortality in Hungary before the modern statistical era', *Population Studies,* 17 (1963–64)

Horváth, R., 'The interdependence of economic and demographic development in Hungary (from the middle of the eighteenth to the middle of the nineteenth century)', in P. Deprez, ed., *Population and economics,* University of Manitoba Press, Winnipeg (1970)

Horváth, R., 'The Malthusian ideas on population in Hungarian demography before World War II', *Journal of European Economic History,* 1 (1972)

Kosa, J., 'A century of Hungarian emigration, 1850–1950', *Slavic Review,* 16 (1957)

Kovacs, A., *The development of the population of Hungary since the cessation of the Turkish rule,* Steiger, New York (1921)

Kovacsics, J., 'The population of Hungary in the eighteenth century (1720–1876)', *Proceedings of the third international economic history conference, Munich, 1965,* Mouton, Paris (1972)

Lengyel, E., *Americans from Hungary,* Lippincott, Philadelphia, Pa. (1948)

Norbert, D. Z., 'Epidemics of smallpox and its mortality at Pressbourg at the end of the eighteenth century', *Torteneti Statisztikai Tanulmanyok,* 3 (1977) [English summary of Hungarian text]

Puskas, J., 'Emigration from Hungary to the United States before 1914', in *Etudes historiques hongroises, 1975. Proceedings of the Fourteenth Congress of Historical Sciences,* Akadémiai Kiadó, Budapest (1975)

Schultheiss, E., and L. Tardy, 'Short history of epidemics in Hungary until the great cholera epidemic of 1831', *Centaurus,* 11 (1966)

Teleki, G., *Ethnographical map of Hungary based on the density of population,* Van Stockum, The

Hague (1920)

Thirring, G., 'Hungarian migration of modern times', in W. F. Willcox, ed., *International migrations*, 2 vols, National Bureau of Economic Research, New York (1929–31)

Vagö, J., 'Unemployment in Hungary. Its causes and cure', *International Labour Review*, 12 (1925)

LABOUR CONDITIONS AND ORGANISATION

Incze, M., 'Condition of the masses in Hungary', *Acta Historica*, 3 (1954) [deals with the 1930s]

International Labour Office, 'The agricultural labourers in Hungary', *International Labour Review*, 1 (1921)

Kovrig, B., 'The reform of social insurance in Hungary', *International Labour Review*, 20 (1929)

Móricz, M., 'Landless agricultural workers in Hungary', *International Labour Review*, 28 (1933)

Pap, D., 'Labour legislation in Hungary', *International Labour Review*, 8 (1923)

INCOMES, WAGES AND PRICES

Horváth, R., 'Monetary inflation in Hungary during the Napoleonic wars', *Journal of European Economic History*, 5 (1976)

Kiss, I. N., 'Money, prices, values and purchasing power from the sixteenth to the eighteenth century', *Journal of European Economic History*, 9 (1980)

Pap, D., 'The adaptation of wages to the cost of living in Hungary', *International Labour Review*, 11 (1925)

URBAN HISTORY

Bacskai, V., and L. Nagy, 'Market areas, market centres and towns in Hungary in 1828', *Acta Historica*, 26 (1980) .

Bart, I., 'Budapest. Birth of a metropolis', *New Hungarian Quarterly*, 21 (1980)

Gutkind, E. A., *et al.*, *International history of city development*, vol. 7, *Urban development in east central Europe. Poland, Czechoslovakia and Hungary*, Collier-Macmillan, London (1972)

Gyimesi, S., 'Incomes, public constructions and investment in the Hungarian towns in the eigh-

teenth century', *Etudes Historiques Hongroises*, 1 (1980)

Passuth, L., 'Sexcentenary of Debrecen', *New Hungarian Quarterly*, 3 (1962) [city development over 600 years]

SOCIAL STRUCTURE AND SOCIAL CONDITIONS

Andorka, R., 'Hungary's long-term social evolution', *New Hungarian Quarterly*, 20 (1979)

Deme, L., 'The Society for Equality in the Hungarian revolution of 1848', *Slavic Review*, 31 (1972)

Farago, T., 'Household structure and development in rural society in Hungary, 1787–1828', *Torteneti Statisztikai Tanulmanyok*, 3 (1977)

Kiraly, B. K., 'Ferenc Deak, the social reformer, in the revolution of 1848–49', *East European Quarterly*, 14 (1980)

Lipsius, F., 'Hungary in 1776. A European frontier', *New Hungarian Quarterly*, 17 (1976) [mainly concerned with social conditions]

McCagg, W. O., 'Ennoblement in dualistic Hungary. An explanation of bourgeois acceptance of "service" status in eastern Europe', *East European Quarterly*, 5 (1971)

McCagg, W. O., 'Hungary's "feudalised" bourgeoisie', *Journal of Modern History*, 44 (1972)

McCagg, W. O., *Jewish nobles and geniuses in modern Hungary*, Columbia University Press, New York (1972)

HISTORIOGRAPHY AND BIBLIOGRAPHY

Kilossa, T., 'The social structure and the peasant class in Austria-Hungary. Statistical sources and methods of research', *East European Quarterly*, 3 (1970)

Pamlényi, E., ed., *Social-economic researches on the history of east central Europe*, Akadémiai Kiadó, Budapest (1970)

Vardy, S. B., 'The Hungarian economic school. Its birth and development', *Journal of European Economic History*, 4 (1975)

Vardy, S. B., 'The social and ideological make-up of Hungarian historiography in the age of dualism (1867–1918)', *Jahrbücher für Geschichte Osteuropas*, 24 (1976)

CZECHOSLOVAKIA

GENERAL ECONOMIC AND SOCIAL HISTORY

Betts, R. R., *Essays in Czech history,* Athlone Press, London (1969)

Brisch, H., and I. Volgyes, eds, *Czechoslovakia. The heritage of ages past,* Columbia University Press, New York (1979)

Brock, P., and H. G. Skilling, eds, *The Czech renascence of the nineteenth century. Essays presented to Otakar Odlozilik in honour of his seventieth birthday.* University of Toronto Press, Toronto (1970)

Busek, V., and N. Spulber, eds, *Czechoslovakia,* Praeger, New York (1957)

Douglas, D. W., *Transitional economic systems. The Polish-Czech example,* Routledge and Kegan Paul, London (1953)

Freudenberger, H. and G. Mensch, 'Regional differences, differential development and generative economic growth', in P. Bairoch and M. Levy-Leboyer, eds, *Disparities in economic development since the industrial revolution,* Macmillan, London (1981)

Gruber, J., *Czechoslovakia. A survey of economic and social conditions,* Macmillan, New York (1924)

Kerner, R. J., *Bohemia in the eighteenth century. A study in political, economic and social history, with special reference to the reign of Leopold II, 1790–1972,* Macmillan, New York (1932)

Kirschbaum, J. K., ed., *Slovakia in the nineteenth and twentieth centuries,* Slovak World Congress, Toronto (1973)

Klima, A., 'Agrarian class structure and economic development in pre-industrial Bohemia', *Past and Present,* 85 (1979)

Komlos, J., *et al.,* 'Thoughts on the transition from proto-industrialization to modern industrialization in Bohemia, 1795–1830', *East Central Europe,* 7 (1980)

Mamatey, V. S., 'The birth of Czechoslovakia. Union of two peoples', in H. Brisch and I. Volgyes, eds, *Czechoslovakia. The heritage of ages past,* Columbia University Press, New York (1979)

Mamatey, V. S., and R. Luza, eds, *A history of the Czechoslovak republic, 1918–48,* Princeton University Press, Princeton, N.J. (1973)

Necas, J., 'Economic and social problems in German Bohemia', *Slavonic and East European Review,* 15 (1937)

Pryor, F. L., *et al.,* 'Czechoslovakia aggregate production in the interwar period', *Review of Income and Wealth,* 17 (1971)

Purs, J., 'The industrial revolution in the Czech lands', *Historica,* 2 (1960)

Purs, J., *The industrial revolution in the Czech lands,* Nokladatestvi Cestoslovenske Akademie Ved., Prague (1960)

Seton-Watson, R. W., *A history of the Czechs and Slovaks,* Hutchinson, London (1943)

Steiner, E., *The Slovak dilemma,* Cambridge University Press, New York (1973)

Teichova, A., *An economic background to Munich. International business and Czechoslovakia, 1919–38,* Cambridge University Press, Cambridge (1974)

Teichova, A., *Forty years after. An economic reassessment,* University of East Anglia, Norwich (1978)

Thomson, S. H., *Czechoslovakia in European history,* Princeton University Press, Princeton, N.J. (1943)

Wanklyn, H. G., *Czechoslovakia,* G. Philip, London (1954)

Whiteside, A., 'Industrial transformation, population movement and German nationalism in Bohemia', *Zeitschrift für Ostforschung* (1961)

AGRICULTURE AND RURAL SOCIETY

International Labour Office, 'Social aspects of land reform in Czechoslovakia', *International Labour Review,* 12 (1925)

Meissner, F., 'Economics of scale in relation to agrarian reforms in Czechoslovakia', *Slavic Review,* 14 (1955)

Spiesz, A., 'Czechoslovakia's place in the agrarian development of middle and east Europe of modern times', *Studia Historica Slovaca,* 6 (1969)

Wright, W. E., *Serf, seigneur and sovereign. Agrarian reform in eighteenth century Bohemia,* University of Minnesota Press, Minneapolis, Minn. (1966)

INDUSTRY AND INTERNAL TRADE

Carter, F. W., 'The industrial development of Prague, 1800–50', *Slavonic and East European Review,* 51 (1973)

Carter, F. W., 'The cotton printing industry in Prague, 1766–1873', *Textile History,* 6 (1975)

Freudenberger, H., 'Industrialization in Bohemia and Moravia in the eighteenth century', *Journal of Central European Affairs,* 19 (1960)

Freudenberger, H., *The Waldstein woolen mill. Noble entrepreneurship in eighteenth century Bohemia,* Baker Library, Boston, Mass. (1963)

Freudenberger, H., 'Records of the Bohemian iron industry, 1694–1875. The basis for a comprehensive study of modern factories', *Business History Review,* 43 (1969)

Freudenberger, H., 'An exploration in entrepreneurial motivation and action', *Explorations in Entrepreneurial History,* 7 (1969–70)

Freudenberger, H., *The industrialization of a central European city. Brno and the fine woollen industry in the eighteenth century.* Edington, Wiltshire (1977)

Haan, H. von, 'Rationalisation in a Czechoslovak glassworks. The Mühlig Union in Teplitz-Schönau', *International Labour Review,* 33 (1936)

Klima, A., 'Industrial development in Bohemia, 1648–1781', *Past and Present,* 11 (1957)

Klima, A., 'Various forms of industrial enterprises in Bohemia in the eighteenth century', *Papers presented to the fourth international conference of economic history, Bloomington, 1968,* Mouton, Paris (1973)

Klima, A., 'The role of rural domestic industry in Bohemia in the eighteenth century', *Economic History Review,* 27 (1974)

Klima, A., 'The beginning of the machine-building industry in the Czech lands in the first half of the nineteenth century, *Journal of European Economic History,* 4 (1975)

Klima, A., 'Industrial growth and entrepreneurship in the early stages of industrialisation in the Czech lands', *Journal of European Economic History,* 6 (1977)

Pounds, N. J. G., 'Planning in the upper Silesian industrial region', *Journal of Central European Affairs,* 18 (1959)

Teichova, A., 'Industrial structure in the twentieth century. Czechoslovakia', *Papers presented to the fourth international conference of economic history, Bloomington, 1968,* Mouton, Paris (1973)

Wright, W. E., 'Neo-serfdom in Bohemia', *Slavic Review,* 34 (1975)

TRANSPORT AND COMMUNICATIONS

Carter, F. W., 'Public transport development in nineteenth century Prague', *Transport History,* 6 (1973)

MONEY, BANKING AND FINANCE

Klima, A., 'English merchant capital in Bohemia in the eighteenth century', *Economic History Review,* 12 (1959–60)

Pryor, Z. P., 'Czechoslovak fiscal policies in the great depression', *Economic History Review,* 32 (1979)

Rasin, A., *Financial policy of Czechoslovakia during the first year of its history,* Clarendon Press, London (1923)

Rudolph, R. L., *Banking and industrialization in Austria-Hungary. The role of banks in the industrialization of the Czech Crown lands, 1873–1914,* Cambridge University Press, Cambridge (1976)

OVERSEAS TRADE AND COMMERCIAL RELATIONS

Andic, V. E., 'The economic aspects of aid to Russian and Ukrainian refugee scholars in Czechoslovakia', *Journal of Central European Affairs,* 21 (1961)

Pryor, Z. P. and F. L., 'Foreign trade and interwar Czechoslovak economic development, 1918–38', *Vierteljahrschrift für Sozial- und Wirtschaftsgeschichte,* 62 (1975)

POPULATION AND MIGRATION

Arato, E., 'Political differentiation in the Hungarian population of Czechoslovakia in the post-World War I years', in *Etudes Historiques Hongroises, 1975, Proceedings of the fourteenth Congress of Historical Sciences,* Akadémiai Kiadó, Budapest (1975)

Baker, H., and F. W. Bulow, *The rural exodus in Czechoslovakia,* Studies and Reports of the I.L.O., Serles K, No. 13, P. S. King, Geneva (1935)

Srb, V., 'Population development and population policy in Czechoslovakia', *Population Studies,* 16 (1962–63)

LABOUR CONDITIONS AND ORGANISATION

Carter, F. W., 'CKD employees in Prague,

1871–1920. Some aspects of their geographical distribution', *Journal of Historical Geography*, 1 (1975)

'Davis, K., 'The modern conditions of agricultural labor in Bohemia', *Journal of Political Economy*, 8 (1899–1900)

Klima, A., 'The role of education in the forming of skilled workers in Bohemia of the eighteenth century', *Papers presented to the fourth international conference of economic history*, Bloomington, 1968, Mouton, Paris (1973)

URBAN HISTORY

Ciborowski, A., *Town planning in Poland, 1845–55*, Polish Publishing House, Warsaw (1956) [introductory background history]

Gutkind, E. A., *et al.*, *International history of city development*, vol. 7, *Urban development in east central Europe. Poland, Czechoslovakia and Hungary*, Collier-Macmillan, London (1972)

Hruza, J., ed., *Town planning in Czechoslovakia*, Association of Czechoslovak Architects, Prague (1958)

SOCIAL STRUCTURE AND SOCIAL CONDITIONS

Cohen, G. B., 'Jews in German society. Prague, 1860–1914', *Central European History*, 10 (1977)

Hajda, J., 'The role of the intelligentsia in the development of Czechoslovak society', in M. Rechcigl, ed., *The Czechoslovak contribution to world culture*, Mouton, The Hague (1964)

Pech, S. A., *The Czech revolution of 1849*, University of North Carolina Press, Chapel Hill, N.C. (1969)

HISTORIOGRAPHY AND BIBLIOGRAPHY

Purs, J., 'New methods and techniques of research into economic history in Czechoslovakia', *Proceedings of the seventh international economic history congress, Edinburgh, 1978*, Edinburgh University Press, Edinburgh (1978)

POLAND

GENERAL ECONOMIC AND SOCIAL HISTORY

Campbell, F. G., 'The struggle for upper Silesia, 1919–20', *Journal of Modern History*, 42 (1970)

Davies, N., *God's playground. A history of Poland*, 2 vols, Oxford University Press, London (1981)

Douglas, D. W., *Transitional economic systems. The Polish-Czech example*, Routledge and Kegan Paul, London (1953)

Fedorowicz, J. K., ed., *A republic of nobles. Studies in Polish history to 1864*, Cambridge University Press, Cambridge (1982)

Frankel, H., *Poland. The struggle for power, 1772–1939*, L. Drummond, London (1946)

Gorecki, R., *Poland and her economic development*, Allen and Unwin, London (1935)

Hagen, W. W., 'The partitions of Poland and the crisis of the old regime in Prussia, 1772–1806', *Central European History*, 9 (1976)

Kann, R. A., 'Case studies on the Habsburg empire and Poland', in B. K. Kiraly and G. E. Rothenberg, eds, *War and society in east central Europe*, Brooklyn College Press, New York (1979)

Kiencewicz, S., and H. Wereszycki, 'Poland under foreign rule, 1795–1918', in A. Gieysztor *et al.*, *History of Poland*, Polish Scientific Publishers, Warsaw (1968)

Kornilowicz, M., ed., *Western and northern Poland. Historical outline, nationality problems, legal aspect, new society, economic survey*, Zachodnia Agencja Prasowa, Posnan (1962)

Landau, Z., and J. Tomaszewski, 'The main social and economic problems of Poland between the wars', *Papers in East European Economics* (1973)

Laszczynski, S., *et al.*, *Polish fisheries statistics, 1820–60*, Central Institute for scientific, Technical and Economic Information, Warsaw (1967)

Leslie, R. F., 'Politics and economics in Congress Poland', *Past and Present*, 8 (1955)

Leslie, R. F., *Polish politics and the revolution of November 1830*, Athlone Press, London (1956)

Leslie, R. F., *Reform and insurrection in Prussian Poland, 1856–65*, Athlone Press, London (1963)

Leslie, R. F., *et al.*, *The history of Poland since 1863*, Cambridge University Press, Cambridge (1980)

Piltz, E., ed., *Poland. Her people, history, industries,*

science, literature, art and social development, H. Jenkins, London (1909)

Pounds, N. J. G., *Poland. Between East and West*, Van Nostrand, New York (1964)

Reddaway, W. F., *The Cambridge history of Poland*, 2 vols, Cambridge University Press, Cambridge (1941–50)

Rose, W. J., *The rise of Polish democracy*, G. Bell, London (1944)

Serczyk, W. A., 'Eastern Europe in the sixteenth to eighteenth centuries. Review article'. *Acta Poloniae Historica*, 32 (1975)

Smogorzewski, K. M., 'Polish economy under Soviet control', *Slavonic and East European Review*, 32 (1954) [useful information on period prior to 1939]

Taylor, J., *The economic development of Poland, 1919–50*, Cornell University Press, Ithaca, N.Y. (1952)

Tomaszewski, J., 'Social and economic relations in western Byeloruthenia, 1921–39', *Papers presented to the third international conference of economic history, Munich, 1965*, Mouton, Paris (1974)

Topolski, J., 'Economic decline in Poland from the sixteenth to the eighteenth centuries', in P. Earle, ed., *Essays in European economic history, 1500–1800*, Clarendon Press, Oxford (1974)

Zielinski, H., 'The role of Silesia in central Europe in the nineteenth and twentieth centuries', *Acta Poloniae Historica*, 22 (1970)

Zweig, F., *Poland between two wars. A critical study of social and economic changes*, Secker and Warburg, London (1944)

AGRICULTURE AND RURAL SOCIETY

Falniowska-Gradowska, A., 'Some remarks on rental system in southern Poland', *Studia Historiae Oeconomicae*, 10 (1975)

Jakobczyk, W., 'The first decade of the Prussian Settlement Commission's activities, 1886–97', *Polish Review*, 17 (1972)

Kaminski, A., 'Neo-serfdom in Poland-Lithuania', *Slavic Review*, 34 (1975)

Kieniewicz, S., *The emancipation of the Polish peasantry*, University of Chicago Press, Chicago, Ill. (1969)

Kula, W., *An economic theory of the feudal system. Towards a model of the Polish economy, 1500–1800*, NLB, London (1976)

Kula, W., 'La seigneurie et la famille paysanne dans la Pologne du 18e siècle', *Annales*, 27 (1972). Translated into English in R. Forster, and O. Ranum, eds, *Family and society*, Johns Hopkins University Press, Baltimore, Md. (1976)

Kula, W., 'Money and serfs in eighteenth century Poland', in E. J. Hobsbawm *et al.*, *Peasants in history. Essays in honour of Daniel Thorner*, Oxford University Press, Calcutta (1980)

Laszczynski, S., *et al.*, *Polish fisheries statistics, 1920–60*, Central Institute for Scientific, Technical and Economic Information, Warsaw (1967)

Leskiewicz, J., 'Land reforms in Poland (1760–1870)', *Journal of European Economic History*, 1 (1972)

Lincoln, W. B., 'N. A. Miliutin and the emancipation of the Polish peasants', *Journal of European Studies*, 7 (1977)

Ludkiewicz, Z., 'The agrarian structure of Poland and France from the point of view of emigration', *International Labour Review*, 22 (1930)

Maczak, A., 'The social distribution of landed property in Poland from the sixteenth to the eighteenth century', *Papers presented to the third international conference of economic history, Munich, 1965*, Mouton, Paris (1968)

Maczak, A., 'Agricultural and livestock production in Poland. International and foreign markets', *Journal of European Economic History*, 1 (1972)

Madurowicz-Urbanska, H., 'The spatial form of industrial settlements. An element of the rural landscape of Polish feudal villages', *Acta Poloniae Historica*, 18 (1968)

Staniewicz, W., 'The agrarian problem in Poland between the two world wars', *Slavonic and East European Review*, 43 (1964–65)

Thomas, W. I., and F. Znaniecki, *The Polish peasant in Europe and America. Monograph of an immigrant group*, R. G. Badger, Boston, Mass.(1918). Reprinted Dover Publications, New York (1958)

Zytkowicz, L., 'The peasant's farm and the landlord's farm in Poland from the sixteenth century to the middle of the eighteenth century', *Journal of European Economic History*, 1 (1972)

INDUSTRY AND INTERNAL TRADE

Cynamon, A., and L. Szlamowicz, 'Economic organisation in small Polish trades and handicrafts', *International Labour Review*, 34 (1936)

Jedlicki, J., 'Industrial state economy in the kingdom of Poland in the nineteenth century', *Acta*

Poloniae Historica, 18 (1968)

Jedlicki, J., 'Social ideas and economic attitudes of Polish eighteenth century nobility. Their approach to industrial policy', *Papers presented to the fifth international economic history conference, Leningrad, 1970*, Mouton, Paris (1979)

Kechova, A., 'Polish salt mines as a state enterprise (XIIIth–XVIIIth centuries)', *Journal of European Economic History*, 10 (1981)

Kuklinska, K., 'Commercial expansion in eighteenth century Poland. The case of Poznan', *Journal of European Economic History*, 6 (1977)

Polish Scientific Publishers, *Outline of the history of Polish science and technology*, Polish Scientific Publishers, Warsaw (1966)

Turnau, I., *Leather for clothes in Poland from the XVIth to the XVIIIth century (techniques and organizaton)*, Zaklad Narowdowy, Warsaw (1975) [English summary]

Wajnryb, M., 'The economic and social importance of the central industrial district of Poland', *International Labour Review*, 38 (1938)

Winston, V. H., 'The Polish bituminous coal-mining industry', *Slavic Review*, 15 (1956)

TRANSPORT AND COMMUNICATIONS

Bochenski, A., *Tracing the development of Polish industry*, Interpress, Warsaw (1971)

May, A. J., 'The Novibazar railway project', *Journal of Modern History*, 10 (1938)

MONEY, BANKING AND FINANCE

Heydel, A., 'The making of Polish state finance', *Slavonic and East European Review*, 18 (1939) [currency and finance after the first world war]

Hilton Young, E., *Report on financial conditions in Poland*, Waterlow, London (1924)

Jedlicki, J., 'Fiscal policy and budget as a factor in capital formation. Polish nineteenth century experience', *Papers presented to the third international conference of economic history, Munich, 1965*, Mouton, Paris (1968)

Mlynarski, F., *The international significance of the depreciation of the zloty in 1925*, Polish Economist, Warsaw (1926)

Pension, J. H., 'The Polish mark in 1921', *Economic Journal*, 32 (1922)

Smith, L., 'The zloty, 1924–35', *Journal of Political Economy*. 44 (1936)

Wellisz, L., *Foreign capital in Poland*, Allen and Unwin, London (1938)

OVERSEAS TRADE AND COMMERCIAL RELATIONS

Best, P. J., 'The Warsaw Insurance Company in the United States', *Polish Review*, 15 (1970)

Cieslak, E., 'Seaborne trade between France and Poland in the eighteenth century', *Journal of European Economic History*, 6 (1977)

Jezierski, A., 'The role of eastern markets in the development of Polish industry in the light of the balance of trade estimate of nineteenth century Poland', *Studia Historiae Oeconomicae*, 4 (1969)

Klimesz, H., 'Poland's trade through the Black Sea in the eighteenth century', *Polish Review*, 15 (1970)

Rusinski, W., 'The role of the Polish territories in the European trade in the seventeenth and eighteenth centuries', *Studia Historiae Oeconomicae*, 3 (1968)

POPULATION AND MIGRATION

Bovowski, S., 'Demographic development and the Malthusian problem in the Polish territories under German rule, 1807–1914', in P. Deprez, ed., *Population and economics*, University of Manitoba Press, Winnipeg (1970)

Copson, Niecko, M. J. E., 'The Polish political emigration in the United States, 1831–64', *Polish Review*, 19 (1974)

Douglass, P. F., *The economic independence of Poland. A study in trade adjustments to political objectives*, Ruter Press, Cincinatti, Ohio (1934)

Greene, V. R., 'Pre-World War I Polish emigrations to the United States. Motives and statistics', *Polish Review*, 6 (1961)

Haiman, M., *Polish past in America, 1608–1865*, Polish Roman Catholic Union Archives and Museum, Chicago, Ill. (1939)

Landau, L., 'Seasonal emigration from Poland to Germany and Latvia', *International Labour Review*, 40 (1939)

Lopata, H. L., 'Polish immigration to the United States of America. Problems of estimation and parameters', *Polish Review*, 21 (1976)

Rabinovitch, G. S., 'The seasonal emigration of Polish agricultural workers to Germany', parts I and II, *International Labour Review*, 25 (1932)

Shulvass, M. A., *From east to west. The westward migration of Jews from eastern Europe during the seventeenth and eighteenth centuries*, Wayne State University Press, Detroit, Mich. (1971)

Stys, W., 'The influence of economic conditions on the fertility of peasant women', *Population Studies,* 11 (1957–58)

Trzeciakowski, L., 'Polish emigrants in the struggle for independence', *Polish Western Affairs,* 20 (1979)

Zubrzycki, J., 'Emigration from Poland in the nineteenth and twentieth centuries', *Population Studies,* 6 (1952–53)

Zubrzycki, J., 'Polish emigration to British Commonwealth countries. A demographic survey', *International Migration Review,* 13 (1979)

LABOUR CONDITIONS AND ORGANISATION

Baumgart, H., 'Polish labour legislation', *International Labour Review,* 7 (1923)

Bilt, L., *The origins of Polish socialism. The history of and ideas of the first Polish socialist party, 1878–86,* Cambridge University Press, Cambridge (1971)

Brock, P., *Nationalism and populism in partitioned Poland. Selected essays,* Orbis Books, London (1974)

Brock, P., *Polish revolutionary populism,* University of Toronto Press, Toronto (1977)

Brozek, A., 'Industrial labour force in a politically divided area. Formation and development of its structures. The upper Silesian example, 1870–1939', in M. W. Flinn, ed., *Proceedings of the seventh International Economic History Association conference, Edinburgh, 1978,* Edinburgh University Pres, Edinburgh (1978)

Dziewanowski, M. K., 'The beginnings of socialism in Poland', *Slavonic and East European Review,* 29 (1950)

Gnoinski, J., 'The conditions of agricultural workers in Poland in 1930 and 1931', *International Labour Review,* 27 (1933)

Lewis, R. D., 'Labour–management conflict in Russian Poland. The Łodz lock-out of 1906–07', *East European Quarterly,* 7 (1974)

Rosner, J., 'An inquiry into the life of unemployed workers in Poland', *International Labour Review,* 27 (1933)

Rosner, J., 'Measures to combat the depression and unemployment in Poland', *International Labour Review,* 30 (1934)

Rosner, J., 'Productive occupation for unemployed young workers in Poland', *International Labour Review,* 31 (1935)

Sokol, F., *Social insurance in Poland,* A. Kundig, Geneva (1925)

Szturm de Sztrem, J., 'Wage problems in Poland during and after the war', *International Labour Review,* 10 (1924)

Zarnowska, A., 'Determinants of the political activity of the working class in the Polish territories on the turn of the nineteenth century', *Acta Poloniae Historica,* 42 (1980)

Zawadzki, B., and P. F. Lazarsfeld, 'The psychological consequences of unemployment', *Journal of Social Psychology,* 6 (1935)

URBAN HISTORY

Dmochowski, Z., *The architecture of Poland. An historical survey,* Polish Research Centre, London (1956) [contains some material on social and urban history]

Fisher, J. C., ed., *City and regional planning in Poland,* Cornell University Press, Ithaca, N.Y. (1966)

Gutkind, E. A., *et al., International history of city development,* vol. 7, *Urban development in east central Europe, Poland, Czechoslovakia and Hungary,* Collier-Macmillan, London (1972)

Kalinowski, W., *City development in Poland up to mid-nineteenth century,* Institute for Town Planning and Architecture, Warsaw (1966)

Stone, D., 'The end of medieval particularism. Polish cities and the Diet, 1764–89', *Canadian Slavonic Papers,* 20 (1978)

Zarebska, T., 'The reconstruction of Kalisz, Poland, following its destruction in 1914', in R. Kain, ed., *Planning for conservation,* Mansell, London (1981) [contains pre-1914 section]

SOCIAL STRUCTURE AND SOCIAL CONDITIONS

Gella, A., and R. A. Wanner, 'Collective status consistency and the Polish intelligentsia. A conceptual elaboration and historical analysis', *Sociology and Social Research,* 63 (1979)

Goldberg, J., 'Poles and Jews in the seventeenth and eighteenth centuries. Rejection or acceptance', *Jahrbucher für Geschichte Osteuropas,* 22 (1974)

Hagen, W. W., 'Impact of economic modernization on traditional nationality relations in Prussian Poland, 1815–1914', *Journal of Social History,* 6 (1972–73)

Heller, C. S., *On the edge of destruction. Jews of Poland between the two world wars,* Columbia University Press, New York (1977)

Kemeny, J., ' "Economic interests" versus "economic pressures". Two case studies of social change', *Social theory and practice,* 2 (1972)

Lewalski, K. F., 'The French medical mission to Poland during the insurrection of 1830–31', *Polish Review,* 10 (1965)

Miaso, J., 'Education and social structures in the kingdom of Poland in the second half of the nineteenth century', *History of Education,* 10 (1981)

Rackauskas, J. A., 'The first national system of education in Europe. The Commission for National Education of the kingdom of Poland and the Grand Duchy of Lithuania, 1773–1914', *Lituanus,* 14 (1968)

Rose, W. J., *'Stanislaw Konarski. Reformer of education in eighteenth century Poland,* Jonathan Cape, London (1929)

Ryszka, F., 'History and the social consciousness', *Polish perspectives,* 21 (1978)

Tazbir, J., and E. Rostworoski, 'The commonwealth of the gentry', in A. Gieysztor, *et al., History of Poland,* Polish Scientific Publishers, Warsaw (1968)

Weinryb, B. D., *The Jews of Poland. A social and economic history of the Jewish community in Poland from 1100 to 1800,* Jewish Publication Society of America, Philadelphia, Pa. (1973)

Wynot, E. D., 'The "service of youth". A Polish experiment in social modernisation, 1937–39', *Canadian-American Slavic Review,* 5 (1971)

Zarnowski, J., 'The role of Polish culture in the Polish nation's liberation striving', *Polish Western Affairs,* 20 (1979)

Zielinski, H., 'The social and political background of the Silesian uprisings', *Acta Poloniae Historica',* 26 (1972)

Zurawicka, J., 'The structure of the Warsaw intelligentsia at the end of the nineteenth century', *Journal of European Economic History,* 5 (1976)

HISTORIOGRAPHY AND BIBLIOGRAPHY

Fryde, M., 'Recent studies in Polish agrarian history', *Polish Review,* 7 (1962)

Gieysztorowa, I., 'Research into demographic history of Poland. A provisional summing-up', *Acta Poloniae Historica,* 18 (1968)

Hensel, J., 'Methods of utilizing notary acts in studies of social history', *Acta Poloniae Historica,* 38 (1978)

Hundert, G., 'Recent studies related to the history of the Jews in Poland from earliest times to the partition of Poland', *Polish Review,* 18 (1973) [contains an extensive bibliography]

Simons, T. W., 'The peasant revolt of 1846 in Galicia. Recent Polish historiography', *Slavic Review,* 30 (1971)

Szulc, S., 'Research on differential fertility in Poland', *Population,* 1 (1934)

Wyczanski, A., 'The annals of Polish social and economic history', *Journal of European Economic History,* 6 (1977)

Wynot, E. D., 'Urban history in Poland. A critical appraisal', *Journal of Urban History,* 6 (1979)

YUGOSLAVIA

GENERAL ECONOMIC AND SOCIAL HISTORY

Allcock, J. B., 'The development of capitalism in Yugoslavia', in F. W. Carter, ed., *An historical geography of the Balkans,* Academic Press, London (1977)

Auty, P., *et al.,* Serbia', in D. Warriner, ed., *Contrasts in emerging societies,* Athlone Press, London (1965) [includes five other Yugoslav states]

Brailsford, H. N., *Macedonia. Its races and their future,* Methuen, London (1906); reprinted by Arno Press, London (1970)

Clissold, S., ed., *A short history of Yugoslavia from early times to 1966,* Cambridge University Press, Cambridge (1966)

Dedijer, V., *The road to Sarajevo,* MacGibbon and Kee, London (1967)

Dedijer, V., *et al., History of Yugoslavia,* McGraw-Hill, New York (1974)

Djordjevic, D., ed., *The creation of Yugoslavia, 1914–18,* Clio Books, Santa Barbara, Cal. (1980)

Dragnich, A. N., *Serbia, Nikola Pasic and Yugoslavia,* Rutgers University Press, New Brunswick, N.J. (1974)

Dvornik, F., *The Slavs in European history and civilisation,* Rutgers University Press, New Brunswick, N.J. (1962)

Gazi, S., *A history of Croatia,* Philosophical Library, New York (1973)

Gestrin, F., 'Slovenia from the sixteenth to the beginning of the twentieth century', *Proceedings of the fourth international economic history conference, Bloomington, 1968,* Mouton, Paris (1973)

Hamilton, F. E. I., *Yugoslavia. Patterns of economic activity,* Praeger, New York (1968) [includes historical section, e.g. on natural resources]

Heppell, M., and F. B. Singleton, *Yugoslavia,* Praeger, New York (1961)

Hočevar, T., *The structure of the Slovenian economy, 1848–1963,* Studia Slovenica, New York (1965)

Hočevar, T., 'Economic determinants in the development of the Slovene national system', *Papers in Slovene Studies,* New York (1975)

Hristov, A., *The creation of Macedonian statehood, 1893–1945,* Kultura, Skopje (1971)

Jelavich, B., 'Servia in 1897. A report of Sir Charles Eliot', *Journal of Central European Affairs,* 18 (1958)

Jelavich, C., 'The revolt in Bosnia-Hercegovina, 1881–82', *Slavonic and East European Review,* 31 (1953)

Lampe, J. R., 'Unifying the Yugoslav economy, 1918–21', in D. Djordjevic, ed., *The creation of Yugoslavia, 1914–18,* Clio Books, Santa Barbara, Cal. (1980)

MacKenzie, D., *The Serbs and Russian pan-Slavism, 1875–78,* Cornell University Press, Ithaca, N.Y. (1967)

Pavlowitch, S. K., 'Early nineteenth century Serbia in the eyes of British travellers', *Slavic Review,* 21 (1962)

Pavlowitch, S. K., *Yugoslavia,* Praeger, New York (1971)

Petrovitch, M. B., *A history of modern Serbia, 1804–1918,* 2 vols, Harcourt Brace Jovanovich, New York (1976)

Rogel, C., *The Slovenes and Yugoslavism, 1890–1914,* Columbia University Press, New York (1977)

Rothenburg, G. E., *The Austrian military border in Croatia, 1522–1747,* University of Illinois Press, Urbana, Ill. (1962)

Rothenburg, G. E., *The military border in Croatia, 1740–1881. A study of an imperial institution,* University of Chicago Press, Chicago, Ill. (1966)

Singleton, F. B., *Twentieth century Yugoslavia,* Macmillan, London (1976)

Singleton, F. B., and B. Carter, *The economy of Yugoslavia,* Croom Helm, London (1982)

Skendi, S., 'Beginnings of Albanian nationalist and autonomous trends. The Albanian League, 1878–81', *Slavic Review,* 12 (1953)

Skendi, S., *The Albanian national awakening, 1878–1912;* Princeton University Press, Princeton, N.J. (1967)

Stevenson, F. S., *A history of Montenegro,* Jarrold, London (1913; reprinted Arno Press, New York (1970)

Sugar, P. F., 'The southern Slav image of Russia in the nineteenth century', *Journal of Central European Affairs,* 21 (1961)

Sugar, P. F., *Industrialisation of Bosnia-Hercegovina, 1878–1918,* University of Washington Press, Seattle, Wash. (1963)

Tomasevich, J., *Peasants, politics and economic change in Yugoslavia,* Stanford University Press, Stanford, Cal. (1955)

Vinski, I., 'National product and fixed assets in the territory of Yugoslavia 1909–59', in P. Deane, ed., *Income and wealth,* No. 9, Bowes and Bowes, London (1961)

Zwitter, F., 'The Slovenes and the Habsburg monarchy', *Austrian History Yearbook,* 3 (1967)

AGRICULTURE AND RURAL SOCIETY

Alexander, P. B., *Land utilisation in the Karst region of Zgornja Pivka, Slovenia,* Studia Slovenica, New York (1967)

Bell, R. M., 'The transformation of a rural village. Istria, 1870–1972', *Journal of Social History,* 7 (1974)

Halpern, J. M., *A Serbian village,* Oxford University Press, Oxford (1958)

Halpern, J. M. and B. K., *A Serbian village in historical perspective,* Holt Rinehart and Winston, New York (1972)

Hoffman, G. W., 'Yugoslavia. Changing character of rural life and rural economy', *Slavic Review,* 18 (1959)

Lodge, O., *Peasant life in Yugoslavia,* Seeley Service, London (1942)

Palairet, M. R., 'Fiscal pressure and peasant impoverishment in Serbia before World War I', *Journal of Economic History,* 39 (1979)

Rasic, P., *Agricultural development in Yugoslavia,* n.p., Belgrade (1955)

Trouton, R., *Peasant renaissance in Yugoslavia, 1900–50. A study of the development of Yugoslav peasant society as affected by education,* Routledge and Kegan Paul, London (1952)

Warriner, D., 'Urban thinkers and peasant policy in Yugoslavia, 1918–59', *Slavonic and East European Review*, 38 (1959)

Wilkinson, H. R., 'Jugoslav Kosmet. The evolution of a frontier province and its landscape', *Transactions of the Institute of British Geographers*, 21 (1955)

INDUSTRY AND INTERNAL TRADE

Anonymous, 'The pork and bacon curing industry in Belgrade', *Journal of the Board of Agriculture*, 10 (1904)

Colanovic, B., *Industrial development in Yugoslavia*, Edition Jugoslavija, Belgrade (1962)

Hamilton, F. E. I., 'The changing pattern of Yugoslavia's manufacturing industry, 1938–61', *Tijdschrift voor Economisch en Sociale Geografie*, 54 (1963)

Palairet, M. R., 'Merchant enterprise and the development of the plum-based trades in Serbia, 1847–1911', *Economic History Review*, 30 (1977)

Patton, K. S., *The kingdom of Serbs, Croats and Slovenes (Yugoslavia). A commercial and industrial handbook*, U.S. Government Printing Office, Washington, D.C. (1928)

TRANSPORT AND COMMUNICATIONS

Beaver, S. H., 'Railways in the Balkan peninsula', *Geographical Journal*, 97 (1941)

May, A. J., 'The Novibazar railway project', *Journal of Modern History*, 10 (1938)

Melik, A., *The development of the Yugoslav railways and their gravitation towards Trieste*, n.p., Belgrade (1945)

Wank, S., 'Aehrenthal and the Sanjak of Novibazar railway project. A reappraisal', *Slavonic and the East European Review*, 42 (1964)

MONEY, BANKING AND FINANCE

Lampe, J. R., 'Serbia, 1818–1912', in R. E. Cameron, ed., *Banking and economic development. Some lessons of history*, Oxford University Press, New York (1972)

Lampe, J. R., 'Finance and pre-1914 industrial stirrings in Bulgaria and Serbia', *Southeastern Europe*, 2 (1975)

OVERSEAS TRADE AND COMMERCIAL RELATIONS

Lorscheider, H. M., 'The commercial treaty between Germany and Serbia of 1904', *Central European History*, 9 (1976)

Pavlowitch, S. K., *Anglo-Russian rivalry in Serbia, 1837–1839*, Mouton, Paris (1961)

Tomasevich, J., 'Foreign economic relations in Yugoslavia, 1918–41', in R. J. Kerner, ed., *Yugoslavia*, University of California Press, Berkeley, Cal. (1949)

Vucinich, W. S., *Serbia between east and west. The events of 1903–08*, Stanford University Press, Stanford, Cal. (1954)

POPULATION AND MIGRATION

Govorchin, G. G., *Americans from Yugoslavia*, University of Florida Press, Gainesville, Fla. (1961)

Kraljic, F., *Croatian migration to and from the United States*, Ragusan Press, Palo Alto, Cal. (1978)

LABOUR CONDITIONS AND ORGANISATION

Haan, H. Von, 'Labour conditions in a rationalised shoe factory. The Bat'a works at Borovo, Yugoslavia', *International Labour Review*, 36 (1937)

Yeremitch, D., 'The problems of agricultural labour in Yugoslavia', *International Labour Review*, 38 (1938)

URBAN HISTORY

Bjelorucic, H., *The Ragusan republic. Victim of Napoleon and its own conservatism*, E. J. Brill, Leiden (1970)

Carter, F. W., 'The decline of the Dubrovnik city state', *Balkan Studies*, 9 (1968)

Carter, F. W., 'Dubrovnik. The early development of a pre-industrial city', *Slavic and East European Review*, 47 (1969)

Carter, F. W., *Dubrovnik (Ragusa). A classic city state*, Seminar Press, London (1972)

Fisher, J. C., 'Urban analysis. A case study of Zagreb, Yugoslavia', *Annals of the Association of American Geographers*, 53 (1963)

Lampe, J. R., 'Modernisation and social structure. The case of the pre-1914 Balkan capitals', *Southeastern Europe*, 5 (1978)

Maksimovic, B., *Urbanizam u Srbiji*, Gradevinska,

Belgrade (1962) [English summary of town planning in nineteenth-century Serbia]

Popovic, D. J., 'Belgrade in 1733–34', *Spomenik (Proceedings of the Royal Serbian Academy)*, 78 (1935)

Violich, F., 'An urban development policy for Dalmatia', *Town Planning Review*, 43 (1972)

SOCIAL STRUCTURE AND SOCIAL CONDITIONS

Anderson, D., *Miss Irby and her friends*, Hutchinson, London (1966) [work of Adeline Irby in relation to housing, education, social conditions and care of refugees, 1860–1911]

Crnja, Z., *Cultural history of Croatia*, Office of Information, Zagreb (1962)

Despalatovic, E. M., 'Ljudevit Gaj and the Illyrian movement', *East European Quarterly*, 8 (1975)

Dyker, D. A., 'The ethnic Muslims of Bosnia – some basic socio-economic data', *Slavonic and East European Review*, 50 (1972)

Gross, M., 'Social structure and national movements among the Yugoslav peoples on the eve of the first world war', *Slavic Review*, 36 (1977)

Halpern, J. M., *Social and cultural change in a Serbian village*, Human Relations Area Files, New Haven, Conn. (1956)

Halpern, J. M., 'Town and countryside in Serbia in the nineteenth century. Social and household structure as reflected in the census of 1863', in P. Laslett, ed. *Household and family in past time*, Cambridge University Press, Cambridge (1972)

Hammel, E. A., 'Social mobility, economic change and kinship in Serbia', *Southwestern Journal of Anthropology*, 25 (1969)

Hammel, E. A., 'The *zadruga* as process', in P. Laslett, ed., *Household and family in past time*, Cambridge University Press, Cambridge (1977) [family structure, sixteenth to twentieth century]

Laslett, P., and M. Clarke, 'Houseful and household in an eighteenth century Balkan city. A tabular analysis of the listing of the Serbian sector of Belgrade in 1733–34', in P. Laslett, ed., *Household and family in past time*, Cambridge University

Press, Cambridge (1972)

Lopashich, A., 'A negro community in Yugoslavia', *Man*, 58 (1958)

McClellan, W. D., *Svetozar, Maskovic and the origins of Balkan socialism*, Princeton University Press, Princeton, N.J. (1964)

Macedonian Review Editions, *The epic of Ilinden*, Macedonian Review Editions, Skopje (1973) [collection of articles on various aspects of the 1903 Ilinden uprising]

Pusic, E., 'The family in the process of social change in Yugoslavia', *Sociological Review*, 5 (1957)

Stoianovich, T., 'The pattern of Serbian intellectual evolution, 1830–80', *Comparative Studies in Society and History*, 1 (1959)

Sugar, P. F., 'The nature of the non-Germanic societies under Habsburg rule', *Slavic Review*, 22 (1963)

HISTORIOGRAPHY AND BIBLIOGRAPHY

Hocevar, T., *Economic history of Slovenia, 1828–1918. A bibliography with subject index*, Society for Slovenic Studies, New York (1978)

Hocevar, T., 'The economic history of Slovenia, 1828–1918. A survey of the literature', *Journal of European Economic History*, 8 (1979)

Petrovich, M. B., 'The rise of modern Serbian historiography', *Journal of Central European Affairs*, 16 (1957)

Petrovich, M. B., 'Dalmatian historiography in the age of humanism', *Medievalia et Humanistica*, 12 (1958)

Petrovich, M. B., 'The rise of modern Slovenian historiography', *Journal of Central European Affairs*, 22 (1963)

Petrovich, M. B., *Yugoslavia. A bibliographic guide*, Library of Congress, Washington, D.C. (1974)

Tadic, J., ed., *Jugoslavija*, Yugoslav National Committee for Historical Studies, Belgrade (1955) [historiography of Yugoslavia]

Wilkinson, H. R., *Maps and politics. A review of the ethnographic cartography of Macedonia*, Liverpool University Press, Liverpool (1951)

BULGARIA

Bell, J. D., 'The genesis of agrarianism in Bulgaria', *Balkan Studies*, 16 (1975)

Bell, J. D., *Peasants in power. Alexander Stambolski and the Bulgarian National Union*,

1899–1923, Princeton University Press, Princeton, N.J. (1977)

Bedrov, L., 'Changes in the social structure of the urban population in Bulgaria from 1878 to 1912', *Southeastern Europe*, 5 (1978)

Damianov, S., 'Political and socioeconomic repercussions of the 1877–78 Russo-Turkish war', *Southeastern Europe*, 6 (1979)

Flaningam, M. L., 'German economic controls in Bulgaria, 1894–1914', *Slavic Review*, 20 (1961)

Gerschenkron, A., 'Some aspects of industrialisation in Bulgaria, 1818–1939' in *Economic backwardness in historical perspective*, Harvard University Press, Cambridge, Mass. (1962)

Gutkind, E. A., *et al.*, *International history of city development*, vol. 8, *Urban development in eastern Europe. Bulgaria, Romania and the U.S.S.R.*, Collier-Macmillan, London (1972)

Hoffman, G. W., 'Transformation of rural settlement in Bulgaria', *Geographical Review*, 54 (1964)

International Labour Office, 'The results of compulsory labour service in Bulgaria from 1925–33', *International Labour Review*, 30 (1934)

International Labour Office, 'The results of compulsory labour service in Bulgaria from 1933 to 1936–37', *International Labour Review*, 38 (1938)

Jensen, J. H., and G. Rosegger, 'British railway builders along the lower Danube, 1856–69', *Slavonic and East European Review*, 46 (1968)

Lampe, J. R., 'Finance and pre-1914 industrial stirrings in Bulgaria and Serbia', *Southeastern Europe*, 2 (1975)

Lampe, J. R., 'Modernization and social structure. The case of the pre-1914 Balkan capitals', *Southeastern Europe*, 5 (1978)

Logio, G. C., *Bulgaria. Problems and politics*, Heinemann, London (1919)

Logio, G. C., *Bulgaria. Past and present*, Sherratt and Hughes, Manchester (1936)

MacDermott, M., *A history of Bulgaria, 1393–1885*, Allen and Unwin, London (1962)

McIntyre, R. J., 'The Bulgarian anomaly. Demographic transition and current fertility', *South-eastern Europe*, 7 (1980)

Meininger, T. A., 'The social stratification of the Bulgarian town in the third quarter of the nineteenth century', *Southeastern Europe*, 5 (1978)

Mishev, D., *The Bulgarians in the past. Pages from the Bulgarian cultural history*, Librairie Centrale des Nationalités, Lausanne (1919)

Monroe, W. S., *Bulgaria and her people. With an account of the Balkan wars, Macedonia, and the Macedonia Bulgars*, Page Company, Boston, Mass. (1914)

Monzelis, N., 'Greek and Bulgarian peasants. Aspects of their sociopolitical situation during the inter-war period', *Comparative Studies in Society and History*, 18 (1976)

Nikoloff, D., 'The trade union movement in Bulgaria', *International Labour Review*, 16 (1927)

Paskeleva, V., 'A contribution to the history of trade in the Bulgarian lands during the first half of the nineteenth century', *Bulgarian Historical Review*, 8 (1980)

Pasvolsky, L., *Bulgaria's economic position*, Brookings Institution, Washington D.C. (1930)

Pinson, M., 'Ottoman Bulgaria in the first Tanzimat period. The revolts in Nish (1841) and Vidin (1850)', *Middle Eastern Studies*, 11 (1975)

Pinto, V. de S., 'Bulgaria', in D. Warriner, ed., *Contrasts in emerging societies*, Athlone Press, London (1965)

Prochazka, Z., *The labour force of Bulgaria*, Bureau of Census, Washington, D.C. (1962)

Sanders, I. T., 'Balkan rural societies and war', in B. K. Kiraly and G. E. Rothenberg, eds, *War and society in east central Europe*, Brooklyn College Press, New York (1979)

Todorov, N., 'The Balkan town in the second half of the nineteenth century', *Etudes Balkaniques*, 2 (1969)

Warriner, D., ed., *Contrasts in emerging societies. Readings in the social and economic history of south-eastern Europe in the nineteenth century*, Athlone Press, London (1965)

Yanouloff, I., 'Labour legislation in Bulgaria', *International Labour Review*, 10 (1924)

ROMANIA

Ardeleanu, I., 'The United Workers' Front. Its historic significance', *Romania*, 4 (1979) [workers' organisations 1843–1944]

Bodea, C., *The Romanians' struggle for unification, 1834–49*, Publishing House of the Academy of the Socialist Republic of Romania, Bucharest (1970)

Boia, L., *Eugene Brote (1850–1912)*, Editura Litera, Bucharest (1974) [broad treatment of economic and cultural development of Romania]

Cernovodeanu, P., 'The setting up of the English consulate in the Romanian principalities (1803) and its activity until 1807', *Revue Romaine d'Etudes Internationales*, 5 (1971)

Cernovodeanu, P., *England's trade policy in the Levant and her exchange of goods with the Romanian countries under the latter Stuarts (1660–1714)*, Publishing House of the Socialist Republic of Romania, Bucharest (1972)

Cernovodeanu, P., 'British economic interests in the lower Danube and the Balkan shore of the Black Sea between 1803–29', *Journal of European Economic History*, 5 (1976)

Cernovodeanu, P., and B. Marinescu, 'British trade in the Danubian ports of Galatz and Braila between 1837–57', *Journal of European Economic History*, 8 (1979)

Chirot, D., and C. Ragin, 'The market. Tradition and peasant rebellion. The case of Romania in 1907', *American Sociological Review*, 40 (1975)

Constantinescu, N. N., 'The problem of industrial revolution in Romania', *Revue Romaine des Sciences Sociales: Série des Sciences Economiques*, 20 (1976)

Constantinescu, N. N., and V. V. Axenciuc, 'The economic development of Romania in the period between 1919–39', *Papers in East European Economics* (1972)

Dutu, A., 'Romanian centres of cultural diffusion in the seventeenth and eighteenth centuries', *Romania*, 4 (1979)

Eidelberg, P. G., *The great Romanian peasant revolt of 1907. Origins of a modern jacquerie*, E. J. Brill, Leiden (1974)

Evans, I. L., *The agrarian revolution in Roumania*, Cambridge University Press, Cambridge (1924)

Fischer-Galati, S., *Twentieth century Romania*, Columbia University Press, New York (1970)

Florescu, R. R., *The struggle against Russia in the Romanian principalities*, Societas Academica Decoromana, Monachii (1962)

Ghiulea, N., 'Labour organisations in Romania', *International Labour Review*, 9 (1924)

Giurescu, C. C., *A history of the Romanian forest*, Editura Academiei Republicii Socialiste Romania, Bucharest (1980)

Giurescu, C. C., *Illustrated history of the Romanian people*, Sport-Turism, Bucharest (1981)

Gorni, O., 'Land reform in Romania', *International Labour Review*, 22 (1930)

Gutkind, E. A., *et al.*, *International history of city development*, vol. 8, *Urban development in eastern Europe. Bulgaria, Romania and the U.S.S.R.*, Collier-Macmillan, London (1972)

Hall, D. J., *Romanian furrow*, Methuen, London (1933)

Herlihy, P., 'Travel accounts as a historical source for nineteenth century Romania', *Revue des Etudes Sud-est Européennes*, 13 (1975)

Hitchins, K., *The Romanian national movement in Transylvania, 1780–1849*, Harvard University Press, Cambridge, Mass. (1969)

Hope, T. J., 'Britain and the Black Sea trade in the late eighteenth century', *Revue Roumaine d'Etudes Internationales*, 7 (1974)

Jensen, J. H., and G. Rosegger, 'British railway builders along the lower Danube, 1856–69', *Slavonic and East European Review*, 46 (1968)

Lampe, J. R., 'Modernization and social structure. The case of the pre-1914 Balkan capitals', *Southeastern Europe*, 5 (1978)

Liveanu, V., 'The socialist movement in a developing country. From the history of socialist ideas in Romania (1905–16)', *Revue des Etudes Sud-est Européennes*, 17 (1979)

Logio, G. C., *Rumania. Its history, politics and economics*, Sherratt and Hughes, Manchester (1932)

Madgearu, V., *Rumania's new economic policy*, P. S. King, London (1930)

Marcu, P., 'A great man. Ioan C. Frimu', *Romania*, 4 (1979) [labour organisation in Romania, 1900–20]

Marinescu, B., 'Economic relations between the Romanian principalities and Great Britain (1848–59)', *Revue Romaine d'Historie*, 8 (1969)

Marinescu, B., 'Aspect of economic relations between Romania and Great Britain (1862–66)', *Revue Romaine d'Histoire*, 18 (1979)

Mitrany, D., *The land and the peasant in Rumania. The war and agrarian reform (1917–21)*, Oxford University Press, London (1930)

Pearton, M., *Oil and the Romanian state, 1895–1948*, Clarendon Press, Oxford (1971)

Radulescu-Zoner, S., 'Contributions to the history of the customs war between Romania and Austria-Hungary', *Revue Romaine d'Etudes Internationales*, 1 (1972)

Riker, T. W., *The making of Roumania. A study of an international problem, 1856–66*, Oxford University Press, London (1931)

Roberts, H. L., *Rumania. Political problems of an agrarian state*, Yale University Press, New Haven,

Conn. (1951)

Roucek, J. S., *Contemporary Roumania and her problems. A study in modern nationalism,* Stanford University Press, Stanford, Cal. (1932)

Seton-Watson, R. W., *A history of the Roumanians,* Cambridge University Press, Cambridge (1934)

Stahl, H. H., *Traditional Romanian village communities. The transition from the communal to the capitalist mode of production in the Danube region,* Cambridge University Press, Cambridge (1980)

Stefanescu, S., 'Independence and modernity in nineteenth century Romania', *Southeastern Europe,* 5 (1978)

Tappe, E. D., *et al.,* 'Rumania', in D. Warriner, ed., *Contrasts in emerging societies,* Athlone Press, London (1965)

Turnock, D., *An economic geography of Romania,* G. Bell, London (1974)

Turnock, D., 'The industrialization of Romania from the unification of principalities to the second world war', in F. W. Carter, ed., *An historical geography of the Balkans,* Academic Press, London (1977)

Turnock, D., 'The Romanian railway debate. A theme in political geography', *Journal of Transport History,* 5 (1979)

Turnock, D., 'Bucharest. Historical perspectives of the Romanian capital', *History Today,* 30 (1980)

Ussoskin, M., *Struggle for survival. A history of Jewish credit co-operatives in Bessarabia, old Rumania, Bukovina and Transylvania,* Jerusalem Academic Press, Jerusalem (1975)

Warriner, D., ed., *Contrasts in emerging societies. Readings in the social and economic history of south-eastern Europe in the nineteenth century,* Athlone Press, London (1965)

RUSSIA/SOVIET UNION

GENERAL ECONOMIC AND SOCIAL HISTORY

Abramovitch, R. R., *The Soviet revolution, 1917–39,* Allen and Unwin, London (1962)

Abramson, A., 'The economic development of the Soviet Union under the second and third Five Year Plans', *International Labour Review,* 41 (1940)

Alexinsky, G., *Modern Russia,* T. F. Unwin, London (1915) [considerable attention to economic and social topics]

Ali, A. S., *Economic development of the Soviet Union,* Ideal Library, Dacca (1966)

Allen, W. E. D., *The Ukraine. A history,* Cambridge University Press, Cambridge (1940)

American Bankers Association, *Russia. A consideration of conditions as revealed by Soviet publications,* Commission on Commerce and Marine of the American Bankers Association, New York (1922)

American-Russian Chamber of Commerce, *Economic handbook of the Soviet Union,* Chamber of Commerce, New York (1931)

American Trade Union Delegation, *Russia after ten years,* Report of the American Trade Union Delegation to the Soviet Union, International Publishers, New York (1927)

Anderson, M. S., 'Russia under Peter the Great and the changed relations of East and West', in J. S. Bromley, ed., *The New Cambridge Modern History,* vol. 6, Cambridge University Press, London (1970)

Anderson, O., 'Economic warfare in the Crimean war', *Economic History Review,* 14 (1961–62)

Balzak, S. S., ed., *Economic geography of the U.S.S.R.,* Macmillan, New York (1949) [covers Tsarist period also]

Baran, P. A., 'National income and product of the U.S.S.R. in 1940', *Review of Economics and Statistics,* 29 (1947)

Baring, M., *The mainsprings of Russia,* Nelson, London (1914)

Baron, S. H., 'The transition from feudalism to capitalism in Russia. A major Soviet historical controversy', *American Historical Review,* 77 (1972)

Barransky, N. N., *Economic geography of the U.S.S.R.,* Foreign Languages Publishing House, Moscow (1956)

Baykov, A., 'Remarks on the experiences in the organisation of "war economy" in the U.S.S.R.', *Economic Journal,* 51 (1941) [considerable data on economic topics 1928–40]

Baykov, A., *The development of the Soviet economic system,* National Institute for Economic and Social Research, London (1946)

Baykov, A., 'The economic development of Russia',

Economic History Review, 7 (1954–55)

Bergson, A., 'Soviet national income and product in 1937', parts 1 and 2, *Quarterly Journal of Economics*, 64 (1950)

Bergson, A., ed., *Soviet economic growth*, Row Peterson, Evanston, Ill. (1953)

Bergson, A., *The real national income of Soviet Russia since 1928*, Harvard University Press, Cambridge, Mass. (1961)

Bergson, A., and S. Kuznets, *Economic trends in the Soviet Union*, Harvard University Press, Cambridge, Mass. (1963)

Black, C. E., *et al.*, *The modernization of Japan and Russia. A comparative study*, Collier-Macmillan, London (1975)

Blackwell, W. L., *The industrialization of Russia. An historical perspective*, AHM Publishing Corporation, Arlington Heights, Ill. (1970)

Blackwell, W. L., ed., *Russian economic development. From Peter the Great to Stalin*, New Viewpoints, New York (1974)

Bromley, J. S., ed., *The rise of Great Britain and Russia, 1688–1715/25*, The New Cambridge Modern History, vol. 6, Cambridge University Press, Cambridge (1970)

Burns, E., *Russia's economic system*, E. P. Dutton, New York (1930)

Carr, E. H., *A history of Soviet Russia*, 3 vols, Macmillan, London, vol. 1, *The Bolshevik revolution, 1917–23* (1950–53), vol. 2, *The interregnum, 1923–24*, (1954), vol. 3, *Socialism in one country, 1924–26*, (1958–64)

Carr, E. H., 'Some random reflexions on Soviet industrialization', in C. H. Feinstein, ed., *Socialism, capitalism and economic growth. Essays presented to Maurice Dobb*, Cambridge University Press, Cambridge (1967)

Carr, E. H., *The Russian revolution. From Lenin to Stalin*, Macmillan, London (1979) [a summary volume of Carr's authoritative fourteen volume work on the 1920s]

Carr, E. H., *From Napoleon to Stalin and other essays*, Macmillan, London (1981)

Carr, E. H., and R. W. Davies, *A history of Soviet Russia*, 3 vols, vol. 4, *Foundations of a planned economy, 1926–29*, Macmillan, London (1969–78)

Central Statistical Administration, *The U.S.S.R. economy. A statistical abstract*, Lawrence and Wishart, London (1957)

Central Statistical Board (U.S.S.R.), *Soviet Union. 50 years. Statistical returns*, Central Statistical Board, Moscow (1969)

Chakrabarti, S. C., *et al.*, *Economic development of the Soviet Union*, Nababharat Publishers, Calcutta (rev. 2nd edn 1965)

Chamberlin, W. H., *Soviet Russia. A living record*, Little Brown, Boston, Mass. (1930)

Chamberlin, W. H., *The Ukraine. A submerged nation*, Macmillan, New York (1944)

Chirovsky, N. L. F., *The economic factors in the growth of Russia. An economic-historical analysis*, Philosophical Library, New York (1957)

Chirovsky, N. L. F., *Old Ukraine. Its socio-economic history prior to 1781*, Florham Park Press, Madison, N.J. (1963)

Clarke, R. A., *Soviet economic facts, 1917–70. A statistical handbook*, Macmillan, London (1972)

Cohen, S. F., 'Stalin's revolution reconsidered', *Slavic Review*, 32 (1973)

Cohn, S. H., 'The Soviet economy. Performance and growth', *Studies on the Soviet Union*, 6 (1967)

Cohn, S. H., *Economic development in the Soviet Union*, D. C. Heath, Lexington, Mass. (1970)

Colton, E., 'The test of communist economic resources', *Slavonic and East European Review*, 11 (1932)

Conquest, R., *The great terror*, Macmillan, London (1973)

Crisp, O., 'The pattern of Russian industrialisation up to 1914', in P. Leon, *et al.*, *L'Industrialisation en Europe au XIXe siècle. Cartographie et typologie*, Editions du Centre national de la recherche scientifique, Paris (1972)

Crisp, O., 'The economic history of pre-reform Russia', *Slavonic and East European Review*, 51 (1973)

Crisp, O., *Studies in the Russian economy before 1914*, Macmillan, London (1976)

DaCosta, E. P. W., *The economic progress of Russia, 1860–1948*, Eastern Economist, New Delhi (1952)

Datta, A., *A century of economic development of Russia and Japan*, World Press, Calcutta (1963)

Dean, V. M., *Soviet Russia, 1917–36*, World Peace Foundation, Boston, Mass., (rev. 3rd edn, 1936) [industrial system and agrarian change considered]

Deane, P., 'Measuring Soviet economic growth', *Soviet Studies*, 14 (1962–63)

Deutscher, I., 'The Russian revolution', in D. Thompson, ed., *The New Cambridge Modern History*, vol. 12, Cambridge University Press, London (1960)

Dymtryshyn, B., ed., *Modernization of Russia under Peter I and Catherine II*, Wiley, New York (1974)

Dmytryshyn, B., *A history of Russia*, Prentice-Hall,

Englewood Cliffs, N.J. (1977)

Dobb, M., 'Comment on Soviet economic statistics', *Soviet Studies*, 1 (1949–50)

Dobb, M., *Soviet economic development since 1917*, Routledge, London (1966)

Dobb, M. H., and H. C. Stevens, *Russian economic development since the revolution*, E. P. Dutton, New York (1928)

Dohan, M. R., 'The economic origins of Soviet autarky, 1927/28–34', *Slavic Review*, 35 (1976)

Dolan, E. G., 'Structural interdependence of the Soviet economy before the industrialization drive', *Soviet Studies*, 19 (1967)

Drage, G., *Russian affairs*, J. Murray, London (1904)

Dyason, J., 'Russia – 1900–36. A statistical interpretation', *Economic Record*, 13 (1937)

Eckstein, A., and P. Gutmann, 'Capital and output in the Soviet Union, 1928–37', *Review of Economics and Statistics*, 38 (1956) [measurement of incremental capital output ratio]

Ellison, H. J., 'Economic modernisation in imperial Russia. Purposes and achievements', *Journal of Economic History*, 25 (1965)

Erlich, A., *The Soviet industrialization debate, 1924–28*, Harvard University Press, Cambridge, Mass. (1967)

Fainsod, M., *How Russia is ruled*, Harvard University Press, Cambridge, Mass. (rev. edn 1965)

Falkus, M. E., 'The beginning of industrial growth in Russia and Japan', in M. E. Falkus, ed., *Readings in the history of economic growth*, Oxford University Press, London (1968)

Falkus, M. E., 'Russia's national income, 1913. A revaluation', *Economica*, 35 (1968)

Falkus, M. E., *The industrialization of Russia, 1700–1914*, Macmillan, London (1972)

Fallenbuchl, Z. M., 'Collectivization and economic development', *Canadian Journal of Economics and Political Science*, 33 (1967)

Feller, A., 'The Soviet Union and the business cycle', *Social Research*, 3 (1936)

Ferguson, A. D., and A. Levin, eds, *Essays in Russian history. A collection dedicated to George Vernodsky*, Archon Books, Hamden, Conn. (1964)

First National City Bank of New York, *Russia and the imperial Russian government. Economic and financial*, First National City Bank, New York (1916)

Florinsky, M. T., *The end of the Russian empire. A study in the economic and social history of the war*, Oxford University Press, London (1931)

Florinsky, M. T., 'Soviet Russia', in J. T. Shorwell, ed., *Governments of continental Europe*, Macmillan, New York (1940)

Florinsky, M. T., *Russia. A history and an interpretation*, 2 vols, Macmillan, New York (1953)

Florinsky, M. T., *Russia. A short history*, Macmillan, New York (1964)

Frank, A. G., 'General productivity in Soviet agriculture and industry. The Ukraine, 1928–55', *Journal of Political Economy*, 66 (1958)

Friedman, E. M., *Russia in transition. A businessman's appraisal*, Viking Press, New York (1932)

Gerschenkron, A., 'An economic history of Russia', *Journal of Economic History*, 12 (1952) [review of Lyashchenko's book]

Gerschenkron, A., 'Problems and patterns of Russian economic development', in C. E. Black, ed., *The transformation of Russian society. Aspects of social change since 1861*, Harvard University Press, Cambridge, Mass. (1960)

Gerschenkron, A., *Economic backwardness in historical perspective. A book of essays*, Belknap Press, Cambridge, Mass. (1962)

Gerschenkron, A., 'The early phases of industrialization in Russia. Afterthoughts and counterthoughts', in W. W. Rostow, ed., *The economics of take-off into sustained growth*, Macmillan, London (1963)

Gerschenkron, A., 'Russia. Patterns and problems of economic development, 1861–1958', in A. Gerschenkron, *Economic backwardness in historical perspective*, Harvard University Press, Cambridge, Mass. (1965)

Gerschenkron, A., 'Agrarian policies and industrialization. Russia 1861–1917', in H. J. Habakkuk and M. M. Postan, eds, *Cambridge Economic History of Europe*, vol. 6(2), Cambridge University Press, Cambridge (1965)

Gerschenkron, A., *Europe in the Russian mirror. Four lectures in economic history*, Cambridge University Press, Cambridge (1970)

Gibson, J. R., 'The significance of Siberia to Tsarist Russia', *Canadian Slavonic Papers*, 14 (1972)

Gibson, J. R., 'Russian expansion in Siberia and America', *Geographical Review*, 70 (1980)

Giesinger, A., 'The first statistical report of the Volga colonies', *Journal of the American Historical Society of Germans from Russia*, 25 (1977)

Goldsmith, R. W., 'The economic growth of Tsarist Russia, 1860–1913', *Economic Development and Cultural Change*, 9 (1961)

Goldstein, J. M., *Russia. Her economic past and future*, Russian Information Bureau, New York (1919)

Gregory, P. R., 'Economic growth and structural change in Tsarist Russia. A case of modern economic growth', *Soviet Studies,* 23 (1971–72)

Gregory, P. R., 'Some empirical comments on the theory of relative backwardness. The Russian case', *Economic Development and Cultural Change,* 22 (1973–74)

Gregory, P. R., 'Russian national income in 1913. Some insights into Russian economic development', *Quarterly Journal of Economics,* 90 (1976)

Gregory, P. R., 'Russian industrialization and economic growth. Results and perspectives of Western research', *Jahrbücher für Geschichte Osteuropas,* 25 (1980)

Gregory, P. R., 'Valueless goods and social goods in the measurement of Soviet output series, 1928–32', *Slavic Review,* 39 (1980)

Gregory, P. R., *Russian national income, 1885–1913,* Cambridge University Press, Cambridge (1982)

Grossman, G., 'The industrialisation of Russia and the Soviet Union', in C. M. Cipolla, ed., *The emergence of industrial societies.* Fontana Economic History of Europe, vol. 4, part 2, Collins Fontana, Glasgow (1973)

H.M.S.O., *A handbook of Siberia and arctic Russia,* H.M.S.O., London (1923?) [contains general account of economic conditions, colonisation, Siberian railways, agriculture]

Hardt, J. P., and C. Modig, *The industrialization of Soviet Russia in the first half-century,* Research Analysis Corporation, McLean, Va. (1968)

Haxthausen, Baron A. von, *The Russian empire. Its people, institutions and resources,* 2 vols, Chapman and Hall, London (1856, rep. 1962)

Heyking, A. B., 'The economic resources of Russia, with special reference to British opportunities', *Journal of the Royal Statistical Society,* 80 (1917)

Hirsch, A., *Industrialized Russia,* Chemical Catalog Company, New York (1934)

Hoeffding, O., *Soviet national income and product in 1928,* Columbia University Press, New York (1954)

Holdsworth, M., 'Soviet central Asia, 1917–40', *Soviet Studies,* 4 (1951–52)

Hoover, C. B., 'Some economic and social consequences of Russian communism', *Economic Journal,* 40 (1930)

Hoover, C. B., *Economic life of Soviet Russia,* Macmillan, New York (1931)

Hourwich, I. A., 'The economic condition of Russia', *Journal of Political Economy,* 12 (1904)

Hovannisian, R. G., *Armenia on the road to independence, 1918,* University of California Press, Berkeley, Cal. (1967)

Hrushevsky, M., *A history of Ukraine,* Archon Books, Hamden, Conn. (1970)

Hunter, H., 'Soviet industrial growth. The early plan period', *Journal of Economic History,* 15 (1955)

Hunter, H., 'The economic costs of the Gulag Archipelago', *Slavic Review,* 39 (1980) [inter-war Soviet economic development]

Hutchings, R., *Soviet economic development,* Blackwell, Oxford (1971)

Iugov, A., *Russia's economic front for war and peace. An appraisal of the three Five Year Plans,* Harper, New York (1942)

Institute of Conjuncture, *Economic conditions in the U.S.S.R. after war and revolution,* Institute of Conjuncture, Moscow (1928)

International Labour Office, 'The problem of labour output in Soviet Russia', *International Labour Review,* 13 (1926)

Jasny, N., 'Intricacies of Russian national income indexes, *Journal of Political Economy,* 55 (1947) [data on aggregate national income 1928–38]

Jatsunsky, V. K., 'Industrialisation of Russia before 1917', *Papers presented to the first international economic history conference, Stockholm, 1960,* Mouton, Paris (1960)

Kafenganz, B. B., 'Some problems of the genesus of capitalism in Russia', in V. V. Mavrodin, ed., *Voprosy genezisa kapitalizma v Rossii,* Leningrad University Press, Leningrad (1960)

Kahan, A., 'The costs of "westernization" in Russia. The gentry and the economy in the eighteenth century', *Slavic Review,* 25 (1966)

Kahan, A., 'Social structure, public policy and the development of education and the economy in Czarist Russia', in C. A. Anderson, and M. J. Bowman, eds, *Education and economic development,* Cass, London (1966)

Kaser, M. C., 'Education in Tsarist and Soviet development', in C. Abramsky, ed., *Essays in honour of E. H. Carr,* Macmillan, London (1974)

Katkov, G., *et al., Russia enters the twentieth century, 1894–1917,* Methuen, London (1973)

Katz, B. G., 'Purges and production. Soviet economic growth, 1928–40', *Journal of Economic History,* 35 (1975)

Kazakevich, V. D., 'The economic strength of the Soviet Union', *Science and Society,* 5 (1941) [data on industrial output 1900–40]

Keep, J., 'Russia', in F. H. Hinsley, ed., *The New*

Cambridge Modern History, vol. 11, Cambridge University Press, London (1962)

Kliuchevskii, V. O., *A history of Russia,* 5 vols, Dent, London (1911–31)

Kochan, L., *The making of modern Russia,* Jonathan Cape, London (1962)

Kononenko, K., *Ukraine and Russia, A history of economic relations between Ukraine and Russia, 1654–1917,* Marquette University Press, Milwaukee, Wis. (1958)

Kovaltchenko, I. D., 'Peculiarities of the genesis of capitalism in Russia in the seventeenth to eighteenth centuries', *Papers presented to the fourth international conference of economic history, Bloomington, 1968,* Mouton, Paris (1973)

Kozmin, P. A., 'Some features of the Russian economic situation', *Journal of Political Economy,* 12 (1904)

Lawton, L., *An economic history of Soviet Russia,* 2 vols, Macmillan, London (1932)

Leites, K., *Recent economic developments in Russia,* Clarendon Press, Oxford (1922)

Litoshenko, L. N., 'The national income of the Soviet Union', *Quarterly Journal of Economics,* 42 (1928)

Lloyd, T., 'The economic condition of Russia', *Economic Journal,* 2 (1892)

Lorwin, L. L., and A. Abramson, 'The present state of economic and social development in the U.S.S.R.', *International Labour Review,* 33 (1936)

Lyashchenko, P. I., *History of the national economy of Russia to the 1917 revolution,* Macmillan, New York (1949)

McCauley, M., *Soviet Union since 1917,* Longman, Harlow, (1981)

MacKenzie, D., 'Turkestan's significance to Russia (1850–1917)', *Russian Review,* 33 (1974)

Madariaga, I., *Russia in the age of Catherine the Great,* Yale University Press, New Haven, Conn. (1981)

Maddison, A., *Economic growth in Japan and the U.S.S.R.,* Allen and Unwin, London (1969)

Mavor, J., *An economic history of Russia,* 2 vols, Russell and Russell, New York (rev. 2nd edn 1965)

Maynard, G., 'Japan and the U.S.S.R.', in G. Maynard, *Economic development and the price level,* Macmillan, London (1963)

Maynard, J., *Russia in flux. Before the October revolution,* Collier, New York (1962)

Mazour, A. G., *Soviet economic development. Operation Outstrip, 1921–65,* Van Nostrand, Princeton, N.J. (1967)

Mieczkowski, Z., 'The economic regionalization of the Soviet Union in the Lenin and Stalin period', *Canadian Slavonic Papers,* 8 (1966)

Miller, M. S., *The economic development of Russia, 1905–14, with special reference to trade, industry and finance,* P. S. King, London (1926)

Minkoff, J., 'Estimating the Soviet wage bill from the receipts of the social insurance system', *Slavic Review,* 20 (1961) [mainly deals with 1937–58]

Montgomery, A., 'Production and ideology in the Soviet Union', *Scandinavian Economic History Review,* 4 (1956)

Moorsteen, R., and R. P. Powell, *The Soviet capital stock, 1928–62,* Richard D. Irwin, Homewood, Ill. (1966)

Mosse, W. E., *Alexander II and the modernization of Russia,* Macmillan, New York (1958)

Munting, R., *The economic development of the U.S.S.R.,* Croom Helm, London (1982)

Nolde, B. E., *Russia in the economic war,* Yale University Press, New Haven, Conn. (1928)

Nordman, N., *Peace problems. Russia's economics,* Putney Press, London (1919) [analyses Russian pre-war and wartime economy]

Notzold, J., 'Agrarian questions and industrialization in Russia on the eve of the first world war', *Saeculum,* 17 (1966)

Nove, A., 'Soviet national income statistics', *Soviet Studies,* 6 (1954–55)

Nove, A., *Was Stalin really necessary? Some problems of Soviet political economy,* Allen and Unwin, London (1964)

Nove, A., 'Russia as an emergent country', in A. J. Youngson, ed., *Economic development in the long run,* Allen and Unwin, London (1972)

Nove, A., *An economic history of the U.S.S.R.,* Penguin, Harmondsworth (1975)

Oberlander, E., *et al., Russia enters the twentieth century, 1894–1917,* Shocken, New York (1971)

Parker, W. H., *An historical geography of Russia,* Athlone Press, London (1968)

Pervushin, S. A., 'Cyclical fluctuations in agriculture and industry in Russia, 1869-1926', *Quarterly Journal of Economics,* 42 (1928)

Pethybridge, R., *A history of post-war Russia,* Allen and Unwin, London (1966)

Pethybridge, R., 'Political repercussions of the supply problem in the Russian revolution of 1917', *Russian Review,* 29 (1970)

Pethybridge, R., 'The Bolsheviks and technical disorder, 1917–18', *Slavonic and East European Review,* 49 (1971)

Pethybridge, R., *The spread of the Russian*

revolution. Essays on 1917, Macmillan, London (1972)

Pierce, R. A., *Russian central Asia, 1867–1917. A study in colonial rule,* University of California Press, Berkeley, Cal. (1960)

Pipes, R., *Russia under the old regime,* Weidenfeld and Nicolson, London (1974)

Pokrovsky, M. N., *Brief history of Russia,* 2 vols, International Publishers, New York (1933) [considerable attention to economic matters]

Popluiko, A., 'The economic development of pre-revolutionary Russia', *Studies on the Soviet Union,* 1 (1957)

Poppe, N., 'The economic and cultural development of Siberia', in E. Oberlander *et al., Russia enters the twentieth century,* Schocken, New York, (1971)

Portal, R., 'The problem of an industrial revolution in Russia in the nineteenth century', in S. Harcave, ed., *Readings in Russian History,* Crowell, New York (1962)

Portal, R., 'The industrialization of Russia', in H. J. Habakkuk and M. M. Postan, eds, *Cambridge Economic History of Europe,* vol. 6(2), Cambridge University Press, Cambridge (1965)

Prokopovitch, S. N., *The economic condition of Soviet Russia,* P. S. King, London (1924)

Prociuk, S. G., 'Russian intervention in early Ukrainian planning', *Soviet Studies,* 15 (1964)

Prybyla, J. S., 'Private enterprise in the Soviet Union', *South African Journal of Economics,* 29 (1961)

Pushkarev, S. G., *The emergence of modern Russia, 1801–1917,* Holt Rinehart and Winston, New York (1963)

Putman, G. E., 'Russian economic situation', *American Economic Review,* 21 (1931)

Raeff, M., *Imperial Russia, 1682–1825,* Knopf, New York (1971)

Rafalovich, A. G., 'Some effects of the war on the economic life of Russia'. *Economic Journal,* 27 (1917)

Riasanovsky, N. V., 'The Russian empire as an under-developed country', *Slavic Review,* 20 (1961)

Riasanovsky, N. V., *A history of Russia,* Oxford University Press, London (2nd edn 1969)

Richards, M., 'Reform, reaction, revolution. Russia, 1894–1917', in H. T. Parker, ed., *Problems in European history,* Moore Publications, Durham, N.C. (1979)

Rigby, T. H., *et al., Authority, power and policy in the U.S.S.R. Essays dedicated to Leonard Schapiro,* St Martin's Press, New York (1980)

Roberts, P. C., 'War communism. A re-examination', *Slavic Review,* 29 (1970)

Ronimois, H. E., 'Soviet experiment with communist economy, 1918–20', *Canadian Slavonic Papers,* 2 (1957)

Roosa, R. A., 'Russian industrialists look to the future. Thoughts on economic development', in J. S. Curtiss, ed., *Essays in Russian and Soviet history in honour of Geroid Tanquary Robinson,* E. J. Brill, Leiden (1963)

Ropes, E. C., 'The statistical publications of the U.S.S.R.', *Russian Review,* 1 (1941) [publications of Central Statistical Administration from 1923]

Rosefielde, S., 'The first "Great Leap Forward" reconsidered. Lessons of Solzhenitsyn's *Gulag Archipelago*', *Slavic Review,* 39 (1980)

Rosovsky, H., ed., *Industrialization in two systems. Essays in honour of Alexander Gerschenkron,* Wiley, New York (1966)

Schweinitz, K. de, 'Industrialization labour controls and democracy', *Economic Development and Cultural Change,* 7 (1958–59)

Serck-Hanssen, J., 'Input–output tables in the U.S.S.R. and eastern Europe', *Economics of Planning,* 3 (1963) [reviews input–output approach from 1920s to 1959]

Seton, F., 'The social accounts of the Soviet Union in 1934', *Review of Economics and Statistics,* 36 (1954)

Seton-Watson, H., *The decline of imperial Russia, 1855–1914,* Methuen, London (1952)

Seton-Watson, H., 'Russia and modernization', *Slavic Review,* 20 (1961)

Singh, V. B., and V. V. Reddy, 'Soviet economic development', in V. B. Singh, ed., *Patterns of economic development. A study of the economic development of the U.K., U.S.A., Japan, the U.S.S.R. and China,* Allied Publishers, Bombay (1970) [covers the period 1861–1960]

Sinzheimer, G. P. G., 'Reflections on Gerschenkron, Russian backwardness and economic development', *Soviet Studies,* 17 (1965–66)

Skerpan, A. A., 'The Russian national economy and emancipation', in A. D. Ferguson and A. Levin, eds, *Essays in Russian history,* Archon Books, Hamden, Conn. (1964)

Sumner, B. H., *Survey of Russian history,* Methuen, London (1961)

Sutton, A. C., *Western technology and Soviet economic development,* vol. 1, *1917–30,* vol. 2, *1930–45,* Stanford University Press, Stanford, Cal. (1968, 1971)

Thalheim, K. C., 'Russia's economic development', in E. Oberlander, ed., *Russia enters the twentieth century, 1894–1917*, Schocken, New York (1971)

Thornton, J. G., 'The index number problem in the measurement of Soviet national income', *Journal of Economic History*, 22 (1962)

Thornton, J. G., 'Factors in the recent decline in Soviet growth', *Slavic Review*, 25 (1966)

Timashev, N. S., *The great retreat. The growth and decline of communism in Russia*, E. P. Dutton, New York (1946) [considerable attention to economic topics]

Trivanovich, V., *Crankshafts or bread*, Acorn Publishing Company, Ridgfield, Conn. (1940)

Turgeon, L., 'Cost-price relationships in basic industries during the Soviet planning era', *Soviet Studies*, 9 (1957–58)

Turin, S. P., *The U.S.S.R. An economic and social survey*, Methuen, London (1944)

Venadsky, G., *A history of Russia*, Yale University Press, New Haven, Conn. (rev. 6th edn 1969)

Venturi, F., *Roots of revolution*, Weidenfeld and Nicolson, London (1960)

Von Laue, T. H., 'Count Witte and the Russian revolution of 1905', *Slavic Review*, 17 (1958)

Von Laue, T. H., 'The state and the economy', in C. E. Black, ed., *The transformation of Russian society. Aspects of social change since 1861*, Harvard University Press, Cambridge, Mass. (1960)

Von Laue, T. H., 'The crises in Russian polity' in J. S. Curtiss, ed., *Essays in Russian and Soviet history in honour of Geroid Tanquary Robinson*, E. J. Brill, Leiden (1963)

Von Laue, T. H., *Why Lenin? Why Stalin? A reappraisal of the Russian revolution, 1900–30*, Weidenfeld and Nicolson, London (1966)

Webster, C. J., 'The economic development of the Soviet Arctic and sub-Arctic', *Slavonic and East European Review*, 29 (1950)

Weissman, B. M., 'The after-effects of the American relief mission to Soviet Russia', *Russian Review*, 29 (1970)

Winterton, P. 'Soviet economic development since 1928', *Economic Journal*, 43 (1933)

Wohlmuth, K., 'The growth of the capital stock in the Soviet Union', *Kyklos*, 23 (1970)

Wolfe, B. D., 'Backwardness and industrialization in Russian history and thought', *Slavic Review*, 26 (1967)

Yarmolinsky, A., ed., *The memoirs of Count Witte*, Doubleday Page, Garden City, N.Y. (1921)

Yatsunsky, V. K., 'Main features of industrialization in Russia before 1917', *Papers presented to the first international economic history conference, Stockholm, 1960*, Mouton, Paris (1960)

Yurievsky, E., 'The development of Russia before 1917', *Studies on the Soviet Union*, 1 (1957)

Zauberman, A., 'Russia and eastern Europe, 1920–70', in C. M. Cipolla, ed., *Contemporary economies*, Fontana Economic History of Europe, vol. 6, part 2, Collins/Fontana, Glasgow (1976)

Zavalani, T., *How strong is Russia?* Hollis and Carter, London (1951)

AGRICULTURE AND RURAL SOCIETY

Anonymous, 'Soviet agricultural legislation', parts 1 and 2, *Slavonic and East European Review*, 10 (1931) [verbatim translations of regulations concerning agriculture]

Anonymous, 'The collectivization of agriculture in the U.S.S.R.', *International Labour Review*, 26 (1932)

Anonymous, 'The collectivization campaign in Uzbekistan, 1927–33', *Central Asian Review*, 12 (1964)

Antsiferov, A. N., *et al.*, *Russian agriculture during the war. Rural economy*, Yale University Press, New Haven, Conn. (1930)

Atkinson, D., 'The statistics on the Russian land commune, 1905–17', *Slavic Review*, 32 (1973)

Auhagen, O., 'Agriculture', in G. Dobbert, ed., *Red economics*, Houghton Mifflin, Boston (1932)

Baikalov, A. V., 'Bolshevist agrarian policy', *Slavonic and East European Review*, 8 (1930)

Baker, A. B., 'Deterioration or development? The peasant economy of Moscow province prior to 1914', *Russian History*, 5 (1978)

Bass, R. H., *Force versus food. A short history of agriculture in the Soviet sphere*, Free Europe Press, New York (1957)

Baykov, A., 'Agricultural development in the U.S.S.R.', *Bulletins on Soviet Economic Development*, 2 (1949)

Belov, F., *The history of a collective farm*, Praeger, New York (1955)

Bennett, M. K., 'Food and agriculture in the Soviet Union, 1917–48', *Journal of Political Economy*, 57 (1949)

Blum, J., 'The early history of the Russian peasantry', *Journal of Economic History*, 11 (1951)

Blum, J., 'Russian agriculture in the last 150 years of serfdom', *Agricultural History*, 34 (1960)

Blum, J., *Lord and peasant in Russia from the ninth to the nineteenth century*, Princeton University

Press, Princeton, N.J. (1961)

Boev, V. R., 'Agricultural production and the rural standard of living in the U.S.S.R. since 1917', *International Labour Review,* 87 (1963)

Brower, D. R., 'Collectivized agriculture in Smolensk. The party, the peasantry, and the crisis of 1932', *The Russian Review,* 36 (1977)

Brown, J. H., 'The publication and distribution of the *Trudy* of the Free Economic Society', *Russian Review,* 36 (1977) [agricultural periodical, 1765–96]

Brubaker, E. R., 'Developments of Soviet agriculture under a vintage model of production', *American Journal of Agricultural Economics,* 51 (1969) [see comments by D. G. Dalrymple, 52 (1970)]

Bulik, J. J., 'U.S.S.R. The fifteen-year afforestation plan', *Land Economics,* 25 (1949) [data on grain acreage and yields, 1917–40]

Carr, E. H., 'The Russian revolution and the peasant', *Proceedings of the British Academy,* 49 (1963)

Chamberlin, W. H., 'The ordeal of the Russian peasantry, *Russian Review,* 14 (1955)

Chayanov, A. V., *The theory of peasant economy,* Richard D. Irwin, Homewood, Ill. (1966)

Crisp, O., 'The state peasants under Nicholas I', *Slavonic Review,* 17 (1959)

Dalrymple, D. G., 'The Soviet famine of 1932–34', *Soviet Studies,* 15 (1963–65), 16 (1964–65)

Dalrymple, D. G., 'American technology and Soviet agricultural development, 1924–33', *Agricultural History,* 40 (1966)

Davies, R. W., *The socialist offensive. The collectivisation of Soviet agriculture, 1929–30,* Macmillan, London (1980)

Davies, R. W., *The Soviet collective farm,* Macmillan, London (1980)

Davison, R. M., Koshelyov and the emancipation of the serfs', *European Studies Review,* 3 (1973)

Dienes, L., 'Pasturalism in Turkestan. Its decline and its persistence', *Soviet Studies,* 27 (1975)

Dow, R., 'Seichas. A comparison of pre-reform Russia and the antebellum south', *Russian Review,* 7 (1947)

Drew, R. F., 'The emergence of an agricultural policy for Siberia in the seventeenth and eighteenth centuries', *Agricultural History,* 33 (1959)

Dubbs, H. H., 'Land hunger and nationalism in the Ukraine, 1905–17', *Journal of Economic History,* 2 (1942)

Dunn, S. P. and E., *The peasants of central Russia,* Holt Rinehart and Winston, New York (1967)

Eason, W. W., *The agricultural labour force and population of the U.S.S.R., 1926–41,* Rand Corporation, Santa Monica, Cal. (1954)

Edmondson, C. M., 'The politics of hunger. The Soviet response to famine, 1921', *Soviet Studies,* 29 (1977)

Ellison, H. J., 'The decision to collectivize agriculture', *Slavic Review,* 20 (1961)

Ely, R. T., 'Russian land reform', *American Economic Review,* 6 (1916)

Emmons, T., *The Russian landed gentry and the peasant emancipation of 1861,* Cambridge University Press, Cambridge (1968)

Emmons, T., 'The Russian landed gentry and politics', *Russian Review,* 33 (1974)

Fallows, T., 'Politics and the war effort in Russia. Union of *zemstvos* and the organization of the food supply, 1914–16', *Slavic Review,* 37 (1978)

Faucher, J., 'The Russian agrarian legislation of 1861', in J. W. Probyn, ed., *Systems of land tenure in various countries,* Cobden Club, London (1881)

Field, D., *The end of serfdom. Mobility and bureaucracy in Russia, 1855–61.* Harvard University Press, Cambridge, Mass. (1976)

Fisher, H. H., *Famine in Soviet Russia, 1919–23,* Macmillan, New York (1927)

Frank, A. G., 'Labour requirements in Soviet agriculture', *Review of Economics and Statistics,* 41 (1959)

Gerschenkron, A., 'An analysis of Soviet agriculture', *Journal of Economic History,* 11 (1951)

Gerschenkron, A., 'Lord and peasant in Russia from the ninth to the nineteenth century', *Journal of Economic History,* 24 (1964) [review article]

Gill, G. J., 'The failure of rural policy in Russia, February–October 1917', *Slavic Review,* 37 (1978)

Gregory, P. R., 'Grain marketing and peasant consumption, Russia, 1885–1913', *Explorations in Economic History,* 17 (1980)

Gubsky, N., 'The land settlement of Russia', *Economic Journal,* 31 (1921)

Haimson, L. H., ed., *The politics of rural Russia, 1905–14,* Indiana University Press, Bloomington, Ind. (1979)

Harris, L., 'Some comparisons of socialist and capitalist agriculture', *Science and Society,* 10 (1946)

Harrison, M., 'Chayanov and the economics of the Russian peasantry', *Journal of Peasant Studies,* 2 (1975)

Harrison, M., 'Resource allocation and agrarian class reform. The problems of social mobility among Russian peasant householders, 1880–1930', *Journal of Peasant Studies,* 4 (1977)

Hine, W., 'American slavery and Russian serfdom. A

preliminary comparison', *Phylon*, 36 (1975)

Hobsbawm, E. J., *et al., Peasants in history. Essays in honour of Daniel Thorner*, Oxford University Press, Calcutta (1980)

Honigsheim, P., 'The roots of the Soviet rural structure. Where and why it has spread', *Agricultural History*, 25 (1951)

Hourwich, I. A., *The economics of the Russian village. Studies in history, economics and public law*, Columbia College, New York (1892)

Hubbard, L. E., *The economics of Soviet agriculture*, Macmillan, London (1939)

International Labour Office, 'The collectivisation of agriculture in the U.S.S.R.', *International Labour Review*, 26 (1932)

Jasny, N., *The socialised agriculture of the U.S.S.R.,* Stanford University Press, Stanford, Cal. (1949)

Johnston, C., 'State advances on corn in Russia', *Economic Journal*, 4 (1894) [tariff war with Germany led to state price support for grain]

Jones, R. E., *The emancipation of the Russian nobility, 1762–85,* Princeton University Press, Princeton, N.J. (1973)

Joravsky, D., 'The merging of *sovkhozes* with *kolkhozes*', *Studies on the Soviet Union,* 3 (1960)

Kachorovsky, K., 'The Russian land commune in history and today', *Slavonic and East European Review*, 7 (1928–29)

Kahan, A., 'A note on estimates of Soviet grain output, 1934–38', *Journal of Political Economy,* 64 (1956)

Kahan, A., 'The collective farm system in Russia. Some aspects of its contribution to Soviet economic development', in C. Eicher, and L. Witt, eds, *Agriculture in economic development,* McGraw-Hill, New York (1964)

Kahan, A., 'Government policies and the industrialization of Russia', *Journal of Economic History,* 27 (1967)

Kahan, A., 'National calamities and their effect upon the food supply in Russia', *Jahrbücher für Geschichte Osteuropas,* 16 (1968)

Kahk, J., and I. Kovalchenko, 'Regional differences in the position of peasants in the European part of Russia in the nineteenth century', in M. W. Flinn, ed., *Proceedings of the seventh international economic history conference, Edinburgh, 1978,* Edinburgh University Press, Edinburgh (1978)

Kahk, J., and I. Kovalchenko, 'Regional differences in the position of peasants in the European part of Russia in the nineteenth century', in P. Bairoch, and M. Levy-Leboyer, eds, *Disparities in economic development since the industrial*

revolution, Macmillan, London (1981)

Karcz, J. F., 'Thoughts on the grain problem', *Soviet Studies,* 18 (1967) [grain marketing in the 1920s. See also R. Beermann in the same issue]

Karcz, J. F., 'Back on the grain front', *Soviet Studies,* 22 (1970) [grain output and marketing 1909–13]

Katkoff, V., 'Financing of agriculture in Russia', *Journal of Farm Economics,* 22 (1940) [activities of Agricultural Bank, 1928–40]

Katkoff, V.., 'The Soviet citrus industry', *Southern Economic Journal,* 18 (1952) [development since 1914]

Kimball, A., 'The First International and the Russian *obshchina*', *Slavic Review,* 32 (1973)

Kingston-Mann, E., 'Proletarian theory and peasant practice. Lenin, 1901–04', *Soviet Studies,* 26 (1974)

Kingston-Mann, E., 'Marxism and Russian rural development. Problems of evidence, experience, and culture', *American Historical Review,* 86 (1981)

Korros, A. S., 'The landed nobility, the state council and P. A. Stolypin (1907–11)', in L. H. Haimson, ed., *The politics of rural Russia, 1905–14,* Indiana University Press, Bloomington, Ind. (1979)

Koslow, J., *The despised and the damned. The Russian peasant through the ages,* Macmillan, New York (1972)

Kovaltchenko, I. D., and L. M. Borodkin, 'Agrarian typology of the *gubernias* (provinces) of European Russia at the turn of the century (an attempt at multidimensional quantitative analysis)', *Soviet Studies in History,* 18 (1980)

Laird, R. D., *Collective farming in Russia. A political study of the Soviet kolkhozy,* University of Kansas Press, Lawrence, Ks. (1958) [considerable attention also to agriculture in Tsarist period]

League of Nations, *Report on economic conditions in Russia, with special reference to the famine of 1921–22 and the state of agriculture,* League of Nations, Geneva (1922)

Lestrade, C. de, 'Present conditions of peasants in Russian empire', *Annals of the American Academy of Political and Social Science,* 2 (1891)

Levasseur, E., 'The Russian famine', *Journal of the Royal Statistical Society,* 55 (1892) [agricultural output 1883–91]

Lewin, M., 'The immediate background of Soviet collectivisation', *Soviet Studies,* 17 (1965–66)

Lewin, M., 'Who was the Soviet kulak?', *Soviet Studies,* 18 (1966–67)

Lewin, M., *Russian peasants and Soviet power. A study of collectivisation,* Allen and Unwin, London (1968)

Lewin, M., 'The *kolkhoz* and the Russian *muzhik*', in E. J. Hobsbawm, *et al., Peasants in history. Essays in honour of Daniel Thorner,* Oxford University Press, Calcutta (1980)

Long, J. W., 'Agricultural conditions in the German colonies of Novouzensk district, Samara province, 1861–1914', *Slavonic and East European Review,* 57 (1979)

Lyashchenko, P. I., 'Technical reconstruction and the growth of production in the agriculture of the U.S.S.R.', *Journal of Farm Economics,* 16 (1934)

Madariaga, I., 'Catherine II and the serfs. A reconsideration of some problems', *Slavonic and East European Review,* 52 (1974)

Maklakov, B., 'The peasant question and the Russian revolution', *Slavonic and East European Review,* 2 (1923–24)

Maklakov, V., 'The agrarian problem in Russia before the revolution', *Russian Review,* 9 (1950)

Male, D. J., 'The village community in the U.S.S.R., 1925–30', *Soviet Studies,* 14 (1963)

Male, D. J., *Russian peasant organisation before collectivisation,* Cambridge University Press, Cambridge (1971)

Millar, J. R., 'Mass collectivisation and the contribution of Soviet agriculture to the first Five Year Plan', *Slavic Review,* 23 (1974)

Miller, R. F., *One hundred thousand tractors. The M.T.S. and the development of controls in Soviet agriculture,* Harvard University Press, Cambridge, Mass. (1970)

Miller, R. F., 'Soviet agricultural policy in the twenties. The failure of co-operation', *Soviet Studies,* 27 (1975)

Mosse, W. E., 'Stolypin's villages', *Slavonic and East European Review,* 43 (1964–65)

Munting, R., 'A note on gentry landownership in European Russia', *New Zealand Slavonic Journal,* 1 (1978)

Munting, R., 'Mechanisation and dualism in Russian agriculture', *Journal of European Economic History,* 8 (1979)

Narkiewicz, O. A., 'Stalin, war communism and collectivization', *Soviet Studies,* 18 (1966–67)

Narkiewicz, O. A., 'Soviet administration and the grain crisis of 1927–28', *Soviet Studies,* 20 (1968–69)

Nasanov, A. N., 'From the history of manorial serfs in the nineteenth century in Russia', *Izvestiva*

Akademii Nauk U.S.S.R., 6 (1926)

Nimitz, N., *Farm employment in the Soviet Union, 1928–63,* Rand Corporation, Santa Monica, Cal. (1965)

Nimitz, N., 'Farm employment in the Soviet Union, 1928–63', in J. F. Karcz, ed., *Soviet and east European agriculture,* University of California Press, Berkeley, Cal. (1967)

Nonomura, K., 'The Soviet agriculture today', *Hitotsubachi Journal of Economics,* 3 (1962) [contains material spanning 1909–60s]

Novak-Decker, N., 'The fate of the grass-arable system', *Studies on the Soviet Union,* 3 (1963)

Nove, A., 'Some problems in Soviet agricultural statistics', *Soviet Studies,* 7 (1955–56)

Nove, A., 'The decision to collectivize', in W. A. D. Jackson, ed., *Agrarian policies and problems in communist and non-communist countries,* University of Washington Press, Seattle, Wash. (1971)

Nove, A., and R. D. Laird, '*Kolkhoz* agriculture in the Moscow *oblast*', *Slavic Review,* 13 (1954)

Olcott, M. B., 'The collectivization drive in Kazakhstan', *Russian Review,* 40 (1981)

Owen, L. A., 'The Russian agrarian revolution of 1917', parts 1 and 2, *Slavonic and East European Review,* 11 (1933), 12 (1934)

Owen, L. A., *The Russian peasant movement, 1906–17,* Russell and Russell, New York (1937)

Pares, B., 'The new crisis in Russia', *Slavonic and East European Review,* 11 (1933)

Pavlovsky, G., *Agricultural Russia on the eve of the revolution,* Routledge, London (1930)

Pearson, T. S., 'The origins of Alexander III's land captains. A reinterpretation', *Slavic Review,* 40 (1981)

Prescott, J. A., 'The Russian Free Economic Society. Foundation years', *Agricultural History,* 51 (1977)

Pushkarev, S. G., 'The Russian peasants' reaction to the emancipation of 1861', *Russian Review,* 27 (1968)

Raeff, M., 'Russia after the emancipation. Views of a gentleman-farmer', *Slavonic and East European Review,* 29 (1950)

Robbins, R. G., 'Russia's system of food supply relief on the eve of the famine of 1891–92', *Agricultural History,* 45 (1971)

Robbins, R. G., *Famine in Russia, 1891–92. The imperial government responds to a crisis,* Columbia University Press, New York (1975)

Robbins, R. G., 'Russia's famine relief law of June 12, 1900. A reform aborted', *Canadian-American Slavic Studies,* 10 (1976)

Robinson, G. T., *Rural Russia under the old regime. A history of the landlord–peasant world and a prologue to the peasant revolution of 1917,* Longmans Green, London (1932)

Rogger, H., 'Government, Jews, peasants and land in post-emancipation Russia', parts 1 and 2, *Cahiers du Monde Russe et Soviétique,* 17 (1976)

Rosovsky, H., 'The serf entrepreneur in Russia', *Explorations in Entrepreneurial History,* 6 (1953–54)

Russell, E. J., 'The farming problem in Russia. How is it being met?', *Slavonic and East European Review,* 16 (1938)

Shaffer, H. G., *Soviet agriculture. An assessment of its contribution to economic development,* Praeger, New York (1977)

Shanin, T., 'Socio-economic mobility and the rural history of Russia, 1905–30', *Soviet Studies,* 23 (1971–72)

Shanin, T., *The awkward class. Political sociology of peasantry in a developing society. Russia, 1910–25,* Clarendon Press, Oxford (1972)

Shinn, W. T., 'The law of the Russian peasant household', *Slavic Review,* 20 (1961)

Simkhovitch, V. G., 'The Russian peasant and autocracy', *Political Science Quarterly,* 21 (1906)

Simms, J. Y., 'The crisis in Russian agriculture at the end of the nineteenth century. A different view', *Slavic Review,* 36 (1977) [see comment by G. M. Hamburg in 37 (1978)]

Simms, J. Y., 'The economic impact of the Russian famine of 1891–92', *Slavonic and East European Review,* 60 (1982)

Smith, R. E. F., *Peasant farming in Muscovy,* Cambridge University Press, Cambridge (1977)

Smith, R. E. F., ed., *The Russian peasant, 1920 and 1984,* Cass, London (1977)

Stepniak, S., *The Russian peasantry,* Swan Sonnenschein, London (1888)

Strauss, E., *Soviet agriculture in perspective,* Allen and Unwin, London (1969)

Struve, P. B., ed., *Food supply in Russia during the world war,* Oxford University Press, London (1930)

Struve, P. B., and C. Zaitzoff, 'Land policy and land conditions in Soviet Russia', in J. Bickermann, ed., *Ten years of Bolshevik domination,* Siegfried Scholem, Berlin (1928)

Suny, R. G., ' "The peasants have always fed us." The Georgian nobility and the peasant emancipation, 1856–1971', *Russian Review,* 38 (1979)

Tchayanov, A., 'Agricultural economics in Russia', *Journal of Farm Economics,* 10 (1928)

Tchayanov, A., 'The organization and development of agricultural economics in Russia', *Journal of Farm Economics,* 12 (1930) [teaching of farm management and research, 1737–1925]

Timoshenko, V. P., 'The new agricultural policy of Soviet Russia', *Journal of Farm Economics,* 13 (1931)

Timoshenko, V. P., *Agricultural Russia and the wheat problem,* Stanford University Press, Stanford, Cal. (1932)

Timoshenko, V. P., *Russia as a producer and exporter of wheat,* Food Research Institute, Stanford, Cal. (1932)

Timoshenko, V. P., 'The wheat problem in the U.S.S.R.', *Journal of Farm Economics,* 14 (1932)

Timoshenko, V. P., 'The agrarian policies of Russia and the wars', *Agricultural History,* 17 (1943) [covers period from emancipation to Stalinist era]

Tokmakoff, G., 'Stolypin's agrarian reform. An appraisal', *Russian Review,* 30 (1971)

Tompkins, S. R., 'Why Witte failed to solve the peasant problem', *Journal of Modern History,* 4 (1932)

Treadgold, D. W., 'Russian expansion in the light of Turner's study of the American frontier', *Agricultural History,* 26 (1952)

Treadgold, D. W., 'Was Stolypin in favor of kulaks?', *Slavic Review,* 14 (1955)

Treadgold, D. W., 'Soviet agriculture in the light of history', in R. D. Laird, ed., *Soviet agriculture and peasant affairs,* University of Kansas Press, Lawrence, Ks. (1963) [survey of seventeenth to twentieth century]

Tschuprow, A. A., 'The break-up of the village community in Russia', *Economic Journal,* 22 (1912)

Tugwell, R. G., 'Russian agriculture', in S. Chase *et al., Soviet Russia in the second decade,* John Day, New York (1928)

Vinogradoff, E. D., 'The "invisible hand" and the Russian peasant', *Peasant Studies Newsletter,* 4 (1975)

Vinogradoff, E. D., 'The Russian peasantry and the elections to the fourth state Duma', in L. Haimson, ed., *The politics of rural Russia, 1905–14,* Indiana University Press, Bloomington, Ind. (1979)

Volin, L., 'Agrarian collectivism in the Soviet Union', *Journal of Political Economy,* 45 (1937)

Volin, L., 'Soviet agricultural policy. Some selected lessons', *Journal of Farm Economics,* 19 (1937)

Volin, L., 'Agrarian individualism in the Soviet Union. Its rise and decline', parts 1 and 2, *Agricultural History,* 12 (1938)

Volin, L., 'The Russian peasant household under the Mir and the collective farm system', *Foreign Agriculture,* 4 (1940)

Volin, L., 'The Russian peasant and serfdom', *Agricultural History,* 17 (1943)

Volin, L., 'Land tenure and land reform in modern Russia', *Agricultural History,* 27 (1953)

Volin, L., 'Agricultural policy of the Soviet Union', in U.S. Congress Joint Economic Committee, *Comparisons of the U.S. and Soviet economies,* Government Printing Office, Washington D.C. (1959)

Volin, L., 'The Russian peasant. From emancipation to Kolkhoz', in C. E. Black, ed., *The transformation of Russian society. Aspects of social change since 1861,* Harvard University Press, Cambridge, Mass. (1960)

Volin, L., 'Land tenure and land reform in modern Russia', in C. K. Warner, ed., *Agrarian conditions in modern European history,* Macmillan, New York (1966)

Volin, L., *A century of Russian agriculture. From Alexander II to Krushchev,* Harvard University Press, Cambridge, Mass. (1970)

Vucinich, W. S., ed., *The peasant in nineteenth century Russia,* Stanford University Press, Stanford, Cal. (1968)

Weinstein, H. R., 'Land hunger and nationalism in the Ukraine, 1905–17', *Journal of Economic History,* 2 (1942)

Weissman, B. M., *Herbert Hoover and famine relief to Soviet Russia, 1921–23,* Hoover Institution Press, Stanford, Cal. (1974)

Wesson, R. G., 'The Soviet communes', *Soviet Studies,* 13 (1962)

Wheatcroft, S. G., 'The reliability of Russian prewar grain output statistics', *Soviet Studies,* 26 (1974)

Whitman, J. T., 'Turkestan cotton in imperial Russia', *Slavic Review,* 15 (1956)

Willetts, H. T., 'The agrarian problem', in E. Oberlander, ed., *Russia enters the twentieth century,* Schocken, New York (1971)

Williams, D. S. M., 'Russian peasant settlement in Semirechye', *Central Asian Review,* 14 (1966)

Williams, D. S. M., 'Land reform in Turkestan', *Slavonic and East European Review,* 51 (1973)

Wolfe, B. D., 'Lenin, Stolypin and the Russian village', *Russian Review,* 6 (1947)

Yaney, G. L., *The urge to mobilize. Agrarian reform in Russia, 1861–1930,* University of Illinois Press, Urbana, Ill. (1982)

Yaney, G. L., 'The concept of the Stolypin land reforms', *Slavic Review,* 23 (1964)

Yaney, G. L., 'Agricultural administration in Russia from the Stolypin land reform to the forced collectivization', in J. R. Millar, ed., *The Soviet rural community,* University of Illinois Press, Urbana, Ill. (1971)

Zaitseff, C., 'Economic aspects of the agrarian question in Russia before and after the Bolshevik revolution', *Journal of Economic and Business History,* 3 (1930–31)

Zaitseff, C., 'The Russian agrarian revolution', *Slavonic and East European Review,* 9 (1930–31)

Zenkovsky, A., 'The emancipation of the serfs in retrospect', *Russian Review,* 20 (1961)

INDUSTRY AND INTERNAL TRADE

Abouchar, A., 'Rationality in the pre-war Soviet cement industry', *Soviet Studies,* 19 (1967–68)

Abouchar, A., *Soviet planning and spatial efficiency. The pre-war cement industry,* Indiana University Press, Bloomington, Ind. (1971)

Ahvenainen, J., 'The paper industry in Finland and in Russia, 1885–1913', *Scandinavian Economic History Review,* 27 (1979)

Alexander, J. T., 'Catherine II, bubonic plague, and the problem of industry in Moscow', *American Historical Review,* 79 (1974)

Amann, R., *et al., The technological level of Soviet industry,* Yale University Press, New Haven, Conn. (1977)

Bailes, K. E., 'Alexei Gastev and the Soviet controversy over Taylorism, 1918–24', *Soviet Studies,* 29 (1977)

Bandera, V. N., 'Market orientation of state enterprises during NEP', *Soviet Studies,* 22 (1970–71)

Barker, G. R., 'A note on the productivity of labour in industry', *Bulletins on Soviet Economic Development,* 7 (1952)

Basseches, N., 'Industry', in G. Dobbert, ed., *Red economics,* Houghton Mifflin, Boston (1932)

Baykov, A., 'The development of industrial production in the U.S.S.R.', *Economica,* 8 (1941)

Baykov, A., 'Industrial development in the U.S.S.R.', *Bulletins on Soviet Economic Development,* 1 (1949)

Beable, W. H., *Commercial Russia,* Constable, London (1918)

Beliajeff, A. S., 'The economic power of the old believers in mid-nineteenth century Moscow', *New Zealand Slavonic Journal,* 1 (1979)

Bernstein, S. A., *The financial and economic results of the working of the Lena Goldfields Company Limited*, Blackfriars Press, London (1930)

Bill, V. T., 'The Morozovs', *Russian Review*, 14 (1955) [rise of entrepreneurial peasant family during the nineteenth century]

Blackwell, W. L., 'The old believers and the rise of private industrial enterprise in early nineteenth century Moscow', *Slavic Review*, 24 (1965)

Blackwell, W. L., *The beginnings of Russian industrialization, 1800–60*, Princeton University Press, Princeton, N.J. (1968)

Bradley, M., 'Franco-Russian engineering links. The careers of Lamé and Clapeyron, 1820–30', *Annals of Science*, 38 (1981)

Bowles, W. D., 'The logging industry. A backward branch of the Soviet economy', *Slavic Review*, 17 (1958) [surveys the period 1928–57]

Burgess, M., 'Fairs and entertainers in eighteenth century Russia', *Slavonic and East European Review*, 38 (1959)

Carver, J. S., '*Tekhnologicheskii Zhurnal. An early Russian technoeconomic periodical*', *Technology and Culture*, 18 (1977)

Chamberlin, W. H., *Russia's iron age*, Little Brown, Boston (1934)

Chase, S., 'Industry and the Gosplan', in *Soviet Russia in the second decade*, John Day, New York (1928) [no ed.]

Clendenning, P. H., 'William Gomm. A case study of the foreign entrepreneur in eighteenth century Russia', *Journal of European Economic History*, 6 (1977)

Crawford, J. M., ed., *The industries of Russia*, 5 vols, Department of Trade and Manufacture, St Petersburg (1893)

Cross, R. D., 'A comparative analysis of urban industrial growth in the Dontesk and Kuznetsh Basins of the U.S.S.R.', *Southern Quarterly*, 10 (1972)

Diakonoff, V. A., 'Industry and accounting in the U.S.S.R.', *Harvard Business Review*, 11 (1933)

Dobb, M., 'Soviet agriculture and the chemical industry', *Slavonic and East European Review*, 24 (1946)

Dodge, N. T., and D. G. Dalrymple, 'The Stalingrad tractor plant in early Soviet planning', *Soviet Studies*, 18 (1966–67)

Drew, R. F., 'The Siberian fair, 1600–1750', *Slavonic and East European Review*, 39 (1961)

Ebel, R. E., *The petroleum industry of the Soviet Union*, American Petroleum Institute, New York (1961)

Fischer, L., *Machines and men in Russia*, Harrison Smith, New York (1932)

Galenson, W., 'Industrial labor productivity', in A. Bergson, ed., *Soviet economic growth*, Row Petersen, Evanston, Ill. (1953)

Gatrell, P., 'Industrial expansion in Tsarist Russia, 1908–14', *Economic History Review*, 35 (1982)

Gerschenkron, A., 'The rate of industrial growth in Russia since 1885', *Journal of Economic History*, Supplement, 7 (1947)

Gerschenkron, A., 'Soviet heavy industry. A dollar index of output, 1927/28–37', *Review of Economics and Statistics*, 37 (1955)

Gerschenkron, A., 'The beginnings of Russian industrialization', *Soviet Studies*, 20 (1970)

Gerschenkron, A., 'Soviet policies versus international cartels. Four historical case studies', *Slavic Review*, 33 (1974) [cartels of 1930s in matches, potash, phosphates and platinum]

Gerschenkron, A., and A. Erlich, *A dollar index of Soviet machinery output, 1927/28–37*, Rand Corporation, Santa Monica, Cal. (1951)

Gerschenkron, A., and N. Nimitz, *A dollar index of Soviet iron and steel output*, Rand Corporation, Santa Monica, Cal. (1953)

Gibson, J. R., *Feeding the Russian fur trade. Provisionment of the Okhotsk seaboard and the Kamchatka peninsula, 1639–1856*, University of Wisconsin Press, Madison, Wis. (1969)

Gibson, J. R., 'The Russian fur trade', in C. M. Judd, and A. J. Ray, eds, *Old trails and new directions. Papers of the third North American fur trade conference*, University of Toronto Press, Toronto (1980)

Giffin, F. C., 'The formative years of the Russian factory inspectorate, 1832–85', *Slavic Review*, 25 (1966)

Goldman, M., 'The relocation and growth of the pre-revolutionary Russian ferrous metal industry', *Explorations in Entrepreneurial History*, 9 (1956)

Goldstein, E. R., 'Vickers Limited and the Tsarist regime', *Slavonic and East European Review*, 58 (1980)

Granick, D., 'Initiative and independence of the Soviet plan management', *Slavic Review*, 10 (1951) [emphasis on heavy industry 1934–41]

Granick, D., *Management of the industrial firm in the U.S.S.R. A study of Soviet economic planning*, Columbia University Press, New York (1954)

Granick, D., *The red executive. A study of the organization man in Russian industry*, Macmillan, London (1960)

Granick, D., 'On patterns of technological choice in

Soviet industry', *American Economic Review*, 52 (1962) [comment by L. G. Reynolds in the same issue]

Harvey, M. L., and M. J. Ruggles, 'The eastward course of Soviet industry and the war', *Russian Review*, 1 (1942)

Heller, A. A., *The industrial revival in Soviet Russia*, Thomas Seltzer, New York (1922)

Hodgman, D. R., 'Soviet machinery output', *Slavic Review*, 12 (1953)

Hodgman, D. R., *Soviet industrial production, 1928–51*, Harvard University Press, Cambridge, Mass. (1954)

Holubnychy, V., *The industrial output of the Ukraine, 1913–56. A statistical analysis,* Institute for Study of the U.S.S.R., Munich (1957)

Holzman, F. D., 'The Soviet Ural-Kuznetsk combine. A study in investment criteria and industrialization policies', *Quarterly Journal of Economics*, 71 (1957)

Hutchings, R., 'The origins of the Soviet industrial price system', *Soviet Studies*, 13 (1961) [covers NEP to World War II]

Hutchings, R., 'Periodic fluctuations in Soviet industrial growth rates', *Soviet Studies*, 20 (1968–69)

Jasny, N., *Indices of Soviet industrial production, 1928–54,* Council for Economic Industry Research, Washington, D.C. (1955)

Jasny, N., *Soviet industrialization, 1928–52,* Chicago University Press, Chicago, Ill. (1961)

Kadomstev, B., *The Russian collapse. A politico-economic essay,* Russian Mercantile and Industrial Corporation, New York (1919)

Kahan, A., 'Entrepreneurship in the early development of iron manufacturing in Russia', *Economic Development and Cultural Change*, 10 (1961–62)

Kahan, A., 'A proposed mercantilist code in the Russian iron industry, 1734–36', *Explorations in Entrepreneurial History*, 2 (1964–65)

Kaser, M. C., 'Russian entrepreneurship', in P. Mathias and M. M. Postan, eds., *Cambridge Economic History of Europe*, vol. 7(2), Cambridge University Press, Cambridge (1978)

Kaufman, A., *Small-scale industry in the Soviet Union,* National Bureau of Economic Research, New York (1962) [concerned with pre-revolutionary period also]

Kelly, W. J., 'Crisis management in the Russian oil industry. The 1905 revolution', *Journal of European Economic History*, 10 (1981)

Kelly, W. J., and T. Kano, 'Crude oil production in the Russian empire, 1818–1919', *Journal of European Economic History*, 6 (1977)

Kirchner, W., 'Western businessmen in Russia. Practices and problems', *Business History Review*, 38 (1964)

Kirchner, W., 'The industrialization of Russia and the Siemens firm, 1853–90', *Jahrbücher für Geschichte Osteuropas*, 22 (1974)

Koropeckkj, I. S., 'Soviet industrial location in practice', *Studies on the Soviet Union*, 1 (1961)

Koropeckkj, I. S., *Location problems in Soviet industry before World War II. The case of the Ukraine,* University of North Carolina Press, Chapel Hill, N.C. (1971)

Koutaissoff, E., 'The Ural metal industry in the eighteenth century', *Economic History Review*, 4 (1951–52)

Krynski, G. I., 'Management problems in Soviet public enterprise as indicated by arbitration awards', *Slavic Review*, 12 (1953)

Lamet, S., 'Soviet fuel and power', *Soviet Studies*, 4 (1952–53)

Lamet, S., 'A survey of the Soviet engineering industries', *Soviet Studies*, 5 (1953–54)

Lavrichev, V. Y., 'The all-Russian union of trade and industry', *Istoricheskie Zapiski*, 70 (1961)

Lenin, V. I., *The development of capitalism in Russia. The process of the formation of a home market for large-scale industry,* Lawrence and Wishart, London (1957)

Leontief, W. W., 'Scientific and technological research in Russia', *Slavic Review*, 4 (1945) [review of progress, 1917–39]

Lewis, R. A., 'Innovation in the U.S.S.R. The case of synthetic rubber', *Slavic Review*, 38 (1979)

Lewis, R. A., 'Some aspects of the research development efforts of the Soviet Union, 1924–35', *Science Studies*, 2 (1972)

Lokshin, E., *Industry in the U.S.S.R.,* Foreign Languages Publishing House, Moscow (1948)

Lonsdale, R. E., 'The Soviet concept of the territorial production complex', *Slavic Review*, 24 (1965) [covers 1920s–60s]

McKay, J. P., 'John Cockerill in southern Russia, 1885–1905. A study of aggressive foreign entrepreneurship', *Business History Review*, 41 (1967)

McKay, J. P., *Pioneers for profit. Foreign entrepreneurship and Russian industrialization, 1885–1913,* Chicago University Press, Chicago, Ill. (1970)

McKay, J. P., 'Foreign businessmen, the Tsarist government and the Briansk Company', *Journal of European Economic History*, 2 (1973)

McKay, J. P., 'Foreign enterprise in Russian and Soviet industry. A long-term perspective', *Busi-*

ness History Review, 48 (1974)

Moorsteen, R. H., *Prices and production of machinery in the Soviet Union, 1928–58*, Harvard University Press, Cambridge, Mass. (1962)

Munro, G. E., 'The Empress and the merchants. Response in St. Petersburg to the regulation of commerce under Catherine II', *Social Science Journal*, 13 (1976)

Naleszkiewicz, W., 'Technical assistance of the American enterprises to the growth of the Soviet Union, 1929–33', *Russian Review*, 25 (1966)

National Bureau of Economic Research, *Statistical abstract of industrial output in the Soviet Union, 1913–55*, 5 vols, N.B.E.R., New York (1956)

Nutter, G. W., 'The structure and growth of Soviet industry. A comparison with the United States', *Journal of Law and Economics*, 2 (1959) [data covering selected years between 1870 and 1955]

Nutter, G. W., *The growth of industrial production in the Soviet Union*, Princeton University Press, Princeton, N.J. (1962)

Ohlobyn, O., *A history of Ukranian industry*, W. Fink, Munich (1971)

Pinter, W. M., 'Government and industry during the Ministry of Count Kankrin, 1823–44', *Slavic Review*, 23 (1964)

Portal, R., 'Muscovite industrialists. The cotton sector', in W. L. Blackwell, ed., *Russian economic development from Peter the Great to Stalin*, Croom Helm, London (1975)

Powell, R. P., 'An index of Soviet construction, 1927/28–55', *Review of Economics and Statistics*, 41 (1959)

Queen, G. S., 'The McCormick Harvesting Machine Company in Russia', *Russian Review*, 23 (1964)

Rafalovich, A. G., 'The state monopoly of spirits in Russia and its influence on the prosperity of the population', *Journal of the Royal Statistical Society*, 64 (1901)

Rafalovich, A. G., ed., *Russia. Its trade and commerce*, P. S. King, London (1918)

Rieber, A. J., 'The Moscow entrepreneurial group. The emergence of a new form in autocratic politics', *Jahrbücher für Geschichte Osteuropas*, 25 (1977)

Robinson, E., 'The transference of British technology to Russia, 1760–1820. A preliminary enquiry', in B. M. Ratcliffe, ed., *Great Britain and her world, 1750–1914. Essays in honour of W. O. Henderson*, Manchester University Press, Manchester (1975)

Rodin, N. W., *Productivity in Soviet iron mining, 1890–1960*, Rand Corporation, Santa Monica, Cal. (1953)

Roellinghoff, W., 'The house market', in G. Dobbert,

ed., *Red economics*, Houghton Mifflin, Boston (1932)

Roosa, R. A., 'Russian industrialists and "state socialism", 1906–17', *Soviet Studies*, 23 (1971–72)

Roosa, R. A., 'United Russian industry', *Soviet Studies*, 24 (1973)

Rudolph, R. L., 'Family structure and proto-industrialization in Russia', *Journal of Economic History*, 40 (1980) [see comments by C. T. Morris and D. Feeny]

Seton, F., 'An estimate of Soviet industrial expansion', *Soviet Studies*, 7 (1955–56)

Seton, F., 'The tempo of Soviet industrial expansion', *Bulletin of the Oxford University Institute of Economics and Statistics*, 20 (1958) [see comment by L. R. Klein in the same issue]

Shimkin, D. B., 'The entrepreneur in Tsarist and Soviet Russia', *Explorations in Entrepreneurial History*, 2 (1949–50)

Shimkin, D. B., *The Soviet minerals-fuels industries, 1928–58. A statistical survey*, U. S. Department of Commerce, Washington, D.C. (1963)

Shul'ga, I. G., 'The development of trade in left bank Ukraine in the second half of the eighteenth century', in V. V. Mavrodin, ed., *Voprosy genezisa kapitalizma v Rossii*, Leningrad University Press, Leningrad (1960)

Snodgrass, J. H., *Russia. A handbook on commercial and industrial conditions*, Government Printing Office, Washington, D.C. (1913)

Sochor, Z. A., 'Soviet Taylorism revisited', *Soviet Studies*, 33 (1981)

Spechler, M. A., 'The regional concentration of industry in imperial Russia, 1854–1917', *Journal of European Economic History*, 9 (1980)

Strumilin, S. G., 'Industrial crises in Russia, 1847–67', in F. Crouzet *et al., Essays in European economic history, 1789–1914.* Edward Arnold, London (1969)

Timacheff, N. S., 'The organisation of state industry in Soviet Russia', *International Labour Review*, 19 (1929)

Tolf, R. W., *The Russian Rockefellers. The saga of the Nobel family and the Russian oil industry*, Hoover Institution Press, Stanford, Cal. (1976)

Trebilcock, C., and G. Jones, 'Russian industry and British business, 1910–30. Oil and armaments', *Journal of European Economic History*, 11 (1982)

Tugan-Baranovsky, M. I., *The Russian factory in the nineteenth century*, Richard D. Irwin, Homewood, Ill. (1898. Repr. 3rd edn 1970)

Veverka, J., 'Long-term measures of Soviet industrial

output', *Soviet Studies*, 16 (1964–65)

Von Laue, T. H., 'The industrialization of Russia in the writings of Sergej Witte', *Slavic Review*, 10 (1951)

Von Laue, T. H., 'The high cost and gamble of the Witte system. A chapter in the industrialization of Russia', *Journal of Economic History*, 13 (1953)

Von Laue, T. H., 'A secret memorandum of Sergei Witte on the industrialization of imperial Russia', *Journal of Modern History*, 26 (1954)

Von Laue, T. H., *Sergei Witte and the industrialization of Russia*, Columbia University Press, New York (1963)

Von Laue, T. H., 'Problems of industrialization', in T. Stavrou, ed., *Russia under the last Tsar*, University of Minnesota Press, Minneapolis, Minn. (1969)

Westwood, J. N., 'John Hughes and Russian metallurgy', *Economic History Review*, 17 (1964–65)

White, J. D., 'Moscow, St. Petersburg and the Russian industrialists', *Soviet Studies*, 24 (1972–73)

Whitman, J. T., 'The Kolkhoz market', *Soviet Studies*, 7 (1956) [deals with growth of market from 1932 legalisation, retail trade, procurement]

Zagorsky, S. O., *State control of industry in Russia during the war*, Yale University Press, New Haven, Conn. (1928)

TRANSPORT AND COMMUNICATIONS

Ames, E., 'A century of Russian railroad construction, 1837–1936', *Slavic Review*, 6 (1947)

Anonymous, 'Early history of the Transcaspian Railway', *Central Asian Review*, 9 (1961)

Bater, J. H., 'The development of public transportation in St. Petersburg, 1860–1914', *Journal of Transport History*, 2 (1973)

Bater, J. H., 'The journey to work in St. Petersburg, 1860–1914', *Journal of Transport History*, 2 (1974)

Baykalov, A. V., 'Siberia since 1894', *Slavic Review*, 11 (1933) [impact of Trans-Siberian Railway on economic development]

Bill, V. T., 'The early days of Russian railroads', *Russian Review*, 15 (1956)

Collins, D. N., 'The Franco-Russian alliance and the Russian railways, 1891–1914', *Historical Journal*, 16 (1973)

Fairlie, S., 'Shipping in the Anglo-Russian grain trade to 1870', *Maritime History*, 1 (1971)

Futrell, M., *Northern underground. Episodes of Russian revolutionary transport and communi-*

cations through Scandinavia and Finland, 1863–1917, Faber and Faber, London (1963)

Garbutt, P. E., *The Russian railways*, Sampson Low, London (1949)

Garbutt, P. E., 'The Trans-Siberian Railway', *Journal of Transport History*, 1 (1953–54)

Gardener, W., 'Peking to Moscow. The trans-Siberian caravan route', *History Today*, 27 (1977)

Haywood, R. M., 'The question of a standard gauge for Russian railways, 1836–60', *Slavic Review*, 28 (1969)

Haywood, R. M., *The beginnings of railway development in Russia in the reign of Nicholas I, 1835–42*, Duke University Press, Durham, N.C. (1969)

Haywood, R. M., 'The "ruler legend". Tsar Nicholas I and the route of the St. Petersburg–Moscow railway, 1842–43', *Slavic Review*, 37 (1978)

Haywood, R. M., 'The development of steamboats on the Volga river and its tributaries, 1817–56', *Research in Economic History*, 6 (1981)

Hunter, H., *Soviet transportation policy*, Harvard University Press, Cambridge, Mass. (1957) [deals with period 1928–55]

Kaplan, N. M., *Soviet transport and communications. Output indexes, 1928–62*, Rand Corporation, Santa Monica, Cal. (1965)

Kelly, W. J., 'Railroad development and market integration in Tsarist Russia. Evidence on oil products and grain', *Journal of Economic History*, 36 (1976)

Kerner, R. J., *The urge to the sea. The course of Russian history. The role of rivers, portages, ostrogs, monasteries and furs*, University of California Press, Berkeley, Cal., (1942)

Krypton, C., *The northern sea route. Its place in Russian economic history before 1917*, Research Programme on the U.S.S.R., New York (1953)

Metzer, J., 'Railroad development and market integration. The case of Tsarist Russia', *Journal of Economic History*, 34 (1974)

Metzer, J., 'Railroads in Tsarist Russia. Direct gains and implications', *Explorations in Economic History*, 13 (1976)

Mirski, M. S., 'The Soviet railway system. Policy and operation', *Russian Review*, 13 (1954) [surveys railway construction before and after the revolution]

Mosse, W. E., 'Russia and the Levant, 1856–62. Grand Duke Constantine Nicolaevich and the Russian Steam Company', *Journal of Modern History*, 26 (1954)

North, R. N., *Transport in western Siberia. Tsarist*

and Soviet development, University of British Columbia Press, Vancouver, B.C. (1979)

Petrov, V. I., and Ushakov, S., *Transport in the U.S.S.R.,* Novosti Press Agency Publishing House, Moscow (n.d.)

Rieber, A. J., 'The formation of La Grand Société des Chemins de Fer Russes', *Jahrbücher für Geschichte Osteuropas,* 21 (1973)

Robbins, M., 'The Balaklava railway', *Journal of Transport History,* 1 (1953)

Rosenberg, W. G., 'The democratization of Russia's railroads in 1917', *American Historical Review,* 86 (1981)

Saller, H., 'Communications', in G. Dobbert, ed., *Red economics,* Houghton Mifflin, Boston (1932)

Spring, D. W., 'Railways and economic development in Turkestan before 1917', in L. Symons and C. White, eds, *Russian transport,* Bell, London (1975)

Spring, D. W., 'The trans-Persian railway project and Anglo-Russian relations, 1904–14, *Slavonic and East European Review,* 54 (1976)

Symons, L., and C. White, eds, *Russian transport,* Bell, London (1975)

Tarsaidze, A., 'American pioneers in Russian railroad building', *Russian Review,* 9 (1950)

Tupper, H., *To the great ocean. Siberia and the Trans-Siberian Railway,* Secker and Warburg, London (1965)

Tverskoi, K. N., *The unified transport system of the U.S.S.R.,* Gollancz, London (1935)

Westwood, J. N., 'Soviet railway development', *Soviet Studies,* 11 (1959–60)

Westwood, J. N., *A history of Russian railways,* Allen and Unwin, London (1964)

Westwood, J. N., 'Vladikavkaz Railway. A case of enterprising private enterprise', *Slavic Review,* 25 (1966)

Westwood, J. N., *Soviet locomotive technology during industrialization, 1928–52,* Macmillan, London (1982)

White, C., 'The impact of Russian railway construction on the market for grain in the 1860s–70s', in L. Symons and C. White, eds, *Russian transport,* Bell, London (1975)

White, C., 'The concept of social saving in theory and practice', *Economic History Review,* 29 (1976)

White, C., 'A Russian attempt to calculate social savings', *Soviet Studies,* 28 (1976)

MONEY, BANKING AND FINANCE

Alexandrov, B., 'The Soviet currency reform', *Russian Review,* 8 (1949)

Anderson, O., 'The Russian loan of 1855. An example of economic liberalism?', *Economica,* 27 (1960)

Apostol, P. N., *et al., Russian public finance during the war,* Yale University Press, New Haven, Conn. (1928)

Arnold, A. Z., *Banks, credit and money in Soviet Russia,* Columbia University Press, New York (1937)

Aronsfield, C. C., 'Jewish bankers and the Tsar', *Jewish Social Studies,* 35 (1973)

Aronsfield, C. C., 'Jewish bankers and the Tsar', *Contemporary Review,* 224 (1974)

Baker, A. B., 'Community and growth. Muddling through with Russian credit co-operatives', *Journal of Economic History,* 37 (1977)

Barkai, H., 'The macro-economics of Tsarist Russia in the industrialization era. Monetary developments, the balance of payments and the gold standard', *Journal of Economic History,* 33 (1973)

Bernatsky, M., 'The problem of Soviet finance', *Slavonic and East European Review,* 9 (1933)

Borovoy, S. Y., 'The state debt as a source of primitive accumulation in Russia', in V. V. Mavrodin, ed., *Voprosy genezisa kapitalizma v Rossii,* Leningrad University Press, Leningrad (1960)

Campbell, M., 'Money, credit and banking', in G. Dobbert, ed., *Red economics,* Houghton Mifflin, Boston (1932)

Carstensen, F. V., 'Myth and reality. A critique of estimates of foreign investments in Russia', in M. Levy-Leboyer, ed., *Position internationale de la France. Aspects économiques et financiers, XIXe–XXe siècles,* Editions de l'Ecole des Hautes Etudes en Sciences Sociales, Paris (1977)

Comstock, A., 'Soviet finance, in S. Chase, *et al., Soviet Russia in the second decade,* John Day, New York (1928)

Crisp, O., 'Russian financial policy and the gold standard at the end of the nineteenth century', *Economic History Review,* 6 (1953–54)

Crisp, O., 'Some problems of French investments in Russian joint-stock companies, 1894–1914', *Slavonic and East European Review,* 35 (1956–57)

Crisp, O., 'French investment in Russian joint-stock companies, 1894–1914', *Business History,* 2 (1959–60)

Crisp, O., 'Russia, 1860–1914', in R. E. Cameron, ed., *Banking in the early stages of industrializa-*

tion, Oxford University Press, New York (1967)

Davies, R. W., *The development of the Soviet budgetary system,* Cambridge University Press, Cambridge (1958)

Dehn, V., 'The Russian currency reform', *Economic Journal,* 8 (1898) [currency reform of 1897]

Demaris, E. J., 'Lenin and the soviet control by the ruble system', *Slavic Review,* 22 (1963)

Drummond, I. M., 'The Russian gold standard, 1897–1914', *Journal of Economic History,* 36 (1976)

Duran, J. A., 'The reform of financial administration in Russia during the reign of Catherine II', *Canadian Slavic Studies,* 4 (1970)

Einzig, P., 'The monetary economy of Bolshevism', *Economic Journal,* 30 (1920)

Falkus, M. E., 'Aspects of foreign investment in Tsarist Russia', *Journal of European Economic History,* 8 (1979)

Fetter, F. W., 'The Russian loan of 1855. A postscript', *Economica,* 28 (1961)

Fisher, R. B., 'American investments in pre-Soviet Russia', *Slavic Review,* 8 (1949)

Frederiksen, D. M., 'Mortgage banking in Russia, 1894', *Annals of the American Academy of Political and Social Science,* 5 (1894–95)

Garvy, G., 'Banking under the Tsars and Soviets', *Journal of Economic History,* 32 (1972)

Garvy, G., 'The financial manifesto of the St. Petersburg soviet, 1905', *International Review of Social History,* 20 (1975)

Garvy, G., 'Advocation of the run on gold as a revolutionary strategy', *Revue Internationale d'Histoire de la Banque,* 10 (1975)

Gillette, P. S., 'American capital in the contest for Soviet oil, 1920–23', *Soviet Studies,* 24 (1972–73)

Goldweiser, A., 'Banking and currency reforms in Russia', *Journal of Political Economy,* 33 (1925) [covers 1924 currency legislation]

Gorlin, R. H., 'Problems of tax reform in imperial Russia', *Journal of Modern History,* 49 (1977)

Gregory, P. R., 'The Russian industrialization experience. Some observations on savings, absorptive capacity and balance of payments', *Soviet Union,* 4 (1977)

Gregory, P. R., 'The Russian balance of payments, the gold standard and monetary policy', *Journal of Economic History,* 39 (1979)

Gregory, P. R., 'A note on Russia's merchandise balance and balance of payments during the industrialization era', *Slavic Review,* 38 (1979)

Gregory, P. R., and J. W. Sailors, 'Russian monetary policy and industrialization, 1861–1913', *Journal*

of *Economic History,* 36 (1976)

Harper, S. N., 'The budget rights of the Russian Duma', *Journal of Political Economy,* 16 (1908)

Holzman, F. D., 'The Soviet budget, 1928–52', *National Tax Journal,* 6 (1953)

Holzman, G. D., 'The ruble exchange rate and Soviet foreign trade pricing policies, 1929–61', *American Economic Review,* 58 (1968)

Hubbard, L. E., *Soviet money and finance,* Macmillan, London (1936)

Kahan, A., 'Capital formation during the period of early industrialization in Russia, 1890–1913', in P. Mathias and M. M. Postan, eds, *Cambridge Economic History of Europe,* vol. 7(2), Cambridge University Press, Cambridge (1978)

Kamendrowsky, V., 'Catherine II's Nakaz, state finances and the *Encyclopédie*', *Canadian-American Slavic Studies,* 13 (1979)

Katzenellenbaum, S. S., *Russian currency and banking, 1914–24,* P. S. King, London (1925)

Kayden, E. M., 'Central co-operative banking in Russia', *Journal of Political Economy,* 32 (1924)

Kohler, G., 'The Soviet-Russian defense burden, 1862–1965', *Bulletin of Peace Proposals,* 11 (1980)

Kohn, S., and A. S. Meyendorff, *The cost of the war to Russia,* Yale University Press, New Haven, Conn. (1932)

Kokovtsev, Count V., 'The financial embarrassments of the Soviet government', *Slavonic and East European Review,* 6 (1927) [former Tsarist Finance Minister's appraisal of 1926–27 budget]

Laughlin, L. J., 'Specie resumption in Russia', *Journal of Political Economy,* 5 (1897)

Le Donne, J. P., 'Indirect taxes in Catherine's Russia. The salt code of 1781', *Jahrbücher für Geschichte Osteuropas,* 23 (1975)

Le Donne, J. P., 'Indirect taxes in Catherine II's Russia. The liquor monopoly', *Jahrbücher für Geschichte Osteuropas,* 24 (1976)

Lewery, L. J., *Foreign capital investment in Russian industries and commerce,* U.S. Bureau of Foreign and Domestic Commerce, Washington, D.C. (1923)

Littlepage, J. D., and B. Demaree, *In search of Soviet gold,* Harcourt, Brace, New York (1937) [USSR gold output 1928–37]

Long, J. W., 'Organized protest against the 1906 Russian loan', *Cahiers du Monde Russe et Soviétique,* 13 (1972)

Long, J. W., 'Russian manipulation of the French press, 1904–06', *Slavic Review,* 31 (1972) [concerned with French loan to Russia]

McGrew, R. E., 'The politics of absolution. Paul I and the Bank of Assistance for the nobility', *Canadian-American Slavic Studies*, 7 (1973)

Melnyk, Z. L., *Soviet capital formation. Ukraine, 1928–32*, Ukrainian Free Press, Munich (1965)

Michelson, A. M., *Russian public finance during the war*, Yale University Press, New Haven, Conn. (1928)

Miklashevsky, A., 'Monetary reform in Russia', *Economic Journal*, 6 (1896)

Millar, J. R., and D. Bahry, 'Financing development and the tax structure in the U.S.S.R.', *Canadian Slavonic Papers*, 21 (1979)

Miller, M. S., 'Taxation in Soviet Russia', *Slavonic and East European Review*, 4 (1925), 5 (1926) and 6 (1927)

Miller, M. S., 'The financing of industry in Soviet Russia', *Slavonic and East European Review*, 9 (1930)

Miller, M. S., 'Financial reform in Soviet Russia', *Slavonic and East European Review*, 10 (1931)

Pavlovsky, G., 'Russia's current monetary problems', *Economic Journal*, 33 (1923)

Pasvolsky, L., and M. G. Moulton, *Russian debts and Russian reconstruction*, McGraw-Hill, New York (1924)

Pickersgill, J. E., 'Hyperinflation and monetary reform in the Soviet Union, 1921–26', *Journal of Political Economy*, 76 (1968)

Pickersgill, J. E., 'A long-run demand function for money in the Soviet Union. Comment', *Journal of Money, Credit and Banking*, 2 (1970)

Powell, R. P., 'Recent developments in Soviet monetary policy', in F. D. Holzman, ed., *Readings on the Soviet economy*, Rand-McNally, Chicago, Ill. (1962) [compares 1932–39 with 1948–57]

Rafalovich, A. G., 'The financial situation in Russia', *Economic Journal*, 14 (1904)

Rafalovich, A. G., 'Russian finance policy (1862–1914)', *Economic Journal*, 26 (1916)

Reddaway, W. B., *The Russian financial system*, Macmillan, London (1935)

Slusser, R. M., 'The budget of the OGPU and the special troops from 1923–4 to 1928–9', *Soviet Studies*, 10 (1958–59)

Sokolnikov, G., *Soviet policy in public finance, 1917–28*, Stanford University Press, Stanford, Cal. (1931)

Sontag, J. D., 'Tsarist debts and Tsarist foreign policy', *Slavic Review*, 27 (1968)

Spring, R. D., 'The north Russian currency', *Economic Journal*, 29 (1919) [currency issue of 1918 in association with British Treasury]

T'ang, L. L., and M. S. Miller, 'The political aspect of international finance in Russia and China', *Economica*, 5 (1925)

Tompkins, S. R., 'Witte as Minister of Finance, 1892–1903', *Slavonic and East European Review*, 11 (1932–33)

Townsend, G. M., 'The Russian-Dutch loan in the press, 1832', *Quarterly Review of Historical Studies*, 17 (1977–78)

Williams, D. S. M., 'Taxation in Tsarist central Asia', *Central Asian Review*, 16 (1968)

Williams, D. S. M., 'Fiscal reform in Turkestan', *Slavonic and East European Review*, 52 (1974)

Willis, H. P., 'Monetary reform in Russia', *Journal of Political Economy*, 5 (1897)

Yeager, L., 'Fluctuating exchange rates in the nineteenth century. The experience of Austria and Russia', in R. A. Mundell, and A. K. Swoboda, eds, *Monetary problems of the international economy*, University of Chicago Press, Chicago, Ill. (1969)

Yurovsky, L. N., *Currency problems and policy of the Soviet Union*, Leonard Parsons, London (1925)

OVERSEAS TRADE AND COMMERCIAL RELATIONS

Anderson, E., 'The U.S.S.R. trades with Latvia. The treaty of 1927', *Slavic Review*, 21 (1962)

Arima, T., 'Foreign markets for Russian iron in the pre-emancipation period (1760–1860)', *Shakai-Keizai–Shigaku*, 44 (1978)

Baykov, A., *Soviet foreign trade*, Princeton University Press, Princeton, N.J. (1946)

Bergquist, H. E., 'Russo-American economic relations in the 1820s. Henry Middleton as a protector of American economic interests in Russia and Turkey', *East European Quarterly*, 11 (1977)

Bolkhovitinov, N. N., 'Russo-American trade relations during the U.S. war of independence', *Soviet Studies in History*, 14 (1975–76)

Bolkhovitinov, N. N., 'Russian-American *rapprochement* and the commercial treaty of 1832', *Soviet Studies in History*, 19 (1980–81)

Bovykin, V. I., 'Russian consular reports to 1917', *Business History*, 23 (1981)

Brutskus, B. D., 'Russia's grain exports and their future', *Journal of Farm Economics*, 16 (1934) [grain exports before 1914, during war, war communism, NEP and collectivisation]

Buist, M. G., 'Russia's entry on the Dutch capital market, 1770–1815', *Papers presented to the fifth* *international economic history conference, Leningrad, 1970,* Mouton, Paris (1979)

Central Statistical Administration, *Soviet trade. A statistical compilation,* State Statistical Publishing House, Moscow (1956)

Cleinow, G., 'Foreign technical assistance', in G. Dobbert, ed., *Red economics,* Houghton Mifflin, Boston (1932) [covers eighteenth to twentieth century]

Conolly, V., *Soviet economic policy in the East. Turkey, Persia, Afghanistan and Tana Tura,* Oxford University Press, London (1933)

Conolly, V., *Soviet trade from the Pacific to the Levant, with an economic study of the Soviet far eastern region,* Oxford University Press, London (1935)

Crisp, O., 'The Russo-Chinese Bank. An episode in Franco-Russian relations', *Slavonic and East European Review,* 52 (1974)

Crosby, A. W., *America, Russia, hemp and Napoleon. American trade with Russia and the Baltic, 1783–1812,* Ohio State University Press, Columbus, Ohio (1965)

Debo, R. K., 'Dutch-Soviet relations, 1917–24. The role of finance and commerce in the foreign policy of the Soviet Russia and the Netherlands', *Canadian-American Slavic Studies,* 4 (1970)

Drummond, I. M., 'Empire trade and Russian trade. Economic diplomacy in the nineteen-thirties', *Canadian Journal of Economics,* 5 (1972)

Ebel, R. E., *Communist trade in oil and gas. An evaluation of the future export capability of the Soviet bloc.* Praeger, New York (1970) [part 1 deals with Tsarist period and the years 1918–40]

Edmondson, C. M., 'An inquiry into the termination of Soviet famine relief programmes and the renewal of grain exports, 1922–23', *Soviet Studies,* 33 (1981)

Entner, M. L., *Russo-Persian commercial relations, 1828–1914,* University of Florida Press, Gainesville, Fla. (1965)

Fairlie, S., 'Anglo-Russian trade, mostly from 1750 to 1830', *Papers presented to the fifth international economic history conference, Leningrad, 1970,* Mouton, Paris (1979)

Falkus, M. E., 'Russia and the international wheat trade, 1861–1914', *Economica,* 33 (1966)

Faas, V. V., *Russia's export trade in timber and the importance of the forest of north European Russia,* Youroveta Home and Foreign Trade Company, New York (1919)

Foster, E. D., 'The trend of Soviet-German commercial relations and its significance', *Harvard Business Review,* 11 (1933) [trend of Russian trade before 1914 and German trade agreements afterwards]

Foust, C. M., 'Russian expansion to the east through the eighteenth century', *Journal of Economic History,* 21 (1961)

Foust, C. M., *Muscovite and mandarin. Russia's trade with China and its setting, 1727–1805,* University of North Carolina Press, Chapel Hill, N.C. (1969)

Frederiksen, O. J., 'Virginia tobacco in Russia under Peter the Great', *Slavonic and East European Review,* 21 (1943)

Gay, J., 'Anglo-Russian economic relations', *Economic Journal,* 27 (1917) [surveys period 1870–1913]

Gibson, J. R., 'The Russian fur trade', in C. M. Judd and A. J. Ray, eds, *Old trails and new directions. Papers of the third North American fur trade conference,* University of Toronto Press, Toronto (1980)

Gopal, S., 'Trading activities of Indians in Russia in the eighteenth century', *Indian Economic and Social History Review,* 5 (1968)

Herlihy, P., 'Russian wheat and the port of Livorno, 1794–1861', *Journal of European Economic History,* 5 (1976)

Herman, L. M., 'Russian manganese and the American market', *Slavic Review,* 10 (1951)

Hermonius, E., 'Russia's agriculture and the repayment of foreign loans', *Economic Journal,* 28 (1918)

Heymann, H., 'Oil in Soviet–Western relations in the inter-war years', *Slavic Review,* 7 (1948)

Himmer, R., 'Rathenau, Russia and Rapallo', *Central European History,* 9 (1976) [Russian-German economic relations]

Hoeffding, W., 'German trade with the Soviet Union', *Slavonic and East European Review,* 14 (1936)

Hubbard, L. E., *Soviet trade and distribution,* Macmillan, London (1938)

Hunczak, T., ed., *Russian imperialism. From Ivan the Great to the revolution,* Rutgers University Press, New Brunswick, N.J. (1974)

Huntingdon, W. C., 'The prospects of American trade with the Soviet Union', *Slavonic and East European Review,* 14 (1935) [examines US–USSR trade in ten years before Five Year Plan]

Johnston, C., 'The Russo-German tariff war', *Economic Journal,* 4 (1894)

Just, C. F., *Reprint of articles dealing with Russian trade,* Department of Trade and Commerce, Ottawa (1916)

Kahan, A., 'Observations on Petrine foreign trade',

Canadian-American Slavic Studies, 8 (1974)

Kaser, M. C., 'A volume index of Soviet foreign trade', *Soviet Studies,* 20 (1969)

Kazemzadeh, F., *Russia and Britain in Persia, 1864–1914. A study in imperialism,* Yale University Press, New Haven, Conn. (1968)

Kirchner, W., ed., *Commercial relations between Russia and Europe, 1400–1800,* Indiana University Press, Bloomington, Ind. (1960)

Kirchner, W., 'Western Europe's role in Russian-American trade in the pre-steam age', *Papers presented to the fifth international economic history conference, Leningrad, 1970,* Mouton, Paris (1979)

Kirchner, W., 'Russian tariffs and foreign industries before 1914. The German entrepreneur's perspective', *Journal of Economic History,* 41 (1981)

Kireev, N. G., 'On the history of Russian-Turkish trade relations via Istanbul in the middle of the eighteenth century', in *Istanbul à la jonction des cultures balkaniques, mediterranéenes, slaves et orientales aux XVIe–XIXe siècles,* A.I.E.S.E.E., Bucharest (1973)

Knoppers, J., *Dutch trade with Russia from the time of Peter I to Alexander I. A quantitative study in eighteenth century shipping,* 3 vols, Interuniversity Centre for European Studies, (1976)

Knoppers, J., 'The changing nature of eighteenth century Dutch trade with Russia', *New Review of East European History,* 15–16 (1976)

Kolz, A. W. F., 'British economic interests in Siberia during the Russian civil war, 1918–20', *Journal of Modern History,* 48 (1976)

Kucherov, S., 'Indigenous and foreign influences on the early Russian legal heritage', *Slavic Review,* 31 (1972)

Lobanov-Rostovsky, A., 'Russian imperialism in Asia', *Slavonic and east European Review,* 8 (1929)

Long, J. W., 'Franco-Russian relations during the Russo-Japanese war', *Slavonic and East European Review,* 52 (1974)

Macmillan, D. S., 'The Scottish-Russian trade. Its development, fluctuations and difficulties, 1750–96', *Canadian-American Slavic Studies,* 4 (1970)

Macmillan, D. S., 'Paul's "retributive measures" of 1800 against Britain. The final turning point in British commercial attitudes towards Russia', *Canadian-American Slavic Studies,* 7 (1973)

Macmillan, D. S., 'The Russia Company of London in the eighteenth century. The effective survival of a "registered" chartered company', *Guildhall Miscellany,* 4 (1973)

Macmillan, D. S., 'Russo-British trade relations under Alexander I', *Canadian-American Slavic Studies,* 9 (1975)

Mikoletzky, L., 'The interdependence of economics and politics. An example from the Austro-Russian alliance during the Napoleonic wars', *Journal of European Economic History,* 2 (1973)

Milgrim, M. R., 'An overlooked problem in Turkish-Russian relations. The 1878 war indemnity', *International Journal of Middle East Studies,* 9 (1978)

Miller, M. S., 'The trade balance of Russia. A critical analysis of the methods of collection of trade statistics', *Slavonic and East European Review,* 1 (1922)

Munting, R., 'Ransome's in Russia. An English agricultural engineering company's trade with Russia to 1917', *Economic History Review,* 31 (1978)

Murby, R. N., 'Canadian economic commission to Siberia, 1918–19', *Canadian Slavonic Papers,* 11 (1969)

Okun, S. B., *The Russian-American Company,* Harvard University Press, Cambridge, Mass. (1961)

Owen, G. L., 'Dollar diplomacy in default. The economics of Russian-American relations, 1910–17', *Historical Journal,* 13 (1970)

Owen, G. L., 'The Metro-Vickers crisis. Anglo-Soviet relations between trade agreements, 1932–34', *Slavonic and East European Review,* 49 (1971)

Pethybridge, R. W., 'British imperialists and the Russian empire', *Russian Review,* 30 (1971) [comparison of imperialist policies in the nineteenth century]

Pikhala, E., 'Finnish iron and the Russian market, 1880–1914', *Scandinavian Economic History Review,* 12 (1964)

Pipping, H. E., 'Trade between Finland and Russia in 1860–1917', *Scandinavian Economic History Review,* 19 (1971)

Price, J. M., 'The tobacco adventure to Russia. Enterprise, politics and diplomacy in the quest for a northern market for English colonial tobacco, 1676–1722', *Transactions of the American Philosophical Society,* 51 (1961)

Putnam, P., *Seven Britons in imperial Russia, 1698–1812,* Princeton University Press, Princeton, N.J. (1952)

Queen, G. S., 'American relief in the Russian famine of 1891–92', *Russian Review,* 14 (1955)

Quested, R., *The Russo-Chinese Bank. A multinational base of Tsarism in China,* University of Birmingham, Birmingham (1977)

Reading, D. K., *The Anglo-Russian commercial treaty of 1734,* Yale University Press, New Haven, Conn. (1938)

Rich, E. E., 'Russia and the colonial fur trade', *Economic History Review,* 7 (1954–55)

Ronimois, H. E., 'The Baltic trade of the Soviet Union. Expectations and probabilities', *Slavic Review,* 4 (1945) [covers period 1913–35]

Ronimois, H. E., *Russia's foreign trade and the Baltic Sea,* Boreas Publishing Company, London (1946)

Ropes, E. C., 'American-Soviet trade relations', *Russian Review,* 3 (1943) [covers period 1918–42]

Rubinow, I. M., *Russian wheat and wheat flour in European markets,* U.S. Department of Agriculture, Bureau of Statistics, Washington, D.C. (1908)

Saul, N. E., *Russia and the Mediterranean, 1797–1807,* University of Chicago Press, Chicago, Ill. (1970)

Sladkovskii, M. I., *History of economic relations between Russia and China,* Israel Programme for Scientific Translations, Jerusalem (1966)

Smith, G. A., *Soviet foreign trade. Organization, operations and policy, 1918–71,* Praeger, New York (1973)

Sokol, A. E., 'Russian expansion and exploration in the Pacific', *Slavic Review,* 11 (1952)

Spring, D. W., 'Russian imperialism in Asia in 1914', *Cahiers du Monde Russe et Soviétique,* 20 (1979)

Taylor, A. E., 'The commerical importance of Russia', *American Economic Review,* 12 (1922)

Thompstone, S., 'Russia's tea traders. A neglected segment of a still neglected entrepreneurial class', *Renaissance and Modern Studies,* 24 (1980)

Tikhmener, P. A., *A history of the Russian-American Company,* University of Washington Press, Seattle, Wash. (1978)

Tillett, L. R., 'Soviet second thoughts on Tsarist colonialism', *Foreign Affairs,* 42 (1964)

Timoshenko, V. P., *Economic background for the post-war international trade of the U.S.S.R.,* Russian Economic Institute, New York (1945) [examines development of Soviet trade 1917–39]

Tuve, J. E., 'Changing directions in Russian-American economic relations, 1912–17', *Slavic Review,* 31 (1972)

Vucinich, W. S., ed., *Russia and Asia. Essays on the influence of Russia on the Asian peoples,* Hoover Institution Press, Stanford, Cal. (1972)

POPULATION AND MIGRATION

Anderson, B. A., 'Who chose the cities? Migrants to Moscow and St. Petersburg cities in the late nineteenth century', in R. D. Lee *et al., Population patterns in the past,* Academic Press, New York (1977)

Anderson, B. A., *Internal migration during modernization in late nineteenth century Russia,* Princeton University Press, Princeton, N.J. (1980)

Armstrong, T., *Russian settlement in the north,* Cambridge University Press, Cambridge (1965)

Baikalov, A. V., 'The conquest and colonisation of Siberia', *Slavonic and East European Review,* 10 (1932)

Bartlett, R. P., 'Foreign settlement in Russia under Catherine II', *New Zealand Slavonic Journal,* 1 (1974)

Bartlett, R. P., *Human capital. The settlement of foreigners in Russia, 1762–1804,* Cambridge University Press, Cambridge (1979)

Bradley, J., 'Patterns of peasant migration to late nineteenth century Moscow. How much should we read into literacy rates?', *Russian History,* 6 (1979)

Chojnacka, H., 'Nuptiality patterns in an agrarian society', *Population Studies,* 30 (1976)

Coale, A. J., *et al., Human fertility in Russia since the nineteenth century,* Princeton University Press, Princeton, N.J. (1979)

Demko, G. J., *The Russia colonization of Kazakhistan, 1896–1916',* Indiana University Press, Bloomington, Ind. (1969)

Duran, J. A., 'Catherine II, Potemkin and colonization policy in southern Russia', *Russian Review,* 28 (1969)

Eason, W. W., *The population of the Soviet Union,* Washington Council for Economic and Industrial Research, Washington, D.C. (1955) [covers period 1890–1955]

Eason, W. W., 'Population changes', in C. E. Black, ed., *The transformation of Russian society,* Harvard University Press, Cambridge, Mass. (1960)

Engman, M., 'Migration from Finland to Russia during the nineteenth century', *Scandinavian Journal of History,* 3 (1978)

Gibson, J. R., 'Russian occupance of the far east, 1639–1750', *Canadian Slavonic Papers,* 12 (1970)

Guinn, U. K., 'A footnote to the 1939 census of the U.S.S.R.', *Soviet Studies,* 14 (1963)

Herlihy, P., 'Death in Odessa. A study of population movements in a nineteenth century city', *Journal of Urban History,* 4 (1978)

Hoch, S. L., and W. R. Augustine, 'The tax censuses and the decline of the serf population in imperial Russia, 1883–1958', *Slavic Review,* 38 (1979)

Johnson, R. E., 'Peasant migration and the Russian

working class. Moscow at the end of the nineteenth century', *Slavic Review*, 35 (1976)

Koop, P. A., 'Some economic aspects of the Mennonite migration, with special emphasis on the 1870s migration from Russia to North America', *Mennonite Quarterly Review*, 55 (1981)

Koshkaryova, L., 'Development and settlement of the Soviet far east', *Far Eastern Affairs*, 2 (1979)

Lautzeff, G. V., and R. A. Pierce, *Eastward to empire. Exploration and conquest on the Russian open frontier to 1750*, McGill-Queens University Press, Montreal (1973)

Leasure, J. W., and R. A. Lewis, *Population changes in Russia and the U.S.S.R. A set of comparable territorial units*, San Diego State College Press, San Diego, Cal. (1966)

Leasure, J. W., and R. A. Lewis, 'Internal migration in Russia in the late nineteenth century', *Slavic Review*, 27 (1968)

Lewis, R. A., and J. W. Leasure, 'Regional population changes in Russia and the U.S.S.R. since 1851', *Slavic Review*, 25 (1966)

Lewis, R. A., and R. H. Rowland, 'East is west and west is east. Population redistribution in the U.S.S.R. and its impact on society', *International Migration Review*, 11 (1977)

Lewis, R. A., and R. H. Rowland, *Population redistribution in the U.S.S.R. Its impact on society, 1897–1977*, Praeger, New York (1977)

Lorimer, F., *The population of the Soviet Union. History and prospects*, United Nations, Geneva (1946)

Mazuv, D. P., 'Reconstruction of fertility trends for the female population of the U.S.S.R.', *Population Studies*, 21 (1967)

Mironenko, Y., 'A demographic survey', *Studies on the Soviet Union*, 7 (1968)

Obolensky-Ossinsky, V. V., 'Emigration from and immigration into Russia', in W. F. Willcox, ed., *International migrations*, 2 vols, National Bureau of Economic Research, New York (1929–31)

Rowney, D. K., and E. G. Stockwell, 'The Russian census of 1897. Some observations on the age data', *Slavic Review*, 37 (1978)

Selegen, G. V., 'Economic characteristics of the population in the Soviet census questionnaire', *Soviet Studies*, 11 (1960) [comparison of 1926 and 1959 census]

Selegen, G. V., 'The first report on the recent population census in the Soviet Union', *Population Studies*, 14 (1960–61)

Siegelbaum, L. H., 'Another "yellow peril". Chinese migrants in the Russian far east and the Russian reaction before 1917', *Modern Asian Studies*, 12 (1978)

Silber, J., 'Some demographic characteristics of the Jewish population in Russia at the end of the nineteenth century', *Jewish Social Studies*, 42 (1980)

Treadgold, D. W., *The great Siberian migration. Government and peasant in resettlement from emancipation to the first world war*, Princeton University Press, Princeton, N.J. (1957)

LABOUR CONDITIONS AND ORGANISATION

Augustine, W. R., 'Russia's railwaymen, July–October 1917', *Slavic Review*, 24 (1965)

Avrich, P. H., 'The Bolshevik revolution and workers' control in Russian industry', *Slavic Review*, 22 (1963)

Bonnell, V. E., 'Radical politics and organized labor in pre-revolutionary Moscow, 1905–14', *Journal of Social History*, 12 (1978)

Bonnell, V. E., 'Trade unions, parties and the state in Tsarist Russia. A study of labor politics in St. Petersburg and Moscow', *Politics and Society*, 9 (1980)

Brodersen, A., *The Soviet worker. Labor and government in Soviet society*, Random House, New York (1966)

Bunyan, J., *The origin of forced labor in the Soviet state, 1917–21. Documents and materials*, Johns Hopkins University Press, Baltimore, Md. (1967)

Conquest, R., ed., *Industrial workers in the U.S.S.R.*, Praeger, New York (1967)

Conquest, R., *Agricultural workers in the U.S.S.R.*, Bodley Head, London (1968) [historical development of collectivization, but mainly post-Stalin]

Crisp, O., 'Labour and industrialization in Russia', in P. Mathias and M. M. Postan, eds., *Cambridge Economic History of Europe*, vol. 7(2), Cambridge University Press, Cambridge (1978)

Crottet, A. A., and S. L. Childs, 'Trade unions in the Soviet state', *Economic History*, 2 (1933)

Dallin, D. J., and B. Nikolaevsky, *Forced labor in Soviet Russia*, Yale University Press, New Haven, Conn. (1947)

Deutscher, I., *Soviet trade unions*, Royal Institute of International Affairs, London (1950)

Dewar, M., *Labour policy in the U.S.S.R., 1917–28*, Royal Institute of International Affairs, London (1956)

Dodge, N. T., 'Fifty years of Soviet labor', *Studies on the Soviet Union,* 7 (1967)

Douglas, P. H., 'Labor legislation and social insurance', in S. Chase *et al., Soviet Russia in the second decade,* John Day, New York (1928)

Duchess of Atholl, *Conscription of a people,* Columbia University Press, New York (1931) [covers forced labour, collectivization]

Dunn, R. W., *Soviet trade unions,* Vanguard Press, New York (1928)

Easton, W. W., *Employment and unemployment in the Soviet Union,* Rand Corporation, Santa Monica, Cal. (1954)

Esper, T., 'The condition of serf workers in Russia's metallurgical industries, 1800–61', *Journal of Modern History,* 50 (1978)

Esper, T., 'Hired labor in the metallurgical industry of the Urals during the late serf period', *Jahrbücher für Geschichte Osteuropas,* 28 (1980)

Florinsky, M. T., 'Stalin's new deal for labour', *Political Science Quarterly,* 56 (1941)

Freeman, J., *The Soviet worker. An account of the economic social and cultural status of labor in the U.S.S.R.,* Liveright, New York (1932)

Galenson, W., 'Industrial training in the Soviet Union', *Industrial and Labour Relations Review,* 9 (1956) [Soviet training schemes, 1928–54]

Giffin, F. C., 'The prohibition of night work for women and young persons. The Factory Law of June 3, 1885', *Canadian Slavic Studies,* 2 (1968)

Giffin, F. C., 'I. I. Yanzuhl, Russia's first district factory inspector', *Slavonic and East European Review,* 49 (1971)

Giffin, F. C., 'The role of the Pleve Commission in the Russian factory laws of 1885 and 1886', *European Studies Review,* 2 (1972)

Giffin, F. C., 'The "First Russian Labour Code". The law of June 3, 1886', *Russian History,* 2 (1975)

Giffin, F. C., 'Improving the conditions of child labour in Russia. The law of 12 June 1884', *European Studies Review,* 7 (1977)

Glickman, R. L., 'Industrialisation and the factory worker in Russian literature', *Canadian-American Slavic Review,* 4 (1970)

Gliksman, J. G., 'The Russian urban worker. From serf to proletarian', in C. E. Black, ed., *The transformation of Russian society. Aspects of social change since 1861,* Harvard University Press, Cambridge, Mass. (1960)

Gordon, M., *Workers before and after Lenin,* E. P. Dutton, New York (1941)

Hammond, T. T., 'Lenin on Russian trade unions under capitalism, 1894–1904', *Slavic Review,* 8 (1949)

Hewes, A., 'Labor conditions in Soviet Russia', *Journal of Political Economy,* 28 (1920)

Hewes, A., 'Russian wage systems under communism', *Journal of Political Economy,* 30 (1922)

Hewes, A., 'Trade union development in Soviet Russia', *American Economic Review,* 13 (1923)

Hewes, A., 'The transformation of Soviet trade unions', *American Economic Review,* 22 (1932)

Hoffding, V., 'Labour conditions in Soviet Russia', parts 1 and 2, *Slavonic and East European Review,* 6 (1928), 7 (1929)

Hubbard, L. E., *Soviet labour and industry,* Macmillan, London (1942)

International Labour Office, 'The employment situation in Russia since the Bolshevist revolution', parts 1 and 2, *International Labour Review,* 3 (1921), 4 (1922)

International Labour Office, 'Unemployment in Russia, 1917–25', *International Labour Review,* 14 (1926)

International Labour Office, *Trade union movement in Soviet Russia,* P. S. King, Geneva (1927)

International Labour Office, 'The problem of hours of work in the Soviet Union', parts 1 and 2, *International Labour Review,* 17 (1928)

International Labour Office, 'Women workers and their protection in Russian industry', *International Labour Review,* 20 (1929)

International Labour Office, 'The provision of work for the unemployed in the U.S.S.R.', *International Labour Review,* 22 (1930)

International Labour Office, 'The seven-hour day in Soviet Russia', *International Labour Review,* 22 (1930)

International Labour Office, 'The continuous working week in Soviet Russia', *International Labour Review,* 23 (1931)

International Labour Office, *Labour conditions in Soviet Russia,* Harrison and Sons, London (n.d.)

Johnson, R. E., 'Strikes in Moscow, 1880–1900', *Russian History,* 5 (1978)

Johnson, R. E., *Peasant and proletarian. The working class of Moscow in the late nineteenth century,* Rutgers University Press, New Brunswick, N.J. (1979)

Kahan, A., 'The "hereditary workers" hypothesis and the development of a factory labor force in eighteenth and nineteenth century Russia', in C. A. Anderson and M. J. Bowman, eds, *Education and economic development,* Cass, London (1966)

Kingsbury, S. M., and M. Fairchild, *Employment*

and unemployment in pre-war and Soviet Russia, International Industrial Relations Association, The Hague (1931)

Kovalchenko, I. D., and N. B. Selunskaia, 'Labor rental in the manorial economy of European Russia at the end of the nineteenth century and the beginning of the twentieth', *Explorations in Economic History*, 18 (1981)

Kuczynski, J., *The condition of the workers in Great Britain, Germany and the Soviet Union, 1932–38*, Gollancz, London (1939)

Lantsev, M., 'Progress in social security for agricultural workers in the U.S.S.R.', *International Labour Review*, 107 (1973)

Levine, I. R., *The new worker in Soviet Russia*, Macmillan, New York (1973) [extensive coverage of pre-1917 years]

Lozovsky, A., ed., *Handbook on the Soviet trade unions*, Co-operative Publishing Society, Moscow (1937)

Lyons, E., *Workers' paradise lost. Fifty years of Soviet communism. A balance sheet*, Funk and Wagnalls, New York (1967)

McFarlin, H. A., 'The extension of the imperial Russian civil service to the lowest office workers. The creation of the Chancery Clerkship', *Russian History*, 1 (1974)

McKinsey, P. S., 'From city workers to peasantry. The beginning of the Russian movement "to the people" ', *Slavic Review*, 38 (1979)

Markus, B. L., 'The abolition of unemployment in the U.S.S.R.', *International Labour Review*, 33 (1936)

Markus, B. L., 'The Stakhanov movement and the increased productivity of labour in the U.S.S.R.', *International Labour Review*, 34 (1936)

Mendel, A. P., 'Peasant and worker on the eve of the first world war', *Slavic Review*, 24 (1965)

Mendelsohn, E., *Class struggle in the Pale. The formative years of the Jewish workers' movement in Tsarist Russia*, Cambridge University Press, Cambridge (1970)

Mixter, T., 'Of grandfather beaters and fat-heeled pacificists. Perceptions of agricultural labour and hiring market disturbances in Saratov, 1872–1905', *Russian History*, 7 (1980)

Moskalenko, G. K., 'Collective agreements in the U.S.S.R.', *International Labour Review*, 85 (1962) [deals with Tsarist period also]

Palat, M. K., 'Tsarist labour policies', *Soviet Studies*, 25 (1973)

Perrins, M., 'Rabkrin and workers' control in Russia, 1917–34', *European Studies Review*, 10 (1980)

Pipes, R., *Social democracy and the St. Petersburg labour movement, 1885–97*, Harvard University Press, Cambridge, Mass. (1963)

Portal, R., 'Serfs in the Urals iron foundries in the eighteenth century', in V. R. Lorwin, ed., *Labor and working conditions in modern Europe*, Macmillan, New York (1967)

Pospielovsky, D., *Russian police trade unionism. Experiment or provocation*, Weidenfeld and Nicolson, London (1971)

Potichnyj, P. J., *Soviet agricultural trade unions, 1917–70*, University of Toronto Press, Toronto (1972)

Price, G. M., *Labor protection in Soviet Russia*, International Publishers, New York (1928)

Redding, A. D., 'Employment and labour productivity in U.S.S.R. railroads, 1928–50', *Soviet Studies*, 5 (1953)

Redding, A. D., 'Comparison of volume and distribution of non-agricultural employment in the U.S.S.R., 1928–55, with the U.S., 1870–1952', *Review of Economics and Statistics*, 36 (1954)

Redding, A. D., 'Volume and distribution of non-agricultural employment in the U.S.S.R., 1928–55', *Slavic Review*, 13 (1954)

Rimlinger, G. V., 'The management of labour protest in Tsarist Russia, 1870–1905', *International Review of Social History*, 5 (1960)

Rimlinger, G. V., 'Autocracy and the factory order in early Russian industrialization', *Journal of Economic History*, 20 (1960)

Rimlinger, G. V., 'The expansion of the labor market in capitalist Russia, 1861–1917', *Journal of Economic History*, 21 (1961)

Rimlinger, G. V., 'The trade union in Soviet social insurance. Historical development and present functions', *Industrial and Labor Relations Review*, 14 (1961)

Robinson, E., 'Birmingham capitalists and Russian workers', *History Today*, 6 (1956)

Roosa, R. A., 'Workers' insurance legislation and the role of the industrialists in the period of the third State Duma', *Russian Review*, 34 (1975)

Roosa, R. A., 'Russian industrialists, politics and labor reform in 1905', *Russian History*, 2 (1975)

Rosefielde, S., 'An assessment of the sources and uses of Gulag forced labour, 1929–56', *Soviet Studies*, 33 (1981)

Rubinow, I. M., 'The new Russian working men's compensation', *Bulletin of the Bureau of Labor*, 10 (1905)

Schwarz, S. M., *Labour in the Soviet Union*, Praeger, New York (1951)

Scott, J., *Behind the Urals. An American worker in Russia's city of steel*, Houghton Mifflin, Boston (1942)

Snow, G. E., 'The Kokovtsov Commission. An abortive attempt at labor reform in Russia in 1905', *Slavic Review*, 31 (1972)

Sorenson, J. B., *The life and death of Soviet trade unionism, 1917–28*, Atherton Press, New York (1969)

Suny, R. G., 'Labour and liquidators. Revolutionaries and the "reaction" in Baku, May 1908–April 1912', *Slavic Review*, 34 (1975)

Surh, G. D., 'Petersburg's first mass labor organization. The assembly of Russian workers and Father Gapon', parts 1 and 2, *Russian Review*, 40 (1981)

Swain, G., 'Bolsheviks and metalworkers on the eve of the first world war', *Journal of Contemporary History*, 16 (1981)

Swain, G., *Russian social democracy and the legal labour movement*, Macmillan, London (1982)

Swianiewicz, S., *Forced labour and economic development*, Oxford University Press, London (1965)

Turnau, I., 'Aspects of the Russian artisan. The knitter of the seventeenth to the eighteenth century', *Textile History*, 4 (1973)

Vasil'ev, B. N., 'The size, composition and territorial distribution of the factory-plant proletariat of European Russia and the Transcaucasus in 1913–14', *Soviet Studies in History*, 19 (1981)

Von Laue, T. H., 'Factory inspection under the Witte system, 1892–1903', *Slavic Review*, 19 (1960)

Von Laue, T. H., 'Russian peasants in the factory, 1892–1904', *Journal of Economic History*, 21 (1961)

Von Laue, T. H., 'Tsarist labor policy, 1895–1903', *Journal of Modern History*, 34 (1962)

Von Laue, T. H., 'Russian labor between field and factory, 1892–1903', *California Slavic Studies*, 3 (1964)

Walkin, J., 'The attitude of the Tsarist government toward the labor problem', *Slavic Review*, 13 (1954)

Ward, B., 'Wild socialism in Russia. Its origins', *California Slavic Studies*, 3 (1964) [factory committees and their economic background]

Weitzman, M. S., and A. Elias, *The magnitude and distribution of civilian employment in the U.S.S.R., 1928–59*, Government Printing Office, Washington, D.C. (1961)

Wheatcroft, S. G., 'On assessing the size of forced concentration camp labour in the Soviet Union, 1929–56', *Soviet Studies*, 33 (1981)

Wildman, A. K., *The making of a workers' revolution. Russian social democracy, 1891–1903*, University of Chicago Press, Chicago, Ill. (1967)

Wolfe, B. D., 'Gosplan and Zubatov. An experiment in police socialism', *Russian Review*, 7 (1948) [police control of trade unions at the turn of the century]

Zelnik, R. E., 'An early case of labor protest in St. Petersburg. The Alexandrovsk machine works in 1860', *Slavic Review*, 24 (1965)

Zelnik, R. E., 'The peasant and the factory', in W. Vucinich, ed., *The peasant in nineteenth century Russia*, Stanford University Press, Stanford, Cal. (1968)

Zelnik, R. E., *Labor and society in Tsarist Russia. The factory workers of St. Petersburg, 1855–70*, Stanford University Press, Stanford, Cal. (1971)

Zelnik, R. E., 'Russian workers and the revolutionary movement. Review essay', *Journal of Social History*, 6 (1972–73)

Zelnik, R. E., 'Two and a half centuries of labor history. St. Petersburg/Petrograd/Leningrad', *Slavic Review*, 33 (1974)

INCOMES, WAGES AND PRICES

Abramson, A., 'Social insurance in Soviet Russia', *Journal of Political Economy*, 37 (1929)

Abramson, A., 'The reorganisation of social insurance institutions in the U.S.S.R.', *International Labour Review*, 31 (1935)

Anonymous, 'Wages and currency reform in Soviet Russia', *International Labour Review*, 10 (1924)

Baster, N., 'Some early family budget studies of Russian workers', *Slavic Review*, 17 (1958)

Bergson, A., 'Distribution of the earnings bill among industrial workers in the Soviet Union, March, 1928, October, 1934', *Journal of Political Economy*, 50 (1942)

Bergson, A., *Structure of Soviet wages. A study of socialist economics*, Harvard University Press, Cambridge, Mass. (1944)

Bergson, A., 'On inequality of incomes in the U.S.S.R.', *Slavic Review*, 10 (1951)

Bergson, A., 'Prices of basic industrial products in the U.S.S.R., 1928–50', *Journal of Political Economy*, 64 (1956)

Bergson, A., *et al.*, *Basic industrial prices in the U.S.S.R., 1928–56. Twenty-five branch series and their aggregation*, Rand Corporation, Santa Monica, Cal. (1956)

Chapman, J. G., *Retail prices of manufactured consumer goods in the U.S.S.R., 1937–48*, Rand Corporation, Santa Monica, Cal. (rev. edn 1952)

Chapman, J. G., 'Real wages in the Soviet Union, 1928–52', *Review of Economics and Statistics,* 36 (1954)

Chapman, J. G., 'Consumption', in A. Bergson, and S. Kuznets, eds, *Economic trends in the Soviet Union,* Harvard University Press, Cambridge, Mass. (1963)

Chapman, J. G., *Real wages in the Soviet Union since 1928,* Harvard University Press, Cambridge, Mass. (1963)

Chapman, J. G., 'Consumption in the Soviet Union', in M. Bernstein, and D. Fusfeld, eds, *The Soviet economy. A book of readings,* Richard D. Irwin, Homewood, Ill. (1966)

Childs, S. L., and A. A. Crottet, 'Wages policy in Soviet Russia', *Economic History,* 2 (1932)

Chossodowsky, E. M., 'Rationing in the U.S.S.R.', *Review of Economic Studies,* 8 (1941) [covers rationing system of 1928–35]

Douglas, P. H., 'Wages in material condition of the industrial workers', in S. Chase, *et al., Soviet Russia in the second decade,* John Day, New York (1928)

Esper, T., 'The incomes of Russian serf ironworkers in the nineteenth century', *Past and Present,* 93 (1981)

Grossman, G., 'Industrial prices in the U.S.S.R.', *American Economic Review,* 49 (1959) [covers period 1929–57]

Hayenko, F., 'Social security in the Soviet Union', *Studies on the Soviet Union,* 4 (1965)

Holzman, F. D., 'Soviet inflationary pressures, 1928–57. Causes and cures', *Quarterly Journal of Economics,* 74 (1960)

Hutt, W. H., 'Two studies in the statistics of Russia', *South African Journal of Economics,* 13 (1945) [covers standard of living before 1914. See comment by C. A. Friedmann in the same issue]

International Labour Office, 'Wages and currency reform in Soviet Russia', *International Labour Review,* 10 (1924)

International Labour Office, 'Social insurance in the U.S.S.R., 1933–37', *International Labour Review,* 38 (1938)

Jasny, N., *Soviet prices of producers' goods,* Stanford University Press, Stanford, Cal. (1952) [covers 1926–27]

Jasny, N., 'Peasant incomes under full-scale collectivization', in N. Jasny, *Essays on the Soviet economy,* Praeger, New York (1962) [considers period 1927/28–37/40]

Kaser, M. C., 'Soviet statistics of wages and prices', *Soviet Studies,* 7 (1955–56)

Knight, C., 'Change in the Soviet diet', *Association for Comparative Economic Studies Bulletin,* 10 (1968) [food tables for selected years, 1928–63]

Kravis, I. B., and J. Mintzes, 'Food prices in the Soviet Union 1936–50', *Review of Economics and Statistics,* 32 (1950)

Miller, J., 'The standard of living in Moscow, 1937', *Soviet Studies,* 4 (1952–53)

Mironov, B. N., 'The "price revolution" in eighteenth century Russia', *Soviet Studies in History,* 11 (1973)

Munting, R., 'Outside earnings in the Russian peasant farm. Tula province, 1900–17', *Journal of Peasant Studies,* 3 (1976)

Nash, E., 'Purchasing power of workers in the Soviet Union', *Monthly Labor Review,* 94 (1971) [comparisons of selected years, including 1928]

Niwa, H., 'Retail and real wages in the U.S.S.R., 1928–59', *Journal of Economic Behaviour,* 1 (1961)

Nove, A., '1926/7 and all that', *Soviet Studies,* 9 (1957–58)

Pintner, W. M., 'Inflation in Russia during the Crimean war period', *Slavic Review,* 18 (1959)

School of Slavonic and East European Studies. *The end of rationing and the standard of living in the Soviet Union,* London University, London (1935)

Schraeder, G. E., 'Consumption in the U.S.S.R. A survey', *Studies on the Soviet Union,* 10 (1970)

Seton, F., 'Pre-war Soviet prices in the light of the 1941 plan', *Soviet Studies,* 3 (1951–52)

Toda, Y., 'An inter-country comparison of the consumption levels of industrial workers' families. Russia 1913–U.S.A. 1901', *Papers presented to the fourth international conference of economic history, Bloomington, 1968,* Mouton, Paris (1973)

Turin, S. P., 'Market prices and controlled prices of food in Moscow', *Journal of the Royal Statistical Society,* 83 (1920) [Moscow prices in 1915, 1919 and 1920]

Turin, S. P., 'Workers' family budget enquiries in Soviet Russia', *International Labour Review,* 20 (1929)

Turin, S. P., *From Peter the Great to Lenin. A history of the Russian labour movement, with special reference to trade unionism,* P. S. King, London (1935)

Vogel, H., 'Satisfaction of consumer needs', *Studies on the Soviet Union,* 7 (1967)

Ward, H. F., *In place of profit. Social incentives in*

the Soviet Union, Scribner, New York (1933)

Wiles, P. J. D., 'Average wages in the U.S.S.R.', *Bulletin of the Oxford University Institute of Economics and Statistics,* 15 (1953) [estimates of average money wages for various years, 1928–50]

Yanowitch, M., 'Trends in differentials between salaried personnel and wage workers in Soviet industry', *Soviet Studies,* 11 (1960)

Yanowitch, M., 'Trends in Soviet occupational wage differentials', *Industrial and Labor Relations Review,* 13 (1960) [covers period from first Five Year Plan]

URBAN HISTORY

Abbott, R. J., 'Crime, police, and society in St. Petersburg, Russia, 1866–78', *Historian,* 40 (1977)

Abbott, W. F., 'Moscow in 1897 as a pre-industrial city. A test of the inverse Burgess zonal hypothesis', *American Sociological Review,* 39 (1974)

Abbott, W. F., 'Social area analysis in comparative perspective. Moscow in 1897 as a pre-industrial city', *Sociological Quarterly,* 19 (1978)

Baron, S. H., 'The town in "feudal" Russia. A review article', *Slavic Review,* 28 (1969)

Bater, J. H., *St. Petersburg. Industrialization and change,* Edward Arnold, London (1976)

Bater, J. H., 'Some dimensions of urbanization and the response of municipal government. Moscow and St. Petersburg', *Russian History,* 5 (1978)

Bater, J. H., 'Transience, residential persistence and mobility in Moscow and St. Petersburg, 1900–14', *Slavic Review,* 39 (1980)

Blackwell, W. L., 'Modernization and urbanization in Russia. A comparative view', in M. F. Hamm, ed., *The city in Russian history,* University Press of Kentucky, Lexington, Ky. (1976)

Blackwell, W. L., 'Geography, history and the city in Europe and Russia', *Journal of Urban History,* 6 (1980)

Block, A., 'Soviet housing. Some town planning problems', *Soviet Studies,* 6 (1954–55)

Brower, D. R., 'Urban Russia on the eve of World War I. A social profile', *Journal of Social History,* 13 (1980)

Eaton, H. L., 'Decline and recovery of the Russian cities from 1500 to 1700', *Canadian-American Slavic Studies,* 11 (1977)

Fedor, T., *Patterns of urban growth in the Russian empire during the nineteenth century,* University of Chicago Press, Chicago, Ill. (1975)

Fox, D. J., 'Odessa', *Scottish Geographical Magazine,* 73 (1963) [city development]

Gozman, G., *Urban networks in Russia 1750–1800, and pre-modern periodization,* Princeton University Press, Princeton, N.J. (1974)

Grekov, B. D., *Kiev Rus,* Foreign Languages Publishing House, Moscow (1959)

Gutkind, E. A., *et al., International history of city development,* vol. 8, *Urban development in eastern Europe. Bulgaria, Romania and the U.S.S.R.,* Collier-Macmillan, London (1972)

Hamm, M. F., ed., *The city in Russian history,* University Press of Kentucky, Lexington, Ky. (1976)

Hamm, M. F., 'The modern Russian city. A historiographical analysis', *Journal of Urban History,* 4 (1977)

Hamm, M. F., 'Riga's 1913 city election. A study in Baltic urban politics', *Russian Review,* 39 (1980)

Herlihy, P., 'Odessa. Staples trade and urbanization in New Russia', *Jahrbücher für Geschichte Osteuropas,* 21 (1973)

Hittle, J. M., *The service city. State and townsmen in Russia, 1600–1800,* Harvard University Press, Cambridge, Mass. (1979)

Kaganovich, L. M., *Socialist reconstruction of Moscow and other cities in the U.S.S.R.,* International Publishers, New York (1931) [general treatment of urban development]

Koenker, D., 'Peasants, proletarians, and Posad people. Social dimension of Russian urban history', *Journal of Urban History,* 7 (1981)

Lincoln, W. B., 'N.A. Miliutin and the St. Petersburg Municipal Act of 1846. A study in reform under Nicholas I', *Slavic Review,* 33 (1974)

Lindenmeyr, A., 'Raskolnikov's city and the Napoleonic plan', *Slavic Review,* 35 (1976)

May, E., 'Cities of the future', in W. Laquerer and L. Labedz, eds, *The future of communist society,* Praeger, New York (1962) [achievements of 1929 town planning schemes]

Petersen, Z. B., 'The architectural heritage of Leningrad', *Slavic Review,* 4 (1945)

Rozman, G., 'Comparative approaches to urbanization. Russia, 1750–1800', in M. F. Hamm, ed., *The city in Russian history,* University of Kentucky Press, Lexington, Ky. (1976)

Rozman, G., *Urban networks in Russia, 1750–1800, and pre-modern periodization,* Princeton University Press, Princeton, N.J. (1976)

Schmidt, A. J., 'William Hastie, Scottish planner of Russian cities', *Proceedings of the American Philosophical Society,* 114 (1970)

Shaw, D. J. B., 'The nature of the Russian city', *Journal of Historical Geography,* 3 (1977)

Siegelbaum, L. H., 'The Odessa grain trade. A case study in urban growth and development in Tsarist Russia', *Journal of European Economic History,* 9 (1980)

Skinner, F. W., 'Trends in planning policies. The building of Odessa, 1794–1917', in M. F. Hamm, ed., *The city in Russian history,* Kentucky University Press, Lexington, Ky. (1976)

Sosnovy, T., 'Town planning and housing', in W. Laquerer and L. Labedz, eds, *The future of communist society,* Praeger, New York (1962)

Thiede, R. L., 'Industry and urbanization in New Russia', in M. F. Hamm, ed., *The city in Russian history,* University of Kentucky Press, Lexington, Ky. (1976)

SOCIAL STRUCTURE AND SOCIAL CONDITIONS

Alexander, J. T., 'Communicable disease, anti-epidemic policies and the role of medical professionals in Russia, 1725–62', *Canadian-American Slavic Studies,* 12 (1978)

Alexander, J. T., *Bubonic plague in early modern Russia. Public health and urban disaster,* Johns Hopkins University Press, Baltimore, Md. (1980)

Alexander, J. T., 'Catherine the Great and public health', *Journal of the History of Medicine and Allied Sciences,* 36 (1981)

Alston, P. L., *Education and the state in Tsarist Russia,* Stanford University Press, Stanford, Cal. (1969)

Ammende, E., *Human life in Russia,* Allen and Unwin, London (1936)

Anderson, M. S., 'Some British influences on Russian intellectual life and society in the eighteenth century', *Slavonic and East European Review,* 39 (1966)

Armstrong, J. A., 'Tsarist and Soviet elite administrators', *Slavic Review,* 31 (1972)

Aronson, I. M., 'The prospects for the emancipation of Russian Jewry during the 1880s', *Slavonic and East European Review,* 53 (1977)

Aronson, I. M., 'Geographical and socioeconomic factors in the 1881 anti-Jewish pogroms in Russia', *Russian Review,* 39 (1980)

Avakumovic, I., 'A statistical approach to the revolutionary movement in Russia, 1878–87', *Slavic Review,* 18 (1959) [deals with class divisions]

Arvich, P. H., *Russian rebels, 1600–1800,* Schocken Books, New York (1972)

Bacon, E. F., *Central Asians under Russian rule. A study in cultural change,* Cornell University Press, Ithaca, N.Y. (1966)

Bailes, K. E., *Technology and society under Lenin and Stalin. Origins of the Soviet technical intelligentsia, 1917–41,* Princeton University Press, Princeton, N.J. (1978)

Baker, A. B., 'Rural education in Russia. Vneshkol'noe Obrazovomie and the co-operatives', *Slavic and European Education Review,* 1 (1977)

Balmuth, D., 'Origins of the Russian press reform of 1865', *Slavonic and East European Review,* 47 (1969)

Baring, M., *The Russian people,* Methuen, London (1911)

Baron, S. W., *The Russian Jew under Tsars and Soviets,* Macmillan, New York (1964)

Bill, V. T., *The forgotten class. The Russian bourgeoisie from the earliest beginnings to 1900,* Praeger, New York (1959)

Black, C. E., ed., *The transformation of Russian society. Aspects of social change since 1861,* Harvard University Press, Cambridge, Mass. (1960)

Black, C. E., 'The nature of imperial Russian society', *Slavic Review,* 20 (1961)

Block, A., 'Soviet housing', *Soviet Studies,* 3 (1951–52)

Block, A., 'Soviet housing – the historical aspect. Problems of amount, cost and quality in urban housing', *Soviet Studies,* 5 (1953–54)

Bobroff, A., 'The Bolsheviks and working women, 1905–20', *Radical America,* 10 (1976)

Brainerd, M., 'The Octobrists and the gentry in the Russian social crisis of 1913–14', *Russian Review,* 38 (1979)

Brower, D. R., 'Fathers, sons, and grandfathers. Social origins of radical intellectuals in nineteenth century Russia', *Journal of Social History,* 2 (1969)

Brower, D. R., 'Student political attitudes and social origins. The Technological Institute of St. Petersburg', *Journal of Social History,* 6 (1972–73)

Brown, J. H., 'The Free Economic Society and the nobility, 1765–96. Some observations', *Canadian-American Slavic Studies,* 14 (1980)

Bushnell, J., 'Peasants in uniform. The Tsarist army as a peasant society', *Journal of Social History,* 13 (1980)

Clements, B. E., 'Bolshevik women. 'The first generation', in T. Yedlin, ed., *Women in eastern Europe and the Soviet Union,* Praeger, New York (1980)

Cowles, V., *The Russian dagger. Cold war in the days of the Czars,* Harper and Row, New York

(1969)

Crummey, R. O., *The old believers and the world of Antichrist. The Vyg community and the Russian state, 1694–1855,* University of Wisconsin Press, Milwaukee, Wis. (1970)

Curtiss, J. S., 'Russian Sisters of Mercy in the Crimea, 1854–55', *Slavic Review,* 25 (1966)

Daniel, W., 'The merchants' view of the social order in Russia as revealed in the town Nakazy from Moskovskaia Guberniia to Catherine's legislative commission', *Canadian-American Slavic Studies,* 11 (1977)

Daniel, W., 'The merchantry and the problem of social order in the Russian state. Catherine II's Commission on Commerce', *Slavonic and East European Review,* 55 (1977)

Dodge, N. T., *Women in Soviet economy. Their role in economic, scientific and technical development,* Johns Hopkins University Press, Baltimore, Md. (1966) [covers 1917–60s]

Dukes, P., *Catherine the Great and the Russian nobility,* Cambridge University Press, Cambridge (1967)

Elkin, B., 'Attempts to revive Freemasonry in Russia', *Slavonic and East European Review,* 44 (1966)

Freeze, G. L., 'Social mobility and the Russian parish clergy in the eighteenth century', *Slavic Review,* 33 (1974)

Freeze, G. L., 'The disintegration of traditional communities. The parish in eighteenth century Russia', *Journal of Modern History,* 48 (1976)

Gill, G. J., 'The mainsprings of peasant action in 1917', *Soviet Studies,* 30 (1978)

Grigorian, L. A., *Soviet society (economic and social structure). A historical survey,* Novosti Press Agency, Publishing House, Moscow (1968) [achievements 1917–67 are assessed]

Grunfeld, J., 'Women's work in Russia's planned economy', *Social Research,* 9 (1942)

Gsovski, V., 'Family and inheritance in Soviet law', *Russian Review,* 7 (1947)

Guroff, G., 'The legacy of pre-revolutionary economic education. St. Petersburg Polytechnic Institute', *Russian Review,* 31 (1972)

Guroff, G., and F. S. Starr, 'A note on urban literacy in Russia, 1890–1914', *Jahrbücher für Geschichte Osteuropas,* 19 (1971)

Haigh, B., 'Urals factory hospitals and surgeons at the dawn of the nineteenth century', *Medical History,* 22 (1978)

Haimson, L. H., 'The problem of social stability in urban Russia, 1905–1917', *Slavic Review,* 23 (1964), 24 (1965)

Halevy, Z., 'Were the Jewish immigrants to the United States representative of Russian Jews?', *International Migration,* 16 (1978)

Hamburg, G. M., 'Russian nobility on the eve of the 1905 revolution', *Russian Review,* 38 (1979)

Hans, N., *A history of Russian educational policy, 1701–1917,* Russell and Russell, New York (1964)

Hassell, J., 'Implementation of the Russian table of ranks during the eighteenth century', *Slavic Review,* 29 (1970)

Heilbronner, H., 'The Russian plague of 1878–79', *Slavic Review,* 21 (1962)

Hingley, R., *The Russian secret police. Muscovite, imperial Russian and soviet political security operations,* Simon and Shuster, New York (1970)

Hollingsworth, B., 'John Venning and prison reform in Russia, 1819–30', *Slavonic and East European Review,* 48 (1970)

Home, R. W., 'Science as a career in eighteenth century Russia. The case of F. M. T. Aepinus', *Slavonic and East European Review,* 51 (1973) [insights into research and development]

Hutchinson, J. F., 'Medicine, morality and social policy in imperial Russia. The early years of the Alcoholism Commission', *Social History,* 7 (1974)

Hutchinson, J. F., 'Science, politics and the alcohol problem in post-1905 Russia', *Slavonic and East European Review,* 58 (1980)

International Labour Office, 'The housing problem in Soviet Russia', *International Labour Review,* 12 (1925)

Jarvesoo, E., 'Agricultural program at the Riga Polytechnic Institute, 1863–1919', *Journal of Baltic Studies,* 11 (1980)

Johnson, A. M., 'Simpson in Russia', *Beaver,* 311 (1980) [daily life in St Petersburg]

Johnson, W. E., *The liquor problem in Russia,* American Issue Publishing Company, Westerville, Ohio (1915)

Jones, R. E., 'Jacob Sievers, enlightened reform and the development of a "Third Estate" in Russia', *Russian Review,* 36 (1977)

Kahan, A., 'Determinants of the incidence of literacy in rural nineteenth century Russia', in C. A. Anderson and M. J. Bowman, eds, *Education and economic development,* Cass, London (1966)

Kahan, A., 'Russian scholars and statesmen on education as an investment', in C. A. Anderson, and M. J. Bowman, eds, *Education and economic development,* Cass, London (1966)

Kahan, A., 'Social aspects of the plague epidemics in eighteenth century Russia', *Economic Development and Cultural Change,* 27 (1978–79)

Keep, J., 'Programming the past. Imperial Russian bureaucracy and society under the scrutiny of Mr. George Yaney', *Canadian–American Slavic Studies,* 8 (1974)

Kingsbury, S. M., and M. Fairchild, *Factory, family and women in the Soviet Union,* Putnam's, New York (1935)

Kochan, M., *Life in Russia under Catherine the Great,* Batsford, London (1969)

Krawchenko, B., 'The impact of industrialization on the social structure of the Ukraine', *Canadian Slavonic Papers,* 22 (1980)

Kudryavtsev, A., 'The past and present of the intelligentsia', *Studies in Soviet Thought,* 17 (1977)

Le Donne, J. P., 'Criminal investigations before the great reforms', *Russian History,* 1 (1974)

Leitsch, W., 'The Russian nobility in the eighteenth century', *East European Quarterly,* 11 (1977)

Levin, A., 'More on social stability, 1905–17', *Slavic Review,* 25 (1966)

Lincoln, W. B., 'The daily life of St. Petersburg officials in the mid-nineteenth century', *Oxford Slavonic Papers,* 8 (1975)

Lincoln, W. B., 'A profile of the Russian bureaucracy on the eve of the great reforms', *Jahrbücher für Geschichte Osteuropas,* 27 (1979)

Longwirth, P., 'Transformations in Cossackdom, 1650–1850', in B. K. Kiraly and G. E. Rothenberg, eds, *War and society in east central Europe,* vol. 1, Brooklyn College Press, New York (1979)

McClelland, J. C., *Autocrats and academics. Education, culture, and society in Tsarist Russia,* University of Chicago Press, Chicago, Ill. (1979)

McGrew, R. E., *Russia and the cholera, 1823–32,* University of Wisconsin Press, Madison, Wis. (1965)

Madison, B., 'The organization of welfare services', in C. E. Black, ed., *The transformation of Russian society. Aspects of social change since 1861,* Harvard University Press, Cambridge, Mass. (1960)

Madison, B., 'Russia's illegitimate children before and after the revolution', *Slavic Review,* 22 (1963)

Madison, B., *Social welfare in the Soviet Union,* Stanford University Press, Stanford, Cal. (1968) [welfare policy formation 1917–66]

Mayzel, M., 'The formation of the Russian general staff, 1880–1917. A social study', *Cahiers du Monde Russe et Soviétique,* 16 (1975)

Meehan-Waters, B., 'The Muscovite noble origins of the Russians in the Generalitet of 1730', *Cahiers du Monde Russe et Soviétique,* 12 (1971)

Meehan-Waters, B., 'Social and career characteristics of the administrative elite, 1689–1761', in W. M.

Pinter and D. K. Rowney, eds, *Russian officialdom. The bureaucratization of Russian society from the seventeenth to the twentieth century,* University of North Carolina Press, Chapel Hill, N.C. (1980)

Menning, B., 'The emergence of a military-administrative elite in the Don Cossack land, 1708–1836', in W. M. Pintner and D. K. Rowney, eds, *Russian officialdom. The bureaucratization of Russian society from the seventeenth to the twentieth century,* University of North Carolina Press, Chapel Hill, N.C. (1980)

Méquet, G., 'Socialist towns. A new development of housing policy in the U.S.S.R.', *International Labour Review,* 25 (1932)

Mirsky, D. P., *Russia. A social history,* Cresset Press, London (1931)

Mosse, W. E., 'Aspects of Tsarist bureaucracy. Recruitment to the Imperial State Council, 1855–1914', *Slavonic and East European Review,* 57 (1979)

Mosse, W. E., 'Russian bureaucracy at the end of the *ancien régime.* The Imperial State Council', *Slavic Review,* 39 (1980)

Mosse, W. E., 'Aspects of Tsarist bureaucracy. The State Council in the late nineteenth century', *English Historical Review,* 95 (1980)

Nash, E., 'The status of women in the U.S.S.R.', *Monthly Labor Review,* 93 (1970) [selected years, 1928–68]

Orlovsky, D. T., 'High officials in the Ministry of Internal Affairs, 1855–81', in W. M. Pintner and D. K. Rowney, eds, *Russian officialdom. The bureaucratization of Russian society from the seventeenth to the twentieth century,* University of North Carolina Press, Chapel Hill, N.C. (1980)

Owen, T. C., *Capitalism and politics in Russia. A social history of the Moscow merchants, 1855–1905,* Cambridge University Press, Cambridge (1981)

Pape, C., 'The "peasant zemstva". Popular education in Vjatka Gubernija, 1867–1905', *Jahrbücher für Geschichte Osteuropas,* 27 (1979)

Papmehl, K. A., *Freedom of expression in eighteenth century Russia,* Nijhoff, The Hague (1971)

Pavlenko, N. I., 'On the question of the evolution of the gentry in the seventeenth and eighteenth centuries', in V. V. Mavrodin, ed., *Voprosy genezisa kapitalizma v Rossii,* Leningrad University Press, Leningrad (1960)

Perrie, M., 'The Russian peasant movement of 1905–07. Its social composition and revolutionary significance', *Past and Present,* 57 (1972)

Perrie, M., 'The Russian peasantry in 1907–08. A survey by the Socialist Revolutionary Party', *History Workshop Journal,* 4 (1977)

Pethybridge, R., *The social prelude to Stalinism,* Macmillan, London (1974)

Pintner, W. M., 'The social characteristics of the early nineteenth century Russian bureaucracy', *Slavic Review,* 29 (1970)

Pintner, W. M., 'The Russian higher civil service on the eve of the "Great Reforms" ', *Journal of Social History,* 8 (1975)

Pintner, W. M., 'Civil officialdom and the nobility in the 1850s', in W. M. Pintner, and D. K. Rowney, eds, *Russian officialdom. The bureaucratization of Russian society from the seventeenth to the twentieth century,* University of North Carolina Press, Chapel Hill, N.C. (1980)

Pintner, W. M., 'The evolution of civil officialdom, 1755–1855', in W. M. Pintner, and D. K. Rowney, eds, *Russian officialdom. The bureaucratization of Russian society from the seventeenth to the twentieth century,* University of North Carolina Press, Chapel Hill, N.C. (1980)

Pintner, W. M., and D. K. Rowney, eds, *Russian officialdom. The bureaucratization of Russian society from the seventeenth to the twentieth century,* University of North Carolina Press, Chapel Hill, N.C. (1980)

Plakans, A., 'Seigneurial authority and peasant family life. The Baltic area in the eighteenth century', *Journal of Interdisciplinary History,* 5 (1975)

Raeff, M., 'Home, school and service in the life of the eighteenth century Russian nobleman', *Slavonic and East European Review,* 40 (1962)

Ransel, D. L., 'Abandoned children of imperial Russia. Village fosterage', *Bulletin of the History of Medicine,* 50 (1976)

Ransel, D. L., ed., *The family in imperial Russia. New lines of historical research,* University of Illinois Press, Urbana, Ill. (1978)

Riasonovsky, N. V., *A parting of ways. Government and the educated public in Russia, 1801–55,* Clarendon Press, London (1976)

Rimlinger, G. V., *Welfare policy and industrialization in Europe, America and Russia,* John Wiley, New York (1971)

Riordan, J. W., 'The development of football in Russia and the U.S.S.R.', *New Zealand Slavonic Journal,* 9 (1972)

Rosenthal, B. G., 'Women under communism. A review article', *Society,* 17 (1979)

Rowney, D. K., 'Higher civil servants in the Russian Ministry of Internal Affairs. Some demographic and career characteristics, 1905–16', *Slavic Review,* 31 (1972)

Rowney, D. K., and W. M. Pintner, 'Organizational change and social adaptation. The pre-revolutionary Ministry of Internal Affairs', in W. M. Pintner and D. K. Rowney, eds, *Russian officialdom. The bureaucratization of Russian society from the seventeenth to the twentieth century,* University of North Carolina Press, Chapel Hill, N.C. (1980)

Schmidt, H., 'Housing problems', in G. Dobbert, ed., *Red economics,* Houghton Mifflin, Boston (1932)

Schnell, R., and H. W. Morris, 'Romanovka. A village in the Caucasus', *Journal of the American Society of Germans from Russia,* 2 (1979)

Sessa, P., 'Social problems and social conditions', in G. Dobbert, ed., *Red economics,* Houghton Mifflin, Boston (1932)

Shapiro, L., *The history of ORT. A Jewish movement for social change,* Schocken, New York (1980)

Sinel, A., 'Educating the Russian peasantry. The elementary school reforms of Count Dmitrii Tolstoi', *Slavic Review,* 27 (1968)

Sinel, A., *The classroom and the chancellery. State educational reform in Russia under Count Dmitry Tolstoi,* Harvard University Press, Cambridge, Mass. (1973)

Skocpol, T., *States and social revolutions. A comparative analysis of France, Russia and China,* Cambridge University Press, New York (1979)

Sorlin, P., *The Soviet people and their society, from 1917 to the present,* Praeger, New York (1968)

Sosnovy, T., 'The Soviet urban housing problem', *Slavic Review,* 11 (1952)

Sosnovy, T., 'Rent in the U.S.S.R.', *Slavic Review,* 18 (1959) [housing rentals]

Spetter, A., 'The United States, the Russian Jews and the Russian famine of 1891–92', *American Jewish Historical Quarterly,* 44 (1975)

Squire, P. S., *The Third Department. The establishment and practices of the political police in the Russia of Nicholas I,* Cambridge University Press, Cambridge (1968)

Stites, R., 'The women's liberation issue in nineteenth century Russia', in T. Yedlin, ed., *Women in eastern Europe and the Soviet Union,* Praeger, New York (1980)

Stscherbakiwskyj, W., 'The early Ukrainian social order, as reflected in Ukrainian wedding customs', *Slavonic and East European Review,* 31 (1953)

Suny, R. G., 'Russian rule and Caucasian society in the first half of the nineteenth century. The Georgian nobility and the Armenian bourgeoisie, 1801–56', *Nationalities Papers*, 7 (1979)

Thaden, E. C., *Russia since 1801. The making of a new society*, John Wiley, New York (1971)

Thurston, R. W., 'Police and people in Moscow, 1906–14', *Russian Review*, 39 (1980)

Timashev, N. S., 'Overcoming illiteracy. Public education in Russia, 1880–1940', *Russian Review*, 2 (1942)

Timoshenko, S. P., 'The development of engineering education in Russia', *Russian Review*, 15 (1956)

Torke, H. J., 'Continuity and change in the relations between bureaucracy and society in Russia, 1613–1861', *Canadian-American Slavic Studies*, 5 (1971)

Vernadsky, G., 'Rise of science in Russia, 1700–1917', *Russian Review*, 28 (1969)

Voyce, A., *Moscow and the roots of Russian culture*, University of Oklahoma Press, Norman, Okl. (1964)

Vucinich, A., *Soviet economic institutions. The social structure of production units*, Stanford University Press, Stanford, Cal. (1952) [discusses *sovkhoz, kolkhoz*, MTS and the factory]

Vucinich, A., *Science in Russian culture. A history to 1860*, Peter Owen, London (1965)

Vucinich, A., *Science in Russian culture, 1861–1917*, Stanford University Press, Stanford, Cal. (1970)

Ware, R., 'Some aspects of the Russian reading public in the 1880s', *Renaissance and Modern Studies*, 24 (1980)

Weissman, N. B., 'Rural crime in Tsarist Russia. The question of hooliganism, 1905–14', *Slavic Review*, 37 (1978)

Winner, I., 'Some problems of nomadism and social organization among the recently settled Kazakhs', parts 1 and 2, *Central Asian Review*, 11 (1963) [covers Tsarist period to collectivization]

Wood, A., 'Russia, 1905. Dress-rehearsal for revolution', *History Today*, 31 (1981)

Yaney, G. L., 'Social stability in pre-revolutionary Russia. A critical note', *Slavic Review*, 24 (1965)

Yedlin, T., ed., *Women in eastern Europe and the Soviet Union*, Praeger, New York (1980)

Zaionchkovsky, P. A., 'Officialdom', *Soviet Studies in History*, 18 (1979) [elites in government administration 1800–1910]

Zuzanek, J., 'Time-budget trends in the U.S.S.R. 1922–70', *Soviet Studies*, 31 (1979) [indicators of social change]

ECONOMIC POLICY AND ADMINISTRATION

Andrew, E., *The new economic policy. Its origin and goal*, Novosti Press Agency Publishing House, Moscow (1969)

Bakhmetov, B., 'The NEP in eclipse', *Slavonic and East European Review*, 3 (1924)

Bandera, V. N., 'The new economic policy (NEP) as an economic system', *Journal of Political Economy*, 71 (1963)

Baron, S. H., 'Plekhanov on Russian capitalism and the peasant commune, 1883–85', *Slavic Review*, 12 (1953)

Baron, S. H., 'Legal Marxism and the "fate of capitalism" in Russia', *Slavic Review*, 16 (1957)

Becker, S., *Russia's protectorates in central Asia. Bukhara and Khiva, 1865–1924*, Harvard University Press, Cambridge, Mass. (1968)

Berkhin, I., *Soviet economic policy. Early years*, Novosti Press Agency Publishing House, Moscow (1970) [deals with NEP]

Buchanan, H. R., 'Lenin and Bukharin on the transition from capitalism to socialism. The Meshchersky controversy, 1918', *Soviet Studies*, 28 (1976)

Conolly, V., 'The "nationalities question" in the last phase of Tsardom", in E. Allworth, ed., *Soviet nationality problems*, Columbia University Press, New York (1971)

Conroy, M. S., 'Stolypin's attitude toward local self-government', *Slavonic and East European Review*, 46 (1968)

Davletshin, T., 'Property law in the Soviet Union', *Studies on the Soviet Union*, 2 (1963) [changes in property law and private ownership from war communism to 1962]

Day, R. B., *Leon Trotsky and the politics of economic isolation*, Cambridge University Press, Cambridge (1973)

Day, R. M., 'The "crisis" and the "crash". Soviet studies of the West (1917–39), N.L.B., London (1981)

Dmytryshyn, B., 'The economic content of the 1767 *Nakaz* of Catherine II', *Slavic Review*, 19 (1960)

Dobb, M., 'The discussion of the twenties on Soviet economic growth', *Soviet Studies*, 17 (1965–66)

Emmons, T., and W. S. Vucinich, *The Zemstvo in Russia. An experiment in local self-government*, Cambridge University Press, Cambridge (1982)

Fisher, R. B., 'Background of the new economic policy', *Russian Review*, 7 (1948)

Griffiths, D. M., 'Eighteenth century perceptions of backwardness. Projects for the creation of a Third

Estate in Catherinean Russia', *Canadian-American Slavic Studies,* 13 (1979)

Gubsky, N., 'Economic law in Soviet Russia', *Economic Journal,* 37 (1927)

Haensel, P. P., *Economic policy of Soviet Russia,* P. S. King, London (1930)

Hardt, J. P., 'Soviet economic development and policy alternatives', *Studies on the Soviet Union,* 6 (1967)

Hoover, C. B., 'The fate of the new economic policy of the Soviet Union', *Economic Journal,* 40 (1930)

Hurt, B., 'Populists and industrializers again', *Canadian Slavonic Papers,* 12 (1970)

Jasny, N., *Soviet economists of the twenties. Names to be remembered,* Cambridge University Press, Cambridge (1972)

Kahan, A., 'Continuity in economic activity and policy during the post-Petrine period in Russia', *Journal of Economic History,* 25 (1965)

Kipp, J. W., 'M. K. Reutern on the Russian state and economy. A liberal bureaucrat during the Crimean era, 1854–60', *Journal of Modern History,* 47 (1975)

Kolchin, P., 'In defense of servitude. American pro-slavery and Russian proserfdom arguments, 1760–1860', *American Historical Review,* 85 (1980)

Koropeckyj, I. S., 'The development of soviet location theory before the second world war', *Soviet Studies,* 19 (1967)

Kresl, P. K., 'Nikolai Bukharin on economic imperialism', *Review of Radical Political Economics,* 5 (1973)

Kurganov, I., 'The problem of nationality in Soviet Russia', *Russian Review,* 10 (1951)

Labedz, L., 'The new CPSU programme', in W. Laquerer and L. Labedz, eds., *The future of communist society,* Praeger, New York (1962)

Lewin, M., *Political undercurrents in Soviet economic debates. From Bukharin to modern reformers,* Princeton University Press, Princeton, N.J. (1974)

Lewitter, L. R., 'Ivan Tikhonovich Pososhkov (1652–1726) and "the spirit of capitalism"', *Slavonic and East European Review,* 51 (1973)

Manning, R. T., '*Zemstvo* and revolution. The onset of gentry reaction, 1905–07', in L. H. Haimson, ed., *The politics of rural Russia, 1905–14,* Indiana University Press, Bloomington, Ind. (1979)

Meehan-Waters, B., 'The Russian aristocracy and the reforms of Peter the Great', *Canadian-American Slavic Studies,* 8 (1974)

Mendel, A. P., *Dilemmas of progress in Tsarist Russia. Legal Marxism and legal population,* Har-

vard University Press, Cambridge, Mass. (1961)

Moravcik, I., 'The Marxian model of growth and the "general plan" of Soviet economic development', *Kyklos,* 14 (1961) [deals mainly with 1920s]

Narkiewicz, O. A., *The making of the Soviet state apparatus,* Manchester University Press, Manchester (1970)

Nove, A., 'New light on Trotskii's economic views', *Slavic Review,* 40 (1981)

Olegina, I. N., 'Capitalist and socialist industrialization in the treatment of A. Gerschenkron', *Istoriya SSSR,* 2 (1971)

Oppenheim, S. A., 'The Supreme Economic Council, 1917–21'. *Soviet Studies,* 25 (1973)

Pethybridge, R., 'Party and society in the new economic policy', *European Studies Review,* 1 (1971)

Pintner, W. M., *Economic policy under Nicholas I,* Cornell University Press, Ithaca, N.Y. (1967)

Pintner, W. M., and D. K. Rowney, eds, *Russian officialdom. The bureaucratization of Russian society from the seventeenth to the twentieth century,* University of North Carolina Press, Chapel Hill, N.C. (1980)

Pipes, R., *Struve. Liberal on the right, 1905–44,* Harvard University Press, Cambridge, Mass. (1980)

Raeff, M., 'Patterns of Russian imperial policy toward the nationalities', in E. Allworth, ed., *Soviet nationality problems,* Columbia University Press, New York (1971)

Raeff, M., 'The bureaucratic phenomena of imperial Russia, 1700–1905', *American Historical Review,* 84 (1979)

Simmons, E. J., ed., *Continuity and change in Russian and Soviet thought,* Harvard University Press, Cambridge, Mass. (1955)

Smith, G. A., 'The political economy of the reform movement', *Critique,* 4 (1975)

Starr, S. F., *Decentralization and self-government in Russia, 1830–70,* Princeton University Press, Princeton, N.J. (1972)

Sternheimer, S., 'Administering development and developing administration. Organizational conflict in Tsarist bureaucracy, 1906–14', *Canadian-American Slavic Studies,* 9 (1975)

Strakhovsky, L. I., 'The statesmanship of Peter Stolypin. A reappraisal', *Slavonic and East European Review,* 37 (1959)

Tanaka, M., 'The Narodniki and Marx on Russian capitalism in the 1870s-80s', *Kyoto University Economic Review,* 39 (1969)

Tuckerman, G., 'Applied Marxism in Soviet Russia', *American Economic Review,* 23 (1933)

Vinogradov, V. A., *Socialist property. Its formation and economic advantages,* Nanka Publishing House, Moscow (1968)

Von Laue, T. H., 'The fate of capitalism in Russia. The Narodnik version', *Slavic Review,* 13 (1954)

Vucinich, A., *Social thought in Tsarist Russia. The quest for a general science of society. 1861–1917,* University of Chicago Press, Chicago, Ill. (1976)

Wagner, W. G., 'Tsarist legal policies at the end of the nineteenth century. A study in inconsistencies', *Slavonic and East European Review,* 54 (1976)

Walicki, A., 'Russian social thought. An introduction to the intellectual history of nineteenth century Russia', *Russian Review,* 36 (1977)

Yaney, G. L., 'Some aspects of the imperial Russian government on the eve of the first world war', *Slavonic and East European Review,* 43 (1964)

Yaney, G. L., *The systematization of Russian government. Social evolution in the domestic administration of imperial Russia, 1711–1905,* University of Illinois Press, Urbana, Ill. (1973)

SOVIET ECONOMIC PLANNING

Baran, P. A., 'National economic planning. The Soviet experience', in M. Bernstein, and D. Fusfeld, eds, *The Soviet economy. A book of readings,* Richard D. Irwin, Homewood, Ill. (1966)

Baykov, A., 'Some observations on planning economic development', in L. J. Zimmerman, ed., *Economic Planning,* Mouton, The Hague (1963)

Brutskus, B. D., *Economic planning in Soviet Russia,* Routledge, London (1935)

Bye, R. T., 'The central planning and co-ordination of production in Soviet Russia', *American Economic Review,* (1929)

Campbell, R., 'What makes a five-year plan feasible?', *Slavic Review,* 32 (1973)

Chamberlin, W. H., *The Soviet planned economic order,* World Peace Foundation, Boston (1931)

Chamberlin, W. H., 'The planned economy', in G. Dobbert, ed., *Red economics,* Houghton Mifflin, Boston (1932)

Coates, W. P., and Z. K., *The second Five Year Plan of Development of the U.S.S.R.,* Methuen, New York (1934)

Counts, G. S., *The Soviet challenge to America,* John Day, New York (1931) [concerned with Five Year Plan]

Cross, S. H., 'The outlook for the Five Year Plan', *Harvard Business Review,* 9 (1931)

Davis, J., ed., *New Russia. Between the first and second Five Year Plans,* John Day, New York (1933)

Davies, R. W., 'Planning for rapid growth in the U.S.S.R.', *Economics of Planning,* 5 (1965)

Davies, R. W., and S. G. Wheatcroft, 'Further thoughts on the first Five Year Plan', *Slavic Review,* 34 (1975)

Davies, R. W., and S. G. Wheatcroft, 'Steven Rosefielde's *Kliukva*', *Slavic Review,* 39 (1980) [debate on first Five Year Plan]

Degras, J., and A. Nove, eds, *Soviet planning. Essays in honour of Naum Jasny,* Blackwell, Oxford (1964)

Dobb, M., 'The significance of the Five Year Plan', *Slavonic and East European Review,* 10 (1931)

Dobb, M., 'Rates of growth under the Five Year Plans', *Soviet Studies,* 4 (1952–53)

Ellman, M., 'Did the agricultural surplus provide the resources for the increase in investment in the U.S.S.R. in the first Five Year Plan?', *Economic Journal,* 85 (1975)

Erlich, A., 'Development strategy and planning. The Soviet experience', in M. Millikan, ed., *National economic planning,* Columbia University Press, New York (1967) [net national product, factor input and productivity data for 1928–58]

Farbman, M. S., *Piatiletka. Russia's 5-year plan,* New Republic, New York (1931)

Florinsky, M. T., *Toward an understanding of the U.S.S.R. A study in government, politics and economic planning,* Macmillan, New York (1939)

Hoeffding, O., 'State planning and forced industrialization', in M. E. Falkus, ed., *Readings in the history of economic growth,* Oxford University Press, London (1968)

Hunter, H., 'Priorities and shortfalls in pre-war Soviet planning', in J. Degras and A. Nove, eds, *Soviet planning. Essays in honour of Naum Jasny,* Blackwell, Oxford (1964)

Hunter, H., 'The overambitious first Soviet Five Year Plan', *Slavic Review,* 32 (1973) [see comments by R. Campbell, S. F. Cohen and M. Lewin in the same issue]

International Labour Office, 'The Five Year Plan and the regulation of the labour market in the U.S.S.R.', *International Labour Review,* 27 (1933)

Jasny, N., *The Soviet economy during the plan era,* Stanford University Press, Stanford, Cal. (1951)

Jasny, N., 'A Soviet planner – V. G. Groman', *The Russian Review,* 13 (1954)

Kaser, M. C., 'The nature of Soviet planning. A critique of Jasny's appraisal', *Soviet Studies,* 14 (1962) [comment on N. Jasny, *Soviet industrialization,*

1928–52]

Knickerbocker, H. R., *The Soviet Five Year Plan and its effect on world trade*, Bodley Head, London (1931)

Lamb, E., *The planned economy in Soviet Russia*, Dorrance, Philadelphia, Pa. (1934)

Lewin, M., 'The disappearance of planning in the plan', *Slavic Review*, 32 (1973)

Miller, J., 'Soviet planners, 1936–37', in J. Degras and A. Nove, eds, *Soviet planning. Essays in honour of Naum Jasny*, Blackwell, Oxford (1964)

Obolensky-Ossinsky, V. V., *et al.*, *Social economic planning in the U.S.S.R.*, International Industrial Relations Association, New York (1932)

Paquet, G., 'The structuration of a planned economy', *Canadian Slavonic Papers*, 8 (1964) [examination of Zaleski's work, dealing with 1918–32]

Prokopovich, S., 'The crisis of the Five Year Plan', *Slavonic and East European Review*, 10 (1931)

Schlesinger, R., 'A note on the context of early Soviet planning', *Soviet Studies*, 16 (1964–65)

Smolinski, L., 'Planning without theory, 1917–67', *Survey*, 64 (1967)

Spulber, N., ed., *Foundations of Soviet strategy for economic growth. Selected essays, 1924–30*, University of Indiana Press, Bloomington, Ind. (1964)

Timoshenko, V. P., 'New Soviet economic plan. Its agricultural aspect', *Journal of Political Economy*, 61 (1953)

Turin, S. P., 'The second Five Year Plan', *Slavonic and East European Review*, 11 (1932)

Zaleski, E., *Planning for economic growth in the Soviet Union, 1918–32*, University of North Carolina Press, Chapel Hill, N.C. (1971)

Zaleski, E., *Stalinist planning and economic growth, 1932–52*, University of North Carolina Press, Chapel Hill, N.C. (1980)

CO-OPERATIVE MOVEMENTS

Antsiferov, A. N., and E. Kayden, *The co-operative movement in Russia during the war*, Yale University Press, New Haven, Conn. (1929)

Baykalov, A. V., 'A brief outline of the Russian co-operative movement', *Slavonic and East European Review*, 1 (1922–23)

Borodaewsky, S. W., 'Co-operation in Russia during the war', *International Labour Review*, 10 (1924)

Kayden, E. M., *Consumers' co-operation The co-operative movement in Russia during the war*, Yale University Press, New Haven, Conn. (1929)

Lee, F. E., *Russian co-operative movement*, Government Printing Office, Washington, D.C. (1920)

Miller, M. S., 'Co-operation in Russia', *Economica*, 1 (1921)

Prokopovitch, M., 'Co-operation in Soviet Russia', *International Labour Review*, 10 (1924)

Totomiantz, V. T., 'Co-operation in Russia before the war', *International Labour Review*, 7 (1923)

HISTORIOGRAPHY AND BIBLIOGRAPHY

Atkinson, D., 'The library of the Free Economic Society', *Slavic Review*, 39 (1980)

Clark, C., *Critique of Russian statistics*, Macmillan, London (1939)

Dickerson, C. J., and W. R. Riddle, 'Russia. Recent Soviet historiography', *Trends in History*, 1 (1979)

East, W. G., 'The economic history of the U.S.S.R.', *Economic History Review*, 2 (1946)

Gerschenkron, A., 'A neglected source of economic information on Soviet Russia', *Slavic Review*, 9 (1950)

Hollingsworth, B., 'Russia through European eyes', *European Studies Review*, 6 (1976)

Holubnychy, V., 'Government statistical observation in the U.S.S.R.', *Slavic Review*, 19 (1960) [history of the organisation of Soviet data collection]

Kahan, A., 'Quantitative data for the study of Russian history', in V. R. Lorwin and J. M. Price, eds, *The dimensions of the past*, Yale University Press, New Haven, Conn. (1972)

Kahk, J., 'Recent results of Soviet historians in use of mathematical methods and computers in agrarian history', *Historisk Tidskrift*, 3 (1974)

Keep, J., 'The agrarian revolution of 1917–18 in Soviet historiography', *Russian Review*, 36 (1977)

Keep, J. L. H., 'From the pistol to the pen. The military memoir as a source on the social history of pre-reform Russia', *Cahiers du Monde Russe et Soviétique*, 21 (1980)

Langer, L. N., 'The historiography of the pre-industrial Russian city', *Journal of Urban History*, 5 (1979)

Leadenham, C. A., 'Sources and resources for teaching about Russia and the USSR', *Social Education*, 45 (1981)

Letiche, J. M., *et al.*, *A history of Russian economic thought. Ninth through eighteenth centuries*, University of California Press, Berkeley, Cal. (1964)

Lincoln, W. B., 'The personal papers of N. A. Miliutin as a source for the economic and social history of mid-nineteenth century Russia', *Cahiers du Monde Russe et Soviétique*, 14 (1973)

McGrew, R. E., 'A note on some European Foreign

Office archives and Russian domestic history, 1790–1812', *Slavic Review,* 23 (1964)

Meisel, J. H., and E. S. Kozera, *Materials for the study of the Soviet system. State and party constitutions, laws, decrees, decisions and official statements of the leaders in translation,* George Wahu, Ann Arbor, Mich. (1950) [particular attention to years 1917–21]

Millar, J. R., and C. A. Guntzel, 'The economics and politics of mass collectivization reconsidered. A review article', *Explorations in Economic History,* 8 (1970–71)

Ransel, D. L., 'Recent Soviet studies in demographic history', *Russian Review,* 40 (1981)

Rosefielde, S., 'Moshe Lewin's interpretation of the industrialization debates, 1921–29, and the postwar literature on economic reform', *Russian Review,* 34 (1975)

Schlesinger, R., 'Discussions on periodization of history', *Soviet Studies,* 4 (1952–53)

Yaresh, L., 'The "peasant wars" in Soviet historiography', *Slavic Review,* 16 (1957)

Zorn, J., 'New Soviet work on the old Russian peasantry', *Russian Review,* 39 (1980)

SOUTHERN EUROPE

ITALY

GENERAL ECONOMIC AND SOCIAL HISTORY

Ackley, F., and L. Sparenta, 'Emigration and industrialisation in southern Italy. A comment', *Banca Nazionale del Lavoro Quarterly Review*, 15 (1962)

Aquarone, A., 'Italy. The crisis and corporative economy', *Journal of Contemporary History*, 4 (1969)

Cafagna, L., 'The industrial revolution in Italy, 1830–1914', in C. M. Cipolla, ed., *The emergence of industrial societies*, Fontana Economic History of Europe, vol. 4, part 1, Collins/Fontana, Glasgow (1973)

Caizzi, B., 'The main themes of the history of the southern question', *Banca Nazionale del Lavoro Quarterly Review*, 15 (1962)

Clough, S. B., *The economic history of modern Italy*, Columbia University Press, New York (1964)

Clough, S. B., and C. Livi, 'Economic growth in Italy. An analysis of the uneven development of north and south', *Journal of Economic History*, 16 (1956)

Cohen, J. S., 'Financing industrialisation in Italy, 1894–1914. The partial transformation of a latecomer', *Journal of Economic History*, 27 (1967)

Cohen, J. S., *Finance and industrialisation in Italy, 1894–1914*, Arno Press, New York (1977)

de Rosa, L., 'Property rights, institutional change and economic growth in southern Italy in the eighteenth and nineteenth centuries', in M. W. Flinn, ed., *Proceedings of the seventh International Congress of Economic History, Edinburgh, 1978*, Edinburgh University Press, Edinburgh (1978)

de Rosa, L., 'Property rights, institutional change and economic growth in southern Italy in the eighteenth and nineteenth centuries', *Journal of European Economic History*, 8 (1979)

Delzell, C. F., ed., *Mediterranean fascism, 1919–45*, Macmillan, London (1971)

di Giovanni, G., 'Economic growth in Tuscany and the Risorgimento', *Journal of European Economic History*, 4 (1975)

Eckaus, R. S., 'The north-south differential in Italian economic development', *Journal of Economic History*, 21 (1961)

Einzig, P., *The economic foundations of fascism*, Macmillan, London (1933)

Fenoaltea, S., 'Railroads and Italian industrial growth, 1861–1913', *Explorations in Economic History*, 9 (1971–72)

Fua, G., *Notes on Italian economic growth, 1861–1964*, Editore Giuffre, Milan (1965)

Gerschenkron, A., 'Notes on the rate of industrial growth in Italy, 1881–1913', *Journal of Economic History*, 15 (1955)

Gerschenkron, A., 'The industrial development of Italy. A debate with Rosario Romeo', *Nord e Sud* (1961)

Gerschenkron, A., 'An index of Italian industrial development', in A. Gerschenkron, *Economic backwardness in historical perspective*, Harvard University Press, Cambridge, Mass. (1982)

Giannone, A., 'Evaluations of Italian national wealth in the last fifty years', *Banca Nazionale del Lavoro Quarterly Review*, 16 (1963)

Gregor, A. J., *Italian fascism and developmental dictatorship*, Princeton University Press, Princeton, N.J. (1980)

Hildebrand, G. H., *Growth and structure in the economy of modern Italy*, Harvard University

Press, Cambridge, Mass (1965)

Hilowitz, J., *Economic development and social change in Sicily*, Schenkman, Cambridge, Mass. (1976)

Lutz, V., 'The growth process in a dual economic system', *Banca Nazionale del Lavoro Quarterly Review*, 11 (1958)

Lutz, V., 'Some structural aspects of the southern problem. The complementarity of emigration and industrialisation', *Banca Nazionale del Lavoro Quarterly Review*, 14 (1961)

Luzzatto, G., 'The Italian economy in the first decade after unification', in F. Crouzet, *et al.*, *Essays in European economic history*, Edward Arnold, London (1969)

McGuire, C. E., *Italy's international economic position*, Allen and Unwin, London (1927)

Marcelletti, M., 'Aspects of planned economy in Italy', *International Labour Review*, 30 (1934)

Matassi, L., 'The Italian economy in the late eighteenth and nineteenth century', *Review of the Economic Conditions in Italy*, 23 (1969)

Matassi, L., 'World War I and the recovery of the Italian economy', *Review of the Economic Conditions in Italy*, 23 (1969)

Matassi, L., 'The great depression and the new recovery of Italian industry', *Review of the Economic Conditions in Italy*, 23 (1969)

Molinari, A., 'Southern Italy', *Banca Nazionale del Lavoro Quarterly Review*, 8 (1949)

Mori, G., 'The genesis of Italian industrialisation', *Journal of European Economic History*, 4 (1975)

Mori, G., 'The process of industrialisation in general and the process of industrialisation in Italy. Some suggestions, problems and questions', *Journal of European Economic History*, 8 (1979)

Mori, G., 'The process of industrialisation in general and the process of industrialisation in Italy. Some suggestions, problems and questions', in P. Bairoch and M. Levy-Leboyer, eds, *Disparities in economic development since the industrial revolution*, Macmillan, London (1981)

Profumieri, P., 'Capital and labour in Italy, 1929–40. An economic interpretation', *Journal of European Economic History*, 1 (1972)

Rath, R. J., 'The Habsburgs and the great depression in Lombardy-Venetia, 1814–18', *Journal of Modern History*, 13 (1941)

Rath, R. J., 'Economic conditions in Lombardy and Venetia, 1813–15, and their effect on public opinion', *Journal of Central European Affairs*, 23 (1963)

Ricossa, S., 'Italy, 1920–70', in C. M. Cipolla, ed., *Contemporary Economies*. Fontana Economic History of Europe, vol. 6, part 1, Collins/Fontana, Glasgow (1976)

Salvemini, G., 'Economic conditions in Italy, 1919–22', *Journal of Modern History*, 23 (1951)

Sarti, R., 'Fascist modernisation in Italy. Traditional or revolutionary?', *American Historical Review*, 75 (1969–70)

Sarti, R., *Fascism and the industrial leadership in Italy, 1919–40*, University of California Press, Berkeley, Cal. (1971)

Saville, L., 'Statistical sampling. An adaptation to Italian economic development', *Economic History Review*, 9 (1956–57)

Saville, L., *Regional economic development in Italy*, Duke University Press, Durham, N.C. (1967)

Schachter, G., *The Italian south. Economic development in Mediterranean Europe*, Random House, New York (1965)

Schmidt, C. T., *The corporate state in action. Italy under fascism*, Gollancz, London (1939)

Seton-Watson, C., *Italy. From Liberalism to fascism*, Methuen, London (1967)

Siegenthaler, J. K., 'Sicilian economic change since 1860', *Journal of European Economic History*, 2 (1973)

Smith, D. M., *A history of Sicily. Modern Sicily after 1713*, Viking Press, New York (1968)

Smith, D. M., *The making of Italy, 1796–1870*, Harper, New York (1968)

Sweet, J. J. T., *Iron arm. The mechanisation of Mussolini's army, 1920–40*, Greenwood Press, Westport, Conn. (1980)

Talamona, M., 'Building fluctuations and business cycles in Italy, 1863–1945'. *Review of Economic Conditions in Italy*, 13 (1959)

Tannenbaum, E. R., 'The goals of Italian fascism', *American Historical Review*, 74 (1967–68)

Tannenbaum, E. R., and E. P. Noether, *Modern Italy*, New York University Press, New York (1974)

Toniolo, G., 'Patterns of industrial growth and Italy's industrialisation from 1894–1913', *Rendiconti*, 1 (1969)

Vaccaro, R., 'Industrialisation in Spain and Italy (1860–1914)', *Journal of European Economic History*, 9 (1980)

Vaudagna, M., 'Structural economic change in fascist Italy', *Journal of Economic History*, 38 (1978)

Vochting, F., 'Industrialisation and "pre-industrialisation" in southern Italy', *Banca*

Nazionale del Lavoro Quarterly Review, 21 (1952)

Wiskemann, E., *Fascism in Italy. Its development and influence*, Macmillan, London (1969)

Zangheri, R., 'The historical relationship between agricultural and economic development in Italy', in E. L. Jones and S. J. Woolf, eds, *Agrarian change and economic development*, Methuen, London (1969)

AGRICULTURE AND RURAL SOCIETY

Bosworth, R. J., 'The Albanian forests of Signor Giacomo Vismara. A case study of Italian economic imperialism during the Foreign Ministry of Antonio di San Giuliano', *Historical Journal*, 18 (1975)

Cohen, J. S., 'Fascism and agriculture in Italy. Policies and consequences', *Economic History Review*, 32 (1979)

Cole, J. W., and E. R. Wolf, *The hidden frontier. Ecology and ethnicity in an Alpine valley*, Academic Press, London (1970) [primarily peasant economy of the Tyrol]

Loubère, L. A., *The red and the white. The history of wine in France and Italy in the nineteenth century*, New York State University Press, Albany, N.Y. (1978)

MacDonald, J. S., 'Agricultural organisation, migration and labour militancy in rural Italy', *Economic History Review*, 16 (1963–64)

MacDonald, J. S. and L. D., 'A simple institutional framework for the analysis of agricultural development potential', *Economic Development and Cultural Change*, 12 (1964)

Rossi-Doria, M., 'The land tenure system and class in southern Italy', *American Historical Review*, 64 (1958–59)

Schmidt, C. T., *The plough and the sword. Labour, land and property in fascist Italy*, Columbia University Press, New York (1938)

Wolf, E., 'The inheritance of land among Bavarian and Tyrolese peasants', *Anthropologica*, 12 (1970)

Woolf, S. J., 'Economic problems of the nobility in the early modern period. The example of Piedmont', *Economic History Review*, 17 (1964–65)

INDUSTRY AND INTERNAL TRADE

Amatori, F., 'Entrepreneurial typologies in the history of industrial Italy (1880–1960). A review article',

Business History Review, 54 (1980)

Anselmi, A., 'Trade associations and corporations in Italy after the recent reforms', *International Labour Review*, 31 (1935)

Chorley, P., *Oil, silk and enlightenment. Economic problems in eighteenth century Naples*, Nella Sede dell' Instituto, Naples (1965)

d'Angelo, M., 'The origins of the Florio. A leading family of Italian entrepreneurs in the nineteenth and twentieth centuries', *Journal of European Economic History*, 9 (1980)

Greenfield, K. R., 'Commerce and new enterprise at Venice, 1830–48', *Journal of Modern History*, 11 (1939)

Olivetti, G., 'Employers' organisations in Italy', *International Labour Review*, 18 (1928)

Pitigliani, F. R., 'The development of Italian cartels and fascism', *Journal of Political Economy*, 48 (1940)

Por, O., 'The Italian corporations at work', *International Labour Review*, 35 (1937)

Tamborra, A., 'The rise of Italian industry and the Balkans (1900–14)', *Journal of European Economic History*, 3 (1974)

Toniolo, G., 'Effective protection and industrial growth. The case of Italian engineering, 1848–1913', *Journal of European Economic History*, 6 (1977)

Webster, R. A., *Industrial imperialism in Italy, 1909–15*, University of California Press, Berkeley, Cal. (1975)

TRANSPORT AND COMMUNICATIONS

Blumberg, A., 'The Second French Empire, Eugène Rouher and the Italian railroads. Documents illustrative of economic imperialism', *Economy and History*, 8 (1965)

Cameron, R. E., 'Problems of French investment in Italian railways. A document of 1868', *Business History Review*, 35 (1961)

Tajani, F., 'Railway nationalisation in Italy', *Economic Journal*, 15 (1908)

MONEY, BANKING AND FINANCE

Anonymous, 'The great banks. Credit Italiano', *Italy. Documents and Notes*, 23 (1974)

Bonelli, F., 'The 1907 financial crisis in Italy. A peculiar case of the lender of last resort in action', in C. P. Kindleberger and J.-P. Laffargue, eds, *Financial crisis. Theory, history and policy*, Cambridge

University Press, Cambridge (1982)

Boyd, E., 'Early Italian accountants', in R. Brown, ed., *A history of accounting and accountants*, Cass, London (1968)

Cameron, R. E., 'French finance and Italian unity. The Cavourian decade', *American Historical Review*, 62 (1956–57)

Carroll, M. B., *Taxation of business in Italy*, U.S. Government Printing Office, Washington, D.C. (1929)

Clough, S. B., 'Taxation and capital formation since 1870 in France, Italy and the United States', *Proceedings of the third international economic history conference, Munich, 1965*, Mouton, Paris (1968)

Cohen, J. S., 'Italy', in R. E. Cameron, ed., *Banking and economic development*, Oxford University Press, London (1972)

Cohen, J. S., 'The 1927 revaluation of the lira. A study in political economy', *Economic History Review*, 25 (1972)

Einaudi, L., 'The public finances of Italy', *Economic Journal*, 25 (1915)

Felloni, G., 'Monetary changes and prices in Italy in the Napoleonic period', *Journal of European Economic History*, 5 (1976)

Foa, B. G., and P. G. Treves, 'Italian finance and investment', *Economica*, 6 (1939)

Klang, D. M., *Tax reform in eighteenth century Lombardy*, Columbia University Press, New York (1977)

Martines, L., 'Early effects of credit mechanisms in Italy', *Journal of Interdisciplinary History*, 4 (1974)

Miller, H. S., 'Italian monetary and exchange policies under fascism', *American Economic Review*, 30 (1940)

Sarti, R., 'Mussolini and the Italian industrial leadership in the battle of the lira, 1925–27', *Past and Present*, 47 (1970)

Sraffa, P., 'The bank crisis in Italy', *Economic Journal*, 32 (1922)

Webster, R. A., 'The political and industrial strategies of a mixed investment bank. Italian industrial financing and the Banca Commerciale, 1894–1915', *Vierteljahrschrift für Sozial- und Wirtschaftsgeschichte*, 61 (1974)

OVERSEAS TRADE AND COMMERICAL RELATIONS

Anonymous, 'The Italian customs and excise police', *Italy Documents and Notes*, 23 (1974)

Coppa, F. J., 'The Italian tariff and the conflict between agriculture and industry. The commercial policy of liberal Italy, 1860–1922', *Journal of Economic History*, 30 (1970)

Csöppus, J., 'The Rome pact and Hungarian agricultural exports to Italy (1920–44)', *Journal of European Economic History*, 11 (1982)

de Cugis, C., ed., *England and Italy a century ago. A new turn in economic relations*, Banca Commerciale Italiana, Milan (1967)

Gendebien, A. W., 'Sardinia and commercial reciprocity, 1819–38', *Journal of Modern History*, 33 (1961)

Glazier, I. A., and V. N. Bandera, 'Terms of trade between south Italy and the United Kingdom, 1817–1869', *Journal of European Economic History*, 1 (1972)

Glazier, I. A., *et al.*, 'Terms of trade between Italy and the United Kingdom, 1815–1913', *Journal of European Economic History*, 4 (1975)

Hess, R. L., 'Italian imperialism in its Ethiopian context', *International Journal of African Historical Studies*, 6 (1973)

Keene, C. A., 'American shipping and trade, 1798–1820. The evidence from Leghorn', *Journal of Economic History*, 38 (1978)

Lane, F. C., *Venice. A maritime republic*, Johns Hopkins University Press, Baltimore, Md. (1973)

McNeill, W. H., *Venice. The hinge of Europe, 1801–1972*, University of Chicago Press, Chicago, Ill. (1974)

Mallia-Milanes, V., 'Some aspects of Veneto-Maltese trade relations in the eighteenth century', *Studi Veneziani*, 16 (1974)

Mallia-Milanes, V., 'Malta and Venice in the eighteenth century. A study in consular relations', *Studi Veneziani*, 17–18 (1975–76)

Nev, I. D., 'An English businessman in Sicily, 1806–61', *Business History Review*, 31 (1957)

Rice, G. W., 'British consuls and diplomats in the mid-eighteenth century. An Italian example', *English Historical Review*, 92 (1977)

Saul, S. B., 'The historical development of the Anglo-Italian trade', *Banca Nazionale del Lavoro Quarterly Review*, 27 (1953)

Smith, R., 'Gianbattista Scala. An adventurer trader, and first Italian representative in Nigeria', *Journal of the Historical Society of Nigeria*, 7 (1973)

Welk, W. G., 'League sanctions and foreign trade restrictions in Italy', *American Economic Review*, 27 (1937)

POPULATION AND MIGRATION

Bell, R. M., *Fate and honour, family and village. Demographic and cultural change in rural Italy since 1800,* University of Chicago Press, Chicago, Ill. (1979)

Briggs, J. W., *An Italian passage. Immigrants to the American cities, 1890–1930,* Yale University Press, New Haven, Conn. (1978)

Cipolla, C. M., 'Four centuries of Italian demographic development', in D. V. Glass and D. E. C. Eversley, eds, *Population in history. Essays in historical demography,* Edward Arnold, London (1965)

Cordasco, F., *Italian mass emigration. The exodus of a Latin people,* Rowman and Littlefield, Totowa, N.J. (1980)

del Panta, L., 'Italy', in W. R. Lee, ed., *European demography and economic growth,* Croom Helm, London (1979)

Dickinson, R. E., *The population problem of southern Italy. An essay in social geography,* Syracuse University Press, Syraceuse, N.Y. (1955)

Dore, G., 'Some social and historical aspects of Italian emigration to America', *Journal of Social History,* 2 (1968)

Foerster, R. F., *The Italian emigration of our times,* Harvard University Press, Cambridge, Mass. (1924)

King, R., 'Italian migration to Great Britain', *Geography,* 62 (1977)

Livi-Bacci, M., *A history of Italian fertility during the last two centuries,* Princeton University Press, Princeton, N.J. (1977)

Livi-Bacci, M., 'Can anything be said about demographic trends when only aggregate vital statistics are available?', in R. D. Lee *et al.,* *Population patterns in the past,* Academic Press, New York (1977) [data on nineteenth-century Tuscany]

Livi-Bacci, M., 'On the frequency of remarriage in nineteenth century Italy. Methods and results', in J. Dupaquier *et al.,* *Marriage and remarriage in populations of the past,* Academic Press, London (1981)

MacDonald, J. S., 'Some socio-economic emigration differentials in rural Italy, 1902–13', *Economic Development and Cultural Change,* 7 (1958–59)

MacDonald, J. S. and L. D., 'Italian migration to Australia', *Journal of Social History,* 3 (1969–70)

Nazzaro, P., 'Italy from the American Immigration Quota Act of 1921 to Mussolini's policy of *Grossraum,* 1921–24', *Journal of European Economic History,* 3 (1974)

Oblath, A., 'Italian emigration and colonisation policy', *International Labour Review,* 23 (1931)

Ratti, A. M., 'Italian migration movements, 1876–1926', in W. F. Willcox, ed., *International migrations,* 2 vols, National Bureau of Economic Research, New York (1929–31)

Serra, E., 'Italian emigration to France during Crispi's first government (1887–91)', *Journal of European Economic History,* 7 (1978)

Vasquez-Presedo, V., 'The role of Italian migration in the development of the Argentine economy, 1875–1914', *Economia Internazionale,* 24 (1971)

Worrall, J. E., 'Italian immigrants in the Peruvian economy, 1860–1914', *Italian Americana,* 2 (1975)

LABOUR CONDITIONS AND ORGANISATION

Agocs, S., 'The road of charity leads to the picket lines. The neo-Thomistic revival and the Italian Catholic labour movement', *International Review of Social History,* 18 (1973)

Davis, J. C., 'A Slovene labourer and his experience of industrialisation, 1888–1976', *East European Quarterly,* 10 (1976) [Italian Slovenia]

Gualtieri, H. L., *The labour movement in Italy,* S. F. Vanni, New York (1946)

Horowitz, D. L., *The Italian labour movement,* Harvard University Press, Cambridge, Mass. (1963)

Hostetter, R., *The Italian socialist movement,* Vol. I (1860–82), Princeton University Press, Princeton, N.J. (1958)

Luraghi, R., 'Wage labour in the "rice belt" of northern Italy and slave labour in the American south – a first approach', *Southern Studies,* 16 (1977)

Procacci, G., 'The Italian workers' movement in the liberal era', in R. Bosworth and G. Cresciani, eds, *A volume of Italian studies,* University of Sydney, Sydney, N.S.W. (1979)

Roberts, D. D., *The syndicalist tradition and Italian fascism,* University of North Carolina Press, Chapel Hill, N.C. (1979)

Snyder, D. S., 'Institutional setting and industrial conflict. Comparative analyses of France, Italy and the United States', *American Sociological Review,* 40 (1975)

Snyder, D., and W. R. Kelly, 'Industrial violence in Italy, 1878–1903', *American Journal of Sociology,* 82 (1976)

Sykes, T. R., 'Revolutionary syndicalism in the Italian labour movement. The agrarian strikes of 1907–08 in the province of Parma', *International Review of Social History,* 21 (1976)

Tilly, L. A., 'I Fatti di Maggio. The working class of Milan and the rebellion of 1898', in R. Bezucha, ed., *Modern European social history*, D. C. Heath, Lexington, Mass. (1972)

INCOMES, WAGES AND PRICES

Biagi, B., 'Family allowances in Italy', *International Labour Review*, 35 (1937)

Giusti, U., 'Methods of recording retail prices and measuring the cost of living in Italy', *International Labour Review*, 4 (1921)

Vigo, G., 'Real wages of the working class of Italy. Building workers' wages (fourteenth to eighteenth century)', *Journal of European Economic History*, 3 (1974)

URBAN HISTORY

Calabi, D., 'The genesis and special characteristics of town-planning instruments in Italy, 1880–1914', in A. Sutcliffe, ed., *The rise of modern urban planning, 1800–1914*, Mansell, London (1980)

Caracciolo, A., 'Some examples of analysing the process of urbanisation. Northern Italy (eighteenth to twentieth century)', in H. Schmal, ed., *Patterns of European urbanisation since 1500*, Croom Helm, London (1981)

Cochrane, E., *Florence in the forgotten centuries, 1527–1800*, University of Chicago Press, Chicago, Ill. (1974)

Costa, F. J., 'The evolution of planning styles and planned change. The example of Rome', *Journal of Urban History*, 3 (1977)

Ghirardo, D. A., 'Mezzanotte in the Mezzogiorno. The urban problems of southern Italy', *Journal of Urban History*, 6 (1980)

Gutkind, E. A.. *International history of city development*, vol. 4, *Urban development in southern Europe. Italy and Greece*, Collier-Macmillan, London (1969)

Kostof, S., *The third Rome, 1870–1950. Traffic and glory*, University Art Museum, Berkeley, Cal. (1973)

Kostof, S., 'The drafting of a master plan for Roma capitale. An exordium', *Journal of the Society of Architectural Historians*, 35 (1976)

Lenzi, L., 'The new Rome', *Town Planning Review*, 14 (1930–31)

Stillman, J., 'British architects and Italian architectural competitions, 1758–80', *Journal of the Society of Architectural Historians*, 32 (1973)

Tilly, L. A., 'Urban growth, industrialisation and women's employment in Milan, Italy, 1881–1911', *Journal of Urban History*, 3 (1977)

Waley, D., *The Italian city republic*, Longman, London (1978)

Weiner, H. R., 'New towns in twentieth century Italy', *Urbanism Past and Present*, 2 (1976)

Wolfe, I. de, *The Italian townscape*, Architectural Press, London (1963)

Woolf, S. J., 'Some notes on the cost of public building in Turin in the eighteenth century', *Atti e Rassegna Tecnica*, 15 (1961)

SOCIAL STRUCTURE AND SOCIAL CONDITIONS

Barbagli, M., *Education for unemployment. Politics, labour markets and the school system. Italy, 1859–1973*, Columbia University Press, New York (1982)

Bell, D. H., 'Worker culture and worker politics. The experience of an Italian town, 1880–1915', *Social History*, 3 (1978)

Bell, R. M., *Fate and honor, family and village. Demographic and cultural change in rural Italy since 1800*, University of Chicago Press, Chicago, Ill. (1979)

Corsini, C. A., 'Why is remarriage a male affair? Some evidence from Tuscan villages during the eighteenth century', in J. Dupaquier *et al.*, *Marriage and remarriage in populations of the past*, Academic Press, London (1981)

Davis, J. C., *The decline of the Venetian nobility as a ruling class*, Johns Hopkins University Press, Baltimore, Md. (1982)

Davis, J. C., 'A Venetian family and its fortune, 1500–1900. The Dona and the conservation of their wealth', *Proceedings of the American Philosophical Society*, 106 (1975)

Douglas, W. A., 'The south Italian family. A critique', *Journal of Family History*, 5 (1980)

Dupaquier, J., and L. Jadin, 'Structure of household and family in Corsica, 1769–71', in P. Laslett, ed., *Household and family in past time*, Cambridge University Press, Cambridge (1972)

Geiger, R. G., 'Democracy and the crowd. The social history of an idea in France and Italy, 1890–1914', *Societàs*, 7 (1977)

Ginsborg, P., 'Peasants and revolutionaries in Venice and the Veneto, 1848', *Historical Journal*, 17 (1974)

Howard, J. J., 'Patriot mothers in the post-Risorgimento. Women after the Italian revolution', in C. R. Berkin and C. M. Lovett, eds, *Women,* *war and revolution*, Holmes and Meier, New York (1980)

Kertzer, D. I., 'European peasant household structure. Some implications from a nineteenth century Italian community', *Journal of Family History*, 2 (1977)

Knoefel, P. K., 'Famine and fever in Tuscany. Eighteenth century Italian concern with the environment', *Physis*, 21 (1979)

Lange, P., and S. Tarrow, eds, *Italy in transition. Conflict and consensus*, Cass, London (1980)

Litchfield, R. B., 'Demographic characteristics of Florentine patrician families, sixteenth to nineteenth centuries', *Journal of Economic History*, 29 (1969)

Lovett, C. M., *The democratic movement in Italy, 1830–76*, Harvard University Press, Cambridge, Mass. (1982) [includes material on social structure]

McArdle, F., *Altopascio. A study in Tuscan rural society, 1587–1784*, Cambridge University Press, Cambridge (1978)

Pristinger, F., 'Ethnic conflict and modernisation in the south Tyrol', in C. R. Foster, ed., *Nations without a state. Ethnic minorities in western Europe*, Praeger, New York (1980)

Shefter, M., 'Party and patronage. Germany, England and Italy', *Politics and Society*, 7 (1977)

Tannenbaum, E. R., *The fascist experience. Italian society and culture, 1922–45*, Basic Books, New York (1972)

Wilson, A., 'Ferrante Aporti. Apostle of infancy', *British Journal of Educational Studies*, 27 (1979) [wider implications of Italian school developments, 1827–60]

Woolf, S., *A history of Italy, 1700–1860. The social constraints of political change*, Methuen, London (1979)

Woolf, S. J., *A history of Italy, 1700–1860. The social Tuscany', Annuario dell' Istituto Storico Italiano*, 23–24 (1971–72)

Zamagni, V., 'The rich in a late industrialiser. The case of Italy', in W. D. Rubinstein, ed., *Wealth and the wealthy in the modern world*, Croom Helm, London (1980)

Zanetti, D. E., 'The *patriziato* of Milan from the domination of Spain to the unification of Italy. An outline of the social and demographic history', *Social History*, 6 (1977)

ECONOMIC POLICY AND THOUGHT

Coppa, F. J., 'Economic and ethical liberalism in conflict. The extraordinary liberalism of Giovanni Giolitti', *Journal of Modern History*, 42 (1970)

Greenfield, K. R., 'Economic ideas and facts of the early period of the Risorgimento', *American Historical Review*, 36 (1930–31)

Greenfield, K. R., *Economics and liberalism in the Risorgimento. A study in nationalism in Lombardy, 1814–48*, Johns Hopkins University Press, Baltimore, Md. (1934)

Oblath, A., 'The campaign against unemployment in Italy', *International Labour Review*, 21 (1930)

Welk, W. G., *Fascist economic policy*, Harvard University Press, Cambridge, Mass. (1938)

Wrigley, D. W., 'Germany and the Turco-Italian war, 1911–12', *Journal of Middle East Studies*, 11 (1980)

HISTORIOGRAPHY AND BIBLIOGRAPHY

Bertelli, S., 'Local history in Italy', *Local History*, 11 (1975)

Cipolla, C. M., 'List of books and articles on Italian economic history published in Italy, 1939–49', *Economic History Review*, 4 (1951–52)

de Felice, R., 'Italian historiography since the second world war', in R. Bosworth and G. Cresciano, eds, *A volume of Italian studies*, University of Sydney Press, Sydney, N.S.W. (1979)

Robertson, R. M., 'Researches in Italian economic history of the period of the Risorgimento', *South African Journal of Economics*, 35 (1967)

Romani, A. M., 'Recent developments of business history in Italy', *Business History Review*, 40 (1966)

SPAIN

GENERAL ECONOMIC AND SOCIAL HISTORY

Carr, R., *Spain, 1808–1939*, Clarendon Press, Oxford (1966)

Chandler, J. A., 'The self-destructive nature of the Spanish restoration', *Iberian Studies*, 2 (1973)

Christelow, A., 'Economic background of the Anglo-Spanish war of 1762', *Journal of Modern History*, 18 (1946)

Cortada, J. W., 'Catalan politics and economics, 1906–11', *Cuadernos de Historia Economica de Cataluna,* 13 (1975)

Cortes, J. B., 'The achievement motive in the Spanish economy between the thirteenth century and the eighteenth century', *Economic Development and Cultural Change,* 9 (1961)

Fontana, J., and J. Nadal, 'Spain, 1914–70', in C. M. Cipolla, ed., *Contemporary economies.* Fontana Economic History of Europe, vol. 6, part 2, Collins/Fontana, Glasgow (1976)

González Encisco, A., and J. Patricio Merino, 'The public sector and economic growth in eighteenth century Spain', *Journal of European Economic History,* 8 (1979)

Hamilton, E. J., 'The decline of Spain', *Economic History Review,* 8 (1938)

Hamilton, E. J., 'Money and economic recovery in Spain under the first Bourbon, 1701–46', *Journal of Modern History,* 15 (1943)

Hamilton, E. J., 'Monetary disorder and economic decadence in Spain, 1651–1700', *Journal of Political Economy,* 51 (1943)

Harper, G. T., *German economic policy in Spain during the Spanish civil war, 1936–39,* Mouton, Paris (1967)

Harrison, R. J., *An economic history of modern Spain,* Manchester University Press, Manchester (1978)

Herr, R., *The eighteenth century revolution in Spain,* Princeton University Press, Princeton, N.J. (1958)

Jackson, G., *The Spanish republic and the civil war, 1931–39,* Princeton University Press, Princeton, N.J. (1965)

Jackson, G., ed., *The Spanish civil war. Domestic crisis or international conspiracy?* D. C. Heath, Boston, Mass. (1967)

Kamen, H., 'The decline of Spain. A historical myth?' *Past and Present,* 81 (1978)

Nadal, J., 'The failure of the industrial revolution in Spain, 1830–1914', in C. M. Cipolla, ed., *The emergence of industrial societies,* Fontana Economic History of Europe, vol. 4, part 2, Collins/Fontana, Glasgow (1973)

Phillips, C. R., *Ciudad Real, 1500–1750. Growth, crisis, and readjustment in the Spanish economy,* Harvard University Press, Cambridge, Mass. (1979)

Pike, F. B., 'Capitalism and consumerism in Spain in the 1890s', *Inter-American Economic Affairs,* 26 (1973)

Sánchez-Albornoz, N., 'Congruence among Spanish economic regions in the nineteenth century', *Journal of European Economic History,* 3 (1974)

Stein, B. H. and S. J., 'Concepts and realities of Spanish economic growth, 1759–89', *Historia Iberica,* 1 (1973)

Trebilcock, C., 'British armaments and European industrialisation, 1890–1914. The Spanish case reaffirmed', *Economic History Review,* 27 (1974)

Vaccaro, R., 'Industrialisation in Spain and Italy (1860–1914)', *Journal of European Economic History,* 9 (1980)

Vicens-Vives, J., *Approaches to the history of Spain,* University of California Press, Berkeley, Cal. (1967)

Vicens-Vives, J., and J. N. Oller, *An economic history of Spain,* Princeton University Press, Princeton, N.J. (1969)

AGRICULTURE AND RURAL SOCIETY

Anes, G., and A. Garcia Sanz, 'Tithes and agricultural production in modern Spain', *Proceedings of the seventh International Congress on Economic History, Edinburgh, 1978,* Edinburgh University Press, Edinburgh (1978)

Gilmore, D., 'Land reform and rural revolt in nineteenth century Andalusia (Spain)', *Peasant Studies,* 6 (1977)

Gorni, O., 'The problem of rural settlement in Spain', *International Labour Review,* 19 (1929)

Greenwood, D. J., *Unrewarding wealth. Commercialisation and collapse of agriculture in a Spanish Basque town,* Cambridge University Press, London (1976)

Harrison, R. J., 'The Spanish famine of 1904–06', *Agricultural History,* 47 (1973)

Hauben, P. J., 'The first decade of an agrarian experiment in Bourbon Spain. The "new towns" of Sierra Morena and Andalusia, 1766–76', *Agricultural History,* 39 (1965)

Herr, R., 'The redistribution of land through royal disentail of Church properties in Spain. 1798–1808', *Proceedings of the fifth international economic history conference Leningrad, 1970,* Mouton, Paris (1979)

Klein, J., *The Mesta. A study in Spanish economic history, 1273–1836,* Kennikat Press, Port Washington, N.Y. (1964; reprint of 1920 edn)

Malefakis, E. E., *Agrarian reform and peasant revolution in Spain. Origins of the civil war,* Yale University Press, New Haven, Conn. (1970)

Rios, F. de los, 'The agrarian problem in Spain', *International Labour Review,* 11 (1925)

Vilar, P., 'Agricultural process and the economic background in eighteenth century Catalonia', *Economic History Review,* 11 (1958–59)

INDUSTRY AND INTERNAL TRADE

Altea, Count de, 'National corporative organisation in Spanish industry', *International Labour Review,* 15 (1927)

Callahan, W. J., 'Crown, mobility and industry in eighteenth century Spain', *International Review of Social History,* 11 (1966)

Callahan, W. J., 'A note on the Real y General Junta de Comercio, 1679–1814', *Economic History Review,* 21 (1968)

Callahan, W. J., 'Don Juan de Goyeneche. Hidalgo industrialist of eighteenth century Spain', *Business History Review,* 43 (1969)

Callahan, W. J., *Honor, commerce and industry in eighteenth century Spain,* Baker Library, Boston (1972)

Checkland, S. G., *The mines of Tharsis. Roman, French and British enterprise in Spain,* Allen and Unwin, London (1967)

Chilcote, R. N., *Spain's iron and steel industry,* Texas University, Austin, Texas (1968)

Felix, D., 'Profit inflation and industrial growth. The historic record and contemporary analogies', *Quarterly Journal of Economics,* 70 (1956)

Harrison, R. J., 'British armaments and European industrialisation, 1890–1914. The Spanish case re-examined', *Economic History Review,* 27 (1974)

Harrison, R. J., 'Catalan business and the loss of Cuba, 1898–1914', *Economic History Review,* 27 (1974)

Harrison, R. J., 'Big business and the failure of the right-wing Catalan nationalism, 1901–23', *Historical Journal,* 19 (1976)

Harrison, R. J., 'Big business and the rise of Basque nationalism', *European Studies Review,* 7 (1977)

Harrison, R. J., 'The origins of modern industrialism in the Basque country', *Sheffield Studies in Economic and Social History,* 2 (1977)

Harvey, C. E., 'Politics and pyrites during the Spanish civil war', *Economic History Review,* 31 (1978)

La Force, J. C., 'Royal joint stock companies in Spain, 1700–1800', *Explorations in Entrepreneurial History,* 1 (1963–64)

La Force, J. C., 'Spanish royal textile factories, 1700–1800', *Journal of Economic History,* 24 (1964)

La Force, J. C., *The development of the Spanish textile industry, 1750–1800.* University of California Press, Berkeley, Cal. (1965)

La Force, J. C., 'The supply of muskets and Spain's war of independence', *Business History Review,* 43 (1965)

Tortella Casares, G., 'Limited liability and industrialisation in Spain, 1829–69', *Proceedings of the fourth international economic history conference, Bloomington, 1968,* Mouton, Paris (1973)

Smith, R. S., *The Spanish guild merchant. A history of the consulado, 1250–1700,* Duke University Press, Durham, N.C. (1940)

TRANSPORT AND COMMUNICATIONS

Ringrose, D. R., 'Transportation and economic stagnation in eighteenth century Castile', *Journal of Economic History,* 28 (1968)

Ringrose, D. R., 'The government and the carters in Spain, 1476–1700', *Economic History Review,* 22 (1969)

Ringrose, D. R., *Transportation and economic stagnation in Spain, 1750–1850,* Duke University Press, Durham, N.C. (1970)

MONEY, BANKING AND FINANCE

Archer, C. I., 'Bourbon finances and military policy in New Spain', *Americas,* 37 (1981)

Barbier, J. A., 'Peninsular finance and colonial trade. The dilemma of Charles IV's Spain', *Journal of Latin American Studies,* 12 (1980)

Barbier, J. A., and H. S. Klein, 'Revolutionary wars and public finances. The Madrid treasury, 1784–1807', *Journal of Economic History,* 41 (1981)

Bazant, J., 'The conqueror's inheritance. The Cortes-Pignatelli Mexican estate', *Journal of European Economic History,* 5 (1976)

Bustelo, F., and G. Tortella-Casares, 'Monetary inflation in Spain, 1800–1970', *Journal of European Economic History,* 5 (1976)

Clough, S. B., 'Taxation and capital formation since 1870 in France, Italy and the United States', *Proceedings of the third international economic history conference, Munich, 1968,* Mouton, Paris (1968)

Hamilton, E. J., 'Monetary problems in Spain and Spanish America, 1751–1800', *Journal of*

Economic History, 4 (1944)

Hamilton, E. J., 'The foundation of the Bank of Spain', *Journal of Political Economy*, 53 (1945)

Hamilton, E. J., 'The first twenty years of the Bank of Spain', *Journal of Political Economy*, 54 (1946)

Hamilton, E. J., 'Plans for a national bank in Spain', *Journal of Political Economy*, 57 (1949)

Harrison, R. J., 'Financial reconstruction in Spain after the loss of the last colonies', *Journal of European Economic History*, 9 (1980)

Hubbard, J. R., 'How Franco financed his war', *Journal of Modern History*, 25 (1953)

Tortella-Casares, G., 'Spain, 1829–74', in R. E. Cameron, ed., *Banking and economic development. Some lessons of history*, Oxford University Press, London (1967)

Whealey, R., 'How Franco financed his war – reconsidered', *Journal of Contemporary History*, 12 (1977)

OVERSEAS TRADE AND COMMERCIAL RELATIONS

Bierck, H. A., 'Tobacco marketing in Venezuela, 1798–99. An aspect of Spanish mercantilistic revisionism', *Business History Review*, 39 (1965)

Cheong, W. E., 'The decline of Manila as the Spanish entrepot in the Far East, 1785–1826. Its impact on the pattern of south-east Asian trade', *Journal of South East Asian Studies*, 2 (1971)

Cuenca, J., 'Statistics of Spain's colonial trade 1792–1820. Consular duties, cargo inventories and balances of trade', *Hispanic American Historical Review* (1981)

Flinn, M. W., 'British steel and Spanish ore, 1871–1914', *Economic History Review*, 8 (1955–56)

Hussey, R. D., *The Caracas Company, 1728–84. A study in the history of Spanish monopolistic trade*, Harvard University Press, Cambridge, Mass. (1934)

Hussey, R. D., and J. S. Bromley, 'The Spanish empire under foreign pressures, 1688–1715', in J. S. Bromley, ed., *The rise of Great Britain and Russia, 1688–1715/25*, The New Cambridge Modern History, vol. 6, Cambridge University Press, Cambridge (1970)

Innis, H. A., 'The rise and fall of the Spanish fishery in Newfoundland', *Transactions of the Royal Society of Canada*, 25 (1931)

Longfield, A. K., 'Irish linen for Spain and Portugal. James Archbold's letters, 1771–79', *Proceedings of the Royal Irish Academy*, 76 (1976)

Lynch, J., *Spanish colonial administration, 1782–1810. The intendant system in the viceroyalty of the Rio de la Plata*, Athlone Press, London (1958)

McLachlan, J. O., *Trade and peace with old Spain, 1667–1750. A study of the influence of commerce on Anglo-Spanish diplomacy in the first half of the eighteenth century*, Cambridge University Press, Cambridge (1940)

Murray, D. R., *Odious commerce. Britain, Spain and the abolition of the Cuban slave trade*, Cambridge University Press, New York (1981)

Noah, M. E., *Old Calabar. The city states and the Europeans, 1880–85*, Scholars, Uyo (Nigeria) (1980) [mainly Spanish slave trade]

Phillips, C. R., 'The Spanish wool trade, 1500–1780', *Journal of Economic History*, 42 (1982)

Sundiata, I. K., 'A note on an abortive slave. Fernando Po, 1778–81', *Bulletin de l' Institute Fondamental d'Afrique Noire* (B), 35 (1973)

Walker, G. J., *Spanish politics and imperial trade 1700–89*, Macmillan, London (1979)

POPULATION AND MIGRATION

Abelson, A., 'Inheritance and population control in a Basque valley before 1900', *Peasant Studies*, 7 (1978)

Din, G. C., 'Spain's immigration policy and efforts in Louisiana during the American revolution', *Louisiana Studies*, 14 (1975)

Gregory, D. D., 'Andalusian migration. A historical perspective', *Iberian Studies*, 4 (1975)

Leasure, W., 'Factors involved in the decline of fertility in Spain, 1900–50', *Population Studies*, 16 (1962–63)

Livi-Bacci, M., 'Fertility and nuptiality changes in Spain from the late eighteenth to the early twentieth century', parts 1 and 2, *Population Studies*, 22 (1968)

Livi-Bacci, M., 'Fertility and population growth in Spain in the eighteenth and nineteenth centuries', in D. V. Glass and R. Revelle, eds, *Population and Social Change*, Edward Arnold, London (1972)

Majoral, R., 'The consequences of depopulation in the western Pyrenees of Catalonia', *Iberian Studies*, 6 (1977)

O'Flanagan, P., 'The changing population structure of Galicia, 1900–70', *Iberian Studies*, 5 (1976)

INCOMES, WAGES AND PRICES

Hamilton, E. J., 'War and inflation in Spain', *Quar-*

terly Journal of Economics, 59 (1944)

Hamilton, E. J., *War and prices in Spain, 1651–1800,* Harvard University Press, Cambridge, Mass. (1947)

Sardà, J., 'Spanish prices in the nineteenth century', *Quarterly Journal of Economics,* 62 (1948)

URBAN HISTORY

Boileau, I., 'La Ciudad Lineal. A critical study of the linear suburb of Madrid', *Town Planning Review,* 30 (1959)

Collins, G. R., 'The Ciudad Lineal of Madrid', *Journal of the Society of Architectural Historians,* 18 (1959)

Gutkind, E. A., *International history of city development,* vol. 3, *Urban development in Spain and Portugal,* Collier-Macmillan, London (1967)

Miller, B., 'Ildefonso Cerda. An introduction', *Architectural Association Quarterly,* 1 (1977) [town planning in Barcelona]

Wynn, M., 'Barcelona. Planning and change, 1854–1977', *Town Planning Review,* 50 (1979)

SOCIAL STRUCTURE AND SOCIAL CONDITIONS

Burke, M. E., *The Royal College of San Carlos. Surgery and Spanish medical reform in the late eighteenth century,* Duke University Press, Durham, N.C. (1977)

Callahan, W. J., 'Corporate charity in Spain. The Hermandad del Refugio of Madrid, 1618–1814', *Social History,* 9 (1976)

Callahan, W. J., 'A sound contract. The poor, the privileged and the Church in eighteenth century Spain', in R. E. Morton, and J. D. Browning, eds., *Religion in the eighteenth century,* Garland, New York (1979)

Casey, J., 'The Spanish anarchist peasant. How primitive a rebel?', *Journal of European Studies,* 8 (1978)

Freeman, S. T., *Neighbours. The social contract in a Castilian hamlet,* University of Chicago Press, Chicago, Ill. (1970)

Garmo, P. H. de, 'Poverty and peasants in the Rioja, 1883–1910', *Agricultural History,* 49 (1975)

Greenwood, D. J., 'Ethnic regionalism in the Spanish Basque country. Class and cultural conflicts', *Iberian Studies,* 5 (1976)

Harrison, R. J., 'The beginnings of social legislation in Spain, 1900–19', *Iberian Studies,* 3 (1974)

Headrick, D. R., 'Spain and the revolution of 1848',

European Studies Review, 6 (1976)

Kamen, H., 'Public authority and popular crime. Banditry in Valencia, 1660–1714', *Journal of European Economic History,* 3 (1974)

Kaplan, T., 'The social base of nineteenth century Andalusian anarchism in Jerez de la Frontera' *Journal of Interdisciplinery History,* 6 (1975–76)

Kaplan, T. *Anarchies of Andalusia, 1868–1903* Princeton University Press, Princeton, N.J. (1977) [social and economic background to political disorder]

Kaplan, T., 'Other scenarios. Women and Spanish anarchism', in R. Bridenthal and C. Koonz., eds. *Becoming visible. Women in European history,* Houghton Mifflin, Boston, Mass. (1977)

Mantelli, R., 'The political and social ideas of an enlightened Catholic. The Catalan Jesuit Juan Francisco Masdeu (1744–1817)', *Archivum Hist. Societatis Iesu,* 50 (1981)

Perry, M. E., ' "Lost women" in early modern Seville. The politics of prostitution', *Feminist Studies,* 4 (1978)

Pescatello, A. M., *Power and pawn. The female in Iberian families.* Greenwood Press, Westport, Conn. (1976)

Rodriguez, L., 'The Spanish riots of 1766', *Past and Present,* 59 (1973)

Rodriguez, L., 'The riots of 1766 in Madrid', *European Studies Review,* 3 (1973)

Thompson, I. A. A., 'The purchase of nobility in Castile, 1552–1700', *Journal of European Economic History,* 8 (1979)

ECONOMIC POLICY AND THOUGHT

Grice-Hutchinson, M., *Early economic thought in Spain, 1177–1740,* Allen and Unwin, London (1978)

Harrison, R. J., 'The regenerationist movement in Spain after the disaster of 1898', *European Studies Review,* 9 (1979)

Harrison, R. J., 'The failure of economic reconstitution in Spain, 1916–23', *European Studies Review,* 13 (1983)

Smith, R. S., 'Economists and the Enlightenment in Spain, 1750–1800', *Journal of Political Economy,* 63 (1955)

Smith, R. S., 'Spanish mercantilism. A hardy perennial', *Southern Economic Journal,* 37 (1971)

Voltes, P., 'Effects of the Spanish government's economic policy in Barcelona between 1884 and

1914', *Journal of European Economic History*, 1 (1972)

HISTORIOGRAPHY AND BIBLIOGRAPHY

Aracil, R., and M. G. Bonafé, 'Contemporary Spanish economic history', *Journal of European Economic History*, 8 (1979) [bibliographical review]

Cortada, J. W., 'Possible uses of computer technology in the study of Spanish history', *Cuadernos de Historia Economica de Cataluna*, 16 (1977)

Harrison, R. J., 'Spanish economic history. From the restoration to the Franco regime', *Economic History Review*, 33 (1980)

Hoffman, P. E., 'The computer, archival data and statistics for the colonial period. A proposal for methodology', *Cuadernos de Historia Economica de Cataluna*, 7 (1972)

McKay, A., 'Recent literature on Spanish economic history', *Economic History Review*, 31 (1978)

Moreda, V. P., 'The journal *Moneda y Credito* and its contribution to Spanish historiography, 1942–74', *Journal of European Economic History*, 4 (1975)

TURKEY

GENERAL ECONOMIC AND SOCIAL HISTORY

Devlet Instatiskik Entitusu, *Fifty years of social and economic development in Turkey*, Devlet Instatiskik Enstitusu, Ankara (1973)

Ergil, D., and R. T. Rhodes, 'Western capitalism and the disintegration of the Ottoman empire', *Economy and History*, 18 (1975)

Hershlag, Z. Y., 'Turkey. Achievements and failures in the policy of economic development during the inter-war period, 1919–39', *Kyklos*, 7 (1954)

Hershlag, Z. Y., *Turkey. The challenge of growth*, E. J. Brill, Leiden (1968)

Issawi, C., 'De-industrialization and re-industrialization in the Middle East since 1800', *International Journal of Middle East Studies*, 12 (1980)

Issawi, C., ed., *The economic history of Turkey, 1800–1914*, University of Chicago Press, Chicago, Ill. (1980)

Karkar, Y. N., 'Economic development in the Ottoman empire, 1856–1914', *Middle Eastern Economic Papers*, (1968)

Karpat, K. H., 'Transformation of the Ottoman state', *International Journal of Middle East Studies*, 3 (1972)

Karpat, K. H., ed., *The Ottoman state and its place in world history*, E. J. Brill, Leiden (1974)

Keyder, C., *The definition of a peripheral economy. Turkey, 1923–29*, Cambridge University Press, Cambridge (1981)

Lewis, B., *The emergence of modern Turkey*, Oxford University Press, London (1961)

McGowan, B., *Economic life in Ottoman Europe. Taxation, trade and the struggle for land, 1600–1800*, Cambridge University Press, Cambridge (1981)

Mears, E. G., ed., *Modern Turkey. A politico-economic interpretation, 1908–23*, Macmillan, New York (1924)

Miller, W., *The Ottoman empire and its successors, 1801–1927*, Cambridge University Press, Cambridge (1936)

Sadat, D. R., 'Rumeli Ayaulari. The eighteenth century', *Journal of Modern History*, 44 (1972) [social structure and economic change in a Turkish province]

Thornburg, M. W., et al., *Turkey. An economic appraisal*, Twentieth Century Fund, New York (1949)

Todorov, N., 'The genesis of capitalism in the Balkan provinces of the Ottoman empire in the nineteenth century', *Explorations in Economic History*, 7 (1969–70)

Warriner, D., ed., *Contrasts in emerging societies. Readings in the social and economic history of south-eastern Europe in the nineteenth century*, Athone Press, London (1965)

Woods, H., *Report on the economic and commercial conditions in Turkey, April, 1924*, H.M.S.O., London (1924)

Woods, H., *Report on the economic and commercial conditions in Turkey, May, 1928*, H.M.S.O., London (1928)

Woods, H., *Economic conditions in Turkey*, H.M.S.O., London (1930)

AGRICULTURE AND RURAL SOCIETY

Hirsch, E. and A., 'Changes in agricultural output *per capita* of rural population in Turkey 1927–60', *Economic Development and Cultural Change*, 11 (1963)

Hirsch, E. and A., 'Changes in terms of trade of farmers and their effects on real farm income *per. capita* of rural population in Turkey, 1927–60', *Economic Development and Cultural Change*, 14 (1966)

Inalcik, H., 'Land problems in Turkish history', *Muslim World*, 45 (1955)

Novichev, A. D., 'The development of commodity-money and capitalist relations in Turkish agriculture', in C. Issawi, ed., *The economic history of the Middle East*, University of Chicago Press, Chicago, Ill. (1966)

Quataert, D., 'Dilemma of development. The agricultural bank and agricultural reform in Ottoman Turkey, 1888–1908', *International Journal of Middle East Studies*, 6 (1975)

INDUSTRY AND INTERNAL TRADE

Osman, M., 'Handicrafts in Turkey', *International Labour Review*, 31 (1935)

Stoianovich, T., 'The conquering Balkan orthodox merchant', *Journal of Economic History*, 20 (1960)

TRANSPORT AND COMMUNICATIONS

Earle, E. M., *Turkey, the great powers, and the Bagdad railway. A study in imperialism*, Macmillan, New York (1924)

Karkar, Y. N., *Railway development in the Ottoman empire, 1856–1914*, Vintage Press, New York (1972)

McLean, D., 'British finance and foreign policy in Turkey. The Smyrna–Aidin railway settlement, 1913–14', *Historical Journal*, 19 (1976)

Quataert, D., 'Limited revolution. The impact of the Anatolian railway on Turkish transportation and the provisioning of Istanbul, 1890–1908', *Business History Review*, 51 (1977)

Schoenberg, P. E., 'The evolution of transport in Turkey (eastern Thrace and Asia Minor) under Ottoman rule, 1856–1918', *Middle Eastern Studies*, 13 (1977)

MONEY, BANKING AND FINANCE

Blaisdell, D. C., *European financial control in the Ottoman empire. A study of the establishment, activities and significance of the administration of the Ottoman public debt*, Columbia University Press, New York (1929)

Kent, M., 'Agent of empire? The National Bank of Turkey and British foreign policy', *Historical Journal*, 18 (1975)

Milgrim, M. R., 'An overlooked problem in Turkish-Russian relations. The 1878 war indemnity', *International Journal of Middle East Studies*, 9 (1978)

Shaw, S., 'The nineteenth century Ottoman tax reforms and revenue system', *International Journal of Middle East Studies*, 6 (1975)

OVERSEAS TRADE AND COMMERCIAL RELATIONS

Bergquist, H. E., 'Russo-American economic relations in the 1820s. Henry Middleton as a protector of American economic interests in Russia and Turkey', *East European Quarterly*, 11 (1977)

Berov, L., 'Change in price conditions in trade between Turkey and Europe in the sixteenth to nineteenth century', *Etudes Balkaniques*, 2–3 (1974)

Kireev, N. G., 'On the history of Russian-Turkish trade relations via Istanbul in the middle of the eighteenth century', in N. G. Kireev, *Istanbul à la jonction des cultures balkaniques, méditerranéenes, slaves et orientales aux XVIe-XIXe siècles*, A.I.E.S.E.E., Bucharest (1973)

Puryear, V. J., *International economics and diplomacy in the Near East. A study of British commercial policy in the Levant, 1834–53*, Stanford University Press, Stanford, Cal. (1935)

Raccagni, M., 'The French economic interests in the Ottoman empire', *International Journal of Middle East Studies*, 11 (1980)

Wood, A. C., *A history of the Levant Company*, Oxford University Press, London (1935)

Wrigley, D. W., 'Germany and the Turko-Iranian war, 1911–12', *International Journal of Middle East Studies*, 11 (1980)

POPULATION AND MIGRATION

Sarc, O. C., 'Changes in the rural–urban distribution of the Turkish population', *Revue de la Faculté des Sciences de l'Université d'Istanbul*, 9 (1948)

LABOUR CONDITIONS AND ORGANISATION

Tuncay, M., 'On the problem of the workers' movement in European Turkey', *Etudes Balkaniques*, 15 (1979)

Weigert, O., 'The new Turkish labour code', *International Labour Review*, 35 (1937)

URBAN HISTORY

Rosenthal, S. T., *The politics of dependency. Urban reform in Istanbul*, Greenwood Press, Westport, Conn. (1980)

SOCIAL STRUCTURE AND SOCIAL CONDITIONS

Ergil, D., 'Class relations and Turkish transformation in historical perspective', *Studia Islamica*, 39 (1974)

Ergil, D., 'Secularisation as class conflict. The Turkish example', *Asian Affairs*, 62 (1975)

Gibb, H. A. R., and H. Bowen, *Islamic society and the West*, Oxford University Press, London (1951)

Inalcik, H., 'The nature of traditional society', in R. E. Ward and D. A. Rustow, eds, *Political modernisation in Japan and Turkey*, Princeton University Press, Princeton, N.J. (1964)

Kazgan, G., 'Peasant movements in Turkish society since the end of the eighteenth century up to our times', *Cahiers Internationales d'Historie Economique et Sociale*, 7 (1977)

HISTORIOGRAPHY AND BIBLIOGRAPHY

Kerner, R. J., *Social sciences in the Balkans and in Turkey. A survey of resources for study and research in these fields of knowledge*, University of California Press, Berkeley, Cal. (1930)

GREECE

Andreades, A., 'The current crisis in Greece', *Economic Journal*, 16 (1906)

Andreades, A., 'Labour legislation in Greece', *International Labour Review*, 6 (1922)

Asdrachas, S. I., 'Problems of economic history of the period of Ottoman domination in Greece', *Journal of the Hellenic Diaspora*, 6 (1979)

Batalden, S. K., 'John Kapodistrias and the structure of Greek society on the eve of the war of independence. An historical essay', *East European Quarterly*, 13 (1979)

Dakin, D., 'The origins of the Greek revolution of 1821', *History*, 37 (1952)

Dakin, D., *The unification of Greece, 1770–1923*, Ernest Benn, London (1972)

Dertilis, P. B., 'Introduction to the stages of the economy of Greece', *Revue Internationale d'Histoire de la Banque*, 2 (1969)

Delivanis, D. J., 'Thessaloniki on the eve of World War I', *Balkan Studies*, 21 (1980)

Diamanduros, N. P., et al., *Helenism and the first Greek war of liberation (1821–30). Continuity and change*, Institute for Balkan Studies, Thessaloniki (1976)

Domestichos, A., 'Productive workers in Greece. Land reclamation and settlement in Macedonia', *International Labour Review*, 30 (1934)

Dumont, P., 'The social structure of the Jewish community of Salonica at the end of the nineteenth century', *Southeastern Europe*, 5 (1978)

Escott, B. A. C. S., *Greece. A political and economic survey, 1939–53*, Royal Institute of International Affairs, London (1954)

Faroqhi, S., 'Agricultural activities in a Bektashi center. The Tekke of Kizil Deli, 1750–1830', *Sudost Forschungen*, 35 (1976)

Forster, E. J., *A short history of modern Greece, 1821–1956*, Praeger, New York (2nd edn 1957)

Geanakoplos, D. J., 'The diaspora Greeks. The genesis of modern Greek national consciousness', in N. P. Diamandouros et al., *Hellenism and the first Greek war of liberation (1821–30). Continuity and change*, Institute for Balkan Studies, Thessaloniki (1976)

Kofas, J. V., *Financial relations of Greece and the great powers, 1832–62*, Columbia University Press, New York (1981)

Kofos, E., 'Dilemmas and orientations of Greek policy in Macedonia, 1878–86', *Balkan Studies*, 21 (1980)

Kyrkilitsis, A., 'The Greek banking system. A historical review', *Revue Internationale d'Histoire de la Banque*, 1 (1968)

Leon, G. B., 'The Greek labor movement and the bourgeois state, 1910–20', *Journal of the Hel-*

lenic Diaspora, 4 (1978)

Levandis, J. A., *The Greek foreign debt and the great powers, 1821–98*, Columbia University Press, New York (1944)

McGrew, W. M., 'The land issue in the Greek war of independence', in N. P. Diamandouros *et al., Hellenism and the first Greek war of liberation (1821–30). Continuity and change*, Institute for Balkan Studies, Thessaloniki (1976)

Miller, W., *Greek life in town and country*, G. Newnes, London (1905)

Miller, W., 'A history of the Greek people (1821–1931), Meltsen, London (1922)

Mouzelis, N., 'Greek and Bulgarian peasants. Aspects of their sociopolitical situation during the inter-war period', *Comparative Studies in Society and History*, 18 (1976)

Mouzelis, N., 'Capitalism and the development of agriculture', *Journal of Peasant Studies*, 3 (1976)

Papadantonakis, K., and R. Rubinson, 'The state as instrument of induction to the periphery. The case of Greece', in R. Rubinson, ed., *Dynamics of world development*, Sage, Beverly Hills, Cal. (1981)

Pepelasis, A. A., 'The legal system and economic development of Greece', *Journal of Economic History*, 19 (1959)

Psomiades, H., 'The economic and social transforma-

Psomiades, H. J., 'The economic and social transformation of modern Greece', *Journal of International Affairs*, 19 (1965)

Psomiades, H. J., 'The character of the new Greek state', in N. P. Diamandouros *et al., Hellenism and the first Greek war of liberation (1821–30). Continuity and change*, Institute for Balkan Studies, Thessaloniki (1976)

Saloutos, T., 'Causes and patterns of Greek emigration to the United States', *Perspectives in American History*, 7 (1973)

Sanders, I. T., *Rainbow in the rock. The people of rural Greece*, Harvard University Press, Cambridge, Mass. (1962)

Sergeant, L., *Greece in the nineteenth century. A record of Hellenic emancipation and progress 1821–97*, T. F. Unwin, London (1897)

Topping, P., 'Greek historical writing on the period 1453–1914. A review article', *Journal of Modern History*, 33 (1961)

Vacalopoulos, C. A., 'Contribution of the Irish philhellene Stevenson to the agricultural development of Greece in 1828', *Balkan Studies*, 13 (1972)

Valaovas, V. G., 'A reconstruction of the demographic history of modern Greece', *Milbank Memorial Fund Quarterly*, 38 (1960)

Zarras, I., 'The organisation of social insurance in Greece', *International Labour Review*, 39 (1939)

PORTUGAL

Alden, D., 'Vicissitudes of trade in the Portuguese Atlantic empire during the first half of the eighteenth century. A review article', *Americas*, 32 (1975)

Boxer, C. R., *The Portuguese seaborne empire*, in H. V. Livermore, ed., *Portugal and Brazil*, Clarendon Press, Oxford (1953)

Boxer, C. R., *The Portuguese seaborne empire', 1415–1825*, Hutchinson, London (1969)

Chapman, A. B. W., 'The commerical relations of England and Portugal, 1487–1807', *Transactions of the Royal Historical Society*, series 3, vol. 1 (1907)

Christelow, A., 'Great Britain and the trades from Cadiz and Lisbon to Spanish America and Brazil, 1759–83', *Hispanic American Historical Review*, 27 (1947)

Clarence-Smith, W. G., 'Slavery in coastal southern Angola, 1875–1913', *Journal of Southern African Studies*, 2 (1976)

Clarence-Smith, W. G., 'The myth of uneconomic imperialism. The Portuguese in Angola, 1836–1926', *Journal of Southern African Studies*, 5 (1979)

Cotta, F., *Economic planning in corporative Portugal*, P. S. King, London (1937)

Dias, J. R., 'Black chiefs, white traders and colonial policy near the Kwanza. Kabuku Kambilo and the Portuguese, 1873–96', *Journal of African History*, 17 (1976)

Fisher, H. E. S., 'Anglo-Portuguese trade 1700–70', *Economic History Review*, 16 (1963–64)

Fisher, H. E. S., *The Portuguese trade. A study of Anglo-Portuguese commerce, 1700–70*, Methuen, London (1971)

Gentil da Silva, J., 'Portugal and overseas expansion from XVIth-XVIIIth centuries', *Journal of European Economic History*, 8 (1979)

Godinho, V. M., 'Portugal and her empire, 1680–1720', in J. S. Bromley, ed., *The rise of*

Great Britain and Russia, 1688–1715/25, Cambridge University Press, Cambridge (1970)

Gutkind, E. A., *International history of city development,* vol. 3, *Urban development in Spain and Portugal,* Collier-Macmillan, London (1967)

Hammond, R. J., *Portugal and Africa, 1815–1910. A study in uneconomic imperialism,* Stanford University Press, Stanford, Cal. (1966)

Hanson, C. A., *Economy and society in baroque Portugal, 1668–1703,* Macmillan, London (1981)

Humphreys, R. A., 'Monarchy and empire', in H. V. Livermore, ed., *Portugal and Brazil. An introduction,* Clarendon Press, Oxford (1953) [material on imperial trade]

Kisch, C. H., *The Portuguese banknote case,* Macmillan, London (1932)

Klein, H. S., 'The Portuguese slave trade from Angola in the eighteenth century', *Journal of Economic History,* 32 (1972)

Kulkarni, A. R., 'Indo-Portuguese history. Perspective and expectations', *Indica,* 16 (1979)

Livermore, H. V., *A history of Portugal,* Cambridge University Press, Cambridge (1947)

Livermore, H. V., *A new history of Portugal,* Cambridge University Press, Cambridge (1966)

Livi Bacci, M., *A century of Portuguese fertility,* Princeton University Press, Princeton, N.J. (1971)

Lodge, R., 'The English factory at Lisbon. Some chapters in its history', *Transactions of the Royal Historical Society,* 16 (1933)

Longfield, A. K., 'Irish linen for Spain and Portugal. James Archbold's letters, 1771–79', *Proceedings of the Royal Irish Academy,* 76 (1976)

Mayer, J., 'Regional development in Portugal (1929–77). An assessment', in P. Bairoch and M. Levy-Leboyer, eds, *Disparities in economic development since the industrial revolution,* Macmillan, London (1981)

Morgado, N. A., 'Portugal', in W. R. Lee, ed., *European demography and economic growth,* Croom Helm, London (1979)

Morrow, D. W., 'Phylloxera in Portugal', *Agricultural History,* 47 (1973)

Newitt, M. D. D., 'Angoche, the slave trade and the Portuguese, c. 1844–1910', *Journal of African History,* 13 (1972)

Oliveira Marques, A. H. de, 'The Portuguese 1920s. A general survey', *Revista de Historia Economica & Social,* 1 (1978)

Parry, J. H., 'Portugal overseas. The search for riches', *Journal of Interdisciplinary History,* 2 (1971–72)

Rau, V., 'Large-scale agricultural enterprise in post-medieval Portugal', *Papers presented to the first international economic history conference, Stockholm, 1960,* Mouton, Paris (1960)

Russell-Wood, A. J., 'Iberian expansion and the issue of black slavery. Changing Portuguese attitudes, 1440–1770', *American Historical Review,* 83 (1978)

Shillington, V. M., and A. B. Wallis Chapman, *The commercial relations of England and Portugal,* Routledge, London (1907)

Sideri, S., 'Secular trends in the terms of trade between Portugal and the United Kingdom, 1854–1957', *Economic Planning and National Accounting Papers,* The Hague (1961)

Sideri, S., *Trade and power. Informal colonialism in Anglo-Portuguese relations,* Rotterdam University Press, Rotterdam (1970)

Smith, W. H. C., 'Anglo-Portuguese relations, 1851–61', *Studia,* 27–8 (1969)

Souza, T. R. de, 'Marine insurance and Indo-Portuguese trade history. An aid to maritime historiography', *Indian Economic and Social History Review,* 14 (1977)

Verlinden, C., 'Virginia Rau and the economic history of Portugal', *Journal of European Economic History,* 4 (1975)

Vincent-Smith, J. D., 'The Anglo-German negotiations over the Portuguese colonies in Africa, 1911–14', *Historical Journal,* 17 (1974)

Vincent-Smith, J., 'The Portuguese economy and the Anglo-Portuguese commercial treaty of 1916', *Iberian Studies,* 3 (1974)

Wagner, M. J., 'Rum, policy and the Portuguese, or, The maintenance of elite supremacy in post-emancipation British Guiana', *Canadian Review of Sociology and Anthropology,* 14 (1977)

MALTA

Bowen-Jones, H., *et al., Malta. Background for development,* Durham University Department of Geography, Durham (1960)

Cavaliero, R., 'The decline of the Maltese Corso in the eighteenth century', *Melita Historica,* 2 (1959) [decline of piracy]

Gardiner, L., 'The steamboat-on-land', *Blackwood's Magazine,* 327 (1980)

Mallia-Milanes, V., 'Some aspects of Veneto-Maltese trade relations in the eighteenth century', *Studi Veneziani,* 16 (1974)

Mallia-Milanes, V., 'English merchants' initial contacts with Malta. A reconsideration', *Melita Historica,* 6 (1975)

Mallia-Milanes, V., 'Malta and Venice in the eighteenth century. A study in consular relations', *Studi Veneziani,* 17–18 (1975–76)

Mallia-Milanes, V., 'Towards an economic history of eighteenth century Malta. Buzzacarini Gonzaga's correspondence to the Venetian Magistracy of Trade, 1754–76', *Journal of European Economic History,* 7 (1978)

Seers, D., 'A fertility survey in the Maltese islands', *Population Studies,* 10 (1957)

SCANDINAVIA

GENERAL WORKS

GENERAL ECONOMIC AND SOCIAL HISTORY

Astrom, S. E., *The economic relations between peasants, merchants and the state in north-eastern Europe in the seventeenth and eighteenth centuries,* University of Helsinki, Institute of Economic and Social History, Research Report No. 8, Helsinki (1976)

Derry, T. K., *A history of Scandinavia,* Allen and Unwin, London (1979)

Dyrvik, S., *et al., The satellite state in the seventeenth and eighteenth centuries,* Universitetsforlaget, Oslo (1979)

Heckscher, E. F., *et al., Sweden, Norway, Denmark and Iceland in the world war,* Oxford University Press, New York (1930)

Hildebrand, K. G., 'Labour and capital in the Scandinavian countries in the nineteenth and twentieth centuries', in P. Mathias, and M. M. Postan, eds, *Cambridge Economic History of Europe,* vol. 7(1), Cambridge University Press, Cambridge (1978)

Hildebrand, K. G., 'Natural resources, preindustrial society and industrialisation in Scandinavia', in M. W. Flinn, ed., *Proceedings of the seventh international economic history congress, Edinburgh, 1978,* Edinburgh University Press, Edinburgh (1978)

Hovde, B. J., *The Scandinavian countries, 1720–1865,* Cornell University Press, Ithaca, N.Y. (1948)

Jörberg, L., 'The industrial revolution in the Nordic countries', in C. M. Cipolla, ed., *The emergence of industrial societies.* Fontana Economic History of Europe, vol. 4, part 2, Collins/Fontana, Glasgow (1973)

Jörberg, L., and O. Krantz, 'Scandinavia, 1914–70', in C. M. Cipolla, ed., *Contemporary economies.* Fontana Economic History of Europe, vol. 6, part 2, Collins/Fontana, Glasgow (1976)

Klingman, D., and G. B. Peters, 'Economic development and the growth of public expenditures in Scandinavia, 1875–1965', *Political Studies,* 28 (1980)

Lindgren, R. E., *Norway-Sweden. Union, disunion and Scandinavian integration,* Princeton University Press, Princeton, N.J. (1959)

Mitchison, R., ed., *The roots of nationalism. Studies in northern Europe,* John Donald, Edinburgh (1980)

Royal Institute of International Affairs, *The Scandinavian states and Finland. A political and economic survey,* Oxford University Press, London (1951)

Westergaard, H. L., *The official statistics of the Scandinavian countries and the Baltic republics,* League of Nations, Geneva (1926)

AGRICULTURE AND RURAL SOCIETY

Bjorkvik, H., 'The farm territories', *Scandinavian Economic History Review,* 4 (1956)

Bunte, R., 'Economic structure and development of Scandinavian fishing, 1870–1960', *Economy and History,* 9 (1966)

Frimanslund, R. 'Farm community and neighbourhood community', *Scandinavian Economic History Review,* 4 (1956)

Löfgren, O., 'Family and household among Scandinavian peasants', *Ethnologica Scandinavica,* 2

(1974)

Osterud, O., 'The transformation of Scandinavian agrarianism. A comparative study of political change around 1870', *Scandinavian Journal of History*, 1 (1976)

INDUSTRY AND INTERNAL TRADE

Drachmann, P., *Industrial development and commercial policies of the three Scandinavian countries*, Clarendon Press, Oxford (1915)

Rowntree, J., and A. Sherwell, *Public control of the liquor traffic. A review of the Scandinavian experiments in the light of recent experience*, Grant Richards, London (1903)

MONEY, BANKING AND FINANCE

Lester, R. A., ed., *Monetary experiments. Early American and recent Scandinavian*, Princeton University Press, Princeton, N.J. (1939)

Wicksell, K., 'The Scandinavian gold policy', *Economic Journal*, 26 (1916)

OVERSEAS TRADE AND COMMERCIAL RELATIONS

Aldridge, D. D., 'The victualling of the British naval expeditions to the Baltic Sea between 1715 and 1727', *Scandinavian Economic History Review*, 12 (1964)

Aström, S. E., 'English timber imports from northern Europe in the eighteenth century', *Scandinavian Economic History Review*, 18 (1970)

Flinn, M. W., 'Scandinavian iron ore mining and the British steel industry, 1870–1914', *Scandinavian Economic History Review*, 2 (1954)

Frederickson, J. W., 'American shipping in the trade with northern Europe, 1783–1860', *Scandinavian Economic History Review*, 4 (1956)

Hautala, K., *European and American tar in the English market during the eighteenth and early nineteenth centuries*, Suomalainen Tiedeakatemia, Helsinki (1963)

Kent, H. S. K., *War and trade in the northern seas. Anglo-Scandinavian economic relations in the mid-eighteenth century*, Cambridge University Press, Cambridge (1973)

Kirby, D., 'The Royal Navy's quest for pitch and tar during the reign of Queen Anne', *Scandinavian Economic History Review*, 22 (1974)

Knoppers, J., 'A comparison of the Sound Accounts and the Amsterdam Galjootsgeldregisters', *Scandinavian Economic History Review*, 24 (1976)

Montgomery, A., 'From a northern customs union to EFTA', *Scandinavian Economic History Review*, 8 (1960)

POPULATION AND MIGRATION

Akerman, S., *et al.*, 'Emigration, family and kinship', in B. Kronborg *et al.*, *Nordic population mobility. Comparative studies of selected parishes in the Nordic countries, 1850–1900*, Oslo University Press, Oslo (1977)

Akerman, S., 'Towards an understanding of emigrational processes', *Scandinavian Journal of History*, 3 (1978)

Akerman, S., *et al.*, *Chance and change. Social and economic studies in historical demography in the Baltic area*, Odense University Press, Odense (1978) [primarily Scandinavia]

Akerman, S., *et al.*, 'Splitting background variables. AID analysis applied to migration and literacy research', *Journal of European Economic History*, 8 (1979)

Dunlevy, J. A., and H. A. Gemery, 'Some additional evidence on settlement patterns of Scandinavian migrants to the United States. Dynamics and the role of family and friends', *Scandinavian Economic History Review*, 24 (1976)

Gaunt, D., and O. Löfgren, 'Remarriage in the Nordic countries. The cultural and socio-economic background', in J. Dupaquier *et al.*, *Marriage and remarriage in populations of the past*, Academic Press, London (1981)

Gille, H., 'The demographic history of the northern European countries in the eighteenth century', *Population Studies*, 3 (1949–50)

Hovde, B. J., 'Notes on the effects of emigration upon Scandinavia', *Journal of Modern History*, 6 (1934)

Hvidt, K., and H. A. Barton, 'Scandinavian discord on emigration', *Swedish Pioneer Historical Quarterly*, 25 (1954)

Jensen, A., 'Migration statistics of Denmark, Norway, and Sweden', in W. F. Willcox, *International migrations*, 2 vols, National Bureau of Economic Research, New York (1929, 1931)

Kronborg, B., *et al.*, *Nordic population mobility. Comparative studies of selected parishes in the Nordic countries, 1850–1900*, Oslo University Press, Oslo (1977)

Ljungmark, L., *For sale. Minnesota. Organized promotion of Scandinavian immigration.*

1866–73, Laromedelsforlag, Gothenburg (1971)

Oden, B., 'Scandinavian emigration prior to 1914', *Scandinavian Economic History Review*, 20 (1972)

Saugstad, L. F., and O. Odegard, 'Crude death rate and infant mortality 1840–1900 in Norway, Sweden, Denmark and England and Wales, with particular attention to the relationship between mortality and population density and urbanization', *Scandinavian Population Studies*, 5 (1979)

Semmingsen, I., 'Emigration from Scandinavia', *Scandinavian Economic History Review*, 20 (1972)

Sogner, S., 'Historical demography in Scandinavia', in *International Population Conference, London, 1969*, vol. 4, International Union for the Scientific Study of the Population, Liège (1971)

Tomasson, R. F., 'Premarital sexual permissiveness and illegitimacy in the Nordic countries', *Comparative Studies in Society and History*, 18 (1976)

Vedder, R. K., and L. E. Gallaway, 'The settlement preferences of Scandinavian emigrants to the United States, 1850–1960', *Scandinavian Economic History Review*, 18 (1970)

LABOUR CONDITIONS AND ORGANISATION

Erichsen, E., 'Scandinavian employers and collective agreements', parts 1 and 2, *International Labour Review*, 26 (1932)

Lafferty, W. M., *Economic development and the response of labor in Scandinavia. A multi-level analysis*, Universitetsforlaget, Oslo (1971)

Montgomery, B. G., *British and continental labour policy. The political labour movement and labour legislation in Great Britain, France and the Scandinavian countries, 1920–22*, Kegan Paul Trench Trubner, London (1922)

INCOMES, WAGES AND PRICES

Krantz, O., and C. A. Nilsson, 'Relative income levels

in the Scandinavian countries', *Economy and History*, 17 (1974)

URBAN HISTORY

Paulsson, T., *Scandinavian architecture. Buildings and society in Denmark, Finland, Norway and Sweden from the Iron Age until today*, Batsford, London (1957)

Rils, T., 'Towns and central government in northern Europe from the fifteenth century to the industrial revolution', *Scandinavian Economic History Review*, 29 (1981)

SOCIAL STRUCTURE AND SOCIAL CONDITIONS

Anthony, K., *Feminism in Germany and Scandinavia*, Holt, New York (1915)

Hovde, B. J., *The Scandinavian countries, 1720–1865. The rise of the middle classes*, Cornell University Press, Ithaca, N.Y. (1948)

HISTORIOGRAPHY AND BIBLIOGRAPHY

Boje, P., *et al.*, 'Select bibliography', *Scandinavian Economic History Review*, 23 (1975), 25 (1977)

Gemzell, C. A., 'Scandinavian history in international research. Some observations on Britain, France, West Germany and East Germany', *Scandinavian Journal of History*, 5 (1980)

Hammarström, I., 'Urban history in Scandinavia. A survey of recent trends', *Urban History Yearbook* (1978)

Imhof, A. E., and O. Larsen, 'Social and medical history. Methodological problems in interdisciplinary quantitative research', *Journal of Interdisciplinary History*, 7 (1977)

Johansen, H. C., *et al.*, 'Current research in economic history in Scandinavia. Historical demography', *Scandinavian Economic History Review*, 20 (1972)

Semmingsen, I., 'Nordic research into emigration', *Immigration History Newsletter*, 11 (1979)

NORWAY

GENERAL ECONOMIC AND SOCIAL HISTORY

Aukrust, O., and J. Bjerke, 'Real capital and economic growth in Norway, 1900–56', in R. Goldsmith and

C. Saunders, eds, *Income and Wealth*, 8, Bowes and Bowes, London (1959)

Derry, T. K., *A short history of Norway*, Allen and Unwin, London (1957)

Hanisch, T., 'The economic crisis in Norway in the

1930s. A tentative analysis of its causes', *Scandinavian Economic History Review*, 26 (1978)

Hodne, F., 'Growth in a dual economy – the Norwegian experience, 1814–1914', *Economy and History*, 16 (1973)

Jörberg, L., 'The industrial revolution in Norway. A reply', *Scandinavian Economic History Review*, 20 (1972)

Jörberg, L., 'The industrial revolution in the Nordic countries', in C. M. Cipolla, ed., *The emergence of industrial societies*. Fontana Economic History of Europe, vol. 4, part 2, Collins/Fontana, Glasgow (1973)

Jörberg, L., and O. Krantz, 'Scandinavia, 1914–1970', in C. M. Cipolla, ed., *Contemporary economies*, Fontana Economic History of Europe, vol. 6, part 2, Collins/Fontana, Glasgow (1976)

Kaartredt, A., 'The economic basis of Norwegian nationalism in the nineteenth century', in R. Mitchison, ed., *The roots of nationalism. Studies in northern Europe*, John Donald, Edinburgh (1980)

Lieberman, S., *The industrialization of Norway, 1800–1920*, Universitetsforlaget, Oslo (1970)

Moe, T., *Demographic developments and economic growth in Norway, 1740–1940. An econometric study*. University of Michigan Press, Ann Arbor, Mich. (1970)

Moe, T., 'Some economic aspects of Norwegian population movements, 1740–1940', *Journal of Economic History*, 30 (1970)

Moe, T., 'The history of economic growth in Norway', *Scandinavian Economic History Review*, 20 (1972) [review of Lieberman's work]

Norwegian Central Bureau of Statistics, *Trends in Norwegian economy, 1865–1960*, Norwegian Central Bureau of Statistics, Oslo (1966)

Ostensjo, R., 'The spring herring fishing and the industrial revolution in western Norway in the nineteenth century', *Scandinavian Economic History Review*, 11 (1963)

Rokkan, S., 'National primary socio-economic data structures. Norway', *International Social Science Journal*, 30 (1978)

Sejersted, F., 'The industrial revolution in Norway', *Scandinavian Economic History Review*, 20 (1972)

AGRICULTURE AND RURAL SOCIETY

Bjorkvik, H., 'The farm territories. Habitation and field systems, boundaries and common ownership', *Scandinavian Economic History Review*, 4
(1956)

Frimannslund, R., 'Farm community and neighbourhood community', *Scandinavian Economic History Review*, 4 (1956)

Holmsen, A., 'The old Norwegian peasant community', *Scandinavian Economic History Review*, 4 (1956)

Holmsen, A., 'The transition from tenancy to freehold peasant ownership in Norway', *Scandinavian Economic History Review*, 9 (1961)

Lunden, K., 'The growth of co-operatives among the Norwegian dairy farmers during the period 1856–1905', *Cahiers Internationaux d'Histoire Economique et Sociale*, 6 (1976)

Semmingsen, I. G., 'The dissolution of estate society in Norway', *Scandinavian Economic History Review*, 2 (1954)

Sogner, S., 'Freeholder and cottar. Property relationships and the social structure in the peasant community in Norway during the eighteenth century', *Scandinavian Journal of History*, 1 (1976)

Soltow, L., 'The distribution of real estate among Norwegian farmers in 1802', *Historisk Tidsskrift* (1978)

Valen-Sendstad, F., 'Two Norwegian agricultural anniversaries', *Scandinavian Economic History Review*, 10 (1962) [agricultural societies]

INDUSTRY AND INTERNAL TRADE

Adamson, O. J., ed., *Industries of Norway*, Dreyer, Oslo (1952)

Basberg, B., 'Patents, innovations and technological development in Norwegian whaling, 1880–1968', *World Patent Information*, 3 (1981)

Hodne, F., and O. Gjolberg, 'Market integration during the period of industrialization in Norway', in P. Bairoch and M. Levy-Leboyer, eds, *Disparities in economic development since the industrial revolution*, Macmillan, London (1981)

Johnsen, A. O., *Norwegian patents relating to whaling and the whaling industry. A statistical and historical analysis*. A. W. Brøggers, Oslo (1947)

Lange, E., 'The Concession Laws of 1906–09 and the Norwegian industrial development', *Scandinavian Journal of History*, 2 (1977)

Svendsen, A. F., *Union, 1873–1973*, Aschehong, Oslo (1973) [English summary of this the second largest Norwegian paper mill]

Tveite, S., 'The Norwegian textile market in the eighteenth century', *Scandinavian Economic History Review*, 17 (1969)

Unwin, S., *Book trade organization in Norway and Sweden*, Augustina, Rock Island, Ill. (1933)

Vamplew, W., 'The paraffin factory at Mandal. A study in business enterprise', *Scandinavian Economic History Review*, 18 (1970)

Wedervang, F., *Development of a population of industrial firms. The structure of manufacturing firms in Norway, 1930–1948*, Universitetsforlaget, Oslo (1965)

TRANSPORT AND COMMUNICATIONS

Gjolberg, O., 'The substitution of steam for sail in Norwegian ocean shipping, 1866–1914. A study in the economics of diffusion', *Scandinavian Economic History Review*, 28 (1980)

Petersen, K., *The saga of Norwegian shipping*, Dreyer, Oslo (1955)

Utaaker, K., 'Norwegian shipping activities between foreign ports, 1815–35', *Sjofartshistorisk Arbok* (1973)

MONEY, BANKING AND FINANCE

Christenson, C. L., 'Gold-parity depression in Norway and Denmark', *Journal of Political Economy*, 45 (1937)

Lester, R. A., 'Gold parity depression in Norway and Denmark', *Journal of Political Economy*, 45 (1937)

Stonehill, A., *Foreign ownership in Norwegian enterprises*, Samfunnokonomiske Studier, Oslo (1965)

OVERSEAS TRADE AND COMMERCIAL RELATIONS

Kent, H. S. K., 'The Anglo-Norwegian timber trade in the eighteenth century', *Economic History Review*, 8 (1955)

Kjaerheim, S., 'Norwegian timber exports in the eighteenth century. A comparison of port books and private accounts', *Scandinavian Economic History Review*, 5 (1957)

Sejersted, F., 'Aspects of the Norwegian timber trade in the 1840s and '50s', *Scandinavian Economic History Review*, 16 (1968)

POPULATION AND MIGRATION

Backer, J. E., 'Population statistics and population registration in Norway', parts 1 and 2, *Population Studies*, 1 (1947–48), 2 (1948–49)

Blegen, T. C., *Norwegian migration to America, 1825–1860*, 2 vols, Norwegian American Historical Association, Northfield, Minn. (1931, 1940)

Drake, M., 'The growth of population in Norway, 1735–1855. Statistical appendix', *Scandinavian Economic History Review*, 13 (1965)

Drake, M., 'Malthus on Norway', *Population Studies*, 20 (1966–67)

Drake, M., *Population and society in Norway, 1735–1865*, Cambridge University Press, Cambridge (1969)

Drake, M., 'Marital age-patterns in peasant societies: Ireland and Norway, 1800–1900', *Papers presented to the third international conference of economic history, Munich, 1965*, Mouton, Paris (1968)

Drake, M., 'Norway', in W. R. Lee, ed., *European demography and economic growth*, Croom Helm, London (1979)

Dyrvik, S., 'Marriage and social norms. A study of Etne, 1715–1801', *Tidsskrift for Samfunnsforkning*, 11 (1970)

Dyrvik, S., 'Historical demography in Norway, 1600–1801. A short survey', *Scandinavian Economic History Review*, 20 (1972)

Dyrvik, S., 'Infant mortality about 1800. A preliminary exploration into Norwegian local material', *Vaestontutkimuksen Vuosikirja*, 13 (1974)

Gedde-Dahl, T., 'Population structure in Norway. Inbreeding, distance and kinship', *Hereditas*, 73 (1973)

Haugen, E., 'Norwegian migration to America', *Norwegian-American Studies and Records*, 18 (1954)

Langholm, S., 'Short-distance migration circles and flows. Movement to and from Ullensaker according to the population census lists of 1865', *Scandinavian Economic History Review*, 23 (1975)

Lieberman, S., 'Norwegian population growth in the nineteenth century', *Economy and History*, 11 (1968)

Ofstad, K., 'Population statistics and population registration in Norway', part 3, *Population Studies*, 3 (1949–50)

Ramholt, P., 'Nuptiality, fertility and reproduction in Norway', *Population Studies*, 3 (1953–54)

Saugstad, L. F., and O. Odegard, 'Marital distance and fertility in remarriages in two parishes in Norway between 1600 and 1850 compared with first marriages during the same period', in J. Dupaquier *et al., Marriage and remarriage in populations of the past*, Academic Press, London (1981)

Semmingsen, I. G., *Norwegian emigration to*

America during the nineteenth century, Norwegian-American Studies and Records, Northfield, Minn. (1940)

Semmingsen, I. G., 'Norwegian emigration in the nineteenth century', *Scandinavian Economic History Review,* 8 (1960)

Semmingsen, I. G., 'Family emigration from Bergen, 1874–93', *Americana Norvegica,* 3 (1971)

Semmingsen, I. G., *Norway to America. A history of migration,* University of Minnesota Press, Minneapolis, Minn. (1978)

Skaug, A., *Fluctuations in migration from Norway since 1900 compared with other countries and causes of those fluctuations,* League of Nations, International Institute of Intellectual Co-operation, Paris (1937)

Sogner, S., 'A demographic crisis averted?', *Scandinavian Economic History Review,* 24 (1976)

Sogner, S., and J. Oldervoll, 'Illegitimate fertility and the marriage market in Norway, 1800–1850. Regional variations', in J. Dupaquier *et al., Marriage and remarriage in populations of the past,* Academic Press, London (1981)

Tveite, S., 'Population and society in Norway', *Scandinavian Economic History Review,* 20 (1972)

LABOUR CONDITIONS AND ORGANISATION

Bull, E., 'Industrial workers and their employers in Norway *c.* 1900', *Scandinavian Economic History Review,* 3 (1955)

Bull, E., 'The Norwegian labour movement', in D. Fauvel-Rouif, ed., *Mouvements ouvriers et dépression économique de 1929 à 1939,* Van Gorcum, Assen (1966)

Galenson, W., *Labor in Norway,* Harvard University Press, Cambridge, Mass. (1949)

Hvidsten, J., 'Unemployment in Norway', *International Labour Review,* 7 (1923)

Voss, F., 'Minimum wage legislation in Norway', *International Labour Review,* 12 (1925)

INCOMES, WAGES AND PRICES

Gjolberg, O., 'A note on wages, standards of living and social stability among Norwegian seamen between 1832 and 1914', *Economy and History,* 21 (1978)

Hodne, F., 'New evidence on the history of tobacco consumption in Norway, 1665–1970', *Economy and History,* 21 (1978)

Soltow, L., *Towards income equality in Norway,* University of Wisconsin Press, Madison, Wis. (1965)

URBAN HISTORY

Gutkind, E. A., *International history of city development,* vol. 2, *Urban development in the Alpine and Scandinavian countries,* Collier-Macmillan, London (1965)

Langholm, S., 'The Christiana project. Historians investigate the making of urban society', *Research in Norway* (1976)

Thowsen, A., 'Bergen. A Norwegian seafaring town', *Maritime History,* 3 (1973)

SOCIAL STRUCTURE AND SOCIAL CONDITIONS

Burke, P., 'Popular culture in Norway and Sweden', *History Workshop Journal,* 3 (1977)

Hale, F., 'Anticlericalism and Norwegian society before the breakthrough of modernity', *Scandinavian Studies,* 52 (1980)

Hangland, K., 'An outline of Norwegian cultural nationalism in the second half of the nineteenth century', in R. Mitchison, ed., *The roots of nationalism. Studies in northern Europe,* John Donald, Edinburgh (1980)

Imhof, A. E., 'The hospital in the eighteenth century. For whom? The Charite hospital in Berlin, the navy hospital in Copenhagen, the Konigsberg hospital in Norway', *Journal of Social History,* 10 (1977)

Odegaard, O., *Emigration and insanity,* Levin and Munksgaards, Copenhagen (1932) [principally concerned with Norwegian settlers in Minnesota but comments on health in Norway in some detail]

Svasand, L., 'The early organization of society in Norway. Some characteristics', *Scandinavian Journal of History,* 5 (1980) [social organisations 1800–50]

HISTIOGRAPHY AND BIBLIOGRAPHY

Semmingsen, I. G., 'Nordic research into emigration', *Scandinavian Journal of History,* 3 (1978)

SWEDEN

GENERAL ECONOMIC AND SOCIAL HISTORY

Ahlstrom, G., 'Price development and economic policy in Sweden, 1776–1802', *Economy and History,* 19 (1976) [reply by H. Lindgren in same volume]

Boethius, B., 'New light on eighteenth century Sweden', *Scandinavian Economic History Review,* 1 (1953)

Childs, M. W., *Sweden. Where capitalism is controlled,* John Day, New York (1934)

Childs, M. W., *Sweden. The middle way,* Pelican Books, New York (1948)

Ek, S. B., 'Economic booms, innovations and the popular culture', *Economy and History,* 3 (1960)

Fridlizius, G., 'The Crimean war and the Swedish economy', *Economy and History,* 3 (1960)

Fridlizius, G., 'Population, enclosure and property rights', *Economy and History,* 22 (1979)

Gaunt, D., 'Natural resources, population and local society. The case of pre-industrial Sweden', *Peasant Studies,* 6 (1977)

Heckscher, E. F., 'The place of Sweden in modern economic history', *Economic History Review,* 4 (1932–34)

Heckscher, E. F., *An economic history of Sweden,* Harvard University Press, Cambridge, Mass. (1954)

Hedlund-Nyström, T., 'The Swedish crisis of the 1850s', *Economy and History,* 6 (1963)

Hildebrand, K. G., 'Sweden', *Proceedings of the first international economic history conference, Stockholm, 1960,* Mouton, Paris (1960)

Johansson, O., *The gross domestic product of Sweden and its composition, 1861–1955,* Acta Universitatis Stockholmiensis, Stockholm Economic Studies, New Series 8, Stockholm (1967)

Jörberg, L., 'Structural change and economic growth. Sweden in the nineteenth century', *Economy and History,* 8 (1965)

Jörberg, L., 'Structural change and economic growth. Sweden in the nineteenth century', in F. Crouzet *et al., Essays in European economic history,* Edward Arnold, London (1969)

Jörberg, L., 'The industrial revolution in the Nordic countries', in C. M. Cipolla, ed., *The emergence of industrial societies,* Fontana Economic History of Europe, vol. 4, part 2, Collins/Fontana, Glasgow (1973)

Jörberg, L., and O. Krantz, 'Scandinavia, 1914–70', in C. M. Cipolla, ed., *Contemporary economies,* Fontana Economic History of Europe, vol. 6, part 2, Collins/Fontana, Glasgow (1976)

Joseffson, M., and J. Ortengren, 'The deflationary crisis in the '20s – a myth?', *Economy and History,* 23 (1980) [reply by O. Krantz in the same issue]

Kindleberger, C. P., 'Sweden in 1850 as an "impoverished sophisticate". A comment', *Journal of Economic History,* 42 (1982)

Koblik, S., ed., *Sweden's development from poverty to affluence, 1750–1970,* University of Minnesota Press, Minneapolis, Minn. (1975)

Kock, K., 'Crisis, depression and recovery in Sweden, 1929–37', in L. Hallendorff and A. Schuck, eds., *A history of Sweden,* C. E. Fritze, Stockholm (1938)

Krantz, O. and C. A. Nilsson, 'National product series in historical analysis. A case study of Sweden, 1861–1975', in P. Bairoch and M. Levy-Leboyer, eds, *Disparities in economic development since the industrial revolution,* Macmillan, London (1981)

Kuuse, J., *Interaction between agriculture and industry. Case studies of farm mechanisation and industrialisation in Sweden and the United States, 1830–1930,* Gothenburg University Institute of Economic History, Gothenburg (1974)

Lindahl, E., *et al., National income of Sweden, 1861–1930,* P. S. King, London (1937)

Lindahl, E., 'The gross domestic product of Sweden, 1861–1951', *Meddelanden fran Konjunkturinstitutet,* 20 (1956)

Lindahl, O., 'Some results of an investigation of the gross product of Sweden for the period 1861–1961', in E. R. Lindahl, *Twenty-five essays in honour of Erik Lindahl,* Ekonomisk Tidskrift, Stockholm (1956)

Milward, A. S., 'Could Swecen have stopped the second world war?', *Scandinavian Economic History Review,* 15 (1967)

Montgomery, G. A., *How Sweden overcame the depression, 1930–33,* Benniers, Stockholm (1938)

Montgomery, G. A., 'Economic fluctuations in Sweden, 1919–21', *Scandinavian Economic History Review,* 3 (1955)

Myrdal, G., 'Population movements and industrialisation. Swedish counties, 1895–1930', *Stockholm Economic Studies,* 2 (1941)

Ohlin, B., 'Economic recovery and labour market problems in Sweden', I and II, *International Labour Review,* 31 (1935)

Sandberg, L. G., 'The case of the impoverished

sophisticate. Human capital and Swedish economic growth before World War I', *Journal of Economic History*, 39 (1979)

Thomas, D. S., *Social and economic aspects of Swedish population movements, 1750–1933*, Macmillan, New York (1941)

Tomaske, J. A., 'International migration and economic growth. The Swedish experience', *Journal of Economic History*, 25 (1965)

Utterström, G., 'Population and agriculture in Sweden *c.* 1700–1830', *Scandinavian Economic History Review*, 9 (1961)

Youngson, A. J., 'The acceleration of economic progress in Sweden, 1850–80', in A. J. Youngson, *The possibilities of economic progress*, Cambridge University Press, Cambridge (1959)

AGRICULTURE AND RURAL SOCIETY

Aspvall, G., 'The sale of Crown land in Sweden. The introductory epoch, 1701–23', *Economy and History*, 9 (1966)

Bjurling, O., 'The barons' revolution', *Economy and History*, 2 (1959) [refers to agricultural land tenure]

Bunte, R., 'The economic structure and development of Scanian fishing, 1870–1960', *Economy and History*, 9 (1966)

Carlsson, S., 'The dissolution of the Swedish estates (1700–1865)', *Journal of European Economic History*, 1 (1972)

Dahl, S., 'Strip fields and enclosure in Sweden', *Scandinavian Economic History Review*, 9 (1961)

Enequist, G., *Geographical changes of rural settlement in north-western Sweden since 1523*, Uppsala University Press, Uppsala (1959)

Ericsson, B., 'Central power and the local right to dispose over the forest commons in eighteenth century Sweden. A micro-study of the decision-making process during Sweden's Age of Freedom', *Scandinavian Journal of History*, 5 (1980) [eighteenth-century rural local government]

Fagerberg, B., 'The transfer of peasant forest to sawmill companies in northern Sweden. A case study of west Bothnia, 1842–75', *Scandinavian Economic History Review*, 21 (1973)

Gaunitz, S., 'Forest resources and forest industry in northern Sweden, 1900–34', *Economy and History*, 12 (1969)

Holgersson, B., 'Cultivated land in Sweden and its growth, 1840–1939', *Economy and History*, 17

(1974)

Norrie, K. H., 'Oats, exports, acreage and production statistics and agricultural depression in Sweden, 1870–1910', *Economy and History*, 22 (1979)

Olsson, C. A., 'Swedish agriculture during the inter-war years', *Economy and History*, 11 (1968)

Olsson, C. A., 'Estimates of the aggregate Swedish farm supply function, 1935–50. Some preliminary results', *Economy and History*, 17 (1974)

Ovesen, T., 'Swedish agricultural policy and agricultural production from 1930 to 1940', *Economy and History*, 1 (1958)

Utterström, G., 'Migratory labour and the herring fisheries of western Sweden in the eighteenth century', *Scandinavian Economic History Review*, 7 (1959)

INDUSTRY AND INTERNAL TRADE

Abrate, M., 'The Swedish iron industry in the 1830s', *Economy and History*, 7 (1964)

Adamson, R., 'Finance and marketing in the Swedish iron industry, 1800–60', *Scandinavian Economic History Review*, 16 (1968)

Arpi, G., 'The Swedish Ironmakers' Association', *Scandinavian Economic History Review*, 8 (1960)

Blomqvist, E., *Hydro-electric power and power supply in Vasternoorland, 1862–1962*, Svenska Vattenkraftforeningen Publikationer, Stockholm (1963)

Boëthius, B., 'Swedish iron and steel, 1600–1955', *Scandinavian Economic History Review*, 6 (1958)

Boëthius, B., ' *Jernkontoret* and the credit problems of the Swedish ironworks. A survey', *Scandinavian Economic History Review*, 10 (1962)

Charlesworth, E. K., 'The contribution of nationalisation to industrial development in Sweden, 1918–39', *Economy and History*, 12 (1969)

Dahl, S., 'Travelling pedlars in nineteenth century Sweden', *Scandinavian Economic History Review*, 7 (1959)

Dahmen, E., *Entrepreneurial activity and the development of Swedish industry, 1919–39*, Richard D. Irwin, Homewood, Ill. (1970)

Flinn, M. W., 'Scandinavian iron ore mining and the British steel industry', *Scandinavian Economic History Review*, 2 (1954)

Frangsmyr, T., 'Swedish science in the eighteenth century', *History of Science*, 12 (1974)

Fritz, M., 'Swedish iron ore and German steel,

1939–40', *Scandinavian Economic History Review*, 21 (1973)

Fritz, M., *German steel and Swedish iron ore, 1939–45*, Gothenburg Institute of Economic History, Gothenburg (1974)

Gaunitz, S., 'Local history as a means of understanding economic development. A study of the timber frontier in northern Sweden during the industrialisation period', *Economy and History*, 22 (1979)

Gerard, O., 'The purchase of agricultural land by the timber industry in Sweden, 1885 to 1906', *Economy and History*, 1 (1958)

Hassbring, L., *The international development of the Swedish Match Company, 1917–24*, Liber Förlag, Stockholm (1979)

Jörberg, L., 'Some notes on competition and co-operation in Swedish industry in the eighteen-seventies and eighteen-eighties', *Economy and History*, 1 (1958)

Jörberg, L., 'Some notes on Swedish entrepreneurs in the 1870s', *Explorations in Entrepreneurial History*, 10 (1958)

Jörberg, L., *Growth and fluctuations of Swedish industry, 1869–1912. Studies in the process of industrialisation*, Almquist and Wiksell, Stockholm (1961)

Krantz, O., 'Production and labour in the Swedish manufactories during the eighteenth century', *Economy and History*, 19 (1976) [two articles]

Kuuse, J., 'Foreign trade and the breakthrough of the engineering industry in Sweden, 1890–1920', *Scandinavian Economic History Review*, 25 (1977)

Lindgren, H., *Corporate growth. The Swedish match industry in its global setting*, Liber Förlag, Stockholm (1979)

Lundström, J., *The history of the Söderfoss anchor works*, Harvard Graduate School of Business Administration, Boston, Mass. (1970)

Montgomery, G. A., *The rise of modern industry in Sweden*, P. S. King, London (1939)

Nilsson, C. A., 'Business incorporation in Sweden. A study of enterprise, 1849–96', *Economy and History*, 2 (1959)

Nilsson, C. A., 'Some notes on the growth of the Swedish iron and steel consumption, 1885–1912', *Economy and History*, 14 (1971)

Nilsson, C. A., 'Foreign trade and the breakthrough of the engineering industry in Sweden. A comment', *Scandinavian Economic History Review*, 26 (1978)

Nilsson, C. A., and L. Schon, 'Factories in Sweden, 1820–70', *Economy and History*, 21 (1978)

Parks, R. W., 'Price responsiveness of factor utilisation in Swedish manufacturing, 1870–1950', *Review of Economic Statistics*, 53 (1971)

Runeby, N., 'Americanism, Taylorism and social integration. Action programmes for Swedish industry at the beginning of the twentieth century', *Scandinavian Journal of History*, 3 (1978)

Sahlin, N. G., *Swedish iron and steel. A historical survey*, Svenska Handelsbanken, Stockholm (1948)

Schön, L., 'Västernorrland in the middle of the nineteenth century. A study in the transition from small-scale to capitalist production', *Economy and History*, 15 (1972)

Schön, L., 'British competition and domestic change. Textiles in Sweden, 1820–70', *Economy and History*, 23 (1980)

Söderlund, E. F., 'Short-term economic fluctuations and the Swedish timber industry, 1850–1900', *Journal of Economic History*, 13 (1953)

Söderlund, E. F., 'The Swedish iron industry during the first world war and the post-war depression', *Scandinavian Economic History Review*, 6 (1958)

Söderlund, E. F., 'The Swedish iron industry, 1932–39', *Scandinavian Economic History Review*, 7 (1959)

Söderlund, E. F., 'The impact of the British industrial revolution in the Swedish iron industry', in L. S. Pressnell, ed., *Studies in the industrial revolution presented to T. S. Ashton*, Athlone Press, London (1960)

Svensson, J., 'A case study in economic retardation', *Economy and History*, 3 (1960) [nineteenth-century textiles]

Tigerschiold, M., *Swedish steel throughout the centuries*, Royal Swedish Commission, Stockholm (1939)

Unwin, S., *Book trade organisation in Norway and Sweden*, Allen and Unwin, London (1932)

Wikander, U., *Krueger's match monopolies, 1925–30. Case studies in market control through public monopolies*, Liber Förlag, Stockholm (1979)

TRANSPORT AND COMMUNICATIONS

Fritz, M., 'Shipping in Sweden, 1850–1913', *Scandinavian Economic History Review*, 28 (1980)

Futrell, M., *Northern underground. Episodes of Russian revolutionary transport and communications through Scandinavia and Finland,*

1863–1917, Faber and Faber, London (1963)

Hansen, F. V., *Canals and waterways of Sweden*, P. A. Norstedt, Stockholm (1915)

Hedin, L. E., 'Some notes on the financing of the Swedish railroads, 1860–1914', *Economy and History*, 10 (1967)

Holgersson, B., and E. Nicander, 'The railroads and the economic development in Sweden during the 1870s', *Economy and History*, 11 (1968)

Krantz, O., 'The competition between railways and domestic shipping in Sweden, 1870–1914', *Economy and History*, 15 (1972)

Lindblad, T., 'Swedish shipping with the Netherlands in the second half of the eighteenth century', *Scandinavian Economic History Review*, 27 (1979)

Modig, H., 'The backward linkage effect of railroads on Swedish industry, 1840–1914', *Swedish Journal of Economics*, 74 (1972)

Söderlund, E. F., 'The placing of the first Swedish railway loan', *Scandinavian Economic History Review*, 11 (1963)

MONEY, BANKING AND FINANCE

Eagly, R. V., ed., *The Swedish bullionist controversy*, American Philosophical Society, Philadelphia, Pa. (1971) [translation of P. N. Christiernin's Lectures on the High Price of Foreign Exchange in Sweden (1761)]

Flux, A. W., *The Swedish banking system*, U.S. Government Printing Office, Washington, D.C. (1910)

Gasslander, O., *History of Stockholms Enskilda Bank to 1914*, Generalstabens Litografiska Anstalts Förlag, Stockholm (1962)

Heckscher, E. F., 'The Bank of Sweden in its connection with the Bank of Amsterdam', in J. G. van Dillen, ed., *History of the principal public banks*, Nijhoff, The Hague (1934)

Hildebrand, K. E. H., *The national debt office, 1789–1939*, P. A. Norstedt, Stockholm (1939)

Hildebrand, K.-G., *Banking in a growing economy. Svenska Handelsbanken since 1871*, Utgiveren, Stockholm (1971)

Kjellstrom, E. J. H., *Managed money. The experience of Sweden*, Columbia University Press, New York (1934)

Lester, R. A., 'Sweden's experiment with managed money, 1931–39', in R. A. Lester, ed., *Monetary experiments. Early American and recent Scandinavian*, Princeton University Press, Princeton, N.J. (1939)

Nilsson, A., 'Study financing and expansion of educa-

tion. An empirical study of study financing of university students in Sweden, 1920–51', *Economy and History*, 20 (1977)

Pipping, H. E., 'Swedish paper currency in Finland after 1809', *Scandinavian Economic History Review*, 9 (1961)

Potter, J., 'The role of a Swedish bank in the process of industrialisation', *Scandinavian Economic History Review*, 11 (1963)

Samuelsson, K., 'The banks and the financing of industry in Sweden, *c*. 1900–27', *Scandinavian Economic History Review*, 6 (1958)

Sandberg, L. G., 'Monetary policy and politics in mid-eighteenth century Sweden. A comment', *Journal of Economic History*, 30 (1970)

Sandberg, L. G., 'Banking and economic growth in Sweden before World War I', *Journal of Economic History*, 38 (1978)

Swedish Banks Association, *Swedish banking companies, 1824–1913*, Swedish Banks Association, Stockholm (1915)

Thomas, B., *Monetary policy and crises. A study of Swedish experience*, Routledge, London (1936)

OVERSEAS TRADE AND COMMERCIAL RELATIONS

Adamson, R., 'Swedish iron exports to the United States, 1783–1860', *Scandinavian Economic History Review*, 17 (1969)

Bjurling, O., 'Sweden's foreign trade and shipping around the year 1700', *Economy and History*, 4 (1961)

Fahlström, J. M., *The history of a Gothenburg house of merchants*, presented on the occasion of the 150th anniversary of the establishment of Ekman and Co., on January 29th, 1802. Ekman, Gothenburg (1952)

Fleisher, E. W., 'The beginning of the transatlantic market for Swedish iron', *Scandinavian Economic History Review*, 1 (1953)

Fridlizius, G., *Swedish corn export in the free trade era. Patterns in the oats trade, 1850–80*, Gleerup, Lund (1957)

Fridlizius, G., 'Sweden's exports, 1850–1960. A study in perspective', *Economic History*, 6 (1963)

Hammarström, I., 'Anglo-Swedish economic relations and the crisis of 1857', *Scandinavian Economic History Review*, 10 (1962)

Hildebrand, K. G., 'Foreign markets for Swedish iron in the eighteenth century', *Scandinavian Economic History Review*, 6 (1958)

Högberg, S., 'Consular reports to the Swedish Board

of Trade', *Business History*, 23 (1981)

Jäger, J. J., 'Sweden's iron ore exports to Germany, 1933–34', *Scandinavian Economic History Review*, 15 (1967)

Jucker-Fleetwood, E. E., *Sweden's capital imports and exports*, Natur och Kultur, Stockholm (1947)

Karlbom, R., 'Sweden's iron ore exports to Germany, 1933–44', *Scandinavian Economic History Review*, 13 (1965); 16 (1968)

Koninckz, C., 'The maritime routes of the Swedish East India Company during the first and second charter (1731–66)', *Scandinavian Economic History Review*, 26 (1978)

Koninckz, C., *The first and second charters of the Swedish East India Company (1731–66). Contribution to the maritime economic and social history of north-western Europe in its relationships with the Far East*, Van Ghemmert Publishing Company, Kortrijk, Belgium (1980)

Kuuse, J., 'Mechanisation, commercialisation and the protectionist movement in Swedish agriculture', *Scandinavian Economic History Review*, 19 (1971)

Modig, H., *Swedish match interests in British India during the interwar years*, Liber Förlag, Stockholm (1979)

Runblom, H., 'Swedish enterprises in Latin America, 1900–40', *American Studies in Scandinavia*, 6 (1971)

Sallius, P. O., 'Swedish-American treaty policy, 1920–35', *Economy and History*, 4 (1961)

Salmon, P., 'British plans for economic warfare against Germany, 1937–39. The problem of Swedish iron ore', *Journal of Contemporary History*, 16 (1981)

Samuelsson, K., 'International payments and credit movements by Swedish merchant houses, 1730–1815', *Scandinavian Economic History Review*, 3 (1955)

Scott, F. D., 'Swedish trade with America in 1920. A letter of advice from Baron Axel Klinkowström', *Journal of Modern History*, 25 (1953)

Söderlund, E. F., ed., *Swedish timber exports, 1850–1950. A history of the Swedish timber trade*, Swedish Wood Exporters Association, Stockholm (1952)

Strandh, J., 'Some notes on the history of international capital movements, 1930–32', *Economy and History*, 5 (1962)

Tilberg, F., *The development of commerce between the United States of America and Sweden, 1870–1925*, Ransom, Moline, Ill. (1930)

Unger, R. W., 'Trade through the Sound in the seventeenth and eighteenth centuries', *Economic History Review*, 12 (1959)

POPULATION AND MIGRATION

Agren, K., *et al.*, *Aristocrats, farmers, proletarians. Essays in Swedish demographic history*, Esselte Studium, Stockholm (1973)

Ahlberg, G., *Population trends and urbanisation in Sweden, 1911–50*, Gleerup, Lund (1956)

Åkerman, S., *et al.*, *Aristocrats, farmers and proletarians. Essays in Swedish demographic history*, University of Uppsala, Studia Historica Uppsaliensia, Uppsala (1973)

Åkerman, S., 'Internal migration, industrialisation and urbanisation (1895–1930). A summary of the Vastmannlund study', *Scandinavian Economic History Review*, 23 (1975)

Åkerman, S., 'Swedish migration and social mobility. The tale of three cities', *Social Science History*, 1 (1977)

Åkerman, S., 'The importance of remarriage in the seventeenth and eighteenth centuries', in J. Dupaquier *et al.*, *Marriage and remarriage in populations of the past*. Academic Press, London (1981)

Åkerman, S., *et al.*, 'Background variables of production mobility. An attempt at automatic interaction detector analysis', *Scandinavian Economic History Review*, 22 (1974)

Åkerman, S., *et al.*, 'Splitting background variables. AID analysis applied to migration and literacy research', *Journal of European Economic History*, 8 (1979)

Appel, E., *et al.*, 'Computerized family reconstitution', in J. Raben and G. Gregory, eds, *Data bases in the humanities and social sciences*, North-Holland Publishing Company, Amsterdam (1980)

Brattne, B., 'The Larsson brothers. A study of the activity of Swedish emigrant agencies during the 1880s', *American Studies in Scandinavia*, 9 (1972)

Carlsson, G., 'The decline of fertility. Innovation or adjustment process', *Population Studies*, 20 (1966)

Carlsson, G., 'Nineteenth century fertility oscillations', *Population Studies*, 24 (1970)

Cole, M., and C. Smith, eds, *Democratic Sweden. A volume of studies prepared by members of the New Fabian Research Bureau*, Routledge, London (1938)

Ellemers, J. E., 'The determinants of migration. An analysis of Dutch studies on migration', *Sociologica Nederlandicae*, 2 (1964)

Eriksson, I., and J. Rogers, *Rural labour and population change. Social and demographic developments in east central Sweden during the nineteenth century,* University of Uppsala, Studia Historica Uppsaliensia, No. 100, Uppsala (1978)

Friberg, N., 'The growth of populations and its economic geographical background in a mining district in central Sweden, 1650–1750', *Geografiska Annaler* (1956)

Friberg, N., 'Population growth in a mining district in Sweden, 1650–1750, and its economic background', *Proceedings of the third international economic history conference, Munich, 1965,* Mouton, Paris (1972)

Fridlizius, G., 'Some new aspects on Swedish population I. A. study at county level. II. A study at parish level', *Economy and History,* 18 (1975)

Fridlizius, G., 'Sweden', in W. R. Lee, ed., *European demography and economic growth,* Croom Helm, London (1979)

Gaunt, D., 'Family planning and the pre-industrial society. Some Swedish evidence', in K. Agren *et al., Aristocrats, farmers, proletarians. Essays in Swedish demographic history,* Esselte Studium, Stockholm (1973)

Gaunt, D., 'Pre-industrial economy and population structure. The elements of variance in early modern Sweden', *Scandinavian Journal of History,* 2 (1977)

Gulberg, B., and B. Oden, 'AID analysis and migration history', *Scandinavian Economic History Review,* 24 (1976)

Hansen, H. O., 'Some age structural consequences of mortality variations in pre-transitional Iceland and Sweden', in H. Charbonneau and A. La Rose, eds, *The great mortalities. Methodological studies of demographic crises in the past,* IUSSP, Ordina Editions, Liege (1979)

Hanssen, B., 'Dimensions of primary group structure in Sweden', in UNESCO *Recherches sur la famille,* vol. 1, Tübingen (1956)

Heckscher, E. F., 'Swedish population trends before the industrial revolution', *Economic History Review,* 2 (1949–50)

Hofsten, E., 'Birth variations in populations which practise family planning', *Population Studies,* 25 (1971)

Hofsten, E., and H. Lundström, *Swedish population history. Main trends from 1750 to 1970,* Statistiska Centralbyran, Stockholm (1976)

Hutchinson, E. P., 'Swedish population thought in the eighteenth century', *Population Studies,* 13 (1959–60)

Hyrenius, H., 'Reproduction and replacement. A methodological study of Swedish population changes during 200 years', *Population Studies,* 4 (1950–51)

Hyrenius, H., 'Fertility and reproduction in a Swedish population group without family limitation', *Population Studies,* 12 (1958)

Institute for Social Sciences, *Population movements and industrialisation. Swedish counties, 1895–1930,* Institute for Social Sciences, Stockholm University, Stockholm (1941)

Janson, F. E., *The background to Swedish immigration, 1840–1930,* Chicago University Press, Chicago, Ill. (1931)

Kalvemark, A. S., 'The country that kept track of its population. Methodological aspects of Swedish population records', *Scandinavian Journal of History,* 2 (1977)

Kumar, J., 'A comparison between current Indian fertility and late nineteenth century Swedish and Finnish fertility', *Population Studies,* 25 (1971)

Lindberg, J. S., *The background of Swedish emigration to the United States. An economic and sociological study in the dynamics of migration,* University of Minnesota Press, Minneapolis, Minn. (1930)

Mosk, C., 'Rural urban fertility differences and the fertility transition', *Population Studies,* 34 (1980)

Myhrman, A., 'The effects of Finland–Swedish emigration upon the homeland', *Swedish Pioneer Historical Quarterly,* 31 (1980)

Nordström, O., 'Population and labour problems in Sweden's depopulated districts', *Economy and History,* 5 (1962)

Olsson, N. W., *Swedish passenger arrivals in New York, 1820–50,* Norstedt, Stockholm (1967)

Quensel, C. E., 'Population movements in Sweden in recent years', *Population Studies,* 1 (1947–48)

Quigley, J. M., 'A model of Swedish emigration', *Quarterly Journal of Economics,* 86 (1972)

Runblom, H., and H. Norman, eds., *From Sweden to America. A history of the migration,* Minnesota University Press, Minneapolis, Minn. (1976)

Scott, F. D., 'Sweden's constructive opposition to emigration', *Journal of Modern History,* 37 (1965)

Thomas, D. S., 'Internal migration in Sweden. A note on their extensiveness compared with net migration gain or loss', *American Journal of Sociology,* 20 (1936)

Utterström, G., 'Some population problems in pre-industrial Sweden', *Scandinavian Economic History Review,* 2 (1954)

Utterström, G., 'Two essays on population in eighteenth century Scandinavia', in D. V. Glass and D. E. C. Eversley, eds, *Population in history. Essays in historical demography,* Edward Arnold, London (1965) [contains some references to Denmark and Norway]

Wargentin, P. W., *Tables of mortality based upon the Swedish population prepared and presented in 1766,* I. Haeggström, Stockholm (1930)

Widen, L., 'Mortality and causes of death in Sweden during the eighteenth century', *Statistik Tidskrift* (1975)

Wilkinson, M., 'Evidence of long swings in the growth of Swedish population and related economic variables, 1860–1965', *Journal of Economic History,* 27 (1967)

LABOUR CONDITIONS AND ORGANISATION

Back, P. E., 'Patriarchalism and the rise of rural labour organisations in Sweden', *Economy and History,* 7 (1964)

Blake, D. J., 'Swedish trade unions and the Social Democratic Party. The formative years', *Scandinavian Economic History Review,* 8 (1960)

Hansson, S., 'The trade union movement in Sweden', *International Labour Review,* 6 (1923)

International Labour Office, 'Agricultural conditions and labour agreements in Denmark and Sweden', *International Labour Review,* 2 (1921)

International Labour Office, 'The labour question in Swedish agriculture', *International Labour Review,* 27 (1933)

International Labour Office, 'Enquiries into conditions of work in Sweden', *International Labour Review,* 39 (1939)

Johansson, A., 'Unemployment in Sweden after the war', *International Labour Review,* 26 (1932)

Montelius, S., 'Recruitment and conditions of life of Swedish ironworkers during the eighteenth and nineteenth centuries', *Scandinavian Economic History Review,* 14 (1966)

Norgren, P. H., 'Collective wage-making in Sweden', *Journal of Political Economy,* 46 (1938)

INCOMES, WAGES AND PRICES

Åkerman, S., 'The Swedish experiment with progressive income tax in 1810', *Economy and History,* 9 (1966)

Allen, G. R., 'Relative real wages in Swedish agriculture and industry, 1930–1950', *Bulletin of the Oxford University Institute of Statistics,* 15 (1953)

Allen, G. R., 'A comparison of real wages in Swedish agriculture and secondary and tertiary industries, 1870–1949', *Scandinavian Economic History Review,* 3 (1955)

Bagge, G., 'Wages and unemployment in Sweden, 1920–30', in *Economic Essays in Honour of Gustav Cassel,* Allen and Unwin, London (1933)

Bagge, G., *et al., Wages, cost of living and national income in Sweden, 1860–1930,* P. S. King, London (1933)

Bengtsson, T., and L. Jörberg, 'Market integration in Sweden during the eighteenth and nineteenth centuries. A spectral analysis of grain prices', *Economy and History,* 18 (1975)

Cederblad, N., 'The Swedish family budget enquiry of 1923', *International Labour Review,* 14 (1926)

Gustafsson, K. E., 'The circulation spiral and the principle of household coverage', *Scandinavian Economic History Review,* 26 (1978)

Institute for Social Sciences, *Wages, cost of living and national income in Sweden, 1860–1930,* P. S. King, London (1937)

International Labour Office, 'Wages and the cost of living in Sweden from 1860 to 1930', *International Labour Review,* 29 (1934)

Jonung, L., and E. Wadensjo, 'A model of the determination of wages and prices in Sweden, 1922–71', *Economy and History,* 21 (1978)

Jörberg, L., *A history of prices in Sweden, 1732–1914,* 2 vols., Gleerup, Lund (1972)

Jörberg, L., 'The development of real wages for agricultural workers in Sweden during the eighteenth and nineteenth centuries', *Economy and History,* 15 (1972)

Jörberg, L., and T. Bengtsson, *Regional wages in Sweden during the nineteenth century,* Lund University, Economic History Institute Publication. No. 3, Lund (1978)

Jörberg, L., and T. Bengtsson, 'Regional wages in Sweden during the nineteenth century', in M. W. Flinn, ed., *Proceedings of the seventh international congress on economic history, Edinburgh, 1978,* Edinburgh University Press, Edinburgh (1978)

Jörberg, L., and T. Bengtsson, 'Regional wages in Sweden during the nineteenth century', in P. Bairoch and M. Levy-Leboyer, eds, *Disparities in economic development since the industrial revolution,* Macmillan, London (1981)

Myrdal, G., *The cost of living in Sweden, 1830–1930,* P. S. King, London (1933)

URBAN HISTORY

Ahlberg, H., *Swedish architecture of the twentieth century,* E. Benn, London (1925)

Åkerman, G., 'The income elasticity of demand for housing', *Scandinavian Economic History Review,* 5 (1957)

Åstrom, K., *City planning in Sweden,* Swedish Institute, Stockholm (1967)

Gutkind, E. A., *International history of city development.* Vol. 2. *Urban development in the Alpine and Scandinavian countries,* Collier-Macmillan, London (1965)

Hahr, A., *Architecture in Sweden. A survey of Swedish architecture throughout the ages and up to the present day,* Bonnier, Stockholm (1938)

Hall, T., 'The central business district. Planning in Stockholm, 1928–78', in I. Hammerström and T. Hall, eds, *Growth and transformation of the modern city,* Swedish Council for Building Research, Stockholm (1979)

Hammarström, I., 'Urban growth and building fluctuations. Stockholm, 1860–1920', in I. Hammerström and T. Hall, eds, *Growth and transformation of the modern city,* Swedish Council for Building Research, Stockholm (1979)

Jutikkala, E., 'Town planning in Sweden and Finland until the middle of the nineteenth century', *Scandinavian Economic History Review,* 16 (1968)

Leighly, J. B., *The towns of Malinden in Sweden. A study in urban morphology,* California University Press, Berkeley, Cal. (1978)

Linden, G., 'Town planning in Sweden after 1850', *Town Planning Review,* 10 (1924)

Lundén, T., 'Stockholm – a hundred years of suburban growth. Agents, flows and restrictions', in I. Hammerström and T. Hall, eds, *Growth and transformation of the modern city,* Swedish Council for Building Research, Stockholm (1979)

Ohngren, B., 'Urbanisation and social change. Report', in M. W. Flinn, ed., *Proceedings of the seventh international congress on economic history, Edinburgh, 1978,* Edinburgh University Press, Edinburgh (1978)

Ohngren, B., 'Urbanisation in Sweden, 1840–1920', in H. Schmal, ed., *Patterns of European urbanisation since 1500,* Croom Helm, London (1981)

Pred, A., *The external relations of cities during the industrial revolution, with a case study of Göteborg, Sweden, 1868–90,* Chicago University Press, Chicago, Ill. (1962)

Raberg, M., 'The development of Stockholm since the seventeenth century', in I. Hammerström and T.

Hall, eds, *Growth and transformation of the modern city,* Swedish Council for Building Research, Stockholm (1979)

Sidenbladh, G., 'Stockholm. A planned city', in K. Davis, ed., *Cities. Their origin, growth and human impact,* Freeman, San Francisco, Cal. (1973)

Sundstrom, T., 'Environmental policies of the city of Stockholm', *Studies in Comparative Local Government,* 6 (1972)

Westerman, H., *Swedish planning of town centres,* Swedish Institute, Stockholm (1965)

SOCIAL STRUCTURE AND SOCIAL CONDITIONS

Burke, P., 'Popular culture in Norway and Sweden', *History Workshop Journal,* 3 (1977)

Frykman, J., 'Sexual intercourse and social norms. A study of illegitimate births in Sweden, 1831–1939', *Ethnologia Scandinavica,* 3 (1975)

Gurr, T. R., 'Contemporary crime in historical perspective. A comparative study of London, Stockholm and Sydney', *Annals of the American Academy of Political and Social Science,* 434 (1977)

Hirsch, A., *Swedish poor laws and charities,* Norstedt, Stockholm (1910)

Johansson, E., *The history of literacy in Sweden in comparison with some other countries,* Umeå University, Umeå (1977)

Johansson, E., 'The history of literacy in Sweden', in H. J. Graff, ed., *Literacy and social development in the West. A reader.* Cambridge University Press, Cambridge (1981)

Lane, R., 'Comparing urban crime. A review article', *Comparative Studies in Society and History,* 21 (1979) [material on eighteenth to twentieth-century Stockholm]

Liedstrand, E., 'Social insurance in Sweden', *International Labour Review,* 9 (1924)

Lundkvist, S., 'The popular movements in Swedish society, 1850–1920', *Scandinavian Journal of History,* 5 (1980)

Martinius, S., *Peasant destinies. The history of 552 Swedes born 1810–12.* University of Stockholm, Studies in Economic History No. 3, Stockholm (1977)

Morell, M., 'On the stratification of the Swedish peasant class', *Scandinavian Economic History Review,* 28 (1980)

Morner, M., 'The process of consolidation in Swedish rural society', *Peasant Studies,* 6 (1977)

Morner, M., 'The evolution of Swedish society,

1620–1920, as reflected in the history of a noble family', *Scandinavian Studies*, 52 (1980)

Myrdal, A., 'A programme of family security in Sweden', *International Labour Review*, 39 (1939)

Persson, G., 'Social mobility in Sweden, 1925–45', *Economy and History*, 17 (1974)

Petersson, L., 'Some aspects of the expansion of education in Sweden', *Economy and History*, 20 (1977)

Qvist, G., 'Policy towards women and the women's struggle in Sweden', *Scandinavian Journal of History*, 5 (1980)

Rice, J. G., 'Indicators of social change in rural Sweden in the late nineteenth century', *Journal of Historical Geography*, 4 (1978)

Samuelsson, K., *From great power to welfare state. Eight hundred years of Swedish social development*, Allen and Unwin, London (1968)

Sandberg, L. G., and R. H. Steckel, 'Soldier, soldier, what made you grow so tall? A study of height, health and nutrition in Sweden, 1720–1881', *Economy and History*, 23 (1980)

Soderberg, J., 'Causes of poverty in Sweden in the nineteenth century', *Journal of European Economic History*, 11 (1982)

Sundin, J., 'Theft and penury in Sweden, 1830–1920', *Scandinavian Journal of History*, 1 (1976)

Vattula, K., 'Women's opportunities in Swedish society', *Scandinavian Economic History Review*, 28 (1980)

Wohl, R., 'What price order?', *Journal of Interdisciplinary History*, 9 (1978) [crime and criminals in Stockholm in the nineteenth century]

ECONOMIC POLICY AND THOUGHT

Clark, H., *Swedish unemployment policy, 1914–40*, American Council on Public Affairs, Washington, D.C. (1941)

Eagly, R. V., 'Monetary policy and politics in mid-eighteenth century Sweden', *Journal of Economic History*, 29 (1969); 30 (1970)

Gerard, O., *The Norrland question. Studies in the government's and the parliament's treatment of the Norrland question*, Skogs, Trelleborg (1971)

Gustafsson, B., 'Keynes and "the Stockholm School" ', *Economy and History*, 16 (1973)

Heckscher, E. F., 'A survey of economic thought in Sweden, 1875–1950', *Scandinavian Economic History Review*, 1 (1953)

Hedlund-Nyström, T., 'The Finance Act of 1862 and its effect on the economy', *Economy and History*, 15 (1972)

Hildebrand, K. G., 'Economic policy in Scandinavia during the inter-war period', *Scandinavian Economic History Review*, 23 (1975)

Huss, E. G., 'The campaign against unemployment in Sweden', *International Labour Review*, 6 (1922)

Huss, E. G., 'The organisation of public works and other measures for the relief of unemployment in Sweden', *International Labour Review*, 26 (1932)

Jonung, L., 'Knut Wicksell's norm of price stabilisation and Swedish monetary policy in the 1930s', *Journal of Monetary Economics*, 5 (1979)

Lundberg, E., *Business cycles and economic policy*, Allen and Unwin, London (1957)

Utterström, G., 'Labour policy and population thought in eighteenth century Sweden', *Scandinavian Economic History Review*, 10 (1962)

Wigforss, E., 'The financial policy during depression and boom', *Annals of the American Academy of Political and Social Science*, 197 (1938)

Winch, D., 'The Keynesian revolution in Sweden', *Journal of Political Economy*, 74 (1966)

HISTORIOGRAPHY AND BIBLIOGRAPHY

di Vittorio, A., ' "Economy and history" and the history of Swedish economic development', *Journal of European Economic History*, 2 (1973)

Kuuse, J., 'The probate inventory as a source for economic and social history', *Scandinavian Economic History Review*, 22 (1974)

Olsson, K., 'Methods and sources for the study of Swedish standards of living', *Scandinavian Economic History Review*, 22 (1974)

DENMARK

GENERAL ECONOMIC AND SOCIAL HISTORY

Bjerke, K., 'The national product of Denmark, 1870–1952' in S. Kuznets, ed., *Income and Wealth*, 5, Bowes and Bowes, London (1955)

Glamann, K., 'Industrialization as a factor in economic growth in Denmark since 1700', *Proceedings of the first international economic history conference, Stockholm, 1960*. Mouton, Paris (1960)

Hagerstrand, T., 'Quantitative techniques for analysis of the spread of information and technology', in C. A. Anderson and M. J. Bowman, eds, *Education and economic development,* Cass, London (1966)

Hansen, S. A., *Early industrialisation in Denmark,* Copenhagen University Institute of Economic History, Copenhagen (1970)

Hornby, O., 'Industrialization in Denmark and the loss of the Duchies', *Scandinavian Economic History Review,* 17 (1969)

Jörberg, L., 'The industrial revolution in the Nordic countries', in C. M. Cipolla, ed., *The emergence of industrial societies.* Fontana Economic History of Europe, vol. 4, part 2, Collins/Fontana, Glasgow (1973)

Jörberg, L., and O. Krantz, 'Scandinavia, 1914–70', in C. M. Cipolla, ed., *Contemporary economies,* Fontana Economic History of Europe, vol. 6, part 2, Collins/Fontana, Glasgow (1976)

Kennedy, K. H., 'The economies of Denmark and Ireland compared', *Eire–Ireland,* 12 (1977)

Olgaard, A., *Growth, productivity and relative prices,* North-Holland Publishing Company, Amsterdam (1966)

Pedersen, J., *Economic conditions in Denmark after 1922,* Copenhagen University Institute of Economics and History, Copenhagen (1931)

Rerup, L., 'The development of nationalism in Denmark, 1864–1914', in R. Mitchison, ed., *The roots of nationalism. Studies in northern Europe,* John Donald, Edinburgh (1980)

Thyssen, A. P., 'The rise of nationalism in the Danish monarchy, 1800–64, with special reference to the socio-economic and historical aspects', in R. Mitchison, ed., *The roots of nationalism. Studies in northern Europe,* John Donald, Edinburgh (1980)

Westergaard, H. L., *Economic development in Denmark before and during the world war,* Clarendon Press, Oxford (1922)

Youngson, A. J., 'The acceleration of economic progress in Denmark, 1865–1900', in A. J. Youngson, *The possibilities of economic progress,* Cambridge University Press, Cambridge (1959)

AGRICULTURE AND RURAL SOCIETY

Bjorn, C., 'The peasantry and agrarian reform in Denmark', *Scandinavian Economic History Review,* 25 (1977)

Bjurling, O., 'The barons' revolution', *Economy and History,* 2 (1959) [refers to agricultural land tenure]

Christiansen, P. O., 'Forms of peasant dependency in a Danish estate 1775–1975', *Peasant Studies,* 7 (1978)

Faber, H., *Agricultural production in Denmark,* Harrison, London (1924)

Faber, H., *Co-operation in Danish agriculture,* Longmans Green, London (1931)

Jensen, E., *Danish agriculture. Its economic development,* J. H. Schultz, Copenhagen, (1937)

Nash, E. F., and E. A. Attwood, *The agricultural policies of Britain and Denmark. A study in reciprocal trade,* Land Books, London (1961)

Pedersen, E. H., 'Towards a theory of agricultural modernization process with special regard to the Danish and American development pattern in the nineteenth century', *Proceedings of the seventh International Economic History Association conference, Edinburgh, 1978,* Ecinburgh University Press, Edinburgh (1978)

Rockwell, J., 'The Danish peasant village', *Journal of Peasant Studies,* 1 (1974)

Skrubbeltrang, F., *Agricultural development and rural reform in Denmark,* Food and Agricultural Organisation, Agricultural Studies, No. 22, Rome (1953)

Skrubbeltrang, F., 'Developments in tenancy in eighteenth-century Denmark as a move towards peasant proprietorship', *Scandinavian Economic History Review,* 9 (1961)

INDUSTRY AND INTERNAL TRADE

Friedmann, K. J., 'Food marketing in Copenhagen, 1250–1850', *Agricultural History,* 50 (1976)

Glamann, K., 'Beer and brewing in pre-industrial Denmark', *Scandinavian Economic History Review,* 10 (1962)

Lind, G., 'Development and location of industry in Danish provincial towns, 1855–82', *Scandinavian Economic History Review,* 27 (1979)

TRANSPORT AND COMMUNICATIONS

Hornby, O., and C. A. Nilsson, 'The transition from sail to steam in the Danish merchant fleet, 1865–1910', *Scandinavian Economic History Review,* 28 (1980)

MONEY, BANKING AND FINANCE

Arnheim, A., 'German court Jews and Denmark during the Great Northern War', *Scandinavian*

Economic History Review, 14 (1966) [finance in early eighteenth century]

Christenson, C. L., 'Gold-parity depression in Norway and Denmark', *Journal of Political Economy*, 45 (1937)

Kindleberger, C. P., 'Competitive currency depreciation between Denmark and New Zealand', *Harvard Business Review*, 12 (1934)

Stancke, B., *The Danish stock market, 1750–1840*, Copenhagen University Institute of Economic History, Copenhagen (1971)

Svendsen, K. E., 'Monetary policy and theory in Denmark, 1784–1800', parts I and 2, *Scandinavian Economic History Review*, 10 (1962); 11 (1963)

OVERSEAS TRADE AND COMMERCIAL RELATIONS

Feldbaek, O., 'The Danish trade in Bengal, 1777–1808. An interim account', *Scandinavian Economic History Review*, 12 (1964)

Feldbaek, O., *Indian trade under the Danish flag, 1772–1808. European enterprise and Anglo-Indian remittance and trade*, C. A. Reitzel, Copenhagen (1969)

Feldbaek, O., 'Dutch Batavia trade via Copenhagen, 1795–1807. A study of colonial trade and neutrality', *Scandinavian Economic History Review*, 21 (1973)

Feldbaek, O., 'Danish East India trade, 1772–1807. Statistics and structure', *Scandinavian Economic History Review*, 26 (1978)

Feldbaek, O., 'The organization and structure of the Danish East India, West India and Guinea companies in the seventeenth and eighteenth centuries', in L. Blusse and F. Gaastra, eds, *Companies and trade*, Leiden University Press, Leiden (1981)

Glamann, K., 'The Danish Asiatic Company, 1732–72', *Scandinavian Economic History Review*, 8 (1960)

Glamann, K., 'The Danish East India Company', in M. Mollat, ed., *Sociétés et compagnies de commerce en orient et dans l'océan indien*, SEVPEN, Paris (1970)

Gobel, E., 'The Danish Asiatic Company's voyages to China, 1732–1833', *Scandinavian Economic History Review*, 27 (1979)

Green-Pedersen, S. E., 'The scope and structure of the Danish negro slave trade', *Scandinavian Economic History Review*, 19 (1971)

Green-Pedersen, S. E., 'Colonial trade under the Danish flag. A case study of the Danish slave trade

in India, 1790–1807', *Scandinavian Journal of History*, 5 (1980)

Hill, J. W., *The Danish Sound dues and the command of the Baltic. A study of international relations*, Duke University Press, Durham, N.C. (1926)

Justesen, O., 'Danish settlements in the Gold Coast in the nineteenth century', *Scandinavian Journal of History*, 4 (1979)

Lange, O., 'Denmark in China, 1839–65. A pawn in a British game', *Scandinavian Economic History Review*, 19 (1971)

Moller, A. M., 'Consular reports. The Danis monarchy, 1797–1904', *Business History*, 23 (1981)

Morrison, R. J., 'The Duchies and the kingdom. Nineteenth century Denmark and the theory of customs unions', *Scandinavian Economic History Review*, 19 (1971)

Ruppenthal, R., 'Denmark and the Continental System', *Journal of Modern History*, 15 (1943)

Tejsen, A. V. S., 'The history of the Royal Greenland Trade Department', *Polar Record*, 18 (1977)

Velschow, T., 'Voyages of the Danish Asiatic Company to India and China, 1772–92', *Scandinavian Economic History Review*, 20 (1972)

Westergaard, W. C., *The Danish West Indies under company rule (1671–1754), with a supplementary chapter, 1755–1917*, Macmillan, New York (1917)

POPULATION AND MIGRATION

Andersen, O., *A malaria epidemic in Denmark*, Institute of Statistics Research Report No. 30, University of Copenhagen, Copenhagen (1976)

Andersen, O., *The population of Denmark*, Institute of Statistics, Copenhagen University, Copenhagen (1977)

Andersen, O., 'Denmark', in W. R. Lee, ed., *European demography and economic growth*, Croom Helm, London (1979)

Dossing, P., *Population changes in Danish agriculture, 1870–1953*, United Nations World Population Conference, vol. 5, United Nations, New York (1954)

Hansen, H. O., 'Migration and population patterns in the parish of Torslev, *c.* 1870–1901', *Vaestontutkimuksen Vuosikirja*, 13 (1974)

Hansen, H. O., 'From natural to controlled fertility. Studies in fertility as a factor in the process of economic and social development in Greenland *c.* 1851–1975', in H. Leridon and J. Menken, eds, *Natural fertility*, Ordina, IUSSP, Liège (1979)

Hansen, H. O., 'The importance of remarriage in

traditional and modern societies. Iceland during the eighteenth and nineteenth centuries and the cohort of Danish women born between 1926 and 1935', in J. Dupaquier *et al., Marriage and remarriage in populations of the past*, Academic Press, London (1981)

Hvidt, K., 'Danish emigration prior to 1914. Trends and problems', *Scandinavian Economic History Review*, 14 (1966)

Hvidt, K., 'Mass emigration from Denmark to the United States, 1868–1914', *American Studies in Scandinavia*, 9 (1972)

Hvidt, K., *Flight to America*, Academic Press, London (1975) [emigration from Denmark to the United States]

Hvidt, K., 'Emigration agents. The development of a business and its methods', *Scandinavian Journal of History*, 3 (1978)

Johansen, H. C., 'The effect on fertility of frequent absences of the husband', in J. Dupaquier *et al., Marriage and remarriage in populations of the past*, Academic Press, London (1981)

Lassen, A., 'The population of Denmark, 1650–1960', *Proceedings of the third international economic history conference, Munich, 1965*, Mouton, Paris (1972)

Lassen, A., 'The population of Denmark, 1660–1960', *Scandinavian Economic History Review*, 14 (1966)

Matthiessen, P. C., *Some aspects of the demographic transition in Denmark*, Copenhagen University, Copenhagen (1970)

Matthiessen, P. C., 'Some aspects of remarriage among Danish women, 1850–1915', in J. Dupaquier *et al., Marriage and remarriage in populations of the past*, Academic Press, London (1981)

Morch, H., 'Population and resources on the minor Danish islands, 1860, 1900 and 1960', *Geografisk Tidsskrift* (1975)

Thestrup, P., 'Methodological problems of a family reconstruction study in a Danish rural parish before 1800', *Scandinavian Economic History Review*, 20 (1972)

LABOUR CONDITIONS AND ORGANISATION

Christiansen, N. F., 'Reformism within Danish social democracy until the nineteen-thirties', *Scandinavian Journal of History*, 3 (1978)

Dubeck, I., 'Female trade unions in Denmark. Freedom of association, the laws of association and women's trade unions in Denmark in the second

half of the nineteenth century', *Scandinavian Journal of History*, 5 (1980)

Hersch, L., 'Seasonal unemployment in the building industry in certain European countries', *International Labour Review*, 19 (1924) [devoted to Denmark]

International Labour Office, 'Agricultural conditions and labour agreements in Denmark and Sweden', *International Labour Review*, 2 (1921)

International Labour Office, 'The working of social insurance in Denmark', *International Labour Review*, 30 (1934)

Johansen, H. C., 'Some aspects of Danish rural population structure in 1787', *Scandinavian Economic History Review*, 20 (1972)

Levine, D., 'Conservation and tradition in Danish social welfare legislation, 1890–1933. A comparative view', *Comparative Studies in Society and History*, 20 (1978)

Steincke, K. K., 'The Danish social reform measures', *International Labour Review*, 31 (1935)

INCOMES, WAGES AND PRICES

Friis, A., and K. Glamann, *A history of prices and wages in Denmark, 1600–1800*, Longmans Green, London (1958)

Rumar, L., 'Assessed average market prices and the prices of cereal grains in Denmark, 1800–50', *Scandinavian Economic History Review*, 18 (1970)

Soltow, L., 'Wealth distribution in Denmark in 1789', *Scandinavian Economic History Review*, 27 (1979)

Thestrup, P., *The standard of living in Copenhagen, 1730–1800. Some methods of measurement*, Institute of Economic History, Copenhagen University, Copenhagen (1971)

URBAN HISTORY

Gutkind, E. A., *International history of city development. Vol. 2, Urban development in the Alpine and Scandinavian countries*, Collier-Macmillan, London (1965)

Hyldtoft, O., 'From fortified town to modern metropolis. Copenhagen, 1840–1914', in I. Hammarström and T. Hall, eds, *Growth and transformation of the modern city*, Swedish Council for Building Research, Stockholm (1979)

Jorgensen, J., 'The economic condition of Zealand provincial towns in the eighteenth century', *Scandinavian Economic History Review*, 19 (1971)

Lind, G., 'Development and location of industry in Danish provincial towns, 1855–82', *Scandinavian Economic History Review*, 27 (1979)

Reumert, J., *The commercial-geographic importance of the situation of Copenhagen*, Royal Danish Geographical Society, Copenhagen (1929)

SOCIAL STRUCTURE AND SOCIAL CONDITIONS

Elklit, J., 'Household structure in Denmark, 1769–1890', in S. Akerman *et al.*, eds, *Chance and change. Social and economic studies in historical demography in the Baltic area*, Odense University Press, Odense (1978)

Hansen, S. A., 'Changes in the wealth and the demographic characteristics of the Danish aristocracy, 1470–1720', *Proceedings of the third international economic history conference, Munich, 1965*, Mouton, Paris (1972)

Imhof, A. E., 'The hospital in the eighteenth century. For whom? The Charite hospital in Berlin, the navy hospital in Copenhagen, the Konigsberg hospital in Norway', *Journal of Social History*, 10 (1977)

Johansen, H. C., 'The position of the old in the rural household in a traditional society', *Scandinavian Economic History Review*, 24 (1976)

Laux, W. E., 'Agricultural interest groups in Danish politics. An examination of group frustration amidst political stability', *Western Political Quarterly*, 21 (1968)

Manniche, P., *The folk high schools of Denmark and the development of a farming community*, Oxford University Press, London (1929)

Manniche, P., *Denmark. A social laboratory. Independent farmers, co-operative societies, folk high schools, social legislation, with 150 photographs illustrating life and conditions in Denmark*, Oxford University Press, London (1939)

Michelson, W., 'From religious movement to economic change. The Grundtvigian case in Denmark', *Journal of Social History*, 2 (1969)

Rordam, T., *The Danish folk high schools*, Danske Selskals, Copenhagen (1965)

Skrubbeltrang, F., *The Danish folk high schools*, Danske Selskals, Copenhagen, (1947)

Wahlin, V., 'The growth of bourgeois and popular movements in Denmark c. 1830–70', *Scandinavian Journal of History*, 5 (1980)

ECONOMIC POLICY AND THOUGHT

Hansen, S. A., 'Danish economic policy, 1784–88', *Nationalokonomisk Tidsskrift*, 106 (1968)

Johansen, H. C., 'J. G. Busch's economic theory and his influence on the Danish economic and social debate', *Scandiavian Economic History Review*, 14 (1966)

Johansen, H. C., 'Carl August Struensee. Reformer or traditionalist', *Scandinavian Economic History Review*, 17 (1969)

HISTORIOGRAPHY AND BIBLIOGRAPHY

Bjorn, C., 'The study of the agrarian history of Denmark. A brief introduction to the literature', *Agricultural History Review*, 22 (1974)

Hansen, H. O., 'Computer methods for production of socio-demographic statistics', *Cuadernos de Historia Economica de Cataluna*, 7 (1972)

Hornby, O., and G. V. Mogensen, 'The study of economic history in Denmark. Recent trends and problems', *Scandinavian Economic History Review*, 22 (1974)

Mogensen, G. V., 'Research into the distribution of prosperity. A Danish comment on some Swedish contributions', *Scandinavian Economic History Review*, 21 (1973)

FINLAND

GENERAL ECONOMIC AND SOCIAL HISTORY

Blomstedt, Y., 'Nationalism in Finland, and the effects of economic factors upon it', in R. Mitchison, ed., *The roots of nationalism. Studies in northern Europe*, John Donald, Edinburgh (1980)

Harmaja, L., *Effects of the war on economic and social life in Finland*, Yale University Press, New Haven, Conn. (1933)

Hjerppe, R., and E. Pikhala, 'The gross domestic product of Finland in 1860–1913. A preliminary estimate', *Economy and History*, 20 (1977)

Jörberg, L., 'The industrial revolution in the Nordic

countries', in C. M. Cipolla, ed., *The emergence of industrial societies.* Fontana Economic History of Europe, vol. 4, part 2, Collins/Fontana, Glasgow (1973)

Jörberg, L., and O. Krantz, 'Scandinavia, 1914–70', in C. M. Cipolla, ed., *Contemporary economies,* Fontana Economic History of Europe, vol. 6, part 2, Collins/Fontana, Glasgow (1976)

Jutikkala, E., 'The economic development of Finland shown in maps', *Proceedings of the Finnish Academy of Science and Letters* (1948)

Jutikkala, E., 'Industrialisation as a factor in economic growth in Finland', *Proceedings of the first international economic history conference, Stockholm, 1960,* Mouton, Paris (1960)

Jutikkala, E., and K. Pirinen, *A history of Finland,* Thames and Hudson, London (1962)

Kiiskinen, A., *The economic growth by regions in Finland, 1926–52,* Economic Research Institute of Finnish Industry, Helsinki (1958) [English summary]

Kiiskinen, A., 'Regional economic growth in Finland, 1880–1952', *Scandinavian Economic History Review,* 9 (1961)

Lundin, C. L., 'Finland', in E. C. Thaden, ed., *Russification in the Baltic provinces and Finland, 1855–1914,* Princeton University Press, Princeton, N.J. (1981)

Rasila, V., 'The Finnish civil war and lend-lease problems', *Scandinavian Economic History Review,* 17 (1969)

Royal Institute of International Affairs, *The Scandinavian states and Finland. Political and economic survey,* Oxford University Press, London (1951)

Stenius, H., 'The breakthrough of the principle of mass organisation in Finland', *Scandinavian Journal of History,* 5 (1980) [deals with industrial and social structure, 1840–1900]

AGRICULTURE AND RURAL SOCIETY

Antilla, V., 'The modernisation of Finnish peasant farming in the late nineteenth and early twentieth centuries', *Scandinavian Economic History Review,* 24 (1976)

Aunola, T., 'The indebtedness of north Ostrobothnian farmers to merchants, 1765–1809', *Scandinavian Economic History Review,* 13 (1965)

Hyvönen, V.,. 'Co-operation in Finland', *International Labour Review,* 8 (1923)

Jutikkala, E., 'Origin and rise of the crofter problem in

Finland', *Scandinavian Economic History Review,* 10 (1962)

Jutikkala, E., 'Peasant movements and agrarian problems in Finland from the end of the nineteenth century to the second world war', *Cahiers Internationaux d'Histoire Economique et Sociale,* 7 (1977)

Jutila, K. T., *The agricultural depression in Finland during the years 1928–35. The measures employed for its alleviation and the results obtained,* Ministry of Agriculture Publications, No. 18, Helsinki (1937)

Kampp, A. H., and K. Rikkinen, 'Farms in a Finnish village (Levanto), 1787–1916', *Geografisk Tidsskrift,* 72 (1973)

Kampp, A. H., and K. Rikkinen, 'A farm in a Finnish village from 1917 to 1973', *Geografisk Tidsskrift,* 73 (1974)

Lefgren, J., 'Famine in Finland, 1867–68', *International Economic Review,* 4 (1973)

Mead, W. R., *Farming in Finland,* Athlone Press, London (1953)

Skrubbeltrang, F., 'The history of the Finnish peasant', *Scandinavian Economic History Review,* 12 (1964)

INDUSTRY AND INTERNAL TRADE

Ahvenainen, J., 'The competitive position of the Finnish paper industry in the inter-war years', *Scandinavian Economic History Review,* 22 (1974)

Ahvenainen, J., *The history of Star Paper, 1875–1960,* Studia Historica, Jyraskylaensia (1976)

Ahvenainen, J., 'The paper industry in Finland – and in Russia, 1885–1913', *Scandinavian Economic History Review,* 27 (1979)

Autio, M., and E. Lodenius, *The Finnish Paper Mills Association, 1918–68,* Helsinki (1968) [no publisher cited in catalogue]

Hjerppe, R., *et al., The growth of extractive and manufacturing industry and of industrial handicrafts in Finland, 1900–65,* Bank of Finland, Helsinki (1976) [summary and table headings only in English

Niitamo, O., 'Development of productivity in Finnish industry, 1925–52', *Productivity Measurement Review,* 15 (1958)

Schybergson, P., 'Joint stock companies in Finland in the nineteenth century', *Scandinavian Economic History Review,* 12 (1964)

Topholm, J., 'Fyns Social-Demokrat, 1896–1920',

Meddelelser om Forskning i Arbejderbetaegelsens Hist. 14 (1980) [history of newspaper]

Virrankoski, P., 'Replacement of flax by cotton in the domestic textile industry of south-west Finland', *Scandinavian Economic History Review*, 11 (1963)

TRANSPORT AND COMMUNICATIONS

Alanen, A. J., 'Maritime trade and economic development in south Ostrobothnia', *Scandinavian Economic History Review*, 1 (1953)

Futrell, M., *Northern underground. Episodes of Russian revolutionary transport and communications through Scandinavian and Finland, 1863–1917*, Faber and Faber, London (1963)

Hautala, K., 'From the Black Sea to the Atlantic. Finnish merchant shipping in the late nineteenth century', *Scandinavian Economic History Review*, 19 (1971)

Jones, M., *Finland. Daughter of the sea*, W. Dawson, Folkestone, Kent (1977)

Jutikkala, E., 'The problem of railway ownership in nineteenth century Finland', *Scandinavian Economic History Review*, 18 (1970)

Kaukiainen, Y., 'Finland's peasant seafarers and Stockholm', *Scandinavian Economic History Review*, 19 (1971)

Kaukiainen, Y., 'The transition from sail to steam in Finnish shipping, 1850–1914', *Scandinavian Economic History Review*, 28 (1980)

Mead, W. R., 'The genesis of waterway improvement in Finland', *Terra*, 81 (1969)

MONEY, BANKING AND FINANCE

Larna, K., *The money supply, money flows and domestic product in Finland, 1910–56*, Finnish Economic Association, Helsinki (1959)

Pipping, H. E., 'Swedish paper currency in Finland after 1809', *Scandinavian Economic History Review*, 9 (1961)

OVERSEAS TRADE AND COMMERCIAL RELATIONS

Aström, S. E., 'The transatlantic tar trade', *Scandinavian Economic History Review*, 12 (1964)

Aström, S. E., 'Technology and timber exports from the Gulf of Finland, 1661–1740', *Scandinavian Economic History Review*, 23 (1975)

Pihkala, E., 'Finnish iron and the Russian market, 1880–1914', *Scandinavian Economic History Review*, 12 (1964)

Pipping, H. E., 'Trade between Finland and Russia in 1860–1917', *Scandinavian Economic History Review*, 19 (1971)

Thaden, E. C., *et al., Russification in the Baltic provinces and Finland, 1855–1914*, Princeton University Press, Princeton, N.J. (1981)

POPULATION AND MIGRATION

Blafield, E., 'Fertility in Finland in the 1900s', *Vaestontutkimnksen Vuosikirja*, (1978)

Engman, M., 'Migration from Finland to Russia during the nineteenth century', *Scandinavian Journal of History*, 3 (1978)

Jutikkala, E., 'Finland's population movement in the eighteenth century', in D. V. Glass and D. E. C. Eversley, eds, *Population in history. Essays in historical demography*, Edward Arnold, London (1965)

Jutikkala, E., 'Migration in Finland in historical perspective', *Proceedings of the third international economic history conference, Munich, 1965*, Mouton, Paris (1972)

Jutikkala, E., 'Finnish mortality in the eighteenth century. The sources and the reality', *Scandinavian Economic History Review*, 26 (1978) [see reply by Pitkanen in 27 (1979)]

Jutikkala, E., and M. Kauppinen, 'The structure of mortality during catastrophic years in a pre-industrial society', *Population Studies*, 25 (1971)

Kero, R., *Migration from Finland to North America in the years between the United States civil war and the first world war*, Turun Yliopisto, Turku, Finland (1974)

Kolehmainen, J. I., 'Finland's agrarian structure and overseas migration', *Agricultural History*, 15 (1941)

Kolehmainen, J. I., 'Finnish overseas emigration from arctic Norway and Russia', *Agricultural History*, 19 (1945) [primarily between 1864 and 1885]

Kumar, J., 'A comparison between current Indian fertility and late nineteenth century Swedish and Finnish fertility', *Population Studies*, 25 (1971)

Myhrman, A., 'The effects of Finland–Swedish emigration upon the homeland', *Swedish Pioneer Historical Quarterly*, 31 (1980)

Pitkanen, K., 'The reliability of the registration of births and deaths in Finland in the eighteenth and nineteenth centuries. Some examples', *Scandinavian Economic History Review*, 25 (1977)

Rosenberg, A., 'Mobility of population in the Finnish

county of Uusimaa (Nyland), 1821–80', *Scandinavian Economic History Review*, 14 (1966)

Turpeinen, O., 'Regional differentials in Finnish mortality rates, 1816–65', *Scandinavian Economic History Review*, 21 (1973)

Turpeinen, O., 'Causal relationships between economic factors and mortality', *Vaestontutkimuksen Vuosikirja*, 15 (1977)

Turpeinen, O., 'Infections, diseases and regional differences in Finnish death rates, 1749–73', *Population Studies*, 32 (1978)

Turpeinen, O., 'Fertility and mortality in Finland since 1750', *Population Studies*, 33 (1979)

Turpeinen, O., 'Infant mortality in Finland, 1749–1865', *Scandinavian Economic History Review*, 27 (1979)

Virkanen, K., *Settlement or return. Finnish emigrants (1860–1930) in the international overseas return migration movement*, Finnish Historical Society, Helsinki (1979)

LABOUR CONDITIONS AND ORGANISATION

Jutikkala, E., 'Finnish agricultural labour in the eighteenth and early nineteenth centuries', *Scandinavian Economic History Review*, 10 (1962)

Korpelainen, L., 'Trends and cyclical movements in industrial employment in Finland, 1885–1952', *Scandinavian Economic History Review*, 5 (1957)

Soikkanen, H., 'Revisionism, reformism and the Finnish labour movement before the first world war', *Scandinavian Journal of History*, 3 (1978)

Stenius, H., 'The breakthrough of the principle of mass organisation in Finland', *Scandinavian Journal of History*, 5 (1980)

INCOMES, WAGES AND PRICES

International Labour Office, 'Wages in Finnish agriculture, 1929–32', *International Labour Review*, 27 (1933)

Jutikkala, E., 'The distribution of wealth in Finland in 1800', *Scandinavian Economic History Review*, 1 (1953)

Markkanen, E., 'Wealth and credit in the Finnish countryside, 1850–1910', *Scandinavian Economic History Review*, 21 (1973)

Markkanen, E., 'The use of probate inventories as indicators of personal wealth during the period of industrialisation. The financial resources of the Finnish rural population, 1850–1911', *Scandinavian Economic History Review*, 26 (1978)

Soltow, L., 'Wealth distribution in Finland in 1800', *Scandinavian Economic History Review*, 29 (1981)

URBAN HISTORY

Aström, S. E., 'Town planning in imperial Helsingfors', in I. Hammerström and T. Hall, eds, *Growth and transformation of the modern city*, Swedish Council for Building Research, Stockholm (1979)

Hertzen, H. von, and P. D. Spreiregen, *Building a new town*, Massachusetts Institute of Technology Press, Cambridge, Mass. (1971; revised edn 1973) [historical development of town planning in Finland]

Jutikkala, E., 'Town planning in Sweden and Finland until the middle of the nineteenth century', *Scandinavian Economic History Review*, 16 (1968)

Niemineva, K., 'The spa at Kupittaa. The development from the end of the seventeenth century to the middle of the nineteenth century', *Nordisk Medicinhistorisk Arsbok* (1978)

SOCIAL STRUCTURE AND SOCIAL CONDITIONS

Jallinoja, R., 'The women's liberation movement in Finland. The social and political mobilisation of women in Finland, 1880–1910', *Scandinavian Journal of History*, 5 (1980)

Kirby, D. G., 'Revolutionary ferment in Finland and the origins of the civil war, 1917–18', *Scandinavian Economic History Review*, 26 (1978)

Klinge, M., ' "Let us be Finns." The birth of Finland's national culture', in R. Mitchison, ed., *The roots of nationalism. Studies in northern Europe*, Edinburgh, John Donald (1980)

Kujala, A., 'The Russian revolutionary movement and the Finnish opposition, 1905. The John Grafton affair and the plan for an uprising in St Petersburg', *Scandinavian Journal of History*, 5 (1980) [arms trade]

Nerdrum, M., 'Household structure in Finstrom parish, Aland, 1760–62 and 1840–42', in S. Akerman et al., *Chance and change. Social and economic studies in historical demography in the Baltic area*, Odense University Press, Odense (1978)

Seppanen, P., 'Dimensions and phases of change in Finnish society', *International Journal of Politics*, 4 (1974)

HISTORIOGRAPHY AND BIBLIOGRAPHY

di Vittorio, A., 'The *Scandinavian Economic History Review* and the economic development of Finland', *Journal of European Economic History*, 5 (1976)

Rasila, V., 'The use of multi-variable analysis in historical studies', *Economy and History*, 13 (1970) [investigation of Finnish civil war and production data *c.* 1900–17]

Vattula, K., 'Finnish growth studies. A review article', *Scandinavian Economic History Review*, 26 (1978)

ICELAND

Baldursson, G., 'Population', in J. Nordal and V. Kristinsson, eds, *Iceland, 874–1974,* Central Bank of Iceland, Reykjavik (1975)

Bjarnason, O., 'Epidemics in Iceland in the eighteenth century', *Nordisk Medicinhistorisk Arsbok* (1980, supplement)

Bjornsson, B. T., 'Building through the centuries', in J. Nordal and V. Kristinsson, eds, *Iceland, 874–1974,* Central Bank of Iceland, Reykjavik (1975)

Blöndal, G., 'The growth of public expenditure in Iceland', *Scandinavian Economic History Review*, 17 (1969)

Chamberlin, W. G., *Economic development of Iceland through World War II*, Columbia University Press, New York (1947) [includes historical introduction]

Hansen, H. O., 'Some age structural consequences of mortality variations in pre-transitional Iceland and Sweden', in H. Charbonneau, and A. La Rose, *The great mortalities. Methodological studies of demographic crises in the past*, I.U.S.S.P., Ordina Editions, Liège (1979)

Hansen, H. O., 'The importance of remarriage in traditional and modern societies. Iceland during the eighteenth and nineteenth centuries and the cohort of Danish women born between 1926 and 1935', in J. Dupaquier, *et al., Marriage and remarriage in populations of the past*, Academic Press, London (1981)

Johannesson, P., 'Iceland. An outline history', in J. Nordal and V. Kristinsson, eds, *Iceland, 874–1974,* Central Bank of Iceland, Reykjavik (1975)

Kampp, A. H., 'Iceland and the Faroes. A comparative demographic study covering the period 1900–70', *Inter-Nord*, 13–14 (1974)

Kjartansson, H. S., 'Emigrant fares and emigration from Iceland to North America', *Scandinavian Economic History Review*, 28 (1980)

Nordal, J., and V. Kristinsson, eds, *Iceland, 874–1974,* Central Bank of Iceland, Reykjavik (1975)

Statistical Bureau of Iceland, *Population census, 1703,* Statistical Bureau of Iceland, Reykjavik (1960) [summary in English; tables in English]

Steffensen, J., 'Smallpox in Iceland', *Nordisk Medicinhistorisk Arsbok* (1977)

Tomasson, R. F., 'Iceland on the brain', *American-Scandinavian Review*, 60 (1972) [travel accounts and transport in eighteenth-century Iceland]

Tomasson, R. F., 'A millennium of misery. The demography of the Icelanders', *Population Studies*, 31 (1977)

Tomasson, R. F., *Iceland. The first new society*, University of Minnesota Press, Minneapolis, Minn. (1980)

THE BALTIC STATES

GENERAL WORKS

Bogucka, M., 'The role of Baltic trade in European development from the sixteenth to the eighteenth centuries', *Journal of European History*, 9 (1980)

Brown, J. C., *Forests and forestry in Poland, Lithuania, the Ukraine and the Baltic provinces of Russia, with notices regarding the export of timber from Memel, Danzig and Riga*, Oliver, Edinburgh (1885)

Eichholz, A. C., *The Baltic states. Estonia, Latvia and Lithuania. A short review of resources, industry, finance and trade*, U.S. Government Printing Office, Washington, D.C. (1928)

Findlay, J. A., *The Baltic exchange, being a short history of the Baltic mercantile and shipping exchange from the days of the old coffee house, 1744–1927*, Witherley, London (1927)

Gazel, A., *Foreign and local trade of the Baltic countries*, J. S. Bergson, London (1936)

Heckscher, E. F., 'Multilateralism, Baltic trade, and the mercantilists', *Economic History Review*, 3 (1950–51)

Hill, J. W., *The Danish Sound dues and the command of the Baltic. A study of international relations*, Duke University Press, Durham, N.C. (1926)

Kirby, D., 'The balance of the north and Baltic trade', *Slavonic and East European Review*, 54 (1976)

Kirby, D., 'A great opportunity lost? Aspects of British commercial policy toward the Baltic states, 1920–24', *Journal of Baltic Studies*, 5 (1974)

Levine, I. D., *The resurrected nations. Short histories of the peoples freed by the Great War and statements of their national claims*, F. A. Stokes, New York (c. 1919)

Newman, E. W. P., *Britain and the Baltic*, Methuen, London (1930)

Page, S. W., *The formation of the Baltic states. A study of the effects of Great Power politics upon the emergence of Lithuania, Latvia and Estonia*, Harvard University Press, Cambridge, Mass. (1959)

Pick, F. W., *The Baltic nations. Estonia, Latvia and Lithuania*, Boreas Publishing Co., London (1945)

Plakans, A., 'Peasants, intellectuals and nationalism in the Russian Baltic provinces, 1820–90', *Journal of Modern History*, 46 (1974)

Plakans, A., 'Seigneurial authority and peasant family life. The Baltic area in the eighteenth century', *Journal of Interdisciplinary History*, 5 (1974–75)

Plakans, A., 'Peasant farmsteads and households in the Baltic littoral, 1797', *Comparative Studies in Society and History*, 17 (1975)

Rasch, A., 'American trade in the Baltic, 1783–1807', *Scandinavian Economic History Review*, 13 (1965)

Raud, V., *The Baltic states as a British market in the past and future*, Women's Printing Society, London (c. 1943)

Raud, V., *The smaller nations in the world's economic life*, P. S. King, London (1943)

Reddaway, W. F., *Problems of the Baltic*, Cambridge University Press, Cambridge (1940)

Ronimois, H. E., 'The Baltic trade of the Soviet Union', *Slavic Review*, 4 (1945) [covers period 1913–35]

Rothelfs, H., 'The Baltic provinces. Some historic aspects and perspectives', *Journal of Central European Affairs*, 4 (1944)

Royal Institute of International Affairs, *The Baltic*

states. *A survey of the political and economic structure and the foreign relations of Estonia, Latvia and Lithuania,* Oxford University Press, London (1938)

Rutter, O., *The new Baltic states and their future. An account of Lithuania, Latvia and Estonia,* Methuen, London (1926)

Senn, A. E., 'The sovietization of the Baltic states', *Annals of the American Academy of Political and Social Science,* 317 (1958)

Spekke, A., *The ancient amber routes and the geog-* raphical discovery of the eastern Baltic, M. Goppers, Stockholm (1957)

Stopczyk, W., *International trade on the Baltic,* Baltic Institute, Torun (Poland) (1928)

Thaden, E. C., *et al., Russification in the Baltic provinces and Finland, 1855–1914,* Princeton University Press, Princeton, N.J. (1981)

Westergaard, H. L., *The official statistics of the Scandinavian countries and the Baltic republics,* League of Nations, Geneva (1926)

ESTONIA

Bagdanoff, G., *Agrarian reform in Estonia,* Baltischer Verlag und Ostbuchhandlung, Berlin (1922?)

Corrsin, S., 'Urbanization and the Baltic peoples. Riga and Tallinn before the first world war', *East European Quarterly,* 12 (1978)

Estonian Co-operative Wholesale Society, *Anglo-Estonian trade relations,* Estonian Co-operative Wholesale Society, Tallinn (1933)

Forgus, S. P., 'Modernization of Estonian primary education, 1860–1905', *Journal of Baltic Studies,* 7 (1976)

Gallienne, W. H., *Economic conditions in Estonia,* H.M.S.O., London (1935)

Gallienne, W. H., *Report on economic and commercial conditions in Estonia,* H.M.S.O., London (1939)

Hill, A. J., *Economic conditions in Estonia,* H.M.S.O., London (1932)

International Labour Office, 'Social insurance in Estonia', *International Labour Review,* 37 (1938)

Jarvesoo, E., 'Early agricultural education at Tartu university', *Journal of Baltic Studies,* 11 (1980)

Jerram, C. B., *Economic conditions in Estonia,* H.M.S.O., London (1929)

Kahk, J., 'New possibilities of using computerized historical analysis in the study of peasant households', *Turun Historiallinen Arkisto,* 28 (1973)

Kahk, J., and H. Ligi, 'The peasant household in Estonia at the eve of industrialization', *Studia Historiae Oeconomicae,* 10 (1975)

Kant, E., *Problems of environment and population in Estonia,* K. Mattieseni, Tartu (1934)

League of Nations, *Report of the Financial Committee of the League of Nations on the economic and financial situation of Estonia,* League of Nations, Geneva (1925)

League of Nations, *Banking and currency reform in Estonia,* League of Nations, Geneva (1927)

Leslie, J. E. P., and W. J. Sullivan, *Report on the economic and industrial conditions in Estonia,* H.M.S.O., London (1923)

Loorits, O., 'The renascence of the Estonian nation', *Slavonic and East European Review,* 33 (1954)

Martna, W., 'The position of the agricultural labourer in Estonia', *International Labour Review,* 5 (1922)

Ministry of Agriculture, (Estonia), *Estonia dairy industry,* Ministry of Agriculture, Tallinn (1923)

Ministry of Agriculture, *Estonian dairy industry,* Ministry of Agriculture, Tallinn (1937)

Ministry of Trade and Industry, *Estonian economic bulletin,* Ministry of Trade and Industry, Tallinn (1923)

Montgomery Grove, H., *Report on the economic and industrial conditions in Estonia,* H.M.S.O., London (1925)

Nodel, E., *Estonia. Nation on the anvil,* Bookman Associates, New York (1964)

Palli, H., 'Parish registers, revisions of land and souls. Family reconstitution and household in seventeenth and eighteenth century Estonia', in S. Akerman *et al., Chance and change. Social and economic studies in historical demography in the Baltic area,* Odense University Press, Odense (1978)

Palli, H., 'Illegitimacy and remarriage in Estonia during the eighteenth century', in J. Dupaquier *et al., Marriage and remarriage in populations of the past,* Academic Press, London (1981)

Parming, T., 'Population changes in Estonia, 1935–70', *Population Studies,* 26 (1972) [contains data on population for whole inter-war period]

Parming, T., 'Long-term trends in family structure in a Soviet republic', *Sociology and Social Research,* 63 (1979)

Pistohlkors, G. von, 'Juhan Kahk's interpretation of feudal agrarian economy in Estonia and northern Livonia, 1825–50', *Journal of Baltic Studies,* 11 (1978)

Raun, T. U., 'The development of Estonian literacy in the eighteenth and nineteenth centuries', *Journal of Baltic Studies,* 10 (1979)

Schumann, H., ed., *Estonian industry, commerce and banks,* Association of Estonian Industrials and the Reval Exchange Committee, Reval (1924)

Tammekann, A., *Outlines of the distribution of population in Estonia,* Tartu Ulikooli Geograafia Instituudi, Toimetused, Tartu (1929)

Tomingas, W., *The Soviet colonization of Estonia,* Kultuur Publishing House, New York (1973)

Uuemaa, E., and F. Valdvere, eds, *Economic development of Estonia,* Ministry of Foreign Affairs, Tallinn (1937)

Uustalu, E., *The history of Estonian people,* Boreas Publishing Company, London (1952)

Vesterinen, E., *Agricultural conditions in Estonia. A short survey,* Tietosanakirya Osakeyhtio, Helsinki (1923)

Voobus, A., *Studies in the history of the Estonian people, with reference to aspects of their social conditions,* 2 vols, Estonian Theological Society in Exile, Stockholm (1969–70)

Weller, A., *The agrarian reform in Estonia from the legal point of view,* Baltischer Verlag und Ostbuchhandlung, Berlin (1922)

LATVIA

Anderson, E., 'The USSR trades with Latvia. The treaty of 1927', *Slavic Review,* 21 (1962)

Balabkins, N., and A. Aïzilnieks, *Entrepreneur in a small country. A case study against the background of the Latvian economy, 1919–40,* Exposition Press, Hicksville, N.Y. (1975)

Bilmanis, A., *History of Latvia,* Princeton University Press, Princeton, N.J. (1952)

Bülow, F. W. von, 'Social aspects of agrarian reform in Latvia', *International Labour Review,* 20 (1929)

Corrsin, S., 'Urbanization and the Baltic peoples. Riga and Tallinn before the first world war', *East European Quarterly,* 12 (1978)

Jarvesoo, E., 'Agricultural program at the Riga Polytechnic Institute', *Journal of Baltic Studies,* 11 (1980)

Jennison, E. W., 'Christian Garve and Garlieb Markel. Two theorists of peasant emancipation during the ages of enlightenment and revolution', *Journal of Baltic Studies,* 4 (1973)

Labsvirs, J., 'The effect of collectivization on Latvian agriculture', *Slavic Review,* 22 (1963) [comparison of pre-1939 and post-1945 agriculture]

Page, S. W., 'Social and national currents in Latvia, 1860–1917', *Slavic Review,* 8 (1949)

Page, S. W., 'Lenin and peasant "Bolshevism" in Latvia, 1903–15', *Journal of Baltic Studies,* 3 (1972)

Plakans, A., 'Peasants, intellectuals and nationalism in the Russian Baltic provinces', *Journal of Modern History,* 46 (1974)

Rutkis, J., ed., *Latvia. Country and people,* Latvian National Foundation, Stockholm (1967)

Sprudzs, A., and A. Rusis, eds, *Res Baltica. A collection of essays in honour of the memory of Dr. Alfred Bilmans (1887–1948),* A. W. Sijthoff, Leiden (1968) [covers peasantry, social structure]

Stares, P., 'The shortage of agricultural labour in Latvia', *International Labour Review,* 40 (1939)

Svabe, A., *Agrarian history of Latvia,* B. Lamey, Riga (1929)

Zeps, V. J., 'Homestead or village. Eighteenth century evidence for the history of Latgalian settlement', *Journal of Baltic Studies,* 5 (1974)

Zvidrins, P., 'The dynamics of fertility in Latvia', *Population Studies,* 33 (1979)

LITHUANIA

Audenas, J., 'The co-operative movement', *Lituanus,* 5 (1959)

Bielinis, K., *The labour problem in Lithuania,*

Mid-European Studies Center, Washington, D.C. (1953)

Chamber of Commerce, Industry and Crafts, *Ten*

years of Lithuanian economy, Chamber of Commerce, Industry and Crafts of Lithuania, Kaunas (1938)

Chicago University, Division of the Social Sciences, *Lithuania in the last thirty years*, Chicago University Press, New Haven, Conn. (1955)

Cronbach, A., 'Social action in Jewish Lithuania', *Hebrew Union College Annual*, 23 (1950–51)

Dainauskas, J., 'Prelude to independence. The great conference of Vilnius, 1905', *Lituanus*, 11 (1965)

Department of Overseas Trade, Economic conditions *in Lithuania*, H.M.S.O., London (1924– irregular series)

Gerutis, A., ed., *Lithuania. 700 years*, Maryland Books, New York (2nd edn 1969)

Gineitis, K., *Lithuanian quality products. A record of remarkable agricultural progress*, The author, London (1938)

International Labour Office, 'Reform of social insurance in Lithuania', *Industrial and Labour Information*, 63 (1937)

Jurgela, C. T., *History of the Lithuanian nation*, Lithuanian Kultural Institut, Historical Research Section, New York (1948)

Kaminski, A., 'Neo-serfdom in Poland–Lithuania', *Slavic Review*, 34 (1975)

Krivickas, D., 'Economic achievements of the Lithuanian state', *Baltic Review*, 13 (1958)

Krivickas, V., 'The Lithuanian populist and the agrarian question. 1918–26', *Journal of Baltic Studies*, 6 (1975)

Krivickas, V., 'The programs of the Lithuanian Social Democrat Party. 1896–1931', *Journal of Baltic Studies*, 11 (1980)

Leslie, R. F., *Polish politics and the revolution of November 1830*, Athlone Press, London (1956)

Leslie, R. F., *Reform and insurrection in Russian Poland, 1856–65*, Athlone Press, London (1963)

Lithuanian Information Bureau, *Economic and financial condition of the Lithuanian Republic at the beginning of 1922*, Lithuanian Information Bureau, London (*c.* 1922)

Manelis, V., 'Agriculture in independent Lithuania. Its progress and problems', *Lituanus*, 5 (1965)

Misiunas, R. J., 'The Sventoji project. Eighteenth century plans for a Lithuanian port', *Journal of Baltic Studies*, 8 (1977)

O'Hara, V. J., 'The Lithuanian forest', *Review of Reviews*, 65 (1922)

Paskiewicz, H., *The making of a Russian nation*, H. Regnery, Chicago, Ill. (1963)

Rackauskas, J. A., 'The first national system of education in Europe. The Commission for National Education of the Kingdom of Poland and the Grand Duchy of Lithuania, 1773–94', *Lituanus*, 14 (1968)

Sabaliunas, L,., 'Social democracy in tsarist Lithuania, 1893–1904', *Slavic Review*, 31 (1972)

Senn, A. E., *The emergence of modern Lithuania*, Columbia University Press, New York (1959)

Senn, A. E., 'Vilna as the cultural centre of Lithuania before 1861', *East European Quarterly*, 2 (1968)

Simutis, A., *The economic reconstruction of Lithuania after 1918*, Columbia University Press, New York (1942)

Smogorzewski, K. M., 'The Russification of the Baltic states', *World Affairs*, 4 (1950)

Trimakas, A., 'Lithuanian co-operative movement in freedom and slavery', *Baltic Review*, 11 (1957)

United States Office of the Commissioner for the Baltic Provinces of Russia, *Lithuanian economic report*, Riga (1920)

Zilinskas, V., 'Independent Lithuania's economic progress', *Baltic Review*, 1 (1946)

INDEX

AALBERS, J. 107
ABBOTT, R. J. 166
ABBOTT, W. F. 166
ABEL, A. 82
ABEL, W. 9
ABELSON, A. 185
ABERCROMBIE, P. 60, 91, 122
ABOUCHAR, A. 150
ABRAHAM, D. 72, 92
ABRAHAMS, P. 36
ABRAMOVITCH, R. R. 139
ABRAMSON, A. 139, 164
ABRAMSON, P. R. 31
ABRATE, M. 200
ACKERKNECHT, E. H., and C. E.
  ROSENBERG 61, 92
ACKERMAN, S. 23
ACKERMANN, E. B. 60
ACKERMANN, E. B., and E. A.
  LANG 61
ACKLEY, F., and L.
  SPARENTA 176
ACOMB, E. M., and M. L.
  BROWN 61
ADAMS, P. V. 71
ADAMS, T. M. 61
ADAMSON, O. J. 196
ADAMSON, R. 200, 202
ADELMAN, I., and C. T.
  MORRIS 1, 9, 35
ADELMANN, G. 77
ADELSON, J. 47
ADLER, J. H. 16
ADLER, P. J. 118
AGHERLI, B. B. 16
AGOCS, S. 180
AGREN, K. 203
AGULHON, M. 61
AHLBERG, G. 203
AHLBERG, H. 206
AHLSTROM, G. 12, 70, 92, 199
AHVENAINEN, J. 150, 212
AITKEN, H. G. J. 1
AKERMAN, G. 206

AKERMAN, S. 194, 203, 205
ALANEN, A. J. 213
ALBERS, G. 91
ALBRECHT-CARRIE, R. 42
ALDCROFT, D. H. 1, 35
ALDEN, D. 190
ALDRIDGE, D. D. 194
ALEXANDER, J. T. 150, 167
ALEXANDER, P. B. 134
ALEXANDROV, B. 155
ALEXINSKY, G. 139
ALI, A. S. 139
ALIBER, R. Z. 16
ALLCOCK, J. B. 133
ALLEN, G. C. 1
ALLEN, G. R. 205
ALLEN, R. C. 84
ALLEN, W. E. D. 139
ALMQUIST, E. L. 35
ALPERT, P. 1
ALSTON, P. L. 167
ALTEA, COUNT DE 184
ALTERMATT, U. 112
AMANN, R. 150
AMATORI, F. 178
AMERICAN BANKERS'
  ASSOCIATION 139
AMERICAN TRADE UNION
  DELEGATION 139
AMERICAN-RUSSIAN CHAMBER
  OF COMMERCE 139
AMERY, L. S. 120
AMES, E. 154
AMINZADE, R. 57, 61, 62
AMMENDE, E. 167
ANDERSEN, O. 209
ANDERSON, B. A. 160
ANDERSON, B. M. 51
ANDERSON, D. 136
ANDERSON, E. 88, 157, 218
ANDERSON, E. N. 92
ANDERSON, E. N. and P. R. 31
ANDERSON, J. L. 9
ANDERSON, M. 31

ANDERSON, M. S. 139, 167
ANDERSON, O. 36, 139, 155
ANDIC, S., and J. VEVERKA 82
ANDIC, V. E. 128
ANDORKA, R. 125, 126
ANDREADES, A. 189
ANDREW, C. M. 53
ANDREW, C. M., and A. S.
  KANYA-FORSTNER 47
ANDREW, E. 171
ANES, G., and A. GARCIA
  SANZ 183
ANGEL-VOLKOV, S. 77, 88
ANGELL, J. W. 72
ANGENOT, L. H. J. 109
ANKARLOO, B. 9
ANONYMOUS 102, 135, 145, 154,
  164, 178, 179
ANSELMI, A. 178
ANSIAUX, M. 102
ANSTEY, R. 19
ANTHONY, K. 92, 195
ANTILLA, V. 212
ANTSIFEROV, A. N. 145
ANTSIFEROV, A. N., and E.
  KAYDEN 174
APOSTOL, P. N. 155
APPEL, E. 203
APPLEBY, A. B. 23, 45
AQUARONE, A. 176
ARACIL, R., and M. G.
  BONAFE 187
ARASARATNAM, S. 108
ARATO, E. 128
ARCHER, C. I. 184
ARDELEANU, I. 137
ARIES, P. 31
ARIMA, T. 157
ARMENGAUD, A. 23
ARMESON, R. B. 77
ARMSTRONG, A. F. 51
ARMSTRONG, J. A. 167
ARMSTRONG, T. 160
ARNDT, H. W. 1

ARNHEIM, A. 208
ARNOLD, A. Z. 155
ARONSFIELD, C. C. 155
ARONSON, I. M. 167
ARPI, G. 200
ARRIAZA, A. J. 31
ARTZ, F. B. 42, 70
ARVICH, P. H. 167
ASDRACHAS, S. I. 189
ASHLEY, P. W. L. 53, 84
ASHLEY, W. J. 88
ASHWORTH, W. 1, 35
ASPVALL, G. 200
ASTROM, K. 206
ASTROM, S. E. 193, 194, 213, 214
ATHEY, L. L. 31
ATKINSON, D. 145, 174
AUBERT, L. 1
AUDENAS, J. 218
AUFFRET, M. 45
AUGE-LARIBE, M. 57
AUGUSTINE, W. R. 161
AUHAGEN, O. 145
AUKRUST, O., and J.
    BJERKE 195
AUNOLA, T. 212
AUSTEN, R. A. 19, 84
AUTIO, M., and E.
    LODENIUS 212
AUTY, P. 133
AVAKUMOVIC, I. 167
AVRICH, P. H. 161
AXE, E. W., and H. M.
    FLINN 72
AYMARD, M. 71, 105

BAADE, F. 72
BACHMANN, G. 112
BACK, P. E. 205
BACKER, J. E. 197
BACON, E. F. 167
BACON, L. B., and F. C.
    SCHLOEMER 20
BACSKAI, V., and L. NAGY 126
BAERWELD, F. 96
BAGDANOFF, G. 217
BAGGE, G. 205
BAIKALOV, A. V. 145, 160
BAILES, K. E. 150, 167
BAILEY, S. 88
BAIROCH, P. 1, 9, 20, 30, 39
BAIROCH, P., and J. M.
    LIMBOR 27, 39
BAIROCH, P., and M.
    LEVY-LEBOYER 1
BAJOHR, S. 92
BAKELESS, J. 36
BAKER, A. B. 145, 155, 167
BAKER, A. R. H. 57
BAKER, D. N., and P. J.
    HARRIGAN 70
BAKER, H., and F. W.
    BULOW 128
BAKHMETOV, B. 171
BALABKINS, N., and

A. AIZILNIEKS 218
BALAWYDER, A. 118
BALDERSTON, T. 72
BALDURSSON, G. 215
BALDWIN, R. E. 1, 20, 39
BALMUTH, D. 167
BALOGH, T. 51, 73
BALTHAZAR, H. 103
BALZAK, S. S. 139
BAMFORD, P. W. 45, 47, 50, 53
BANDERA, V. N. 117, 150, 171
BANE, S. L., and R. H. LUTZ 36,
    73
BANFIELD, T. C. 77
BARAN, P. A. 139, 173
BARBAGLI, M. 181
BARBER, E. D. 62
BARBERA, H. 1
BARBIER, J. A. 184
BARBIER, J. A., and H. S.
    KLEIN 184
BARCLAY, D. E. 96
BARING, M. 139, 167
BARKAI, H. 155
BARKER, E. 12
BARKER, G. R. 150
BARKER, R. J. 47, 51
BARKHAUSEN, M. 77, 100, 111
BARKIN, K. D. 77
BARLEY, M. W. 30
BARNES, T. G., and G. D.
    FELDMAN 1
BARON, S. H. 139, 166, 171
BARON, S. W. 167
BARRANSKY, N. N. 139
BARROWS, S. 62
BARSBY, S. L. 35
BART, I. 126
BARTEL, R. J. 16
BARTLETT, R. P. 160
BARUCH, B. M. 36, 97
BASBERG, B. 196
BASCH, A. 84, 117
BASS, R. H. 145
BASSECHES, N. 150
BASTER, A. S. J. 1, 16, 73
BASTER, N. 164
BATALDEN, S. K. 189
BATER, J. H. 154, 166
BATTY, P. 77
BAUDET, H., and H. VAN DER
    MEULEN 1
BAUDET, H., and I. J.
    BRUGMANS 108
BAUDHUIN, F. 1
BAUGHMAN, J. J. 51
BAUMERT, G. 92
BAUMGART, H. 132
BAYKALOV, A. V. 154, 174
BAYKOV, A. 139, 145, 150, 157,
    173
BAZANT, J. 184
BEABLE, W. H. 150
BEAUROY, J. 45
BEAVER, S. H. 135

BECK, T. D. 62, 71
BECKER, S. 171
BECKER, W. 38
BEDARIDA, F. 71
BEER, J. J. 77
BEHRENS, B. 31, 45
BELIAJEFF, A. S. 150
BELL, A. C. 37
BELL, D. H. 181
BELL, J. D. 136
BELL, R. M. 134, 180, 181
BELOV, F. 145
BENDA, G. 124
BENEVOLO, L. 30
BENGTSSON, T., and L.
    JORBERG 205
BENHAM, F. 12
BENKIN, R. L. 118
BENNATHAN, E. 73
BENNETT, E. W. 73, 82
BENNETT, M. K. 9, 145
BERDAHL, R. M. 76
BERDROW, W. 77
BEREND, I. T. 38, 117, 123, 124
BEREND, I. T., and G. RANKI 1,
    114, 118, 123, 124, 125
BERENSON, E. 45
BERGER, S. 45
BERGERON, L. 42, 47
BERGHOUSE, E. 15
BERGIER, J. F. 27
BERGMAN, C. 97
BERGMAN, M. 111
BERGQUIST, H. E. 157, 188
BERGSON, A. 140, 164
BERGSON, A., and S.
    KUZNETS 140
BERKER, L. K., and J. W.
    SHAFFER 62
BERKHIN, I. 171
BERKNER, L. K. 31, 38, 76, 87,
    122
BERKNER, L., and F. F.
    MENDELS 23
BERLANSTEIN, L. R. 62
BERNATSKY, M. 155
BERNSTEIN, P. 68
BERNSTEIN, S. A. 151
BEROV, L. 20, 117, 118, 137, 188
BERRIL, K. 20
BERTELLI, S. 182
BESSEL, R. 73
BESSEL, R., and E. J.
    FEUCHTWANGER 92
BEST, P. J. 131
BETERAMS, F. G. C. 104
BETTS, R. R. 127
BEYEN, J. W. 16
BEZUCHA, R. J. 31, 57, 71
BIAGI, R. 181
BICANIC, R. 2
BIDEAN, A. 56
BIDWELL, R. L. 16, 39
BIELINIS, K. 218
BIERCK, H. A. 185

BILL, V. T. 151, 154, 167
BILMANIS, A. 218
BILT, L. 132
BIRABEN, J. N. 56
BIRNIE, A. 2
BIUCCHI, B. M. 112
BIZIERE, J. M. 31
BJARNASON, O. 215
BJELORUCIC, H. 135
BJERKE, K. 207
BJORKVIK, H. 193, 196
BJORN, C. 208, 211
BJORNSSON, B. T. 215
BJURLING, O. 200, 202, 208
BLACK, C. E. 140, 167
BLACKBOURN, D. 92
BLACKER, J. G. C. 62
BLACKWELL, W. L. 30, 140, 151, 166
BLAFIELD, E. 213
BLAISDELL, D. C. 117, 188
BLAKE, D. J. 205
BLANCHARD, M. 50
BLANNING, T. C. W. 92, 96
BLASCHKE, K. 87
BLAUG, M. 35
BLAYO, Y. 62
BLEGEN, T. C. 197
BLESSING, W. K. 88
BLITZ, R. C. 35
BLOCH, J. F. 51
BLOCH, M. 45
BLOCK, A. 166, 167
BLOCK, H. 77, 96
BLOCKMANS, W. 104
BLODGETT, R. H., and D. L. KEMMERER 2
BLOK, P. J. 105
BLOMQVIST, E. 200
BLOMSTEDT, Y. 211
BLONDAL, G. 215
BLOOMFIELD, A. I. 16
BLUM, J. 2, 9, 45, 116, 120, 145
BLUMBERG, A. 51, 178
BLUMENFELD, H. 30
BLUSSE, L., and F. GAASTRA 20
BOBROFF, A. 167
BOCHENSKI, A. 131
BODEA, C. 137
BOETHIUS, B. 199, 200
BOETTLER, H. E. 2
BOEV, V. R. 146
BOG, I. 84
BOGART, E. L. 37
BOGUCKA, M. 12, 216
BOHACHEVSKY-CHOMIAK, M. 118
BOHME, H. 73, 84
BOIA, I. 114, 138
BOILEAU, I. 186
BOIME, A. 47
BOJE, P. 195
BOLKHOVITINOV, N. N. 157
BOLLEREY, F., and K. HARTMANN 91

BONELLI, F. 178
BONN, M. J. 82
BONNELL, A. T. 84
BONNELL, V. E. 161
BOOGMAN, J. C. 105
BORCHARDT, K. 73
BORGHESE, A. 57
BORKIN, J., and C. A. WELSH 96
BORN, K. E. 90
BORODAEWSKY, S. W. 174
BOROVOY, S. Y. 155
BORSEL, A. 112
BORSKY, G. 97
BOSHER, J. F. 48, 51, 53, 62, 71
BOSWELL, J. L. 37
BOSWORTH, R. J. 178
BOUCHER, M. 102
BOULDING, K. E. 37
BOULLE, P. H. 54, 60
BOUMAN, P. J. 106
BOURDE, A. J. 45
BOURGEOIS-PICHAT, J. 56
BOUVIER, J. 51
BOVOWSKI, S. 131
BOVYKIN, V. I. 157
BOWDEN, W. 2
BOWEN-JONES, H. 191
BOWEN, R. H. 77
BOWLES, W. D. 151
BOWLEY, A. L. 37
BOWMAN, M. J., and C. A. ANDERSON 2
BOXER, C. R. 108, 190
BOXER, M. J. 62
BOXER, M. J., and J. H. QUATAERT 31
BOYD, E. 179
BRAATZ, W. E. 84
BRACHER, K. D. 98
BRADLEY, J. 160
BRADLEY, M. 48, 51, 70, 151
BRADY, R. A. 73, 77, 96, 98
BRAILSFORD, H. N. 133
BRAINERD, M. 167
BRAKE, W. TE 111
BRANCA, P. 31
BRANDT, K. 9, 76, 96
BRATTNE, B. 203
BRAUDEL, F. 2
BRAUDEL, F., and F. C. SPOONER 29
BRAUN, H. J. 96
BRAUN, R. 112
BRAUNTHAL, A. 104
BRAUNTHAL, G. 88
BREITLING, P. 91, 122
BREMER, S. 23
BRENNER, R. 9
BRENNER, Y. S. 2
BRENTANO, L. 76
BRESCIANI-TURRONI, C. 90
BRIDENTHAL, R., and C. KOONZ 31
BRIGGS, A. 2, 12

BRIGGS, J. W. 180
BRINKMANN, C. 73
BRINTON, C. 68
BRISCH, H., and I. VOLGYES 127
BRITISH ELECTRICAL AND ALLIED MANUFACTURERS' ASSOCIATION 77
BROCK, P. 132
BROCK, P., and H. G. SKILLING 127
BRODER, A. 54
BRODERSEN, A. 161
BROEZE, F. J. A. 20, 108
BROMLEY, J. S. 108, 140
BROMLEY, J. S., and E. H. KOSSMAN 105, 108
BRONDEL, G. 12
BROWER, D. R. 146, 166, 167
BROWN, J. C. 216
BROWN, J. H. 146, 167
BROWN, R. 12
BROWN, W. A. 16, 37
BROWNING, O. 54
BROZEK, A. 88, 132
BRUBAKER, E. R. 146
BRUCK, W. F. 73
BRUFORD, W. H. 31, 92
BRUGMANS, I. J. 105, 111
BRUIJN, J. R. 110, 111
BRUNN, G. 2
BRUNNER, K. 2
BRUTSKUS, B. D. 157, 173
BRUYNS, C. M. 110
BRY, G. 90
BRY, G., and BOSCHAN, C. 90
BRYANT, L. 82
BUCHANAN, H. R. 171
BUCHANAN, N. S., and H. S. ELLIS 2
BUCHHEIM, C. 84
BUCKLEY, P. J., and B. R. ROBERTS 20
BUCKLEY, R. N. 54
BUISSINK, J. D. 109
BUIST, M. G. 16, 107, 157
BULIK, J. J. 146
BULL, E. 198
BULOW, F. W. VON 218
BUNLE, H. 56
BUNTE, R. 193, 200
BUNYAN, J. 161
BURCH, T. K. 23
BURCHARDT, L. 96
BURGDORFER, F. 87
BURGESS, M. 151
BURGIN, A. 112
BURKE, M. E. 186
BURKE, P. 30, 198, 206
BURNETT, P. M. 97
BURNS, E. 140
BURY, J. P. T. 2
BUSE, D. K. 92
BUSEK, V., and N. SPULBER 127
BUSH, J. W. 70

BUSHNELL, J. 167
BUSTELO, F., and G. TORTELLA-CASARES 184
BUTLER, R. 37
BUTTER, I. H. 111
BYE, R. T. 173
BYNUM, W. F. 62, 92
BYRNES, R. F. 48

CAFAGNA, L. 176
CAGAN, P. 16
CAHILL, J. R. 42
CAHM, E. 62
CAIN, P. J. 20
CAIRNCROSS, A. K. 2, 20, 36, 39
CAIRNCROSS, A. K., and J. FAALAND 20, 39
CAIZZI, B. 176
CALABI, D. 181
CALDWELL, J. C. 23
CALDWELL, T. B. 57
CALLAHAN, W. J. 184, 186
CALLAHAN, W. J., and D. HIGGS 31
CAMERON, I. A. 62
CAMERON, R. E. 2, 12, 16, 36, 38, 42, 51, 54, 78, 82, 102, 117, 178, 179
CAMPBELL, F. G. 78, 129
CAMPBELL, M. 155
CAMPBELL, R. 173
CAPLAN, J. 92
CARACCIOLO, A. 181
CARDEN, G. L. 12, 102
CARLISLE, R. B. 68
CARLSSON, G. 23, 203
CARLSSON, S. 200
CARNEGIE ENDOWMENT FOR INTERNATIONAL PEACE & INTERNATION CHAMBER OF COMMERCE 2
CARON, F. 42, 48, 50
CARR, E. H. 140, 146
CARR, E. H., and R. W. DAVIES 140
CARR, R. 182
CARR, W. 84
CARROLL, B. A. 98
CARROLL, M. B. 16, 51, 112, 179
CARROLL, M. R. 96, 122
CARSTEN, F. L. 98, 114
CARSTENSEN, F. V. 155
CARTER, A. C. 104, 107, 108, 110, 111
CARTER, E. C. 48
CARTER, F. W. 114, 117, 127, 128, 135
CARVER, J. S. 151
CASEY, J. 186
CASPARD, P. 112
CASSEL, G. 16, 73
CASTAN, N. 62
CASTELOT, E. 56
CAVALIERO, R. 191
CAVANAUGH, G. J. 45

CECIL, L. 78
CEDERBLAD, N. 205
CENSER, J. R. 12, 62
CENTRAL STATISTICAL ADMINISTRATION 140, 158
CENTRAL STATISTICAL BOARD U.S.S.R. 140
CERMAKIAN, J. 50
CERNOVODEANU, P. 138
CERNOVODEANU, P., and B. MARINESCU 138
CHAKRABARTI, S. C. 140
CHALONER, W. H. 50
CHAMBER OF COMMERCE, INDUSTRY AND CRAFTS 218
CHAMBERLIN, W. G. 215
CHAMBERLIN, W. H. 12, 140, 146, 151, 173
CHAMOUX, A. 62
CHANDLER, A. D. 12
CHANDLER, A. D., and H. DAEMS 12
CHANDLER, J. A. 182
CHANG, H. J. 42, 73
CHAPIN, F. S. 31
CHAPMAN, A. B. W. 190
CHAPMAN, B. 60
CHAPMAN, J. G. 165
CHAPMAN, S. D. 20
CHAPMAN, S. D., and S. CHASSAGNE 48
CHARLESWORTH, E. K. 200
CHARTRES, J. 15
CHASE, S. 151
CHAUDURI, K. N. 20
CHAYANOV, A. V. 146
CHECKLAND, S. G. 36, 184
CHENERY, H. B. 36
CHENERY, H. B., and L. TAYLOR 36
CHEONG, W. E. 185
CHEVALIER, L. 23, 62
CHICAGO UNIVERSITY, DIVISION OF THE SOCIAL SCIENCES 219
CHILCOTE, R. N. 184
CHILD, F. C. 84
CHILDERS, T. 90
CHILDS, M. W. 199
CHILDS, S. L., and A. A. CROTTET 165
CHIROT, D. 31
CHIROT, D., and C. RAGIN 138
CHIROVSKY, N. L. F. 140
CHISICK, H. 70
CHOAY, F. 30
CHOJNACKA, H. 23, 160
CHORLEY, G. P. H. 9
CHORLEY, P. 178
CHOSSODOWSKY, E. M. 165
CHOUDHRI, E. U., and L. A. KOCHIN 17
CHRISTELOW, A. 182, 190
CHRISTENSON, C. L. 197, 209
CHRISTIANSEN, N. F. 210

CHRISTIANSEN, P. O. 208
CHRISTOFFERSON, T. R. 48, 60
CHRISTOPHER, J. C. 62
CHURCH, R. A. 112
CIBOROWSKI, A. 129
CIESLAK, E. 54, 131
CIPOLLA, C. M. 2, 23, 180, 182
CITROEN, H. A. 23
CLAPHAM, J. H. 37, 42, 73
CLAPP, V. W. 12
CLARENCE-SMITH, W. G. 190
CLARK, C. 2, 174
CLARK, G. N. 20
CLARK, H. 207
CLARK, J. G. 51
CLARK, J. J. 42
CLARK, J. M. 37
CLARK, L. L. 62, 68
CLARK, T. N. 68
CLARKE, R. A. 140
CLARKE, S. V. O. 17, 52, 68
CLEINOW, G. 158
CLEMENTS, B. E. 167
CLEMHOUT, S. 36
CLENDENNING, P. H. 151
CLISSOLD, S. 133
CLOGG, R. 118
CLOUGH, S. B. 2, 42, 52, 176, 179, 184
CLOUGH, S. B., and C. G. MOODIE 38
CLOUGH, S. B., and C. LIVI 176
CLOUGH, S. B., and C. W. COLE 2
CLOUT, H. D. 42, 45
CLOUT, H. D., and K. SUTTON 71
COALE, A. J. 23, 160
COATES, W. P., and Z. K. 173
COBB, R. C. 62
COBBAN, A. 42, 62
COCHRANE, E. 181
COCKS, P. 35
COHEN, D. K. 69
COHEN, G. B. 129
COHEN, J. E. 24
COHEN, J. S. 176, 178, 179
COHEN, S. F. 140
COHN, G. 15, 82, 87
COHN, S. H. 140
COLANOVIC, B. 135
COLE, C. W. 69
COLE, G. D. H., and M. 2
COLE, J. W., and E. R. WOLF 178
COLE, M., and C. SMITH 203
COLE, W. A., and P. DEANE 2
COLEMAN, W. 62
COLLINET, M. 57
COLLINS, D. N. 54, 154
COLLINS, E. J. T. 9
COLLINS, G. R. 30, 186
COLLINS, G. R., and C. C. 30
COLM, G. 96
COLTON, E. 140

COLTON, J. G. 57
COMMISSION OF ENQUIRY INTO NATIONAL POLICY IN INTERNATIONAL ECONOMIC RELATIONS 20
COMSTOCK, A. 97, 155
CONACHER, H. M. 27
CONDLIFFE, J. B. 20
CONOLLY, V. 158, 171
CONQUEST, R. 140, 161
CONRADS, U., and H. G. SPERLICH 30
CONROY, M. S. 171
CONSTANTINESCU, N. N., and V. V. AXENCIUC 138
CONZE, W. 99, 116
COONS, R. E. 120
COOPER, J. M. 37
COOPER, J. P. 9
COPPA, F. J. 179, 182
COPSON-NIECKO, M. J. E. 131
CORCIA, J. DI 62
CORDASCO, F. 180
CORNEBISE, A. E. 97
CORNISH, W. R. 12
CORRSIN, S. 217, 218
CORSINI, C. A. 181
CORTADA, J. W. 183, 187
CORTES, J. B. 183
CORTI, E. C. 17
COSTA, F. J. 181
COSTIGLIOLA, F. 73
COTTA, F. 190
COTTRELL, P. L. 52, 120
COUNTS, G. S. 173
COUPERIE, P. 60
COWAN, L. G. 42, 78
COWARD, D. A. 62
COWLES, V. 167
COYNER, S. 92
CRAEYBECKX, J. 100, 104, 111
CRAFTS, N. F. R. 48
CRAIG, G. A. 2
CRAWFORD, J. M. 151
CRAWLEY, C. W. 2
CREAMER, D. 96
CREW, D. F. 88, 91
CREW, D. F., and E. ROSENHAFT 99
CRISP, O. 54, 140, 146, 155, 158, 161
CRNJA, Z. 136
CRONBACH, A. 219
CROOT, P., and D. PARKER 42
CROSBY, A. W. 158
CROSLAND, M. 70, 71
CROSS, G. S. 56
CROSS, R. D. 151
CROSS, S. H. 173
CROTTET, A. A., and S. L. CHILDS 161
CROUZET, F. 2, 17, 37, 42, 50
CROWHURST, P. 108
CROWHURST, R. P. 51
CROWLEY, R. W. 17

CRUMMEY, R. O. 168
CRUMP, N. 98
CSATO, T. 116
CSERNOK, A. 3
CSOPPUS, J. 125, 179
CUENCA, J. 185
CULLEN, L. M., and F. FURET 45
CULLITY, J. P. 88
CUMMINGS, M. 62
CURL, J. S. 30
CURTISS, J. S. 168
CUSHING, G. F. 123
CYNAMON, A., and L. SZLAMOWICZ 130
CZEKNER, J. 120, 124

D'ABERNON, VISCOUNT 82
D'ANGELO, M. 178
DAALDER, H. 111
DACOSTA, E. P. W. 140
DAELEMANS, F. 101
DAEMS, H. 102
DAEMS, H., and H. VAN DER WEE 12
DAHL, S. 200
DAHMEN, E. 200
DAINAUSKAS, J. 219
DAKIN, D. 189
DALLAS, G. 45
DALLIN, D. J., and B. NIKOLAEVSKY 161
DALRYMPLE, D. G. 146
DAMIANOV, S. 137
DANHOF, C. H. 9
DANIEL, W. 168
DANIERE, A. 60
DARBY, H. C., and H. FULLARD 3
DASEY, R. 92
DATTA, A. 140
DAUMARD, A. 60, 62
DAVIES, A. 45
DAVIES, N. 129
DAVIES, R. B. 20
DAVIES, R. W. 146, 156, 173
DAVIES, R. W., and S. G. WHEATCROFT 173
DAVIS, G. H. 31
DAVIS, J. 173
DAVIS, J. C. 180, 181
DAVIS, J. S. 3, 17, 42, 73
DAVIS, K. 129
DAVIS, K., and J. E. ISAAC 24
DAVIS, R. 3
DAVISON, R. M. 146
DAVISSON, W. I., and J. E. HARPER 3
DAVLETSHIN, T. 171
DAWES, R. C. 37
DAWSON, P. 78
DAWSON, W. H. 73, 76, 78, 84, 88, 91, 92, 96, 97, 112
DAY, C. 3, 20
DAY, C. R. 70

DAY, J. P. 3
DAY, R. B. 35, 171
DAY, R. M. 171
DE BRABANDER, G. L. 100
DE CECCO, M. 17
DE CUGIS, C. 179
DE FELICE, R. 182
DE GROOT, A. H. 20
DE JONG, A. M. 107
DE JONGE, J. A. 105
DE ROSA, L. 176
DE VITTORIO, A. 123
DE VRIES, J. 3, 30, 100, 105
DEAN, V. M. 140
DEANE, P. 140
DEATON, A. S. 29
DEBIEN, G. 45
DEBO, R. K. 108, 158
DECHESNE, L. 103
DEDIJER, V. 133
DEGLER, C. N. 3
DEGRAS, J., and A. NOVE 173
DEHN, R. M. R. 78
DEHN, V. 156
DEL PANTA, L. 180
DELDLYCKE, T. 27, 39
DELIVANIS, D. J. 189
DELLE DONNE, O. 20
DELZELL, C. F. 176
DEMARIS, E. J. 156
DEME, L. 126
DEMENY, P. 121, 125
DEMETER, K. 92
DEMKO, G. J. 160
DENBY, E. 31
DEPARTMENT OF OVERSEAS TRADE 219
DEPREZ, P. 24, 102, 103, 109
DERRY, T. K. 193, 195
DERRY, T. K., and T. I. WILLIAMS 12
DERTILIS, P. B. 189
DESAI, A. V. 90
DESAMA, C. 103
DESPALATOVIC, E. M. 136
DEURBO, M. C., and G. A. HOEKVELD 109
DEUTSCH, K. W., and A. ECKSTEIN 3
DEUTSCHER, I. 140, 161
DEVLET INSTATISKIK ENSTITUSU 187
DEWAR, M. 161
DEYON, P., and P. GUIGNET 48
DHONDT, J. 27, 102, 104
DHONDT, J., and M. BRUWIER 100, 105
DI GIOVANNI, G. 176
DI VITTORIO, A. 207, 215
DIAKONOFF, V. A. 151
DIAMANDUROS, N. P. 189
DIAS, J. R. 190
DIBBLE, V. 92
DICKERSON, C. J., and W. R. RIDDLE 174

DICKINSON, R. E. 73, 180
DICKLER, R. A. 76
DICKSON, P. G. M., and J.
  SPERLING 37
DIEDERICKS, H., and P. H. J.
  VAN DER LAAN 111
DIEDERIKS, H. 30, 111
DIENES, L. 146
DIEPHOUSE, D. J. 38
DIETRICH, E. B. 12, 54
DIETZEL, H. 82, 84
DILLARD, D. 20
DIN, G. C. 185
DIXON, R. A., and E. K.
  EBERHART 32
DJORDJEVIC, D. 116, 133
DLUGSBORSKI, W. 116
DMOCHOWSKI, Z. 132
DMYTRYSHYN, B. 140, 171
DOBB, M. 3, 141, 151, 171, 173
DOBB, M., and H. C.
  STEVENS 141
DODGE, N. T. 162, 168
DODGE, N. T., and D. G.
  DALRYMPLE 151
DOERFLINGER, T. M. 54
DOHAN, M. R. 141
DOLAN, E. G. 141
DOMESTICHOS, A. 189
DOMINICK, R. 93
DON, Y. 121, 125
DONAGHAY, M. 54
DONALD, R. 123
DONALDSON, J. 20
DORE, G. 180
DORN, W. L. 73
DOSSING, P. 209
DOUGALL, H. E. 51
DOUGILL, W. 110
DOUGLAS, D. W. 127, 129
DOUGLAS, P. H. 60, 162, 165
DOUGLAS, W. A. 181
DOUGLASS, P. F. 131
DOUKAS, K. A. 51
DOVRING, F. 10, 24, 38
DOW, R. 146
DOWD, D. F. 3
DOWE, D. 93
DRACHMANN, P. 194
DRAGE, G. 141
DRAGNICH, A. N. 133
DRAKE, M. 24, 197
DRESCHER, S. 62
DREW, R. F. 146, 151
DRUMMOND, I. M. 52, 156, 158
DU BOFF, R. B. 69
DUBBS, H. H. 146
DUBECK, I. 210
DUBREUIL, H., and J. P.
  LUGRIN 48
DUCHESS OF ATHOLL 162
DUKES, P. 168
DULLES, E. L. 52
DULLES, J. F. 97
DUMAS, J. 45

DUMKE, R. H. 78
DUMONT, P. 189
DUNHAM, A. L. 15, 43, 48, 51,
  54, 57, 71
DUNLEVY, J. A. 24
DUNLEVY, J. A., and H. A.
  GEMERY 194
DUNN, R. E. 20
DUNN, R. W. 162
DUNN, S. P. and E. 146
DUNNE, J. 71
DUNNING, J. H. 20
DUPAQUIER, J. 24, 56, 63
DUPAQUIER, J., and L.
  JADIN 181
DUPEUX, G. 56, 63
DURAN, J. A. 156, 160
DURHAM, M. E. 118
DUTU, A. 138
DVORNIK, F. 133
DYASON, J. 141
DYKER, D. A. 136
DYMOND, T. S. 124
DYMTRYSHYN, B. 140
DYRVIK, S. 193, 197
DZIEWANOWSKI, M. K. 132

EAGER, J. M. 32
EAGLY, R. V. 43, 73, 202, 207
EARLE, E. M. 43, 188
EARLE, P. 3
EASON, W. W. 146, 160, 162
EAST, W. G. 174
EASTERLIN, R. 24
EASTMAN, M. 12
EATON, H. L. 166
EBEL, R. E. 151, 158
EBENSTEIN, W. 98
EBERSOLE, J. F. 37
ECKAUS, R. S. 176
ECKER-RACZ, L. 123
ECKER, L. L. 125
ECKHART, F. 123
ECKSTEIN, A. 123
ECKSTEIN, A., and P.
  GUTMANN 141
EDDIE, S. M. 120, 121, 124, 125
EDMONDSON, C. M. 146, 158
EDWARDS, G. W. 35
EDWARDS, S. 63
EAGLE, W. 78
EHRMANN, H. W. 48, 71
EICHHOLZ, A. C. 216
EIDELBERG, P. G. 138
EINAUDI, L. 179
EINZIG, P. 3, 17, 37, 52, 84, 98,
  156, 176
EK, S. B. 199
ELDRIDGE, H. T. 24
ELEY, G. 32, 93, 99
ELEY, G., and K. NIELD 99
ELKIN, B. 168
ELKLIT, J. 211
ELLEMERS, J. E. 110, 203
ELLIS, G. 54

ELLIS, H. S. 82, 117, 120, 125
ELLISON, H. J. 141, 146
ELLMAN, M. 173
ELLSWORTH, P. T. 3
ELSAS, M. 82
ELSTER, J. 3
ELWITT, S. 57, 63
ELY, R. T. 146
EMDEN, P. H. 17
EMERY, C. R., AND K. W.
  SWART 104, 111
EMMER, P. C. 108
EMMONS, T. 146
EMMONS, T., and W. S.
  VUCINCH 171
EMSLEY, C. 3
ENDE, A. 93
ENDREI, W. 117
ENDS, T. 71
ENEQUIST, G. 200
ENGELS, W., and H. POHL 78
ENGERMAN, S. L. 20, 24
ENGLESING, R. 93
ENGMAN, M. 160, 213
ENTNER, M. L. 158
ERGIL, D. 189
ERGIL, D., and R. T.
  RHODES 187
ERICHSEN, E. 195
ERICKSON, C. 24
ERICSSON, B. 200
ERIKSSON, I., and J.
  ROGERS 204
ERLICH, A. 141, 173
ESCOTT, B. A. C. S. 189
ESPER, T. 162, 165
ESTEY, J. A. 27
ESTONIAN CO-OPERATIVE
  WHOLESALE SOCIETY 217
ETIENNE, B. 56
EUCKEN, W. 96, 98
EVANS, I. L. 138
EVANS, R. J. 32, 88, 93
EVANS, R. J., and W. R. LEE 93
EVENSON, N. 60
EVERAERT, J., and C.
  VANDENBROEKE 104
EVERSLEY, D. E. C. 24
EYRE, E. 3

FAAS, V. V. 158
FABER, H. 208
FABER, J. A. 105, 106
FAGE, J. D. 20
FAGERBERG, B. 200
FAHLSTROM, J. M. 202
FAINSOD, M. 141
FAIRCHILDS, C. C. 57, 63
FAIRLIE, S. 154, 158
FALKUS, M. E. 3, 17, 73, 141,
  156, 158
FALLENBUCHL, Z. M. 141
FALLOWS, T. 146
FALNIOWSKA-GRADOWSKA,
  A. 130

FANNO, M. 17
FARAGO, T. 126
FARBMAN, M. S. 173
FARNSWORTH, H. C. 29
FAROQHI, S. 189
FARQUHARSON, J. E. 76
FARRAR, M. M. 43
FASEL, G. 57
FAUCHER, J. 146
FAURE, O. 63
FAY, H. VAN V. 20
FEARON, P. 3
FEDOR, T. 166
FEDOROWICZ, J. K. 129
FEELEY, D. 63
FEINERMAN, F. M. 63
FEIS, H. 3, 17
FELD, M. D. 3
FELDBAEK, O. 108, 209
FELDMAN, G. D. 73, 78, 90
FELDMAN, G. D., and U.
   NOCKEN 78
FELDMAN, G. R. 3
FELIX, D. 97, 184
FELLER, A. 141
FELLONI, G. 179
FENOALTEA, S. 176
FERENCZI, I. 24, 39
FERGUSON, A. D., and A.
   LEVIN 141
FERGUSSON, A. 82
FETTER, B. S. 84
FETTER, F. W. 156
FICEK, K. F. 96
FIELD, D. 146
FIELDHOUSE, D. K. 3, 20
FINDLAY, J. A. 216
FINLAY, R. 24
FIRST NATIONAL CITY BANK
   OF NEW YORK 141
FIRTH, S. 84
FISCHER-GALATI, S. 138
FISCHER, E. 122
FISCHER, F. 96
FISCHER, L. 151
FISCHER, R. 82
FISCHER, W. 12, 32, 38, 73, 82,
   84, 99
FISCHER, W., and P. CZADA 78
FISHER, H. A. L. 54
FISHER, H. E. S. 190
FISHER, H. H. 146
FISHER, J. C. 132, 135
FISHER, R. B. 156, 171
FISHMAN, J. S. 112
FISK, H. E. 3, 37, 39
FLANDRIN, J. L. 32
FLANINGHAM, M. L. 45, 76, 85,
   137
FLEISCHER, M. P. 76
FLEISHER, E. W. 202
FLEISIG, H. 3, 97
FLETCHER, R. 73
FLINK, J. 73
FLINN, M. W. 24, 185, 194, 200

FLORESCU, R. R. 138
FLORINSKY, M. T. 3, 43, 97, 98,
   141, 162, 173
FLUX, A. W. 85, 202
FOA, B. G., and P. G.
   TREVES 179
FOERSTER, R. F. 180
FOHLEN, C. 43, 48, 71
FONTANA, J., and J. NADAL 183
FORBES, I. D. 93
FORBES, I. L. D. 85
FORCHHEIMER, C. 122
FORD, F. L. 63
FOREMAN-PECK, J. 12
FORER, P. S. 57
FORGUS, S. P. 217
FORMAN, P. 93
FORNARI, H. D. 20
FORREST, A. 63
FORRESTER, R. B. 48
FORSTENZER, T. R. 63
FORSTER, E. and R. 32
FORSTER, E. J. 189
FORSTER, R. 45, 63, 71
FORSTER, R. and E. 32
FORSTER, R., and O. RANUM 63
FORTY, A. 63
FOSTER, E. D. 85, 158
FOURASTIE, J. 24
FOUST, C. M. 158
FOX-GENOVESE, E. 54, 69
FOX, D. J. 166
FOX, R. 63
FOX, R., and G. WEISZ 70
FRADER, L. L. 57
FRANGSMYR, T. 200
FRANK, A. G. 3, 141, 146
FRANK, L. 99
FRANKEL, H. 129
FRANKO, L. G. 12
FREDERICKSON, J. W. 194
FREDERIKSEN, D. M. 156
FREDERIKSEN, O. J. 158
FREEDEMAN, C. E. 48, 71
FREEMAN, J. 162
FREEMAN, S. T. 186
FREEZE, G. L. 168
FREMDLING, R. 82
FREMDLING, R., and R.
   TILLY 73
FRENCH, C. J. 15
FRENKEL, J. A. 17, 82
FRANKEL, J. A., and K. W.
   CLEMENTS 17
FREUDENBERGER, H. 12, 119,
   120, 128
FREUDENBERGER, H., and F.
   REDLICH 12
FREUDENBERGER, H., and G.
   MENSCH 127
FREY, S. L. 38
FRIBERG, N. 204
FRIDLIZIUS, G. 199, 202, 204
FRIEDMAN, E. M. 141
FRIEDMAN, P. 3, 4, 85, 125

FRIEDMANN, H. 10
FRIEDMANN, K. J. 208
FRIEDRICHS, C. R. 78, 91, 93
FRIIS, A., and K. GLAMANN 210
FRIMANNSLUND, R. 193, 196
FRITZ, M. 78, 200, 201
FRUMKIN, G. 27
FRYDE, M. 133
FRYKMAN, J. 206
FUA, G. 176
FUKUO, T. 78
FULLERTON, R. A. 78
FURET, F., and J. OZOUF 63, 70
FURSENKO, A. 20
FUSS, H. 27
FUSSELL, G. E. 10, 106
FUTRELL, M. 154, 201, 213
FUTUGAWA, Y. 32

GAGLIARDO, J. G. 76
GAGNIER, D. 54
GALBRAITH, J. K. 4
GALENSON, W. 28, 29, 151, 162,
   198
GALLIENNE, W. H. 217
GARBUTT, P. E. 154
GARDENER, W. 154
GARDINER, L. 192
GARGAN, E. T., and R. A.
   HANNEMAN 63
GARMO, P. H. DE 186
GARRATY, J. A. 28, 96
GARVY, G. 96, 156
GASKIN, K. 24
GASSLANDER, O. 202
GATES, R. A. 99
GATRELL, P. 151
GATTRELL, V. A. C. 32
GAUNITZ, S. 200, 201
GAUNT, D. 199, 204
GAUNT, D., and O.
   LOFGREN 194
GAY, J. 158
GAYER, A. D. 17
GAZEL, A. 216
GAZI, S. 134
GEANAKOPLOS, D. J. 189
GEARY, D. 28, 88, 93
GECK, L. H. A. 96
GEDDE-DAHL, T. 197
GEHLING, D. 85
GEIGER, R. G. 48, 181
GEISENBERGER, S., and J. H.
   MULLER 90
GEISS, I. 85
GELFAND, T. 63
GELLA, A., and R. A.
   WANNER 132
GELLATELY, B. 93
GEMZELL, C. A. 195
GENDEBIEN, A. W. 179
GENTIL DA SILVA, J. 190
GERARD, O. 201, 207
GERBOD, P. 70
GEREMEK, B. 28

GERETSEGGER, H., and M. PEINTNER 30
GERRETSON, F. 106
GERRITSZ, J. 111
GERSCHENKRON, A. 4, 32, 35, 36, 38, 43, 76, 119, 137, 141, 146, 151, 174, 176
GERSCHENKRON, A., and A. ERLICH 151
GERSCHENKRON, A., and N. NIMITZ 151
GERUTIS, A. 219
GESSNER, D. 76
GESTRIN, F. 134
GHIRARDO, D. A. 181
GHIULEA, N. 138
GIANNONE, A. 176
GIBB, H. A. R., and H. BOWEN 189
GIBSON, J. R. 141, 151, 158, 160
GIBSON, R. 63
GIDE, C. 43, 45, 52, 54
GIESEY, R. E. 63
GIESINGER, A. 141
GIEYSZTOROWA, I. 133
GIFFIN, F. C. 151, 162
GIGNILLIAT, J. L. 21
GILBERT, C. 37
GILBERT, M. 4, 17
GILDEA, R. 63
GILL, G. J. 146, 168
GILLE, B. 17
GILLE, H. 194
GILLESPIE, C. C. 70
GILLET, M. 48
GILLETTE, P. S. 156
GILLINGHAM, J. 102
GILLIS, J. R. 32
GILMORE, D. 183
GINEITIS, K. 219
GINSBORG, P. 181
GIRARD, L. 16
GIRAULT, A. 54
GIURESCU, C. C. 138
GIUSTI, U. 181
GJOLBERG, O. 197, 198
GLAMANN, K. 21, 108, 207, 208, 209
GLAMANN, K., and H. VAN DER WEE 4
GLASS, D. V. 24
GLASS, D. V., and D. E. C. EVERSLEY 24
GLASS, D. V., and E. GREBENIK 24
GLASS, D. V., and R. REVELLE 24
GLAZIER, I. A. 179
GLAZIER, I. A., and V. N. BANDERA 179
GLICKMAN, R. L. 162
GLIKSMAN, J. G. 162
GLYNN, S., and A. L. LOUGHEED 17
GNOINSKI, J. 132

GOBEL, F. 209
GODECHOT, J. 63
GODINHO, V. M. 190
GOLDBERG, H. 45
GOLDBERG, J. 132
GOLDIN, C. D. 10
GOLDMAN, M. 151
GOLDSHEIDER, C. 24
GOLDSMIDT, P. 103
GOLDSMITH, R. W. 141
GOLDSTEIN, E. R. 151
GOLDSTEIN, J. M. 141
GOLDWEISER, A. 156
GOLOB, E. O. 54
GOMEZ-MENDOZA, A. 16
GOMPERS, S. 28
GONZALEZ ENCISO, A., and J. PATRICIO MERINO 183
GOOD, D. F. 17, 114, 117, 119, 120, 122, 123
GOODWIN, A. 4, 32, 43
GOODY, J. 32
GOPAL, S. 158
GORDON, B. M. 122
GORDON, E. 32
GORDON, M. 162
GORDON, M. S. 21
GORDON, N. M. 85
GORECKI, R. 129
GOREUX, L. M. 43
GORLIN, R. H. 156
GORNI, O. 138, 183
GOTTLIEB, B. 71, 100
GOTTLIEB, L. R. 37
GOTTSCHALK, M. 28, 103
GOUBERT, P. 56, 63, 71
GOULD, J. D. 4, 24
GOUREVITCH, P. A. 54, 85
GOUTALIER, R. 21
GOVORCHIN, G. G. 135
GOY, J., and E. LE ROY LADURIE 10
GOZMAN, G. 166
GRABAU, T. W. 69
GRAFF, H. J. 32
GRAHAM, F. D. 90, 97
GRAMM, W. P. 4
GRANICK, D. 114, 151
GRANTHAM, G. W. 45, 46
GRAS, N. S. B. 10
GRASSBY, R. B. 63
GRASSMAN, S. 21
GRATZ, G. 123
GRATZ, G., and R. SCHULLER 121, 125
GREBING, H. 88
GREBLER, L. 12
GREBLER, L. 96
GREBLER, L., and W. WINKLER 82, 120
GREEN-PEDERSEN, S. E. 209
GREEN, A., and M. C. URQUHART 21
GREENBAUM, L. S. 64
GREENE, E. T. 91

GREENE, V. R. 131
GREENFIELD, K. R. 178, 182
GREENWOOD, D. J. 183, 186
GREER, D. 56
GREER, G. 48, 97
GREGOR, A. J. 176
GREGORY, D. D. 185
GREGORY, P. R. 142, 146, 156
GREGORY, P. R., and J. W. SAILORS 156
GREGORY, T. E. 17
GREKOV, B. D. 166
GRICE-HUTCHINSON, M. 186
GRICE, J. W. 52, 83, 102
GRIFFITHS, D. M. 171
GRIFFITHS, R. 57
GRIFFITHS, R. T. 105, 106
GRIGG, D. B. 10
GRIGORIAN, L. A. 168
GROSS, M. 136
GROSS, N. T. 114, 119, 120, 123
GROSSMAN, G. 142, 165
GRUBER, J. 127
GRULL, G. 120
GRUNBERGER, R. 88, 93
GRUNFELD, J. 90, 168
GRUNIG, F. 73
GRUNWALD, K. 83
GRUNWALD, M. 122
GRUTTNER, M. 93
GSOVSKI, V. 168
GUALTIERI, H. L. 180
GUBSKY, N. 146, 172
GUERIN, D. 99
GUERLAC, H. 43
GUIGNET, P. 57
GUILLEBAUD, C. W. 73, 96, 98
GUILLET, E. C. 24
GUILLOT-LAGEAT, G. 46
GUINN, W. K. 160
GULBERG, B., and B. ODEN 204
GULIK, C. A. 119
GULLICKSON, G. L. 57
GUNARSSON, G. 38
GUNST, P. 10, 114
GUPTA, S. P. 17
GUROFF, G. 168
GUROFF, G., and F. S. STARR 168
GURR, T. R. 206
GURVITCH, G. 64
GUSTAFSSON, B. 207
GUSTAFSSON, K. E. 205
GUTKIND, E. A. 30, 60, 91, 103, 110, 112, 118, 122, 126, 129, 132, 137, 138, 166, 181, 186, 191, 198, 206, 210
GUTMANN, M. P. 101, 103
GUTMANN, M. P., and E. VAN DE WALLE 104
GUTTMAN, W., and P. MECHAN 90
GUTTSMAN, W. L. 73
GUYE, R. 12, 32
GUYOT, Y. 12, 54

GYIMESI, S. 126

H.M.S.O. 142
HAAN, H. VON 128, 135
HABAKKUK, H. J. 4, 24, 32, 35
HABAKKUK, H. J., and M. M.
  POSTAN 4
HABER, L. F. 12, 13
HABERLER, G. 4
HACKMAN, W. D. 106
HAENSEL, P. P. 172
HAFTER, D. M. 48
HAGEN, E. E. 24
HAGEN, W. W. 129, 132
HAGERSTRAND, T. 208
HAHN, A. 78
HAHR, A. 206
HAIDER, C. 4, 99
HAIG, R. M. 52
HAIGH, B. 168
HAIGHT, F. A. 54
HAIMAN, M. 131
HAIMSON, L. H. 146, 168
HAINES, M. R. 24, 32, 76, 87
HAJDA, J. 129
HAJNAL, H. 117
HAJNAL, J. 24, 25
HALASZ, A. 114
HALE, F. 198
HALEVY, Z. 168
HALL, D. J. 138
HALL, P. 91
HALL, T. 206
HALLE, E. VON 78
HALLER, W. M. 78
HALLGARTEN, G. W. F. 78
HALPERN, J. M. 134, 136
HALPERN, J. M. and B. K. 134
HALSTEAD, J. L. 28
HAM, W. T. 89
HAMBURG, G. M. 168
HAMBURGER, L. 78, 89
HAMEROW, T. S. 73, 93
HAMILTON, E. J. 13, 21, 183,
  184, 185, 186
HAMILTON, F. E. I. 134, 135
HAMILTON, K. A. 54
HAMM, M. F. 166
HAMMARSTROM, I. 195, 202,
  206
HAMMARSTROM, I., and T.
  HALL 30
HAMMEL, E. A. 136
HAMMEN, O. J. 73
HAMMOND, R. J. 191
HAMMOND, T. T. 162
HAMMOND, W. E. 51, 82
HAMPSON, N. 64
HANAGAN, M. P. 57, 64
HANAK, P. 123
HANGLAND, K. 198
HANISCH, T. 195
HANNAH, L. 13, 78
HANS, N. 168
HANSEN, A. H. 4, 25, 73

HANSEN, B., and K. TOURK 51
HANSEN, E. 104, 105, 110, 111
HANSEN, E., and P. A.
  PROSPER 110
HANSEN, F. V. 202
HANSEN, H. O. 204, 209, 211,
  215
HANSEN, K. 93
HANSEN, M. L. 87
HANSEN, S. A. 208, 211
HANSON, C. A. 191
HANSSEN, B. 204
HANSSON, S. 205
HARDACH, G. 37
HARDACH, K. 74, 100
HARDENBERG, H. 112
HARDIE, D. W. F. 78
HARDT, H. 93
HARDT, J. P. 172
HARDT, J. P., and C.
  MODIG 142
HARKINS, J. R. 54
HARMAJA, L. 211
HARMS, R. 102
HARPER, G. T. 85, 183
HARPER, S. N. 156
HARRIGAN, P. J. 64, 70, 72
HARRIS, C. R. S. 98
HARRIS, J. R. 48
HARRIS, J. R., and PRIS, C. 48
HARRIS, L. 146
HARRIS, P. M. G. 32
HARRIS, R. C. 21
HARRIS, R. D. 52
HARRIS, S. E. 17, 52
HARRISON, A. 4
HARRISON, M. 146
HARRISON, R. J. 183, 184, 185,
  186, 187
HART, H. W. 82
HART, H., and H. HERTZ 93
HARTMAN, M. S. 64
HARTMANN, H. 78
HARTSOUGH, M. L. 78, 91
HARTWELL, R. M. 4, 13
HARVEY, C. E. 184
HARVEY, M. L., and M. J.
  RUGGLES 152
HASSBRING, L. 201
HASSELL, J. 168
HAUBEN, P. J. 183
HAUG, C. J. 60, 72
HAUGEN, E. 197
HAUNER, M. 99
HAUSER, H. 43, 78, 85
HAUSER, P. M. 25
HAUTALA, K. 194, 213
HAWTREY, R. G. 17, 52
HAXTHAUSEN, BARON A.
  VON 142
HAYASHI, K. 74
HAYENKO, F. 165
HAYWOOD, R. M. 154
HEADRICK, D. R. 21, 186
HEATH, J. S. C. 96

HEATON, H. 4
HECHTER, M. 32
HECKSCHER, E. F. 4, 21, 43,
  107, 193, 199, 202, 204, 207, 216
HEDIN, L. E. 202
HEDLUND-NYSTROM, T. 199,
  207
HEILBRONNER, H. 168
HEILPERIN, M. A. 29
HEINEMANN, J. L. 96
HELCZMANOVSKI, H. 121, 125
HELD, J. 124
HELIN, E. 104
HELLEINER, K. F. 25, 121
HELLER, A. A. 152
HELLER, C. S. 132
HELLERSTEIN, E. 64, 72
HELMREICH, J. E. 70
HENDERSON, W. O. 4, 13, 28,
  43, 54, 70, 74, 78, 79, 82, 85, 93,
  96, 98, 99, 112
HENDERSON, W. O., and W. H.
  CHALONER 48
HENRY, L. 56
HENSEL, J. 133
HEPPELL, M., and F. B.
  SINGLETON 134
HERBER, C. J. 122
HERBST, J. 89
HERLIHY, D. 30
HERLIHY, P. 138, 158, 160, 166
HERLITZ, F. 25
HERMALIN, A. I., and E. VAN
  DE WALLE 56
HERMAN, L. M. 158
HERMONIUS, E. 158
HERR, R. 183
HERSCH, L. 25, 28, 210
HERSHLAG, Z. Y. 36, 187
HERTZ, F. 114
HERTZEN, H. VON, and P. D.
  SPREIREGEN 214
HERWIG, H. H. 93
HESS, R. L. 179
HESSELBACH, W. 79
HEWES, A. 162
HEXNER, E. 13
HEYDEL, A. 131
HEYKING, A. B. 142
HEYL, J. D. 96
HEYMANN, H. 158
HEYWOOD, C. M. 48, 57
HICKEY, S. 89
HIDEN, J. W. 74
HIDY, R. 79
HIGGS, D. 46
HIGGS, H. 46
HILDEBRAND, G. H. 176
HILDEBRAND, K. E. H. 202
HILDEBRAND, K. G. 193, 199,
  202, 207
HILFERDING, R. 4
HILGENGA, J. 110
HILGERDT, F. 13
HILL, A. J. 217

HILL, J. W. 209, 216
HILL, M. 4
HILL, M. J. 69
HILL, R. L. 17
HILLMANN, H. C. 85
HILOWITZ, J. 177
HILTON YOUNG, E. 131
HIMMER, R. 85, 158
HINE, W. 146
HINGLEY, R. 168
HINSLEY, F. H. 4
HIRSCH, A. 142, 206
HIRSCH, E. and A. 188
HIRSCH, F., and P.
    OPPENHEIMER 18
HITCHINS, K. 138
HITTLE, J. M. 166
HJERPPE, R. 212
HJERPPE, R., and E.
    PIKHALA 211
HOBSBAWM, E. J. 4, 147
HOBSBAWM, E. J., and J. W.
    SCOTT 32
HOBSON, J. A. 35
HOCEVAR, T. 35, 134, 136
HOCH, S. L., and W. R.
    AUGUSTINE 160
HODGMAN, D. R. 152
HODNE, F. 196, 198
HODNE, F., and O.
    GJOLBERG 196
HODSON, W. V. 4
HOEFFDING, O. 142, 173
HOEFFDING, W. 85, 158
HOFFDING, V. 162
HOFFMAN, G. W. 134, 137
HOFFMAN, P. E. 187
HOFFMAN, R. J. S. 85
HOFFMAN, S. R. 43
HOFFMANN, W. G. 4, 74
HOFFNER, C. 29
HOFSTEE, E. W. 110
HOFSTEN, E. 204
HOFSTEN, E., and H.
    LUNDSTROM 204
HOGAN, M. J. 37
HOGBERG, S. 202
HOHENBERG, P. M. 4, 13, 46
HOLBORN, H. A. 74
HOLDSWORTH, M. 142
HOLGERSSON, B. 200
HOLGERSSON, B., and E.
    NICANDER 202
HOLLAN, A. 125
HOLLINGSWORTH, B. 168, 174
HOLMSEN, A. 196
HOLT, R. 64
HOLTFRERICH, C. L. 90
HOLTON, R. J. 32
HOLUBNYCHY, V. 152, 174
HOLZMAN, F. D. 152, 156, 165
HOME, R. W. 168
HOMZE, E. L. 79, 89
HONEYCUTT, K. 93
HONIGSHEIM, P. 147

HOOKER, A. A. 21
HOOVER, C. B. 142, 172
HOPE, T. J. 138
HOPFINGER, K. B. 79
HORN, N., and J. KOCKA 13, 49,
    74, 79
HORNBY, O. 208
HORNBY, O., and C. A.
    NILSSON 208
HORNBY, O., and G. V.
    MOGENSEN 211
HORNER, J. 13
HOROWITZ, D. L. 180
HORSEFIELD, J. K. 18
HORSFALL, T. C. 93
HORVATH, J. 123
HORVATH, R. 123, 125, 126
HOSELITZ, B. 36, 49
HOSTETTER, R. 180
HOUMANIDIS, L. 21
HOURWICH, I. A. 142, 147
HOVANNISIAN, R. G. 142
HOVDE, B. J. 193, 194, 195
HOWARD, E. D. 79
HOWARD, J. J. 181
HOWORTH, J., and P. G.
    CERNY 64
HRISTOV, A. 134
HRUSHEVSKY, M. 142
HRUZA, J. 129
HUBBARD, J. R. 185
HUBBARD, L. E. 147, 156, 158,
    162
HUBBARD, W. H. 122
HUERTAS, T. F. 119
HUFTON, O. 32, 46, 60, 64
HUGGETT, F. E. 10
HUGHES, D. J. 93
HUGHES, J. R. T. 4, 36
HUGHES, M. 90
HUGHES, T. P. 79
HUMPHREYS, R. A. 191
HUNCZAK, T. 158
HUNDERT, G. 133
HUNT, D. 64
HUNT, J. C. 76, 85
HUNT, P. 58
HUNT, V. R. 28
HUNTER, H. 142, 154, 173
HUNTER, J. C. 56
HUNTINGDON, W. C. 158
HURST, W. 102, 107, 112
HURT, B. 172
HURWITZ, E. F. 32
HUSI-HUEY LIANG 93
HUSS, E. G. 207
HUSSEY, R. D. 185
HUSSEY, R. D., and J. S.
    BROMLEY 185
HUSTON, J. A. 74
HUTCHINGS, R. 142, 152
HUTCHINSON, E. P. 25, 204
HUTCHINSON, J. F. 168
HUTT, W. H. 165
HVIDSTEN, J. 198

HVIDT, K. 25, 210
HVIDT, K., and H. A.
    BARTON 194
HYLDTOFT, O. 210
HYRENIUS, H. 204
HYVONEN, V. 212

IGGERS, G. G., and H. T.
    PARKER 38
ILIASU, A. A. 54
ILLES, A. E., and A.
    HALASZ 123
IMHOF, A. E. 87, 93, 100, 198,
    211
IMHOF, A. E., and O.
    LARSEN 195
IMLAH, A. G. 112
INALCIK, H. 188, 189
INCZE, M. 126
INGRAHAM, B. L. 64, 93
INNIS, H. A. 185
INSTITUTE FOR SOCIAL
    SCIENCES 204, 205
INSTITUTE OF
    CONJECTURE 142
INTERNATIONAL
    CONFERENCE OF ECONOMIC
    SERVICES 4, 39
INTERNATIONAL ECONOMIC
    HISTORY ASSOCIATION 4
INTERNATIONAL INSTITUTE
    OF AGRICULTURE 10
INTERNATIONAL LABOUR
    OFFICE 5, 13, 25, 28, 29, 32,
    49, 76, 89, 110, 112, 116, 126, 127,
    137, 142, 147, 162, 165, 168, 173,
    205, 210, 214, 217, 219
ISAAC, J. E. 25
ISHERWOOD, R. M. 64
ISHIZAKA, A. 102
ISSAWI, C. 187
IUGOV, A. 142
IVANYI, B. G. 123
IVERSON, C. 18

JACK, D. T. 18
JACKSON, G. 183
JACKSON, G. D. 116
JACKSON, J. H. 93
JACKSON, R. V. 16
JACOBS, N. 94
JACOBS, R. L. 90
JACOBSSON, P. 18
JAEGER, H. 100
JAFFE, W. 112
JAGER, J. J. 203
JAHODA, M. 122
JAKOBCZYK, W. 130
JALLINOJA, R. 214
JAMES, H. 79, 96
JANKOWSKI, M. D. 79
JANSEN, J. C. G. M. 101, 106
JANSEN, P. 111
JANSON, F. E. 204
JARAUSCH, K. H. 94

JARVESOO, E. 168, 217, 218
JASNEY, M. P. 76
JASNY, N. 142, 147, 152, 165, 172, 173
JATSUNSKY, V. K. 142
JEDLICKI, J. 130, 131
JEDRUSZCZAK, H. 116
JEFFERSON, C. 70
JEFFERSON, M. 29, 39
JELAVICH, B. 114, 134
JELAVICH, C. 134
JELAVICH, C. and B. 114, 118
JEMNITZ, J. 28
JENNINGS, L. C. 54, 55
JENNISON, E. W. 97, 218
JENSEN, A. 194
JENSEN, C., and D. BITTON 64
JENSEN, E. 208
JENSEN, J. H., and G. ROSEGGER 117, 137, 138
JEQUIER, F. 112
JEROME, H. 25
JERRAM, C. B. 217
JEWKES, J. 5
JEWSIEWICKI, B. 102
JEZE, G. 52
JEZIERSKI, A. 131
JOHANNESSON, P. 215
JOHANSEN, H. C. 195, 210, 211
JOHANSSON, A. 205
JOHANSSON, E. 206
JOHANSSON, O. 199
JOHN, B. H. 97
JOHNSEN, A. O. 196
JOHNSON, A. M. 168
JOHNSON, C. H. 46, 58, 72
JOHNSON, D. 64
JOHNSON, H. G. 35, 98
JOHNSON, R. E. 160, 162
JOHNSON, W. E. 168
JOHNSTON, C. 85, 147, 158
JOLAS, T., and F. ZONABEND 46
JOLL, J. 38
JONES, A. N. 60
JONES, C. 64
JONES, E. 13
JONES, E. L. 5, 32, 36
JONES, E. L., and S. J. WOOLF 10
JONES, L. E. 90
JONES, M. 213
JONES, P. M. 46, 64
JONES, R. A., and R. M. ANSERVITZ 69
JONES, R. E. 147, 168
JONES, R. L., and K. W. SWART 104, 112
JONG, T. P. M. DE 108
JONGE, J. A. DE 105
JONUNG, L. 207
JONUNG, L., and E. WADENSJO 205
JORAVSKY, D. 147
JORBERG, L. 193, 196, 199, 201, 205, 208, 211
JORBERG, L., and O. KRANTZ 193, 196, 199, 208, 212
JORBERG, L., and T. BENGTSSON 205
JORDAN, W. M. 55, 98
JORGENSEN, J. 210
JOSEFFSON, M., and J. ORTENGREN 199
JOSTOCK, P. 74
JUCKER-FLEETWOOD, E. E. 203
JUDT, T. 46, 58
JURGELA, C. T. 219
JUST, C. F. 158
JUSTESEN, O. 209
JUTIKKALA, E. 206, 212, 213, 214
JUTIKKALA, E., and K. PIRINEN 212
JUTIKKALA, E., and M. KAUPPINEN 213
JUTILA, K. T. 212

KAARTREDT, A. 196
KACHOROVSKY, K. 147
KADOMSTEV, B. 152
KAELBLE, H. 30, 38, 49, 79, 94
KAFENGANZ, B. B. 142
KAGAN, R. L. 64
KAGANOVICH, L. M. 166
KAHAN, A. 10, 35, 116, 142, 147, 152, 156, 158, 162, 168, 172, 174
KAHK, J. 174, 217
KAHK, J., and H. LIGI 217
KAHK, J., and I. KOVALCHENKO 147
KAIN, R. 10
KAISER, C. 64
KAISER, D. E. 37
KALDOR, N. 119
KALECKI, M. 69
KALINOWSKI, W. 132
KALLY, I. 124
KALVEMARK, A. S. 204
KAMEN, H. 183, 186
KAMENDROWSKY, V. 156
KAMENKA, E., and F. B. SMITH 32
KAMINSKI, A. 130, 219
KAMPP, A. H. 215
KAMPP, A. H., and K. RIKKINEN 212
KANIPE, E. S. 64
KANN, R. A. 119, 122, 124, 129
KANT, E. 217
KAPLAN, N. M. 154
KAPLAN, S. L. 43, 46, 64
KAPLAN, T. 186
KAPLOW, J. 64
KAPP, K. W. 5
KARADY, V. 70
KARCZ, J. F. 147
KARKAR, Y. N. 117, 187, 188

KARLBOM, R. 203
KARPAT, K. H. 187
KASER, M. C. 142, 152, 159, 165, 173
KASER, M. C., and E. A. RADICE 114
KATKOFF, V. 147
KATKOV, G. 142
KATUS, L. 124
KATZ, B. G. 142
KATZENBACK, E. L. 69
KATZENELLENBAUM, S. S. 156
KATZENELLENBOGEN, S. E. 85
KAUFMAN, A. 152
KAUKIAINEN, Y. 213
KAWANO, K. 43
KAYDEN, E. M. 156, 174
KAZAKEVICH, V. D. 142
KAZEMZADEH, F. 159
KAZGAN, G. 189
KECHOVA, A. 131
KEENE, C. A. 179
KEEP, J. 142, 169, 174
KEHR, E. 74
KEIGHLY, J. B. 206
KELE, M. H. 89
KELLENBENZ, H. 13, 16
KELLER, M. 13, 49
KELLEY, A. C. 25
KELLY, W. J. 152, 154
KELLY, W. J., and T. KANO 152
KELSO, M. R. 58
KEMENY, J. 133
KEMP, T. 5, 43
KENNEDY, K. H. 208
KENNEDY, P. M. 85
KENT, H. S. K. 194, 197
KENT, M. 188
KENWOOD, A. G., and A. L. LOUGHEED 5, 13
KERNER, R. J. 119, 127, 154, 189
KERO, R. 213
KERTZER, D. I. 182
KESSLER, W. C. 79
KEYDER, C. 187
KEYNES, J. M. 37, 74, 98
KIENIEWICZ, S., and H. WERESZYCKI 129
KIENIEWICZ, S. 130
KIERNAN, V. 21
KIESWETTER, H. 90
KIISKINEN, A. 212
KILDEBRAND, K. G. 202
KILOSSA, T. 126
KIMBALL, A. 147
KIMBALL, S. B. 122
KIMMICH, C. M. 74
KINDLEBERGER, C. P. 5, 13, 18, 21, 25, 43, 52, 69, 70, 74, 199, 209
KING, R. 180
KINGSBURY, S. M., and M. FAIRCHILD 162, 169

KINGSTON-MANN, E.   147
KIPP, J. W.   172
KIRALY, B. K.   37, 124, 126
KIRALY, B. K., and G. E.
   ROTHENBERG   114
KIRBY, D.   194, 214, 216
KIRCHNER, W.   21, 85, 152, 159
KIREEV, N. G.   159, 188
KIRK, D.   25, 56
KIRKPATRICK, C.   94
KIRSCHBAUM, J. K.   127
KISCH, C. H.   191
KISCH, H.   49, 79
KISS, I. N.   29, 126
KITAMURA, J.   79, 85
KITCHEN, M.   74, 99
KJAERHEIM, S.   197
KJARTANSSON, H. S.   215
KJELLSTOM, E. J. H.   202
KLANG, D. M.   179
KLASS, G. VON   79
KLEIN, B. H.   74
KLEIN, H. S.   191
KLEIN, J.   183
KLEIN, J. J.   83
KLEIN, P. W.   105
KLEP, P. W. W.   103
KLEZL, F.   121
KLIMA, A.   13, 117, 127, 128, 129
KLIMESZ, H.   131
KLINGE, M.   214
KLINGMAN, D., and G. B.
   PETERS   193
KLIUCHEVSKII, V. O.   143
KLOBERDANZ, T. J.   87
KLOMPMAKER, H.   112
KNAPP, J.   122
KNAPP, V. J.   28
KNAPTON, D. R.   72
KNAUERHASE, R.   82, 83, 99
KNICKERBOCKER, H. R.   174
KNIGHT-PATTERSON, W. M.
   74
KNIGHT, C.   165
KNIGHT, M. M.   5
KNODEL, J.   25, 87
KNODEL, J., and C. WILSON   87
KNODEL, J., and E. SHORTER
   87
KNODEL, J., and E. VAN DE
   WALLE   87
KNODEL, J., and M. J.
   MAYNES   87
KNODEL, J., and S. DEVOS   87
KNOEFEL, P. K.   182
KNOLL, A. J.   85
KNOPPERS, J.   108, 159, 194
KNOWLES, L.   5, 43
KOBLIK, S.   199
KOCHAN, L.   143
KOCHAN, M.   169
KOCK, K.   199
KOCKA, J.   79, 89, 100, 123
KOEBNER, R.   21
KOEHL, R. L.   99

KOENKER, D.   166
KOEPKE, R. L.   49
KOFAS, J. V.   189
KOFOS, E.   189
KOHLER, E. D.   97
KOHLER, G.   156
KOHN, S., and A. S.
   MEYENDORFF   156
KOISTINEN, P. A. C.   13
KOKOVTSEV, COUNT V.   156
KOLCHIN, P.   172
KOLEHMAINEN, J. I.   213
KOLLMANN, W.   79, 87, 91
KOLOSSA, T.   123
KOLZ, A. W. F.   159
KOMLOS, J.   83, 119, 120, 124,
   127
KONINCKX, C.   203
KONONENKO, K.   143
KOOIJ, P.   30
KOOP, P. A.   161
KOOY, M.   5
KORNILOWICZ, M.   129
KOROPECKYJ, I. S.   152, 172
KORPELAINEN, L.   214
KORROS, A. S.   147
KOSA, J.   125
KOSHKARYOVA, L.   161
KOSLOW, J.   147
KOSSMAN, E. H.   101, 105
KOSTOF, S.   181
KOUTAISSOFF, E.   152
KOVACS, A.   125
KOVACSICS, J.   25, 125
KOVALCHENKO, I. D.   143
KOVALCHENKO, I. D., and L. M.
   BORODKIN   147
KOVALCHENKO, I. D., and N. B.
   SELUNSKAIA   163
KOVRIG, B.   126
KOZMIN, P. A.   143
KRALJIC, F.   135
KRANTZ, O.   201, 202
KRANTZ, O., and C. A.
   NILSSON   195, 199
KRANZBERG, M., and C.
   PURSELL   5
KRAVIS, I. B.   21
KRAVIS, I. B., and J.
   MINTZES   165
KRAWCHENKO, B.   169
KRESL, P. K.   172
KRIEDTE, P.   13
KRIVICKAS, V.   219
KRIZ, M. A.   18
KRONBORG, B.   194
KRUIJT, B.   110
KRYNSKI, G. I.   152
KRYPTON, C.   154
KUCHAROV, S.   159
KUCZYNSKI, J.   28, 58, 74, 89,
   99, 163
KUCZYNSKI, J., and M.
   WITT   99
KUCZYNSKI, R. R.   25, 83, 88, 90

KUDRYAVTSEV, A.   169
KUISEL, R. F.   43, 49, 69
KUJALA, A.   214
KUKLINSKA, K.   118, 131
KULA, W.   130
KULISCHER, E. M.   25
KULKARNI, A. R.   191
KULSTEIN, D. I.   58
KUMAR, J.   204, 213
KURGANOV, I.   172
KUUSE, J.   199, 201, 203, 207
KUZNETS, S.   5, 18, 21, 25, 29,
   38, 39
KYRKILITSIS, A.   189

LA BERGE, A. F.   64
LA FORCE, J. C.   184
LABEDZ, L.   172
LABISCH, A.   89
LABORDERE, M.   52
LABROUSSE, E.   43, 46, 72
LABSVIRS, J.   218
LAFFERTY, W. M.   195
LAFFEY, J. F.   55, 60
LAGO, A. M.   36
LAIRD, R. D.   147
LAMAR, C.   82
LAMB, E.   174
LAMBERT, A. M.   106
LAMBI, I. N.   76, 79, 86
LAMET, S.   152
LAMFALUSSY, A.   102
LAMONT, T.   98
LAMPARD, E. E.   30
LAMPE, J. R.   114, 118, 119, 134,
   135, 137, 138
LAMPE, J. R., and M. R.
   JACKSON   115, 119
LANDAU, Z., and J.
   TOMASZEWSKI   129
LANDAU, L.   131
LANDER, J. E.   5
LANDES, D. S.   5, 13, 43, 49, 52,
   72, 74, 79, 94, 112
LANDSBERGER, H. A.   10, 118
LANE, B. M.   30, 91
LANE, F. C.   35, 179
LANE, F. C., and J. C.
   RIEMERSMA   13
LANE, R.   206
LANGE, E.   196
LANGE, O.   209
LANGE, P., and S. TARROW   182
LANGER, L. N.   174
LANGER, W. L.   25
LANGHOLM, S.   197, 198
LANTHIER, P.   49
LANTSEV, M.   163
LANTZEFF, G. V., and R. A.
   PIERCE   161
LAQUEUR, T. W.   70
LARNA, K.   213
LASLETT, P.   25, 32
LASLETT, P., and M.
   CLARKE   136

LASSEN, A. 210
LASZCZYNSKI, S. 129, 130
LAUGHLIN, L. J. 156
LAURENT, R. 72
LAURSEN, K., and J.
  PEDERSEN 90
LAUX, J. M. 49
LAUX, W. E. 211
LAVELEYE, E. L. V. DE 101,
  106
LAVES, W. H. G. 86
LAVRICHEV, V. Y. 152
LAWLEY, F. E. 5
LAWRENCE, P. A. 83
LAWTON, L. 143
LAYTON, W., and C. RIST 119
LE DONNE, J. P. 156, 169
LE GOFF, T. J. A. 49, 61
LE GOFF, T. J. A., and D. M. G.
  SUTHERLAND 46
LE GUIN, C. A. 46
LE ROY LADURIE, E. 10, 38, 46
LE ROY LADURIE, E., and J.
  GOY 10, 46
LE ROY LADURIE, E., and M.
  BAULANT 10
LEACH, R. H. 105
LEADENHAM, C. A. 174
LEAGUE OF NATIONS 5, 6, 10,
  14, 16, 18, 21, 22, 29, 37, 39, 40,
  115, 120, 125, 147, 217
LEASURE, J. W., and R. A.
  LEWIS 161
LEASURE, W. 185
LEBOVICS, H. 74
LEDERER, M. 119
LEE, E. S. 25
LEE, F. E. 174
LEE, J. J. 89, 91, 97
LEE, R. D. 25
LEE, W. R. 25, 74, 88, 94, 100
LEES, A. 91, 94
LEES, A. and L. 31
LEES, L. 61
LEET, D. R., and D. A.
  SHAW 43
LEFEBVRE, G. 43, 46, 61
LEFFLER, M. P. 6, 44
LEFGREN, J. 212
LEFRANC, G. 51
LEGMAN, D. 89
LEGOUIS, J. 103
LEHFELDT, R. A. 18
LEHNING, J. R. 64
LEIBENSTEIN, H. 25
LEIFMANN, R. 14
LEITES, K. 143
LEITSCH, W. 169
LEMEY, E. 65
LENGYEL, E. 125
LENIN, V. I. 152
LENZI, L. 181
LEON, G. B. 189
LEONARD, C. M. 61
LEONTIEF, W. W. 152

LEQUIN, F. 108
LEQUIN, Y. 58
LERCH, O. 65
LESKIEWICZ, J. 130
LESLIE, J. E. P., and W. J.
  SULLIVAN 217
LESLIE, R. F. 129, 219
LESLIE, T. E. C. 46
LESTER, R. A. 194, 197, 202
LESTHAEGHE, R. J. 103
LESTRADE, C. 147
LETICHE, J. M. 174
LEUILLIOT, P. 72
LEVANDIS, J. A. 190
LEVASSEUR, E. 147
LEVI-STRAUSS, L., and H.
  MENDRAS 72
LEVIN, A. 169
LEVINE, D. 210
LEVINE, I. D. 216
LEVINE, I. R. 163
LEVY-LEBOYER, M. 44, 49
LEVY-LEBOYER, M., and P.
  BAIROCH 6
LEVY, H. 14, 79
LEWALSKI, K. F. 133
LEWERY, L. J. 156
LEWIN, M. 147, 148, 172, 174
LEWIS, B. 187
LEWIS, B. W. 97
LEWIS, C. 22
LEWIS, C., and J. C.
  MCCLELLAND 86
LEWIS, G. 120
LEWIS, M. J. T. 14
LEWIS, R. A. 152
LEWIS, R. A., and J. W.
  LEASURE 161
LEWIS, R. A., and R. H.
  ROWLAND 161
LEWIS, R. D. 132
LEWIS, W. A. 6, 22, 40
LEWIS, W. A., and P. J.
  O'LEARY 6, 40
LEWITTER, L. R. 172
LIDTKE, V. 94
LIEBEL, H. 91
LIEBEL, H. P. 94, 117, 121
LIEBERMAN, S. 6, 196, 197
LIEBMAN, R. 58
LIEBOWITZ, J. J. 44, 74
LIEDSTRAND, E. 206
LIEFMANN, R. 80
LIEPMAN, H. 22
LIEPMANN, K. 32
LIESSE, A. 52
LIFKA, M. L. 58
LILLEY, S. 14
LINCOLN, W. B. 130, 166, 169,
  174
LIND, G. 208, 211
LINDAHL, E. 199
LINDAHL, O. 199
LINDBERG, J. 28
LINDBERG, J. S. 204

LINDBLAD, T. 107, 202
LINDEN, G. 206
LINDENMEYR, A. 166
LINDERT, P. 18
LINDGREN, H. 201
LINDGREN, R. E. 193
LINDSAY, J. O. 6, 32
LINK, E. M. 120
LIPSIUS, F. 126
LIS, C., and H. SOLY 32, 103
LITCHFIELD, R. B. 182
LITCHFIELD, R. B., and D.
  GORDON 65
LITHUANIAN INFORMATION
  BUREAU 219
LITOSHENKO, L. N. 143
LITTLEPAGE, J. D., and B.
  DEMAREE 156
LIVEANU, V. 138
LIVERMORE, H. V. 191
LIVI BACCI, M. 180, 185, 191
LJUNGMARK, L. 194
LLOYD GEORGE, D. 37, 98
LLOYD, G. I. H. 89
LLOYD, T. 143
LOBANOV-ROSTOVSKY, A. 159
LOCHORE, R. A. 25
LOCKE, R. R. 49
LOCKRIDGE, K. A. 25
LODGE, E. C. 69
LODGE, O. 118, 134
LODGE, R. 191
LODHI, A. O., and C. TILLY 65
LOFGREN, O. 193
LOGAN, T. H. 91
LOGIO, G. C. 137, 138
LOKKE, C. L. 55
LOKSHIN, E. 152
LONG, D. C. 55, 86, 120, 121
LONG, J. W. 52, 76, 148, 156, 159
LONGFELLOW, D. 58
LONGFIELD, A. K. 185, 191
LONGWIRTH, P. 169
LONSDALE, R. E. 152
LOORITS, O. 217
LOPASHICH, A. 136
LOPATA, H. L. 131
LOPES, R. P. 32
LORCH, A. 32
LORENCE, B. W. 33
LORIMER, F. 161
LORSCHEIDER, H. M. 86, 135
LORWIN, L. L. 35, 58
LORWIN, L. L., and A.
  ABRAMSON 143
LORWIN, V. R. 28, 58
LOTZ, W. 80
LOUBERE, L. A. 46, 58, 178
LOUGES, C. C. 70
LOVEDAY, A. 22, 83
LOVETT, C. M. 182
LOVIN, C. R. 76, 119
LOWENSTEIN, S. M. 94
LOZOVSKY, A. 163
LUCAS, H. S. 110

LUDKIEWICZ, Z. 46, 130
LUNDBERG, E. 6, 207
LUNDEN, K. 196
LUNDEN, T. 206
LUNDGREEN, P. 80
LUNDIN, C. L. 212
LUNDKVIST, S. 206
LUNDSTROM, J. 201
LURAGHI, R. 180
LURIE, S. 83
LUTGE, F. 99
LUTHY, H. 22
LUTZ, H. L. 37
LUTZ, V. 177
LUZA, R. 86, 121
LUZZATTO, G. 177
LYASHCHENKO, P. I. 143, 148
LYNCH, J. 185
LYNCH, K. A. 28, 65
LYONS, E. 163

MACARTNEY, C. A. 115, 119, 122, 124
MACCLINTOCK, S. 52
MACDERMOTT, M. 137
MACDONALD, C. A. 74
MACDONALD, J. S. 178, 180
MACDONALD, J. S. and L. D. 178, 180
MACEDONIAN REVIEW EDITIONS 136
MACGREGOR, D. H. 80
MACIVER, R. M. 6
MACKENZIE, D. 134, 143
MACKENZIE, K. 52, 83
MACKRELL, J. Q. C. 46
MACLEOD, R. and K. 14
MACMILLAN, D. S. 159
MACURA, M. 26
MACZAK, A. 6, 22, 115, 130
MACZAK, A., and W. N. PARKER 6
MADARIAGA, I. 143, 148
MADDISON, A. 6, 14, 35, 40, 143
MADGEARU, V. 138
MADISON, B. 169
MADUROWICZ-URBANSKA, H. 130
MAEHL, W. H. 89, 97
MAGNUS, E. 28
MAIER, C. 74
MAIER, C. S. 6, 14, 29, 37
MAITRA, P. 6
MAIZELS, A. 22
MAJORAL, R. 185
MAKKAI, L. 116
MAKLAKOV, B. 148
MAKLAKOV, V. 148
MAKSIMOVIC, B. 135
MALCOLMSON, R. W. 33
MALE, D. J. 148
MALEFAKIS, E. E. 183
MALENBAUM, M. 22
MALLIA-MILANES, V. 179, 192

MAMATEY, V. S. 127
MAMATEY, V. S., and R. LUZA 127
MANCERON, C. 65
MANCHESTER, W. 80
MANDEL, E. 6
MANDELBAUM, K. 75
MANELIS, V. 219
MANNICHE, P. 211
MANNING, R. T. 172
MANTELLI, R. 186
MANTOUX, E. 98
MARBURG, T. F. 97
MARCELLETTI, M. 177
MARCU, P. 138
MARCZEWSKI, J. 44
MARGADANT, T. W. 46, 58, 65, 71
MARINESCU, B. 138
MARJOLIN, R. 69
MARKKANEN, E. 214
MARKOVITCH, T. J. 49
MARKS, S. 98
MARKUS, B. L. 163
MARRUS, M. R. 65
MARSCHALK, P. 26
MARTEL, G. 82
MARTIN, B. F. 65
MARTIN, D. A. 18
MARTIN, E. W. 33
MARTIN, G. 44
MARTIN, K., and F. G. THACKERAY 22
MARTIN, P. W. 35
MARTINES, L. 179
MARTINIUS, S. 206
MARTNA, W. 217
MARWICK, A. 37
MARZ, E. 115, 119
MASCHKE, E. 80
MASON, T. 89, 99
MASON, T. W. 37
MASUR, G. 91
MATASSI, L. 177
MATHIAS, P. 14, 33
MATHIAS, P., and M. M. POSTAN 6
MATHIAS, P., and P. O'BRIEN 52
MATOLESY, M., and S. VARGA 124
MATOSSIAN, M. K., and W. D. SCHAFER 65
MATTHEWS, G. T. 52
MATTHIESSEN, P. C. 210
MATTHIESSEN, P. C., and J. C. MCCANN 26
MATZERATH, H. 92
MAUCO, G. 56, 58
MAURETTE, F. 28, 69
MAURO, F. 22
MAURO, F., and J. O'LEARY 22
MAVOR, J. 143
MAY, A. J. 117, 119, 120, 124, 131, 135

MAY, E. 166
MAYER, A. J. 6, 33
MAYER, J. 191
MAYER, K. B. 112
MAYEUR, F. 65
MAYHEW, A. 77
MAYNARD, G. 143
MAYNARD, J. 143
MAYNES, M. J. 33, 65, 71, 94
MAYZEL, M. 169
MAZOUR, A. G. 143
MAZUV, D. P. 161
MCARDLE, F. 182
MCBRIDE, T. M. 58, 65
MCCAGG, W. O. 126
MCCAULEY, M. 143
MCCLELLAN, W. D. 136
MCCLELLAND, C. 94
MCCLELLAND, J. C. 169
MCCLOSKEY, D. N. 52
MCCLOY, S. T. 65, 69, 71
MCCOLLIM, G. 52
MCCONAGHA, W. A. 58, 89
MCCORMMACH, R. 94
MCCREARY, E. C. 94
MCCUSKER, J. J. 18, 40
MCDONALD, F. 46
MCDOUGALL, M. L. 58, 65
MCDOUGALL, W. A. 44, 98
MCFARLIN, H. A. 163
MCGOWAN, B. 115, 187
MCGREW, R. E. 157, 169, 174
MCGREW, W. M. 190
MCGUIRE, G. E. 177
MCHALE, V. E., and E. A. JOHNSON 94
MCINTOSH, D. C. 98
MCINTYRE, R. J. 137
MCKAY, A. 187
MCKAY, D. C. 49
MCKAY, J. P. 16, 152
MCKEOWN, T. 26
MCKINSEY, P. S. 163
MCLACHLAN, J. O. 185
MCLAREN, A. 65, 69
MCLEAN, D. 188
MCMILLAN, J. F. 65
MCNEILL, W. H. 14, 26, 115, 124, 179
MCNEILL, W. H., and M. KAMMEN 38
MCNEILL, W. H., and R. S. ADAMS 26
MCPHEE, P. 61, 65
MEAD, W. R. 212, 213
MEADE, J. E. 102
MEAKIN, W. 14
MEARS, E. G. 187
MEDALEN, C. 80
MEDICK, H. 33
MEEHAN-WATERS, B. 169, 172
MEIER, G. M. 6
MEIER, G. M., and R. O. BALDWIN 7
MEIJ, J. L. 10

MEININGER, T. A. 137
MEISEL, J. H., and E. S. KOZERA 175
MEISSNER, F. 127
MELIK, A. 135
MELLER, H. 31
MELLOR, J. W. 10
MELNYK, Z. L. 157
MELSON, K. L. 75
MELTING, R. M. 112
MELVN, F. E. 51
MENDEL, A. 80
MENDEL, A. P. 118, 163, 172
MENDELS, F. F. 7, 14, 26, 33, 38, 101, 103
MENDELS, F. F., and L. K. BERKNER 33
MENDELSOHN, E. 163
MENDERSHAUSEN, H. 14, 37, 75
MENDRAS, H. 46
MENNING, B. 169
MEQUET, G. 33, 169
MEREDITH, H. O. 55
MERITT, H. P. 86
MERKIN, G. 91
MERLIN, S. 97
MERRIMAN, J. M. 33, 58, 61, 65
MERRINGTON, J. 31
METHORST, H. W. 110
METZER, J. 154
MEUVRET, J. 7, 44, 56
MEYER, H. C. 117
MEYER, R. H. 18
MEYERS, P. V. 71
MIASO, J. 133
MICHELSON, A. M. 157
MICHELSON, W. 211
MIDDELHOVEN, P. J. 110
MIDLAND BANK REVIEW 91
MIECZKOWSKI, Z. 143
MIKLASHEVSKY, A. 157
MIKOLETZKY, L. 121, 159
MILEYKOVSKY, A. 33
MILGRIM, M. R. 159, 188
MILKEREIT, G. 80
MILLAR, J. R. 148
MILLAR, J. R., and C. A. GUNTZEL 175
MILLAR, J. R., and D. BAHRY 157
MILLER, B. 186
MILLER, H. E. 53
MILLER, H. S. 179
MILLER, J. 165, 174
MILLER, J. W. 97
MILLER, M. S. 143, 157, 159, 174
MILLER, R. F. 148
MILLER, W. 187, 190
MILWARD, A. S. 75, 199
MILWARD, A. S., and S. B. SAUL 7
MINCHINTON, W. E. 22, 29
MINCHINTON, W. E., and E. E. WILLIAMS 86

MINGE-KALMAN, W. 33
MINISTRY OF AGRICULTURE 217
MINISTRY OF AGRICULTURE (ESTONIA) 217
MINISTRY OF TRADE AND INDUSTRY 217
MINKES, A. L. 117
MINKOFF, J. 143
MIQUELON, D. 55
MIRINGOFF, M. L. 94
MIRONENKO, Y. 161
MIRONOV, B. N. 165
MIRSKI, M. S. 154
MIRSKY, D. P. 169
MISES, L. VON 121, 125
MISHEV, D. 137
MISHINSKY, M. 28
MISIUNAS, R. J. 219
MITCHELL, A. R. 10
MITCHELL, B. R. 7, 40
MITCHELL, H. 65
MITCHELL, H., and P. N. STEARNS 28
MITCHISON, R. 193
MITNITZKY, M. 124
MITRANY, D. 115, 138
MITTELMAN, E. B. 89
MITTERAUER, M., and R. SIEDER 33
MITZMAN, A. 58
MIXTER, T. 163
MLYNARSKI, F. 131
MOCH, L. P. 56
MODIG, H. 202, 203
MOE, T. 196
MOELLER, R. G. 77
MOGENSEN, G. V. 211
MOGENSEN, W. 65
MOGGRIDGE, D. E. 18
MOISUC, V., and I. CALAFETEANU 115
MOKYR, J. 7, 101, 104, 105, 111
MOLENDA, D. 118
MOLINARI, A. 177
MOLLER, A. M. 209
MOLLER, H. 26
MOLODOWSKY, N. 86
MOMMSEN, W. J. 86, 94
MOMMSEN, W. J., and G. HIRSCHFELD 33
MOMTCHILOFF, N. 117
MONACO, P. 65, 94
MONNET, G. 69
MONROE, A. E. 53
MONROE, W. S. 137
MONTELIUS, S. 205
MONTER, E. W. 113
MONTGOMERY GROVE, H. 217
MONTGOMERY, A. 143, 194
MONTGOMERY, B. G. 58, 195
MONTGOMERY, G. A. 199, 201
MONZELIS, N. 137
MOODY, V. A. 10
MOON, P. T. 98

MOON, S. J. 58
MOORE, W. E. 118
MOORSTEEN, R. H. 153
MOORSTEEN, R. H., and R. P. POWELL 143
MORAVCIK, I. 172
MORCH, H. 210
MOREDA, V. P. 187
MORELL, M. 206
MORGADO, N. A. 191
MORGAN, O. S. 116
MORGENSTERN, O. 18
MORI, G. 14, 177
MORICZ, M. 126
MORIER, R. D. B. 77
MORINEAU, M. 46
MORK, G. R. 82
MORNER, M. 26, 206
MORRISON, R. J. 102, 209
MORROW, D. W. 191
MORROW, J. H. 80
MOSK, C. 204
MOSKALENKO, G. K. 163
MOSS, B. H. 58
MOSSE, W. E. 97, 143, 148, 154, 169
MOULTON, H. G. 7, 37, 98
MOULTON, H. G., and C. E. MCGUIRE 98
MOULTON, H. G., and C. LEWIS 53
MOULTON, H. G., and L. PASVOLSKY 37
MOUSNIER, R., and B. PEARCE 65
MOUZELIS, N. 190
MOWAT, C. L. 7
MUHLEN, N. 83
MUINCK, B. E. DE 110
MULLER, D. K. 94
MULLER, K. J. 44
MULLER, M. 109
MULLIN, J. R. 92
MULTHAUF, R. P. 14
MUNCY, L. 94
MUNRO, G. E. 153
MUNRO, W. B. 31
MUNTING, R. 143, 148, 159, 165
MURBY, R. N. 159
MURPHY, O. T. 55
MURPHY, R. C. 89
MURPHY, T. D. 66
MURRAY, D. R. 185
MUSGRAVE, P. W. 80
MUTH, H. 77
MUTHESIUS, S. 92
MYERS, M. G. 18, 53
MYHRMAN, A. 204, 213
MYRDAL, A. 207
MYRDAL, G. 7, 199, 205

NADAL, J. 183
NAGY, T. 124
NAGY, Z. L. 115
NALESZKIEWICZ, W. 153

NAPIER, E. S. 83
NARKIEWICZ, O. A. 148, 172
NASANOV, A. N. 148
NASH, E. 165, 169
NASH, E. F., and E. A.
ATTWOOD 208
NATHAN, O. 75, 83, 91, 97
NATIONAL BUREAU OF
ECONOMIC RESEARCH 18,
26, 153
NATIONAL INDUSTRIAL
CONFERENCE BOARD 80
NAZZARO, P. 180
NEAL, L. 14, 26, 86
NECAS, J. 127
NEF, J. U. 7, 14
NEISSER, H. 7
NEITZEL, G. 91
NELSON, W. H. 80
NERDRUM, M. 214
NEUBERGER, H. M. 83
NEUBURGER, H. M., and H. H.
STOKES 18, 83, 86
NEUMAN, R. P. 88, 94
NEUMANN, F. 99
NEUMEYER, F. 49
NEV, I. D. 179
NEVILLE, R. G. 58
NEWBOLD, J. T. W. 7
NEWBURY, C. W. 55
NEWCOMER, M. 83
NEWELL, W. H. 44, 46
NEWITT, M. D. D. 191
NEWMAN, A. R. 88
NEWMAN, E. W. P. 216
NEWMAN, M. D. 86, 121
NEWMAN, P. C. 80
NEWTON, G. 105
NICHOLLS, A. J. 99
NICHOLSON, M. 33
NICOLLE, A. 53
NIEDERHAUSER, E. 118
NIEMINEVA, K. 214
NIITAMO, O. 212
NIKOLOFF, D. 137
NILSSON, A. 202
NILSSON, C. A. 201
NILSSON, C. A., and L.
SCHON 201
NIMITZ, N. 148
NIPPERDAY, T. 75
NIWA, H. 165
NOAH, M. E. 185
NODEL, E. 217
NOLAN, M. 94
NOLDE, B. E. 143
NOLTE, E. 80
NONOMURA, K. 148
NORBERT, D. Z. 125
NORDAL, J., and V.
KRISTINSSON 215
NORDMAN, N. 143
NORDSTROM, O. 204
NORGREN, P. H. 205
NORRIE, K. H. 200

NORTH, D. C. 18, 36, 39
NORTH, D. C. and R. P.
THOMAS 36
NORTH, R. N. 154
NORTHROP, M. B. 83
NORWEGIAN CENTRAL
BUREAU OF STATISTICS 196
NOTEL, R. 117
NOTESTEIN, F. W. 26
NOTZOLD, J. 143
NOURSE, E. G. 22
NOVACK, D., and M. SIMON 22
NOVAK-DECKER, N. 148
NOVE, A. 143, 148, 165, 172
NOVE, A., and R. D. LAIRD 148
NOVICHEV, A. D. 188
NOYES, P. H. 89
NUGENT, J. B. 18
NURSKE, R. 7
NUSSBAUM, F. L. 35
NUTTER, G. W. 153
NZEMEKE, A. D. 22

O'BOYLE, L. 33
O'BRIEN, P. K. 7, 16, 46, 61
O'BRIEN, P. K., and C.
KEYDER 44
O'FARRELL, H. H. 53, 83
O'FAURELL, H. H. 86
O'FLANAGAN, P. 185
O'HARA, V. J. 219
OBERLANDER, E. 143
OBERLE, W. E. 37
OBERMANN, K. 88
OBLATH, A. 180, 182
OBOLENSKY-OSSINSKY, V. V.
161, 174
ODEGAARD, O. 198
ODEN, B. 195
OERLEMANS, J. W. 111
OFFEN, K. M. 66
OFSTAD, K. 197
OGBORN, W. F., and W.
JAFFE 44
OHLIN, B. 36, 98, 199
OHLOBYN, O. 153
OHNGREN, B. 206
OHNO, E. 75, 94
OKEY, R. 115
OKOCHI, A., and H. VCHIDA 14
OKUN, B., and R. W.
RICHARDSON 7
OKUN, S. B. 159
OLCOTT, M. B. 148
OLEGINA, I. N. 172
OLGAARD, A. 208
OLIVEIRA MARQUES, A. H. DE
191
OLIVETTI, G. 178
OLIVIERI, A. 61
OLSON, J. M. 94
OLSSON, C. A. 200
OLSSON, K. 207
OLSSON, N. W. 204

OPPENHEIM, S. A. 172
OPPENHEIMER-BLUHM, H. 91
ORDE, A. 86, 121
ORGANISATION FOR
ECONOMIC CO-OPERATION
AND DEVELOPMENT 14, 40
ORLOVSKY, D. T. 169
ORSAGH, T. J. 91
OSBORNE, T. R. 66
OSMAN, M. 188
OSMOND, J. 77
OSTENSJO, R. 196
OSTERUD, O. 194
OTSUKA, H. 19
OUALID, W. 59, 69
OUDENDIJK, J. K. 22
OUTHWAITE, R. B. 39
OVERY, R. J. 75, 80, 99
OVESEN, T. 200
OWEN, G. L. 159
OWEN, L. A. 148
OWEN, T. C. 169

PACHTER, H. M. 94
PAGE, S. W. 216, 218
PAIGE, D. C. 7
PAINE, S. 28
PALAIRET, M. R. 134, 135
PALAT, M. K. 163
PALGRAVE, R. 19
PALLI, H. 217
PALMADE, G. P. 44
PALMER, B. D. 28
PALMER, R. S. 46
PALYI, M. 19, 60, 99
PAMLENYI, E. 126
PAP, D. 126
PAPADANTONAKIS, K., and R.
RUBINSON 190
PAPAYANIS, N. 59
PAPE, C. 169
PAPMEHL, K. A. 169
PAQUET, G. 174
PARES, B. 148
PARET, P. 75
PARETTI, V., and G. BLOCH 14,
40
PARISH, W. L. 26
PARISH, W. L, and M.
SCHWARTZ 66
PARKER, G. 33
PARKER, H. T. 50, 69
PARKER, W. 53
PARKER, W. H. 143
PARKER, W. N. 7, 14, 80
PARKER, W. N., and E. L.
JONES 10
PARKS, R. W. 201
PARMING, T. 217, 218
PARRINI, C. P. 22
PARRY, J. H. 191
PASKELEVA, V. 137
PASKIEWICZ, H. 219
PASSANT, E. J. 75

PASSUTH, L. 126
PASVOLSKY, L. 19, 115, 137
PASVOLSKY, L., and M. G.
  MOULTON 157
PATEL, S. J. 14, 40
PATTON, K. S. 135
PAUL, H. W. 71
PAULAT, V. J. 117
PAULIN, V. 50
PAULSSON, T. 195
PAVLENKO, N. I. 169
PAVLOVSKY, G. 148, 157
PAVLOWITCH, S. K. 134, 135
PAYNE, H. C. 66
PEARSON, T. S. 148
PEARTON, M. 138
PECH, S. A. 129
PEDERSEN, E. H. 208
PEDERSEN, J. 83, 208
PEEL, A. G. V. 53, 69
PEET, R. 22
PEETS, E. 31, 61, 92
PEITER, H. 50
PELAEZ, C. M. 19
PELENSKI, J. 33, 118
PELLER, S. 26
PELLICELLI, G. 14
PENSION, J. H. 131
PEPELASIS, A. A. 190
PERKINS, J. A. 77, 109
PERRIE, M. 169, 170
PERRINS, M. 163
PERROT, M. 59, 72
PERRY, M. E. 186
PERSELL, S. M. 55
PERSSON, G. 207
PERVUSHIN, S. A. 143
PESCATELLO, A. M. 186
PESEK, B. P. 14, 40
PESELZ, B. 115
PESEZ, J. M., and E. LE ROY
  LADURIE 47
PETER, J. P. 66
PETERSEN, K. 197
PETERSEN, W. 110
PETERSEN, Z. B. 166
PETERSON, E. N. 75, 83
PETERSON, L. 100
PETERSSON, L. 207
PETHYBRIDGE, R. 143, 159, 170,
  172
PETRITSCH, L. 121
PETROV, V. I., and S. USHAKOV
  155
PETROVICH, M. B. 136
PETROVITCH, M. B. 134
PETZINA, D. 75
PFEIFER, G. 118
PFISTER, C. 113
PHAYER, J. M. 33, 94
PHELPS BROWN, E. H. 29, 40
PHELPS BROWN, E. H., and M.
  H. BROWNE 29, 40
PHELPS BROWN, E. H., and S. V.
  HOPKINS 30, 40

PHILIPPOVICH, E. VON 121,
  125
PHILIPS, A. 37
PHILIPS, F. 107
PHILLIPI, G. 91
PHILLIPS, C. R. 183, 185
PHILLIPS, R. 66
PICARD, R. 59, 69, 97
PICK, F. W. 216
PICK, P. W. 82
PICKERSGILL, J. E. 157
PIERARD, R. V. 86
PIERCE, R. A. 144
PIERENKEMPER, T. 80
PIETERS, L. J. 107
PIKE, F. B. 183
PIHKALA, E. 159, 213
PILBEAM, P. 66
PILLORGET, R. 72
PILTZ, E. 129
PINDER, J. 7
PINKNEY, D. H. 56, 59, 61
PINSON, M. 137
PINTER, W. M. 153, 165, 170,
  172
PINTNER, W. M., and D. K.
  ROWNEY 170, 172
PINTO, V. DE S. 137
PIPES, R. 144, 163, 172
PIPPING, H. E. 159, 202, 213, 218
PISTOHLKORS, G. VON 218
PITIGLIANI, F. R. 178
PITKANEN, K. 213
PITTS, J. R. 44
PIUZ, A. M. 113
PLAKANS, A. 33, 170, 216, 218
PLUMMER, A. 14
POGGE VON STRANDMANN, H.
  86
POKROVSKY, M. N. 144
POLACH, J. G. 118, 122
POLAK, J. J. 19
POLISENSKY, J. 122
POLISH SCIENTIFIC
  PUBLISHERS 131
POLITICAL AND ECONOMIC
  PLANNING 22, 115
POLLARD, S. 7
POLLARD, S., and C.
  HOLMES 39
POLONSKY, A. 115
POOLE, K. E. 83
POOR, H. L. 92
POPE, B. C. 66
POPLUIKO, A. 144
POPOVIC, D. J. 136
POPPE, N. 144
POR, O. 178
PORTAL, R. 144, 153, 163
POSPIELOVSKY, D. 163
POST, J. D. 10, 11, 26, 44
POSTAN, M. M., and J.
  HATCHER 11
POSTHUMUS, N. W. 110
POSTMA, J. 109

POTICHNYJ, P. J. 163
POTTER, J. 202
POULSON, B. W., and J.
  HOLYFIELD 26
POUNDS, N. J. G. 7, 75, 80, 128,
  130
POUNDS, N. J. G., and W. N.
  PARKER 14
POWELL, R. P. 153, 157
PRAKASH, O. 109
PRED, A. 206
PRESCOTT, J. A. 148
PRESTON, H. H. 19
PRESTON, S. H. 26
PRESTON, S. H., and E. VAN DE
  WALLE 56
PRESTWICH, P. E. 51, 66
PRICE, A. H. 86
PRICE, G. M. 163
PRICE, J. M. 159
PRICE, R. 44, 47, 66
PRIEBE, H. 11
PRINGLE, W. H. 7
PRISTINGER, F. 182
PRITCHARD, J. S. 51
PROBYN, J. W. 11
PROCACCI, G. 180
PROCHASKA, D. R. 55
PROCHAZKA, Z. 137
PROCUIK, S. G. 144
PROFUMIERI, P. 177
PROKOPOVICH, S. 174
PROKOPOVITCH, M. 174
PROKOPOVITCH, S. N. 144
PRYBYLA, J. S. 144
PRYOR, F. L. 127
PRYOR, Z. P. 128
PRYOR, Z. P., and F. L. 128
PRZEWORSKI, A. 66
PSOMIADES, H. J. 190
PUHLE, H. J. 100
PUNDT, A. G. 47
PURS, J. 127, 129
PURYEAR, V. J. 188
PUSHKAREV, S. G. 144, 148
PUSIC, E. 136
PUSKAS, J. 125
PUTMAN, G. E. 144
PUTNAM, P. 159
PYENSON, L., and D. SKOPP 94
PYLE, K. B. 75

QUATAERT, D. 188
QUATAERT, J. H. 94
QUEEN, G. S. 153, 159
QUENSEL, C. E. 204
QUESTED, R. 159
QUIGLEY, H., and R. T.
  CLARK 75
QUIGLEY, J. M. 204
QVIST, G. 207

RABB, T. K., and R. T.
  ROTBERG 33
RABERG, M. 206

RABINBACH, A. G. 80
RABINOVITCH, G. S. 131
RABINOWITCH, H. 14
RACCAGNI, M. 55, 188
RACKAUSKAS, J. A. 133, 219
RADULESCU-ZONER, S. 121, 138
RAEFF, M. 33, 144, 148, 170, 172
RAFALOVICH, A. G. 144, 153, 157
RAGER, F. 28, 122
RAM, K. V. 51
RAMHOLT, P. 197
RANKI, G. 115, 124, 125
RANSEL, D. L. 170, 175
RANUM, O. 61
RAPPAPORT, R. 69
RAPPARD, W. E. 22
RASCH, A. 216
RASIC, P. 134
RASILA, V. 212, 215
RASIN, A. 128
RATCLIFFE, B. M. 51, 53, 55, 69
RATH, R. J. 120, 177
RATTI, A. M. 180
RAU, V. 191
RAUD, V. 216
RAUMER, H. VON 80
RAUN, T. U. 218
RAUPACH, H. 115
RAVEN-HART, R. 109
RAVENHOLD, H. 26
RAWLINS, D. 75
RAZZELL, P. E. 26
READING, D. K. 160
REARDON, J. A. 59, 103
REBENTISCH, D. 92
REDDAWAY, W. B. 157
REDDAWAY, W. F. 130, 216
REDDING, A. D. 163
REDDY, W. M. 59, 66
REDLICH, F. 14, 19, 53, 66, 75, 80, 83, 94, 100
REDLICH, F., and H. FREUDENBERGER 15
REED, I. H. 15
REES, G. 7
REID, D. 59
REIMANN, G. 7, 80, 99
REINGOLD, N., and A. MOLELLA 15
REINHOLD, P. 75
REINKE, H. 39
REMAK, J. 120
REMPEL, D. G. 86
RERUP, L. 208
REUIECKE, J. 92
REUMERT, J. 211
RHODES, B. 53
RIASANOVSKY, N. V. 144, 170
RICE, G. W. 179
RICE, J. G. 207
RICH, E. E. 160
RICH, E. E., and

C. H. WILSON 8
RICHARD, A. R. 77
RICHARDS, M. 144
RICHARDS, T. 88
RICHARDSON, J. H. 30
RICHARZ, M. 95
RICKLEFS, M. C. 109
RICOSSA, S. 177
RIDLEY, F. F. 75
RIEBER, A. J. 153, 155
RIEHL, W. H. 95
RIESSER, J. 83
RIGBY, T. H. 144
RIKER, T. W. 138
RILEY, J. C. 53, 107, 109
RILEY, P. F. 66
RILS, T. 195
RIMLINGER, G. V. 8, 28, 29. 33, 59, 89, 163, 170
RINGER, F. K. 33, 91, 95
RINGROSE, D. R. 36, 184
RIORDAN, J. W. 170
RIOS, F. DE LOS 184
RIST, M. 55
RISTOW, W. W. 106
RITTER, G. A. 95
RIVET, F. 51
ROBBINS, H. H., and F. DEAK 33
ROBBINS, L. 8, 38
ROBBINS, M. 82, 155
ROBBINS, R. G. 148
ROBERTS, C. A. 30
ROBERTS, D. D. 180
ROBERTS, H. L. 138
ROBERTS, J. S. 89
ROBERTS, M. 11
ROBERTS, P. C. 144
ROBERTS, R. O. 16
ROBERTSON SCOTT, J. W. 106
ROBERTSON, E. M. 99
ROBERTSON, R. M. 182
ROBINSON, E. 153, 163
ROBINSON, G. T. 149
ROBINSON, N. 86
ROBINSON, R. A. H. 8
ROBINSON, S. 36
ROBISHEAUX, E. 53
ROCHE, D. 72
ROCWELL, J. 208
RODIN, N. W. 153
RODRIGUEZ, L. 186
ROEHL, R. 44
ROELLINGHOFF, W. 153
ROESSINGH, H. K. 106
ROGEL, C. 134
ROGER, C. 104
ROGERS, J. H. 60
ROGERS, J. W. 47
ROGGER, H. 149
ROHR, D. G. 95
ROHRLICH, G. F. 97
ROKKAN, S. 196
ROLL, E. 75
ROMANI, A. M. 182

RONALL, J. 86, 121
RONDOLSKY, R. 116
RONIMOIS, H. E. 144, 160, 216
ROOSA, R. A. 144, 153, 163
ROPES, E. C. 144, 160
ROPKE, W. 8, 97
RORDAM, T. 211
ROSE, A. 118
ROSE, A. M. 26
ROSE, J. H. 55
ROSE, R. B. 53, 66
ROSE, W. J. 130, 133
ROSEFIELDE, S. 144, 163, 175
ROSENBAUM, E., and A. J. SHERMAN 83
ROSENBERG, A. 213
ROSENBERG, C. 33
ROSENBERG, H. 75, 97, 115
ROSENBERG, N. 15
ROSENBERG, W. G. 155
ROSENHAFT, E. 89
ROSENSTEIN-RODAN, P. 115, 118
ROSENTHAL, B. G. 170
ROSENTHAL, B. M. 80
ROSENTHAL, S. T. 189
ROSNER, J. 132
ROSOVSKY, H. 144, 149
ROSSI-DORIA, M. 178
ROSSITER, M. W. 11
ROSTAS, L. 80
ROSTOW, W. W. 8, 36
ROTBERG, R. I., and T. K. RABB 26
ROTHELFS, H. 216
ROTHENBERG, J. 116
ROTHENBURG, G. E. 122, 134
ROTHSCHILD, J. 115
ROTHSCHILD, K. W. 120
ROUBIN, L. 66
ROUCEK, J. S. 115, 139
ROW-FOGO, J. 83
ROWBOTHAM, S. 33
ROWLAND, B. M. 19
ROWNEY, D. K. 170
ROWNEY, D. K., and E. G. STOCKWELL 161
ROWNEY, D. K., and W. M. PINTNER 170
ROWNTREE, J., and A. SHERWELL 194
ROWNTREE, S. 101
ROYAL INSTITUTE OF INTERNATIONAL AFFAIRS 11, 19, 29, 115, 193, 212, 216
ROZMAN, G. 166
RUBINOW, I. M. 160, 163
RUDE, G. E. 31, 33, 44, 66
RUDOLPH, R. L. 115, 120, 121, 123, 124, 125, 128, 153
RUFF, J. 66
RUMAR, L. 210
RUNBLOM, H. 203
RUNBLOM, H., and

H. NORMAN 204
RUNEBY, N. 201
RUPIEPER, H. J. 98
RUPPENTHAL, R. 209
RURUP, R. 95
RUSINSKI, W. 131
RUSSELL-WOOD, A. J. 191
RUSSELL, C. 34
RUSSELL, D. 55
RUSSELL, E. J. 149
RUTKINS, J. 218
RUTLEDGE, J. S. 122
RUTTEN, V. W. 47
RUTTER, O. 217
RUDD, C. A. 34
RYCHNER, J. 113
RYSZKA, F. 133

SAALMAN, H. 61
SABALIUNAS, L. 219
SABEAN, D. 11, 34, 77, 95
SADAT, D. R. 187
SAGARRA, E. 95
SAHLIN, N. G. 201
SALEMI, M. K. 83
SALIN, E. 15
SALLER, H. 155
SALLIUS, P. O. 203
SALMON, J. H. M. 66
SALMON, P. 203
SALOUTOS, T. 190
SALTER, A. 8
SALVEMINI, B. 16
SALVEMINI, G. 177
SAMUEL, H. B. 53
SAMUELSSON, K. 202, 203, 207
SANCHEZ-ALBORNOZ, N. 183
SANDBERG, L. G. 199, 202
SANDBERG, L. G., and R. H.
    STECKEL 207
SANDERS, I. T. 119, 137, 190
SANDERSON, G. N. 22
SARC, O. C. 188
SARDA, J. 186
SARGENT, F. O. 47
SARGENT, T. J., and N.
    WALLACE 91
SARTI, R. 177, 179
SAUCERMAN, S. A. 38
SAUER, W. 99
SAUGSTAD, L. F. 197
SAUGSTAD, L. F., and O.
    ODEGARD 195
SAUL, N. E. 160
SAUL, S. B. 15, 179
SAUVY, A. 44
SAVILLE, L. 8, 177
SAWYER, J. E. 44, 67
SCHACHT, H. H. G. 83, 84, 98
SCHACHTER, G. 177
SCHAEPER, T. J. 39, 50
SCHAMA, S. 107, 111
SCHEELE, G. 75
SCHELBERT, L. 113
SCHIEDER, T. 34

SCHIFF, E. 105, 111, 113
SCHIFF, W. 86
SCHINDLER, E. 80
SCHLESINGER, K. 121
SCHLESINGER, R. 174, 175
SCHLUMBOHM, J. 95
SCHMAL, H. 31
SCHMID, R. J. 98
SCHMIDT, A. J. 166
SCHMIDT, C. T. 75, 177, 178
SCHMIDT, G. C. 53
SCHMIDT, H. 170
SCHMIDTBAUER, P. 123
SCHMILT, J. M. 50
SCHMITZ, C. J. 80
SCHMOLDERS, G. 91
SCHMOOKLER, J. 8
SCHNEIDER, J. 55
SCHNELL, R., and H. W.
    MORRIS 170
SCHOENBAUM, D. 95
SCHOENBERG, P. E. 188
SCHOFER, L. 39, 89
SCHOFFER, I. 109, 111
SCHOFIELD, R. 26
SCHOMERUS, H. 95
SCHON, L. 201
SCHOOL OF SLAVONIC AND
    EAST EUROPEAN
    STUDIES 165
SCHOONOVER, T. 22
SCHORE, D. J. 11
SCHORSCH, L. L. 39
SCHORSKE, C. 31, 122
SCHRAEDER, G. E. 165
SCHRECKER, E. 53
SCHREMMER, E. 15, 80
SCHUKER, S. A. 53, 75
SCHULTHEISS, E., and L.
    TARDY 125
SCHULZ, G. 38
SCHULZE GAEVERNITZ, G. 15
SCHUMACHER, H. 84, 98
SCHUMANN, H. 218
SCHUMPETER, J. A. 8
SCHUSTER, E. 81
SCHUTTE, G. 109
SCHWARTZ, A. J. 30, 40
SCHWARZ, S. M. 163
SCHWEINITZ, K. DE 89, 144
SCHWEITZER, A. 81, 84, 86, 95,
    99
SCHWOB, P. 69
SCHYBERGSON, P. 212
SCOTT, F. D. 26, 203, 204
SCOTT, J. 164
SCOTT, J. B. 38
SCOTT, J. W. 59, 67
SCOTT, J. W., and L. A.
    TILLY 34
SCOVILLE, W. C. 44, 50, 59, 71
SCOVILLE, W. C., and J. C. LA
    FORCE 8
SCULL, A. T. 34
SEE, H. 44, 50, 55, 72

SEEBER, E. D. 69
SEEBOHM, F. 47
SEERS, D. 192
SEGALEN, M. 34, 67
SEIDMAN, M. 59
SEJERSTED, F. 196, 197
SELEGEN, G. V. 161
SELIGMAN, E. R. A. 38
SEMMINGSEN, I. G. 26, 195,
    196, 197, 198
SENKOWSKA-GLUCK, M. 22
SENN, A. E. 217, 219
SEPPANEN, P. 214
SERCK-HANSSEN, J. 144
SERCZYK, W. A. 130
SERGEANT, L. 190
SERING, M. 98
SERRA, E. 56, 180
SESSA, P. 170
SETON-WATSON, C. 177
SETON-WATSON, H. 115, 144
SETON-WATSON, R. W. 127,
    139
SETON, F. 144, 153, 165
SEWELL, W. H. 59, 67
SEXAUER, B. 47
SHAFFER, H. G. 149
SHAFFER, J. W. 47, 67
SHANAHAN, E. W. 11
SHANIN, T. 149
SHANKLEMAN, J. 89
SHAPIRO, A. L. 67
SHAPIRO, L. 170
SHARLIN, A. 81, 103, 121
SHAW, D. J. B. 166
SHAW, S. 188
SHAW, S. J. 115
SHEEHAN, J. J. 75, 92, 95, 97,
    100
SHEFTER, M. 95, 182
SHEPHERD, H. L. 102
SHEPPARD, T. F. 47
SHERIDAN, G. J. 50
SHERMAN, D. 69
SHIELDS, R. A. 55
SHILLINGTON, V. M., and A. B.
    WALLIS CHAPMAN 191
SHIMKIN, D. B. 153
SHINN, W. T. 149
SHORROCK, W. I. 55
SHORTER, E. 26, 34, 95
SHORTER, E., and C. TILLY 59
SHOWATTER, D. E. 81
SHUL'GA, I. G. 153
SHULVASS, M. A. 131
SIBALIS, M. D. 59
SICHEL, F. H. 81
SIDENBLADH, G. 206
SIDERI, S. 191
SIEGELBAUM, L. H. 161, 167
SIEGENTHALER, H. 113
SIEGENTHALER, J. K. 177
SIEGENTHALER, K. 113
SIEGHART, R. 121
SIENGENTHALER, J. K. 15

SIEPMANN, H. A. 8
SILBER, J. 161
SILVER, J. 44, 67
SILVERMAN, D. P. 8, 44, 75, 95
SIMKHOVITCH, V. G. 149
SIMMONS, E. J. 172
SIMMS, J. Y. 149
SIMONI, P. 47
SIMONS, T. W. 133
SIMPSON, A. E. 75, 84
SIMUTIS, A. 219
SINEL, A. 170
SINGER, B. 67
SINGER, C. 15
SINGER, H. 8
SINGER, J. D., and M. SMALL 8, 40
SINGH, V. B., and V. V. REDDY 144
SINGLETON, F. B. 134
SINZHEIMER, G. P. G. 144
SIRINELLI, J. F. 67
SITTE, C. 31
SITZLER, F. 89, 91
SKAUG, A. 198
SKENDI, S. 134
SKERPAN, A. A. 144
SKINNER, F. W. 167
SKLAR, J. L. 118
SKOCPOL, T. 67, 170
SKRUBBELTRANG, F. 208, 211, 212
SLADKOVSKII, M. I. 160
SLICHER VAN BATH, B. H. 11, 101, 105, 106, 110
SLUSSER, R. M. 157
SMITH-GORDON, L., and C. O'BRIEN 8
SMITH, A. E., and D. M. SECOY 11
SMITH, B. G. 67
SMITH, C. N. 81
SMITH, D. M. 177
SMITH, D. S. 26
SMITH, G. A. 160, 172
SMITH, J. E. 26
SMITH, J. G. 50
SMITH, J. H. 59, 67
SMITH, L. 131
SMITH, M. S. 50, 55
SMITH, R. 179
SMITH, R. E. F. 149
SMITH, R. J. 71
SMITH, R. L. 67
SMITH, R. S. 77, 184, 186
SMITH, W. D. 86
SMITH, W. H. C. 191
SMOGORZEWSKI, K. M. 130, 219
SMOLINSKI, L. 174
SNODGRASS, J. H. 153
SNOW, G. E. 164
SNYDER, D. S. 59, 180
SNYDER, D., and W. R. KELLY 180

SNYDER, L. L. 86
SOBOUL, A. 47
SOCHOR, Z. A. 153
SODERBERG, J. 207
SODERLUND, E. F. 201, 202, 203
SOGNER, S. 195, 196, 198
SOGNER, S., and J. OLDERVOLL 198
SOHN-RETHEL, A. 99
SOIKKANEN, H. 214
SOKOL, A. E. 160
SOKOL, F. 132
SOKOLNIKOV, G. 157
SOKOLOFF, S. 47
SOLIDAY, G. L. 100
SOLTOW, L. 103, 196, 198, 210, 214
SOMAN, A. 34
SOMOGYI, S. 29
SONENSCHER, M. 50
SONTAG, J. D. 157
SORENSON, J. B. 164
SORLIN, P. 67, 170
SUSNOVY, T. 167, 170
SOUBEYROUX, N. 47
SOUTHARD, F. A. 15
SOUZA, T. R. DE 191
SOWERWINE, C. 67
SPAGNOLI, P. G. 56
SPATES, T. G. 122
SPEARS, J. 67
SPECHLER, M. A. 153
SPEER, A. 99
SPEKKE, A. 217
SPENCELEY, G. F. R. 75
SPENCER, B. 103
SPENCER, E. G. 81, 89
SPENGLER, J. J. 26, 29, 35, 56, 69, 72
SPERLING, J. G. 19
SPETTER, A. 170
SPIESZ, A. 127
SPOONER, F. C. 30, 53
SPREE, R. 95
SPRING, D. 11
SPRING, D. W. 155, 160
SPRING, R. D. 157
SPRUDZS, A., and A. RUSIS 218
SPULBER, N. 115, 174
SQUIRE, P. S. 170
SRAFFA, P. 179
SRB, V. 128
STADLER, K. R. 120
STAEHLE, H. 30
STAHL, H. H. 139
STALEY, E. 8, 38
STAMBROOK, F. G. 86, 117, 121
STAMP, J. 38
STANCKE, B. 209
STANIEWICZ, W. 130
STANKIEWICZ, Z. 11
STARES, P. 218
STARR, S. F. 172
STATISTICAL BUREAU OF

ICELAND 215
STAVRIANOS, L. S. 116
STEARNS, P. N. 29, 34, 50, 59, 67, 89, 90, 103
STEEFEL, L. D. 121
STEENSON, G. P. 90
STEFANESCU, S. 139
STEFFENSEN, J. 215
STEIGENGA, W. 111
STEIN, B. H. and S. J. 183
STEIN, R. L. 50, 55
STEINBERG, H. J. 95
STEINBERG, J. 95, 113
STEINCKE, K. K. 210
STEINER, E. 127
STENIUS, H. 212, 214
STEPHENSON, J. 95
STEPNIAK, S. 149
STERN, F. 81
STERN, G. 81
STERN, R. M. 22
STERN, S. 19
STERN, W. M. 100
STERNBERG, F. 29
STERNHEIMER, S. 172
STEVENSON, F. S. 134
STEVENSON, I. 47
STEVENSON, J. A. 34
STILLMAN, J. 181
STITES, R. 170
STOCKDER, A. H. 44, 81
STOIANOVICH, T. 116, 117, 118, 119, 136, 188
STOJANOVIC, M. D. 116
STOLNITZ, G. J. 26
STOLPER, G. 75
STOLS, E. 102, 109
STONE, D. 132
STONEHILL, A. 197
STOPCZYK, W. 217
STRAKHOVSKY, L. I. 172
STRANDH, J. 19, 203
STRAUSS, E. 149
STREBEL, E. G. 67
STRIETER, T. W. 67
STRUMILIN, S. G. 153
STRUMINGHER, L. S. 59, 67, 71
STRUVE, P. B. 149
STRUVE, P. B., and C. ZAITZEFF 149
STSCHERBAKIWSKYJ, W. 170
STUART, A. J. C. 107
STUDENSKI, P. 8
STURMER, M. 34
STURMTHAL, A. F. 29
STYS, W. 132
SUGAR, P. F. 116, 119, 134, 136
SULEIMAN, E. N. 67
SUMNER, B. H. 144
SUNDIATA, I. K. 185
SUNDIN, J. 207
SUNDSTROM, T. 206
SUNY, R. G. 149, 164, 170
SUPPLE, B. E. 8, 15
SURH, G. D. 164

SUSSMAN, G. D.   67
SUTCLIFFE, A.   31, 39, 61, 92
SUTTON, A. C.   144
SVABE, A.   218
SVASAND, L.   198
SVENDSEN, A. F.   196
SVENDSEN, K. E.   209
SVENNILSON, I.   8, 22
SVENSSON, J.   201
SWAIN, G.   164
SWEDISH BANKS
    ASSOCIATION   202
SWEET, J. J. T.   177
SWEEZY, M. Y.   81, 91
SWIANIEWICZ, S.   164
SWIERENGA, R. P.   110
SWIERENGA, R. P., and H. S.
    STOUT   110
SYKES, T. R.   180
SYMONS, L., and C. WHITE   155
SZABO, E.   124
SZAJKOWSKI, Z.   88
SZTURM DE SZTREM, J.   132
SZULC, S.   133

T'ANG, L. L., and M. S.
    MILLER   157
TADIC, J.   136
TAJANI, F.   178
TAKAYAMA, S.   15
TALAMONA, M.   177
TALBOTT, J.   68
TAMASON, C. A.   68
TAMBORRA, A.   117, 178
TAMMEKANN, A.   218
TAMPKE, J.   81
TAMSE, C. A.   102, 105, 109
TANAKA, M.   172
TANN, J., and M. J.
    BRECKIN   15
TANNENBAUM, E. R.   177, 182
TANNENBAUM, E. R., and E. P.
    NOETHER   177
TAPPE, E. D.   139
TARDIEU, S.   98
TARSAIDZE, A.   155
TASCA, H. J.   22
TAYLOR, A. E.   160
TAYLOR, A. J. P.   120
TAYLOR, G. V.   44, 50, 53
TAYLOR, H. C. and A. D.   23
TAYLOR, J.   130
TAYLOR, P.   27
TAZBIR, J., and E.
    ROSTWOROSKI   133
TCHAYANOV, A.   149
TEICH, M.   15
TEICHOVA, A.   116, 117, 127, 128
TEJSEN, A. V. S.   209
TELEKI, G.   125
TEMIN, P.   15, 19, 76
TEMPERLEY, H. W. V.   38
TENFELDE, K.   34, 95
TEUTEBERG, H. J.   34
THADEN, E. C.   171, 213, 217

THALHEIM, K. C.   145
THAYER, G.   23
THELWALL, J. W. F., and C. J.
    KAVANAGH   76
THESTRUP, P.   210
THIBERT, M.   29
THIEDE, R. L.   167
THIES, J.   97, 99
THIRRING, G.   126
THIRSK, J.   11
THISTLETHWAITE, F.   27
THOMAS, B.   27, 202
THOMAS, D. S.   200, 204
THOMAS, K.   95
THOMAS, L. B.   19
THOMAS, W. I., and F.
    ZNANIECKI   130
THOMAS, W. L.   34
THOMPSON, D. G.   53
THOMPSON, I. A. A.   186
THOMPSTONE, S.   160
THOMSON, D.   8, 34, 44
THOMSON, J. K. L.   61
THOMSON, S. H.   127
THORNBURG, M. W.   187
THORNER, D.   11
THORNTON, J. G.   145
THOWSEN, A.   198
THURSTON, R. W.   171
THYSSEN, A. P.   208
TIGERSCHIOLD, M.   201
TIKHMENER, P. A.   160
TILBERG, F.   203
TILLETT, L. R.   160
TILLY, C.   8, 11, 27, 34, 56, 68
TILLY, C., and E. A.
    WRIGLEY   27
TILLY, L. A.   27, 34, 68, 72, 181
TILLY, L. A. and C.   34
TILLY, L. A., and J. W.
    SCOTT   34
TILLY, R.   76, 81, 84, 95
TILTMAN, H. H.   8
TIMACHEFF, N. S.   153
TIMASHEV, N. S.   145, 171
TIMOSHENKO, S. P.   171
TIMOSHENKO, V. P.   11, 149,
    160, 174
TIPPS, D. C.   34
TIPTON, F. B.   76, 77, 81, 97
TIRRELL, S. R.   77
TITS-DIEUAIDE, M. J.   101, 103
TOBLER, H. W.   86
TODA, Y.   165
TODD, J. A.   15
TODOROV, N.   116, 137, 187
TODSAL, H. R.   81
TOKMAKOFF, G.   149
TOLF, R. W.   153
TOMASEVICH, J.   134, 135
TOMASKE, J. A.   27, 200
TOMASSON, R. F.   195, 215
TOMASZEWSKI, J.   130
TOMINGAS, W.   218
TOMLOS, R.   68

TOMPKINS, S. R.   149, 157
TONIOLO, G.   177, 178
TONSOR, S. J.   72
TOPHOLM, J.   212
TOPOLSKI, J.   8, 130
TOPPING, P.   190
TORKE, J. H.   171
TORTELLA-CASARES, G.   184,
    185
TOTH, T.   124
TOTOMIANTZ, V. T.   174
TOUTAIN, J. C.   60
TOWNSEND, G. M.   157
TOWNSEND, M. E.   86
TRACHTENBERG, M.   53, 69, 98
TRACY, M.   11
TRAYNOR, D. E.   19
TREADGOLD, D. W.   149, 161
TREBILCOCK, C.   8, 15, 183
TREBILCOCK, C., and G.
    JONES   153
TRESCOTT, M. M.   8
TREUE, W.   76
TRIFFIN, R.   19
TRIMAKAS, A.   219
TRIVANOVICH, V.   76, 145
TRIVANOVITCH, V.   81
TROUTON, R.   38, 134
TROW-SMITH, R.   11
TRUANT, C. M.   59
TRZECIAKOWSKI, L.   132
TSCHUPROW, A. A.   149
TSIANG, S. C.   19
TUCKERMAN, G.   172
TUGAN-BARANOVSKY, M. I.
    153
TUGWELL, R. G.   70, 149
TUMA, E. H.   8, 11
TUNCAY, M.   189
TUPPER, H.   155
TURGEON, L.   145
TURIN, S. P.   145, 165, 174
TURK, E. L.   95
TURNAU, I.   30, 119, 131, 164
TURNER, H. A.   76, 81, 99
TURNOCK, D.   116, 139
TURPEINEN, O.   214
TUVE, J. E.   160
TVEITE, S.   196, 198
TVERSKOI, K. N.   155
TYSZYNSKI, H.   23, 41

UNGER, R. W.   107, 203
UNINSKY, P. B., and C. A.
    TAMASON   61
UNITED NATIONS   15, 19, 27, 41
UNITED STATES OFFICE OF
    THE COMMISSIONER FOR
    THE BALTIC PROVINCES OF
    RUSSIA   219
UNWIN, S.   197, 201
USELDING, P.   30
USHER, A. P.   8, 47
USSOSKIN, M.   139
UTAAKER, K.   197

UTTERSTROM, G. 200, 204, 205, 207
UUEMAA, E., and F. VALDVERE 218
UUSTALU, E. 218

VACALOPOULOS, C. A. 190
VACCARO, R. 177, 183
VACHER, L. C. 27
VAGO, J. 126
VAGTS, A. 84
VAGTS, D. F. 82
VAIZEY, J. 8
VALAOVAS, V. G. 190
VALEN-SENDSTAD, F. 196
VALLENTIN, A. 29
VAMPLEW, W. 197
VAN DE WALLE, E. 57, 101
VAN DEN BERG, G. VAN B. 34
VAN DEN BRINK, T. 110
VAN DER FLIER, M. J. 107
VAN DER POEL, J. M. G. 106
VAN DER POLS, K. 107
VAN DER WAL, S. L. 109
VAN DER WEE, H. 8, 19, 60, 101, 102, 103, 106
VAN DER WEE, H., and E. AERTS 102, 107
VAN DER WEE, H., and E. VAN CAUWENBERGHE 101, 106
VAN DER WOUDE, A. 27, 104, 106, 111, 112
VAN DIJK, H. 111
VAN DIJK, H., and D. J. ROORDA 111
VAN DILLEN, J. G. 19, 107, 109
VAN DONGEN, F. 109
VAN ENGELSDORP GASTELAARS, R., and W. WAGENAAR 111
VAN HELTEN, J. J. 86, 109
VAN HOUTTE, J. A. 101, 105
VAN NOESKE, P. 102
VAN PRAAG, P. 103, 110
VAN STUIJVENBERG, J. H. 101
VAN STUYVENBERG, J. H. 15
VAN TIJN, T. 110, 111
VAN WINTER, P. J. 107
VANDENBROEKE, C. 11, 101
VANN, J. A. 100
VANN, R. T. 34
VARDY, S. B. 126
VASIL'EV, B. N. 164
VASQUEZ-PRESEDO, V. 180
VASUDEVAN, C. P. A. 23
VATTULA, K. 207, 215
VAUDAGNA, M. 177
VAUGHAN, M. 71
VAUGHAN, M., and M. S. ARCHER 71
VEBLEN, T. 76
VEDDER, R. K., and L. E. GALLAWAY 195
VETT-BRAUSE, I. 72, 100
VELSCHOW, T. 209

VENADSKY, G. 145
VENTURI, F. 145
VERAGHTERT, K. 104
VERLINDEN, C. 191
VERNADSKY, M. 171
VERNON, R. 15
VERRIJN STUART, G. M. 107
VESS, D. M. 68
VESTERINEN, E. 218
VEVERKA, J. 153
VICENS-VIVES, J. 183
VICENS-VIVES, J., and J. N. OLLER 183
VIGO, G. 181
VILAR, P. 9, 19, 184
VILES, P. 55
VILJOEN, S. 9
VINCENT-SMITH, J. 191
VINCENT, P. E. 57
VINER, J. 38
VINOGRADOFF, E. D. 149
VINOGRADOV, V. A. 173
VINSKI, I. 134
VIOLICH, F. 136
VIRKANEN, K. 214
VIRRANKOSKI, P. 213
VISSER, D. 81
VISSERING, G. 9, 108
VIVARELLI, R. 39
VOCHTING, R. 177
VOELTZ, R. A. 95
VOGEL, H. 165
VOLGYES, I. 116
VOLIN, L. 149, 150
VOLKOV, S. 95
VOLLANS, E. C. 104
VOLLWEILER, H. 90
VOLTES, P. 186
VON HIPPEL, H. 88
VON LAUE, T. H. 145, 154, 164, 173
VOOBUS, A. 218
VOSS, F. 198
VOYCE, A. 171
VRIES, J. DE 103, 105, 106, 107, 110
VRIES, P. DE 112
VUCINICH, A. 171, 173
VUCINICH, W. S. 119, 135, 150, 160

WABEKE, B. H. 110
WACHTER, K. W. 34, 41
WAELBROECK, P. 59, 90
WAELBROECK, P., and I. BESSLING 95
WAGENFUHR, R., and W. VOSS 29, 90
WAGNER, M. J. 191
WAGNER, W. G. 173
WAHLIN, V. 211
WAJNRYB, M. 131
WALEY, D. 181
WALICKI, A. 173

WALK, J. 95
WALKER, F. 81
WALKER, G. 98
WALKER, G. J. 185
WALKER, M. 88
WALKIN, J. 164
WALLER, B. 86, 117
WALLERSTEIN, I. M. 9
WALRE DE BORDES, J. VAN 121
WANGERMANN, E. 120
WANK, S. 135
WANKLYN, H. G. 116, 127
WARD, B. 35, 164
WARD, H. F. 165
WARE, R. 171
WARGENTIN, P. W. 205
WARNER, C. K. 11, 47
WARRINER, D. 11, 81, 116, 135, 137, 139, 187
WASSERMAN, M. J. 50, 60
WATKINS, S. C. 27, 103
WATSON, C. 70
WAZ, D. D. 23
WEARY, W. A. 68
WEAVER, F. S. 36
WEBB, A. D. 9, 41
WEBB, S. B. 77, 81
WEBER, A. F. 31, 92
WEBER, E. 47
WEBER, E. J. 34
WEBER, H. F. 41
WEBER, M. 95
WEBER, R. E. J. 107
WEBSTER, C. J. 145
WEBSTER, J. H. 55
WEBSTER, R. A. 178, 179
WECHSBERG, J. 34
WEDERVANG, F. 197
WEHLER, H. U. 76
WEIGERT, O. 97, 189
WEILLER, J. S. 56
WEINER, D. 68
WEINER, H. R. 181
WEINRYB, B. D. 133
WEINSTEIN, H. R. 150
WEISBROD, B. 81, 95
WEISKEL, T. C. 56
WEISS, J. H. 72
WEISSER, M. R. 35
WEISSMAN, B. M. 145, 150
WEISSMAN, N. B. 171
WEISZ, G. 71
WEITMAN, S. 57
WEITZMAN, M. S., and A. ELIAS 164
WELK, W. G. 179, 182
WELLER, A. 218
WELLISZ, L. 131
WELLMANN, I. 11
WENDEL, H. C. M. 90
WESSELING, H. L. 23
WESSON, R. G. 150
WEST, H. 95
WESTERGAARD, H. L. 193, 208, 217

WESTERGAARD, W. C. 209
WESTERMAN, H. 206
WESTWOOD, J. N. 154, 155
WEVER, F. DE 102
WHALE, P. B. 84
WHALEY, J. 95
WHEALEY, R. 185
WHEATCROFT, S. G. 150, 164
WHEATON, R. 35
WHEATON, R., and T. K.
  HAREVEN 68
WHEELER-BENNETT, J. 98
WHEELER-BENNETT, J., and H.
  LATIMER 98
WHEELER, R. F. 29
WHITE, A. D. 53
WHITE, C. 155
WHITE, D. S. 77
WHITE, H. D. 56
WHITE, J. D. 154
WHITESIDE, A. 127
WHITMAN, J. T. 150, 154
WIATROWSKI, L. 116
WICKSELL, K. 194
WIDEN, L. 205
WIEBENSON, D. 50
WIENER, J. M. 96
WIGFORSS, E. 207
WIGGS, K. I. 90
WIKANDER, U. 201
WILDMAN, A.K. 164
WILES, P. J. D. 166
WILKE, G., and K. WAGNER 96
WILKEN, P. H. 15
WILKINS, M. 15
WILKINS, W. H. 68, 71
WILKINSON, H. R. 135, 136
WILKINSON, M. 27, 205
WILKS, P. 50
WILLCOX, W. F. 27, 41
WILLETTS, H. T. 150
WILLIAMS, A. 61
WILLIAMS, D. 19
WILLIAMS, D. S. M. 150, 157
WILLIAMS, E. E. 81
WILLIAMS, E. N. 35
WILLIAMS, G. 23
WILLIAMS, J. H. 98
WILLIAMS, M. 86, 121
WILLIAMSON, J. G. 27, 36, 84
WILLIS, F. R. 61
WILLIS, H. P. 157
WILLIS, H. P., and B. H.
  BECKHART 19
WILLIS, H. P., and J. M.
  CHAPMAN 91
WILLOUGHBY, W. F. 59, 60, 102

WILSON, A. 182
WILSON, C. H. 9, 15, 16, 23, 106,
  109
WILSON, C. H., and G. PARKER
  39
WILSON, L. C. 68
WILSON, S. 68, 72
WINCH, D. 35, 207
WINCHESTER, H. P. M. 57
WINER, J. 35
WINKLER, H. A. 81
WINNER, I. 171
WINSTON, V. H. 131
WINTER, J. M. 27, 38
WINTERTON, P. 145
WIRTH, M. 19
WISCHNITZER, M. 27
WISKEMANN, E. 178
WITT, T. E. J. DE 96
WITTE, E. 104
WOHL, R. 207
WOHLMUTH, K. 145
WOLF, E. 77, 178
WOLF, P. M. 61
WOLFE, B. D. 145, 150
WOLFE, I. DE 181
WOLFE, M. 23, 53, 84
WOLFF, K. H. 81
WOLOCH, I. 68, 72
WOOD, A. 171
WOOD, A. C. 188
WOOD, G. L. 38
WOODRUFF, W. 9, 15, 23
WOODRUFF, W. and H. 15
WOODS, H. 187
WOOLF, S. J. 9, 99, 178, 181, 182
WOOLSTON, M. B. Y. S. 99
WORRALL, J. E. 180
WOYTINSKY, W. S. 35, 90
WOYTINSKY, W. S. and E. S. 9
WRIGHT, G. 45, 47, 56
WRIGHT, H. R. C. 109
WRIGHT, P. Q. 19, 29
WRIGHT, W. E. 127, 128
WRIGLEY, D. W. 86, 182, 188
WRIGLEY, E. A. 15, 35
WUNDERLICH, F. 90, 97, 99
WYCZANSKI, A. 133
WYNN, M. 186
WYNNE, W. H. 53
WYNOT, E. D. 133

YAMEY, B. S. 107
YANEY, G. L. 150, 171, 173
YANOULOFF, I. 137
YANOWITCH, M. 166
YARESH, L. 175
YARMOLINSKY, A. 145
YATES, P. L. 11, 23
YATES, P. L., and D.
  WARRINER 11
YATSUNSKY, V. K. 145
YEAGER, L. 19, 121, 157
YEDLIN, T. 119, 171
YEREMITCH, D. 135
YOUNG, D. B. 50
YOUNG, E. 29
YOUNG, J. P. 19
YOUNGSON, A. J. 9, 23, 200, 208
YURIEVSKY, E. 145
YUROVSKY, L. N. 157

ZACCHIA, C. 23
ZAGOROFF, S. D. 116
ZAGORSKY, S. O. 154
ZAIONCHKOVSKY, P. A. 171
ZAITSEFF, C. 150
ZALESKI, E. 174
ZAMAGNI, V. 182
ZANETTI, D. E. 182
ZANGHERI, R. 178
ZAREBSKA, T. 132
ZARNOWSKA, A. 132
ZARNOWSKI, J. 133
ZARRAS, I. 116
ZAUBERMAN, A. 116, 117, 145
ZAVALANI, T. 145
ZAWADSKI, B., and P. F.
  LAZARSFELD 122, 132
ZEHR, H. 68, 96
ZELDIN, T. 45
ZELNIK, R. E. 164
ZENKOVSKY, A. 150
ZEPS, V. J. 218
ZIELINSKI, H. 76, 90, 130, 133
ZILINSKAS, V. 219
ZIMMERMAN, L. J. 9, 41
ZOLBERG, A. R. 27, 104
ZOPHY, J. W. 92
ZORN, J. 175
ZUBRZYCKI, J. 132
ZUCKER, S. 90
ZUPKO, R. E. 50
ZURAWICKA, J. 133
ZUZANEK, J. 171
ZVIDRINS, P. 218
ZWEIG, F. 130
ZWITTER, F. 134
ZYTKOWICZ, L. 130